The Indigenous Voice

Volume 1

The Indigenous Voice

Visions and Realities

Volume 1

Edited by Roger Moody

IWGIA

Zed Books Ltd
London and New Jersey

International Work Group for Indigenous Affairs
Copenhagen

The Indigenous Voice: Visions and Realities (Volumes 1 and 2)
was first published by Zed Books Ltd, 57 Caledonian Road, London N1 9BU, UK,
and 171 First Avenue, Atlantic Highlands, New Jersey 07716, USA,
and by The International Work Group for Indigenous Affairs, Fiolstræde 10,
DK 1171 Copenhagen K, Denmark, in 1988.

Cover designed by Andrew Corbett.
Typeset by EMS Photosetters, Rochford, Essex.
Printed and bound in the United Kingdom
by Biddles Ltd, Guildford and King's Lynn.

British Library Cataloguing in Publication Data

The Indigenous voice: visions and realities.
1. Indigenous persons. Civil rights
I. Moody, Roger
323.1'1

ISBN 0-86232-305-3 V.1
ISBN 0-86232-306-1 V.1 Pbk
ISBN 0-86232-518-8 V.2 Cased
ISBN 0-86232-519-6 V.2 Pbk

Library of Congress Cataloging-in-Publication Data

The Indigenous voice.
1. Native races. 2. Minorities. 3. Culture conflict.
I. Moody, Roger.
GN380.I54 1988 305.8 88-17177
ISBN 0-86232-305-3 (v. 1)
ISBN 0-86232-306-1 (pbk. : v. 1)
ISBN 0-86232-518-8 (v. 2)
ISBN 0-86232-519-6 (pbk. : v. 2)

Contents

Part 3: Present Struggles *(continued)*

Dedicated to Helge Kleivan,
co-founder of IWGIA and WCIP,
soulmate and teacher. Also to
Joyce, Winona and Angie.

IWGIA = International Workgroup for Indigenous Affairs, Copenhagen
WCIP = World Council of Indigenous People

Acknowledgements

The International Workgroup for Indigenous Affairs, Copenhagen (IWGIA) – and particularly the indefatigable Andrew Gray – finally made possible the publication of this book, by securing a substantial sum of money from the Norwegian government's aid agency Norad. The money was accepted with gratitude, although in the 1970s this same government had oppressed its Sami people when they tried, unsuccessfully, to halt construction of the Alta-Kautokeino dam (see page 207).

The initiative for the project came from Robert Molteno of Zed Books, and it is only due to his enduring patience, and the zeal and tenacity of Anna Gourlay of Zed, that the work is now in print. Anna and Ralph Smith (also of Zed) had the unenviable task of reading and marking-up what must have been the most unwieldy and perplexing manuscript their publishing house had seen. For their efforts – and to the typesetter, Ken Morgan, for his fortitude and imagination – a special word of thanks.

My colleagues at Colonialism and Indigenous Minorities Research/Action (CIMRA) co-operated fully over about ten years in eliciting and filing away the thousands of documents from which this anthology draws. Thank you – Angie Aldridge, John Holliday, Karen George, Andrew Peel, Sue Newland, Phil Wilson, Alys Swan in Britain; and Jan Roberts and Stan Pelcyznski in Australia.

Peter, my brother, sustained me throughout the three years of the book's gestation, by unobtrusively tidying up my constant chaos, keeping the household from cracking apart, and refreshing me whenever necessary. Mick Licarpa greatly assisted in translating from German several *Pogrom* articles reproduced in the text. Stephen Corry of Survival International provided interpretations from Spanish when necessary, as well as other invaluable advice.

Mamunur Rahman spent hours photocopying the manuscript – a crucial task in the light of the fact that a third of the manuscript disappeared during the early stages. Many thanks to him, and to Shanaj Rahman for similar assistance.

Lastly, my gratitude to the People against Rio Tinto Zinc and Subsidiaries (Partizans) collective, and sharers in my London household, who tolerated a virtual takeover of much work and domestic space, as well as my own bad and good humours.

Roger Moody

Sources and Selections

A personal note

Compiling this anthology has been one of the most gratifying — and frustrating — literary tasks I've performed. In giving the customary apology for collections of this kind — that the shortcomings are mine and not that of the peoples represented, the publisher, or those who advised me — I realise I must say more than that about this work.

First, I can legitimately be faulted for being the wrong person to produce such a work. I have no indigenous forebears — at least, none traceable — have lived for only short periods among native nations and can claim neither a youth's callowness, nor an elder's wisdom in making my selections.

Second, my choice is clearly that of one man (and I say "man" deliberately, since a woman, a women's collection, and certainly an indigenous women's collection would have gone to some different sources and many incidental emphases would have changed). It is true I presented the initial outline to others — notably Winona La Duke, Anishnabe researcher, activist and superb commentator, and Stephen Corry of Survival International. I learned much from them; some of the material from Peru and Colombia is here for the first time published in English, thanks to Stephen's assistance. But the final structure and selection is mine alone.

Third, I have depended heavily on English-language material which has already appeared in some form. The anthology is, of its nature, eclectic and very diverse: to the extent that I may be accused of mounting my hobby horse and riding off in all directions at once. There could have been room for original articles but I did not feel competent to commission them. There is probably a need for more than the half dozen longer, analytical pieces included here; regretfully I considered there was no space for them. Above all, there are gaping holes which a more resourceful, wider-travelled anthologist (with no other commitments for several years) would certainly have filled. Such a woman or man might now be introducing the reader to historic statements made by Kol or Santhal guerrilla leaders in 19th Century India, *samizdat*-like protests from Soviet aboriginal peoples, or authentic declarations made by Mexican Indians on their forcible integration into the United States.

Fourth, despite methodical attempts to get formal permission to use many of the contributions, I have signally failed in several important instances. There has usually been no problem obtaining the endorsement of native peoples' support groups which have themselves used the material in printed form. In this respect I owe a very special debt, to both the International Work Group for Indigenous

Affairs (IWGIA) in Copenhagen, and Survival International in London, who gave me *carte blanche* to reprint anything I wished. But, despite writing twice to the addresses of several indigenous organisations or journals, there has been no response.

If this were a conventional portmanteau of other peoples' offerings, my lacunae would probably condemn it out of hand. But of course it is not. Although there exist several good collections of indigenous peoples' writings and oratory, these are either limited by geography (like Frederick Turner's *North American Indian Reader*, Shirley Hill Witt and Stan Steiner's *The Way*, or Paul Jacobs, Saul Landau and Eve Pell's brilliant *To Serve the Devil*); or occasion (for example, the cases brought to the Fourth Russell Tribunal which are cited in *Akwesasne Notes*/ARC's *Native Peoples in Struggle*). To my knowledge, this book represents the first time anyone — in any language — has tried to convey both the form and the substance of indigenous realities, without any brief, except that all contributions should come from indigenous people. If no native anthologist has done this job before, it may only point up my own rashness. On the other hand, many of them do have more important immediate tasks. Those who run newspapers inevitably — and rightly — stress their own concerns or those of the federations they represent. Even *Akwesasne Notes* — one of the most courageous and tenacious publishing ventures of recent times — has tended to concentrate on the US, rather than Canada, on North America rather than South America, on the Americas rather than Australasia, and so on. Indigenous spokespeople recognise at least two functions that non-native journalists can perform, provided they listen carefully, respect privacy and sacred ceremony and do not profit excessively from their expression. The first is to broadcast their concerns to a wider, sympathetic public. For example, the Six Nations Confederacy wanted their *Hau de no sau nee* Declaration (Part 4, Chapter 11) circulated worldwide. Unfortunately it wasn't, and I'm very happy to include it in these pages now. Similarly, the conclusions of the 1983 Nuclear Free and Independent Pacific Conference — the latest to be held before this book went to press — were tailored for broadcast around the globe. (In fact, I know of no group outside the NFIP organising committee which reprinted these important resolutions in full. Once again, I am gratified that the scope of this anthology enables a key social and political document of the 1980s to reach a wider audience, intact.)

But the sympathetic outsider can perform a second, less obvious function. She or he inevitably edits "indigenous" texts, even when they are re-presented in full. The editor's personal biases are more obvious when the article is translated, cut, and juxtaposed with other contributions. Despite the obvious pitfalls, this task is often welcomed by native spokespeople and their communities. Since 1978, I have been co-ordinating editor of an English-language newspaper which is exchanged with many indigenous peridicals around the world. Not once has *Native Peoples News* been called to order for its often controversial editorials — or news coverage which leans heavily to anti-nuclear, libertarian and radical ecological viewpoints. Indeed, on a visit to England in 1981, Boolidt Boolidtba (Les Russell) of the Aboriginal Mining Information Centre (AMIC) pointed out how important it was for Aborigines to "see ourselves as others see us". A number of other indigenous writers and groups represented in this anthology (for example, Marie-Helene Laraque, Winona La Duke, the Pacific Concerns Resource Center) have made similar comments; while the Dene leader, George Erasmus, in a major speech some years ago, stressed that, just as aboriginal origin was no guarantee of an anti-colonial praxis, so being non-native was no automatic bar to fighting for indigenous rights. "You actually have native and non-native interests coming together and talking about a common society . . . Indeed, we're talking about a single world." (see Part 5, Chapter 1).

Of course it is possible for an outsider to make blunders. This was brought home to me during the early days of selecting material for this work. I earmarked for inclusion a statement by the Aboriginal community of Welatye Therre (Alice Springs), just before learning that one of the families involved in this occupation of a sacred site lost some of its members in a grievous fire. Aboriginal customary law demands that no material, printed or photographic, be circulated which might identify, or "image", the dead, for a year after the tragedy. This was something of which I was not aware, until receiving an urgent message release, put out by the community's support group; not only was the particular piece pulled out, but I destroyed all photographs and references to members of the Welatye Therre occupation and asked others to do likewise. (A small quote from Rosie Ferber of Welatye Therre was put in to the "dams" chapter, after the year's mourning was over.) Naturally it is possible that I have unwittingly infringed another peoples' privacy or customary law — perhaps *sanctuary* is the best term for concepts which cannot be adequately phrased in English. More likely, I have included some redundant (though not necessarily repudiated) statements; quoted spokespeople who are no longer such; missed the right emphases (especially in translated passages), and even placed contributions in the wrong context.

One way of avoiding such errors would have been to decline publishing any statement which did not bear the *imprimatur* of its author(s), together with explicit permission to print in this anthology. This would have made for a quite slender and — in my view — thoroughly unrepresentative work. As I have already said, I did my best to obtain conventional permissions from groups and individuals I know to be active and functioning. I also concluded that there was no need to seek separate permissions for work recently published by trusted support and solidarity groups. But it was often impossible — and surely meaningless — to determine the copyright for most of the historical contributions. The sources of some more recent material — notably Aboriginal student newspapers of the 1970s — have also apparently disappeared without trace.

The result of these problems, and my own failings, is a presentation which will stick out like a gnarled trunk among the groves of Academe and earn its editor few conventional plaudits. It will no doubt be accused of inaccuracy, repetitiveness, and worst of all, a lack of objectivity. Some critics will ask why there are no *pro*-nuclear voices, no Aborigines praising mining, no forest-dwellers welcoming dams. Others, with more justification, might wonder why "obscure" issues such as the killings in the Chittagong Hill Tracts are given prominence, while historic events — like the Wounded Knee confrontations of the early 1970s — get only a mention and a footnote.

There *are* valid reasons for these apparent imbalances: pro-nuclear natives there undoubtedly are, but they rarely publish statements or make public declarations; Aboriginal communities have never welcomed corporate miners on their land but they have, within carefully laid-down parameters, tolerated some of them. I also felt justified in restricting over-subscribed space (both Zed Press and myself originally intended a single-volume work) when it came to issues dealt with lengthily and accessibly elsewhere. Hence, the detailed annotated introduction to the contributions on missionising among indigenous peoples — a subject still crying out for comprehensive book-length treatment — but the slim briefing on Indians in Guatemala. After all this is an issue covered in three excellent works, numerous shorter publications, a superb recent documentary film (*When the Mountains Tremble*, Prod. Yates/Sigel, Skylight Pictures, New York) and a riveting, if over-romanticised, feature film (*El Norte*).

In the final event, however, I make no pretence that this is an objective anthology; no more than the response (say) of West Papuans to the Indonesian-sponsored "re-settlement" of Javanese peasant families can be measured and reasonable, in the face of ethnocide. The oral tradition which essentially distinguishes linear, extended societies from multicultural ones, depends on revelation, insight, profound observation of the natural world, and collective conscientisation. This is not to say that indigenous communities repudiate intellect or individual endeavour: on the contrary. But these are rooted in a "sense of who we already are" rather than a disoriented search for who-we-might-have-been, or what we might become. It is the existential, not the scientific or supposedly cultural bases, of ab-original society which defines them properly for the rest of us. It would have been possible to paint a portrait of native North America, resplendent in its anthropological headdress, yet which had no bearing on contemporary Indian existence or struggles. If these volumes are accepted as one Westerner's valid tribute to the liberation struggles of millions of largely-unrecognized peoples, he will be well-pleased.

Roger Moody

Introduction

In 1967, as co-editor of a small but influential magazine I almost missed six column inches on an inside page of the *Guardian* newspaper, summarizing the findings of a Brazilian government commission into the operations of its Indian Protection Service (SPI). Responsible for poisoning, aerially bombing, uprooting, prostituting and enslaving hundreds of thousands of the country's original inhabitants, the SPI had apparently been transformed into the antithesis of the project of its founder, Marshal Rondon. "Die, but do not kill" had been Rondon's demand on his agency officials. But their protectionism effectively opened up the interior of Amazonia, facilitating possession by rubber tappers, prospectors, nut collectors, ranchers and land speculators. What had been revealed in mid-20th century Brazil seemed finally to dissolve the dubious boundary between an 18th century "enlightened" view of primitive man as a childlike wastrel, and the Darwinist view that paved the way for the atrocities of 19th century colonial conquest.

My immediate response to those half-dozen column inches was to contact the *Guardian*. They knew nothing more; the story had come over the wire from São Paulo. Next stop was the Brazilian senator, Antonio Figueiredo, whose eponymous commission had first made these appalling revelations. He offered me the entire, bulky document, but it would have taken a crate to transport it and a battery of translators for me to make sense of it. Perhaps, he added, I should contact an anthropologist living in France who had helped the Commission to make its report? And there was always Claude Levi-Strauss, the world-famous anthropologist who in the 1930s had carried out his fieldwork among the Caduveo, Bororo, the Nambikwara and the Tupi-Kawahib peoples of Mato Grosso.

Levi-Strauss blessed my enterprise with a charming note from the Left Bank. But it was Vilma Chiara-Schultz, in the first article I had ever commissioned as an editor, who not only set my adrenalin flowing but put me on a course from which I have hardly deviated in the past 20 years. For, said Chiara-Schultz, not only were the methods of destruction described by Figueiredo still employed on Amazonian communities, but the entire edifice his commission had so passionately indicted was about to be resurrected.

A Foundation for the Indians (Funai) was to be set up, controlled by the very officers within the army and Interior Ministry who were now planning to criss-cross the Amazon with highways, open up indigenous lands to multinational mining and meat corporations, and resettle thousands of poor families from the north-east, where their propensity for revolt was not much appreciated by the military regime.

My special issue of *Peace News*, glibly entitled "We, the tribes" duly appeared in 1968: a modest proposal for looking at indigenous liberation as an issue apart, *sui generis*, by an author who was scarcely aware that others had recently gone further along the same path. Within months, a more compelling writer had published his own account of "Genocide in Brazil" in the London *Sunday Times*. While neatly encapsulating the Figueiredo conclusions, Norman Lewis trounced the Brazilian regime, and called for a new international campaign to save the last forest Indians of Amazonia. Lewis' appeal brought an immediate and overwhelming response. By then, I had made contact with radical anthropologists in the USA and Europe and was in touch with pro-Aboriginal groups in Australia and New Zealand. I was also beginning to understand something about the deficiencies of my own political development and the limitations of anti-imperialism, as defined by the anti-war, social revolutionary movement of the late 1960s. Was it really possible that whole nations had been left off the Western revolutionary agenda, simply because they were too discrete, sent no delegates to the UN, had not learned the appropriate rhetoric, or received no armed or economic help from the Soviet Union? Had the territorial marginalization engineered by colonial forces on tribal or nomadic peoples become an automatic justification for their marginalization by political activists?

Ironically, at the very heart of the struggle dominating radical thought and activity at that time (but lost to our view) was the predicament of the original peoples of Laos, Cambodia, Thailand and Vietnam. Many of these – such as the Hmong who fought under General Vang Pao – sided with the United States in its ignominy: that was sufficient to damn them in the eyes of most observers. Few (if any) scrutinized the pressures applied to the hill peoples of South-East Asia, or asked whether (like some native nations of northern America which allied with the French or English colonists in the 17th and 18th centuries) they might be making desperate pragmatic decisions to support the more powerful of the parties to a conflict that manifestly was not of their own making.

Slowly it dawned upon me, as it did on a number of sociologists and anthropologists at this time, that the struggles of indigenous peoples were burningly relevant simply because they were in danger of extinction, but to set up support organizations, or despatch missions of investigation and mercy was not enough. These could either turn out to be facile expressions of *civilisado* guilt, or confirm the victim stereotype of people who fundamentally required direct access to agencies of public opinion or power. First, we Westerners had to recover our own diminishing capacity to be rooted in one place and time. No mean feat in a world rapidly being characterized by what the founder of intermediate technology, E. F. Schumacher, called "footlooseness". But mobility as such was not to blame: after all, travel in its widest sense – a component of Marshall McLuhan's "global village" consciousness – was giving many of us a view of "remote" and "exotic" peoples, radically different from the classificatory systems handed down by anthropologists, the patronizing stereotypes of ex-colonial administrators, or the assimilationist images projected by numerous governments. Rather, we had to create a complex balance between offering legitimate assistance to peoples subsisting "in the face of ethnocide" (to borrow the title of an important work by Jacques Lizot on the Yanomami, published in 1976), keeping our distance from communities which might crack up under the influence of alien norms or pressures, and opening non-coercive, culturally compatible channels of communication, travel, trade and aid to communities that sought them. These were by no means neatly-packaged options, between which indigenous peoples could choose: all three are intimately connected, as has been shown by native peoples' declarations at international tribunals, from 1977 onwards.

Second, we had to reject the acquisitive, utilitarian, justification for *protecting* indigenous peoples. This became something of a vogue in the early 1970s, as interest increased in jungle medicines, and alarms were sounded over the monopolization by multinationals, such as Shell and Union Carbide, of seed strains and cultivars. This was the point at which environmental groups began to show concern for indigenous peoples. It was a concern shorn of real commitment or political comprehension; an attitude sustained to the mid-1980s when the British Friends of the Earth launched an international campaign on saving rainforests without reference to their inhabitants, and Greenpeace International clamoured for a halt to all whaling and fur-trapping, until forcibly made aware that the survival of many northern peoples depended on them. The "deep ecology" movement, which emerged in this same period, borrowed (often without being aware of the fact) holistic concepts and practices understood and employed by indigenous peoples for many generations. But supporters of wilderness at any cost were bound to clash with forest-dwellers demanding management of national parks, while some of the programmes advocated recently by "deep ecologists" (as exemplified by the Earth First organization in the USA) have meshed-in closely with demands from the New Right. A platform of restricted immigration, blanket sterilization of poor peoples, and depopulation (by letting nature have its way with disease, disaster and starvation) has no place in the ideology of any indigenous rights organization that I know of, although superficially some of these demands might appeal to some indigenous groups. More problematic is the newer hypothesis of Gaia, which depends on several strands of "deep" ecological thinking. As formulated by geochemist James Lovelock, and developed by other scientists, this hypothesis views the earth as a living entity, the biosphere as a single system, and Gaia as a physical, psychological and spiritual reality that is both within, and without, all living things. Since it derives from observation of the natural world and, in particular, from anomalies that cannot be explained by contemporary scientific disciplines, the Gaia hypothesis purports to be not a political programme, but rather a cosmology. The fundamental roles in Gaia ascribed to the air, sea and earth, certainly resemble the significance given to these elements in indigenous cosmologies (see Part 1, Chapter 1). Both posit a symbiotic, if not egalitarian, relationship between human beings and animals; and both exclude *homo sapiens* from its pivotal role in instrumental science or manipulative technology.

Third, it was becoming increasingly clear through the 1970s that other radical Western-oriented tenets had to be revised to meet the analyses of the emergent international indigenous movement – the "fourth world" movement, as some called it, using the title of Canadian Chief George Manuel's book, which partly inspired the setting-up of the World Council of Indigenous Peoples (see Part 4, Chapter 9). Racism could no longer be regarded in simple white-on-black terms, nor did the term "black" politically encapsulate the way that many aboriginal people now saw themselves. (See Part 3, Chapter 11.) Indigenous communities shared with many Third World communities a profound mistrust of conventional development aid, administered by central government or foreign agencies and regional elites: they were even more imperilled by monolithic agri-business, civil engineering or hydro-electric schemes (see Part 3, Chapters 4, 5, 6). A technical fix of any kind – including "appropriate" or intermediate ones – could prove damaging and unacceptable. Paradoxically, despite their impoverishment, and in some cases virtual enslavement (Part 3, Chapter 12), native peoples, given title to their land and resources, might be better able to subsist than apparently more prosperous communities surrounding them.

Above all, the way in which indigenous organizations analysed and confronted colonialism, though having much in common with the perceptions of Frantz Fanon, and certainly with those of Walter Rodney or Malcolm Caldwell, finally parted company with conventional Marxism (but *not* the unadulterated Marx of his early economic and social manuscripts) over attitudes towards the land, the function of political parties, the role of ritual, the presence of outsiders and, of course, the seizure of national power (see Part 5).

It is worth looking more closely at how native peoples have received the agents of colonialism and the legacy of those fateful first contacts. The general outline is now fairly well known. Over the space of about 300 years, five mercantile powers – vying with each other to control the spice routes, to grab fabled *el dorados* and harness whole subcontinents of human power – colonized a majority of the world's populated land mass. In the process, millions died in central and south America; north American tribes were decimated as their prairies were stripped of bison and their warriors succumbed on the battlefield. Great nations of indigenous peoples – the Maori of Aotearoa ("New Zealand"), the Incas of south America – were inveigled out of their resources and their polity. In parts of Australia, and northern Canada, where soldiers were incompetent to venture, the settlers, gold-diggers, hunters, buccaneers and speculators rolled back the frontier, forcing the aboriginal landowners into enclaves where they starved, or died from smallpox, dysentery, influenza and venereal disease.

Only where the original inhabitants had already suffered conquest and enforced assimilation (such as India and China) did the white imperial machine temper its onslaught. Conquering for the king, which had typified the invasion of Mexico, Peru and the land of the Maya (Guatemala), gave way to conquering by the company; the corruption of local satraps and regents substituted for the imposition of direct rule.

Until the late 19th century Africa's vastness, its impenetrable rainforest and parched hinterland, protected many central tribal peoples, but not those of the coastal states, from slave raiding which, from sub-Saharan Africa alone, snatched around 30 million people. The militant African nations in the southern cone of the continent who co-existed with the original inhabitants – the Kungi and San ("Bushmen") – eventually succumbed in battle, to join Indian and Chinese dirt-cheap labour as servants of the industrializing empire. (Those bedrocks of apartheid, the pass laws and the homelands, were introduced by the mining magnates, the Randlords, to maintain a steady supply of "kaffirs" for the mines.)

By the early 20th century – except for parts of the Pacific, the Arctic and deepest Amazonia – the indigenous worlds of precolonial times had all but ceased to exist.

Of course, all this has some truth in it. But, useful though it is in stressing the enormity of crimes committed through colonial expansionism, this broad brush obscures other realities only recently recognized, thanks largely to the work and statements of indigenous peoples as exemplified in this anthology.

Probably the most startling revelation is that native peoples won almost as many battles against the (largely) white invaders, as they lost. Even where outnumbered and outgunned, they were rarely outflanked. As early practitioners of guerrilla warfare, Australia's Aborigines would vanish into the outback, to conduct lightning raids on British settlements. In parts of northern Australia – especially Queensland – black communities avoided contact with whites until the late 19th century, when many themselves chose to approach the missions, bartering their labour in exchange for tools, flour and tobacco. Although the soldiers of Christ eventually carried out the assimilation that soldiers of the Queen had failed to perform, while many blacks succumbed to imported disease, these aboriginal communities were not subjected to the genocide perpetrated elsewhere on the continent. Even in New South Wales, Victoria and Tasmania – where Aboriginal culture was all but obliterated – black Australians proved themselves highly organized, militarily disciplined and self-confident.

> Aborigines were neither apathetic in face of the European invasion nor incurious about the newcomers' lifestyles. The historical record indicates that they were not locked into a rigid unchanging culture. They showed themselves just as capable of adapting to altered circumstances as the European pioneers . . . Yet there were aspects of Aboriginal culture and philosophy which proved remarkably resistant to change. Traditional society was, therefore, both more conservative and more innovative than standard accounts have suggested with their picture of a culture too rigid to bend, collapsing suddenly and completely under the European invasion. [Henry Reynolds, *The Other Side of the Frontier: Aboriginal resistance to the European Invasion of Australia*, Penguin, 1982, p. 59.]

Henry Reynolds' ground-breaking work, together with that of other recent historians, paints a picture of Aboriginal society far removed from the popular romanticized notion of Stone-Age people, devoid of resources, crushed by the weight of convicts and Crown. Of the 500 or more tribal peoples on the continent at the time of the invasion, many were excellent farmers, fishers, even miners; living in houses, tending crops and following the dreaming paths which linked settlement to settlement, and each person to their own "country" as its unique spiritual custodian. They traded with whites, stole from them, blandished them, outwitted them, co-operated with them. Certainly there were massacres, and thousands of Aborigines were killed: official shootings of blacks continued well into the present century. But resistance was intense and prolonged. Here one "explorer" recounts how, in the 1870s, his party was met in the Musgrove Ranges by 200 armed Aborigines, crying (in pidgin) "Walk, whitefeller, walk!":

> At a first glance this force was most imposing . . . they looked like what I should imagine a band of Comanche Indians would appear when ranged in battle line. The men were closely packed in serried ranks and it was evident they formed a drilled and perfectly organised force . . . approached in a solid phalanx of five or six rows, each row consisting of eighteen or twenty warriors. [Quoted in S. Stone, *Aborigines in White Australia*, Heinemann, Melbourne, 1974, p. 149.]

The very compactness and intricacy of Aboriginal societies, however, enabled disease to spread like the proverbial bush fire. Almost certainly, this was the biggest single factor in the destruction of indigenous communities, compounded by what Noel Butlin rather euphemistically calls, "the removal of resources by whites from blacks", in other words, slow starvation. According to Butlin, previous estimates of the number of Aborigines in Australia in 1788 – the common baseline for the start of the invasion – are probably underestimated severalfold. This means that the number of killings has itself been underestimated, as has the degree to which the original peoples of the continent, largely dependent on agriculture and food-gathering, were affected both by the seizure of land and the fatal viruses accompanying such massive theft. (Noel Butlin, *Our Original Aggression: Aboriginal Populations of Southeastern Australia 1788–1850*, George Allen and Unwin, Sydney, 1983.)

We can extrapolate this conclusion to south and central America where it becomes obvious that the Inca empire was not a vast unyielding monolith, which simply caved in under Spanish assault. The Western authority on the Incas, John Hemming, despite lapses into ethnocentrism, has convincingly demonstrated that the Conquistadores were often outfought by the Incas; that their rebellions almost succeeded. The military "Conquest" lasted half a century and involved intrigue, in-fighting and betrayal on both sides. While the descendants of the Inca royal family, the Huayna-Capac, survived into the 18th century and were by and large firm supporters of Spanish rule, modern Peruvian and Colombian Indian organizations, claiming descendancy from the Incas and *their* own enslaved minorities, are among the most militant of south America's indigenous groups. As in Australia, it was almost certainly disease, greatly assisted by land-grab, which dealt the deadliest blows. In 1971, Eduardo Galeano had mistakenly assumed that "The unequal development of the two worlds [Spanish and indigenous] explains the relative ease with which native civilisations succumbed". (Eduardo Galeano, *Open Veins of Latin America: Five centuries of the Pillage of a Continent*, Monthly Review Press, New York, 1973, p. 27.) That millions of women, children and men died working the mines, and later as a result of the *encomienda* system of forced peonage cannot be disputed. But many millions more died, simply from being in contact with virulent invaders.

Indeed, recent demographic studies suggest that Galeano's own estimate of the havoc wreaked by Spanish colonialism (a total of 70 million people reduced to around four million over a century and a half) may be much too low, because both the extent of indigenous habitation, and the effects of disease, have been under-calculated. Out of the 49 million people believed to be living in South America alone in 1492, some 96% were probably wiped out in the first few decades (J. Wilbert, *Survivors of El Dorado*, Praeger, New York, 1972). Add to this, the number who died over the next 400 years, and the full toll is closer to 100 million people, not including those dying today from imported whooping cough, measles and influenza. (A word of caution here: we should not confuse radical reassessment of the reason why indigenous people suffered so calamitously from colonialism with any attempt to minimize its intent or effect. Far from being revisionism – like the contemporary apologia for fascism, or the holocaust "numbers game" – data stressing the importance of introduced genocidal agents, rather than outright massacre, or the inherent weaknesses of aboriginal society, *strengthens* the case for today's land rights movements. Australia was anything but a *terra nullius*, purloined from a handful of Stone Age blacks, who fled into the bush at the first sign of superior force. The Amerindians with their complex, well-adapted societies, vast repositories of cultivars and medicines, thriving agriculture and irrigation systems were so resilient, that they could *only* be destroyed by a non-human agency.)

The second conclusion destined to upset our stereotype of the noble, doomed, savage has been prompted more directly by the research of indigenous historians, lawyers, and activists. This is that many native nations decisively gained their independence only to have it eroded in succeeding years by the one tactic the colonists could better deploy than their victims: deceit. Of the approximately 400 treaties concluded between settlers, the Federal administration and north American Indian leaders throughout the 19th century, many were signed from positions of strength by the indigenous nations.

The 1868 Fort Laramie Treaty is perhaps the best example, drafted by a colonial administration trying to cut its losses after coming off worst in many encounters with the Lakota (Sioux) during the previous ten years. (In fact, the original treaties between the Lakota and the usurping state were signed half a century before. These supposedly "guaranteed" 30 million acres of land – steadily eroded until the "Great Sioux Uprising" of 1862, when the Lakota land base was down to a mere 10 by 15 mile plot.)

Gold was discovered in the sacred Paha Sapa (Black Hills) in 1874; a year later a government commission sent to buy up the region was angrily repulsed by the Lakota. Then, in 1876, Custer's punitive expedition was wiped out by the Indians at the legendary battle of Little Big Horn. The following year, an illegal appropriations Bill was rushed through the Senate, with the nominal support of just ten percent of the Lakota. The contemporary native American historian, Roxanne Dunbar Ortiz, in *Indians of the Americas* (Zed Press, 1984) asks the obvious question, why the Lakota signed a Treaty effectively cutting their land base, when they had not been defeated in war: "on the contrary, the US sued for peace". Her answer indicates that the most pernicious impact of colonialism on the plains Indians was the progressive erosion of their economy, as they increasingly traded with the "good whites" along the frontier:

> During the 19th century, the Sioux had been gradually enveloped in the fur trade, their product being bison hides. In order to produce this marketable

xxiv *Introduction*

commodity, a subsistence item in unending supply, the Sioux had to acquire European manufactured guns and ammunition. As commerce took precedence, manufactured goods from foreign countries were required to take the place of items no longer produced. The Sioux abandoned agricultural production, and turned entirely to bison hunting for their own subsistence and for hides to trade for manufactured goods. [Dunbar Ortiz, p. 143.].

But, as the bison herds were depleted by ruthless white destruction, the dependence of the Lakota on their erstwhile enemies became near-absolute.

This predicament obtained through much of the country, especially after the 1884 Dawes Commission decreed the break-up of treaty land into small allotments. There was now little sanctity even for the reserves which had been set up by the administration (sometimes genuinely) as a protection against the "final solution" being carried out by prospectors, ranchers, railroad barons and later oilmen. By 1934, when the Indian Reorganization Act introduced tribal councils – the rubric for final assimilation – more than half the Indian land base of a century before had been illegally seized or sequestered (90 million out of 150 million acres).

That this was a genocidal process in effect, and often in intent, goes without saying. But although, in the 1930s, the existence of Treaties might have seemed merely academic, over the following years they became crucial weapons in the hands of tribal nations threatened first with "termination" of their reservations, later with new invasions from mining and energy multinationals and a second wave of forced relocations. Although termination was officially ended under the Kennedy administration after militant protests by the emerging American Indian Movement (see Part 4, Chapter 5), some tribes have since exchanged their treaty claims for cash. Others – notably the Lakota – supported by the International Indian Treaty Council (which has UN consultative status) so far resist the blandishments, and demand nothing less than self-determination, guaranteed by international law.

Half way across the globe, a similar radical indigenous movement among New Zealand Maoris today focuses on the way successive colonial administrations have flagrantly contravened the Treaty of Waitangi. Signed in 1840, the Treaty is another major example of a contract drawn up between two undefeated nations, whereby the indigenous partners were supposedly guaranteed rights in perpetuity to their lands, forests and fisheries, while the Crown was given the first option of purchasing these resources. Once again, it was breaches of the Treaty that provoked native communities into attacks on the colonists, thus providing the pretext for land snatching on a huge scale. Betty Whaitiri Williams, a Maori activist who has carried out major research into the Treaty and its aftermath, points out that ". . . the course for Maori land alienation and subsequent colonisation followed an extensive, cleverly contrived, plan aimed at pakeha (white) supremacy and British control". (Betty Whaitiri Williams, *The Passage of Maori Land into Pakeha Ownership, A Maori View*, Cabbage Tree Publications, Sumner, Christchurch, 1985, p. 1.)

In the first instance, missionaries from the Church Missionary Society set about denigrating Maori concepts of spirituality and weakening their custodial relationship to the land; the first "sale" of land in Aotearoa was the 1814 exchange of 200 acres for a dozen axes. The Waitangi Treaty was, says Betty Williams "an empty promise which the Pakeha had no intention of honouring". But it served to allay fears, while the colonists built up their numbers. In the 1860s, confiscation of land by immigrants intensified, assisted by English land laws and corrupt courts whose decisions violated the principle of communal ownership. Maoris were invited to appoint ten or less "share holders" for their landholdings and given to understand that these were trustees for the tribe. In reality, they were absolute owners: "As soon as the titles were registered, land sharks picked off individuals and pirated their shares . . . Conveniently the [Maori Land] Court had not been vested with the jurisdiction to intervene". This process of fragmentation – combined with Maori failure to pay for surveys of their land, and the rates clapped on to it – ensured that, within less than three decades, six-sevenths of all Maori land had passed under European dominion. The 20th century brought further, more subtle and pernicious depredations: such as the 1967 Maori Affairs Amendment Act, which automatically appropriated land owned by four or fewer Maoris, and nullified Maori "shares" worth less than $50. Six years later the Town and Country Planning Act substituted single ownership for all communal land titles. Many Maoris quitted the land for relative poverty in the cities during the 1950s and 1960s, exposing so-called "idle Maori land" to speculators and compelling those left to grow cash crops instead of staples. As Betty Whaitiri Williams puts it, these became "dependent upon the export conglomerate for seed, fertiliser, insecticides and sprays, transport and storage, which all underlie the control that is exerted over them and the dangers involved in competing on the export market". (Betty Williams, p. 14.)

It is worth studying the theft of indigenous land in New Zealand in some detail. By no means unique (the Chilean junta subjected Mapuche land holdings to similar single-owner privatization in one of its first acts after seizing power) it illustrates how extensive the colonial manipulations have had to become, in order to legally justify the violations of treaties once signed with an equal power.

Then there is a third, surprising, conclusion to which recent research points us. In many instances indigenous societies and colonists never went to war with each other, or they reached an accommodation which has sometimes survived to this day. This is not to say the native communities came off best in the encounter. On the contrary the 19th century "protection" the British afforded the Miskitos on Nicaragua's Atlantic coast, has deepened the hostility with which the Sandinista government regards some of their land claims, and has precipitated today's tragic situation, where indigenous leaders are fighting on both sides of the war. The Aché (Guayaki) of Paraguay were also afforded a rigorous, ascetic, shield from the worst horrors of invasion, by their Jesuit masters. But what they gained as "children" in the 16th and 17th centuries ill-prepared them to resist the onslaught of land-robbers, supported by the fanatical New Tribes Mission in the 1960s and 1970s; some were killed on "pig hunts", and survivors were dragged into virtual concentration camps.

The Cherokee occupy the other end of the spectrum: an indigenous nation so intent on gaining the benefits of civilization that, by the 1820s they had inscribed their own language, were publishing their own newspaper and, in many cases, willingly sending their children to mission schools to gain advancement. The integuments of Cherokee society, and the quasi-philosophical positions adopted by the missionaries who rushed to civilize them, are so complex that it is meaningless to speak of one community exploiting more than the other. (For example, some Cherokee "owned" black slaves while some of the more liberal missionaries disapproved of the practice.) When, in the late 1820s, the state of Georgia, supported by Andrew Jackson's reactionary government, arranged the "removal" of the Cherokee to desolate "Indian territory" in Oklahoma – the destiny and the graveyard for numerous Indian nations in this period (Part 1, Chapter 2) – the Cherokee responded with a nationwide campaign, based on their treaty rights.

> They had learned to expect the worst in their dealings with the whiteman. In the end, it was their able, determined and courageous efforts on their own behalf which made the Cherokees the focus of national attention during the removal crisis. Their leaders proved extremely skillful in manipulating white public opinion and the white political and legal structure. [William G. McLoughlin, *Cherokees and Missionaries, 1789–1839*, Yale University Press, New Haven and London, 1984, p. 245.]

The missionaries were split in their attitudes to removal. Most eventually (if grudgingly) supported it, as white settlers encroached on Cherokee land, but a few – notably Congregationalists – heroically sided with the Indians, and two missionaries spent a year in prison, refusing to give in to the state. In 1835, there were more whites – some 15,000 – on Cherokee land, than the people themselves, although the nation still refused to sign the removal treaty. By this time, some of the mixed-blood chiefs had concluded there was no chance of reversing the genocidal policy and they openly supported relocation. Five years later 14,000 Cherokee were marched on foot westwards to Oklahoma. On this infamous "Trail of tears" – a barbarity that finds few parallels, even in the rest of US colonial history – nearly one-third of the nation died from cold and starvation; some, because government contractors pocketed the food ration funds.

It is clear that the *modus vivendi* reached between the missionaries and their reluctant hosts was at best uneasy, and bought the Cherokee no more than a few years respite from the settler onslaught. There are, however, numerous instances in indigenous experience where co-existence with immigrants has not resulted in total negation, but rather developed dialectically; certain aspects of both societies undergoing transformation, but the fundamental aboriginal values – religious, cultural, familial and even economic – persisting and sometimes strengthening. The Cuna of Panama are sometimes held up as the only native central Americans who fully survived the Spanish Conquest. This is hardly accurate: the reason they migrated to the Caribbean coast of Panama was to avoid killing and enslavement by the *conquistadores*. They did, however, enter into alliances with marauding French and English pirates (to the advantage of all parties) and, after the successful repulsion of the Panamanian police force in 1925, have managed ever since to preserve their autonomy on the islands of San Blas. Their fate stands in marked contrast to that of the Ciboney, Arawaks and Caribs, only a few of whose descendants are living today anywhere in the Caribbean region they once occupied. (See Part 3, Chapter 16.)

The Inuit of Canada and Alaska were able to survive alongside a minority of settlers without dramatic disturbance, until well into the 20th century. Militarization opened up the north during the Second World War and the previous trickle of trappers and missionaries became a stream. The discovery of oil on the Alaskan north slope, accompanied by a Land Claims Settlement (still unique in indigenous histories) which funnelled royalties into new native-run corporations, ensured that lengthy migrations became a thing of the past for the American "Eskimo". As one Alaskan Inuit woman has expressed the transformation of the past few decades:

> A long time ago, our people used to move a lot; but then they settled down. They built homes and stayed in one place. They followed the fish and caribou, but came back to their houses. I guess they stopped being a herd of Eskimos, moving and moving and moving! But now we're moving again! Soon we won't be a people. We'll be Mr Joseph and Mrs Thomas and all the names we've got from the missionaries and the fur trappers and the gold-crazy, money-drunk explorers! [Robert Coles, *The Last and First Eskimos*, New York Graphic Society, Boston, 1978, p. 141.]

But the pessimism with which some northern peoples view recent enforced changes is neither universal nor unalleviated. Unlike their sisters and brothers in the Soviet Arctic, whose cultural extinction since the 1920s has been so methodical that many are no longer even aware of their Inuit origin (see Part 3 Chapter 5), native peoples in Alaska enjoy some control over their resources, while the Inuit of Greenland are moving – inevitably, if far too slowly – towards full independence from Denmark, having rejected uranium mining and membership of the EEC. Despite continued failure to negotiate their land claims settlements, the Federal Canadian government has permitted both the Dene and the Inuit of the North West Territories to draw up plans for limited autonomy in the form of the new provinces, Denendeh and Nunavut (see Part 6, Chapter 3). Also involved in negotiations over land claims in this region are the Metis, descendants of Indian/white marriage whose former leader, Louis Riel, led a major rebellion against colonial rule in the 19th century: another illustration of the fact that in areas of sparse habitation and few apparent natural resources, there were often to be found settlers who rejected the logic and racism of frontier colonization.

Such rewritten histories of the impact of colonialists on indigenous societies, crucially supported by positions adopted at regional and international meetings from 1975 onwards (see Part 4) should propel contemporary radicals to several conclusions, some of which may not be very palatable to dogmatic leftists. Separatism (the "reservation" mentality), enslavement, enforced assimilation and integration all come to be seen as aspects of the same phenomenon. Similarly, the differences between old-style colonialism, contemporary internal colonization, neo-colonialism (as in the Pacific – see Part 4, Chapter 13) and neo-imperialism, appear paper-thin and largely irrelevant to indigenous communities in their present struggles; ones of degree and motivation, rather than kind.

If we view colonialism as characteristic only of a certain breed of person, we ignore the fact that, imbued with similar materialist aims, human societies of all kinds have engaged in pillaging, ethnocide and peonage (if not actual enslavement): this includes some indigenous societies as well. Similarly, throughout history, there have been individuals and communities who actively opposed the barbarities perpetrated by the states of which they were citizens: Bartolomé Las Casas in 16th century Peru, Augustin Farabundo Marti and other *mestizo* leaders of the El Salvador Indian uprising of 1932, Don Macleod, a white man accepted as an honorary Aborigine, who helped organize the first Aboriginal strike in the Pilbara in 1946.

The idea that colonialism is largely a thing of the past and that we now have new, more virulent, global forces with which to contend, ignores the fundamental link between militarization, the de-development of the Third World, the spread of corporate capitalism, the continuing seizure of indigenous peoples' lands, and the adulteration of their spirituality and culture. More important, it seriously underestimates the resilience and consciousness of indigenous nations who today (like the peoples of the Pacific) struggle for final independence, or against obliteration (like the Maya of Guatemala and the Maubere of East Timor) or discrimination (like India's 30 million aboriginal people, and those of Australia).

Out of such thoughts and perceptions – essentially a redefinition of the radical social and political agenda needed for the next few decades – this anthology emerged. Of course, the overwhelming substance of it has already stood on its own merits, in a multiplicity of forms – newspaper articles, letters to government agencies, interviews, statements of negotiating positions, and above all, declarations before local, regional, or international forums. I am, however, sure that, as a collection, it could have found shape and audience only as the result of a crucial, 20-year old, dialectic. On the one hand, indigenous communities are discovering or reaffirming their unique identities and systems; analysing for themselves their real oppressors and laying claim to whole regions of activity, ideology and definition usurped by others – for example, what it is to be "native" or "Indian"; what constitutes a true "nation"; what are the actual preconditions for "self determination". (See Part 4.)

In addition, communities once typified as "traditional" and therefore conservative (not so long ago a euphemism for "doomed") are forging unprecedented alliances with individual "Indians", radical action groups such as AIM (American Indian Movement), indigenous-led liberation movements (FLNKS – Front de Libération Nationale Kanak et Socialiste – in Kanaky, Fretilin and OPM – Operasi Papoea Merdeka – in Indonesia) and political pressure groups run by younger men and women who, not so long ago, were considered detribalized. The young people – often university-educated, urban-based, in some cases never having seen their tribal country – perceive the barrenness of the institutions which raised them up, while keeping their people down. Yet, while clearly lacking neither courage nor self-assertion, they see themselves as denied a vital understanding of their own creation histories, sacred places, prophecies, the best ways to fish, hunt, cultivate the land or gather medicinal plants and food in lean times. It is these wisdoms that their elders preserved and practised, even when the odds were heavily stacked against them.

It is possible to conclude, then, that today's indigenous resurgence ("native power" as it is characterized in a book of the same title: *Native Power; the Quest for Autonomy and Nationhood of Indigeous Peoples*, ed. Jens Brøsted et al., Universitetsforlaget AS, Oslo, 1985) has depended on the forging of numerous coalitions between individuals who have come dangerously close to absorption in white society, and communities which have come dangerously close to extinction, because they chose to resist such absorption.

At the same time, neither AIM nor the traditional Hopis (Part 6, Chapter 10), neither Cheryl Buchanan (Part 3, Chapter 13) nor the Yungngora or Mapoon people (Part 3, Chapter 4), neither the skilful young Igorot lawyer nor the community he left behind him in the Cordillera (Part 3, Chapter 5), would have achieved the same degree of mutual recognition, or gone so far along similar paths, had they not drawn strength from organizations and institutions in the outside world. The reason that poverty-stricken, isolated, oppressed native groups go to the United Nations, endorse the setting-up of support and solidarity organizations, apply to development agencies for funding (or, as in Canada, rely largely on government funding for their survival) should be self-evident. More difficult is to find compatibility between those taking an ostensibly pro-indigenous stance, who are as diverse as the World Council of Churches and President Ghadafi, the Norwegian government and the Women's Nuclear Free and Independent Pacific movement, the Sahabat Alam (FoE) Malaysia and Cultural Survival of the USA. Perhaps all that can safely be said is that the motives for taking up indigenous causes are hugely mixed (ranging from the highly-serious intent of the UN Working Group on Indigenous Populations, to the frivolous practices of whites donning native American headdress and learning sun-dances, to the manifest self-serving of the Reagan administration condemning the "repression" of Nicaragua's Miskitos, and apartheid spokespeople unfavourably comparing the status of Canadian Indians or Australian Aborigines to that of South Africa's black majority). But welcome and perceptible changes *have* occurred as some organizations take on board indigenous rights and injustices. These include state universities (viz. Bolivia) that fund the promotion of indigenous languages; public bodies supporting aboriginal-run radio and TV stations (Australia); churches increasingly willing to sell their shareholdings in companies trespassing on native lands; left-wing newspapers (such as the Marxist Humanist Detroit-based monthly *News and Letters*) giving regular space to an indigenous viewpoint; and aid agencies becoming more ready to intervene directly on behalf of oppressed indigenous peoples, despite the opposition of the central government (as in Ethiopia or Guatemala).

But this does not mean that indigenous peoples are somehow dependent on external organizations in formulating their demands, let alone in taking specific action. What it does mean is that they are increasingly employing well-tested channels of communication and representation or institutions for change, previously considered outside their reach or capabilities, while transforming their *modus operandi* – and sometimes their objectives. Native people now run their own newspapers, have their own electronic mail-boxes, invest in their own corporations, trade their own agricultural products (not just their "crafts"), found their own schools and universities, appoint their own ambassadors. (See Part 6.) Indigenous worlds are no longer flies in amber, human zoos, or islands set apart. Perhaps most surprising is their ability to survive, despite an escalation in the assaults visited upon them. They have confounded those widespread predictions, made a bare two decades ago, that they would either disappear completely, or survive solely in the memories, dreams and the redundant ritual of their assimilated remnants.

But there has been a price to pay: namely exposure to the conflicting and contradictory possibilities that face the rest of us. While it is patronizing, and palpably untrue, to suggest that indigenous peoples are less able to deal with these choices, they are nevertheless especially vulnerable to certain of them: large-scale tourism, for example, or commercialized fishing and trapping. Acceptance of some overtly attractive options can lead to the denial of more fundamental ones: taking money in exchange for the extinction of treaty rights, or surrendering land to mining in return for the cash to build a training centre or run a Toyota pick-up.

Differences between indigenous leaders, and between communities of the same people, can be read between the lines in several pieces in this book: they are spelt out quite specifically in some of the conclusions reached by the Second Conference of Indian Nations and Organisations from South America, held in Bolivia in 1983: "Some Indians are exploiters as well as exploited, oppressors as well as oppressed ... Ideological, political, and military authoritarian leaders develop among Indians to suppress others" (see Vol. 2, pp. 143-7).

On the other hand, what prevents a complete breakdown in the majority of indigenous communities, between (say) pro-militarists and pacifists, corporate high-flyers and advocates of low-technology, or missionary-converted and "pagan" believers, is a recognition of common origin – of *indiginousness*. Despite many worthy, no doubt inevitable, attempts in recent years to satisfactorily define this concept for non-indigenous people (not least member-states of the UN and members of the ILO) a compact, universal description is bound to prove a chimera. It would have to be a catch-all for numerous human societies under all historical circumstances; this it clearly cannot be. Just as colonialism can only be defined as a *process*, deriving from the structural domination of certain peoples by others, by the nature of the contact between them and by the one-directional flow of resources and cultural values, so indigenousness – the major target and casualty of colonial projects – can only be defined from specific events and perceptions. Indeed, one working description could be that where historical origins (first comings, first emergences, dreamtime) and individual perceptions (being "of the people") coalesce, there indigenousness begins. But this cannot be the whole story, for there are many contemporary communities rightly termed (and calling themselves) aboriginal, who do not trace a primogeniture – certainly not on the lands they now occupy (the Adivasis of Indian, Inuit of northern America, the descendants of the Caribs and Arawaks). If these peoples fall within the terms of reference of the special priorities, rights and recognition they are now demanding, it is not primarily because they were once in a particular place at a particular time, practising certain beliefs or livelihoods. It is because they are in their *present* place (or demanding a present place from which they have been uprooted) at *this* point in time. By granting them special recognition – whether we call it indigenousness or tribal status, and they call it "being Indian" or "living as an Aborigine" – we pave the way for their own liberation, or for them to practise their self-chosen way of life.

"Indigenousness" then, partly becomes a self-fulfilling prophecy; presenting for administrators the unwelcome prospect of thousands of people previously labelled half-caste, assimilated – or "peasant" rather than "Indian" – crossing-over and claiming indigenous heritage. In those regions where the colonizing regime has virtually eradicated native peoples' knowledge of their own histories (perhaps especially in the Soviet Union) the administration has good reason to be alarmed and (*glasnost* notwithstanding) to suppress all discussion of the issue. Elsewhere, attempts to fix "degrees" of aboriginality become increasingly important for state officials determining who is eligible for which hand-outs, who is entitled to negotiate land claims or the custodianship of sacred sites and to sit on commissions or corporative boards. While in certain nation-states there has been an obvious shift away from respecting the degree of indigenous status conceded by a previous administration – including measures by the Chilean junta to wipe out Mapuche rights altogether and a recent proposal by the Brazilian government to discard special protection for "acculturated" Indians (see Postscript) – the militancy and consciousness-raising of other indigenous peoples is actually helping to move the balance of power in an opposite direction. It is now likely that, in absolute terms, there are more Australian Aborigines than at any time since the early 19th century – certainly more than the last census concedes. This is not simply because of a mounting birthrate, but because part-Aborigines are more ready to own up to their black parentage, while descendants of the small band of Aborigines forcily removed from Tasmania in the 1840s, or from the south Australian desert as a result of weapons and rocket testing 20 to 30 years ago, are now rewriting the white textbooks which consigned their people to the very edge of history.

In India too there has been increasing identification between so-called untouchables (dalits) and scheduled and non-scheduled tribes (Adivasis, Adim Jati, Jankati, Banabasi), although there is a considerable way to go. (See Part 4, Chapter 3.)

This recovery of origins (explored at length in Part 4) has not only confirmed indigenous peoples' self-definitions, but meant the revival of names they gave themselves before colonization – names that often mean "We, the people" or "We, the first". Thus, the Navajo affirm their reality as Diné, the Sioux as Lakota, the "Bushmen" as San or Kungį, the Guayaki (a Paraguayan word which means "rabiate rats") as Aché, the Eskimos as Inuit or Innu, the Lapps as Sami (Saami).

*   *   *

There are no contributions in this anthology from Africa – the continent with the longest-surviving and most diversely organized indigenous peoples on this planet. There is both a short and a long explanation for this anomaly. The short is that no statements could be obtained from Africa addressing any of the themes considered central by indigenous people on other continents. This cannot be explained away merely by citing the lack of literacy among, for example, the San, the Bedu, the Maasai, or the forest-dwellers of Zaire (the so-called "Pygmy"): that has been no bar in the case of many communities elsewhere. Rather, it is bound up with an absence of consciousness that to deliver statements, present cases before external tribunals – identify as *indigenous*, rather than ethnic or nomadic – is the best way to meet the often extreme threats to their traditional ways of life. (And there is no doubting the pressure facing the San in Namibia, where the South African army uses them as trackers, or the Bedu, who are being relocated away from their ancient sites, to make way for tourists.) This lack of indigenous consciousness is by no means fixed: it is possible to conceive of the Kung; San one day addressing the UN Working Group on Indigenous Populations; or a session of the WCIP in Africa; or the Anuak of Illubabor, persecuted by the Ethiopian regime, calling for political support, as well as relief assistance, from indigenous support groups. But the very extent, and sheer length in time, of the invasions, removals, and encroachments on the land of Africa's "first peoples" has set them apart in several ways from land-based communities in Asia, America and Australasia. It has meant that very few African peoples can identify their original "homeland"; producing the paradox that nomadism, and a "shifting" economy are perhaps the lifestyles most identifiable as indigenous to indigenous peoples elsewhere. Second, there is rarely a sense of being uniquely threatened by outsiders, of being at the frontier in a scramble for resources, or belonging to a single self-contained social system, the surrender of which would mean cultural annihilation or spiritual death. Third, and most important, colonialism reached its climax as a rapacious, ruthless, transforming project on the African continent: forcing entire communities into enslavement overseas, eradicating traditional agricultures and religion, and, at a later stage, enforcing servitude upon the spot. The "tribe" came to be the dominant colonial administrative unit and inevitably "tribalism" was both the basis and the bane of later 19th century colonial expansionism. By not modifying the territorial boundaries agreed by the Western powers, but with the imperative to overcome tribal divisions and intra-tribal antagonism, and advance towards a modernizing state, the independence movements of the 1950s – later, the independent African governments – have often successfully created a state, or even national, identity which, for most purposes, supercedes tribal identity. Nonetheless, political parties (in Nigeria for example) continue to recruit on a tribal or clan basis, and the number of appalling tribal/ethnic based conflicts in Africa has manifestly increased in the past 30 years.

From the continent where the human species almost certainly originated, we must continue to draw experience and conclusions about the nature of indigenousness itself, and its role in the contemporary world. It must be acknowledged that this vital task has hardly begun.

Roger Moody

Part 1
The Species of Origin

1.   The Species of Origin

Introduction

The title of this section is intended as more than a pun on the title of one of the most influential books ever written. For, although Darwin ultimately rejected the purely biological, as opposed to cultural, explanation for human evolution[1] his Origin of Species *provided an intellectual basis for much of the racist and imperialist anthropology which was to blight the world from the mid-19th Century onwards. At its most insidious and tendentious, the cult of "natural selection", via the false science of eugenics, could justify genocide.[2] More commonly, it became a self-fulfilling prophecy: Western white males should be entitled to colonise brown and black peoples, usurp their resources and sterilise their women, because they were the natural world traders, planters of seed, miners of metal, religious and secular instructors of the young and, ultimately, political rulers.*

Indigenous peoples have rarely taken sides in the nurture/nature debate that has preoccupied countless social engineers for the past 100 years. To many of them, there is no fundamental difference between the genetic and cultural bases of their societies, because — as Jean Marie Tjibaou expressed it in a recent speech (reprinted below) — "It's the Earth that implants the genealogy". However, while traditional societies may successfully transcend the anti-theses which prevent more heterogeneous or dispersed peoples from adequately defining themselves, their senses of self have not been immune to internal contradictions or fraction, let alone outside interventions. Ironically, the portrayals of "original" existence, given in the first contributions to this section (largely drawn from the records of sympathetic 19th Century white observers) must now seem over-idealised, while those written by indigenous spokespeople can seem over-pessimistic, over-influenced by the need to counter alien influences. "We are what we are" yet "We can never be the same again" can be a recipe for hopelessness and the abandonment of origins. On the other hand, to assert that "though we can never be what we were . . . We are always what we are" may be a resounding affirmation.

The Creation of Beginning (Navajo/Diné)[3]

This version of the Navaho creation story was told to Aileen O'Bryan in late

November 1928 by Sandoval, Hastin Tlo'tsi hee (Old Man Buffalo Grass), a principal Navaho chief. "You look at me," he said, "and you see only an ugly old man, but within I am filled with great beauty. I sit as on a mountaintop and I look into the future. I see my people and your people living together. In time to come my people will have forgotten their early way of life unless they learn it from white men's books. So you must write down what I tell you; and you must have it made into a book that coming generations may know this truth."

The First World

These stories were told to Sandoval, Hastin Tlo'tsi hee, by his grandmother, Esdzan Hosh kige. Her ancestor was Esdzan at a', the medicine woman who had the Calendar Stone in her keeping. Here are the stories of the Four Worlds that had no sun, and of the Fifth, the world we live in, which some call the Changeable World.

The First World, Ni'hodilqil, was black as black wool. It had four corners, and over these appeared four clouds. These four clouds contained within themselves the elements of the First World. They were in color, black, white, blue, and yellow.

The Black Cloud represented the Female Being or Substance. For as a child sleeps when being nursed, so life slept in the darkness of the Female Being. The White Cloud represented the Male Being or Substance. He was the Dawn, the Light-Which-Awakens, of the First World.

In the East, at the place where the Black Cloud and the White Cloud met, First Man, Atse'hastqin was formed; and with him was formed the white corn, perfect in shape, with kernels covering the whole ear. Dohonot i'ni is the name of this first seed corn, and it is also the name of the place where the Black Cloud and the White Cloud met.

The First World was small in size, a floating island in mist or water. On it there grew one tree, a pine tree, which was later brought to the present world for firewood.

Man was not, however, in his present form. The conception was of a male and a female being who were to become man and woman. The creatures of the First World are thought of as the Mist People; they had no definite form, but were to change to men, beasts, birds, and reptiles of this world.

Now on the western side of the First World, in a place that later was to become the Land of Sunset, there appeared the Blue Cloud, and opposite it there appeared the Yellow Cloud. Where they came together First Woman was formed, and with her the yellow corn. This ear of corn was also perfect. With First Woman there came the white shell and the turquoise and the yucca.

First man stood on the eastern side of the First World. He represented the Dawn and was the Life Giver. First Woman stood opposite in the West. She represented Darkness and Death.

First Man burned a crystal for a fire. The crystal belonged to the male and was the symbol of the mind and of clear seeing. When First Man burned it, it was the mind's awakening. First Women burned her turquoise for a fire. They saw each other's lights in the distance. When the Black Cloud and the White Cloud rose higher in the sky First Man set out to find the turquoise light. He went twice without success, and again a third time; then he broke a forked branch from his tree, and, looking through the fork, he marked the place where the light burned. And the fourth time he walked to it and found smoke coming from a home.

"Here is the home I could not find," First Man said.

First Woman answered: "Oh, it is you. I saw you walking around and I wondered why you did not come."

Again the same thing happened when the Blue Cloud and the Yellow Cloud rose higher in the sky. First Woman saw a light and she went out to find it. Three times she was unsuccessful, but the fourth time she saw the smoke and she found the home of First Man.

"I wondered what this thing could be," she said.

"I saw you walking and I wondered why you did not come to me," First Man answered.

First Woman saw that First Man had a crystal for a fire, and she saw that it was stronger than her turquoise fire. And as she was thinking, First Man spoke to her. "Why do you not come with your fire and we will live together." The woman agreed to this. So instead of the man going to the woman, as is the custom now, the woman went to the man.

About this time there came another person, The-Great-Coyote-Who-Was-Formed-in-the-Water, and he was in the form of a male being. He told the two that he had been hatched from an egg. He knew all that was under the water and all that was in the skies. First Man placed this person ahead of himself in all things. The three began to plan what was to come to pass, and while they were thus occupied another being came to them. He also had the form of a man, but he wore a hairy coat, lined with white fur, that fell to his knees and was belted in at the waist. His name was Atse'hashke', First Angry or Coyote. He said to the three: "You believe that you were the first persons. You are mistaken. I was living when you were formed."

Then four beings came together. They were yellow in color and were called the *tsts' na* or wasp people. They knew the secret of shooting evil and could harm others. They were very powerful.

This made eight people.

Four more beings came. They were small in size and wore red shirts and had little black eyes. They were the *naazo' zi* or spider ants. They knew how to sting, and were a great people.

After these came a whole crowd of beings. Dark colored they were, with thick lips and dark, protruding eyes. They were the *wolazhi'ni*, the black ants. They also knew the secret of shooting evil and were powerful; but they killed each other steadily.

By this time there were many people. Then came a multitude of little creatures. They were peaceful and harmless, but the odor from them was unpleasant. They were called the wolazhi'ni nlchu nigi, meaning that which emits an odor.

And after the wasps and the different ant people there came the beetles, dragonflies, bat people, the Spider Man and Woman, and the Salt Man and Woman, and others that rightfully had no definite form but were among those people who peopled the First World. And this world, being small in size, became crowded, and the people quarreled and fought among themselves, and in all ways made living very unhappy.

The Second World

Because of the strife in the First World, First Man, First Woman, The-Great-Coyote-Who-Was-Formed-in-the-Water, and the Coyote called First Angry, followed by all the others, climbed up from the World of Darkness and Dampness to the Second or Blue World.

They found a number of people already living there: blue-birds, blue hawks, bluejays, blue herons, and all the blue-feathered beings. The powerful swallow people lived there also, and these people made the Second World unpleasant for those who had come from the First World. There was fighting and Killing.

The First Four found an opening in the World of Blue Haze; and they climbed through this and led the people up into the Third or Yellow world.

The Third World

The bluebird was the first to reach the Third or Yellow World. After him came the First Four and all the others.

A great river crossed this land from north to south. It was the Female River. There was another river crossing it from east to west, it was the Male River. This Male River flowed through the Female River and on; and the name of this place is tqo alna'osdli, the Crossing of the Waters.

There were six mountains in the Third World. In the East was Sis nájin, the Standing Black Sash. Its ceremonial name is Yol gai'dzil, the Dawn or White Shell Mountain. In the South stood Tso'dzil, the Great Mountain, also called Mountain Tongue. Its ceremonial name is Yodolt i'zhi dzil, the Blue Bead or Turquoise Mountain. In the West stood Dook'oslid, and the meaning of this name is forgotten. Its ceremonial name is Dichi'li dzil, the Abalone Shell Mountain. In the North stood Debe'ntsa, Many Sheep Mountain. Its ceremonial name is Bash'zhini dzil, Obsidian Mountain. Then there was Dzil na'odili, the Upper Mountain. It was very sacred; and its name means also the Center Place, and the people moved around it. Its ceremonial name is Ntl'is dzil, Precious Stone or Banded Rock Mountain. There was still another mountain called Chol'i'i or Dzil na'odili choli, and it was also a sacred mountain.

There was no sun in this land, only the two rivers and the six mountains. And these rivers and mountains were not in their present form, but rather the substance of mountains and rivers as were First Man, First Woman, and the others.

Now beyond Sis na'jin, in the east, there lived the Turquoise Hermaphrodite, Ashon nutli'. He was also known as the Turquoise Boy. And near this person grew the male reed. Beyond, still farther in the east, there lived a people called the Hadahuneya'nigi, the Mirage or Agate People. Still farther in the east there lived twelve beings called the Naaskiddi. And beyond the home of these beings there lived four others — the Holy Man, the Holy Woman, the Holy Boy, and the Holy Girl.

In the West there lived the White Shell Hermaphrodite or Girl, and with her was the big female reed which grew at the water's edge. It had no tassel. Beyond her in the West there lived another stone people called the Hadahunes'tqin, the Ground

Heat People. Still farther on there lived another twelve beings, but these were all females. And again, in the Far West, there lived four Holy Ones.

Within this land there lived the Kisa'ni, the ancients of the Pueblo People. On the six mountains there lived the Cave Dwellers or Great Swallow People. On the mountains lived also the light and dark squirrels, chipmunks, mice, rats, the turkey people, the deer and cat people, the spider people, and the lizards and snakes. The beaver people lived along the rivers, and the frogs and the turtles and all the underwater people in the water. So far all the people were similar. They had no definite form, but they had been given different names because of different characteristics.

Now the plan was to plant.

First Man called the people together. He brought forth the white corn which had been formed with him. First Woman brought the yellow corn. They laid the perfect ears side by side; then they asked one person from among the many to come and help them. The Turkey stepped forward. They asked him where he had come from, and he said that he had come from the Grey Mountain. He danced back and forth four times, then he shook his feather coat and there dropped from his clothing four kernels of corn, one gray, one blue, one black, and one red. Another person was asked to help in the plan of the planting. The Big Snake came forward. He likewise brought forth four seeds, the pumpkin, the watermelon, the cantaloupe, and the muskmelon. His plants all crawl on the ground.

They planted the seeds, and their harvest was great.

After the harvest the Turquoise Boy from the East came and visited First Woman. When First Man returned to his home he found his wife with this boy. First Woman told her husband that Ashon nutli' was of her flesh and not of his flesh. She said that she had used her own fire, the turquoise, and had ground her own yellow corn into meal. This corn she had planted and cared for herself.

Now at that time there were four chiefs: Big Snake, Mountain Lion, Otter, and Bear. And it was the custom when the Black Cloud rose in the morning for First Man to come out of his dwelling and speak to the people. After First Man had spoken the four chiefs told them what they should do that day. They also spoke of the past and of the future. But after First Man found his wife with another he would not come out to speak to the people. The Black Cloud rose higher, but First Man would not leave his dwelling; neither would he eat or drink. No one spoke to the people for four days. All during this time First Man remained silent, and would not touch food or water. Four times the White Cloud rose. Then the four chiefs went to First Man and demanded to know why he would not speak to the people. The chiefs asked this question three times, and a fourth, before First Man would answer them.

He told them to bring him an emetic. This he took and purified himself. First Man then asked them to send the hermaphrodite to him. When he came First Man asked him if the *metate* and brush were his. He said that they were. First Man asked him if he could cook and prepare food like a woman, if he could weave, and brush the hair. And when he had assured First Man that he could do all manner of woman's work First Man said: "Go and prepare food and bring it to me." After he had eaten, First Man told the four chiefs what he had seen, and what his wife had said.

At this time The-Great-Coyote-Who-Was-Formed-in-the-Water came to First Man and told him to cross the river. They made a big raft and crossed at the place where the Male River followed through the Female River. And all the male beings left the female beings on the river bank; and as they rowed across the river they looked back and saw that First Woman and the female beings were laughing. They were also behaving very wickedly.

In the beginning the women did not mind being alone. They cleared and planted a small field. On the other side of the river First Man and the chiefs hunted and planted their seeds. They had a good harvest. Nadle ground the corn and cooked the food. Four seasons passed. The men continued to have plenty and were happy; but the women became lazy, and only weeds grew on their land. The women wanted fresh meat. Some of them tried to join the men and were drowned in the river.

First Woman made a plan. As the women had no way to satisfy their passions, some fashioned long narrow rocks, some used the feathers of the turkey, and some used strange plants (cactus). First Woman told them to use these things. One woman brought forth a big stone. This stone-child was later the Great Stone that rolled over the earth killing men. Another woman brought forth the Big Birds of Tsa bida'hi; and others gave birth to the giants and monsters who later destroyed many people.

On the opposite side of the river the same condition existed. The men, wishing to satisfy their passions, killed the females of mountain sheep, lion, and antelope. Lightning struck these men. When First Man learned of this he warned his men that they would all be killed. He told them that they were indulging in a dangerous practice. Then the second chief spoke: he said that life was hard and that it was a pity to see women drowned. He asked why they should not bring the women across the river and all live together again.

"Now we can see for ourselves what comes from our wrong doing," he said. "We will know how to act in the future." The three other chiefs of the animals agreed with him, so First Man told them to go and bring the women.

After the women had been brought over the river First Man spoke: "We must be purified," he said. "Everyone must bathe. The men must dry themselves with white corn meal, and the women with yellow."

This they did, living apart for four days. After the fourth day First Woman came and threw her right arm around her husband. She spoke to the others and said that she could see her mistakes, but with her husband's help she would henceforth lead a good life. Then all the male and female beings came and lived with each other again.

The people moved to different parts of the land. Some time passed; then First Woman became troubled by the monotony of life. She made a plan. She went to Atse'hashke', the Coyote called First Angry, and giving him the rainbow she said: "I have suffered greatly in the past. I have suffered from want of meat and corn and clothing. Many of my maidens have died. I have suffered many things. Take the rainbow and go to the place where the rivers cross. Bring me the two pretty children of Tqo holt sodi, the Water Buffalo, a boy and a girl."

The Coyote agreed to do this. He walked over the rainbow. He entered the home of the Water Buffalo and stole the two children; and these he hid in his big skin coat with the white fur lining. And when he returned he refused to take off his coat, but pulled it around himself and looked very wise.

After this happened the people saw white light in the East and in the South and West and North. One of the deer people ran to the East, and returning, said that the white light was a great sheet of water. The sparrow hawk flew to the South, the great hawk to the West, and the kingfisher to the North. They returned and said that a flood was coming. The kingfisher said that the water was greater in the North, and that it was near.

The flood was coming and the Earth was sinking. And all this happened because the Coyote had stolen the two children of the Water Buffalo, and only First Woman and the Coyote knew the truth.

When First Man learned of the coming of the water he sent word to all the people, and he told them to come to the mountain called Sis na'jin. He told them to bring with them all of the seeds of the plants used for food. All living beings were to gather on the top of Sis na'jin. First Man traveled to the six sacred mountains, and, gathering earth from them, he put it in his medicine bag.

The water rose steadily.

When all the people were halfway up Sis na'jin, First Man discovered that he had forgotten his medicine bag. Now this bag contained not only the earth from the six sacred mountains, but his magic, the medicine he used to call the rain down upon the earth and to make things grow. He could not live without his medicine bag, and he wished to jump into the rising water; but the others begged him not to do this. They went to the kingfisher and asked him to dive into the water and recover the bag. This the bird did. When First Man had his medicine bag again in his possession he breathed on it four times and thanked his people.

When they had all arrived it was found that the Turquoise Boy had brought with him the big Male Reed; and the White Shell Girl had brought with her the big Female Reed. Another person brought poison ivy; and another, cotton, which was later used for cloth. This person was the spider. First Man had with him his spruce tree which he planted on the top of Sis na'jin. He used his fox medicine to make it grow; but the spruce tree began to send out branches and to taper at the top, so First Man planted the big Male Reed. All the people blew on it, and it grew and grew until it reached the canopy of the sky. They tried to blow inside the reed, but it was solid. They asked the woodpecker to drill out the hard heart. Soon they were able to peek through the opening, but they had to blow and blow before it was large enough to climb through. They climbed up inside the big male reed, and after them the water continued to rise.

The Fourth World

When the people reached the Fourth World they saw that it was not a very large place. Some say that it was called the White World; but not all medicine men agree that this is so.

The last person to crawl through the reed was the Turkey from Gray Mountain. His feather coat was flecked with foam, for after him came the water. And with the water came the female Water Buffalo who pushed her head through the opening in the reed. She had a great quantity of curly hair which floated on the water, and she had two horns, half black and half yellow. From the tips of the horns the lightning flashed.

First Man asked the Water Buffalo why she had come and why she had sent the flood. She said nothing. Then the Coyote drew the two babies from his coat and said that it was, perhaps, because of them.

The Turquoise Boy took a basket and filled it with turquoise. On top of the turquoise he placed the blue pollen, tha'di'thee do tlij, from the blue flowers, and the yellow pollen from the corn; and on top of these he placed the pollen from the water flags, tquel aqa'di din; and again on top of these he placed the crystal, which is river pollen. This basket he gave to the Coyote who put it between the horns of the Water Buffalo. The Coyote said that with this sacred offering he would give back the male child. He said that the male child would be known as the Black Cloud or Male Rain, and that he would bring the thunder and lightning. The female child he would keep. She would be known as the Blue, Yellow, and White Clouds or Female Rain. She would be the gentle rain that would moisten the earth and help them to live. So he kept the female child, and he placed the male child on the sacred basket between the horns of the Water Buffalo. And the Water Buffalo disappeared, and the waters with her.

After the water sank there appeared another person. They did not know him, and they asked him where he had come from. He told them that he was the badger, nahashch'id, and that he had been formed where the Yellow Cloud had touched the Earth. Afterward this Yellow Cloud turned out to be a sunbeam.

The Fifth World

First Man was not satisfied with the Fourth World. It was a small, barren land; and the great water had soaked the earth and made the sowing of seeds impossible. He planted the big Female Reed and it grew up to the vaulted roof of this Fourth World. First Man sent the newcomer, the badger, up inside the reed, but before he reached the upper world water began to drip, so he returned and said that he was frightened.

At this time there came another strange being. First Man asked him where he had been formed, and he told him that he had come from the Earth itself. This was the locust. He said that it was now his turn to do something, and he offered to climb up the reed.

The locust made a headband of a little reed, and on his forehead he crossed two arrows. These arrows were dressed with yellow tail feathers. With this sacred headdress and the help of all the Holy Beings the locust climbed up to the Fifth World. He dug his way through the reed as he digs in the earth now. He then pushed through mud until he came to water. When he emerged he saw a black water bird swimming toward him. He had arrows crossed on the back of his head and big eyes.

The bird said: "What are you doing here? This is not your country." And continuing, he told the locust that unless he could make magic he would not allow him to remain.

The black water bird drew an arrow from back of his head, and shoving it into his mouth drew it out of his nether extremity. He inserted it underneath his body and drew it out of his mouth.

"That is nothing," said the locust. He took the arrows from his headband and pulled them both ways through his body, between his shell and his heart. The bird believed that the locust possessed great medicine, and he swam away to the East, taking the water with him.

Then came the blue water bird from the South, and the yellow water bird from the West, and the white water bird from the North, and everything happened as before. The locust performed the magic with his arrows; and when the last water bird had gone he found himself sitting on land.

The locust returned to the lower world and told the people that the beings above had strong medicine, and that he had great difficulty getting the best of them.

Now two dark clouds and two white clouds rose, and this meant that two nights and two days had passed, for there was still no sun. First Man again sent the badger to the upper world, and he returned covered with mud, terrible mud. First man gathered chips of turquoise which he offered to the five Chiefs of the Winds who lived in the uppermost world of all. They were pleased with the gift, and they sent down the winds and dried the Fifth World.

First Man and his people saw four dark clouds and four white clouds pass, and then they sent the badger up the reed. This time when the badger returned he said that he had come out on solid earth. So First Man and First Woman led the people to the Fifth World, which some call the Many-Colored Earth and some the Changeable Earth. They emerged through a lake surrounded by four mountains. The water bubbles in this lake when anyone goes near.

Now after all the people had emerged from the lower worlds First Man and First Woman dressed the Mountain Lion with yellow, black, white, and grayish corn and placed him on one side. They dressed the Wolf with white tail feathers and placed him on the other side. They divided the people into two groups. The first group was told to choose whichever chief they wished. They made their choice, and, although they thought they had chosen the Mountain Lion, they found that they had taken the Wolf for their chief. The Mountain Lion was the chief for the other side. And these people who had the Mountain Lion for their chief turned out to be the people of the Earth. They were to plant seeds and harvest corn. The followers of the Wolf chief became the animals and birds; they turned into all the creatures that fly and crawl and run and swim.

And after all the beings were divided, and each had his own form, they went their ways.

This is the story of the four Dark Worlds and the Fifth, the World we live in. Some medicine men tell us that there are two worlds above us, the first is the World of the Spirits of Living Things, the second is the Place of Melting into One.

Source: Aileen O'Bryan, "The Dîné: Origin Myths of the Navaho" *Bureau of American Ethnology*, Bulletin 163 (Washington, 1956).

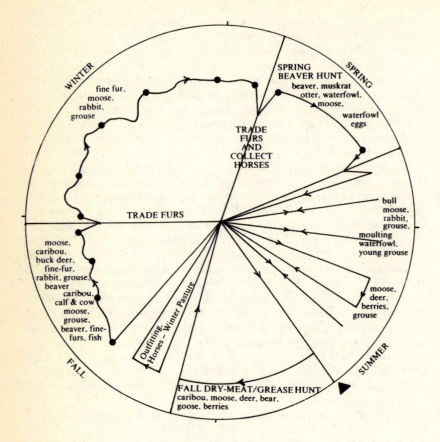

OUR YEAR — PRE-1960

The centre of the circles represents the summer meeting place, and the black dots represent cabins on traplines. The arrows indicate movement. Back and forth arrows on one line indicate short term hunting trips. The principal resources and activities of each season are indicated near the perimeter. (After Brody, 1981).

Source: WCIP Newsletter No. 3, August 1983, Lethbridge.

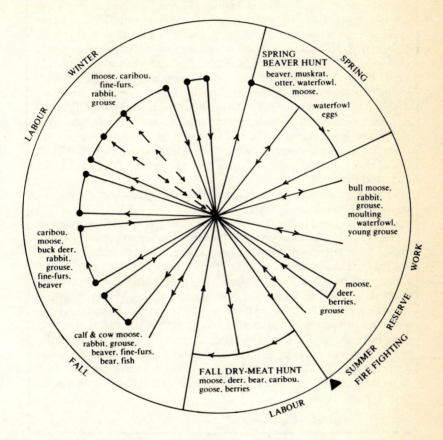

Inside the circle (clockwise from top):

SPRING
BEAVER HUNT
beaver, muskrat,
otter, waterfowl,
moose.

waterfowl
eggs

bull moose,
rabbit,
grouse,
moulting
waterfowl,
young grouse

moose,
deer,
berries,
grouse

FALL DRY-MEAT HUNT
moose, deer, bear, caribou,
goose, berries

calf & cow moose,
rabbit, grouse,
beaver, fine-furs,
bear, fish

caribou,
moose,
buck deer,
rabbit,
grouse,
fine-furs,
beaver

moose, caribou,
fine-furs,
rabbit,
grouse

Outside the circle:

WINTER

SPRING

LABOUR

WORK

SUMMER
RESERVE
FIRE FIGHTING

LABOUR

FALL

OUR YEAR — POST-1960

In this figure, seasonal wage labour is marked outside the circle.

Source: WCIP, ibid.

Gudatrigakwitl and the Creation (Wishosk)

At first there were no trees nor rivers and no people on the earth. Nothing except ground was visible. There was no ocean. Then Gudatrigakwitl was sorry that it was so. He thought, "How is it that there are no animals?" He looked, but he saw nothing. Then he deliberated. He thought, "I will try. Somebody will live on the earth. But what will he use?" Then he decided to make a boat for him. He made things by joining his hands and spreading them. He used no tools. In this way he made people. The first man was *wat*, the abalone. The first people were not right. They all died. Gudatrigakwitl thought that they were bad. He wanted good people who would have children. At first he wanted every man to have ten lives. When he was an old man he was to become a boy again. Afterwards Gudatrigakwitl found that he could not do this. He gave the people all the game, the fish, and the trees. . . .

Gudatrigakwitl used no sand or earth or sticks to make the people; he merely thought and they existed.

Gudatrigakwitl thought: "When something is alive, like a plant, it will not die. It will come up again from the roots and grow again and again. So it will be with men, and animals, and everything alive. . . ."

Gudatrigakwitl left the people all kinds of dances. He said: "When there is a festivity, call me. If some do not like what I say, let them be. But those to whom I leave my instructions, who will teach them to their children, will be well. Whenever you are badly off, call me. I can save you in some way, no matter how great the difficulty. If a man does not call me, I will let him go. . . ."

Gudatrigakwitl went all over the world looking. Then he made everything. When he had finished everything he made people.

Gudatrigakwitl is not called on every day. He is called only when a man is in difficulty.

Source: A. L. Kroeber, "Wishosk Myths," *Journal of American Folklore*, Vol. 18.

Myth of Creation (Osage)

Way beyond, a part of the Osage lived in the sky. They desired to know their origin, the source from which they came into existence. They went to the sun. He told them that they were his children. Then they wandered still farther and came to the moon. She told them that she gave birth to them, and that the sun was their father. She told them that they must leave their present abode and go down to the earth and dwell there. They came to the earth, but found it covered with water. They could not return to the place they had left, so they wept, but no answer came to them from anywhere. They floated about in the air, seeking in every direction for help from some god; but they found none. The animals were with them, and of all these the elk was the finest and most stately, and inspired all the creatures with confidence; so they appealed to the elk for help. He dropped into the water and began to sink. Then he called to the winds, and the winds came from all quarters and blew until the waters went upward as in a mist.

At first rocks only were exposed, and the people travelled on the rocky places that produced no plants, and there was nothing to eat. Then the waters began to go down until the soft earth was exposed. When this happened, the elk in his joy rolled over and over on the soft earth, and all his loose hairs clung to the soil. The hairs grew, and from them sprang beans, corns, potatoes, and wild turnips, and then all the grasses and trees.

Source: Alice Fletcher and Francis LaFléche, *The Omaha Tribe.*

A MAYA PROPHECY
(Yucatán)

Eat, eat, while there is bread,
Drink, drink, while there is water;
A day comes when dust shall darken the air,
When a blight shall wither the land,
When a cloud shall arise,
When a mountain shall be lifted up,
When a strong man shall seize the city,
When ruin shall fall upon all things,
When the tender leaf shall be destroyed,
When eyes shall be closed in death;
When there shall be three signs on a tree,

      Father, son, and grandson hanging dead
         on the same tree;
      When the battle flag shall be raised,
      And the people scattered abroad in the forests.

Translated from D. G. Brinton, "The Books of Chilam Balam," in *Essays of an Americanist*,
p. 303. The Books of Chilam Balam are the sacred books of the Maya of Yucatán.

PRAYER TO THE ANCIENTS AFTER HARVESTING
(Zuñi)

      From where you stay quietly,
      Your little wind-blown clouds,
      Your fine wisps of clouds,
      Your massed clouds you will send forth
            to sit down with us;
      With your fine rain caressing the earth,
      With all your waters
      You will pass to us on our roads.
      My fathers,
      With your great pile of waters,
      With your fine rain caressing the earth,
      You will pass us on our roads.
      Add to your hearts.
      Your waters,
      Your seeds,
      Your long life,
      Your old age
      You will grant to us.
      Therefore I have added to your hearts,
      To the end, my fathers,
      My children:
      You will protect us.
      All my ladder-descending children
      Will finish their roads;
      They will grow old.
      You will bless us with life.

Source: Ruth Bunzel, *Zuñi Ritual Poetry*, pp. 622–3.

Songs of the People (Anishinabe Nagamon)

Gerald Vizenor, the author of this piece, is an Anishinabe (Chippewa) of the White Earth Reservation, Minnesota. He is one of the younger generation of native scholars, who are reviving and reinterpreting their people's traditional literature. For another contribution from White Earth see Winona La Duke (Vol. 2, p. 219).

The sacred *migis* shell of the *Anishinabe* spirit arose from the eastern sea and moved along the inland waters guiding *the people* through the sleeping sun of the woodland to *bawitig* — the long rapids in the river.

The *Anishinabe* — the *original people* of the woodland — believe they were given wisdom and life color from the sun reflecting on the sacred shell during this long migration. Five hundred years ago, the *migis* shell appeared in the sun for the last time at *Moningwanekaning* in *Anishinabe kitchigami* — the great sea of the *Anishinabe*.

The people measured living through time in the circles on the sun and moon and human heart. Trailing the summer shores of *kitchigami* to the hardwoods and swamps, drawing *sisibakwat*, and gathering *manomin*, the *Anishinabe* returned each winter to *Moningwanekaning* — Madeline Island in Lake Superior — and told stories of the summer heat.

In the seventeeth century, voyagers and the first missionaries of the old world established a Christian fur trading post on *Moningwanekaning* near the sacred community of *the people*. While showing the new world discoverers how to endure the long woodland winters, only half of the *Anishinabe* survived the first pestilence of the white man — a severe smallpox epidemic.

Fulgurant missionaries latinized the woodland dead and thundered through the Epistles that *the people* were only children learning the hymns of a new civilization. The hymns were peddled like military secrets to the nervy voyagers who learned the language and life style of the woodland and enmeshed *the people* in the predatory economics of peltry.

The expanding interests of the fur trade — spurred by the old world bourgeois demand for felt hats — drew *the people* to other fur trading posts with beaver peltry in exchange for firearms and diluted intoxicants.

> moving forward and back
> from the woodland to the prairie
> Dakota women
> weeping
> as they gather
> their wounded men
> the sound of their weeping
> comes back to us

With rifles the *Anishinabe* easily defeated the woodland *Dakota* and drove them from the rich wild rice lands in northern Minnesota.

The fur trade interposed an economic anomaly between the intuitive rhythm of

woodland life and the equipoise of the *Anishinabe* spirit. While *the people* were
resuming the human unity of tribal life, thousands of sainted white settlers procured
the land with new laws and enslaved the *Anishinabe* in the fury of discovery.

> honoring your brave men
> like them
> believing in myself

The rhythm of the land was broken by the marching cadence of Christian
patriotism. *Anishinabe* orators of the *mang odem*, legions of the *makwa odem*, and
the people of the *amik odem*, were colonized and mythologized and alienated from
their woodland life and religion while the voices of the conquerors rang with
freedom.

> brave warriors
> where have you gone
> *ho kwi ho ho*

The *Anishinabe* did not have a written history. The past was a visual memory and
oratorical gesture of dreams plaiting an endless woodland identity between the
conscious and unconscious worlds of *the people.*

I am a bird . . . if you wish to know me you must seek me in the clouds . . . the
Anishinabe orator *Keeshkemun* told the *jaganash* military officers who had asked
him to explain his position in the new world territorial wars. *Keeshkemun*
responded to the question with a personal dream song.

The song poems of the *Anishinabe* are intuitive lyrical images of woodland life.

> the first to come
> epithet among the birds
> bringing the rain
> crow is my name

The *Anishinabe* hears music not only in the human voice, but in the sounds of
animals and trees and ice cracking on the lakes. *The people* are surrounded by life.
They are not alone.

> the wind
> only
> fearing him

Anishinabemowin is a language of verbal forms and word images. The spoken
feeling of the language is a moving image of tribal woodland life: *nibi*—water,
mang—loon, *makwa*—bear, *amik*—beaver, kingfishers at dusk, the owls at night,
and maple syrup in the snow.

The language is euphonious: *Anishinabe nagamon*—songs of the people,
pipigwan—flute, *manomin*—wild rice, *gimiwan*—rain, *sibi*—river, *memengwa*—
butterfly, *nibawin*—sleeping, *sisibakwat*—maple sugar, *ishkote*—fire, *papakine*—
grasshopper, *wawatessi*—firefly.

And the words are descriptive: *missanwi*—snow falling from the branches,
kijiga—maple sap is running fast from the trees, *onabani gisiss*—the month of the
moon on the crust of the snow, *sagashka*—grass begins to grow, *papakine magad*
ishkote—crackling fire.

The *Anishinabe* drew pictures of ideas and presentient dreams. The song pictures of the *midewiwin* — the sacred life of *the people* — were incised on the soft inner bark of the birch. These scrolls of pictomyths and sacred songs are taught and understood only by members of the *midewiwin* who believe that music and the knowledge and use of herbal medicine prolong life.

Anishinabe song poetry is a symphony of cosmic rhythms and tribal instincts, memories and dream songs, expressing the contrasts of life and death, day and night, man and woman, courage and fear.

> my feathers
> sailing
> on the breeze

The song words of the woodland poet are like the feathers of birds lifting one by one on the wind — the shadows of death escaping through avian dreams.

> the clear sky
> loves to hear me sing

The presentient dreams of the *Anishinabe* are expressed in songs like the spontaneous rhythm of breathing.

> overhanging clouds
> echoing my words
> with a pleasing sound

The people do not fear silence and space. In the past the *Anishinabe* knew self-reverence and disciplined himself against the excesses of human desires and possessions. Visions were imperfect and dreams were the songs of history.

> across the earth
> everywhere
> making my voice heard

The song poems of the *Anishinabe* are songs of individual freedom. The dreams are not forgotten. The woodland voice of *the people* may still be heard wavering over the mourning bell of decadent promises for peace.

Gerald Vizenor

Cry of the Earth

Forty thousand years ago I came to this land from the Dreamtime. I came with knowledge that this land would care for me and I in return would acknowledge it as my Saviour.

I looked upon my surroundings and saw a land, like none other, with majestic mountains — so high their tops blended with the sky in blissful content. The gum trees whispered to me that they would shelter me from winds and rains and I understood and said 'Yes, I will honour you and take only what you give, we will live here together. You will drink from the heavens and I will drink from the earth — the rivers and the streams.'

The years passed and my people grew to be many tribes who share the land. Homes were made for each tribe; all must obey that is our law, all tribes must honour their birthright, their inheritance, their land. As we grew, nature supplied us with food fit for our consumption and our bodies grew accustomed to the food nature provided, making us unique. Nature was good to us and looked after us well. We honoured our traditional land in song and ceremonies and kept sacred its secrets. We praised the creation that was ours in corroboree each day so our children could pass them on to their children. We lived thus for many years — until the white man came.

We saw the ships come bearing England's shame, a shame which they flaunted at us. We did not understand these murderers, beggars and thieves; nor did we understand the arrogant free settlers. We did not have anything in common with them. Their interests in us grew into greed as they saw how rich our land was. They spread across our country destroying and devouring fauna and wildlife until there was nothing left untouched above the earth. They found the treasures buried deep within its heart, a treasure so beautiful and priceless beyond the imagination — gold, silver, diamonds, and opals — given to us by the Creator. But now the earth's back is scraped by steel, harvest ploughs and tractor wheels. The old gum tree whose life spans hundreds of years, stripped of its bark and left to die in shame — when once its limbs reached the sky.

With its shame emerged our destruction. We were utterly confused, the white man hunted us down like dogs. Our death became their freedom. Our old ones, the keepers of the laws, slaughtered along with our Dreamtime, and sacred rules were left to weather and perish over the plains we roamed.

Soon our conquerors' blood mingled with our own, inflicting us with diseases. Added to our misery and despair we were detribalized and left confined in lands that were not our own; we became trespassers on sacred ground owned by other tribes. Our spirit could not condone; as the years passed our children lost their identity. Without our tradition we became aliens, soon we were victims of anthropologists' lust, archaeologists' insanity, and a museum's delight. We were open prey to every devious topic in the world; under scrutiny of every social curriculum. With our environment turned topsy turvy our spirits rebelled. We began 'to fight for peace'; with our backs to the sea we could not be pushed any further; we advanced, gathering together our mutilated race; we emerged on shaky legs to rectify the white man's disaster; we started the repairs.

Soon our individual organizations sprouted and started to bloom, kindling in our old ones a burning desire to delve into their memories for cultural strength to sustain us through the following years. Our slow reincarnation strengthened us to bury the colonialism that has plagued us over the last two centuries. In its place came patriotism moulding us into a political ball with new awareness. Departments grabbed us with iron claws cementing us into categories, squeezing us into societies where we don't belong. The mighty farce of oppression sapped our strength, we searched for spiritual guidance and left ourselves open to prey for other holy doctrines. With our spirits thrusting for holy guidance we devoured Christianity, a force so powerful and destructive to our cultural beliefs we were listless. Christianity showered over our own spiritual beliefs, turning us into believers of white man's Christian doctrine, alienating us completely from the Dreamtime faith.

As a shattered race, we emerge in this new era and we are afraid. In the atomic age we see ourselves slowly disintegrating into a highly sophisticated state of systematic people confined to a system that is not our inheritance. We have stepped into a future that will ultimately be our destruction as our people become riddled with the concepts of the Western world, vice, and social mutilation.

For us to survive this new century we must have full control over our destiny, revive our culture and fulfil our inheritance, own our land; to restore us to the proud people that we are.

Loraine Mafi Williams

Source: Asian Action, Newsletter of Asian Cultural Action for Development (ACAD), No. 24 Bangkok, date unknown.

The Aboriginal Question

Most non-Aborigines think that the term 'Dreamtime' refers to a long distant era of the past when Aborigines languorously drew patterns on the walls of caves and generally moved in a dream-like trance through life, without constraint of law and regulation and generally slept in the sunshine. The zenith of alien thinking is one of sable kings of native areas or the 'Noble Savage' and there, in the minds of most, further thought ceases. But when we compare the stability and level of true civilisation, the ennobled estate of Aborigines, the length of our civilisation, to the British, Chinese, Germans etc. we find that we rank not only amongst the most civilised and most socialised, but also as the longest unchanged, continuing civilisation in the world.

The Dreaming, the Dreamtime, not only refers to an historic heroic era in the long distant past but is a living continuation of spiritual life and instruction that continues today.

The real history, or rather, the historic place of Aborigines in this land has not yet been written nor, unfortunately, even dimly perceived by the most learned anthropologists and archaeologists of the day. This non-perception of Aboriginal beginnings, the Dreamtime, by anthropologists is not so surprising if we keep in mind that, by undergoing their own educational initiations, they are blinded to any probability that could upset their own value judgements, their philosophy, their religious beliefs or the vested interests of the society that feeds them. For instance, the anthropologist, even though he may reject a religious perspective, will be so imbued with the beliefs of his society that other possibilities are excluded. Surely it is illogical that man, *Homo sapiens*, the wise, originated solely 'somewhere in Africa or Europe'. Neither is it logical that God created the Arabic man within seven kilometres of Mecca and then the race bred, developed and dispersed; nor is it logical to accept the Biblical assertion of a singular 'Garden of Eden', where one Jewish man and one woman were created, then over millenia diversified, hybridised and multiplied into the many genetically different racial structures we see today. Yet the concept that in many lands there were many 'Gardens of Eden', or places where simultaneous development of *Homo sapiens* occurred, mingled and hybridised with pre-human types is rarely considered. (It is important to note that the Neanderthals only stopped flourishing as a type some short 50,000 years ago.)

Aboriginal pre-history, archaeologically speaking, extends some 45,000 years and the actual period of any intensive archaeological study of Aborigines is a mere forty years or so. Their studies, their findings, have not gone far past the top midden heap of supportive evidence which will, one day, establish the fact of the Dreamtime history, The Beginning.

The Beginning, the Time before time began, when the world was a twilight zone. The Great Creative Essence of Life, the Creator, had filled the land with creative spirits and, in a transmorphosis, these spirits took on physical shapes and became the progenitors of the modern mammals, animals, earthforms we see today, imbuing them with spiritual being. Amidst this creative spiritual chaos humankind was created and spiritually generated. The 'modern' type being came as a generative leap in physical and mental development. The Aboriginal Australian has been in this land from the Beginning. The migration theory will prove to be a wrong conclusion.

The people formed tribes. The tribes developed their civilisation. Land ownership rules regulated their daily lives, the Council of the Elders effectively maintained the government, created laws and gave judgement against the law breakers. They ascertained their land areas with neighbouring tribes and kept to their borders according to the Law.

As it was in the Beginning, the laws are such that every person, every sacred created thing has a precious valued status, for, since creation is sacred it follows that all things created are significantly sacred as well.

There were no barbaric wars, no slaves, no debasement of other humans, no prisoners.

The 'culture' developed when Aborigines formed co-operative tribal/family groups, setting up laws, expressing their daily lives through dance, creating artifacts, following the law, husbanding the resources of the land. They carried out communication by symbolised drawings, carvings, configurations on rocks, smoke fires, telepathy, inter-tribal symbols, initiation cycles, dance exchange and complex language patterns. All are part of a refined civilisation in existence long before written language was developed, a mere 5,000 years ago.

The Aboriginal religion, deemed animistic, is more akin to the Eastern religions in so far as the belief of spiritual return, telepathy, the silken cord, astral travelling, the third eye, tele-transportation, hypnosis and telekinesis are very much the basic part of Aboriginal religion. Most important is the spiritual knowledge, not only of creation and the Great Creative Spirit who maintains the soul, but also the fact that we are spiritually and physically co-existent and part of everything containing the life force; trees, soil, rocks, water, grass, clouds, celestial bodies etc.

When tribes discovered Captain Cook, they discovered not only the man, but the injustice, the viruses and bacteria that had travelled with him from his barbaric, heathen world of England.

Then came Philip and the colonists. The world of magic and love, equal status, value for life and peaceful co-existence soon was shattered. The Council, the wisest of the wise men, sang and danced and cried but the remedies, the checks, the law against the law breakers and harbingers of evil did not work against the barbarians who were not only killing by sword and gun, but were burning, flogging, poisoning the people and killing with some invisible magic which they, the whites, called the flu, the pox, pneumonia, tuberculosis, syphilis, gonorrhea and leprosy. The old men, the old magic couldn't stop these less-than-men, these barbaric invaders, from slaughtering the hunter as he sought food, then raping and murdering the women and children. They couldn't understand a society that raped and murdered, for the sake of murder. They understood even less why their magic wouldn't work. Their spirit law-keepers and their God had recoiled in horror, leaving them to become hapless victims of these colonists and convicts, these dregs of English society who were amongst the most rapacious scum on earth.

Two hundred years has elapsed since our land was invaded by white Australians. 200 years of victimisation, debasement of our humanity, attempts at physical and cultural genocide and undeclared war.

The tribes, physically decimated and

kept from their sacred areas and hunting/farming land, faced starvation and the terror of merciless unrelenting race murder. They hid in the remote areas, some finding protection and humanity with a few white settlers who, moved in human pity by the atrocities dealt the people, acted against the mainstream of opinion of their own white society. They nursed, fed, guarded and preserved the lives of the people.

After the land theft was accomplished by the whites, they placed the Aboriginal people into concentration camp areas, which they called 'Aboriginal Reserves'. When cries of outrage against the land theft and murders were raised in other nations, Australia defended its action by declaring to the world that the land was actually 'waste land and unoccupied' and that the undeclared war was 'peaceful settlement'. Also, that Aborigines had no civilisation, no law, no artifact, no agriculture or economic use of the land, no status as human beings and latterly, that 'Aborigines belong to the land, the land does not belong to the Aborigines'.

But in 1981 the spiritual essence has returned. The old men are re-linking the chain of law through initiation. Revelation is amongst the people. The ceremony is having effect and the whiteman's God (his crops and cattle), reel under the drought dance.

Soon the land will be used as our ally to regain the land and our people, now numbering only 150,000 (less than a quarter of the number that populated this land when the white terror struck) are demanding a rightful share in the affluence of wealth ripped out of our country and forming the rich, high standard of health and living enjoyed by whites and rated as one of the highest in the world. A living standard gained by ill-gotten means; the murder, deprivation and denial of the original owners, the Aborigines, who have suffered an intense psychological battering over 200 years. Australians should remember that the last government-sponsored massacre occurred less than 60 years ago, within living memory, and the most recent attempt at individual massacre was the strychnine poisoning at Alice Springs in March 1981. Physical and health conditions approximate those of Bangladesh. Aborigines suffer amongst the highest infant mortality, leprosy, curable blindness (Trachoma), malnutrition and tuberculosis rates in the world, in a country where whites claim they have eliminated these eighteenth century diseases in *their* society.

To whom do we turn for justice? The heads of white society? Do we humbly beg the thief to act as judge? Do we ask the grazier, who fattens his cattle, his family, on land that was robbed from us in the most dastardly manner, for the return of our rightful property or at least a viable land base and reparation throughout Australia? No. It is not logical to expect the tyrant, the thief, to relinquish his unlawful gains.

We need the force of conscience and law to achieve justice. We need to let the other peoples of the world know the reality, the scumminess and lack of morality of white Australia. We need to gain allies. We need to teach young white Australians about the spiritual flow of our lives and, in accordance with aboriginal Law, warn the offender, as I do, that if justice does not come soon from the offenders' quarter, come it will with terror and fire from another quarter; for from other corners of the world there are men and women who have a vested interest in justice and preserving the rights of humanity as conferred by the Great Creator.

Kevin Gilbert

Source: Social Alternatives Vol. 2 No. 2, Brisbane 1981.

New Caledonia's broad national liberation party, the Front de Libération Nationale Kanak et Socialiste (FLNKS) *was formed in 1984, after a congress which brought together many Kanak independence parties, organisations and committees. It organised the effective boycott of the 'internal autonomy' elections in November 1984 and set up a provisional government under Jean-Marie Tjibaou in December the same year.*[4]

In response the French government appointed a special envoy, Edgard Pisani who soon presented a plan for 'internal independence' for New Caledonia, with the metropolitan power retaining control over defence and security.[5] *The plan was rejected by the white settlers, and in January 1985 two members of the Kanak provisional government, Eloi Machoro and Marcel Nonaro were gunned down while peacefully surrendering to police sharp-shooters, during a meeting of the FLNKS. This, and further killings, precipitated the FLNKS into a solid pro-sovereignty position.*[6]

This speech was delivered by Tjibaou at a less stormy period, a few years before these events.

"I am always dual"

The Melanesian world has tried to give answers to the questions which work on the guts of all the human family . . . And the answer to the question 'where do we come from?' — on the soil of Caledonia — people have translated in the genealogies. It's 'the folk of a certain clan', 'it's the clan . . . Aramoto' . . . well, the Aramato, they left the straw, a certain family of straw, pushed on some mountain, and from this straw comes a certain clan, and in this clan . . .' Remember, those who believe the Bible, the genealogy of Jesus, 'son of David, son of Abraham, son of Adam' . . . we again find the same plan. But we find in the term genealogy a tree or an animal or a rock or thunder. It is the relation with the Earth, with the environment, with the countryside, with the soil. We aren't people otherwise. We are people who came out of this Earth. The ethnologists, the psychologists, the psychiatrists could speak at length on the psychoanalytical significance of this way of 'self-originating', but that isn't my purpose. I want to simply say: that's how it happens.

People come from a tree, from a rock, from a turtle, from an octopus, a stone, they come from thunder, and the thunder is the totem. It's important to point out that the connection with the totem is something sacred. If you are a descendant of a shark, you have the shark's protection . . . if you come from a pine tree you don't have the right to destroy this tree. Because these totems are your spirits. They are a part of you. You give them your respect and veneration . . .

In many places still, this connection with the totem remains a connection with the divinity. Through this relation comes the religious dimension with those that are 'behind the mirror'. To give an example: in our country in the month of March we dig out the new yams. We are going to eat the new yams. In many clans, in many families, there is a ceremony for eating the new yams. And it's forbidden to eat them before. Friday, when I went to my uncle's, he gave me something I call a medicine. This isn't a magical potion of Asterix (a character in a French cartoon on ancient Gaul) but it's a beverage made of herbs, of leaves, etc. He told me: 'Good, you drink this so that when you go into the world on your journeys, if you eat yams, the ancestors won't be harsh on you, because you'll have carried out the custom beforehand.' It's something sacred. Last year, at the time of digging up the new yams, my uncle brought us all together. At that time, we were struggling for the independence of our country. Well, he cooked the yams, opened the pot, and then he asked the ancestors to give us strength in our fight, to make us strong in our convictions and in our speech. So that our voices would be heard. Because sometimes one says true things but ears are closed.

The Bible says that there are hearts that are closed to the truth, where the spirit isn't open to the light. Well, this is a little in that direction . . . Next he made us eat . . . We drank several beverages for such and such precise thing. Next we got authorization to dig up the new yams and to eat them. Before, we couldn't. In all rural societies there are those things. But I believe that what's important is that it's *today*. How much longer? Twenty-five years, 15 years, the year 2000? I studied at the faculty of Lyon, in the Catholic schools. Then when I went back there, 1968 didn't 'liberate' me. And I am very happy for not being 'liberated'.

At the origin, there's the tree, the thunder, etc. Then there's a series of ancestors, and then there's us. And life passes through this genealogy, and this genealogy is that of my fathers, but it is also the clan which gave my mother, and that, in giving my mother, gives me life. The father gives the character, the social rule, the Earth. Life is given by blood. It's the mother who gives the blood. And the owner of the blood, it's her, her brothers, her fathers. I'm always *dual*. I'm never *individual*. I can't be individual. The body isn't a principle of individualization. The body is always the *connection*. The body, it's blood. And the blood, it's the mother. And the owner of this part of me, it's my maternal uncles.

It's for that reason that when a child comes into the world, we give presents to the mother to pay homage to her, to bless her because she is fertile, because she has given life, she has enlarged our clan. My children have my name. They have the social rule that my name gives them. We have in the clan four or five names. They're like the equivalent of roles in some social affairs. They aren't names which anyone can use like a key. They aren't public names. The names are the property of the clans. If you take the names I give . . . we will make war! Or you will receive the curse of the ancestors, you will become sick, you will die. Well, the children receive the name, receive the paternal rule, unless they're retaken by the mother, in compensation. My mother comes from your home, she can retake one of her sons for herself. For she guards the rule, her line in her family, and she guards her name . . .

That is the principle of life, and I believe that it's fundamental for understanding the difference and also the difficulties of adaptation of Melanesians to the modern world. We are never . . . I am never *me*. 'Me' is tied to the individual. I am always someone *in reference to.* In reference to my fathers, in reference to my uncles. That is very serious in modern society for making decisions, and especially rapid decisions. Well, we are always in the process of consulting, holding councils, palavers. And one has problems because one isn't rapid enough. That's important. It's important because this connection that exists at the level of the individual, of the man, finds itself in the society. There is only someone *in reference to.* Always. In that context, I spoke of the person who comes out of this, it's the person who guards alliances well on one side or the other. With the fathers, and with the uncles. The maternal uncles and the mothers. One little detail: my mother, with all her sisters, these are 'mamas', and my father with his brothers, his cousins, these are 'papas'. European businesses in Caledonia sometimes have problems when an employee goes to bury a grandfather. And afterwards it's another grandfather, and then another grandfather! Finally, it's his/her mother, and there are many mothers. Because all sisters of the mother, the first cousins of the mother, etc, are 'mamas'.

There's also the conception of life's outcome: where is the prestige? This is a very gross idea. In the Melanesian system, to be a prestigious person, it's necessary to 'have', of course, like everyone else. It is thus necessary to work, or to have a large family that permits you to 'have' a lot. A 'having' that renews itself with work. But to have doesn't make prestige. The prestige is in giving, of giving a lot, and of giving it everywhere. It is the opposite of the capitalist world!

The soil is very important because it constitutes the *archives.* It is this that contains the archives of the group . . . It's the Earth that implants the genealogy. The genealogies don't have a direction if they aren't inscribed in space, in a precise spot. 'Jesus, son of David', it is people that are from a *certain place.* Take away this genealogy from this soil, and it no longer has direction . . . Me, today, I have a notebook, on which I've written the things that I wanted to say. Later on, my children will be able to look at this paper, and see that I said all this in Geneva. In the earth of my country, in my tribe, genealogy . . . the notebook, it's the Earth, it's a certain stone with a certain spring. And at a certain place that has a certain name, there begins history. One continues, one continues, down to the water, and one has a root, a spatiality, one is historical with regard to this space. Otherwise, one has no history. One is a citizen of the world and of nowhere.

Jean-Marie Tjibaou

Source: A 1981 speech by the President of the FLNKS (Kanaky) transcribed by *Esprit* magazine and translated from a shortened version in *Le Monde*, Paris, 3 December 1984, by Zoltan Grossman.

Notes: Part 1

1. Charles Darwin, *The Descent of Man*, London 1901 (originally 1871) page 945.
2. For an intelligent summary of the connection between Darwin's new biology and the racist eugenics movement see Derek Freeman's *Margaret Mead and Samoa, the making and unmaking of an anthropological myth*, Harvard University Press, 1983, especially pages 3-18. Reprinted by Penguin Books, Harmondsworth, with a new preface, in 1984.
It is worth noting that Joseph Mengele, who refined biological determinism for the National Socialist Party of Germany into practices which defy expletive, was given refuge in recent years by at least two South American regimes that have openly practised ethnocide against their indigenous peoples — Paraguay and Brazil.
3. Voluminous explanations of the proper names used in this oral account are to be found in the Aileen O'Bryan article from which this piece is taken. They are not included here.
4. Pacific Peoples Anti-nuclear Action Committee *Newsletter*, Auckland, 1984.
5. Ingrid A. Kirche *The Kanaks of New Caledonia*, Minority Rights Group Report No. 71, London, 1986 p. 11.
6. *Pacific Bulletin*, PCRC, Honolulu, Vol. 5, No. 1, February 1985.

Part 2
Dispossession

1.   The Avenging Angel

A letter by Francisco de Montejo Xiu, 1567 (Maya)

After we learned the good, in knowing God our Lord as the only true God, leaving our blindness and idolatries, and Your Majesty as temporal lord, before we could well open our eyes to the one and the other, there came upon us a persecution of the worst that can be imagined; and it was in the year '62, on the part of the Franciscan religious, who had taken us to teach the doctrine, instead of which they began to torment us, hanging us by the hands and whipping us cruelly, hanging weights of stone on our feet, torturing many of us in a windlass, giving the torture of the water, from which many died or were maimed.

Being in these tribulations and burdens, trusting in Your Majesty's Justice to hear and defend us, there came the Dr. Quijada to aid our tormentors, saying that we were idolators and sacrificers of men, and many other things against all truth, which we never committed during our time of blindness and infidelity. And as we see ourselves maimed by cruel tortures, many dead of them, robbed of our property, and yet more, seeing disinterred the bones of our baptized ones, who died as Christians, we came to despair.

Not content with this, the religious [i.e. the friars] and the royal Justice held at Mani a solemn auto of inquisition, where they seized many statues, disinterred many dead and burned them there in public; made slaves of many to save Spaniards, . . . the one and the other gave us great wonder and fear, because we did not know what it all was, having been recently baptized, and not informed; and when we returned to our people and told them to hear and guard justice, they seized us, put us in prison and chains, like slaves, in the monastery at Merida, where many of us died; and they told us we would be burned, without our knowing the why.

At this time came the bishop whom Your Majesty sent, who, although he took us from prison and relieved us from death and the *sambenitos,* has not relieved us from the shame of the charges that were made against us, that we were idolaters, human sacrificers, and had slain many men; because, at the last, he is of the habit of San Francisco and does for them. He has consoled us by his words, saying that Your Majesty would render justice.

A receptor came from Mexico, and made inquiry, and we believe it went to the Audiencia, and nothing has been done.

Then came as governor Don Luis de Céspedes, and instead of relieving us he has increased our burdens, taking away our daughters and wives to serve the Spaniards, against their wills and ours; which we feel so greatly that the common people say that not in the time of our infidelity were we so vexed or maltreated, because our ancestors never took from one of his children, nor from husbands their wives to make use of them, as today does Your Majesty's Justice, even to the service of the Negroes and mulattoes.

And with all our afflictions and labors, we have loved the fathers and supplied their necessities, have built many monasteries for them, provided with ornaments and bells, all at our cost and that of our vassals and fellows; although in payment of our services they have made of us their vassals, have deprived us of the signories we inherited from our ancestors, a thing we never suffered in the time of our infidelity. And we obey Your Majesty's Justice, hoping that you will send us remedy.

One thing that has greatly dismayed and stirred us up, is the letters written by Fray Diego de Landa, chief author of all these ills and burdens, saying that Your Majesty has approved the killings, robberies, tortures, slaveries and other cruelties inflicted on us; to which we wonder that such things should be said of so Catholic and upright a king as is Your Majesty. If it is told that we have sacrificed men after we received baptism, it is a great and false witness invented by them to gild their cruelties.

And if there have been or are idols among us, they are but those we have gathered to send to the religious as they required of us, saying that we had confessed to their possession under the torture; but all know that we went many leagues to gather from places where we knew that they had been kept by those before us, and which we had abandoned when we were baptized; and in good conscience they should not punish us as they have done.

If Your Majesty wishes to learn of all, send a person to search the truth, to learn of our innocence and the great cruelty of the *padres*; and had not the bishop come, we should all have been brought to an end. And though we cherish well Fray Diego and the other *padres* who torment us, only to hear them named causes our entrails to revolt. Therefore, Your Majesty, send us other ministers to teach us and preach to us the law of God, for we much desire our salvation.

The religious of San Francisco of this province have written certain letters to Your Majesty and to the general of the order, in praise of Fray Diego and his other companions, who were those who tortured, killed and put us to scandal; and they gave certain letters written in the Castilian language to certain Indians of their familiars, and thus they signed them and sent them to Your Majesty. May Your Majesty understand that they are not ours, we who are chiefs of this land, and who did not have to write lies nor falsehoods nor contradictions. May Fray Diego de Landa and his companions suffer the penance for the evils they have done to us, and may our descendants to the fourth generation be recompensed the great persecutions that came on us.

May God guard Your Majesty for many years in his sacred service and for our good and protection.

From Yucatán, the 12th of April, 1567.

Francisco de Montejo Xiu

Source: William Gates, *Yucatán before and after the Conquest*, pp. 115–7.

2. Indian Wars

"LET THEM COME THEN. I HEAR THEM AND SEE
THEM IN THE SOUTH AND IN THE EAST. THEY COME
LIKE THE SUMMER LEAVES ROLLING AND RUSTLING
IN THE BREEZE. IT IS WELL. SHALL TECUMSEH
TREMBLE? SHALL THEY SAY THAT HE HATED THE
WHITE MAN AND FEARED HIM? NO! THE MOUNTAINS
AND PLAINS WHICH THE GREAT SPIRIT GAVE ARE
BEHIND AND AROUND ME. I, TOO, HAVE MY
WARRIORS AND HERE, WHERE WE WERE BORN, ARE
WE NOW PREPARED TO DIE — ON THE RIVERS OF
THE SCIOTO, THE WABASH, AND ON THE BROAD
WATERS OF THE NORTH. OVER THESE SHALL MY
VOICE BE HEARD!'

Tecumseh's war-cry on hearing of the Americans' threat to
exterminate both him and his people, the Shawnees.

*More treaties were signed between the white invaders and Indian nations in
the United States than in any other country; indeed, more than in all other
colonial territories put together. Yet every one of these has been broken,
and in all cases the violators have been white — the military, cattle-barons,
gold-seekers, the US Congress and more recently mining companies.*[1]

*The full story of America's violation of its own Constitution may not yet
have been told: a wave of right-wing legislation broke on Congress in the
1970s and early 1980s attempting to extinguish Indian land titles once and
for all. Although these bills did not succeed, the Reagan administration has
made it abundantly clear that it wants an end to land reclamation, the
abnegation of outstanding treaty claims, and the opening-up of huge tracts
of public land to oil, gas, coal, uranium and other mineral exploitation.*[2]

*In the years of colonisation, Indian nations living near the sea-board,
particularly in Florida and California, were decimated — though others
have been militant and skilful in pushing their demands.*[3] *Further north, the
Six Nations and the Ojibway held out against the invaders longer and more
successfully than other Indian communities, largely because of the nature
of their terrain, the ambivalent attitudes of the first settlers*[4] *and native
diplomatic and guerrilla skills.*[5]

For the great majority of America's original inhabitants, however, the white man's 'Manifest Destiny'[6] offered no quarter and no compromise. The Cherokee, Chickasaw, Choctaw, Creek and Seminole were given the choice of assimilation (taking an allotment of land and living on it) or compulsory removal. The Cherokee — who, by 1827, had their own constitutional republic, schools, written language and newspaper (The Cherokee Phoenix) *resisted. Although the US Supreme Court upheld an early Treaty guaranteeing their land[7] the Georgia legislature banned the Cherokee from mining it, and eased the way for thousands of white prospectors to invade the reservation. In the ensuing forced march to 'Indian Territory' — newly opened up on barren land in Oklahoma — 4,000 out of 14,000 Cherokee died. This was the infamous 'Trail of Tears'. Other tribes were uprooted and compelled to march to Oklahoma well into the last quarter of the 19th Century.[8]*

Over the next 30 years the railroad, gold-diggers, property speculators, ranchers and other settlers, moved against the Apache and Navajo in the south-west and the Lakota, Cheyenne and other nations on the Plains.[9] What open genocide did not accomplish by 1880, the Dawes Act did in 1887, with the 'allotment' of reservation land to turn ignorant and recalcitrant Indians into 'good whites'.[10] By the time this legislation was officially ended in 1934 (with the Indian Reorganization Act) almost two thirds of the Indian land base had been surrendered: 90 out of 150 million acres.[11]

The pieces which follow trace the effects of this genocidal process through the words of the chiefs who survived what many of their comrades could not endure. Unfortunately we usually are not aware what the followers felt and spoke and the statements of the chiefs all come through the medium of officials, missionaries or other whites who interpreted them. For this reason they must be viewed with caution, but should not be dismissed. Indeed, they are often quoted by today's native Americans in support of their own struggles to regain the land and treaty rights stripped from them over the past 200 years.

Beware of friends as these

I admit that there are good white men, but they bear no proportion to the bad; the bad must be the strongest for they rule. They do what they please. They enslave those who are not of their color, although created by the same Great Spirit who created them. They would make slaves of us if they could; but as they cannot do it, they kill us. There is no faith to be placed in their words.

They are not like the Indians who are only enemies while at war, and are friends in peace. They will say to an Indian, 'My friend; my brother!' They will take him by the hand and, at the same moment destroy him. And you will also be treated by them before long. Remember that this day I warned you to beware of such friends as these. I know the Long-knives. They are not to be trusted.

Pachgantachilias, Delaware 1787

Source: To Serve the Devil, edited by Paul Jacobs and Saul Landau with Eve Pell, Vol. I, p. 12, Vintage Books, New York, 1971.

In an address to George Washington at Philadelphia (then the seat of colonial government) in 1791, Seneca Chief Cornplant begged the President to restore lands taken from his people by the Treaty of Fort Stanwix, signed a few years earlier.

"That we may know if you are just",

FATHER! THE VOICE OF THE SENECA NATION SPEAKS TO YOU, the Great Counsellor, in whose heart the wise men of all the thirteen fires [thirteen states], have placed their wisdom. What we may have to say may appear small in your ears and we therefore entreat you to hearken with attention, for we are about to speak of things of very great importance.

When your army entered the country of the Six Nations we called you the TOWN DESTROYER, and to this day, when that terrible name is heard, our women look behind and turn pale, and our children cling to the breasts of their mothers. Our Counsellors and Warriors are men, and cannot be afraid, but their hearts are grieved on account of the distress of our women and children.

Father! when that great country was surrendered, there were but few Chiefs present, and they were compelled to give it up and it is not the Six Nations only that reproach these Chiefs with giving up that country; the Chippewas, and all the Nations who lived on those lands, westward, call to us and ask us, 'brothers of our fathers, where is the place you have reserved for us to lie down upon?'

Father! you have compelled us to do that which has made us ashamed. We have nothing to answer to the children of the brothers of our fathers. When, last Spring, they called upon us to go to war, to secure a bed to lie upon, the Senecas entreated them to be quiet, until we had spoken to you . . .

Father! we will not conceal from you, that the Great God, and not man, has preserved Cornplant from the hands of his own Nation; for they ask continually: 'where is the Land which our children, and their children after them are to lie upon?' You told us, they say, 'that the line drawn from Pennsylvania to Lake Ontario, would mark it forever on the East; and the line running from Beaver Creek to Pennyslvania, would mark it on the West, and we see that it is not so. For first one, and then another, comes and takes it away, by order of that people which *you* tell us promised to secure it to us.' He is silent, for he has nothing to answer. When the Sun goes down, he opens his heart before his God, and earlier than the Sun appears upon the hills, he gives thanks for his protection during the night; for he feels that among men, made desperate by their wrongs, it is God alone that can preserve him. He loves peace, and all that he had in store he has given to those who have been robbed by your people, lest they should plunder the innocent to repay themselves. The whole season, while others have been employed in providing for their families, he has spent in his endeavours to preserve peace, and at this moment his wife and children are lying on the ground, and in want of food; his heart is pained for them, but he perceives that the Great God will try his firmness in doing what is right.

Father! you have said we are in your hand, and that by shutting it you could crush us to nothing. Are you determined to crush us?

Father! innocent men of our Nation are killed, one after another, and of our best families, but none of your people who have committed these murders have been punished. We now ask you, was it intended that your people should kill the Senecas, and not only remain unpunished by you, but be protected by you against the revenge of the next of kin?

Father! these are to us very great things. We know that you are very strong — we have heard you are wise — and we now wait to receive your answer to what we have said, that we may know if you are just.

Chief Cornplant

Farewell, My Nation! Farewell!

Soon after our return home, news reached us that a war was going to take place between the British and the Americans.

Runners continued to arrive from different tribes, all confirming the reports of the expected war. The British agent, Colonel Dixon, was holding talks with, and making presents to, the different tribes. I had not made up my mind whether to join the British or remain neutral. I had not discovered yet one good trait in the character of the Americans who had come to the country. They made fair promises but never fulfilled them, while the British made but few, and we could always rely implicitly on their word.

One of our people having killed a Frenchman at Prairie du Chien, the

British took him prisoner and said they would shoot him next day. His family were encamped a short distance below the mouth of the Wisconsin. He begged for permission to go and see them that night as he was to die the next day. They permitted him to go after he had promised them to return by sunrise the next morning.

He visited his family, which consisted of his wife and six children. I cannot describe their meeting and parting so as to be understood by the whites, as it appears that their feelings are acted upon by certain rules laid down by their preachers, while ours are governed by the monitor within us. He bade his loved ones the last sad farewell and hurried across the prairie to the fort and arrived in time. The soldiers were ready and immediately marched out and shot him down . . .

Why did the Great Spirit ever send the whites to this island to drive us from our homes and introduce among us poisonous liquors, disease, and death? They should have remained in the land the Great Spirit allotted to them. But I will proceed with my story. My memory, however, is not very good since my late visit to the white people. I have still a buzzing noise in my ears . . . I may give some parts of my story out of place, but will make my best endeavor to be correct.

[*Some chiefs were called upon to go to Washington to see the Great Father, who wanted them in case of war to remain neutral, promising them to let the traders sell to them in the fall goods on credit, that they might hunt and repay with furs in the spring, as the British had arranged it up to then. Everything depended for the Sac upon this institution. But — the trader refused bluntly to sell on credit.*]

The war chief said the trader could not furnish us on credit, and that he had received no instructions from our Great Father at Washington. We left the fort dissatisfied and went to camp. What was now to be done we knew not . . . Few of us slept that night. All was gloom and discontent.

[*As a result of this treatment they joined the British.*]

Our lodges were soon taken down, and we all started for Rock Island. Here ended all hopes of our remaining at peace, having been forced into war by being deceived . . .

We continued our march, joining the British below Detroit, soon after which we had a battle. The Americans fought well and drove us back with considerable loss. I was greatly surprised at this, as I had been told that the Americans would not fight . . .

On my arrival at the village I was met by the chiefs and braves and conducted to the lodge which was prepared for me. After eating, I gave a full account of all that I had seen and done. I explained to my people the manner in which the British and Americans fought. Instead of stealing upon each other and taking every advantage to kill the enemy and save their own people as we do, which with us is considered good policy in a war chief, they march out in open daylight and fight regardless of the number of warriors they may lose. After the battle is over they retire to feast and drink wine as if nothing had happened. After which they make a statement in writing of what they have done, each party claiming the victory and neither giving an account of half the number that have been killed on their own side.

[*The British lose constantly. After a long time of consideration and many councils Black Hawk decides to make a treaty of peace with the 'chief at St. Louis.'*]

The great chief at St. Louis having sent word for us to come down and confirm the treaty, we did not hesitate but started immediately that we might smoke the peace pipe with him. On our arrival we met the great chiefs in council. They explained to us the words of our Great Father in Washington, accusing us of heinous crimes and many misdemeanors, particularly in not coming down when first invited. We knew very well that our Great Father had deceived us and thereby forced us to join the British, and could not believe that he had put this speech into the mouths of those chiefs to deliver to us. I was not a civil chief and consequently made no reply, but our civil chiefs told the commissioners: 'What you say is a lie. Our Great Father sent us no such speech, he knew that the situation in which we had been placed was caused by him.' The white chiefs appeared very angry at this reply and said, 'We will break off the treaty and make war against you, as you have grossly insulted us.'

Our chiefs had no intention of insulting them and told them so, saying, 'We merely wish to explain that you have told us a lie, without any desire to make you angry, in the same manner that you whites do when you do not believe what is told you.' The council then proceeded and the pipe of peace was smoked.

Here for the first time I touched the goose quill to sign the treaty, not knowing, however, that by the act I consented to give away my village. Had that been explained to me I should have opposed it and never would have signed their treaty, as my recent conduct will clearly prove. What do we know of the manners, the laws, and the customs of the white people? They might buy our bodies for dissection, and we would touch the goose quill to confirm it and not know what we were doing. This was the case with me and my people in touching the goose quill the first time.

We can only judge of what is proper and right by our standard of what is right and wrong, which differs widely from the whites', if I have been correctly informed. The whites may do wrong all their lives and then if they are sorry for it when about to die, all is well, but with us it is different. We must continue to do good throughout our lives. If we have corn and meat, and know of a family that have none, we divide with them. If we have more blankets than we absolutely need, and others have not enough, we must give to those who are in want.

[*As Black Hawk could not yield to the demand of the 'white chiefs' and leave his village and his graveyard, a war ensued, the so-called Black Hawk War, lasting from 1831–2. Chief Keokuk, his great antagonist, who was willing to negotiate with the whites and persuaded part of the tribe to abandon the village, caused thus a rift among the Sac.*]

I looked upon Keokuk as a coward and no brave . . . What right had these people [*the whites*] to our village and our fields, which the Great Spirit had given us to live upon? My reason teaches me that land cannot be sold. The Great Spirit gave it to his children to live upon and cultivate as far as necessary for their subsistence, and so long as they occupy and cultivate it they have the right to the soil, but if they voluntarily leave it, then any other people have a right to settle on it. Nothing can be sold but such things as can be carried away.

[*It was at Fort Crawford that Black Hawk, in the despair of defeat, said:*

'*Farewell, my nation! Farewell, Black Hawk!*']

The massacre which terminated the war lasted about two hours. Our loss in killed was about sixty, besides a number that was drowned . . .

I was now given up by the agent to the commanding officer at Fort Crawford, the White Beaver [*General Atkinson*] having gone down the river.

On our way down I surveyed the country that had cost us so much trouble, anxiety, and blood, and that now caused me to be a prisoner of war. I reflected upon the ingratitude of the whites when I saw their fine houses, rich harvests, and everything desirable around them; and recollected that all this land had been ours, for which I and my people had never received a dollar, and that the whites were not satisfied until they took our village and our graveyards from us and removed us across the Mississippi.

On our arrival at Jefferson Barracks we met the great war chief, White Beaver, who had commanded the American army against my little band. I felt the humiliation of my situation; a little while before I had been leader of my braves, now I was a prisoner of war. He received us kindly and treated us well.

We were now confined to the barracks and forced to wear the ball and chain. This was extremely mortifying and altogether useless. Was the White Beaver afraid I would break out of his barracks and run away? Or was he ordered to inflict this punishment upon me? If I had taken him prisoner on the field of battle I would not have wounded his feelings so much by such treatment, knowing that a brave war chief would prefer death to dishonor. But I do not blame the White Beaver for the course he pursued, as it is the custom among white soldiers, and I suppose was a part of his duty.

Black Hawk

Source: The Autobiography of Black Hawk, dictated by himself to Antoine LeClair 1833, edited by J. B. Patterson, US, 1882.

The **Testimony of Chief Sealth** *(usually called Seattle) has probably become the most-quoted single statement by any native American. Although it tends not to feature in early anthologies of American Indian oratory, it now has a secure place in numerous small-press editions, on calendars, postcards, greetings cards and posters. It is not hard to see why: in his rounded condemnation of white urban society and evocation of a holist, environmentally sacrosanct native alternative, Sealth crystallises the fears and yearnings of the new 'green' movement like none other. But the historical context of the Declaration is equally important: Sealth was welcoming the whites to his native Duwamish country (now in Washington state) at a tribal assembly held in 1854 to prepare for the signing of the Treaties. By the time of his death in 1866, Sealth had converted to Christianity.*

THE GREAT CHIEF IN WASHINGTON
sends word that he wishes to
buy our land.

The Great Chief also sends us words
of friendship and good will. This
is kind of him, since we know he
has little need of our friendship
in return.

But we will consider your
offer. For we know that if
we do not sell, the white
man may come with guns and
take our land.

How can you buy or sell the
sky, the warmth of the land?
The idea is strange to us.

If we do not own the freshness

of the air and the sparkle of
the water, how can you buy them?

Every part of this earth is
sacred to my people. Every
shining pine needle, every
sandy shore, every mist in
the dark woods, every clearing
and humming insect is holy in
the memory and experience of
my people. The sap which courses
through the trees carries the
memories of the red man.

The white man's dead forget
the country of their birth
when they go to walk among
the stars. Our dead never forget
this beautiful earth, for
it is the mother of the red man.
We are part of the earth and it
is part of us.

The perfumed flowers
are our sisters;
the deer, the horse, the great eagle,
these are our brothers.
The rocky crests,
the juices of the meadows,
the body heat of the pony, and man
— all belong to the same family.
So, when the Great Chief in
Washington sends word that he
wishes to buy our land, he asks
much of us.

The Great Chief sends word he
will reserve us a place so that
we can live comfortably to
ourselves, he will be our father
and we will be his children.

So we will consider your offer
to buy our land. But it will not
be easy. For this land is sacred
to us.

This shining water that moves
in the streams and rivers is not
just water but the blood of our
ancestors. If we sell you land,
you must remember that it is
sacred, and you must teach your
children that it is sacred and
that each ghostly reflection in
the clear water of the lakes
tells of events and memories in
the life of my people. The water's
murmur is the voice of my father's
father.

The rivers are our brothers,
they quench our thirst. The
rivers carry our canoes, and
feed our children. If we sell
you our land, you must remember,
and teach your children, that
the rivers are our brothers,
and yours, and you must henceforth
give the rivers the kindness
you would give any brother.

The red man has always retreated
before the advancing white man,
as the mist of the mountains runs
before the morning sun. But the
ashes of our fathers are sacred.
Their graves are holy ground,
and so these hills, these trees,
this portion of the earth is
consecrated to us. We know that
the white man does not understand
our ways. One portion of land is
the same to him as the next, for
he is a stranger who comes in the
night and takes from the land
whatever he needs. The earth is
not his brother, but his enemy,
and when he has conquered it, he
moves on. He leaves his fathers'
graves behind, and he does not
care. He kidnaps the earth from
his children. He does not care.
His fathers' graves and his children's
birthright are forgotten.
He treats his mother, the earth,
and his brother, the sky, as
things to be bought, plundered,
sold like sheep or bright beads.
His appetite will devour the
earth and leave behind only a
desert.

I do not know. Our ways are
different from your ways. The
sight of your cities pains the
eyes of the red man. But perhaps
it is because the red man is a
savage and does not understand.

There is no quiet place in the
white man's cities. No place to
hear the unfurling of leaves in
spring or the rustle of insect's
wings. But perhaps it is because
I am a savage and do not
understand. The clatter only seems to
insult the ears. And what is there
to life if a man cannot hear the
lonely cry of the whippoorwill or
the arguments of the frogs around
a pond at night? I am a red man
and do not understand. The Indian
prefers the soft sound of the
wind darting over the face of a
pond, and the smell of the wind
itself, cleansed by a midday rain
or scented with the piñon pine.

The air is precious to the red
man, for all things share the
same breath — the beast, the tree,
the man, they all share the same
breath. The white man does not

seem to notice the air he breathes.
Like a man dying for many days,
he is numb to the stench. But if
we sell you our land, you must
remember that the air is precious
to us, that the air shares its
spirit with all the life it
supports. The wind that gave our
grandfather his first breath also
receives his last sigh. And the
wind must also give our children
the spirit of life. And if we sell
you our land, you must keep it
apart and sacred, as a place where
even the white man can go to taste
the wind that is sweetened by the
meadow's flowers.

So we will consider your offer to
buy our land. If we decide to
accept, I will make one condition:
The white man must treat the beasts
of this land as his brothers.

I am a savage and I do not
understand any other way. I
have seen a thousand rotting
buffalos on the prairie, left
by the white man
who shot them
from a passing train. I am a

savage and I do not understand
how the smoking iron horse can
be more important than the buffalo
that we kill only to stay
alive.

What is man without the beasts?
If all the beasts were gone, men
would die from a great loneliness
of spirit. For whatever happens
to the beasts, soon happens to
man. All things are connected.

You must teach your children that
the ground beneath their feet is
the ashes of our grandfathers. So
that they will respect the land,
tell your children that the earth
is rich with the lives of our kin.
Teach your children what we have
taught our children, that the
earth is our mother. Whatever
befalls the earth befalls the
sons of the earth. If men spit
upon the ground, they spit upon
themselves.

This we know. The earth does not
belong to man; man belongs to the
earth. This we know. All things
are connected like the blood
which unites one family. All
things are connected.

Whatever befalls the earth befalls
the sons of the earth. Man did not
weave the web of life, he is merely
a strand in it. Whatever he
does to the web, he does to himself.

But we will
consider your
offer to go to
the reservation
you have for my
people. We will
live apart, and
in peace. It matters
little where we

spend the rest of our days. Our
children have seen their fathers
humbled in defeat. Our warriors
have felt shame, and after defeat
they turn their days in idleness
and contaminate their bodies with
sweet foods and strong drink. It
matters little where we pass the
rest of our days. They are not
many. A few more
hours, a few more
winters, and none
of the children of
the great tribes
that once lived on
this earth or that
roam now in small
bands in the woods
will be left to
mourn the graves
of a people once
as powerful and
hopeful as yours.
But why should I
mourn the passing
of my people?
Tribes are made
of men, nothing
more. Men come and go, like the
waves of the sea.

Even the white man, whose God
walks and talks with him as
friend to friend, cannot be
exempt from the common destiny.
We may be brothers after all;
we shall see. One thing we know,
which the white man
may one day discover
— our God is the same
God. You may think
now that you own Him
as you wish to own
our land, but you
cannot. He is the God
of man and His compassion is

equal for the red man
and the white. This earth is
precious to Him and to harm
the earth is to heap contempt
on its Creator. The whites too
shall pass; perhaps sooner than
all other tribes. Continue to
contaminate your bed, and you
will one night suffocate in
your own waste.

But in your perishing you will
shine brightly, fired by the
strength of the God who brought
you to this land and for some
special purpose gave you dominion
over this land and over the red
man. That destiny is a mystery
to us, for we do not understand
when the buffalo are all
slaughtered, the wild horses are
tamed, the secret corners of the
forest heavy with the scent of many
men and the view of the ripe
hills blotted by talking wires.

Where is the thicket? Gone.
Where is the eagle? Gone.
And what is it to say goodbye

to the swift pony and the hunt?
The end of living and the
beginning of survival.

So we will consider your offer
to buy our land. If we agree
it will be to secure the
reservation you have promised.
There, perhaps, we may live out our
brief days as we wish. When the
last red man has vanished from
this earth, and his memory is
only the shadow of a cloud
moving across the prairie,
these shores and forests will
still hold the spirits of my
people. For they love this earth
as the new-born loves its mother's
heartbeat. So if we sell you
our land, love it as we've loved it.
Care for it as we've cared
for it. Hold in your mind the
memory of the land as it is
when you take it. And with all

your strength, with all your
mind, with all your heart,
preserve it for your children
and love it . . . as God loves us all.

One thing we know. Our God
is the same God. This earth is
precious to Him. Even the
white man cannot be exempt
from the common destiny. We
may be brothers after all.
We shall see.

Chief Seattle

The Poncas were removed from their land in Dakota in the early 1870s and force-marched to 'Indian Territory' in Oklahoma. After a horrendous attrition, some of them, led by Chief Standing Bear, made their way to Nebraska, where the Omahas gave them a piece of their own reserve. Here they were arrested and brought before a local court where the US government contended that they were not 'entitled to protection of the writ of habeas corpus not being a person or citizen under the law'.[12] The judge ruled against the government, however: a Presidential commission galvanised by public disquiet later settled 600 of the Poncas in Oklahoma and 250 on the reservation in Nebraska. As John Upton Terrell commented on this criminal episode:

'The Government was the victor. It had succeeded in breaking and dividing a small peaceful people whose loyalty to the United States had never wavered. It had killed some two hundred of them . . . men, women and children.'[13]

"We would rather have died"

'We lived on our land as long as we can remember. No one knows how long ago we came there. The land was owned by our tribe as far back as memory of men goes.

'We were living quietly on our farms. All of a sudden one white man came. We had no idea what for. This was the inspector. He came to our tribe with Rev. Mr. Hinman. These two, with the agent, James Lawrence, they made our trouble.

'They said the President told us to pack up — that we must move to the Indian Territory.

'The inspector said to us: "The President says you must sell this land. He will buy it and pay you the money, and give you new land in the Indian Territory."

'We said to him: "When two persons wish to make a bargain, they can talk together and find out what each wants, and then make their agreement."

'We said to him: "We do not wish to go. When a man owns anything, he does not let it go till he has received payment for it."

'We said to him: "We will see the President first."

'He said to us: "I will take you to see the new land. If you like it, then you can see the President, and tell him so. If not, then you can see him and tell him so." And he took all ten of our chiefs down. I went, and Bright Eyes' uncle went. He took us to look at three different pieces of land. He said we must take one of the three pieces, so the President said. After he took us down there he said: "No pay for the land you left."

'We said to him: "You have forgotten what you said before we started. You said we should have pay for our land. Now you say not. You told us then you were speaking truth." All these three men took us down there. The man got very angry. He tried to compel us to take one of the three pieces of land. He told us to be brave. He said to us: "If you do not accept these, I will leave you here alone. You are one thousand miles from home. You have no money. You have no interpreter, and you cannot speak the language." And he went out and slammed the door. The man talked to us from long before sundown till it was nine o'clock at night.

'We said to him: "We do not like this land. We could not support ourselves. The water is bad. Now send us to Washington, to tell the President, as you promised."

'He said to us: "The President did not tell me to take you to Washington; neither did he tell me to take you home."

'We said to him: "You have the Indian money you took to bring us down here. That money belongs to us. We would like to have some of it. People do not give away food for nothing. We must have money to buy food on the road."

'He said to us: "I will not give you a cent."

'We said to him: "We are in a strange country. We cannot find our way home. Give us a pass, that people may show us our way."

'He said: "I will not give you any."

'We said to him: "This interpreter is ours. We pay him. Let him go with us."

'He said: "You shall not have the interpreter. He is mine, and not yours."

'We said to him: "Take us at least to the railroad; show us the way to that."

'And he would not. He left us right there. It was winter. We started for home on foot. At night we slept in haystacks. We barely lived till morning, it was so cold. We had nothing but our blankets. We took the ears of corn that had dried in the fields. We ate it raw. The soles of our moccasins wore out. We were barefoot in the snow. We were nearly dead when we reached the Otoe Reserve. It had been fifty days. We stayed there ten days to strengthen up, and the Otoes gave each of us a pony. The agent of the Otoes told us he had received a telegram from the inspector, saying that the Indian chiefs had run away; not to give us food or shelter, or help in any way. The agent said: "I would like to understand. Tell me all that has happened. Tell me the truth."

'Then we told our story to the agent and to the Otoe chiefs —how we had been left down there to find our way.

'The agent said: "I can hardly believe it possible that any one could have treated you so. That inspector was a poor man to have done this. If I had taken chiefs in this way, I would have brought them home; I could not have left them there."

'In seven days we reached the Omaha Reservation. Then we sent a telegram to the President: asked him if he had authorized this thing. We waited three days for the answer. No answer came.

'In four days we reached our own home. We found the inspector there. While we were gone, he had come to our people and told them to move.

'Our people said: "Where are our chiefs? What have you done with them? Why have you not brought them back? We will not move till our chiefs come back."

'Then the inspector told them: "Tomorrow you must be ready to move. If you are not ready you will be shot." Then the soldiers came to the doors with their bayonets, and ten families were frightened. The soldiers brought wagons; they put their things in and were carried away. The rest of the tribe would not move.

'When we got there, we asked the inspector why he had done this thing, and he got very angry.

'Then we said to him: "We did not think we would see your face again, after what has passed. We thought never to see your face any more. But here you are."

'We said to him: "This land is ours. It belongs to us. You have no right to take it from us. The land is crowded with people, and only this is left to us."

'We said to him: "Let us alone. Go away from us. If you want money, take all the money which the President is to pay us for twelve years to come. You may have it all, if you will go and leave us our lands."

'Then, when he found that we would not go, he wrote for more soldiers to come.

'Then the soldiers came, and we locked our doors, and the women and children hid in the woods. Then the soldiers drove all the people the other side of the river, all but my brother Big Snake and I. We did not go; and the soldiers took us and carried us away to a fort and put us in jail. There were eight officers who held council with us after we got there. The commanding officer said: "I have received four messages telling me to send my soldiers after you. Now, what have you done?"

'Then we told him the whole story. Then the officer said: "You have done no wrong. The land is yours; they had no right to take it from you. Your title is good. I am here to protect the weak, and I have no right to take you; but I am a soldier and I have to obey orders."

'He said: "I will telegraph to the President, and ask him what I shall do. We do not think these three men had any authority to treat you as they have done. When we own a piece of land, it belongs to us till we sell it and pocket the money."

'Then he brought a telegram, and said he had received answer from the President. The President said he knew nothing about it.

'They kept us in jail ten days. Then they carried us back to our home. The soldiers collected all the women and children together; then they called all the chiefs together in council; and then they took wagons and went round and broke open the houses. When we came back from the council we found the women and children surrounded by a guard of soldiers.

'They took our reapers, mowers, hay-rakes, spades, ploughs, bedsteads, stoves, cupboards, everything we had on our farms, and put them in one large building. Then they put into the wagons such things as they could carry. We told them that we would rather die than leave our lands; but we could not help ourselves. They took us down. Many died on the road. Two of my children died. After we reached the new land, all my horses died. The water was very bad. All our cattle died; not one was left. I stayed till one hundred and fifty-eight of my people had died. Then I ran away with thirty of my people, men and women and children. Some of the children were orphans. We were three months on the road. We were weak and sick and starved. When we reached the Omaha Reserve the Omahas gave us a piece of land, and we were in a hurry to plough it and put in wheat. While we were working the soldiers came and arrested us. Half of us were sick. We would rather have died than have been carried back; but we could not help ourselves.'

Standing Bear

Source: Testimony of Chief Standing Bear. Indian Bureau Report, Washington DC, 1876.

Behold, my brothers, the Spring has come; the earth has received the embraces of the sun and we shall soon see the results of that love!

Every seed is awakened and so has all animal life. It is through this mysterious power that we too have our being and we therefore yield to our neighbors, even our animal neighbors, the same right as ourselves, to inhabit this land.

Yet hear me, people, we have now to deal with another race —small and feeble when our fathers first met them but now great and overbearing. Strangely enough they have a mind to till the soil and the love of possession is a disease with them. These people have made many rules that the rich may break but the poor may not. They take tithes from the poor and weak to support the rich and those who rule. They claim this mother of ours, the earth, for their own and fence their neighbors away; they deface her with their buildings and their refuse. That nation is like a spring freshet that overruns its bank and destroys all who are in its path.

Sitting Bull

In 1877, Chief Joseph and his small group of Nez Percé Indians left their traditional land in the Wallowa Valley to journey to the Lapwai reservation. After clashes with white settlers – which the Nez Percé resoundingly won – the group was pursued by General Nelson Miles, as it attempted to trek 1,500 miles to sanctuary in Canada. Cut off, Joseph surrendered on 5 October 1877. His people were removed to Indian territory in Oklahoma.

'I Will Fight No More Forever'

I am tired of fighting. Our chiefs are killed. Looking Glass is dead. Toohulsote is dead. The old men are all dead. It is the young men who say no and yes. He who led the young men is dead. It is cold and we have no blankets. The little children are freezing to death. My people, some of them, have run away to the hills and have no blankets, no food. No one knows where they are – perhaps they are freezing to death. I want to have time to look for my children and see how many of them I can find. Maybe I shall find them among the dead. Hear me, my chiefs, I am tired. My heart is sad and sick. From where the sun now stands I will fight no more forever.

Highn'moot Tooya'akeet (Chief Joseph)

Source: Herbert J Spindend, *The Nez Percé Indians*, The American Anthropological Association, Memoirs, Vol 2. Pt. 3 p. 243, Lancaster, Pa., 1917.

The Dawes Commission (1884) — initially established by the US government to investigate life among reservation Indians –effectively privatised ('allotted') nearly half of all native American reservation land, reducing the Indian territorial base by half.[14] The following response to the Commission was later presented by Choctaw and Chickasaw delegates to the President and Congress.

Sacrificing Homes and Children

We desire to recall a little history of our people. The Choctaw and Chickasaw people have never cost the United States a cent for support. They have always and are now self-sustaining. It will be admitted that but little over a half a century ago the Choctaws and Chickasaws were happily located east of the Mississippi River. Their possessions were large and rich and valuable. The whites began to crowd around and among us in the east, as they now are in the west. The Government of the United States urged us to relinquish our valuable possessions there to make homes for their own people and to accept new reservations west of the great river Mississippi, assuring us that there we would be secure from the invasion of the white man. Upon condition that the Government would protect us from such renewed invasion and would give us the lands in fee and convey them to us by patent, and would, by solemn treaty guarantee that no Territorial or State Government should ever be extended over us without consent, and as it was to yield up and surrender our old homes, we consented, and with heavy hearts we turned our backs upon the graves of our fathers and took up the dismal march for our new western home in a wilderness west of the Mississippi River. After long and tedious marches; after suffering great exposure and much loss of life, we reached the new reservation, with but one consolation to revive our drooping spirits, which was that we were never again to be molested. There, in the jungle and wilds, with nothing but wild animals and beasts for neighbors, we went to work in our crude way to build homes and Governments suited to our people.

In 1855, at the request of the United States we leased and sold the entire west part of our reservation amounting to over 12 million acres, for the purpose of homes for the white man and of locating thereon other friendly Indians. Again in 1866, at the urgent request of the Government we gave up all that part leased for the occupancy of friendly Indians, and ceded it absolutely for the same purpose. And again, in 1890 and 1891, we relinquished . . . 3 million acres . . . to be occupied by the whites. Now in less than five years we are asked to surrender completely our tribal governments and to accept a Territorial Government in lieu thereof; to allot our lands in severalty, and to become citizens of the United States and what is worse, an effort is being made to force us to do so against our consent. Such a radical change would, in our judgement, in a few years annihilate the Indian . . .

We ask every lover of justice, is it right that a great and powerful government should, year by year, continue to demand cessions of land from weaker and dependent people, under the plea of securing homes for the homeless. While the great government of the United States, our guardian, is year by year admitting foreign paupers into the Union, at the rate of 250,000 per annum, must we sacrifice our homes and children for this pauper element?

We have lived with our people all our lives and believe that we know more about them than any Commission, however good and intelligent, could know from a few visits . . . on the railroads and towns, where but a few Indians are to be seen and where but few live . . . They [the white man] care nothing for the fate of the Indian, so that their own greed can be gratified.

THE INDIAN VOICE

I am the Indian Voice.
I long to be heard across our land.
I have been a prisoner of war for more than two hundred years
on my very own soil!
I am a captive of hate, greed, lies, prejudice, indifference,
ignorance, injustice
by men who outnumber me and my people
since they have landed on my shores
and have overrun my home land. They have wrought on me
their society, their religion, and their laws,
all of which have caused the number of my people
to be less today than when he first came
with his false promises to our shores.

I am the collective Indian Voice
and I cry out from a million graves of unresting souls
and another million cries that ask the questions:
where does my future belong and to whom:
Does it belong to my people?
Is it to prosper on the land that is rightfully mine?
Yes, it does and it shall.
For my voice shall not be stilled
nor my spirit stopped from soaring
to the heights of greatness
which my people have known and shall know again.

I am the Indian Voice —
I shall be heard and my people shall see
the coming of a new day.
The Mother Earth provides and the Great Spirit guides
so that truth is known from shore to shore
by the Voice of a proud Indian Race.

Leonard Peltier
from Oakalla Prison
1976

3.   The Massacres

Australian academics continue to hotly debate the nature of the colonial destruction of Aboriginal society. Although something of a numbers game has developed and, more importantly, disagreement over the relevant importance to the genocidal effect of warfare and disease,[15] no historians dispute the broad picture. Before the arrival of British and Dutch settlers, hundreds of original Australians lived in small communities, scattered throughout the continent; they hunted and fished, gathered food, practised agriculture, lived in fixed settlements, or were nomadic.[16] Some 500 nations had all been on this land since the Dreamtime – that crucial point of origin, which is both a past existence, a present fulfilment, and a future guaranteed.

Whether, in whitemen's terms, this period could be represented by 40,000 or 100,000 years,[17] and whether there were 200,000 or more than 500,000 women, children and men[18] is less vital than the fact that virtually all the land was, in some way, occupied by Aboriginal Australians who, by the early years of this century, after heroic resistance were on the point of final extinction.

Although Dutch sailors and mercenaries arrived on the continent's north-western cape (significantly, close to Mapoon, site of the biggest post-war land-grab of Aboriginal territory – see p. 177) a century and a half before Cook and his crew invaded the south east,[19] it was the British who took formal possession, and so promoted one of the most grotesque and infamous myths ever enshrined as public policy. This was terra nullius *– the idea that Australia was effectively free of people, and could therefore be claimed by whoever had the firepower to do so.[20]*

In 1837 a British House of Commons Select Committee repudiated this obscene doctrine in no uncertain terms, invoking the 'incontrovertible right [which Aborigines have] to their own soil; a plain and sacred right . . .' and deploring the fact that the original inhabitants had been '. . . driven back into the interior as if they were dogs or kangaroos':[21] the committee instructed the new colonisers not to take any further land that 'is now actually occupied or enjoyed by [the natives]'.[22]

But the legislators were 12,000 miles away: on the spot, the settlers, backed by police, conducted genocidal operations against the tribes, which ranged from idle skirmish to murderous expedition.[23] *It was primarily the militancy, organisation, wit and superior knowledge of the Aborigines which prevented the entire destruction of those in the north; on the island of Tasmania, only a few tribal descendants escaped a terrible slaughter.*[24] *Elsewhere dubious respite was gained from the killings by the institution of reserves, which not only segregated white from black, but also black from black (able-bodied from the weak; half caste from 'full blood', children from parents) and provided dirt-cheap labour for cattle stations and converts to the missionary version of Christianity.*

The contributions to this chapter come from Aboriginal people remembering massacres in the Northern Territory, Western Australia and northern Queensland. Ninibi was about ten-years-old when other members of her community were slaughtered, for shooting a horse as food: her account was given 45 years later, in 1965.

Grant Ngabidj led a violent life during his youth in the East Kimberley region of Western Australia, and was responsible for the deaths of some fellow Aborigines.[25] *But these were nothing compared to the round-ups and wholesale murders perpetrated by police and white cattle-station owners, intent on 'cleaning up' 'bush blacks' who were 'wild'. A few years after the incident described by Grant Ngabidj, a larger number of Aborigines was massacred, ostensibly in retaliation for the murder of a white man by an aborigine named Lumbulumbia, at Forrest River in the same region. A Royal Commission was set up to investigate the Onmalmeri massacre, and an outcry provoked among southern whites over the treatment of northern blacks.*[26] *Further south and west, other less publicised atrocities had recently taken place, as recounted by Lenny Leonard in his contribution to this chapter.*

We also hear from some of the people of Mapoon, who recounted similar events to sympathetic white journalists up to 80 years after they had occurred.

(In order to preserve continuity, the brief linking passage by J. Roberts and D. Mclean is retained.)

"Bin kill all them children"

'The horse was get away from the yard. It belong *guddia* [white man] Jack Beasley and Ted Saddlin. One pack horse had a bell. Them blackfella get down and find out that horse. They bin chase him and spear him that horse for their meat.

Then *guddia* bin follow that track to find that horse. Blood they bin see on the track. That horse got hobbles and he jump along with spear in him. Them *guddia* find the body, one head and feet, that's all they find. They gone looking for them blackfella and go back and get all the things – rope, strap, swag strap, bridle reins, anything.

They bin come back and tie up them blackfella. They bin tie up half of them. They could not tie up boy and girl and old people. They couldn't run away, them *guddia* bin watch them. They shoot all the fellas bin stop no chain and all those girls. They bin start shooting from just 6 o'clock and clear all those without chain, and bin kill all them children.

Then they start and shoot all those bin tied up. He bin leaves 20 blackfella people to throw all those dead bodies in the well. And then shoot them 20 last fella later. They get a lot of wood those last blackfella and chuck it over the dead bodies in the dry well and them last blackfella get shot.

My cousin Neimo bin ask me when I bin grow up if I bin muster that country high up the Linacre River, up to the gorge. This side of the gorge on the limestone ridges. He bin ask me if I bin see that old well. I did find it. I could not see right down that well.

Long time after this happen, the manager, Mr Coniker, the travelling manager, he bin hear this story. He said to Jack Beasley, I won't give you any more boy, you will have to have *guddia* work with you. He bin go and look that well – he never believe it much how many people bin shot down. He pick up dead men teeth and bones just for proof. Mr Coniker bin give them to aboriginal man. Those teeth bin talk language to aboriginal man. Them teeth bin say we never bin knows that horse we reckon different billock. We bin starvination and had to kill him. Mr Coniker bin say no more shooting of aboriginal man from now on. We save those people to work for me.'

Source: Unknown.

The Massacres
Mapoon

The cattlemen Lachlan Kennedy and Frank Jardine were the first Europeans to settle the area.

'Jardine and Kennedy came through Batavia River (now called the Wenlock on Government maps). Jardine wanted to put his station 50 miles up — you can still see the stone walls he made for his footpath. They were killing people all the way up. At Dingle Dingle Creek they killed most of a tribe. That's the Batavia River people. Billy Miller and Andrew Archie are of that tribe. Only 50 left out of 300,' said Jerry Hudson. But the Aboriginal people were a fighting people and not easily cowed. 'About this Moreton Station. Well we people took spears, people from Mapoon and Weipa and all them places. They came together from Coen Creek to go to Moreton. They were fighting there with the spears. They killed one bloke. He fell down. He was out of the mission, but they were very strong in the mission,' said Harry Toeboy.

Jerry Hudson continues, 'They were chased out by the Mapoon people and had to go up to Somerset' (on the tip of Cape York).

On the way up, they passed through the territory known as the Seven Rivers, (which extends from Mapoon up to Somerset. The massacring continued. 'You see,' says Mrs Jimmy, 'from all the Seven Rivers, that was all wiped out. Mr Jardine took over from up at Catfish Creek (on the Ducie River due east of Mapoon) right up to Somerset. They were wiped out completely. The only child he saved, he grew up as his son, but the rest were wiped out. They had no chance because Mr Jardine had his armour on. That's how they could not spear him. The spears were broken on his armour.'

Frank Don tells how 'The time when we were cutting timber for fence rails at the old mission, the story was told to me that they climbed up into the ti-tree, anything that had leaves, bushy you know. When they see them, they shoot them down. They fall like birds on the ground — and that's how the Seven River Men got killed. If they run away, they caught them for a tracker go with these men to find them so they can be shot. They had rifles too.' That is how today there are no Aboriginal people living along the rivers North of Mapoon, even though this region is as yet Aboriginal Reserve as it is mostly unwanted by the mining companies.

Mrs Jimmy tells about her uncle: 'What my Mother told me was that people got killed at the time when Rev Hey and Rev Ward — James Gibson Ward — was here (around 1893). The first child they picked up was my uncle. My Grandmother had to hide him inside a waterhole and cover him with a skin bark, but Lachlan Kennedy heard the little baby crying. I think the baby was about two years old. They took the child into the mission and gave him to Mrs Ward and she grew my Uncle Barkly, and that's how he was one of the young chaps that built up the Church that is burnt down here today at Old Mapoon.'

Up at Cowal Creek, at the other end of Seven River territory, they remember how Jardine used to kill black children by knocking their heads against trees, and how he and Kennedy together exterminated hundreds of Aboriginals.

Lachlan Kennedy, according to the Mapoon people, eventually mended his ways and started helping the people. Mrs Jimmy said, 'About the cattle now, it was given by Lachlan Kennedy in exchange for the lives of our Aboriginal people.' He married a local Aborigine. They say he asked to be buried in a vertical position as a sign of his disgrace as a murderer. He had some 20 notches on his gun for the Blacks he had killed.

J. Roberts & D. McClean

Source: Mapoon Books, IDA, Melbourne, 1976, Vol. I, p. 6.

Gadia

The white men when they came in took over the land. One said, 'Oh it's good country down here, good water', so he made the first station at Auvergne. Another bloke came along with a big mob of horses and said, 'How about we make a cattle station?' They went back somewhere to find bullocks and fetched a hundred — bulls, weaners and cows — which they let go to breed after making a bit of a yard and a paddock. One year they had the bullocks and the next year they would brand the calves. In the early days they had wagons, drays and buggies, that was all. The next time again, another man came along and found Newry, 'Oh good water here, good country'.

The blackfellers who were born very early were shot everywhere, from Auvergne, Bullita and Newry Stations in the Northern Territory right down to Kununurra. At first out in the bush the blackfellers used to kill and eat the kangaroo. Later they hunted the bullocks, and in those days the white men did not like to see the bullocks killed. They would come along, find the tracks and say, 'Oh, blackfeller bin kill a bullock', and they would chase after them and shoot them.

I will tell you now how the shooting happened with my people, when the white men put the chains around their necks. The white men came along with a big mob of pack horses and they found tracks. 'Oh, them blackfeller. You look. That's the blackfeller track.' They came on and met one old man called Pompey and another called Ding Ding. 'Ah. Is that a old man there, a old man there?' Gddip, gddip, gddip, gddip, he rode up. 'Ah, ullo old man?' [in a falsetto voice]. That white man knew him very well too. 'Ullo Pompey. Ullo, old man. I'll give you tobacco.' He had it in his pocket, and gave him some to chew. 'Ah old man, where this mob?' 'Ah boss, you seeim that one fire there? They on island. Big mob blackfeller there.' This was a round island near the marsh. 'Ah right old man, I'll go 'way now.' 'Oh yeah.' Pompey did not know what he was doing, that they were going to shoot them. He was very sorry about it afterwards.

The white men came along then, riding, and looked. 'Oh, somebody ere.' They were at a billabong which the white men call Moogarooga Hole; its blackfeller name is Madbaranga. 'Ah', an old man looked out, '*gadia, gadia.*' They call the white man *gadia* you know. There were old women and one young feller. And the young feller was a bloody fool; he cut out into the plain, running all the way, trying to reach the marsh, to get into the mangroves. Those white men, Ted Lockland and Billy Weaber, had two dogs. They could not catch up the blackfellers on their horses but, my word, those dogs could gallop. They were wild dogs from Queensland, bull dogs with yellow hair. They smelled that young feller and chased him, and before he could reach the mangroves they grabbed him and pulled him down, one on the throat and the other tailing him on the leg. At a hill the *gadia* Ted Lockland got off from his horse, sat down and, bang, cut him, finished him. That blackfeller was Ding Ding's own uncle, and Ding Ding's brother was shot later with another mob. Two girls were shot dead and that one bloke in the middle of the plain. Another two blokes in the middle all passed running and the white men galloped up all the way. This was trouble which had been caused earlier. A bullock had been killed before in the paddock. Those blackfellers had been with us; the bullock was in our camp. It happened right in the marsh country, a little to the east of where I was born, on the sun rise. That was the first boy to be killed; they had not found my mob yet.

The dogs came back then and sat down when Ted Lockland whistled to them. That *gadia* caught them and brought them back to the billabong where he gave them a drink and cooled them down from their chase after that blackfeller. They went on then and camped right up at another place called Gilibirringari, Mud Spring. After that they travelled on like you would drive a motor car and came out at Ngulyarryu and took a drink of water there. 'Ah, what I see? Fresh one track? Ah might be alla go tha way.' This was at a round water hole. They looked further. 'Oh, lota big moba blackfeller ere.' They could see them a little way off cutting up a bullock they had killed.

At that moment I was playing near a billabong with a big mob of dogs belonging to my mother. I was getting that lily water, the pretty flower in the water, for her, my granny and my sister. The people who were in the camp saw the horses then. 'Oh', they said, 'Oh *gadia, gadia. Yowadabang, yowadabang.* A white man is coming on horseback.' The *gadia* galloped to them shouting 'Eh eh eh eh'. Somebody galloped up to stop the pack horses. They had already rounded up all the blackfellers on the front who had killed that bullock out in the bush. They chucked the bullock away to one side, pulled out big long chains, tied them all by the neck and padlocked them. All the old women ran away, all heaped up. The white men brought those blackfellers into our camp near the lily hole where we had stopped to eat all that tucker.

And I ran off with that mob of dogs and took them all to the billabong. There were a lot of trees around there and I climbed up a little leaning one so the *gadia* would not see me. And then this bloody Paddy and a half-caste boy called Jacko (who died later at Ruby Plain) galloped up. 'Ah, little boy, come ere, come ere'. I sat there looking out at those two fellers. 'Hey boy, come on lad', Paddy said to me. Paddy was a Miriwong boy and just big enough to ride a horse. His country was higher up from this river here. Ngalmarinmi is the hill where he was born, near the Gorge close to Yiralalam. His country, called Gobuama, was his father's and mother's too and started from the Top Dam. The river from the Top Dam to Ivanhoe is called Widam. That boy got off then from his horse. 'Come on mate', he called to me like that. 'Come on, come on.' I held onto the tree. He pulled at me. 'Come on mate', he beckoned to me. I did not understand language or

English you know. 'Ah, come on.' This half-caste got off then, caught hold of my shoulders and lifted me down. 'Ah huh, Ah, whatsa matter?' I did not talk; I did not understand. Anyhow, Paddy mounted his horse and rode back. Jacko said, 'We go now', and followed him up. We went to look for the big mob.

My mother was running around looking for me. I told her. 'I'm here, hiding in the long grass with a big moba dogs so the white man can't shoot me.' 'Ahh now', mother sang out, 'my son, me an you'll ave to go, get shot together.' She gave me a kiss, put me on her shoulder and went to meet my sister. I saw a large mob of blackfellers there tied up. I stood alongside my mother. The white man had them all, my elder sister Natbarria, my aunty, my mother Wurrai, my half-brother, and my uncle. They had cut out all the boys, the blackfellers, and put them on one side. They fetched bullets from the pack horses.

There were three white men, Billy Weaber, the Ningbing boss (he had a big moustache), his brother Jimmy Weaber, Ted Lockland and only Topsy, a Queensland girl from Borroloola. Topsy could ride a horse and had learnt very well to shoot blackfellers too. She was a school girl I think, brought up on a mission station like at Port Keats or Kalumburu. She used to carry two side revolvers and all bullets around her belt. Oh she was fucking dangerous I tell you. Those white men were sort of a German breed, a different mob who came from that country they were fighting in the war. They were looking for cattle country. There were also three boys, Nipper, Banjo and Charlie who came from the same place in Queensland as Topsy.

We all walked down to a big leaning boab tree. The white men were there with their horses. They had brought those blackfellers to that bottle tree, made them sit down, and put chains on their necks like the policemen. We sat down and my uncle and my granny gave us some matches and tobacco. The second day we all went up Grant Creek until one of the boys saw a big white gum. I was on top of a horse, holding on and riding behind that mate of mine, old Paddy, who carried me all the way. We went ahead up the creek a long way, about a mile or so, with some of the blackfellers then. The others stopped back by the big tree. Old Topsy, Billy Weaber, Ted Lockland and Jacko the half-caste stood all the other blackfellers up and tied them to the tree. They did not want me to see them, and when we got into the scrub we never saw them again. We were about half a mile away when we heard the shots behind: bang, bang, bang, bang, bang, bang; ptoo, ptoo, ptoo, ptoo, ptoo. We reckoned, 'Ah, they shootin all the blackfeller'. They were using rifles and they shot what you call twenty, and another twenty; all the young fellers and two women and two men. These were all Gadjerong who were shot, not different blackfellers.

All those white men came along then. They did not pull out the chains but left them there. They just left them there standing, all the bodies, all dead right round the tree. You cannot find them now; their bones were buried I think and burned in a grass fire. They let the rest of the women and children go, and they stayed behind. My granny, my uncle and my aunty were sent back to Pompey at Skull Creek. My eldest brother Marrmarr and my other sisters Ngarayilmi, Wudju and Yau were scattered when I was rounded up. They had run away and hidden in the mangroves. Natbarria, my mother and I were taken back to Ningbing Station, where my sister became Billy Weaber's stud.

On our way to the station we stopped where they had a camp at a big spring on Surprise Creek or Garimala, named for the Rainbow Snake, and had dinner. In the morning we went on to the station. I was only a little bugger, just playing about. I did not know anything; I was really myall. I did not know English; I did not know how to talk to the white men. White men would talk to me and I would go, 'Ha ha ha ha ha'. And you know that big long washing soap? When we stopped for dinner I thought it was fat and ate it up. Oh you should have seen it. And that old woman, Borroloola Topsy who shot a lot of blackfellers, looked at me, 'Eh, little boy tuckout [eat] fat. Little boy tuckout fat'. She ran and wiped my mouth with a handkerchief and water to clean me out.

I was given my white man name from where they picked me up, at Grant Creek. Billy Weaber gave it to me when I was a big boy. My sister reared me up on the station. She was the only one left out of my mob; the rest were either killed or they died out later. All the old people on Carlton and Ningbing died off from sickness in the early days. My mother passed away at Carlton. Of all those people who did that killing, Billy Weaber went to Brisbane, became blind and died there. Jimmy Weaber died at Tennant Creek near Queensland where you get that gold. Ted Lockland died at Auvergne, and that woman Topsy died at Rosewood. So those three *gadia* and

that one black girl from Borroloola are all dead now. The Gadjerong people who were left sang them, but they died a good while after that. 'Singing' was done by getting the boots, trousers or shirt belonging to the white man, rubbing in bullock fat mixed with blackfeller fat taken from the kidney of a live man while he sleeps — he dies later — and burning the clothes. The white man's body swells up.

And Pompey died by poisoning. Davison, who was the Ningbing manager after Billy Weaber, sent Pompey off with a letter and put strychnine in the bread he carried to eat on the journey. Pompey sat down under a *marrman*, lay back awhile, then he thought about eating and having a drink. After that he lay back and was finished; passed away like a dog, like a dingo [dingoes are routinely poisoned with strychnine. However, Jack Sullivan remarked that Pompey did not die in this way].

That other relation of mine who was killed — my half-father by the skin [subsection classification] was looking after me and my mother while my proper father was away. It did not matter under that skin Law who looked after you, whether a sister, which daddy or uncle [provided the relationship called for it]. My proper father Budbirr was with a big mob of different blackfellers up Legune way. He followed us to Ningbing when he heard that my granny and my uncle had been shot, and he cried with us. My sister told me, 'That's our father', and he lived with us then.

Source: Ngabidj & Shaw, *My Country of the Pelican Dreaming*, (AIAS, Canberra, 1981) pp. 36, 40. (Reprinted with permission)

"They shoot all the native people"

"One time, long time ago, two man, one white man and one Chinese man come up here and take one girl from here [One Arm Point]. Then one day them same two man go to fix their dingy on other side Cygnet Bay. Then all the fella from here go across there and kill the whiteman for taking that girl. We only wound the Chinaman, who then run and swim to his dingy. He then go for three mile on other side of Cygnet Bay where he was staying. Then he got one big mirror out so he can signal the fleet of lugger out in Cygnet Bay. One boat come in and pick him up. Then these fella go to where the whiteman got kill. They pick him up too and make arrangement for one boat to go to Derby to tell the story of the whiteman death. From there all the policemen come with packhorse. They ride all the way to Cygnet Bay where they find people on Skeleton Point. They shoot all the man there. When they ride more, they find more people. This time they shoot all the native people there. Maybe 200 or 300. Something like that.

After that, they ride up to One Arm Point and then go across with one lugger to Sunday Island. In Sunday Island they shoot maybe two man. When they come back from Sunday Island, they find one old man there at Swan Point and they shoot him too. Then they start to go back to Derby when they find one more man spearing fish. When the sargeant call him he look up and see many policeman coming for him. They throw all his fish away and spear and then surround him. He was a clever man, so when they try to shoot him they miss. He then jump up other side of them and run along the beach. When they chase him he run and hide in the bush. When they can't find him, they go back to Swan Point and kill all the people there. Then they go back to Derby.

All the people they killed is from the Baardi tribe, between Pender Bay and Caledon Point.

Lenny Leonard
(transcribed by Des Hill)

Source: Kimberley Land Council Newsletter, Derby, April 1980.

4. The Last Days

Probably the most deeply pessimistic document in this anthology, the following account was recorded in the early 1970s among a people who have since disappeared from the face of the earth.

Until the late 1960s the Guarasug'we lived in the Bolivian seíva, near the border with Brazil.[27] *Eighty years ago they numbered at least 300 people — by 1964 only 50 remained. Three years later the Bolivian military regime tried to recruit soldiers from the remaining Guarasug'we and their chief (captain) was killed by* mestizos. *The remnants of the tribe (around 25 people) fled into Brazil, and nothing has been heard about or from them since.*[28]

"Our End Has Come"

It shall soon be the end of us, and therefore I want to tell you the last part. This part is sad and not as entertaining as the stories you already know. It goes like this:

Before there were many kinfolks that also called themselves Guarasug'we like we do.

Some lived near the River Paraguá, others lived on the other side of the River Iténez.

Long before that, we all lived together on the banks of the River Pauserna.

There, there were big villages and we lived happily. There, there were no white men, like today.

The whites call us 'pauserna'. We don't like that name, because we are not savages. We got the name of Guarasug'we from our ancestors. The name 'pauserna' was given to us by the whites. My father and the elders say that they called us 'pauserna' for the following reason: In the villages of the past, we used to plant big trunks of hard wood. These trunks were there in memory of the ancestors. The trunks stood either in the village itself or outside. With the trunks, it was as if a person who had died or been absent for a long time were present.

Later on, the Brazilians came to the villages of the River Pauserna. They brought with them the terrible flu and the fever, diseases we had not known before.

People left the villages of the River Pauserna. They say there were ten big villages, each one of them with its own captain [*capitán*] and two assistants.

We left the villages of the River Pauserna. Some went to the River Iténez, others to the River Paraguá, others still went as far as beyond Suviuhu, the big pampa, to a lagoon that is to be found there. It was a great mass of people that left the River Pauserna. Many wept, many died, and many others did not know what would happen now. There, by the River Pauserna, we had lived in happiness. Yes, before we were happy, but today our end has come. But our story has not ended yet.

My friends and I, we went to the River Paraguá. There I was born. It was while I still was a small child that the men looking for rubber came. These men made us suffer a great deal. The elders say that we were a big tribe when we left the River Pauserna and moved to the River Iténez. We came to the place where the Bella Vista River runs out into the lagoon. There, many of us died of the fever. They simply fell dead: while fetching water, talking with friends . . . They tell that my mother's sister got up one morning, went out for water and never came back. The Guarasug'we went out to look for her and found the poor woman near the waterhole. Blood came out of her mouth. She had fever and you could hardly hear what she was saying: 'The fever comes from the whites. We shall all die if we don't get away soon.' Thus many of us died. Yes, before we had many kinfolks.

I am the son of Kunumis. My mother's name is Pesu. Savui is my brother and Hapik'wa, my sister. In those days my father was captain. Today the captain is Tarecuve, his son and our elder brother.

The captain of our kinfolks on the other side of the River Iténez was called Ovopyte. The whites called him by his other name, Fortunato.

While we were still living on the banks of the River Pauserna, there was no war between us, but afterwards when a part of the tribe was living by the River Iténez and another by the River Paraguá, then the war between us started. The Guarasug'we from the River Iténez were very bad; we are nicer than they are. We suffered a great deal because of them. Those from the River Iténez were very aggressive but we can also fight and we can also be brave. Those from the River Iténez fought with us on account of our women. They used to come over to steal our women but we would attack them and make them flee. My father told me that those of the River Iténez suffered a lot from the flu. He said that they suffered more than we did and when Fortunato died, there were only a few kinfolks left by the River Iténez. My wife Yeruv'sa is from the River Iténez. Tariku also. All the kinfolks from the River Iténez came over to us when Fortunato died. Now we all live together, as we did before by the River Pauserna. The only difference is that now there are less kinfolks, now we are only a few. My mother Pesu told me that the ancestors had not always lived on the River Pauserna but had come from the place where the great Barraca of San Ignacio is found. The ancestors travelled a lot, not as today when the Guarasug'we no longer want to walk. They have become lazy and tired. They walk a little and stop to rest, walk a little more and finally stay in one place. Before, the Guarasug'we were good and brave travellers: they did not stay in one place, but moved a great deal. Long before that time, the Guarasug'we, guided by their Karai [*shaman*] came to the district of the Barraca of San Ignacio. This happened a long time ago as it was told by my mother's ancestors and they should know . . .

When my father Kunumis still was not very old, the white men came. They came to the village and all the Guarasug'we fled up into the hills. There they stayed for a while without getting out. The whites went to the Big House and there they left axes, knives, and iron machetes, dresses made of cloth, combs and many other things. After that they left. Then the Guarasug'we came down from the hills and went to the Big House. What joy, my father told, when they saw all the things in the Big House! Now my kinfolks had iron tools, and now also they were lost.

Some days later, the whites came back. This time the Guarasug'we did not flee to the hills, except for a few women, children and some men. Most of the Guarasug'we stayed in the village. Once more the whites left beautiful things in the Big House and my people went inside. When almost all the Guarasug'we had gone into the house, the whites surrounded it and shot at those who tried to escape. Many were deadly wounded. Afterwards the whites left with all those who had been in the Big House, men, women and children. The Guarasug'we who had not been in the Big House, stayed in the hills until the whites had gone.

The whites let my people walk all the way to Santa Cruz de la Sierra, which, they say, is further away than the Barraca of San Ignacio. In Santa Cruz the whites sold the Guarasug'we. They say that almost all of the young boys and girls died on the way to Santa Cruz. The whites raped the women and the young girls still virgins. The whites do not respect women. They were very cruel to us.

A few kinfolks have returned from Santa Cruz and told what had happened. They told us about the city and the road to it. Those who managed to come back say that there are many things in that big city. They came back by way of the Guarayo territory. The Guarayo speak almost the same language as we . . . In their country, there were also white men who sold our kinfolks, as you sell rubber. Those who were able to escape from the Guarayo territory say that the whites took our kinfolks to the Beni River.

For all of these reasons, the Guarasug'we of today do not like the whites because they are bad and treacherous. Look for instance at Sr . . . who lives with his own daughter and each year kills the child he begets with his daughter.

Yaneramai [The almightiest god of the Guarasug'we] does not want us to live with the whites . . . When the end of the world comes, we do not want our souls to die. Yes, the end of the world will soon come, more or less in 2 x 13 years [to be understood as in the very near future]. Then it is really going to be terrible for the people of the Earth. In a short time, the Earth will be completely destroyed. That will be our end too. You can see for yourself how small our tribe is now, and that our end is near. It will only last another 2 x 13 years. But before that, we have to leave and go to live far away from the whites . . .

Tesere

Source: Jurgen Riester. *Los Guarasug'we — Cronica de sus ultimos dias Los Amigos de Libro.* (Publicacion del Mueseo Nacional de Etnografia y Folklore, La Paz, 1977) trans. by IWGIA Copenhagen, published in IWGIA Newsletter No. 20–27. 1978 pp. 44–9.

5.   Assimilation Soviet-style

Russian colonisation of Siberia started at the end of the 16th Century, and by the end of the following century, Russians outnumbered the indigenous inhabitants. In 1897 some 4.7 million Russians made up 80% of the population. The brutalities of Tzarism, followed by the 1917 Revolution and civil war decimated the Inuit even further; by the early 1930s the Soviet Union's control of its huge eastern peninsula was more or less complete. Although some Soviet ethnologists in the Committee of the North tried benevolently to save tribal cultures,[29] government policies were clear and uncompromising: shamanism was to be ruthlessly suppressed, young 'Eskimos' inducted into boarding schools, and indigenous languages to be 'liquidated' (an official term).[30] Tikhon Semushkin, a Young Communist Leaguer who joined the Soviet kultbaz ('cultural base') in Chukotskiykhrebet (the land of the Chukchee Inuit) in 1928, to set up a boarding school, had no doubt that despite their strenuous resistance to deculturation,[31] the Chukchee children were being 'saved':

The Chukchees are an individual and freedom-loving people and these characteristics are also predominant in the children. A great deal of tact and intuition was needed in our struggle against their harmful traditions and customs.[32]

The Itelemenes are also an Inuit people who originally occupied what is now Kamchatka in the Sea of Okhotsk. Traditionally they hunted and fished, gathering in sedentary villages. During the Stalinist era, they were compulsorily grouped into five settlements and by 1979 only around 1,400 Itelmene-speaking Inuit were left in the entire region.[33] Tyan Zaochynaya is an Itelmene who, in 1973, began to study this dying culture and language on her own account. Seven years later her papers were confiscated by the KGB as a 'security risk for the state'.[34] She then left the country and has since been living in West Germany, where the following interview was taped with Alex Diedrich of the Gesellschaft für bedrohte Völker (GfbV).

Attempts have been made by the Inuit Circumpolar Conference (ICC) (see p. 132) to keep the Soviet regime informed of regional initiatives made by aboriginal Arctic peoples in the past few years: Soviet staff attended a reception given by the ICC in 1984.[35] *However, the regime refused to allow Siberian Inuit to attend the previous year's ICC conference in Iqaluit (Frobisher Bay) because of alleged 'political undertones at the conference'.*[36]

As Tyan Zaochynaya points out, Kamchatka itself is heavily militarised, while Murmansk, on the Sami land of the Kola peninsula – the most north-westerly tip of the Soviet Union – is headquarters for no less than half the country's strategic nuclear armed submarine forces.[37]

Suppressed and humiliated for ever

Diedrich: *In most ethnographic literature one finds two different names for the original peoples of Kamchatka, 'Itelmenes' and 'Kamchadals', usually adding that Kamchadals are actually Russians. What do you think of this?*

Zaochynaya: I am an Itelmene but deep in myself I have the feeling I'm not a genuine Itelmene. Where my parents have been living and my mother still is, we used to call ourselves Kamchadals and not Itelmenes. For us, Itelmenes are the people of the west coast of Kamchatka. They still call themselves by their own name because they have been on the flight from the Russians for 300 years and have been thus able to hold on to their own name. We, who stayed on under the Russians, have been calling ourselves Kamchadals, as the authorities used to call us, for a long time now. For me, it took a long process of consciousness-finding to start calling myself an Itelmene. Officially, there are no Kamchadals, only Itelmenes. Anybody calling themselves a Kamchadal is officially a Russian.

Is there a difference, for a stranger, between Kamchadals and Itelmenes — for example in their way of life, in the way they build their houses, in their looks?

A very difficult question, this. There are russified Kamchadals and, on the other hand, also Russians and people of other origins who have lived a long time already on Kamchatka and call themselves Kamchadals. This is a mixed population, but not genuinely Russian. Think of the parallel of the Sibiryaks in Siberia, also officially non-existent and called Russians; they, too, are a mixture of aboriginals and immigrants. And then, there are genuine Itelmenes from the still existing five Itelmene villages on the west coast of Kamchatka who call themselves Kamchadals. Really, this is a question of great complexity. My father, for example, has been calling himself a Kamchadal as well as the language he was using, never Itelmene. But it wasn't Russian either. I'm afraid I don't really know what he was actually speaking — which dialect — as each village has its own. I only know from history that people from the west coast had, some time ago, come to the village where we later used to live. My mother, on the other hand, didn't speak anything else than Russian as she had grown up in a village with Russian inhabitants for more than 300 years. Kamchatka was conquered during the 17th Century, and the land was repeatedly settled with Cossacks and Russians. Small in numbers first and from many places, they still managed to push out the Itelmenes.

Data on the number of Itelmenes differ. What are the census criteria to establish ethnic affiliation? Is it up to the individual person to define their ethnic affiliation or is this established by the census interviewer?

It is the police who decide one's ethnic affiliation. Police have strong authority over us, and if policemen interrogated somebody, they would never call themselves an Itelmene or Kamchadal if their identity card said 'Russian'. I myself was registered as Russian, too, but as my consciousness has been developing I wanted to define my ethnic affiliation for myself, and succeeded under great duress in being registered as an Itelmene.

Hard to tell how many Itelmenes still exist. Ms Starkova's and other ethnographists' figures are lower than those of the 1979 census. Evidently it is in somebody's (I don't know whose) interest to let the figures appear higher than they are. The figure given in one specialist author's most recent book[38] is lower, too, than 1,400 – the 1979 census figure. But this is the case not only with regard to the Itelmenes. I've learnt it is similar with the Aleuts, a specialist author giving lower figures than the census.

Yes, this seems to be the case with regard to the Sami of the Soviet peninsula Kola too. Could it be that a specialist, a linguist would use the language as criterion of ethnic affiliation and count only those as Itelmenes who are still speaking it?

Well, language . . . That is the great difficulty with us. Our parents' generation was so very much under the influence of the authorities that they've been ashamed to speak their own language. One didn't speak it well but one spoke Russian! After moving to another village my father didn't speak any Kamchadalian any more! He only ever mumbled in that language when he was drunk. With us children he has never used it. One brother of mine wanted to learn Kamchadalian but my father was dead before he could do so. And my father was the youngest of all his brothers and relatives I've known. There might have been others left but I've never met them. And I do know that my father was the last of them to die.

Could it be he was afraid of it becoming a hindrance for the future of his children if they spoke Kamchadalian? Might this have been one of his reasons not to pass on the language?

Well, I don't know if he was afraid; self-reproach, though, is quite pronounced with the people. Maybe he had some complex about it.

Is it correct to conclude, from what you are telling, that nothing whatsoever is produced now in Itelmenian or Kamchadalian — no books, no magazines, no broadcasts?

That is so, there is no written language. There have been some specialists studying the language of the Itelmenes but nobody to do so thoroughly. These were just people interested in comparing Itelmenian with other languages, studying it for a couple of weeks or months. Others neglected it totally; they only said: there are Itelmenes, they have their own language, and that's it. Recently there was just one linguist studying Itelmenian intensively and publishing about it. Itelmenian has no alphabet, no spelling, most people only know its [Russian] transcription. There was once an attempt to develop a common alphabet for Itelmenian and the other Siberian languages, but this was by using Latin letters and was no good.

Was this in the '20s?

Yes, in the '20s and '30s, and the committees engaged in this were not able to continue their work later on.

Other small peoples of the Soviet Union, too, were alphabetised in Latin letters in the '20s, and this was discontinued by Stalin.

Yes, many of those working on this were accused of being 'cosmopolites', convicted and often executed. For the Itelmenes this latinising written language was thus no good. Previously they were analphabetic and they didn't suddenly manage to learn both Russian with its Cyrillic alphabet and the Latin alphabet of their own language. I don't know if it was actually so but one is told that there were more important things than learning languages: war and the bad post-war years. And the Itelmenes stood up under strong pressure to forget their language: it wouldn't sound nice, it contained too many useless or bad ethnic traditions, it would be of no use to keep it. And so it comes about that we still don't have a written language. This has its historical consequences and consequences for the further development of language and culture.

Maybe it wouldn't be that bad not to have a written language; it can be passed on orally, too. But the gap between generations, between the old and the young is wide. With Itelmenes, when children start school, they automatically go to boarding school; they cannot see their parents more than one or two hours a day and they sleep at school, too. Parents and children cannot meet even if living in the same village. This causes generations to be isolated from one another. Another problem is that militarisation on Kamchatka makes it hard for villages to keep in touch. People may not travel, may not visit one another, need permits. Even now having the most modern transportation, planes and so on, relations between people are not becoming better. In olden times, with dog slides, it took three days, a week or more to make a visit, and still we came together more often than in this epoch of modern transportation. This is another reason for declining language and culture. Add to this that there is no consciousness of this in the people. Information we are fed with from morning to night is biased to the extent that we don't understand anything any more; that we don't wish for anything any more.

Life is too hard, and there's just simply no time left to think of something as abstract as culture. We have to care for our daily bread first. True, that has never been easy. But going to fish, hunt or gather in woods or elsewhere, working in that way one could be sure to get something to eat. Now, it's more difficult. We are receiving food from other parts of Russia, but it's scarcely anything else than tins. It's difficult to go hunting, and it's forbidden (as is fishing). It's difficult also to gather berries, roots and herbs.

Difficult because the freedom of movement is limited through militarisation?

Yes, certainly.

What, then,. are the people living off, what occupations are they pursuing?

Well, they still try, without a permit, to fish or to hunt. They can also try to go gathering. And then, there's stock-farming and agriculture.

Is agriculture then the usual occupation?

Yes, we now have stock-farming *sovkhozes*, cattle-breeding for meat. In my mother's village for example, they have some 1,000 cattle for meat production. Still, meat is a rarity there. Many people work on the stock-farm, so do my brother and my sisters, but they don't have any meat at home. We used to eat tinned food, tinned meat, even that's a rarity. If meat gets delivered to the shops once in a while, a queue forms at once and everybody tries to get some. After all one has to cook next day too. Fish, also, has become rare.

Are there industries on Kamchatka, are raw materials being exploited? What is the environmental situation?

There are no large industries on Kamchatka, financially it wouldn't do to allocate them there. Recently, there has been some exploration for gold. And there are some fishing industries on the coastline. Otherwise, there is no industry. Still, even these small industries have negative effects on ecology.

Don't the fishing industries allow for ecological factors; are they catching too many fish?

Well, it's now forbidden to fish the rivers as they think fish resources in the sea are decreasing. And, allegedly, more fish have now bred since the ban. Another problem: agriculture is being intensified, and fertilisers are sprayed in great amounts. Because of the fertilisers sometimes there are now no berries at all as spraying takes place in spring with snow still lying.

And when the snow melts, this fertiliser poison goes with the melting snow into streams and rivers and into subsoil water?

Yes. But Kamchatka is very large so that this is not too bad for the territory as a whole. Only small parts of it are in agricultural use.

And what about forestry?

Unfortunately, I haven't been in parts where wood is cut, I'm from a district where this isn't done, so I cannot judge.

Perhaps something more about militarisation?

In Kamchatka there are many military installations, and I'm afraid there's no resistance against them. This is something one doesn't discuss, nobody talks about it. People are confronted with accomplished facts. And they don't usually ask whether the authorities are doing the correct thing or not.

One is powerless against this. More and more installations are being constructed, freedom of movement is ever more limited, and nobody offers resistance.

How are relations amongst the different aboriginal peoples of Siberia? Is there something like a common identity of aborigines against the Russians?

For one thing the Itelmenes have the feeling of doing more with Russia, they see themselves as a part of something large. Still, this is just one side of it. It is too abstract, and it is too far away, and it isn't possible to make up one's mind about this on one's own. One has the feeling of being a part of something larger. One has the feeling everything is all right. And if something went wrong, if something bad happened, one would be looking to oneself for the guilt and not to those high up. People are not of age there, you could say. I see it as if the people living on Kamchatka, the Itelmenes and Kamchadals, felt themselves not to be of age, to be minors, to be unable to make any decisions. This is why there's no resistance, nothing, they don't even think of it. This small people has been suppressed and humiliated forever, has never felt itself to be the equal of the Russians or of Kamchatka's other peoples. Naive and childish they are all! I do know my parents have been naive, just taking everything as it came. My mother, for example: she was using all her strength since she was 13, and even having now problems, great hardship, having to go on fighting for survival, still she doesn't worry about deeper causes. I'm very much a pessimist about my people.

Source: Pogrom, 109, September 1984, GfbV, Gottingen.

Notes: Part 2

1. Among the considerable literature documenting this mammoth land grab, see especially: Alvin M. Josephy, jnr. *The Indian Heritage of America*, Jonathan Cape, London 1972 especially pp. 89–105; Bruce Johansen and Roberto Maestas. *Wasi'chu; the continuing Indian Wars*, Monthly Review Press, New York and London 1979, pp. 17–55; John Upton Terrell. *Land Grab: the truth about the 'winning of the west'*. Dial Press, New York 1972.

2. For an account of historical legislation seeking to 'contain' the Indian 'problem' from the late 19th Century to the Reagan era, see Roxanne Dunbar Ortiz, *Indians of the Americas; Human Rights and Self-determination*, Zed Press, London 1984, pp. 141–2 and 173–84.

For a running account of contemporary legislation seeking to terminate Indian rights, once and for all, see the excellent Friends Committee on National Legislation (FCNL)'s *Indian Report* published quarterly from Washington DC. On 24 January 1984, Reagan reaffirmed the importance of Indian treaties, while cutting back severely on Federal programmes — especially health — and leaving the implementation of much of the remainder in the hands of the Bureau of Indian Affairs (BIA)-appointed tribal governments. See FCNL *Indian Report*, 1–20,

Summer 1984, p. 4, also FCNL *Washington Newsletter* No. 47, July 1984, pp. 1–2. For a good summary of the impact of Reaganomics on reservation America, see *Onaway*, 36, early 1985, Leeds, pp. 8–13, 26.

On the impact of mineral exploitation on the Indian land base, see Bruce Johansen and Roberto Maestas, *Wasi'chu: The continuing Indian Wars*, Monthly Review Press, New York, 1979; also Richard Nafziger, *Uranium: a brief overview*, Americans for Indian Opportunity, Albuquerque, 1978; *Native Americans and Energy Development*, Anthropology Resource Center (ARC), Boston, 1978; *Native Americans and Energy Development KK*, ARC, Boston, 1984; David Weiss, *The Hour is Late: Native Americans and Energy Resource Development*, University of California at Santa Cruz, 9 March 1979, (cyclostyled, available from the author).

3. Josephy estimates that out of 100,000 Indians living in California when it was acquired by the USA in 1848, only 15,000 remained by the end of the century. However, both on and off reservations, the population has grown during the 20th Century, and in the early 1970s was estimated at around 40,000 people, Josephy, op cit p. 150.

4. Karen Ordahl Kupperman, *Settling with the Indians: the Meeting of English and Indian Cultures in America, 1580–1640*, J. M. Dent and Sons, London 1980, especially pp. 169–88.

5. While the French and English colonisers manipulated some Indian 'bands' to prosecute their territorial warfare, north-eastern Indian groups often concluded willing alliances with the invaders, in pursuit of their aims. The Ojibway, Huron and Ottawa joined with the French to fight the Iroquois in the early 17th Century; the Five Nations made pacts with the English in their wars against the Algonquians and other Iroquois. See James Houston, *Ojibwa Summer*, Barre publishers, Massachusetts, 1972, pp. 5–6; also Josephy, pp. 104–106.

6. Johansen and Maestas p. 25.

7. Ibid. p. 27

8. Ibid p. 29

9. Ortiz, p. 134.

10. Johansen and Maestas, p. 31.

11. Ibid.

12. Terrell, p. 84.

13. Ibid. p. 85.

14. Ortiz, pp. 141, 143.

15. Two recent contributions stand out in the debate: Henry Reynolds' highly readable, and well documented study concludes that in north Australia, 10,000 Aborigines died as a direct result of white action and 20,000 in the continent as a whole. (Reynolds, *The Other Side of the Frontier: Aboriginal Resistance to the European Invasion of Australia*, James Cook University of North Queensland Press, 1981; reprinted, Penguin, Ringwood, 1982, pp. 123, 201.) Reynolds concludes 'An overemphasis on the significance of massacres tends to throw support behind the idea that the blacks were helpless victims of white attack . . .' (p. 124). Of course they weren't, but to me, Reynolds seems not to provide very sound evidence for a figure which is exceedingly low, if intended to cover a century and a half. Noel Butlin in *Our Original Aggression: Aboriginal Populations of Southeastern Australia 1788–1850* (George Allen and Unwin, Sydney, 1983) advances the argument that white robbery of black resources was as critical a factor in the destruction of blacks and their society, as outright murder, while deaths from smallpox and venereal disease may have been the biggest killer of all. This is not, of course, a very novel or radical thesis, but by extrapolation of some quite impressive calculations, Butlin

concludes that the 'pre-contact' Aboriginal population was larger, by several factors, than now commonly supposed — consequently the destruction is all the more shocking, accounting for between 90% and 95% of the original population (Butlin, page xi). If this is the case, it renders even more repugnant the *terra nullius* justification for colonisation and (I would think) actually substantiates the contemporary battle for justice and land rights better than might Reynolds' main argument.

16. Jan Roberts, *Massacres to Mining, the Colonisation of Aboriginal Australia* (Dove Communications, Blackburn, 1981) pp. 1–6. See also Geoffrey Blainey *Triumph of the Nomads, a History of Ancient Australia* (Macmillan, Melbourne, 1975).

17. The generally quoted figure is 40,000 years, but two scientists attached to the Western Australia museum conjectured 100,000 years in May 1978 (see Roberts, op cit page 6).

18. See note 15 above. Al Grassby, the Australian Commissioner for Community Relations, pointed out in his 1977 report that the low, but commonly preferred figure of 200,000, 'conveniently saved explaining the massacres' (quoted in Roberts, p. 2).

19. Roberts, pp. 7–10.

20. At the 1984 UN Working Group on Indigenous Peoples' session in Geneva, the New South Wales (NSW) Aboriginal Legal Service and other Aboriginal organisations presented a memorandum urging UN rejection of this concept, once and for all.

21. *Report from Select Committee on Aborigines*, Commons Papers, London 1834, Vol. 7 pp. 212 ff., as quoted in Barrie Pittock, *Aboriginal Land Rights*, IWGIA Copenhagen, 1972 p. 9. The liberal attitude of the Select Committee seems to have been at least 150 years ahead of its time. In 1984, at the annual general meeting of Rio Tinto Zinc (RTZ) Roderick Carnegie, the chairman of its Australian subsidiary, CRA, justified continued depredation of Aboriginal resources with the memorable words: 'The right to land depends on the ability to defend it.' (See *RTZ Uncovered*, Partizans, London 1985, p. 16).

22. *Report from Select Committee on Aborigines*, 1834.

23. See Roberts, pp. 12–27. Among recent books dealing in an enlightened way with both the European invasion and the Aboriginal resistance to it, see M. F. Christie, *Aborigines in Colonial Victoria 1835–86* (Sydney University Press, 1979) especially pp. 74–80; Ross Fitzgerald, *From the Dreaming to 1915* (University of Queensland Press, St Lucia, 1982) especially pp. 36–70; Graham Jenkin's *Conquest of the Ngarrindjeri, the Story of the Lower Murray Lakes Tribes* (Rigby, Adelaide, 1979) is a model of committed scholarship tracing the history of the confederated Ngarrindjeri nation of 3,000 people from 'first contact' to an accomplished assimilation which, nonetheless, has not completely extinguished their identity. Also on Aboriginal struggles against white invasion, see Fergus Robinson and Barry York, *The Black Resistance* (Widescope, Camberwell, Victoria, 1977). The best general histories of the colonial process in Australia are those of Henry Reynolds, Jan Roberts, and Lorna Lippmann's *Generations of Resistance: The Aboriginal Struggle for Justice* (Longman, Cheshire, Melbourne 1981). The latter two concentrate on 20th Century developments; Reynolds gets closest to Aboriginal life. The Aboriginal-written history of Australia still has to be made.

24. A myth has arisen that all Tasmania's Aborigines were massacred, poisoned, or died of disease; Queen Truganini is said to have been the 'last of her people'. It is a quite convenient misreading of history for those who want to deny land rights to

any of the island's contemporary black, or part-Aboriginal descendants. In fact, Truganini was the last of the members of the 'official' reserve established on Oyster Island; other Aborigines managed to remain behind in the white community, when the 1847 removals took place. (Roberts, pp. 29–30).

25. See *My Country of the Pelican Dreaming: The Life of an Australian Aborigine of the Gadjerong. Grant Ngabidj 1904–1977*, as told to Bruce Shaw, (Australian Institute of Aboriginal Studies, Canberra, 1981) p. 19.

26. Ibid, pp. 157–63. See also C. D. Rowley, *The Destruction of Aboriginal Society* (Penguin, Harmondsworth, 1970).

27. See Jurgen Riester, *Indians of Eastern Bolivia: Aspects of their present situation,* IWGIA document No. 18, Copenhagen, 1975.

28. *IWGIA Newsletter*, 20–21, Copenhagen, 1978, p. 42.

29. Alex Diedrich in *Pogrom*, 109. (Gesellschaft für bedrohte Völker, Göttingen, September 1984).

30. Tikhon Semushkin, *Children of the Soviet Arctic* (Hutchinson, London *no date*, though clearly published during the Second World War) p. 138.

31. Soon after setting up the school, some of the children tried to run away (Semushkin, p. 52–7). Despite her total lack of sensitivity to traditional Chuckchee life, Semushkin is forced to acknowledge the strength of the 'old ways', especially among the young. 'Years of hard work were spent inculcating cultural habits into Chukot children, and when they returned to their homes the primitive conditions of life in the *yarangas* [Chuckchee traditional houses] compelled them to renounce their newly-acquired habits from the moment they crossed the threshold'. Ibid. p. 163.

32. Ibid. p. 69.

33. Diedrich.

34. Ibid.

35. *Inuit Arctic Policy Review* (ICC, Nuuk, No. 2, 1984) p. 7.

36. Ibid. No. 3, 1983, p. 3

37. *Nuclear Free Press*, (Peterborough, Ontario, Spring 1984) p. 15.

38. G. K. Starkova *Itelmenii* (Moscow 1976). (Ms Starkova is herself an Itelmene).

Part 3
Present Struggles

1. Invasions and Genocide

The war being prosecuted by the Indonesian military regime against the Maubere (and other) people of East Timor has become the second deadliest in the world.[1] Up to a quarter of a million east Timorese have died from bullets, torture, and starvation induced by military occupation.[2]

Napalm, defoliants, and torture have been explicitly employed[3] along with enforced 'resettlement' of a traditional agricultural people in concentration camps.[4]

The Timorese are largely a people of Melanesian and Malay origin, many of whom have intermarried with Chinese, Arab and African traders searching for sandalwood some time before the arrival of European colonisers. By the middle of the 19th Century, the Dutch controlled western Timor and the Portuguese the eastern half of the island.[5]

After the Portuguese revolution in 1974, European administration on East Timor virtually collapsed, and the most militant and popular liberation movement, Fretilin (Frente Revolucionaria de Timor Leste Independente), *declared independence on 28 November 1975. Nine days later the Indonesian army invaded East Timor in an apparently spontaneous act, which, in reality, was carefully and lengthily prepared.[7]*

The aim was to crush Fretilin at virtually any cost. In the years since, the Indonesian military has devastated large areas of the island, broken – or appropriated — much of the power of the traditional chiefs (liurais) *and successfully 'Timorised' the leadership of the occupying army, through attrition, bribery and terrorism.[8]*

It has been the biggest military operation ever mounted by the Indonesian army.[9]

Indonesia's key strategy has been to break up the Maubere settlements, destroy their crops and livestock, and force them — starving and diseased — into encampments. Where the people have not died from starvation in guerrilla-held areas, they have often collapsed and died from neglect under Indonesian hands.[10] It was not until early 1979, three years after the invasion, that the International Red Cross was allowed to enter the island.[11] In addition — like the people of West Papua — the Timorese had to suffer from encroachment, this time by Balinese families drafted in as part of Indonesia's notorious 'transmigration' programme.[12]

During 1977 and 1978 Fretilin suffered enormous losses: in the succeeding two years, though the liberation movement regrouped and replanned its resistance strategies, many civilians died from starvation. At the beginning of 1983, the Indonesian military flirted with the idea of a truce. The regime displayed its true colours, however, when General Benny Murdani (who organised the 1975 takeover of East Timor) was appointed Commander-in-Chief of Indonesia's armed forces. By the end of that year, Murdani was pledged to crush resistance 'without mercy'.[13]

Few other contemporary 'crisis' situations reveal the dereliction of democratic principles among Western and Third World powers as vividly as in East Timor. In a succession of votes at the United Nations on recognition of the Maubere people's right to self-determination, the US, Britain[14] and — most scandalously — Australia[15] voted with their thumbs down, for reasons of self-interest, as did India, Japan, Saudi Arabia and several Pacific nations blandished by the Suharto regime.[16] China, the USSR, Tanzania, Cuba, Eire and Nicaragua are among those to have condemned the invasion.[17]

Kay Rala Xanana, the President of Fretilin's Revolutionary Council of National Resistance (CRRN) has on several occasions delivered eloquent testimony against the occupation.[18] I have, however, chosen here statements made by two lesser-known Fretilin commanders. The first was delivered by Roque Rodrigues, Fretilin's representative in Luanda, at the UN Special Committee on Decolonization in August 1979, soon after Fretilin suffered huge defeats. The second is part of an interview Fretilin's commander-in-chief and defence minister gave to Afrique-Asie, *in April 1980. This points out the way in which the East Timorese have adapted traditional health-care and village economics to fight a prolonged war whose tactics owe a great deal to other liberation struggles in south-east and southern Asia.*

"Time is on our side"

The history of East Timor and the struggle for national self-determination of our people is already known to members of this Committee [UN Special Committee on Decolonization, 16 August 1979]. Documents abound that can offer an excellent historical background of East Timor. For this reason, we shall refrain from repeating what has been said here in order to save time for other useful purposes. It is clear to everyone that Indonesia invaded East Timor on December 7, 1975. Indonesia's invasion of East Timor was a breach of the United Nations charter and international law. Indonesia's arguments for its intervention in East Timor are the very same arguments used by other colonial expansionist and racist regimes to justify armed aggression and military occupation of other people's lands, be they in Africa, the Middle East or Asia. The people of East Timor have the right and ought to be granted the opportunity to exercise freely their right to self-determination and independence. Indonesia's continuing armed aggression and occupation of East Timor constitute an impediment to the full implementation of Resolution 1514 and other General Assembly and Security Council resolutions on the question of East Timor. As a matter of fact, Indonesia has not complied with the four General Assembly and two Security Council resolutions calling for the withdrawal of Indonesian forces from East Timor.

It has been almost four years since the Government of Indonesia launched a full-scale invasion of East Timor with many thousands of troops, airplanes, helicopters, tanks, and warships. In the course of this savage war of aggression, more than 10 per cent of the entire East Timor's population has been killed. However, the war of national liberation and resistance against foreign domination has continued unabated in East Timor. In spite of overwhelming odds, lack of material support from third world countries, serious shortage of medical supplies and clothing, the people of East Timor, under the leadership of FRETILIN, have not succumbed to Indonesia's attempted annexation.

Indonesia is spending almost a half million dollars a day on the war in East Timor. Several thousand Indonesians have been killed or wounded. In the meantime, Indonesia is experiencing a serious economic, social and political crisis. There is starvation in many parts of Indonesia. Unemployment is at about 30 per cent. Corruption is widespread and has become an institution and a means of survival for many millions of Indonesians. The Central Committee of FRETILIN is fully aware that the war in East Timor might continue for many years to come. The people of East Timor are prepared for this war. One thing is certain however: time is on our side. Just as the Shah Mohammad Reza Pahlavi with all his imperial might was crushed by a simple popular uprising by unarmed people, the regime of General Suharto and his corrupt and repressive clique of generals will follow the Shah's fate. Whatever military and economic aid that the Western countries — particularly the USA — might give to their puppets in Jakarta will not save the regime. The Shah of the old Iran had the most powerful army in the Third World. No one in the Western capitals would have dreamed that Reza Pahlavi could be ousted by any opposition, let alone by unarmed peasants, students, workers and intellectuals. The Iran that was the so-called bastion of the 'free world' in the Middle East has now been freed from Western neo-colonialism.

The international community cannot accept the politics of *fait accompli* for it would set a very serious precedent. If armed intervention and annexation are to be condoned by the United Nations, the very survival of many small States around the globe will no longer be guaranteed by the rule of law. Armed aggression, military intervention in other countries' affairs, violation of colonial and established boundaries must be opposed by the international community as a whole and must be condemned. Indonesia's invasion and attempted annexation of East Timor has been a gross violation of the United Nations charter and international law and, therefore, it must be condemned and opposed by member states. The failure to enforce existing international laws will set very serious precedents that will threaten the very survival of many countries in Latin America, Africa, Europe and Asia. No country should call upon itself the role of policeman of the world, for no country can justify military incursions into the territory of other states.

Indonesia's invasion of East Timor is a clear-cut case of military aggression and attempted conquest. It has been a case in which the international community has been mocked by an arrogant power. Indonesia, a United Nations member state, has been defying the entire international community and by its actions has contributed to the sorry discredit of this organization in the eyes of millions of people around the world. It is high time for other member states to stand firm on the noble principles that inspired the creation of the United Nations Organization and to enforce its resolutions. Only by doing so, can peace and order be safeguarded.

The Central Committee of FRETILIN, and the people of East Timor, will continue their armed resistance to Indonesia's military occupation. The Central Committee of FRETILIN will not accept any cosmetic solution short of total and complete national independence. To achieve these ends, the FRETILIN military command will strike on every single Indonesian military, economic and political target. The lives of many thousands of East Timorese people — women, children and men — would not have been lost in vain. East Timor will be free, independent and sovereign.

Roque Rodrigues

Source: IWGIA *Newsletter*, No.20, 1979.

"We teach our people to count on themselves"

Afrique-Asie: *What is your assessment of the present situation in East Timor?*

Lebato: The invasion of 7 December 1975 yielded 200,000 victims, killed by the Indonesians. 100,000 continue to live in miserable conditions, suffering from starvation; 300,000 others — who stayed in the territories occupied by Indonesia — live in constant terror.

The rest of the people fled to the jungle: the situation is weak because we're trying to resist on an island completely encircled by Indonesian warboats. It is difficult fighting under such conditions.

Despite this, we have — as of now — put about 30,000 Indonesian soldiers out of action. But our losses have also been considerable.

The Indonesian regime is proposing to bring 300,000 people from Bali and Java to replace the decimated population on East Timor. Suharto's objective is to implant a foreign population, so as to cut Fretilin off from the people.

Today the Red Cross has access only to those areas controlled by Fretilin. In the past, humanitarian aid was delivered to the Indonesian Red Cross, but that had to be stopped because the Indonesian generals organised a racket to sell the food for their profit.

We are witnessing a holocaust on the island. The Indonesians have every intention of exterminating the entire population.

How do the refugees survive in the zones that you control?

East Timor wasn't a very developed country, but it does have the potential of being a rich one. The rainy season lasts nine months, so we could have three harvests a year. We also have lots of cotton, both wild and cultivated. Moreover, Fretilin has developed production units and, in spite of the Indonesian invasion, we had the island's biggest harvest in 1976.

In order to hinder us, the invaders use defoliants and napalm, supplied by the USA. In mid-1978 we had serious production problems, but if our people are not starving, we shall continue to fight for 20 or 30 years if necessary.

How, more precisely, can you organise an armed resistance in such isolation?

For a long time it was thought impossible to fight in the desert — but look what the Polisario Front are doing! In East Timor, they said 'you're mad to try and carry out a campaign on an island'. But we don't have any choice . . . Remember, in 1975, we took 15,000 arms from the Portuguese colonial army . . . we've used these in order to capture Indonesian arms.

But it would be lying to say that we've had no problems. To develop an armed struggle on half an island, totally cut-off by sea and air, isn't easy. However, we are surviving and resisting without any outside help. And, paradoxically, the arms we obtain come from the black market operated by Indonesian officers!

How does the Indonesian army look in East Timor?

The Indonesian army, which has 247,000 men, deploys 55,000 alone in East Timor — which occupies a little triangle of 19,000 square kilometres.

The geographical conditions force us to be extremely mobile. If we're attacked in the mountains, we have to retreat to the coast. When we're attacked on the coast, we disappear into the jungle. In five years, we've understood the Indonesians' weaknesses. They don't dare to attack Fretilin in the interior of the island . . .

We have declared our independence and several countries have recognised our state as sovereign . . . There is absolutely no reason for Indonesia to consider a Free Timor as a threat. What threat can one million of us offer to 140 million of them?

What is happening with the other separatist movements of the Indonesian archipelago?

Look! Sukarno promised federalism, but never promoted it. Then Suharto decided to destroy all liberation movements in Sumatra, Borneo, Sulawesi, the Moluccan islands and in Irian Jaya [West Irian].

What type of social organisation is Fretilin creating in the zones it occupies?

In 1976, when Indonesia was getting bogged down in the war, General Benimurani — the officer who organised the invasion of East Timor — confirmed to the Pentagon that it would be difficult to win a war in East Timor, because Fretilin had had its own organisation in the free zones for a long time.

Our social structures, in the free areas, enabled us in the thick of the fighting in 1976, to teach literacy to 60,000 children and adults in our schools. We have developed traditional medicines, producing them in our own factories.

There is no money in East Timor. We produce cotton, rice and cereals: the coffee producers exchange with the rice producers. And we make our clothes from wild cotton, in traditional workshops.

In a word, our political principle is self-sufficiency. We don't exclude outside aid, but we teach our people to count only on themselves.

Don't you feel isolated?

We are not. Fretilin is beginning to find an international audience. Our audience will grow as the armed struggle intensifies. At present, we have diplomatic relations with all the Portuguese ex-colonies, several African countries — Congo, Zambia, Ethiopia, Tanzania — as well as with South Yemen, Albania, Cuba, Guyana and Jamaica. The moral and political support of the whole socialist bloc is behind us . . .

Source: Afrique-Asie. April 1980. Trans. Roger Moody.

The First National Consultation of Minority Peoples in the Philippines was held in September 1983, when representatives from many indigenous organisations and groups in the archipelago came together in Quezon under the auspices of the National Council of Churches. From the Cordillera there were Ifuao, Bontoc, Kalinga, Kankanai, Tingguian and Tuwali representatives; from la Sierra Madre, Dumagat and Remontado, and from Mindanao, Banwaon, Higaonon, Mandaya, Mangguangan, Manobo, Mansaka and Subanon people.

The organisations agreed to conclude a bodong *— or 'peace pact', similar to the one which had already united the Kalinga and Bontoc in opposition to the Chico dams (see Part 3, chapter 5). They also decided to form the first National organisation of all tribal peoples in the Philippines.[18] Their Declaration is reprinted below.*

One of the main concerns of the conference was the increased militarisation of tribal areas by the Marcos regime, under the pretext of rooting-out 'communists'. Within a few months of this historic consultation, the Bontoc and Kalinga areas of Luzon were subjected to huge 'search and destroy' operations conducted by the army: 3,000 soldiers were reportedly supported by armoured personnel carriers, and many settlements were bombarded.[19] The aggression continued well into 1984.[20]

On 9 July 1984 the Kalinga-Bontoc Peace Pact Holders Association put out an urgent statement of protest, which was sent around the world.

Since the toppling of the Marcos regime in February 1986, there has been little diminution in aggression against indigenous Filipinos. As the Episcopal Commission on Tribal Filipinos commented in Spring that year: '. . . even while the government possesses liberal tendencies, no basic structures in society have changed. Specifically among the minority peoples, their actual conditions remain the same.'[21]

This section ends with the resolutions to the Aquino government jointly submitted in February 1986 by the Council of Leaders of Minority Peoples of the Philippines (CAMPP) and three support organisations (The Episcopal Commission on Tribal Filipinos, the Philippine Association for Inter-cultural Development Inc., and the Ugnayang Pang-Agham Tao).

"Common problems . . . Common struggles"

Pact Declaration

'We affirm our belief in the minority peoples' just and inalienable rights to life, to the defence of our ancestral lands and the protection of our environment, to the preservation of our indigenous cultures as distinct peoples, to self-determination in our process of development.

'We, the minority peoples of the Philippines, now gathered in the First National Consultation of Minority Peoples, cognizant of our common problems and common struggles, hereby declare our national solidarity.

'We reiterate our unanimous opposition to the grabbing of our lands, the exploitation and plunder of our human and natural resources, the commercialisation and destruction of our culture, and the atrocious attacks against our peoples, as perpetrated by the collusion of multinational corporations, local big business, the government and the military.

'We, the peoples of the Cordillera, the Sierra Madre and Mindanao, are forging a peace pact with the Lumads of Mindanao, Agta of the Sierra Madre and groups in the Cordillera.

'In this peace pact, we have agreed to abide by the following rules:

1) Unity in thought and sentiment.
2) Defence of life, honour and property.
3) Regular consultations to strengthen our unity every two years.
4) Mutual respect and protection of visitors.
5) Establishment of a support structure with a board and secretariat to implement our common agreements.
6) Whoever harms the well-being of the community will be excluded from the peace pact.
7) Whoever violates these rules shall be penalised according to the decision of the peacepact holders.'

Source: Tribal Forum November/December 1983, Vol. IV. No. 7.

"Defy the Armed Invasion On Our Land, Resist this New Colonialisation"

We speak to our Brother Filipinos in the midst of an ongoing war being waged by the Armed Forces of the Philippines on the tribal Kalinga and Bontoc people. For the past month up to the present, we have witnessed an atrocious military campaign designed to coerce our tribes into acceding to a new colonisation of our ancestral lands.

Starting from the last week of June, our people have suffered from the escalating military abuses being dealt by the AFP.

Using helicopters and warplanes, our villages and our lands have been strafed and bombed. A number of Kalinga have already been killed during the military campaign. Our Kalinga women, whom the criminal AFP troops treat so lowly, have been subjected to worse indignities such as body searches and gang-rapes. And in the midst of their genocidal campaign, we have been ordered to stop harvesting the *palay* from our fields. Our mere presence outside our homes is being used as pretexts for wholesale manslaughter.

We raise a call to all our brother Filipinos to help us put an end to this bloody carnage being perpetrated on our people. No amount of government and military effort to win back our 'hearts and minds' will convince us to accept this unlawful intrusion into our domain.

The government and its military criminals have acquired a notorious reputation to the mountain tribes of Bontoc and Kaliga-Apayao. In the mid-70s they tried, unsuccessfully to construct four huge dams over the Chico River that would destroy our crops, desecrate the burial grounds of our ancestors and leave us homeless, all for the benefit of transnational corporations in need of hydroelectric power.

Our brother Tingguians, in Abra, together with the Kalinga and Bontoc people also resisted the planned deforestation of over 400,000 hectares of pine land for the Cellophil Resources Corporation, a local partner of transnational paper companies.

Our leader, Macliing Dulag, who valiantly resisted all bribes and threats made by PANAMIN [Presidential Assistant on National Minorities — government agency charged with responsibility for the national minorities of the Philippines], the local government and the military, was felled by assassins bullets in April 1980 and up to now his assassins have not been punished.

The consistency with which the government and the military have persecuted our people have taught us to be more vigilant and courageous despite exploitation and oppression. We shall face this new attempt at colonization in the same manner that we did for the Spanish, Japanese and American colonizers.

In the face of all these atrocities, we demand the immediate and total withdrawal of all military detachments and troops in the areas of Bugnay, Basao, Ngibat, Buscalan, Tinglayan, Kalinga-Apayao and in the villages of Annabel, Aguid, Agawa, Sagada and Bontoc.

We demand justice for all victims of military atrocities. Punish the military men, their officers and field commands, and the AFP chiefs of staff who planned, participated in and led the attacks on our sacred land. General Ver has reported that heavy casualties have been inflicted on NPA rebels operating in the area. The fact is that Kalinga and Bontoc people are those that suffer most from such an operation.

We reiterate a call to all Filipinos, individuals, groups and organisations to help the Kalinga and Bontoc people in their struggle against this insanity of the AFP.

Kalinga-Bontoc Peace Pact holders
July 9th 1984

An Open Letter to President Ferdinand E. Marcos

August 1984

Mr President,
Is it war and we are such enemies that you must send so many soldiers to our barrios? If the soldiers are here to sow peace and instill order in our midst, why have they come dressed and geared for battle?

Fear, not peace Mr President, is what militarisation has brought to our barrios. We fear the soldiers because we have come to associate them with abuse: torture, rape and looting; arbitrary arrests and killings. Lieutenant Adalen's murder of Macli-ing is still fresh in our memories.

Hunger, not order, Mr President, is the impending result we perceive. We are hindered from roaming our own forests for game. We can no longer freely tend our swidden fields, where we grow basic crops. Even our rice terraces, we hesitate to frequent. If this continues, Mr President, we will surely starve. Even your soldiers will have nothing to take from our granaries any more.

We know, Mr President, that we have time and again opposed your policies and programs. Is this why you have sent your soldiers to our barrios?

Our land is rich in natural resources. Through the years, government laws and policies have always outlined the Cordillera as a resource area for extractive industries, such as mining and logging, and for infrastructure support, such as hydroelectric dams and other energy projects. We oppose these programmes and policies because they threaten our very existence.

We oppose, Mr President, because to us land is not just a commodity. Land to us, is life itself. And not just any land, either, for we are rooted in only one: the Cordillera. To separate us from it would be to deprive us of our existence and identity as a people. We belong to this land and to no other.

We have the constitutional right to oppose. The highest law of the land provides that 'the State shall consider the customs and traditions, beliefs and interests of national cultural communities in the formulation and implementation of state policies' (Article XV Section 11). Yet, when we oppose policies and programs that threaten our interests, the military quickly brands us as subversives.

Our right as a people to self determination is recognised by international law, The United Nations Covenant on Civil and Political Rights provides that 'all peoples have the right to self-determination. By virtue of this right, they freely determine their political status and freely pursue their economic, social and cultural development' (Article 1 Section 1). Yet, when we assert this right in one voice and as one people, the military steps in to sow fear and disunity among us.

You, yourself Mr President have stated that 'there can be no trade-off of human rights with economic development.' We thus call on you Mr President to heed our voice as we struggle to protect, assert, and uphold our rights as a people:

1. Put an end to massive militarisation, which undermines our capacity as a people to protect, assert and uphold our rights to our ancestral land. Withdraw all military and paramilitary units operating in the Cordillera.

2. Punish all who have inflicted harm and brought death on the civilian population. Grant indemnity to communities for lost production, disruption of livelihood, and social dislocation bought about as a consequence of militarisation. All stolen or destroyed property should, in addition be paid for.

3. Put an end to the plunder of the Cordillera and its use as a mere resource base. Stop the incursions and indiscriminate operations of state and private corporations, installations and projects. Repeal all

laws and withdraw all programs that violate our territorial prerogative to our ancestral domain and that deprive us of benefits of our land and resources.

The Cordillera People's Alliance for the Defense of the Ancestral Domain.
Cordillera Consultative Committee
Room 304 Laperal Building
Session Road, Baguio City, Philippines.

Resolutions of CAMPP to the Aquino Government, 1986

1. Disband and order the removal of military and paramilitary units engaged in military operations and acts of terrorism within the ancestral lands of national minorities.

2. Indemnify tribal communities displaced through infrastructure projects, militarization, agri-business, multinationals, etc.

3. Rehabilitate released political detainees who are members of national minorities.

4. Investigate, expose and stop projects and programs which are gravely detrimental to the interests and well-being of national minorities.

5. Expose and stop the malpractice of non-national minorities who mis-represent themselves as members of national minority groups in order to obtain favors and privileges granted to national minorities alone.

6. Implement laws favorable to tribal communities while recognizing their customary laws and practices; and repeal or abrogate all repressive and discriminatory laws.

7. Codify customary laws.

8. Return to the national minorities all ancestral lands declared as such, while likewise reviewing illegally acquired titles involving ancestral domains.

9. Cancel, remove and/or redirect all ongoing and planned infrastructure development projects and programs, all multinational enterprises and all forms of landgrabbing within the domain of national minorities that are gravely harmful to their existence and survival as a people, and are destructive of their ancestral lands, culture and lifestyle.

10. Include in the formal educational system appropriate indigenous cultural elements.

11. Support self-directing cultural development.

12. Make immediately operative regional autonomy for the Cordillera peoples as planned and recommended by the Cordillera People's Alliance; and thereafter for other national minorities, particularly those in Mindanao.

13. Bring and make accessible to national minorities basic social services as well as opportunities and services provided by appropriate government and non-government bodies toward enhancing and sustain-

ing land and resource productivity.

14. Remove the Nuclear Power Plant in Bataan as it is definitely a threat to the life and limb of our Negrito brothers and sisters in Bataan.

15. Investigate the harmful effects on national minorities of the RP–US bases agreement, specifically the Subic Bay–Clark Field military complexes.

16. Recommend to the Cory Aquino government the recognition and acceptance of a body composed of genuine, non-government national minorities' organizations/communities to be consulted on all matters pertaining to the national minorities.

Source: Tribal Forum, Manila, Vol. VII, No. 2, March–April 1986.

Among the many tribal communities of Bangladesh,[22] *the most distinctive and independent live in the Chittagong Hill Tracts (CHT) — a sliver of territory sandwiched between India, south-eastern Bangladesh and Burma. Under the British raj the area was administered as a 'backward tract' until 1935, and an 'excluded area' until independence in 1947.*[23] *Seventeen years later, the dictator, Ayub Khan of Pakistan, annulled the CHT's special status — a double-edged sword which, while it had partially infantilised the people and left untouched the power of the Chakma king, did at least protect them from the worst indignities of direct rule. After Bangladesh won its independence in 1971, the Tracts were handed over to a non-tribal District Commissioner with virtually 'unlimited powers'.*[24] *From 1964, the region had been exposed to uncontrolled encroachment from Bengalis living on the plains. But in 1979, the Bangladesh military regime set in motion a secret plan to settle thousands of outsiders on tribal land. Most Bengalis appear not to have objected to the scheme — especially in view of the lucrative inducements made to them to move.*[25] *These financial carrots are remarkably similar to those offered poor families in Brazil's north-east when the Brazilian government was opening-up Indian land in Amazonia during the late 1960s and 1970s.*[26] *And the governmental motives would appear to be the same: instead of tackling the endemic problems of poverty caused by inequitable land ownership in the rest of the country, the regime found it easier to shift the problem — and a potentially rebellious peasant force — to the relatively inaccessible hinterland.*

In 1980, there were about 590,000 indigenous Hill Tracts residents out of a total population of 815,000, the largest tribal communities, the Chakmas and Marmas, comprising more than half the total of indigenous people in the territory. The alarm with which these Buddhists have viewed the incursion of largely Muslim immigrants can be imagined — it far outstrips the rate at which the Indonesian military is resettling Javanese and Balinese families in West Papua (see Vol. 2, p. 120). At first sight, the objections of the Hill Tracts tribes seem to have something in common with the prejudices displayed by some white Europeans against migrants from Asia, Africa and the Caribbean. It is true that some Chakma spokespeople have tended to see their struggle against the newcomers in narrowly religious terms. But, in reality, the two situations cannot be compared. What the Hill Tracts people strenuously object to is not outsiders as such, but incursions which are clearly designed to deprive them of their means of subsistence and, after 1982, of their cultural values, when Bengali was imposed as the tribespeoples' 'mother tongue'.[27]

In 1963 the huge Kaptai hydroelectric scheme displaced 100,000 people — about a sixth of the entire tribal population. The majority have still received no compensation for this assault. Although mainly sedentary rice farmers, they were forced into the jhum (shifting) cultivation typical of most of the hill tracts. The dam precipitated an ecological disaster which has been compounded by the settlement of Bengali families in the past five years[28] *who have themselves failed in lowland methods of agriculture and had to resort to* jhum. *In addition, the Swedish International Development Agency (SIDA) was contracted to develop a large commercial forestry programme which would have reduced the tribal land-base even further. The Australian Development Assistance Bureau was commissioned to build a 32-foot wide road, ostensibly as part of the forestry programme, but probably to facilitate access (especially by the Bangladesh army) to recalcitrant tribespeople in the north.*[29] *After international concern was expressed to the Swedish government about human rights abuses in the Hill Tracts, SIDA pulled out in 1981. That year the Australian team also withdrew after attacks by armed tribesmen.*

The military occupation of the Chittagong Hill Tracts began very soon after Bangladesh independence.[30] *On 26 May 1979, Brigadier Hannan and Lieutenant-Colonel Salam of the Bangladesh army declared at a public meeting in Panchari that they wanted 'the soil and not the people of the Chittagong Hill Tracts'.*[31] *Less than a year later, 300 unarmed women, children and men were massacred by army units, assisted by Bengali settlers, at Koakhali.*[32] *The same year, the Bangladesh government passed the Disturbed Areas Bill which gave almost unlimited powers to the police — including licence to army NCOs to fire upon any person in an area declared to be a 'politically disturbed zone'.*[33] *In 1981 there was another army massacre of tribespeople at Matiranga.*[34]

Tribal Resistance to absorption by the raj, *Pakistan and Bangladesh, enjoys a long pedigree. In 1777, for example, the Chakma Raja, Jan Bux Khan declared war on the East India Company; it lasted for ten years, and led to the Fort William treaty under which the semi-autonomous status of the region was supposedly guaranteed.*[35]

In 1972, the Parbottya Chattagram Jana Sanghati Samity (PCJSS) — or Chittagong Hill Tracts Peoples Solidarity Committee — was founded by Manobendra Narayan Larma and his brother Bodhi Priyo (Shantu) Larma. Its armed wing, the Gono Mukti Fouj — more commonly known as the Shanti Bahini — opened an offensive against the Bangladesh military which intensified after 1975. An appeal made by the Shanti Bahini in 1980 (see below) marked the first occasion on which its struggle was recognised outside the Indian sub-continent.

In the past four years, there has been little evidence of the Marxist — or indeed the Maoist — strands of the original PCJSS.[36] *(A smaller Marxist-Leninist group called the Mukti Parishad, formed mainly of young people from the Tanchangya tribe, seems to have disappeared altogether.) Recent reports from Bangladesh suggest that faction fighting has broken out within the Shanti Bahini, and that Manadendra Lal Chakma was killed by another group of Chakmas in late 1983.*[37] *Upendra Lal Chakma was made an 'adviser on freedom fighters' by Bangladesh President Ershad in 1984.*[38] *Some members of the Shanti Bahini have also allegedly attacked Bengali settlers with considerable savagery.*[39] *Thousands of tribal refugees fled to India where they sought the aid of the United Nations.*[40]

But a year later, the Indian government began pushing back refugees, precipitating new fighting and — in May 1986 — renewed attacks by the Shanti Bahini on Bengali settlers. One of the guerrilla factions was said to have surrendered in 1985, while talks between the Bangladesh government and the other factions broke down. [41]

An appeal to the Governments of all peace-loving countries, all conscientious people, all humanitarian organizations including Amnesty International and the democratic forces of the world to compel governments of Bangladesh to stop genocide in Chittagong Hill Tracts

Dear Friends,

The Chittagong Hill Tracts, the largest district in Bangladesh with an area of 5,199 sq. miles, is inhabited mostly by the tribal people, who are ethnically different from Bengalees. These tribal people are also not Muslims by faith. They are mostly Buddhists, Hindus and Christians. In 1947, when India was divided, 97.5 percent of the population of the district were non-Muslims and tribals. During the British period it was governed directly by the Governor of Bengal and administered under Chittagong Hill Tracts Regulation of 1900. There was separate police administration and except Deputy Commissioner, who was British, and a few other high officials, all other Govt. functionaries including police personnel were locally recruited. There were also three tribal Chiefs, who used to help the Deputy Commissioner in administering the district. All local administration was run by the tribal people. According to Chittagong Hill Tracts Regulation of 1900, the non-tribal people were not allowed to settle in the district permanently nor they could purchase land from the tribal people and under rule 51 of the said Regulation, they could be expelled from the district when they were thought undesirable or found doing anything prejudicial to the interest of the tribal people.

But after 1947, when this district became part of Pakistan, the situation gradually changed. Though the Chittagong Hill Tracts Regulation was not abrogated or nullified, its rules were not followed. The Government of Pakistan systematically put the Regulation into disuse and started to bring Muslim population into the district in order to increase the Muslim population. The Government of Pakistan disbanded Chittagong Hill Tracts Police Force, which was previously constituted with only the tribal people, and transferred all tribal police officers to other districts of the East Pakistan. The Government also transferred all civilian tribal officers from this district to other districts.

In the name of getting cheap power supply, the Govt. built a huge dam at Kaptai as a result of which about 100,000 tribal people were uprooted from their ancestral homes and were given only nominal compensation for the lands and houses. Tribal people were not given any jobs in the Karnaphuli Project (where the dam was built) though they were evicted almost without any compensation. There is not a single tribal man in the project now.

In the name of creating jobs for the people and industrialisation the Govt. established a huge paper-mill at Chandraghona. But here also practically no tribal people are employed. The then Govt. of Pakistan established other industries in the district acquiring the lands of the tribal people but the tribal people were not employed in any of the industries. The then Govt. of Pakistan systematically increased the Muslim population in the district by bringing them from other districts and allowing them to settle and acquire lands in violation of Chittagong Hill Tracts Regulation which was still not abrogated or nullified, and technically the district was still administered in accordance with this old Regulation.

In 1961, there was serious riot in the district against the tribal people when about 60,000 tribal people fled to India. The riot was stopped by the Govt. only when the Indian Govt. lodged a strong protest with the Govt. of Pakistan. The Govt. of Srilanka also lodged a protest with the Pakistani Govt.

During the liberation war of Bangladesh, many Muslims from neighbouring districts of Chittagong and Noakhali occupied the lands of the tribal people with the help of the Pakistan Army. The tribal people never got their lands back even after liberation of Bangladesh. But the real tragedy came to the tribal people only after liberation of Bangladesh.

Soon after independence of Bangladesh about 400 tribal people were killed by Bangladesh Army in the name of their so called 'search for Rajakars and Albadars' (supporters of Pakistan), hundreds of houses were burnt and looted, many girls and women were raped and tortured. Their reckless killings and oppression compelled the tribal people to organize resistance and demand autonomy. Their leader, Mr. M. N. Larma, an MP, led a delegation to Mr. Sheikh Mujibur Rahman and submitted a memorandum demanding regional autonomy.

But Sheikh Mujib did not pay any heed and instead increased oppression in the name of establishing law and order. In the name of 'search for Rajakars and Albadars', he started combing operation with his army and police forces in the district. His Airforce also made heavy bombing raids on the tribal villages.

During Mujib's regime more non-tribal people were allowed to settle in the district permanently. Repatriated Bengalees were rehabilitated in different parts of the district by expelling the tribal people from their homes and agricultural lands. The policy of Sheikh Mujib's Govt. was to force the tribal people to lose their identity in the greater Bengalee society of the country and outnumber them by the Bengalee settlers in order to destroy the possibility of any political unrest or popular movement by the tribal people in the district.

After the overthrow of Sheikh Mujib, a delegation consisting of 67 representatives from the district met Justice A. S. Sayem, the then President of Bangladesh, on 19 Nov., 1975, and submitted a memorandum to him demanding regional autonomy.

Now a total of 57,000 armed forces (also including Bangladesh Rifles, Police and

Ansars) are deployed in Chittagong Hill Tracts. Three military cantonments have been established at Dighinala, Ruma and Alikadam, and three Brigade Command Offices have been established at Rangamati, Kaptai and Bandarban. One Naval base has been established at Kaptai. Two special Police battalions have been posted at Barkal and Mahalchari. The Sector Headquarters for Bangladesh Rifles has been established at Rangamati while two Wing Headquarters for the same have been established at Kaptai and Ramgarh. Three Ansar battalions have also been posted — one at Khagrachari, the other at Ghagra and the third at Bandarban.

Previously there were only 12 Police Stations in the district. Now the number has been increased to 28 and the strength of the Police Force has also been increased greatly. Now the total strength of the armed forces is such that there is one armed personnel for every ten hillmen. In the name of establishing law and order and searching for the miscreants, Army/Police camps have been set up in every market place and in all places where there are Govt. establishments. Most of the schools in the countryside are under their occupation.

The military also occupied many Govt. offices and Rest Houses. Even the old office of the Deputy Commissioner at Rangamati is now under the occupation of the Bangladesh Rifles. Now the total number of armed forces at Rangamati, the Headquarters of the district, exceeds the total number of civilian population of the town.

In order to coerce the public to withdraw their support from 'Shantibahini' (tribal resistance group) and to liquidate the guerrillas by starvation, the Bangladesh Govt. let loose a reign of terror in the district. The Army and Police carried out inhuman repressive measures against the tribals and burnt down the villages.

The following are only a few examples of crimes carried out by the Bangladesh Army and Police against the tribal people:—

(a) In the early months of 1977, the Govt. sent troops to massacre the inhabitants of Matiranga, Guimara, Manikchari, Lakshmichari etc. 50 tribals were shot dead, 23 women were tortured to death, 54 men died in pits, many women were raped, the villagers were robbed of their property and the houses were set on fire. Five thousand tribals were pushed into Tripura, India. But the Govt. of India sent them back to the hostile Bangladeshi Army's disposal after negotiating for their safety with the Bangladesh Govt.
(b) In December 1978, and January 1979, the Bangladeshi troops invaded a big area comprising Dumdumya Mouza (*No* 150 Mouza; 'Mouza' is an administrative unit which includes a number of villages), Maidong Mouza (*No* 138) and Panchari Mouza (*No* 137). The total area is about 175 sq. miles; it includes about 50 villages and its population is about 75,000.

- On 22 Dec., 1978, all the 22 villages of the Dumdumya Mouza were completely burnt to ashes;
- On 9 Jan., 1979, all the houses of the Maidong Mouza were set on fire;
- On 16 Jan., 1979, Panchari Mouza and all the Subalong valley villages were wiped out;

- Basanta Muni Tontongya. 30 yrs old. son of Bayanta. village Bagakhali. Dumdumya Mouza. was shot dead;
- Roalsoang Pankho. 42 yrs. old. son of Dulkhob. village Noapara. Dumdumya Mouza. was shot dead;
- Mrs Chandramala Chakma. 25 yrs. old. wife of Meyaram. village Mandira Chara Mukh. Dumdumya Mouza. was kidnapped by Army. No trace;
- Miss Gurimila Chakma. 18 yrs. old. daughter of Bansiram. village Mandira Chara Mukh. Dumdumya Mouza. was kidnapped by Army. No trace;
- Mrs Anal Devi Chakma. 22 yrs. old. w/o Mangal Chandra. village Denha Tejori Bhuatalichara. was shot dead;
- Mrs. Bunga Kajhi Chakma. 71 yrs. old. w/o Kesharmuni. village Chakrakada Mone. Panchari Mouza. was burnt alive in her house by the Army;
- All the cattle. poultry and foodstuff were taken away or destroyed by the troops.

The young men of village Gargajyachari, 4 miles south of Sub-Divisional Headquarters, Khagrachari, were on village defence duty against childlifters on March 5, 1979. Some Army men moving incognito came and arrested them and took them to the Khagrachari military camp. The Army made meat of them by cutting them to pieces with their own tagals (broad knife), first separating the muscles from the bones in peculiar joy. The victims were:

- Samiran Talukder, 16 yrs. old boy, 1st. year I. A. student, Khagrachari College, s/o Mr Chittomuni;
- Alomoy Talukder, 17 yrs. old boy, 2nd year I. A. student, Khagrachari College, s/o Mr Jatindra Bikash;
- Hallwa Chakwa, 16 yrs. old boy, farmer, s/o Mr Bangali Chand;

On 9 April 1979, at 0200 hours, the Army raided civilian quarters of the District Headquarters, Rangamati, and took away 70 people among whom were:—

- Mr Chandra Mohan Dewan, aged 91, retired Police Officer;
- Mr Pulin Chandra Dewan, aged 72, retired District Engineer;
- Mrs Dewan, w/o Mr Pulin Chandra Dewan, aged 60. All of them were thrown into pits. Even tribal Govt. servants were not exempted.
- Mr Jagat Jyoti Chakma, Accounts Officer, Bangladesh Small Industry Corporation, Rangamati;
- Mr Purnendu Chakma, Sub-Divisional Co-operative Officer, Rangamati;
- Mr Ramesh Chandra Chakma, Clerk, Forest Office;
- Mr Gnanendriya Chakma, Public Relations Officer. Rangamati Development Board, were tortured.

Among other prominent tribal people who were arrested and detained in the Army camp were:

- Mr Puranjoy Khisa and his family.
- Mr Arabinda Chakma and members of his family;
- Mr Santimoy Dewan, Chairman, Balukhali Union Parishad;

- Mr Kalpa Ranjan Chakma, who was a prominent Member of President Zia's Bangladesh Nationalist Party, was also arrested and inhumanly beaten;
- Mrs Ramani Chakma, w/o a senior Govt. Officer, was detained by the Army for about a fortnight leaving her four month old breast-fed baby at her home. Her fault was that her elder brother has joined the 'Shantibahini', the tribal resistance organization, which is demanding autonomy for their district.

On 5 Jan. 1979, one Mrs Kandari Chakma, 57 yrs. old, village Rengkhyang, Kaptai Sub-Division, was burnt alive in her own house by the Army. The house was closed from outside and then it was burnt to ashes.

But the most tragic incident occurred at Kamalchari, $2\frac{1}{2}$ miles south of Khagrachari (Sub-Divisional Headquarters). During the liberation war of Bangladesh, while President Ziaur Rahman (then he was a Major) was fleeing away to India in a hurry by a jeep, his jeep fell into the Chengi River at Kamalchari. It was a knee-deep water. The villagers of Kamalchari rescued the jeep and one Mr Mriganka Chakma s/o Mr Kali Kumar Chakma, Kamalchari, carried Ziaur Rahman on his back to the other side of the river. On 12 Aug., 1979, Zia's Army shot Mriganka Chakma dead on suspicion, in front of his father.

Early on 23 April 1979, in Kamugopara village, 16 miles south of Khagrachari, the Army led by Captain Abul Kalam Mahmud shot dead:

(1) Mr Shindhu Kumar Chakma, aged 40 yrs., (2) Mr Anabil Chakma, aged 25 yrs., (3) Anabil's younger brother, aged 18 yrs., (4) the only son of Sarada Chakma, aged 20 yrs., (5) Mr. Arun Kanti Chakma, a student of Class VIII of Pujgang High School.

The bodies of the victims were burnt in the presence of the members of the bereaved families. Before leaving the place Captain Abul Kalam gave stern warning and said 'such shall be the fate of every Chakma, remember this, all right?'

On 16 March 1979, Bangladesh Army rounded up all men, women and children of the two villages, Khagrachari and Khabong Paria, adjacent to Khagrachari Sub-Divisional Headquarters, and beat every one of them mercilessly. Some of them were hung from the trees and beaten.

Even senior and old tribal officers of the Govt. like (1) Mr Satya Brata Chakma, Sub-Divisional Food Controller, (2) Mr Debabrata Chakma, Thana Agriculture Officer, and teachers of Khagrachari College like (3) Prof. Bodhisatta Dewan, (4) Prof. Progabir Chakma, and (5) Prof. Madhu Mongal Chakma were badly beaten.

On 21 Feb. 1979, the Army burnt down the entire village of Pujgang 20 miles north of Khagrachari. **In Feb. 1979,** the Army burnt down villages of Dhudukchara and Logang area about 26 miles north of Khagrachari. **On 7 March 1979,** the entire village of Babuchara under Dighinala Police Station was destroyed. **On 13 March 1979,** Udalbagan village about 22 miles east of

Khagrachari was burnt down. On the same day the Army burnt down Logang village for the 2nd time. On **29 March 1979,** Durgachara village was also burnt down.

On 15 Oct., 1979, about 40 members of the Mahalchari Police battalion went to Mubhachari village, about 16 miles south of Khagrachari, and were attacked by Guerrilla group and about 30 of them were killed. In retaliation the Army burnt down several villages within a radius of 16 sq. miles. Many men and women were arrested and their fate is still not known. The Army also killed several people who were passing through the place by river/road not knowing anything about the incident beforehand.

In early Nov., 1979, about 30 personnel of the Army were killed at Adharakchara while returning from combing operation by the members of the 'Shantibahini'. In retaliation the Army burnt down the entire area covering about 50/60 sq. miles. They killed even the cattle of the villagers and roasted some of them for their feast. Now the entire area is still abandoned and the people have been in the forest.

On 23 Dec., 1979, the Army also destroyed the villages of Bangahata, Thakujyamakalak, Gulshakhali Kala and killed many tribal people including Buddhist priests Ven. Bannitananda Bhikkhu of Thakujyamakalak and Ven. Ajara Bhikkhu. The entire family consisting of 7 members of Rangabap Chakma was also killed by the Army. One Mrs Kamala Chakma was raped and then put to death. Now about 40–50,000 inhabitants of these villages in jungles in great distress. The Govt. are settling Bengalee Muslims, from outside the district, in all these villages.

In August 1979, the Govt. issued a secret circular to all District Commissioners of the country and advised them to prepare the list of the landless people in their respective districts. Now these landless people from other districts are being taken to Chittagong Hill Tracts in Govt.-hired buses, trucks and trains in large numbers and are being settled on the lands of the tribal people. These people are supplied with wheat free of cost, house building grant and a pair of cattle for ploughing by the Govt. It was learnt that the Govt. have been distributing the wheat, which they received for Food for Work Projects. It was also learnt that the Govt. is distributing about 60,000 maunds of wheat every month to these people.

Since the Bengalee Muslims have occupied the lands of the tribals there had been clashes and riots and 30 Bengalees were killed. Now the Army has established camps near the new settlers and has been training them with small arms. Many of them have been recruited as Ansars (Islamic Guards) and they are being given training in the use of small arms by the Army.

In the early part of Jan., 1980, the Army burnt down several villages of Matiranga Police Station and about 4,000 tribal people fled to India. This news was broadcast by All India Radio from Delhi.

Previously there were only three Sub-Divisions in the District. Now the Govt. have created three more Sub-Divisions. This has been done with a view to making the administrative unit smaller and to bringing more Bengalees in the district. Chittagong Hill Tracts Development Board was established ostensibly to make quick development but as a matter of fact to get the development funds granted easily for the Army. With this money of the Board, strategic roads for the use of the Army are being built. New school buildings, office buildings and Rest Houses are being built but all for the Army's use only. Any Army personnel who are transferred to Rangamati, can claim these buildings for their use. No foreigner is allowed to go to the countryside. The Bangladesh Govt. preach maintenance of world peace, equal treatment for all, cry in support of the black people of Rhodesia and South Africa but in their own country they are trying to exterminate the entire tribal population (six hundred thousand) of the Chittagong Hill Tracts. As a matter of fact, on 26 May, 1979, Brigadier Hannan and Lt. Col. Salam declared in a public meeting at Panchari, 16 miles north of Khagrachari, 'We want only the soil, and not the people of the Chittagong Hill Tracts'. District Commissioner, Mr Ali Haider Khan, and Mr Abdul Awal, previously Divisional Commissioner of Chittagong Division, warned the tribal leaders several times by saying that they could be extinct in the next 5 yrs.

At present 12,000 to 15,000 tribals are in detention inside and outside the Chittagong Hill Tracts jails including underground pits attached to every Military camp in the Chittagong Hill Tracts. They have been detained and imprisoned without charge and without trial and under routine and most inhuman torture.

It is estimated that about 25,000 to 30,000 tribal people were put to death or crippled.

We appeal to all peace-loving Governments, all humanitarian organizations and all conscientious people to come forward to save the 600,000 tribal people of the Chittagong Hill Tracts from total extinction.

"Jana Sanghati Samiti"
(Chittagong Hill Tracts People's League)
16 January 1980

This document included a list of 31 men and boys crippled, and 35 women and girls raped by members of the Bangladesh Army and Police in the Chittagong Hill Tracts on the instruction of the Bangladesh Government.

Lino Pereira, of the Miranha people, issued the following indictment on behalf of the Indians of Brazil, during a conference on Aboriginal rights and the operations of multinational corporations, held in Washington in 1982.

"Without its native people, Brazil does not exist"

"The indigenous people of Brazil wish to express their solidarity with their brothers in Guatemala, Nicaragua, Australia, Canada and other countries because of oppressions and massacres presently committed against them and because of the situation in which they find themselves, and to publicly condemn these things which are now occurring. At the same time, we want to inform the other indigenous peoples attending this conference in Washington of some of the principal problems caused by multinationals in Brazil and by the Brazilian government itself. We protest the following:

1. The construction of the highway from Cuiaba to Porto Velho, financed by the World Bank, which will cut through the territory of the Nambiquara Indians;

2. The invasion of the Satere-Mawe territory in the state of Amazonas by the French Elf Aquitaine petroleum corporation, which has destroyed a large part of hunting, fishing, forest resources and the traditional culture of these people;

3. The development of the ProAlcool (gasahol) program in the Brazilian northeast, which will affect various indigenous groups including the Wacu, Tinguiboto, Xoxo-Cariri, whose lands will be destroyed by sugar cane plantations;

4. The invasion of the Kaingang lands in the state of Parana in southern Brazil by the company of Slavero and Son, which has already cut down a large part of their forest for export;

5. The lack of legal recognition of Yanomami lands and the constant threats by politicians both of the government and opposition parties to reopen the Yanomami lands to prospecting. Besides leading to land loss and illegal mineral exploitation, these mines will also subject the Yanomami to diseases to which they have no resistance;

6. The absurd removal of the Pataxo people of the Brazilian northeast to inferior lands where they have no food stocks. Those who will suffer most are mothers and children. All this is in benefit of some big land owners under the protection of politicians who foresee the coming elections. All this is an affront to basic human dignity;

7. The construction of the Tamandua hydroelectric dam on the Cotingo River in the northern part of the Amazon, which will flood the Macuxi and Wapixana Indian lands. There is also an effort on the part of the government of Roraima to settle homeless Brazilian families on part of the lands that the Indians will lose;

8. The construction of the Balbina hydroelectric plant on the Uatuma River, which will flood the territory of the Waimiri-Atroari;

9. The transfer of the Guarani people of Ocoi on the Parana River to an area less than half the size of their own,

because of the construction of the Itaipu hydroelectric project;

10. The threat of the termination of the special legal status of the Indian and the imposition of special criteria to establish who is a member of the Indian community, both projects undertaken by the president of a special planning commission of FUNAI (National Indian Foundation), Colonel Ivan Zanoni;

11. The method used by FUNAI as a weapon to quiet indigenous people – the large-scale contracting of Indian people as its employees;

12. The implementation of large-scale economic projects to introduce Indians to capitalism, thus diverting their attention from their own subsistence farming activities;

Confronted by these aggressions, the indigenous people of Brazil join together in body and spirit with the other indigenous peoples of other countries. Together, we may see our rights respected and achieve a peace similar to that which existed among us before the rise of capitalism.

To conclude, we should remember that a large part of the world's resources are in indigenous areas, and that the indigenous peoples are the best keepers of their lands; that it is all peoples – not just the indigenous ones – that the forces of capitalism, especially in the form of multinational corporations want to exploit for their own enrichment.

Therefore we invite you to come to learn with us.

Without its native people, Brazil does not exist."

Source: Multinational Monitor, Washington, December 1982.

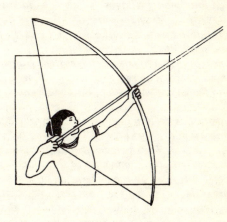

Ten years ago, anyone outside Central America could be forgiven their ignorance about the victimisation of indigenous Guatemelans.[42] Since 1978, however, and the Massacre at Panzos[43] it has been quite clear that successive military regimes are determined to wipe out all representations of Maya history and culture which cannot be appropriated and neutralised.[44] Since a culture is, in a broad sense, its people, this means genocide (a word whose meaning is still intact, even though it has often been mis-used).

With the fall of the Rios Montt regime and the rise of Oscar Mejia Victores, some observers purported to detect an improvement in human rights in Guatemala. Certainly there appears to have been a drop in murder squad assassinations in the towns;[45] a human rights organisation, comprising relatives of the 'disappeared' has surfaced, though not without difficulty[46] and civilian elections were held in late 1985, which brought the Christian Democrats nominally to power.[47]

However, objective reports foresee no overall improvement in a land where, over 30 years, more than 100,000 largely unarmed people have been killed by the military, 38,000 have disappeared, large numbers of trade unionists, teachers and students are abducted every month: a 'nation of widows and orphans',[48] and 'a nation of prisoners', indeed.[49]

Twenty per cent of the military's budget currently goes on the military establishment,[50] with the US contribution quadrupling under the Reagan administration.[51] Much other US aid goes towards a 'civilian' aid programme which simply assists the army's penetration of highland regions. In two respects particularly, indigenous Guatemalans have become the targets of a recently-introduced civil/military containment strategy: they are grouped into 'model villages' which owe much to the notorious 'strategic hamlets' of the Vietnam war[52] and they are being drafted, at accelerating rates, into civilian militias which, by early 1984, had already claimed over one-tenth of the entire population.[53]

Huge numbers of Mayan people have fled Guatemala and found a precarious toehold in Mexican refugee zones.[54] Many others remain behind as guerrillas, and leaders of various liberation movements (see Vol. 2, Part 5, ch. 2 for further details).

The statements in this section begin with a message delivered to the Guatemalan Federation of Workers in 1979, during a visit to the capital paid by native campesinos/campesinas *from El Quiche, after army beatings and arrests (with the connivance of local land-owners) drove them to take direct action. Hosted by the Federation of Workers, the Mayans met eight Congress deputies, and the Congress President, in Guatemala City. When they left, however, they were hounded by the military who cordoned off the streets, taking advantage of the confusion to arrest many students, workers and Indians. At the end of the day, another 13 Guatemalans joined the ranks of the 'disappeared'.[55]*

Following this is an account given by two native Guatemalans (who wish to remain anonymous for fear of reprisals) of the growth of repression in

Guatemala, ending with a partial list of atrocities covering a mere four month period in 1982. The third and fourth statements were delivered in the USA later the same year.

Underpinning the massacres and invasion of indigenous lands has been an alliance between external capitalists (specifically American) and the military élite which, from the monopoly days of United Fruit, through to the USAID projects of the 1960s and early 1970s, was probably stronger and more aggressive than anywhere else south of the Mexican border.[56]

As the liberation movements grew during the late 1970s, while Congress support for government-sponsored terrorism waned in the face of increasing condemnation by human rights organisations,[57] *the US State Department resorted to more subtle and subversive means of undermining the popular resistance. One of these — a proposed 'anthro–political' study on Guatemalan Indians — was resoundingly debunked by the World Council of Indigenous peoples in Central America.*

The chapter ends with a statement issued — also in late 1982 — by the Mexican-based CORPI which highlights the current oppression of all indigenous peoples in Central America.

In the midst of grief, a hundred Indians take their message to the capital

'This is to inform you that the Army came to San Pablo, arriving at our homes, and obliged the men and children to leave, while they kept the women inside to cook for them the little food we had; coffee, tortillas, and they killed the chickens. A captain walked on the roof of a house as they robbed us. They divided up the food among themselves while we put our hands in the air. Afterwards, from a distance of 30 meters, they fired on us. We tried to defend ourselves as best we could with machetes, hoes, firewood and stones. At the same moment, there were five soldiers in the bush. They also fired on us. Those soldiers who were near us were shot by their own comrades. One of the injured soldiers shouted at them to stop firing, that disgracefully they had misunderstood the order, and that later they would get what they deserved.

'The same captain pointed to an injured soldier and said, "With him, we're going to suffer because he can't walk." They decided to kill him, and did so with 3 shots. They pulled up two poles and hung the body and carried it towards El Rosario plantation. They told the colonel that the soldier had been killed in a battle with the Poor People's Guerrilla Army (EGP).

'We later asked this colonel to come and investigate the place where the gunfight happened, and to take into account what was happening to us, the Indians of San Pablo Baldio. If they had killed all of us, the guerrillas would have been blamed.

'What we heard on the radio is a lie. They are violating the laws, and yet it is us who are vilified. What has to be said is that they are attacking our homes.

'These are the details that we give you, friends, to pass along a thousand times on the radio so all the people of Guatemala will know what the soldiers are doing with the poor and exploited campesinos. Thanks for your attention, friends.'

Repression of the Indian peoples of Guatemala

We present first a short summary of our history in order to lead to an understanding of our life in the country called Guatemala. Here we shall speak of those who have always been oppressed, silenced, discriminated against, denied, exploited and massacred.

The first thing to bear in mind is that Guatemala is a country where the population does not belong to the same ethnic group. One cannot think about changes in the social structure without taking account of the majority which is the Indian. One must also take account of the millions of cultural and historical roots before there can be a full liberation. We are a people with a different foundation due to our way of living, understanding and seeing things. Because of that we are accused of being unadapted socially, the cause of under-development, the reason for cultural backwardness and other descriptions.

We express ourselves little for in all manner of ways we have been taken advantage of. However, we believe that it is time that we should talk as a people. Already there exist documents concerning the Indian people but they have not been expressed by ourselves. There have been studies, investigations, analyses and experiments by specialists in social studies and they have used us like rabbits for their experiments and their results have been of more use to the powerful than to us.

At the present time we still live within a culture which has reached us from the past in which spiritually we maintain our love and togetherness with nature with the same fervour as always. Our sufferings and struggle have lasted 500 years in which we have shown many forms of resistance to the invader. That resistance has allowed us to subsist and in Guatemala we are still the majority. The aims of our fight throughout all periods has been and continues to be for the right to land, to life, to our culture and to justice.

Our situation began to change in 1492 when the Spaniards arrived in our lands and was aggravated in 1524 when the ambitious invaders arrived in what is now Guatemala to take away our lands, eliminate our leaders and impose a different system of life through an excessive use of force and other means such as religion to subjugate us. In the whole of Central America there were round about 25 millions of inhabitants at the time of the arrival of the invaders. After a mere century, we were only 1 million; we had suffered the worst of human genocide.

At present the Guatemalan population is formed mainly of Mayan Indians (70%), who have suffered most from all kinds of ill-treatment and domination in the many aspects of life: social, economic, political and religious, etc. In the economic sphere, the spoliation of land was institutionalised, and slavery was established to give landowners access to Indian workers. In the religious sphere, the Inquisition was employed to select victims from our people from among the wisemen, governors and priests. Ethnocide and genocide have been part of our history from the time of the invasion. For 458 years the Spanish invaders have violated our women, single or married, young or old and the same happens at the present day. The Government has in its service repressive squads which with no scruple whatever rape and kill pregnant women. The Indian woman has never been respected by the invaders; on the contrary they have been even more exploited.

In Guatemala there exists an institution for tourism, INGUAT, an institution dedicated to the exploitation of the Indian, especially women as an object of tourist attraction and tool for publicity. All this without any benefit whatever. This can easily be seen in magazines, picture postcards for tourist promotion overseas, photographs, films such as *Nimak'ij en Sololá*, (archaeological zones) in which the actor is an Indian, but the economic benefit goes to the hotel chain, travel agencies, restaurants, middlemen selling local textiles, owners of transport networks etc. In many years these sectors earn a larger amount of income in foreign currency than the national economy. As can be demonstrated, we have always been made use of economically, with no thought given to our human value. Another of the serious abuses is the discrimination with which we live daily. They insult us calling us wild animals, barbarians, pagans, infidels, uncivilised, summing up all these epithets in the word INDIAN. Our religion is not respected; it is treated as a spectacle for tourists as in the case of Santo Tomas Chichicastenango. Another spectacle used to exploit Indian women is the festival of Cobán where women are presented as objects reaching the gross extreme of showing partially clothed girls in front of television cameras.

The colonial system in Guatemala was supported fundamentally by the exploitation of the land through the labour of Indian slaves. With the grants of land and labour, whole families were forced to migrate to the productive zones and received in exchange, starvation wages, disease and death. And at present, another cause of death is through intoxication brought by insecticides contaminating the environment and the water in the rivers. In Guatemala, an agricultural country, 3% of the population control 75% of the cultivable land and the Indians have been relegated to the least fertile areas where modernisation is difficult due to the steep slopes. On the few lands we possess for cultivation, the national oligarchy and transnational corporations have discovered rich resources under ground. They are defrauding our Indian brothers through false papers in order to get hold of this land. If we try and stop them they threaten us; they burn our crops, houses, poison our water supplies and in the end they massacre us like they did to the Ixiles in Quiché, to the Quechies in Panzós, in Chimaltenango, Solola, Huehuetenango, etc.

Our participation in politics has been nil; never have we had a representative in the Government who could communicate our socio-economic and socio-cultural interests. With regards to us, they remember only in each electoral campaign to use our language in their propaganda offering us things that they never do later.

Soldiers in the army are brother Indians captured in the streets and in their houses. Once in the army they alienate them from their roots, rob them of their moral principles in order to turn them into criminals prepared to massacre their own people to defend the interests of the oligarchy.

We have seen in broad sweeps, part of our history, we have served only to accelerate the enrichment of the dominant oligarchy which is associated with the transnationals. We must make it clear that we do not want to fall into ethnocentricism, but to demand respect for our identity . . .

With respect to the recent elections, we must say at the outset that none of the candidates offered any solutions to the people. All were basically a response to the interests of the dominant class; they varied only in their subsidiary characteristics. Conditions in the country were highly conflictive with a high degree of repression exercised by the army and other repressive bodies. A large number of leaders were eliminated as they could not find support from parties such as the FUR.

The people were threatened with gaol or fines if they refused to take part in the voting. Above all, those not voting were accused of being subversive. All who worked in the state apparatus as well as those working for private enterprise were threatened with the loss of their jobs if they did not vote. According to electoral registers, 2 million citizens were entitled to vote; but in the election only 1.2 millions cast their votes.

In the face of an extremely conflictive situation, candidates came into collision with each other and even killed each other. On the other side, many popular organisations continued their work because clearly the elections were but a game. Under these circumstances young officers in the military staged a so-called coup. In reality all that has happened is that the young officers who have been shooting and massacring the people have gone into the Palace while the old officers have left the Palace to return to their barracks. Those now belonging to the present Military Junta are also responsible for the many crimes in Guatemala. Ríos Montt is himself responsible for the massacre in Sansirisay, eastern province. The other two military chiefs are equally responsible for murders and massacres in different parts of the country.

Repression in Guatemala has not stopped; indeed more savage methods are now being used. The army is shooting and massacring people in the region of Huehuetenango, San Marcos, Quiché, Sololá, Chimaltenango and they are setting fire to the woods and jungle. Settlements are being occupied by the army where all sorts of crimes are committed by them: robbery, rape, murder.

The clandestine indigenous organisation has attempted to document and record the atrocities perpetrated against the people of Guatemala. We reproduce their findings for a two and a half month period: April to mid June, 1982.

April

2   54 killed in Aldea Pujujil, Sololá (25 women, 20 men and 9 children).

3   people killed when 5 villages between Tecpan and Santa Apolonia were burnt down.

6	an old woman of over 100 was killed by the army in Aldea Palamá, San José Poaquil, Chimaltenango.
12	12 killed in Santa Rosa and Chubuyub.
15	25 killed and 3 kidnapped in Agua Caliente, San Juan Comalapa, Chimaltenango.
15	20 killed in Semejá Primero, Chichicastenango.
16	35 killed in Aldea Covadonga, Barrillas, Huehuetenango.
16	8 killed in Chiché, Quiché.
17	40 killed in Pujujil, Sololá.
17	14 killed in San José Poaquil.
17/22	67 killed in Aldea Xesic, Chocoaman, Tobil, Quiché.
19	13 killed in Aldea Tziquinay, San Martín Jilotepeque, Chimaltenango.
25	13 killed in Aldea Varituc, San Martín Jilotepeque, Chimaltenango.
26	20 killed in Aldea Chipiacul, Patzún, Chimaltenango.
29	houses burnt in Aldea Xecoxol, Tecpan, Chimaltenango.

May

2	several families killed in Aldea Chijocon.
3	15 killed in Parramos, Chimaltenango.
5	2 women (one with a twelve-day old child) killed in Tecpan, Chimaltenango.
8	46 killed in Aldea Saquixa II, Chichicastenango (15 women, 25 children and 6 men).
10	4 killed in Aldea Sacualin, Chisec, Alta Verpaz (3 women and 1 child).
14	5 brothers killed in Aldea El Granadillo, Colotenango, Huehuetenango.
14	4 men killed in San Ildefonso Ixtahuacán, Huehuetenango.
14	3 women killed in Aldea Majtilabaj, San Cristóbal, Alta Verapaz.
15	8 men killed in Aldea Semeja II Chichicastenango; 2 men killed in Santa Cruz and 3 women killed in Mulua.
18	100 to 150 killed in Aldea El Pajarito, Pichiquil, Patzul San Juan Cotzal, el Quiché.
18	6 men killed in Aldea Chillel, el Quiché.
18	8 killed in Aldea Pocoil Matzul Cuarto, el Quiché.
18	bodies of 84 men, women and children found in Aldea Chuatalun, San Martin Jilotepeque, Chimaltenango.
19	bodies of 62 men, women and children found in the amphitheatre of el Quiché.
19	many killed in Paraxtut, El Pajarito and Tobil, el Quiché during destruction of the villages.

June

2	2 killed and 1 burned in Aldea las Pacayas, San Cristóbal Verapaz.
4	32 students kidnapped in various parts of the country by kidnappers driving police cars.
5	12 students kidnapped and later released due to recent amnesty.
6	10 women killed in Aldea Chijuc, Alta Verapaz; 7 had been decapitated and 2 young girls raped before being killed.
7	15 men kidnapped from Aldea Chijuc, Alta Verapaz.

7	mutilated body of a man found at Colonia el Encinal, Mixco.
9	2 students disappear in Sanarate, Santa Rosa.
9	17 students tried in the capital accused of terrorism.
10	18 killed (8 women, 6 men and 4 children) and 34 wounded in Las Pacayas, Alta Verapaz.
10	13 students (3 girls and 9 boys) kidnapped and accused of being members of subversive organisations (such as the FP-31). They were later released due to amnesty.

The residents of the Río Usumacinta and Pasion region have been asking the government to stop work on the hydro-electric power project which will inundate more than 12,000 square kilometres. Though official studies describe the zone as arid and unpopulated, more than 25,000 families and 30 million trees live there. The action is seen as an attempt by the government to throw out these families as a measure of repression.

Guatemala, June 1982

The dimension of Indian peasants

When I was six, my parents used to tell us kids stories from the past. They did this as the tamales were being cooked and in this way related to us the sufferings of our ancestors and what people were going through at that time as well. We lived in such conditions of poverty that it is very difficult for people in this country to understand. As I watched my parents, I realized at the age of ten that I would have to leave my family and make my own way so that there would be less of a burden on them. So I went to the city and there I realized that the city people too lived in terrible conditions. I became aware that the situation of exploitation was one against an entire people.

And so it came to me at the age of 14 that I had to do something — that I had to work something out so I could work for my people. But being so young, many people would not listen to me or to my friends who thought as I did. What could we do against such forces? And I carried this with me, this feeling of wanting to do something for my people and rising against all that was against us. When I reached the age of 19, I was able to talk to people and thus began the work.

We started by talking with my cousins and people close to us. Little by little we had some success; first in our home province of Quiché. By 1978, there was some strength in three areas of the country and on the 1st of May, 1978, we formed our Committee of Peasant Unity. This was the first time in the history of Guatemala that an organization had been formed under the direct leadership of peasants. It should be pointed out that of the 7.5 million people in Guatemala, 5 million are peasants.

Most of the Indian population does not know how to read or write. But those of us who do have been teaching the others. When I left my town the people didn't have blackboards, chalk or anything like that, so we used the ground and a stick to teach people how to read and write and a large number of my comrades can now write their name even though they can't totally read and write. Increasingly it is the women and children who must plant the crops on which we live because the men are either dead or working in some other place.

In addition, many many women have left their towns and directly involved themselves and their children into the armed struggle. And also the children had a growing consciousness that we are involved in a crucial struggle. One day we were sleeping in a ditch and one of the children woke up and said that he was hungry. And his mother said not to cry because the military were coming and they will hear us and from that moment on the child did not cry. He endured his hunger and the cold in silence.

By the time the children are eight years old they are ready to play very important roles in the struggle. They serve as couriers and are organized into groups. When they observe something about the military, they form a line and pass the word so that the last child in line can take the message into the village.

And so our appearance at this time was a blow to the government. Especially since never before had the most exploited sector of the country, the peasant class, joined together to voice their concerns. Another point that should be made is that it was very frightening to the government that on the first of May, we appeared in demonstrations — Indians and Ladino workers — side by side. Because for a long time, one method for continuing the system of exploitation was to use divisions between Indian and Ladino peoples.

In 1979, the government began a systematic series of massacres in Quiché. When Montt replaces Lucas, the repression gets worse — a scorched earth policy that destroys entire towns, establishes strategic hamlets which are living hells, poisons the rivers and burns crops, kills and tortures the people.

We realize that these are acts of desperation because they can't destroy our organizations, nor the level of struggle of the people. We have been unifying all organizations. After the massacre at the Spanish Embassy, our organization began to unite the mass groups. Now all four major armed organizations are involved. We never wanted to have a war. But the response of the government has created a war. For the future, we want a government that will respect all people. This must be a government that includes Indians. It is the people who are now involved in the struggle — Indians, peasants, workers — from which a new government will come.

Domingo Hernandez Iztoy

The dimension of Indian women

For many years now we the Indian people have been exploited and oppressed in Guatemala; and we are more than 70 percent of the country's population. In the rural areas we don't have sanitary water, roads or schools.

The young boys are forcibly taken away to military barracks to serve in the army. Many people have to migrate to the coastal plantations to work in coffee, cotton, and sugar cane. They are so poorly paid that when they come back they have nothing.

In my village, my father was president of Catholic Action, and every Sunday people would get together and talk. Out of these meetings there came other meetings to talk about village problems, the formation of co-ops, and the distribution of food.

As the people met, the question of land ownership came up, the fact that few people had access to any land. Out of this came the formation of the Committee for Peasant Unity (CUC). As people participated in the development of CUC, they became more aware of the rich and what they were doing to us.

The rich have always treated us Indians as people who are crazy, who can't think. They think of Indians as animals, who don't have the capacity to learn and the capacity to become conscious. But we've demonstrated in practice that we can organize and do things and we're not crazy like they say.

And it's not just we Indians who are suffering exploitation and oppression. It's also the majority of the Ladinos (non-Indians) who are poor and suffer. For example, the slum dwellers in Guatemala City live in houses made of cardboard, and have no running water and no electricity. Thus we Indians are struggling alongside the Ladinos in Guatemala, against the rich.

We knew there were also guerrilla forces who were struggling with arms. And on the big coastal farms, thousands of agricultural workers were organizing demonstrations and strikes, while in Guatemala City, student and union organizations were beginning to get strong. So it wasn't just in one place that people were organizing. It was all over Guatemala, in all sectors.

The more we organized, the more the government replied with massacres. You'd find dead bodies in gorges and valleys and alongside of roads.

At first the army used to persecute only men. They never paid any attention to the women; they thought we were invisible. But when the men would leave the village, the army noticed that we still had organizations and protests. They discovered that the women were organized too.

For example, in one town, women were making explosives out of fruit cans, with gasoline inside. When the army came in and saw that there were only women there, they started to laugh — but when the women threw the explosives the soldiers started to cry! And these women held off the army long enough to allow the rest of the village to escape.

In May of this year, thirteen of us from the group FP31, including myself, decided to take over the Brazilian Embassy, because that was the only way of forcing the attention of the world press on the massacres in the rural areas. When we occupied the Embassy, the government said that under no circumstances would they negotiate with us. They said they would burn us alive, like what had happened two years before in the Spanish Embassy.

We are asking for the broadest possible solidarity to stop the U.S. from sending arms to Guatemala. The Reagan Administration is sending military aid to Rios Montt. The helicopter parts the American government sends are for the same helicopters that bomb our towns.

The government is massacring us because we're organizing and rising up. They have massacred a lot of people, but there are still many people left. The strength of the movement is that both the mass organizations are united and the four guerrilla organizations are united. We have great hope that we will arrive in power and create a new Guatemala.

Manuela Sequic

Source: News and Letters, Denver, July 1982

More Penetration Anthropology by the U.S. Government

The WCIP has learned that the U.S. Department of State in Arlington Virginia recently requested proposals for a research study, 'The Guatemalan Indians: An Anthro–Political Study'. The closing date for proposals was June 24, 1983. The study is to take place over five months and we assume that the study has been or soon will be awarded. The work statement of the request for proposals reads as follows:

Purpose: To describe the interaction of Indian culture with internal warfare and political struggle in Guatemala.

Although they constitute half its population, Guatemala's Indians have not, historically, been active in national political or economic systems. Not only have ladino elites excluded the Indians; many Indian communities have deliberately sought isolation as a mechanism to preserve their cultural integrity. Now, though still marginal beneficiaries of recent Guatemalan economic growth, the Indians have become central to the political struggle which will determine Guatemala's future.

The current generation of guerrillas have cast their struggle in terms of Indian rights. Why? Was this decision based upon a valid appreciation of racial, historical, linguistic or other distinctive features of Indian culture? Was this a tactical decision primarily to increase international support? Does it reflect or facilitate Indian participation in guerrilla ranks? How, in sum, do the guerrillas view the Indian, both ideologically and tactically?

Government and political elite (including military) attitudes toward and perceptions of the Indians are similarly crucial. How do they parallel or differ from the guerrillas'? How has the Government attempted to deal with the Indian question? Do political and military elites support these efforts? With superior resources, has it had any more success than the guerrillas in obtaining Indian allegiance? If the government successfully integrates the Indians into national political and economic life, what will be the result? Was such an integration occurring after the 1976 earthquake and before the onset of the war in 1979? What were the activities of the Lucas government in the highlands? Of the Rios Montt government?

The proposal further stated that the contracting team will be required 'to consult, in particular, materials originating in Guatemala — from the guerrillas, the government, and Guatemalan scholars'. In addition the request for proposal calls for a report in four major sections analyzing:

1. The historical elements and features of Indian culture which are most relevant to an understanding of the current conflict, including a description of Indian social, cultural, economic and political grievances and aspirations;
2. Relations between the guerrillas and the Indians;
3. Relations between government and political elites and the Indians; and,
4. The factors most likely to determine the outcome of the struggle for Indian allegiance.

An annotated bibliography of the 25 most policy relevant mongraphs were also to be included in the appendix.

Comments and Observations

This study is a clear case of penetration anthropology designed to serve U.S. intervention in Guatemala. We note that Guatemala has the highest U.S. business investment of any of the Central American countries.

The U.S. government will use this study, together with other intelligence, to improve their strategy for penetrating the indigenous areas of Guatemala to exploit the indigenous peoples' lands and resources without regard to human life.

This study, together with other sources will inform the aid policies and programs of such agencies as the Inter-American Development Bank, the World Bank, U.S.A.I.D., the U.S. Foreign Policy Commission on Central America chaired by Henry Kissinger, among others. We sincerely doubt that they have the indigenous interest at heart.

This case is yet another example of the U.S. exploiting Indians within the context of a popular revolutionary struggle by gathering and manipulating strategic information so that the U.S. government and its agents can attempt to manipulate the Indian resistance now and in the future.

The obvious goal is to break the guerrilla warfare in the indigenous areas of Guatemala using indigenous anthropology/sociology to implement the conqueror's rules based on division and provoking internal conflicts within Guatemala.

There is an obvious parallel to the strategy that the United States is using in Nicaragua.

This study underlines the U.S.'s attempt to tailor a 'hearts and minds' campaign to win the support of the indigenous people so as to follow up to Rios Montt's 'scorched earth' and subsequent 'tortilla, shelter and work' policies designed to push the people to the limits of survival by attacking their economic and cultural systems and values. The study is very specific in its emphasis on how to integrate the Indians into the nation's economic life. In this, the struggle of the Indians' allegiance is viewed as crucial.

In addition to underrepresenting the Indigenous peoples as half rather than 70% of the national population, to say that the Indians are 'marginal beneficiaries of recent Guatemalan economic growth' is a lie. Rather, they are the victims and will continue to be the victims as long as the U.S. government, the transnationals and the ruling elites within Guatemala continue to act out their plans for exploitation of the lands and resources of the indigenous people. Given the recent replacement of presidents by the Guatemalan military we are likely to continue to see food and medical supplies used as a weapon for securing Indian allegiance together with the usual battery of kidnapping, torture and assassination.

Source: WCIP (World Council of Indigenous Peoples) Bulletin No. 3, (Lethbridge) August 1983, pp. 1–2.

Bulletin from the Regional Coordinating Body of Indian People (CORPI) (Central America and Mexico) Tlahuitoltepec, Oaxaca, Mexico, 11 October 1982

1. We the Indian people of the Central American region, are experiencing at the present time, massacre and total extermination by the military governments who support those who have the economic power in the area and who are supported by North American Imperialism. This unjust situation is the result of the colonial system that has been imposed upon us since the arrival of the Europeans in America and has evolved into what is known as Liberal Capitalism.

2. We Indian people in America live the same reality that other Indian people colonized by Europe in other parts of the world are suffering, although there are cultural and historical differences.

3. In America, we the Indian people are suffering a situation that is the result of more than 450 years of Economic Exploitation, Cultural Domination, Social Marginalisation and Racial Discrimination. Particularly in Central America we have been struggling in one way or another, directly or indirectly, for our complete liberation from the Exploitation, Marginalisation and Discrimination to which we have been and we are still subjected.

4. Today Central America is a very convulsive region, because of the people's struggle for liberation — among them Indigenous Peoples. Efforts are being made by governments together with U.S. Imperialism to suppress the struggle.

5. The victory of the Nicaraguan Revolution in 1979 is internationally known as is the liberation struggle of the Salvadorean and Guatemalan people against a situation that is the result of centuries of oppression, exploitation and social injustice.

6. The military governments in Central America, massacre, repress and exploit in an inhuman way the majority of the population in order to maintain their sovereignty and protect the interests of a few families and certain groups in the country. The Salvadorean and Guatemalan governments, with the support of the U.S. government and other dictatorships, are carrying out a policy of extermination in the area. The Indian people are the main victims of this extermination policy. As well, the U.S. government is attempting by all means to disrupt the Nicaraguan Revolution.

7. In Guatemala, where at least 70% of the total population is Indian, the policy of repression that has been followed by former governments and the present one is especially against Indian peoples. Hundreds of Indian people have been massacred and many communities wiped out in different provinces. There are more than one hundred thousand refugees in Mexico and other countries. Some days ago, the President of Guatemala, Efrain Rios Montt, declared that it is necessary to exterminate Indian people in order to bring peace to the country.

8. In order to put an end to this situation, the participation of Indigenous peoples, particularly in the Guatemala struggle, is the deciding factor in the attempt to build up a just and equal society.

9. In El Salvador, the government purports to have a democratic image while it continues to massacre and exterminate the Salvadorean people who are struggling for liberation. The U.S. government continues to give economic and military support to the Salvadorean government. In each military barrack the number of U.S. military advisers is increasing. The sole purpose of these atrocities is to protect the interests of the 14 families who are the bourgeoisie and the oligarchy of El Salvador.

10. The Agrarian Reform, very well advertised by the U.S. as a generous gesture on the part of the Salvadorean government, has worsened the massacres of the Salvadorean people.

11. In Nicaragua the revolutionary development has been in progress for three years; led by the Sandinista Front of the National Liberation (FSLN). This revolution is a decisive step in Central America's history and must be supported due to the threats of American Imperialism that promotes the counterrevolution and is threatening to destroy that which the Nicaraguan people has achieved.

12. Due to manipulation by counterrevolutionaries and the mistakes committed in the revolutionary process, Nicaraguan Indian communities of the Atlantic Coast are confronted with very difficult situations at the present time. This situation has led to the migration in large numbers of Miskito and Sumo Indians to Honduras and other countries.

13. The counterrevolutionaries and the U.S. government have manipulated for their own interests the events of the Atlantic Coast and have used the Indian brothers as cannon fodder to undermine the revolutionary process of the Nicaraguan people.

14. Representing the organizational efforts of Indian people in Central America, Mexico and Panama is the Regional Coordinating Body of Indian People (CORPI); a member of the WCIP which is a non-governmental organization within the United Nations. CORPI denounces:

a) The extermination of our Indian brothers in Guatemala and El Salvador by the respective governments, with the direct support of the U.S. government and with the complicity of other dictatorships.

b) The manipulation of the real demands of Indian people of the Nicaraguan Atlantic Coast by the counterrevolutionary and Imperialist groups, with the purpose of destroying the popular Sandinista revolution.

c) The enforced participation of Indian representatives in the Guatemalan government, just to give the image of a Democracy that doesn't exist.

15. The Regional Coordinating Body of Indian People (CORPI) is in solidarity with the liberation struggle that our brothers of Guatemala and El Salvador are carrying out. They are not alone, our voice, our spirit, our mind and the Indian support are with them.

16. CORPI supports also the real struggle of our Indian brothers of the Atlantic Coast of Nicaragua for their historical and cultural rights within a popular revolutionary process. In the meantime CORPI calls upon the Nicaraguan Government to start a true dialogue with the Indian communities in order to inspire their trust in the revolution and to find effective mechanisms of participation for

Indian people in the construction of a just and equal society for everybody.

17. CORPI urges all democratic governments in America and other countries of the world to help reduce the strain of the Central American region; to demand the U.S. government and other governments who are involved to stop their political and especially their military intervention in the internal matters of the region. To let our people assume with responsibility their future in the best way.

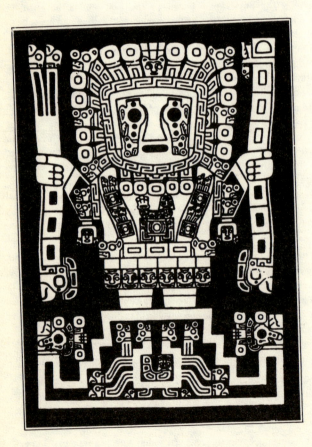

Since the bloody coup which toppled the democratically elected Allende government in 1973, the Mapuche nation (about 9% of the total population) has received the brunt of military oppression in the rural areas of Chile. In particular, 1984 was a year of despojo *(plunder) during which many Mapuche leaders were arrested and beaten; the* Alianza Chilena Anticomunista *issued threats against the lives of several leaders of the Mapuche AD-Mapu movement.*

Six years after the Pinochet takeover, the regime promulgated Decree Law 2568, which sought to deny Mapuche traditional access to — and inheritance of — their lands, by dividing them into plots and consigning many of these to non-indigenous land holders.[58] *In December 1984, a member of AD-Mapu addressed the United Nations Special Rapporteur for Chile in the following words:*

"The Pinochet regime has implemented, since the beginning, an open and systematic policy of racial discrimination and genocide against the Mapuche people. This has been in the form of killings, arrests, exile, and disappearances of many members and leaders of the Mapuche communities from different regions of the country. This is generally unknown to organizations committed to human rights investigations.

"We want to call the attention of human rights organizations to the Mapuche situation. In order to do this, it is important to keep in mind the vision of the cosmos and the cultural values of the Mapuche, which are not generally considered in reports.

"We would like to point out that the Mapuches have a SACRED and COLLECTIVE concept of the earth and all it produces. There are no concepts like private property, commercial value, or constantly changing technology that industrial societies have. The religious and sacred dimensions have a global and general quality in Mapuche culture. To alter any aspect of Mapuche culture is to alter the sacred spirituality of Mapuche people.

"Traditionally, for the Mapuche the earth is part of life itself and it also has a sacred dimension which encompasses the existence and culture as a whole of Mapuche society.

"With this in mind, it is easy to see the vast damage caused to the spirit of the Mapuche people by the division of sacred and collective land. The consequences are unpredictable for the future of the culture of this people.

"In documents recently issued by the AD-Mapu Mapuche organization, the current situation of the Mapuche people is characterized as the most critical in history. This is based on the weakening of social and cultural unity as a direct consequence of the arbitrary and unjust division of Indian communities. INDAP (Instituto Nacional de Desarrollo Agropecuario) representatives, with no consideration of the legitimate rights of the community, grant land titles to the OCCUPANTS, whether or not they have rights to the land. Many times these titles are granted to non-Mapuche individuals and landholders.

"When Decree Law 2568 was written in 1979, 2,066 Indian reservations covering 375,000 hectares existed within the 8th and 10th regions. According to INDAP, by late 1983, 1,365 reservations totalling 235,000 hectares had been divided. This means that only 701 reservations have not yet been divided . . .

"The implementation of this law has meant that several thousand Mapuches have been robbed of their lands and have been left without territorial rights . . .

"One of the immediate effects which can be seen by the implementation of this new law is the severe social and economic situation. There is a high percentage of unemployment, hunger, and misery in all communities, both those which have been divided and those which have not. This is leading towards a situation of racial explosion of unforeseeable consequences, caused by the neglect, discrimination, and repression suffered during these years of military rule."

This chapter ends with an interview given by the Director of the National Association of Salvadorean Indians to the Mapuche Information Bulletin (Boletin Informativo Mapuche) in 1982.

Introduction: I am the leader of the Salvadorean Indian Association. This organisation has 14,865 members organised for the most part in agrarian co-operatives. Why agrarian co-operatives and not in communities or reserves like other ethnic groups in our continent? Well, brother, the treatment that we received from the colonizers and from those who followed them and who still hold the power, was more brutal and inhumane than in the other Indoamerican countries.

Here, in my country there were no special or protectory laws for the Indian peoples. The traditional communities were violently incorporated into a new social order based fundamentally on the feudal system of land tenure, the Spaniards appropriated our land. And our people, we the Indians remain on small patches situated in or on the edge of our former land, and on the worst land, for we had no alternative but to serve as serfs on the estates of the white exploiters. Thus our culture began to disappear, our traditions have also been slowly disappearing as have our languages. Yes, it must be accepted that the process of cultural domination has been violent and rapid.

Q. What percentage of the Salvadorean population do you think is Indian?
A. I think that 40% of the Salvadorean population is Indian, however the official statistics deny our existence, they say that we are less than 3%. This is not true, we are 40%. Of course from the cultural point of view we have lost ground but from the biological point of view we are a large population.

Q. What Indian heroes do you remember as a people, and what are your struggles now?

A. Well our best known heroes are Anastacio Aquino and Lucio Alama. These men along with many others fought for our rights, our land and our freedom. But the enemy was stronger and having defeated us took all our land away, we are given no reserve nor any kind of common land in this country — and because of this they now say that we don't exist or that there are very few of us. However, my friend, I say that on a national level we represent a great strength. Now as far as our struggle goes I'll only go back a few decades to the time when I began to struggle for my race. As I told you we Indians are peasants for the most part, we live on the edge of the big estates and more often on the estates themselves. The houses have cardboard roofs, some are tiles and others are simply palm huts. As far as medicine goes it has never been given to us and we just depend on traditional domestic medicines — as you realise in these modern times scientific medicine has achieved great advances, but we have had no access to these services. It is because of this that we have gone on struggling to regain our cultural values, our language and our community life which has gradually been disappearing — that's why we formed the co-operatives to work, live and struggle together. We continue the struggle to recover the land stolen from our ancestors and I am sure that with the unity of the Indians and the support of the Salvadorean people we shall win.

Q. As everyone knows El Salvador is at this moment in the throes of war — can you tell us how far the Indians are participating and why?

A. Well the war has been growing in dimension all the time. The number of dead is steadily growing as is the number of victims. In the course of the last year, 1980, there were 13,000 deaths and the number of victims reached 80,000. What hurts most is to have to see the bestiality of the military against innocent people. Only a few days ago when I was walking through the streets of my village I saw the heads of corpses on both sides of the street on the pavements. These criminals do it to threaten and scare us but they don't succeed. In my case, for example, just seeing this and realising the abuses they commit against the people gives me courage and a stronger desire to fight against this brutal tyranny. As you know the enemy is strong and counts on the foreign support of the U.S.A. For the people the struggle is a hard one. To make clear the point that the struggle of the Salvadorean people is our struggle, I emphasise that we the Indian peoples are involving ourselves in it, and aligning ourselves with the Farabundo Marti Front for National Liberation — and we shall win, my friend.

Q. Can you describe geographically which areas populated by Indians are being destroyed by the air forces of the Junta?. According to one report in the Washington Star *of 29 January 1982 the U.S. military have given the El Salvador air force a substantial amount of Napalm?*

A. We the Indians of El Salvador comprise the poorest section of the people, we are without land but we still keep alive the Indian names for our geographical regions. The protectors of the dictatorship are now destroying the forests and the fertility of the land — this action will bring fatal consequences in the future. They don't care if they destroy everything, they just want to put an end to the resistance of the people. I now want to show with examples those Indian places that have been destroyed by them, the enemy of the poor in El Salvador. In the north, in the Chalatelango and Zacateluca region the Guazapa highlands have been heavily bombed and also the San Vicente volcano region. In the East they have bombed Morazan in Coscagopera, Torola and

Tototile, La Union and Mapalita. In the west Santa Ana, Chualchapa, Metapang, Zuchitoto, Tecomatepe, Oratorio and Istagua. The areas where there is now the greatest Indian population are in the districts round Zonzonate and after that, Zacatecoluca, Cuzcatlan, Zalco, Nahuazalco, Zucazate, Belanguijac and Cuyuapa.
Q. What message would you send to the Chilean Mapuches and to the readers of our bulletin?
A. Well brother, what I would say is SOLIDARITY, solidarity with the people of El Salvador, solidarity is brotherhood, solidarity is peace, solidarity is Victory. Thank you.

Source: Survival International Review, London, Spring 1982.

2. Militarisation

United by a circle of death

". . . When years before they had first come to the people living on the Cebolleta land grant they had not said what kind of mineral it was. They were driving US Government cars, and they paid the land grant association $5,000 not to ask questions about the test holes they were drilling . . . Early in the spring of 1943, the mine began to flood with water from subterranean springs. They hauled in big pumps and compressors on flat-bed trucks from Albuquerque . . . But later in that summer the mine flooded again, and this time no pumps or compressors were sent. They had enough of what they needed, and the mine was closed, but the barbed-wire fences and guards remained until August 1945. By then they had other sources of uranium, and it was not top-secret any more. . . He had been so close to it, caught up in it for so long that its simplicity struck him deep inside his chest; Trinity Site, where they had exploded the first atomic bomb, was only 300 miles to the southeast, at White Sands. And the top-secret laboratories, where the bomb had been created, were deep in the Jemez Mountains on land the Government took from Cochiti Pueblo: Los Alamos, only 100 miles northeast of him now, still surrounded by high electric fences. There was no end to it; it knew no boundaries; and he arrived at the point of convergence where the fate of all living things, and even the earth had been laid. From the jungles of his dreaming he recognized why the Japanese voices had merged with Laguna voices . . . converging in the middle of witchery's final ceremonial sand-painting. From that time on, human beings were one clan again, united by the fate the destroyers planned for all of them, for all living things; united by a circle of death that devoured people in cities 12,000 miles away, victims who had never known these mesas, never seen the delicate colors of the rocks that had boiled up their slaughter . . .'

Leslie Marmom Silko, *Ceremony*, 1977
Laguna Pueblo

*For a period of 20 years British RAF Vulcans — more recently Tornados —
have been exploiting an area of Ntesinan (Quebec–Labrador) about the size
of Eire for low-level training flights.*[59] *Joined by the West German Luftwaffe
in 1980*[60] *these supersonic military aircraft have 'strafed' Innut villages as far
north-east as Utshimsit (Davis Inlet) and south-west as Esipit (Les
Escoumins). The effects — though consistently ignored and downplayed by
the military*[61] *— have been profound, and are becoming worse. The Innu —
supported by scientific opinion — are confronted with the worst dislocation of
their lives, and interference with their hunting, that many of them, especially
the women and children, have ever experienced. The most damaging impact
has been on those communities, such as La Romaine, which recently started
returning to the bush and trying to recover their traditional skills.*[62] *As
Francois Bellefleur put it, in September 1984:*

> *"My life is at stake here and the life my father and my father's father
> lived is also at stake. I want to teach my children the kind of life the Innu
> People have always lived — it is this, the continuation of the Innu way of
> living, that is at stake.'*[63]

*The Naskapi-Montagnais Innu Association, the Innu National Council and
the Labrador Inuit Association*[64] *are unanimously opposed to all militarisation
of land which, as David Nuk of Sheshatshit puts it '. . . has never been the
object of any transfer of sovereignty from the Innu People to any foreign
power and remains legitimately our country'.*[65]

*In October 1984 the national associations and villagers from many of the
affected areas united in an international campaign to halt the flights.*[66] *They
received considerable publicity in West Germany: two years later their cause
was taken up in Britain.*[67]

*Camile Mestanapeo lives in La Romaine, in the Quebec part of Ntesinan. The
following statement was delivered at a Toronto public meeting in October
1984 as part of this campaign.*

The Innu Declaration was released a few days earlier.

"A clear violation of Commitments"

Press Release: 8 October 1984
Released by: Innu band councils of Mingan, Natashaquan, La
Romaine, Schefferville, and St. Augustine; the Naskapi-Montagnais
Innu Association (NMIA); the Conseil Attikamek-Montagnais (CAM);
and the Innu National Council (Innu Kanantuapatshet).

**Topic: Low-Level Military Aircraft Training Flights and Bombing
Ranges**

Note: the term 'Innu' (Innut — plural) refers to the Indian people previously labelled Montagnais-Naskapi.

The Innu people wish to state their total opposition to the use of their territory (Quebec–Labrador Peninsula), most of which is actual or potential caribou range, for the purposes of low-level military flight training and bombing practice. This opposition is absolute and arises from a number of considerations. Pre-eminent amongst these are:

1.   The territory over which these exercises are being conducted remains the territory of the Innu people and is inhabited for most of the year by Innu families scattered across the country.

2.   We firmly believe that the low-level flights have been seriously harming the caribou population in our territory. Evidence of the impact of these flights is seen in the widespread disruption of natural caribou migration patterns, calving range abandonment, and a decreasing live-birth rate.

3.   Innut and biologists have witnessed the negative effects of low-level flights on other animals as well, including waterfowl, osprey, beaver, porcupine and small game.

4.   Innu families have been repeatedly traumatized by very low-level, high-speed flights over their camps, with suffering imposed on children and old people in particular. (This has occurred even when it has been evident that the military are aware of the location of Innu camps.)

5.   The Innu people, legitimate owners of the territory in question (Ntesinan) have never entered into any treaty or other agreements yielding up their collective rights to self-determination and permanent sovereignty over their natural resources.

6.   The collective rights of the Innu people are guaranteed in international agreements to which Canada is a signatory. The imposition of intensive low-level high-speed military flight training over Ntesinan against the wishes of the Innu constitutes a clear violation of these commitments.

The Innu people living in the region in question, the Innu populations based in Schefferville, Davis Inlet, Sheshatshit, St Augustin, La Romaine, Mingan, and Natashquan, are united in their opposition to the use of their territory for such exercises and will employ all peaceful means at their disposal to bring this abuse to an end.

During constitutional talks in 1965 for the independence of Mauritius between the British government under Harold Wilson and a Mauritian delegation led by Sir Seewoosagur Ramgoolam, part of the Chagos archipelago was bartered away for Mauritian independence. The island of Diego Garcia was detached from Mauritius, formed into the British Indian Ocean Territory (BIOT) and then leased to the USA.[68] Just over eleven million dollars was paid for what has become America's largest military and nuclear base outside of mainland USA.[69]

The islanders on Diego Garcia — The Ilwa — were all removed from their homeland between 1965 and 1972 and dumped in slums in Mauritius, where they now live — in atrocious conditions.[70] None of them has been able to return to their island.

For several years, the Ilwa maintained a strident campaign to force the Mauritian government to reopen negotiations with the British government for compensation and eventual resettlement. Petitions, sit-ins, and a women's hunger strike forced their government's hand and in 1983, £4 million was paid in 'final' compensation by Britain. The following year, in talks with the country's Prime Minister, Aneerod Jugnauth, the Thatcher government dismissed any idea of Mauritius' claim to Diego Garcia.[71] The Reagan administration also rejected any idea of responsibility for meaningful compensation.[72]

Memorandum to the UK Government 19 March 1981

1. Please find enclosed a copy of a memorandum submitted to the Government of Mauritius today. Also enclosed, a copy of a 'Special Report of the Public Accounts Committee of the 1980 session' on the 'Financial and other aspects of the "sale" of Chagos Islands and the resettlement of the displaced Ilois.

2. As you must already be aware, a certain number of Ilois women, one of them nearly 70 years old, have gone on a hunger strike as from last Monday, 16th March 1981, and mean to carry on to the bitter end if necessary. One of them, aged 60 years old, had to be taken to hospital today but is holding on.

3. You must also already be aware of the desperate situation the Ilois community has been in since they were torn from their native land between 1965 and 1973.

4. We are aware of the reply given to Mr McNamara in the House of Commons (Vol 978 No. 114) on the 11th February 1980 by Mr Luce when he said that: 'In November 1979 the legal representative for the Ilois community presented to them Her Majesty's Government's offer of £1.25 million. We understand it is still under consideration. Since the main object of the offer is to facilitate the resettlement of the former islanders of Mauritius, those who accept will be required to abandon any claim to return to the Chagos Archipelago'.

5. As you are already aware, the Ilois refused to sign at the end of 1979 the 'deed of acceptance' presented to them by Mr B. Sheridan because of that part of it which

referred to their 'prohibition from ever returning to the Islands composing British Indian Ocean Territory'.

6. It is clear that this offer of £1.25 million from Her Majesty's Government is an admission on its part that the £650,000 it paid in 1973 to the Government of Mauritius for the resettlement of the Ilois people was totally inadequate.

7. It is our contention that this offer of £1.25 million is itself totally inadequate and should not be tied in any way with the rights to return one day to their native island.

8. In view of the above, we urge Her Majesty's Government to make available as rapidly as practicable the sum of £8 millions as a final compensation for the proper resettlement of the Ilois community. We need not refer again here to the urgency of the matter being given that the Ilois women referred to above have reached today their 5th day on hunger strike and mean to carry on until they will have obtained a positive reply to the requests to the government of Mauritius and to Her Majesty's Government.

9. This sum of £8 millions has been calculated on the following basis:

(a) Each Ilois Family should receive the following:

   (i) A plot of land of 100 toises = Rs 35,000.
   (ii) A house of 1,000 sq. ft. = Rs 100,000.
   (iii) An allowance to start a family business = Rs 15,000.

(b) This per family compensation should be made available to 900 families (number quoted by Mr Hervé Silva, who has just completed the official survey of the Ilois community, at the last meeting of the official Ad Hoc Committee on the Resettlement of Ilois, held on Monday the 9th of March 1981).
This therefore amounts to a total sum of Rs 135,000,000 (i.e. 900 x Rs 150,000).

(c) Furthermore, the Ilois community considers that an additional amount should be paid to cover the collective needs of the Ilois community (such as for a Community Centre, for a training and education programme etc., amounting to a sum of Rs 15 millions).

(d) The individual and collective elements of the compensation amount to a total sum of Rs 150,000,000 which comes to just over £8 millions at the current rate of exchange.

(10) We undertake to provide further information about the mechanism for receiving and distributing the money, when the British Government informs us of its willingness to negotiate on the above proposals.

(11) We however reserve our right to add to those proposals after further discussions among the Ilois representatives

Elie Michel   **Mrs C. Alexis**   **Mrs L. Naick**

(for the *Comité Ilois-O.F.*, being the 3 Ilois representatives on the above committee)

Kishore Mundil   **Alain Laridon**

for the *Front National de Soutien aux Ilois* (consisting of the following organisations: MMM, PSM, GWF, FTU, OUA, CDMO, IDP, *Linion Etidian Moris*, MCPS, The Joint Ilois Committee and the *Comité Soutien Ilois*).

Source: The Struggle of the Chagos People for their rights and their Home Islands, National Support Front for the Ilois, Mauritius, June 1981 appendix pps. 1–2.

Kaho'olawe, a sacred Hawaiian island, was first used for bombing practice in 1982 by the RIMPAC (Rim of the Pacific) countries, USA, Canada, Australia, New Zealand and Japan. That year, a Hawaiian based organisation embracing many individuals and organisations (including the Pacific Concerns Resource Center and Greenpeace) opposed the RIMPAC 'exercises' with an international pressure campaign.[73] However, both RIMPAC and the bombing of Kaho'olawe have continued. This statement was released by 'Protect Kaho' olawe' Ohana, just before the 1984 bombardments.

Stop RIMPAC 1984!

RIMPAC stands for both the nations which rim the Pacific and the large-scale military training exercise sponsored by the United States in which these nations participate. Beginning in 1971, the United States has invited the nations of Australia, New Zealand, Canada, and, since 1980, Japan, to participate in this joint military training exercise, an exercise which has included the bombing of Kaho'olawe, one of the eight major islands of Hawaii. In 1984, France will join the RIMPAC nations in these military maneuvers.

The size of the RIMPAC exercises is awesome. In 1978 it included the nuclear aircraft carrier USS Enterprise and 41 other warships, 255 military planes and 22,000 personnel. In 1980 it included 41 naval ships, 200 aircraft and 20,000 personnel. In 1982 the exercises involved 60 warships and submarines, including the aircraft carrier USS Ranger, 120 aircraft, and 29,000 sailors and marines.

The RIMPAC lasts nearly one month and integrates a variety of actions, including ship-to-shore shelling, anti-submarine, torpedo and counter vessel actions, as well as the jamming of 'enemy' intelligence actions.

The RIMPAC military training exercises culminate with the coordinated shelling and bombing of the Hawaiian Island of Kaho'olawe.

Under the control of the U.S. military since 1941, Kaho'olawe has been used primarily as a bombing target for Navy ships. However, in 1976 Kaho'olawe became the focus for a Hawaiian cultural reawakening, when a group of Native Hawaiian activists and their supporters began a series of 'illegal' occupations of the island to protest the Navy's control and abuse of the land. The protesters presented a clear indigenous response to the Navy's violent destruction. From the strength of a traditional Hawaiian relationship to the land, the Protect Kaho'olawe 'Ohana (extended family) was born.

Historically, Kaho'olawe has played a significant, if not major role in ancient Hawaiian religion and life. The western-most part of the Island, *Lae o ke ala i kahiki* (Pathway to Tahiti) was said to be a key directional point forming a navigational triangle for journeys to Tahiti, Aotearoa and other southerly islands.

Through the efforts of the 'Ohana, Kaho'olawe has been recognized as an important historical site, when the entire island was placed on the U.S. National Register of Historical Places. The 'Ohana has restored Kaho'olawe's cultural integrity by reviving traditional Hawaiian practices, skills and crafts through the construction of traditional house structures, continued pursuit of further research from native resources to reveal the Hawaiian significance of Kaho'olawe.

In questioning the military's jurisdiction to bomb Kaho'olawe the 'Ohana exposed the heart of American military domination of the Pacific. Because of its strategic location in the mid Pacific, Hawaii historically has played a crucial role in the expansionist foreign policies of the United States. Prior to World War II, Hawaii became the first line of defense for the U.S. as it fought for control of the Pacific with Japan. Today, the sphere of American military domination stretches across the Pacific and well beyond into the Indian Ocean and the oil-rich Persian Gulf.

In order to secure its control of the Pacific region, the U.S. must maintain strong alliances in the region and get them to bear a greater share of the cost of military protection against insurgent national liberation struggles. The RIMPAC exercises are the largest naval exercises conducted in the Pacific and Indian Oceans. These exercises are an important part of the U.S. strategy to secure the command of the seas of the Pacific region. Their significance can be better appreciated when we recall that prior to the U.S. invasion of Grenada, the Ranger forces which invaded Grenada had just recently conducted the 'Ocean Venture' training exercises at Vieques in which the invasion of Grenada was simulated. In the context of the Pacific, RIMPAC is excellent training for intervention by the U.S., France, Australia, New Zealand, Japan or Canada in any of the major national liberation movements in the region, from the Fretilin in East Timor, to the Kanak Independence Front in New Caledonia and the National Democratic Front in the Philippines.

If successful, our efforts to stop the RIMPAC '84 military exercises, especially to stop the bombing of Kaho'olawe during those military exercises, can make a significant contribution to the de-militarization of the Pacific.

Source: Pacific Bulletin (PCRC, Hawaii) Vol. 3, No. 7, 1984.

3.   The Nuclear State

When the Western press announced the flight of a Soviet cruise missile over Norway (which shattered on Finnish Samiland at the end of its trajectory),[74] there was no hint that a US Cruise missile test had taken place nine months before. On 6 March 1984 the rockets — minus warheads — were flown over Dene land in Canada's North-West Territories (NWT). Although missiles were not launched on that occasion, there are plans to make the tests 'real' in the near future.[75] Meanwhile B-52 low-flight bomb tests are also in the offing.[76]

The MacKenzie Valley is predominantly occupied by the Dene. In the 1970s they fought a long and hard battle against the laying of pipelines on their land and won a moratorium.[77] Their territory has, however, long been militarised: Norman Wells pipelines supplied fuel to US forces during the Second World War, and uranium mined in the Great Lake area was used in the Hiroshima and Nagasaki bombs.[78]

The majority of people in the region — native and non-native — are implacably opposed to Cruise missile testing. Both in 1977 and 1983 the Inuit Circumpolar Conference (ICC) which represents the vast majority of northern Inuit, passed nuclear-free zone resolutions,[79] which have received little attention, even from anti-nuclear movements in the world at large.

Marie-Helene Laraque is a native writer who contributes regularly to the Dene Nation's Native Press, *from which the following article is reprinted. This is followed by the ICC resolution passed in 1983.*

Missile tests will change the North

My children are asleep. The house is quiet and peaceful. Outside there is no sign of the new moon. It's warm for a winter night, overcast. There's that homey smell of wood smoke in the air. But after tomorrow the North will never be the same.

They have decided that on March 6, the Cruise missile would be tested for the first time over this land. 'They' are the Armed Forces and governments of the United

States and Canada. We who live here have taken every opportunity to say NO to the tests. Every major Northern and national Native organization has said NO. The Legislative Assembly of the Northwest Territories has said NO. We are left to conclude that what the people want does not really matter. Trudeau's peace initiative could've really meant something if he had started at home by refusing to allow testing of the Cruise.

As you read this, everything may appear the same as usual. But as we enter this new era, our surroundings, our reality and our selves will have been altered in a disturbing and profound way — our security shattered.

Actually, the security of the world was shattered in 1945. With the first nuclear explosion, we learned that there is no such thing as a safe place left. The nervous fingers of mortal men now hold the power to make decisions over life and death of the planet. The North used to seem relatively safe from this madness. It's not.

As the man from the Department of National Defense told an overflowing and concerned crowd at Yellowknife City Hall last week, our survival is being threatened so as to insure our survival. Although there's already enough arms and bombs to destroy the world many times over, we are being asked to cooperate with a process that promotes the threat of death to — as they tell us — protect life. The spokesmen for the Armed Forces tried to convince us with a rational approach for an argument that does not make sense. Wouldn't it be simpler just to work for peace?

Testing the Cruise missile here is 'Canada's contribution to NATO.' It could provide 'our side' with more lethal weapons to achieve what is called, in their language, 'mutually-assured destruction.' That means if there's a war, no one wins because neither side will be left alive. Peace by default? My 6-year old boy wanted to know 'Are we all going to die, mom?' How does a mother answer that?

The Cruise flies at 2000 feet, 500 miles an hour, down from the Beaufort Delta area, following the course of the Mackenzie River (why?) to Alberta, then east to Cold Lake. It will need a corridor 80 metres wide and the test flight is supposed to avoid, by at least 5 miles, any settlement or development site. The present agreement between the U.S. — producers of the missiles — and Canada (just being neighbourly good guys) allows for 4 to 6 tests a year between January and March, for the next 5 years. It was reluctantly admitted that this agreement and testing could be extended to 20 years. The Cruise is said to be unarmed for now. But it is designed to carry nuclear war-heads.

To those who made these decisions, this is just another game, a war game. The little boys have become men. The scientists, generals and leaders — recognized, paid, honored, and treated as learned and knowledgeable men in this society, though obviously not necessarily wise man — are playing little boys' games with our lives and the lives of unborn generations of human, plant, and animal life.

These big boys are members of a special club based on power. The world is their stage. That's why it's natural for them to speak of different places on the earth as 'theatres' for war. They think in terms of moves and counter-moves, attack and retreat, winning and losing.

My first real insight into this way of relating to the world was at a meeting between Native organizations and Indian Affairs officials a few years back. The Minister said he understood Native concerns and he supported them, but personally he couldn't make any guarantees. His cabinet colleagues would have to bounce it around. It seemed the decision would have to be worked out as a deal amongst each other. The Dene lost that one. I don't know who won. The Norman Wells pipeline was approved shortly after.

The crash of the Soviet Union's Cosmos 954 over the Great Slave Lake area in 1978 gave us the first indication that the N.W.T. has a place in the war plans of the super powers. By the way, whatever became of all the research the military conducted here as a result?

Testing the Cruise marks our official designation as a new 'theatre' for war. That means we can be attacked. Last summer at the Inuit Circumpolar Conference, Inuit of 3 countries declared their land a Nuclear Free Zone. I can still hear the clear powerful voice of Makka Kleist sharing a parting gift at the end of the gathering: the cold wind that blows in the north she said, is the same wind that blows in the east and west and south. It is felt in every part of the Mother Earth. Remember, she said, all that lives is related.

Marie-Helene Laraque

Source: Native Press, Yellowknife, 9 March 1984.

"A nuclear free zone in the Arctic"

Whereas, the Inuit Circumpolar Conference developed a fundamental policy restricting the arctic and sub-arctic to those uses which are peaceful and environmentally safe;

Whereas, this policy is reflected in the several resolutions adopted by the general Assembly and the Executive Council since the formation of the Inuit Circumpolar Conference in 1977;

Whereas, the governments of the United States and Canada intend to co-operate with each other to test the cruise missile in our northern Canadian homeland;

Whereas, the government of the United States has entertained the idea of basing the massive MX missile system in our Alaskan homeland;

Whereas, Atomic Energy Canada Limited plans to test the environmental and economic feasibility of the mini-**Candu** and the **Slowpoke 3** (small nuclear reactors for generating electricity) in the Canadian north since they are prohibited from testing them in the Canadian south due to environmental restrictions; and

Whereas, the arctic and sub-arctic shall not be used for any nuclear testing or as a nuclear dump-site;

Now, therefore be it resolved that the Inuit Circumpolar Conference emphatically restates its nuclear position:

1. that the arctic and sub-arctic be used for purposes that are peaceful and environmentally safe;
2. that there shall be no nuclear testing or nuclear devices in the arctic or sub-arctic;
3. that there shall be no nuclear dump-sites in the arctic or sub-arctic;

4. that exploration and exploitation of uranium, thorium, lithium or other materials related to the nuclear industry in our homeland be prohibited.

Furthermore be it resolved that the Canadian government be notified of our opposition to the testing of the Cruise missile in our Canadian homeland and that they be requested to refrain from such tests;

Furthermore be it resolved that Atomic Energy Canada Limited be notified of our opposition to the testing of nuclear reactors in the Canadian arctic or sub-arctic and that they be notified to refrain from such tests;

Furthermore be it resolved that the United States government be notified of our opposition to the placement of the MX missile in our Alaskan homeland and that they be requested to cease with any such plans;

Furthermore be it resolved that the Inuit Circumpolar Conference study and research current international treaties to determine whether or not they comply with the Inuit Circumpolar Conference Arctic Policy;

Furthermore be it resolved that the Executive Council of the Inuit Circumpolar Conference lobby the United Nations and various international organizations to encourage members of the United Nations to adopt a policy for a nuclear free zone in the Arctic.

Source: ICC Arctic Policy Review, Nuuk, No. 3, 1983 pp. 6–7.

Nuclear-free constitution (Vanua-Aku)

The 'condominium' territory of the New Hebrides (jointly colonised by Britain and France) achieved independence in 1981.[80] The Independence Party Vanua-aku Pati, was (and is) one of the strongest supporters of a nuclear free and independent Pacific (see Part 4, ch. 13). One of its first acts, after independence, was to refuse 'visitation rights' to US navy ships.[76]

A nuclear-free motion was passed by the country's parliament in 1983.

A. To safeguard the health and well-being of all citizens of Vanuatu, both now and in the future.

B. To declare to all countries our desire to live in peace and our total abhorrence of all ways and means of propagating a nuclear war.

Now, therefore, Parliament hereby resolves: That the following be banned or prohibited within the territorial land, sea and airspace of Vanuatu:

1. All tests of nuclear explosives devices.
2. All nuclear test facilities.
3. All tests of nuclear weapon delivery vehicles and systems.
4. All storage, transit, deployment or any other form or presence of nuclear weapons.
5. All bases carrying out command control, communication, surveillance, navigation, and any other functions which aid the performance of a nuclear weapon delivery system.
6. All nuclear power reactors, all nuclear powered satellites, surface and sub-surface vessels, and all transit, storage, release or dumping of radioactive material except for that which is strictly used inside Government approved medical and educational institutions for medical and/or educational purposes.
7. Uranium mining, processing and transport.

Nuclear-free Belau

Belau, in Micronesia, was the world's first nuclear-free state. In 1978 the 15,000 islanders enshrined rejection of all things nuclear in their Constitution. Since then — on ten occasions — they have gone to the polls and either confirmed the Constitution, or voted down a bilateral military and economic Compact of Free Association with the United States.[82] *On each occasion the US government has disputed the peoples' decision and massed huge legal forces to overturn it: Belau is a plum in America's military pie — the principal port for Trident nuclear submarines and other warships.*[83]

Roman Bedor is internationally known as a chief defender of his people's nuclear free constitution. In this article he describes the tortuous process by which a handful of Micronesians have jeopardised the military intentions of the world's most powerful state.[84]

We Appeal for Life

For centuries Belau and the rest of Micronesia have been subject to foreign colonization. Their peoples have witnessed and experienced the imposition and exercise of the rules and laws of four different colonial masters at different times.

Spain was the first to arrive, during the age of discovery, and remained on the islands for a century. On their departure they sold the islands, their peoples and the ocean between them to Germany for about 4.5 million US dollars. This was done without the knowledge or consent of the native people but, since it was approved by the Pope in Rome, it was considered to be a lawful transaction.

Under Spanish rule, the people of the islands were forced to adopt a Spanish lifestyle, with the main emphasis being on Christianity, which served as the basic instrument in the alienation of the islands from the natives, allowing total foreign domination. This was, and still is, a very foreign concept to the islanders — the idea that land is considered as property like anything else and can be sold, traded or given away, is an attitude with no place in local tradition. Land is considered rather as a gift of life. The title of the land remains with clan, lineage or family and rights of use are assigned to members of same.

With German succession, lifestyles adopted under the Spanish were continued, though Protestantism replaced Catholicism. The islanders could see no difference in the two, both of which believed in Christ as the Son of God and based their teachings on the bible. The only difference they came to realise was that a Catholic priest cannot marry while a Protestant priest can have a wife and children.

Land was again appropriated by the ruling power, but this time going to the Protestant rather than the Catholic church. Most of the land given by the native clans was done so under the impression that only right of use was being transferred and the actual title remaining with the clan. The natives believed they still had ultimate control. But several years later the church claimed that the transaction had been executed according to the practise of the western world. Thus, title ownership along with rights and privileges concerning the land, were all relinquished.

When Germany left the islands, any native traditional way of life had been virtually destroyed. There remained, and still exists today, a law system which, as a result of both German and Spanish imposition, greatly contradicts itself. There are thus many problems in abiding by and enforcing the law.

When Germany was defeated in the first World War, the Treaty of Versailles forced Germany to give up its overseas territories. To the people of Micronesia this implied a new freedom — a freedom to control their own destiny and be masters of their own land. But, in reality, it meant another colonial master, with its own laws and lifestyles to impose.

During the subsequent period of Japanese control, the islanders witnessed the alienation of their land to a new power. This time, the Japanese claimed to be establishing a military defense for Belau and Micronesia from the 'enemy'. Thus it proceeded to condemn land for utilisation by the Japanese government. Military bases were introduced and land used by Japanese companies in their economic 'development' of the islands.

Before the outbreak of World War II, more than half of the islands were in the hands of Japanese companies and the Government. The influx of Japanese nationals and other Asians employed by Japanese companies, steadily increased to the figure of 300,000. Thus the native peoples were overrun and displaced in their own land.

The existence of extensive military installations in Belau made it the target for heavy American offensives and one of the major battlefields of the second World War. Many Belauans, promised protection and defense, died in their sleep as American and Japanese soldiers fought for the victory of World War II. Others died in their fishing grounds searching for food to feed their families.

In the written history of the battle for Belau and other Micronesian islands, as well as other parts of the Pacific, there is no mention by American or Japanese authors of the decimation suffered by the native people.

The defeat of Japan in the war meant victory to the US and a freedom for some people. But to the people of Belau it meant neither freedom nor victory. It meant complete reconstruction of Belau from the smoke and ashes of the war. It had now also received another imperial master, one completely different to the Spanish, German or Japanese.

In 1947, the United Nations handed to the United States the right to colonize Belau and the other Micronesian Islands. Again, the knowledge and consent of the Belauans was non-existent. According to the United Nations Trusteeship Agreement, the US is charged with a responsibility to promote the economy of the islands until such time as they may become a self-sufficient or independent nation. Similarly, they are charged with the protection of the land and the islands' resources. Although this agreement is binding (as the US exercises its authority over the islands under these conditions), it is never adhered to when compliance seems to be against its own interests.

When the US moved into the Marshall Islands it exiled the native peoples to nearby islands. It then proceeded to conduct nuclear tests on the islands, causing the complete annihilation of some. Originally healthy and beautiful environments have thus been contaminated for the next thousand years or more. Such projects and experiments are justified by the US as being 'for the good of mankind'.

The US also pledged to establish a democratic principle of government on the islands. It guaranteed the right to self-determination and the freedom to exercise this right to form a structure of government of the peoples' choice.

For more than 34 years the islanders have subscribed to this right and belief and now the time has come for them to exercise it and to practise this democratic form of government that they have been taught by the US government.

Referendum as an Act of Self Determination

The right of self-determination is a fundamental one and was reaffirmed to the Micronesian islanders by the US government, where previous colonial powers had denied them this right. Accordingly, the people of Belau, in 1978, elected their representatives to form a democratic government. Thirty-eight delegates were elected throughout Belau on a democratic voting system. Belau had not had its own government since colonisation by Spain. Immediately prior to this, the island had been under the control of the Trust Territory Government, an extension of the Department of the Interior in Washington DC.

The newly elected delegates formed the Palau Constitutional Convention and, within three months, created what is now the Constitution of Belau with a governmental structure similar to that of the US. During the course of the Convention, public hearings were conducted throughout the islands to solicit the views of the people on what form the new government should take. The majority feeling was that it should be a democratic style of government on the lines of that of America. The populace demanded that Belau be a nuclear-free nation, that it ban the use of Belau for a military base for the storage of nuclear weapons or for nuclear power plants. If the people ever considered changing any of these restrictions, a referendum would be conducted and a minimum of three out of four must be in favour of such a change of policy.

Before the constitution was ever submitted to the people for ratification through referendum, the US government issued strong objections — particularly to those provisions that would render Belau a nuclear-free state and all other rulings that would hinder US military plans in the area. Five days before the referendum US ambassador Peter R. Rosenblatt sent a strongly worded telegram to the Palau Constitutional Convention offering provisions to replace certain plans unfavourable to the US.

Ratification of the Constitution

Despite US objections and demands for amendments, the Palau Constitutional Convention went ahead and the Constitutional referendum was submitted to the people. Delegates to the Convention advised the US ambassador that it was not America's place to amend the constitution before it was ratified — this would be a violation of Belau's fundamental right of self-determination. The constitution had a mechanism for amendments which would be considered after the referendum. This principle and the insistence that such rights should be exercised free from any interference or threat is, after all, part of American teaching in Belau practiced for the last 30 years.

On 9 July 1979, three months after the Constitutional Convention concluded their work, the referendum was held, observed by representatives of the UN. An intensive campaign had been launched on both sides — both for and against the constitution. The result was 92% in favour, the constitution ratified and the people of Belau delighted with their long sought-after chance to determine their destiny.

Several weeks later the US Trust Territory Court declared the enabling act, that had created the opportunity for referendum, invalid. Hence, the results of the referendum were not legally binding and the Belauans' wish not recognised.

The Palau Constitutional Drafting Commission was established to draft another constitution and nine members were abitrarily chosen by the then Speaker of the Palau Legislature — a staunch supporter of the US military role in Belau. Within 15 days the second constitution was drafted, identical in every way to the original with the exception of an absence of the Nuclear-Free clause and all those provisions to which the US had previously objected. On 23 October a second referendum was held and this time the UN refused to send representation. The sum of $100,000 was appropriated for the endorsement of this second constitution. The monies were all spent and the people of Belau rejected the constitution with an 80% majority.

Unfortunately this exercise of 'self-determination' was again not recognised. The US define that right to self-determination as a conditional one — one which must meet with US interests in the Pacific. This definition is slightly different to that taught by the Americans in Belau for the last 34 years.

With the first constitution rejected by the US Trust Territory Court and the second by the Belauan people, the destiny of Belau was now in the hands of the US Trust Territory Government. Now the future of Belau could be easily navigated by American officials to satisfy US demands on Belau.

The Belauans demanded implementation of their original constitution but there were problems with the dates included which would have to be adjusted. This, however, would be unconstitutional and as such would not be binding. The only possible way to implement the original constitution was to conduct a third referendum. It was suggested that legislation be enacted to provide for this implementation but the legal experts who worked with the people of Belau advised that this could still be challenged. Thus it was decided to conduct a third referendum.

On 9 July 1980, a year after the first referendum, this third one was ratified with a majority of 80%. (This included the Nuclear-Free clauses.)

Compact of Free Association

The Compact of Free Association is a treaty between Belau and the United States which offers financial and economic assistance to Belau. In return, Belau must grant the US the right to use Belau for its military guerrilla training, permission to station naval bases and to store nuclear weapons. It also authorises the US government to invite any nation to Belau for military training exercises, similar to such joint exercises as Team Spirit in Korea or Rimpac.

On 25 August 1982, the Compact of Free Association was signed by representatives of the governments of Belau and the United States. The signing of the Compact was not an acceptance or ratification, as it is a constitutional requirement that ratification be decided by a peoples' vote. In the US, ratification is left to the Congress.

Article II, section 3 of the Belauan constitution provides that any treaty or compact shall be approved by not less than two-thirds of the members of each house and by a majority of the votes cast in a nation-wide referendum. Any such agreement which authorises the use, testing, storage or disposal of nuclear, toxic chemical, gas or biological weapons requires the approval of not less than three-quarters of the vote cast. A compact of free association shall be ratified by both houses in the Belauan Congress, requiring a two-thirds majority and by at least 75% of the people's votes. Without these requirements, the compact should not be ratified and hence not be allowed to take effect.

The result of the referendum for this Compact, on 10 February 1983, fell short of the requirement. The US, however, claimed that the compact had been ratified, again exhibiting their refusal to recognise the expressed wish of the people of Belau. It has become obviously clear that the government of the United States has no intention of allowing the people of Belau the right to self-determination or to make any decision affecting their lives. Such concessions by America would obviously threaten US military plans in the region.

At the present time, with the Compact having been rejected, the government of the United States must not be permitted to force the Belauan people to renegotiate the Compact. Rather, as the 'champion of human rights and right of self-determination', the United States must be forced to adhere to its democratic preachings. Is it not highly ironical that the US support the people of the Falkland Islands in their demands for self-determination while refusing to recognise the same for the people of Belau who have been under US administration since 1947?

J. Roman Bedor

Source: Gensuikin News (Japan) No. 107, Autumn 1983.

"The Next Test Could be Fatal"

In 1946 the US uprooted 167 Marshallese from Bikini island, Micronesia, then blasted the island with an atomic bomb. Over the next 12 years there were 23 nuclear tests at Bikini.

In 1963 the French also removed indigenous people from an island and blasted it into lifelessness. But, while Bikini stands as a disgraceful monument to aggression, colonialism and nuclear madness — Muroroa is still today in the firing line and the French are continuing to explode nuclear weapons in the Pacific.

MYRON MATAO is a Tahitian opposition leader. In this interview with the Dutch radical weekly De Groene, *he describes the ways in which French testing have affected his people. The only alternative to a nuclear Pacific — in his view and that of many Polynesians — is independence from France.*

Matao: Our islands are in a dangerous situation. Recently a couple of our people went underwater to look at the Mururoa atoll, after an underground test. They discovered cracks appearing in the ocean floor. As the tests proceed, so the island sinks. And I believe that, as it sinks, so the accumulated radiation gets free. It will poison our entire environment.

In January 1963, a delegation of Tahitian political leaders went to Paris to protest [at the start of atomic tests]. What the former President De Gaulle told them is still one of the greatest insults paid to our people. He said: 'Since Tahitian soldiers fought so bravely in our army during two world wars, I haven't forgotten you. I've therefore decided to hold the tests in your territory.' De Gaulle regarded it as a great honour for the inhabitants of French Polynesia.

[After 1963 the French carried out 41 tests around Tahiti. Following protests by various countries at the UN, the French turned to underground testing in 1975. Since then, they have carried out no fewer than 30 so-called peaceful explosions. A French engineer, who has asked that his name be withheld for fear of reprisals, recently declared that the next test will prove extremely powerful and dangerous.]

Matao: The French have now built a number of platforms. They want the people to use them during the next explosion. They know how dangerous that is, but want us to take the risks. What's their plan? Do they now want to eradicate us? The French think to themselves: 'Only 160,000 people live on the islands, and in France there's about 50 million. What pressures can we apply, as against that of just a few people? We are whites, and they're just natives.'

De Groene: *What have been the consequences of the atomic tests?*

Since they started, there have been signs of contamination among the people. Many cases of cancer have been discovered, some of which have resulted in death.

That sort of thing never happened before. There was always cancer, but certainly not as much as now. Out of 1,093 people who died in a three year period, 70 died because of cancer. That's much too many. Right up to today people are dying from it. An uncle of mine died from it. He lived on an atoll about 100 miles from Mururoa. I'm sure he was contaminated because of the atomic tests. Cancer had never existed on that island before.

Polynesians eat a lot of fish. Every day my uncle ate fish. Can you get cancer from healthy fish? Around Mururoa you can no longer eat anything that comes from the land or the sea. So what should we do? Do the French now want us to eat steaks and tinned meat and sardines, like the north American Indians who no longer have buffaloes for their food supplies?

Are the people aware of the effects of eating contaminated fish from the area?

The French have informed them. They had to. Otherwise, there would have been a violent reaction. Some natives didn't observe the rule and touched contaminated stuff. They were taken to hospital. Some recovered, but others died.

It's not only our people who are endangered. Many species of fish from our territory travel great distances. They swim everywhere — Greenland, Australia, Peru. In Peru, they've caught radioactive turtles.

Is there any possibility that the French tests will be called off?

Only through independence, in my opinion. At the present time, there are several independence movements. I don't believe any single other country can stop France. Nor the UN. Just look at how things are in the UN. France sits there, with the USA, the USSR, China, Indian, Great Britain — all countries which have the atomic bomb . . . We are making an appeal to the governments of West Germany, the Netherlands, and all other countries which don't have atomic weapons, to support our case. That includes support for our independence struggle. Otherwise a whole people, an entire race will be wiped out. It may take 20 or 30 years, who can say? It is difficult to assess the effects of radioactivity over a long period.

I hope that a fifth Russell Tribunal for the people of the Pacific can help us.

It's very difficult for us to undertake something against France. If we're troublesome, they'll send the army against us. When *Greenpeace* once sailed a ship towards Tahiti, the French navy almost sunk it. The crew was arrested and sent to gaol. We've held protest marches on the islands. The French usually don't react at all . . . We are merely a band of a hundred thousand natives with stones. They have atom bombs!

How would you feel if you knew there was a bomb right over your head? How would you feel if an atom bomb was made or tested over your home? . . . If the French experimented in France itself, a revolution would break out!

What happens to Tahitians who openly protest?

Since a new independence movement has got underway, the French have been shamelessly trying to buy it off. On Tahiti there are two social classes — a small group of rich and a large group of poor. Recently a middle class has grown up. The poor see what the rich have and eagerly want prosperity as well.

When you go to act against the government, someone comes up to you and says: 'If you're peaceful we'll find you jobs. Then you can buy a beautiful house and nice car.' Put yourself in the position of a poor man with a wife and family. What should you do? I know very few men who wouldn't accept such an offer. Most say: 'Okay, I'll take it and work for you.'

Independence is our one goal. The so-called 'treaties' signed here and there don't resolve anything. No one observes them. Countries like France, the USSR and the

USA . . . just put their foot through them. I'm sure that a world war will break out soon. The small nations would do well to set themselves against it. In Tahiti, we don't really understand why Europe has chosen a French person as President of the European Parliament. Simone Veil won't stop the tests.

We can only fight with words. But words are sometimes too weak. A couple of times the secret police have come to me asking why I don't stop my activities with the independence movement. They asked me why I wanted to break away from France. I answered: 'I want freedom for my people and myself'. They know I'm the vice-president of an independence movement. That's why they come back each time, with more and more money, asking if I won't give up. But that I'll never do.

I only ask for justice!

Myron Matao
Source: De Groene, Amsterdam, 8 August 1981, trans. Roger Moody.

Opposing MX (Shoshone)

> **"During the last school year, one of our 12 year old children drew a picture of the MX. The MX was shown going right through his house. What is going through the minds of our children?"**
>
> **Jerry Millett,** Chairman, Duckwater Shoshone Tribe, quoted *Akwesasne Notes*, Spring 1981.

When Ronald Reagan tried to foist his pre-Star Wars extravaganza — the MX missile — on people in America's south-west, in 1981, the mammoth project met unprecedented criticism from people and Congress. Almost unheard, however, were the voices of 2,000 Western Shoshone, several of whose reservations would have been in the path (rather, the bed) of the missiles, and whose total land-base would have been severely affected by diversion and misuse of their water supplies.[85]

But more important, under the 1863 Ruby Valley Treaty, the Shoshone had never surrendered rights to their land, even though they have long given access to white ranchers and miners.

By 1983, the original, grandiose, MX-missile proposal was grounded. A year later, two sisters Carrie and Mary Lann Dann won legal rights to 24 million acres of Nevada and Utah for the Western Shoshone in a court case which, temporarily, safeguarded their future.[86] *Two years later, however, the US Supreme Court ruled that the Federal government had merely to place $26 million in a trust fund, for compensation to be legally paid, and the traditional Shoshone land to be thus forfeited.*[87]

The following three statements were made by native residents of the south west USA between 1979 and 1981. The fourth is a press release issued by the Western Shoshone National Council in early 1986.

"All will be destroyed"

"The MX will use a lot of water. Water is life. Water is not just used for consumption, but is also used in spiritual ways — for purification like in sweat ceremonies. The hot springs are spiritual and are used to purify the body before attending ceremonies.

"Another thing the MX will destroy is the natural vegetation and the herbs. Medicine herbs like the be de ba, doz, sagebrush, chaparral, Indian tea — all these things will be destroyed. Not only the herbs but other medicines, like lizards in the south which are used to heal the mentally sick and arthritis.

"Whatever is used as a defense system to protect the missiles will also destroy the natural habitat — such as electrical fences, nerve gas, or even the use of security personnel — will disturb the natural environment. The natural habitat of the eagles and hawks will be destroyed. The pine trees, a staple food of the Shoshone, will be destroyed. Other natural foods will be destroyed; the rock chuck, ground-squirrel, rabbit, deer, sagegrouse, and rattlesnake.

"Some of the areas designated for the MX are recognized by Indians throughout Nevada, as being spiritual lands. These areas were used regularly for praying, until the Bureau of Land Management came in to control the public lands. Ceremonies such as the round dance, bear dance, cry dance and now new Indian doctors use these places to fast as part of their ceremonies."

Glen Holley
(Battle Mountain Indian Community)

Source: Akwesasne Notes, Spring, 1981

"If our land is taken — where will we go as Indian people? For the non-Indian it is different, a non-Indian can go back to their home country — where their ancestors are. But we as an Indian, if we do not have the land, we have nowhere else to go. This has always been our land, for I would say a million years. If the non-Indian buys the land from us — he can tell us to move on. Where will we go? . . . How can we lose something that is a part of us — something that is tied to our lives. You cannot take this away from the Shoshone people."

Corbin Harney
(Duck Valley Reservation)

Source: Akwesasne Notes, ibid.

"The land is most sacred, as is the water flowing upon it. The growing things of the land. The air we breathe. The food that grows for us to eat. All of these things were put here for our use by the Great Spirit and respect is given them by all Indian people of this land. The Western Shoshone have a duty to protect these things . . . We declare that we are opposed to the installation of the MX missile system or any other offensive weapon of war."

Western Shoshone Sacred Lands Association 3 November 1979

Source: Akwesasne Notes, ibid.

"A Nation bent on its own destruction"

"On this 35th anniversary of the opening of the Nevada Test Site the Western Shoshone National Council marks this date by publicly expressing our opposition to continued nuclear testing at the Nevada Test Site as well as world wide.

"The lands which contain the Test Site are within the borders of the Western Shoshone Nation's Homelands. The Western Shoshone aboriginal title to those lands remains unextinguished.

"Although the Western Shoshone wish to emphasize the fact of our nation's unextinguished title to the lands, our opposition to nuclear testing is not based on legal or nationalistic self-interest. The continuing detonation of nuclear devices, the majority of which are weapons, endangers Shoshone and Americans alike. Those who have suffered the effects of exposure to fall-out that has vented from the tests and travelled downwind to Nevada and Utah communities are painfully aware of the terrible consequences connected to nuclear testing. Leukemia and other cancer-related diseases plague the communities as a direct result of uncontained fall-out.

"While people who live within the Test Site's path of fall-out know of nuclear testing's dangers through experience, those of us who live outside of that path are not outside the shadow that is cast by nuclear testing. In this latter half of the twentieth century, all human beings live under the imminent threat of nuclear holocaust. As a nation indigenous to this continent, continuing here for thousands of years, the Western Shoshone watch with horror as powerful nation-states such as the United States and the USSR work to perfect and stockpile life-destroying technologies.

"Because the Western Shoshone National Council understands that the American people are humans, just as we are, and are capable of understanding the need for a peace that is not based on military might, we wish to remind you of this: When a nation's direction is determined by the desires of its warriors, that nation is bent on its own destruction. The threat of death that your government holds over the heads of its enemies does not stop at your enemy's borders. It knows no national boundaries, but circles the earth, returning to hang over America's own head.

"Because the Nevada Test Site operates at the expense of the Western Shoshone Nation's homelands, at the expense of the lives of fall-out victims, and at the expense of possible mass destruction by way of perfection of nuclear weapons through testing, the Western Shoshone National Council declares its opposition to the continuation of the Nevada Test Site."

(Western Shoshone National Council, PO Box 68, Duckwater NV 89314, USA.)

1984: Appeal to all people who believe in a non-nuclear future

A Call for a Global Petition Campaign To Effectively Halt Uranium Mining and Stop the Perpetuation of the Nuclear Cycle

On behalf of the Indigenous Peoples of the Americas, Australia, Namibia, and all concerned parents of future generations we appeal for support to stop the illegal mining of uranium for the perpetuation of the nuclear cycle.

The Indigenous Peoples of the Americas, Australia, and Namibia have been implicated as unwilling and unknowing partners in the crime of genocide. Explicit examples of these inhumanities are: the uranium that was used in the Hiroshima bomb was extracted from the illegally alienated lands of the Indigenous Peoples of Upper North America (Port Radium, N.W.T., Canada): the construction of the Roxby Downs Uranium Mine on Sacred Aboriginal land in Australia, the continuing illegal extraction and export of uranium from Namibia by the racist South African regime.

The illegal and immoral exploitation of the extremely hazardous 'fuel of the future' is a cause of great concern to peoples in every phase of the infamous nuclear cycle: those from whose lands it is stolen, those in whose waters and lands it is transported, those in whose lands it is used, and those in whose lands or waters the wastes are dumped.

The Indigenous Peoples of Australia and the Americas in solidarity with the Indigenous Peoples of Namibia have now joined lands and minds with the Peoples of the Pacific, Japan, and also Peoples from all parts of the globe to launch a universal campaign against uranium mining.

The success of effectively stopping uranium mining will also mean the curtailing of the supply of this nuclear explosive mineral to the apocalyptic nuclear arms race which is with each passing minute bringing us to the brink of oblivion.

Therefore, we urgently appeal to all Peoples of the world who respect Mother Earth and envision a lasting future for mankind to support this worthwhile campaign. With **your** support we **will** succeed, we shall overcome and ensure a beautiful and lasting Mother Earth for those yet unborn.

Let us join hands and minds in a united global effort to stop uranium mining and thereby stop the perpetuation of the nuclear cycle.

Shortly O'Neill	**Ron Lameman**	**Michael Lane**
National Federation of Land Councils	Coalition of First Nations (Canada)	Internation Indian Treaty Council

* Please translate the appeal and the petition form into your own language and distribute it in your country. If possible, please make your own copies.

* We would appreciate any financial support you may wish to offer to help in this campaign. Please send donations by a check or an international postal money order payable to National Federation of Land Councils, Australia

Although nuclear fission has been exploited commercially for less than three decades,[88] *the mining of uranium on indigenous peoples' land is one of the most bitter bones of contention between contemporary landholders and governments and mining companies. Currently around half the production of the USA derives from the Four Corners region, where it centres on Navajo, Pueblo and other native American communities.*[89]

Canada, now the Western world's most important producer, gains its yellowcake from huge mines on native land in northern Saskatchewan and Ontario.[90] *The two main operating mines in Australia are situated in the heart of Aboriginal country in the Arnhemland region of the Northern Territory;*[91] *a third, massive copper–uranium project, planned for the 1990s, trespasses on Kokatha territory.*[92] *Elsewhere in the Western sphere of influence, the French-dominated uranium mines of Niger radiate a landscape used by Tuareg nomads — who also provide cheap labour under the most appalling conditions.*[93]

While nuclear programmes, both military and 'civil', do not now promise the uranium industry the eldorado it envisaged before the Three Mile Island disaster shook the confidence of nuclear barony,[94] *they remain substantial and, in some countries, are growing.*[95] *Native peoples' lands — which already provide an estimated two-thirds of the West's primary nuclear fuel supplies*[96] *— are destined to remain crucial to the survival of the industry until well into the next century.*[97]

Whether or not corporate uranium grabbers, the International Atomic Energy Agency, and the various governments and electricity utilities prominent in yellowcake exploration, deliberately target native territory (and there is some evidence they do) they have benefited in the past from weak and disorganised opposition, the impoverishment of American-Indian and Australian Aboriginal societies, and the general care-lessness of an anti-nuclear movement which put the relatively remote dangers on its own doorstep above the proven hazards of mining.[98]

All this is changing, however, due overwhelmingly to the militancy of indigenous peoples. Projected mines will never be opened, thanks to local opposition, headed by native organisations.[99] *Several existing mines, especially in the USA, have closed down recently; not just because of a collapsing market, lower grades of ore and increasing costs, but also because the price of heading-off the opposition is simply too prohibitive.*

The statements which follow reflect this new-found militancy, and (as with the last three articles in this section) the determination of indigenous organisations to work together, and with support groups, against what they see as a unique, universal threat.

"After the water is contaminated, what will we live on?"

Open letter to Band Councils, Community Councils, Anti-Nuclear Groups, other concerned groups and individuals (13 July 1984).

Dear Friends:

We are concerned about the uranium mine development that is taking place on the west side of Wollaston Lake, only 20 miles across the lake from our community of 700 people. The Rabbit Lake Mine was operated by Gulf Minerals from 1975 to 1983 when they sold it to Eldorado Resources Limited, a federal crown corporation. From 1975 to 1977 untreated wastes were released into Hidden Bay of Wollaston Lake. These wastes are now 'treated'; however, the settling ponds they pass through have no leakage-proof liners so radioactive contaminants are still leaking into Wollaston Lake through the groundwater channels. A study by Environment Canada in 1978 determined that 'the water quality of Horseshoe Lake has deteriorated considerably since 1972' and 'elevated radionuclide levels were detected in the Rabbit Creek system especially in the Sedimentation Lake sediments.' Tests by the Environmental Protection Services on several occasions found ammonia levels high enough to kill trout in the tailings effluent which goes into Effluent Creek and on to Hidden Bay.

Eldorado Resources is now developing the Collins Bay B-Zone orebody, six miles north of the Rabbit Lake Mine. This mine operation is even more dangerous because ore is under the lake. They have already built a dyke between two islands, drained the water from this area, and have begun to dig the open pit. They will soon begin to dig out the ore. The dyke is made with thin sheet-steel pipes, rocks and earth and is only four feet above the water level. If water from the lake comes into contact with the ore in the pit, the radiation will spread to the whole lake. This dyke will be removed when the mine closes in six years. The radioactive tailings from this mine will be placed in the old Rabbit Lake pit. No leakage-proof liners will be installed. Radium 226 and other radioactive 'daughters' will leach into the groundwater channels which flow into Wollaston Lake for possibly thousands of years.

Explorations by the Saskatchewan Mining Company, Gulf Minerals, Anaconda Canada Explorations, SERU Nucleare (Canada), Asamera Incorporated, and other companies have discovered at least 10 other uranium orebodies in this area. The uranium mines that were operated by Eldorado at Uranium City, Saskatchewan, have permanently contaminated the land and water. Three lakes are now dead: nothing will grow in them. Huge piles of waste rocks and mine buildings have been left to release radiation into the air, land and water. Most of the people moved out when the mines closed in 1982. We do not want the same thing to happen here.

We have always used this land for hunting, trapping, fishing, and berry-picking. We still obtain most food from hunting and fishing. About 50 people still trap and about 50 commercial fish. The exploration and mining is destroying these livelihoods. At least 10 men have their traplines in the area where mining and exploration is being done. As Councillor Martin Josie has stated: 'Now because of the white people like the Department of Northern Saskatchewan, prospectors and mining companies, the animals are becoming scarce. Even the moose are hard to kill now and because of the mines the animals are not fit to eat.' Only two men received any compensation for the losses on their traplines. Contamination of the lake may destroy commercial fishing.

Elder Helen Besskaytare has also expressed concern about the mines. 'Nowadays if you kill some ducks they're skinny, not like they used to be. I hear now you can get cancer from eating the waterfowl. People used to live to be in their 60s or 70s. People lived off fish and berries. But now people are dying from cancer and we know it's from the mines. Now we can't even eat bears because we're afraid what they may have eaten from the mines. What I'm really concerned about is the kids in the future. If the water is contaminated and not fit to drink and the fish are not fit to eat, what are the children going to live on?'

Only five people have permanent jobs at Rabbit Lake and five are now employed at Collins Bay. People from Wollaston Lake are often refused jobs because they lack training, but the mining companies won't provide any training. Employment for a few people is not adequate compensation for the destruction of the environment. As then Chief Joseph Besskaystare stated: 'At a meeting here in 1977 with the government and mining company officials, I told them NO to the mine because of what it might do to the lake. In about 35 years you people will be finished mining. All the workers will go but we still be here. After the water is contaminated, what are going to live on?'

Many workers from uranium mines have died from cancer. Over 30 miners from Uranium City and over 400 miners from the Elliot Lake, Ontario, mines have died from cancer. We do not want this to happen to Wollaston Lake people.

The people of Wollaston Lake opposed the opening of the Rabbit Lake Mine at meetings held here with the government and mining companies in 1972 and 1977. We unanimously opposed the opening of Collins Bay B-Zone at Hearings held here and La Ronge in 1981. The Government of Saskatchewan refuses to listen to us and allows uranium exploration and mining to continue.

At a community meeting here on 13 June 1984 people again expressed opposition. Band Councillor Martin Josie stated: 'We, the Chief and Band Councillors will not agree to have the Collins Bay Mine opened. This mine concerns everybody because Wollaston Lake flows everywhere, North, South, East and West. We will be very happy for any people that protest against Collins Bay B-Zone Development. If people protest in other places, not only Wollaston Lake, it will be good.'

We are sending petitions to the Government of Saskatchewan Department of the Environment demanding that the Collins Bay B-Zone Development and all uranium explorations and mining in this area be stopped immediately.

Please send your petitions of support to:

Lac La Hache Band
Wollaston Lake, Saskatchewan
SOJ 3CO

We will present them to Honorable Neil Hardy, Minister of the Department of the Environment, Government of Saskatchewan.

PROTEST actions can also be directed against Eldorado at:

Eldorado Nuclear Limited   AND   Eldorado Resources
Suite 400   2115-11th Street
255 Albert Street   Box 2070
Ottawa, Canada KIP 6A9   Saskatoon, Saskatchewan S7K 3S7
613- 238-5222   306- 382-0505
(Head Office)

It is important that we act now to stop uranium mining and exploration before the environment is destroyed. We do not have much time to stop the Collins Bay Development. We urge your community or organization to support our protests and organize your own protests against uranium mining and exploration.

Lac La Hache Chief and Band Councillors
Hector Kkailther, Chief
Martin Josie, Councillor
Jimmy Kkaikka, Councillor
Rosalie Tsannie, Councillor

Wollaston Lake Local Advisory Council
Emil Hansen, Secretary-Treasurer
Flora Natomagan, Councillor
Gabriel Benonie, Councillor

Native Peoples Oppose Uranium

The reason for the trip was the 35th Anniversary of Japan Congress Against A — and H — Bombs or Gensuikin as it is better known. Conferences were held in Tokyo, Hiroshima and Nagasaki but unfortunately because of visa problems I did not get to Japan to make the Tokyo and Hiroshima Conferences. I arrived in Tokyo on the 6/8/80 — Memorial Day in Hiroshima, — and travelled by Shinkansen 'Bullet Train' to Nagasaki. Here I met other members of the Gensuikin delegation and was pleased to see 'Grassroots' people. Representatives came from the Pacific Islands of Guam, Palau, Marshall Islands and Hawaii as well as a North American Navajo Indian woman, and people from U.S.A., Holland, France and Australia.

The first Conference at which I spoke was at Nagasaki 8/8/80 and was primarily on Land Rights, mining and in particular to the stopping of Uranium Mining. The reception I received from the 100 or so people that were there was very good, a sign (I believe) that we have their support. After I had finished speaking, the Navajo woman, Elsie Peshlakai, spoke and she said that after listening to me speak, it was as if we came from the same reservation. I had the privilege of speaking to Elsie many times about our peoples and soon it appeared to me that perhaps the major difference between the Aborigines and the North American Indians is that they live in America while we live in Australia.

Listening to the Pacific Islanders speak was also very educational. These people are mainly controlled by the United States and as a result of this they have been used as Nuclear testing sites. Many people have suffered, are suffering and very probably will suffer in the future. The Marshallese were displaced when their Island and their home was chosen as a testing site. Since this has taken place many of their people suffer from kidney and liver disorders and just recently a thirteen-year-old boy died from the effects of the nuclear testing. This boy was one-year-old when the testing took place. The results of other related diseases are still to be seen in the future.

Palau and Guam are fighting another part of the nuclear war. They are strongly opposing the dumping of nuclear wastes in their waters. I listened to many people talk on this subject, including Japanese and the Pacific Islanders, and from the results of surveys etc. that have been done, there is still no safe way to dump wastes in the oceans or indeed store them on land. The Japanese have made it clear that they cannot store large quantities of nuclear wastes on land anyway, because land is very precious and must be used for more productive means.

I spoke again on 9/8/80 at another Gensuikin Conference and this time called for the support of the Japanese people to stop the beginning of the nuclear cycle by supporting we, the Aboriginal people, in our fight against uranium mining. I felt quite honoured to speak at this particular Conference because I was one of two chosen to do so and also because this meeting was the Memorial Day for Nagasaki and after my speech we observed the one minute silence for those who died in the atomic bombing of that city.

Later that afternoon the delegates of Gensuikin were invited to attend the World Conference put on by a group called Gensuiquo. This group had invited many people who were not from the grass-roots level. There were representatives from the United Nations and other 'do-gooders' also who spoke on behalf of indigenous peoples. For this reason and also because of the Constitution that was presented, the Native peoples 'walked-out'. The Constitution was very general and made no references at all to the stopping of uranium mining or the banning of nuclear plants that are currently situated on Indian Land. We immediately got together to write up a protest and walked back on the stage where the protest was presented by a Commanche Indian, Karen Koshacona.

We, the Native peoples, representing our people in Japan gave a Press Conference that night to local and national newspapers. We were able to support each other in our fight against nuclear power etc, because we realised that the uranium is first mined on Aboriginal and Indian land and then at the end of the cycle, the nuclear waste is dumped in Pacific waters in the territory of other Native people. Therefore, to stop waste-dumping it is first necessary to unite in the struggle against uranium mining. This is one particular issue that the whole of Australia can unite in. Support the Aboriginal people to stop mining to promote a nuclear free Australia, nuclear free Pacific and a nuclear free world.

Sandra Levers

Source: North Queensland Messagestick, North Queensland Land Council (NQLC) Cairns, September 1980

"The white fellas never learn"

We been fight for Yeelirrie. The sacred ground is each side of Yeelirrie. 'Yeelirrie' is white man's way of saying, right way is 'Youlirrie'. Youlirrie mean by Aboriginal word means 'death', dead, Wongi way. Anything been shifted from there means death. People been finished from there, early days, all dead, but white fella can't see it. How the Wongi's know it? But it's there.

Uranium, they say uranium they make anything from it, invent anything, yet during the War when Americans flew over, what happened to Hiroshima? And that'll happen here too if they're messing about with that thing. They never learn.

We just hope that they stand their grounds at Noonkanbah and don't let the Government take 'em. We the Aboriginal people of Leonora support them.

Roley Hill whose tribal name is Nulli
Peter Hogarth whose tribal name is Yambilli,
Croydon Beaman, Aboriginal tribesmen 8 mile out of Leonora, Western Australia
21 June 1980[100]

Uranium mining in the Black Hills

Six Oglala Lakota women were buried in late September, all from the Pine Ridge Indian reservation: all died of uterine cancer. Ted Means sits in his prison cell, paying in precious time for his 1974 riot conviction: the American Indian Movement leader has only a few months left. Leonard Peltier will be paying for the rest of his two consecutive life sentences. Prison time allows for plenty of reflection on victims of war and prisoners of war.

It is a strange idea to be born and raised on land someone else is trying to steal. This year, the United States is 'officially stealing' the Black Hills, or Paha Sapa as it is called by the Lakota nation. The offer: $105 million for the Black Hills, plus a bargain of $40 million for the adjoining five state area. Since the time of the 1868 Fort Laramie Treaty, which guaranteed this land to the Lakota 'in perpetuity', the people have fought for the hills. Today the stakes are higher than ever.

The heart and soul of a nation is being weighed against massive mineral resources — uranium is the key. In 1977, the United States Indian Claims Commission offered the Lakota nation $17.5 million for the Black Hills — final settlement in a 35-year-old legal suit. The lawsuit was for money, initiated by white Washington lawyers, but money is something the Lakota will never accept. The 1979 offer of $105 million is the $17.5 million *plus* interest on a century's illegal occupation.

In 1977, Frank Fools Crow, Lakota leader, answered the US government definitively: 'The Black Hills are sacred to the Lakota people . . . How can you expect us to sell our church and our cemeteries . . . ?'

The United States is putting its entire bureaucratic military power into forcing the Lakota to sell the hills — offering more money to colonially impoverished people is a common tactic. The price increase can be attributed to two factors: the increasing Lakota resistance to further colonisation (combined with outside pressure on the US to respect Lakota sovereignty); and the publicly known increase in the value of the Hills (besides iron ore and gold, there's some 8 million tons of uranium). On this basis, $105 million is very little to pay. One half of the US annual gold production comes from the Black Hills — the backbone of American capitalism. In other words, the US economic base is owned by the Lakota nation.

Money is out of the question, Mother Earth is what the struggle is about. After the most genocidal colonisation possible — massacres, germ war-fare, sterilisation, stock exhaustion, incarceration and radiation — the people continue fighting. As Russell Means, Oglala Lakota, said, 'No white man is going to run me out of Lakota country.' Neither will any Wasichu ('he who eats the fat') corporations.

In 1973, the Lakota nation stood up in front of the world by taking control of Wounded Knee on the Pine Ridge reservation. The independent Oglala Nation was formed, and the cries of liberation from the American Indian Movement echoed throughout the Indigenous colonies. Today, the warriors — men, women and children of Wounded Knee — maintain their resistance. The resource war is formally declared.

On 25 June 1975, FBI forces attacked a traditional camp on the reservation. The women and children would surely have perished if not for four brave warriors. At the end of the day, 2 FBI agents had been killed — as had one Oglala man, Joe Stuntz. The year coincided with a government mineral resources survey of Pine Ridge reservation — finding a large uranium deposit in the northwest corner of the reservation, near the Sheep Mountain Gunnery Range. The day coincided with Dick Wilson (government installed Tribal Chairman) having negotiated the secret transfer of one-eighth of the reservation to the US government. The area was the Gunnery Range; the tactic is diversion. Today, Leonard Peltier is paying for the land with his life — framed for the killing of two FBI agents, who probably died in their own crossfire. No one is doing time for the death of Joe Stuntz, after all he is only an Indian.

The one-eighth of the reservation is killing the Oglala Lakota people. Since World War II, the Sheep Mountain area has been dominated by the US government. Nearby Ellsworth Air Force base used the corner of the reservation for bombing. Dick Wilson only made government occupation official. All title and control over the gunnery range was transferred to the US. No one knows exactly what the government does behind the well-guarded fences of the range, one can only speculate. In 1974, two helicopters hauling a large cask between them were seen entering the gunnery range. The witness was driven off with jeeps and dogs. More strange occurrences have followed, with unmarked trucks going in.

Radiation may be the key. Union Carbide thought radiation meant uranium when they offered the Pine Ridge Tribal Council a uranium mine in 1978, but it is more likely that the radiation in that corner is from waste disposal — a frightening possibility. Five women from one family who live next to the Gunnery Range have cancer — breast, colon and uterine cancer — every woman in the family. Sterility, miscarriages, cancer and diseases are at epidemic levels in the reservation. No one knows where it comes from, or why it is happening now, but the people know that something very bad is going on. The six women buried in late September were victims of someone's war.

From the Hills comes all life in the Northern Plains. The Paha Sapa is the source of the aquifer (underground water table). East and west flows the water, through the Gunnery range, to Pine Ridge, expanding as it gets further from the source. The Lakota people have always understood this, the ranchers of South Dakota are beginning to understand, but the government and the companies never will — it goes against the grain of profits. When you are sitting on $400 million-worth of uranium, you go about your life with a sort of terrifying determination to win. Uranium exploration is underway, with Tennessee Valley Authority (government owned), Union Carbide, Kerr McGee and Gulf Oil leading the way. Cattle have died from eating radioactive grass in the areas of uranium exploration, people are getting sick, and the water wells are getting low.

When the Corporate state slaps you in the face, and tells you that you're going to give up the only life you ever knew, you look for allies, and join the battle.

Two former foes in south Dakota have come together — the Cowboys and the Indians. They call themselves The Black Hills Alliance. They have come to understand that the corporations and the government are betting on racism to pull off their energy plan. If the companies win, all that will remain of the Black Hills after iron ore, coal and uranium mining will be Mount Rushmore — America's shrine to democracy.

If the companies lose, the people's victory will be appreciated world wide. Those millions of tons of uranium represent a lot of radiation, something best kept in the ground.

Winona La Duke

Source: Peace News, Nottingham, 7 December 1979.

"We come here in our last breath"

A message to you from the elders of the Navajo Nation! From those who have lived a long life, we grant you a wish for happiness. We come from a country that is devastated by radiation. Not a day goes by but another one dies from cancer — cancer contained at the beginning of the nuclear chain. We live in an area which is a bole to life. Four thousand years we lived there, because we chose to live there. When granted the opportunity for treaties with the USA we chose the Four Corners (New Mexico, Colorado, Utah, Arizona). We were there centuries before anyone from Europe. We knew there was a power point in this earth, in the Four Corners. But because the government sees us as 'their children, their wards' they have reverted our treaties into the subjugation of control.

When we asked: why do we feel the nausea, why does our hair fall out, why do our teeth weaken and fall out, why do our children sleep all the time and get no rest, why do we get up in the morning and have no breath? — we went to the books, looked back into history, as had the Japanese people. We went to Enewiatok atoll and asked them: why don't you return to the land? We went to the Nevada Platte: they gave us the same answer. We had four people who suffered from the same illness. They gave us answers to take back to the têpee. Our whole land is devastated by radon-222; a vacuum draws it up and blows it over everything. There is crying in the wind. We're in a bowl so it rests in that bowl; people, trees, herbs are dying.

We're talking about survival, not souvenirs. Not talking about warm toilet seats powered by electricity, which they choose to have in Beverly Hills, nor electric blankets, electric eyes, handles, curling irons – we're talking about life and death. We come here only in our last breath. We know our time is short. Even my own grandchildren have a very short life to look at. But I'll defy every government on this earth to know we have a chance for survival. And we will, no matter what their laboratories tell us. We know what the earth is all about. The chain for us has never been broken. We go underground at times, but we surface, knowing what powers there are. We don't have to take it apart to know how it works.

There are powerlines in this land which only a knowing, penetrating eye can see. Most of all, we believe there is an insatiable will to believe, among all human beings. Because of that we are the objects of discrimination and racism. I can only appeal to you: downwind from where we live, so do you! Your children will suffer the same as our's – unless . . . unless . . . Unless!

Herb Blatchford, 19 October 1980, Copenhagen.

No mines on our land

It was a very happy thing that happened two or three years ago when the non-Indian people saw it was necessary to ally with our Indian people, Santo Domingo. We joined forces and we battled against the Occidental (Corp.) This is a very good coalition because the non-Indian citizens within the area couldn't do anything on their own without the help of us and we couldn't succeed without the help of them. So it's a good alliance and we should maintain that momentum. We got to make a united front against those corporations. We're not afraid of anybody. I think we know the strategies so we can whip them. With knowledge and faith and trust, you can go a long way.

Ernest Lavato, Spokesperson
Santa Domingo Pueblo
23 September, 1978

No waste on our land

Native American lands have not only unwillingly provided uranium for nuclear weapons and 'civil' nuclear power, but also the sites for atomic reactors[101] and the dumping-ground for nuclear and other toxic wastes. In the late 1970s Chicano/Indian lands at Carlsbad, New Mexico, were earmarked for a high-level nuclear waste depository, and a few years later the Menominee Reservation in Wisconsin was designated a potential waste-site [confirmed in 1987].[102] The majority of US nuclear wastes is currently stored at Hanford Nuclear Reservation (sic!) only 20 miles from the Yakima reservation and well within their 1855 guaranteed Treaty lands.[103] *The following statement was delivered by Yakima councilman, Russel Jim, in 1980, to a Senate Subcommittee on the Environment.*

The Yakima Indian nation is deeply disturbed by the future plans for the Hanford Nuclear Reservation as presently put forward by the representatives of Rockwell International . . . We feel strongly that steps of vital importance to the very existence of our people are being taken, and are about to be taken without proper regard . . . for the safety of all peoples within the area, and for the federal obligations contained in the treaty with the Yakima Indian people . . . the Yakima Indian nation is an important part of the fifty-mile circle around the Hanford reservation within which the law requires that workable plans for evacuation be developed. The Yakima Indian nation sees this concept of evacuation as a cynical and empty phrase when applied to our Indian reservation . . . By placing hazardous radioactive wastes near our reservation, they may well undermine our Treaty rights by threatening a destruction which the implications of the Treaty show to be illegal. Our lands may be contaminated irretrievably by action on nearby non-Indian land or from faulty transportation of radioactive wastes. I believe any of you gentlemen will realize that for Native Americans, 'Evacuation' from their lands is meaningless . . .

Russel Jim

Source: Senate Subcommittee on the Environment, US GPO, 12 January 1980.

Statement by World Council of Indigenous Peoples
"An indefinite moratorium on uranium mining"

The greatest danger to Indigenous peoples throughout the world is that of nuclear attack. The first regions to be attacked would inevitably be those areas where nuclear energy is mined. These areas, of course, are on or close to Indigenous land and communities. Needless to state, the results would be disastrous.

The ultimate destruction of Indigenous land and resources will mean the destruction of Indigenous economic and political communities. The short term economic, social and political gains resulting from such exploitation masks the long term spoliation of ecosystems essential to the survival of Indigenous Peoples.

The following recommendations are being put forth by the World Council of Indigenous Peoples with the hope of immediate action by the international community:

1) That a moratorium on the development of uranium mines on Indigenous homelands be enacted to be in effect for an indefinite period of time.

2) That all Indigenous People have exclusive jurisdiction over the management of all Indigenous lands which includes all resources both above and below the surface. This also includes the safeguarding of all Indigenous sacred land sites on or off Indigenous held land.

3) That nation-states shift away from military and nuclear aid to developing countries to socio-economic aid for Indigenous People of the Third and Fourth World.

4) That nation-states guarantee full Indigenous involvement in the process of making laws which effect Indigenous People directly and/or indirectly.

5) That an international agreement be made against the further proliferation of nuclear weapons and further agreements to be drawn up on the necessary measures for arms control and disarmament.

6) That all current uranium and nuclear development be subject to very strict occupational health, safety and environmental regulations and the approval of the Indigenous communities affected.

7) That a disarmament program for all nation-states begin immediately.

Source: WCIP/NAC (National Aboriginal Conference of Australia) joint submission to the International NGO Conference on Indigenous Peoples and the Land, September 1981.

Statement of Fourth and Third World Nations against uranium mining

"Our most serious concern"

Cabled message (21.10.79) to: kurt waldheim secretary general united nations new york

following the conference quote uranium mining a new threat to the peoples of the third and fourth world unquote held in copenhagen denmark eighteenth to twentieth october 1979 the representatives of invited delegations representing the indigenous peoples of north america (american indian environmental council and international indian treaty council) comma the aboriginal peoples of australia comma the north queensland land council comma swapo of namibia and representatives of the people of greenland wish to express their most serious concern over the effects of uranium mining upon their respective peoples their land and their environment stop

we call upon the secretary general to use his personal influence to establish the most effective means available for all our peoples representatives to present their case to united nations general assembly through a specially appointed body of inquiry stop

we urge that this body of inquiry be established with all possible urgency through communication between the above peoples representatives and the secretary general personally stop

we therefore request your earliest possible response through the danish organisers of this conference namely international work group for indigenous affairs comma organisation for information on nuclear energy and danish association for international cooperation stop

signed: conference delegations representing the above third and fourth world organisations and peoples

(Following the International Conference on Uranium Mining and Peoples of Third and Fourth World, Copenhagen, 1979.)

4. Mining and Multinationals

In May 1982, just before an annual general meeting at which his company faced the biggest barrage of criticism experienced by any mining company in recent times[104] the chairman of Rio Tinto Zinc (RT-Z) encapsulated his views on the benefits mining could bring to indigenous peoples.

Any foreign investor has a clear responsibility to its employees and their families, and in the case of a mining company, to the local community, especially the indigenous population [wrote Sir Anthony Tuke].[105] The question both we as investors and indeed the people who will be affected by a new operation must ask, is whether the benefits of a major investment outweigh the disadvantage change may bring. We do believe that the advantages overwhelmingly outweigh the disadvantages as we see the rising standards of living in the areas where we operate. These are evidenced by the high quality of housing, education, health and medical care, training and opportunity for advancement as well as benefits to the wider community, especially in third world countries, of new sources of revenue and foreign exchange, together with educational and training opportunities from the independent foundations that have been established locally from the profits earned. It is interesting to note that the most vociferous critics of these investments are often many thousands of miles away from the operation itself and know little about the actual conditions there.

In fact, the most vociferous critics of RT-Z have always been found close to (or literally on) land coveted by the Corporation's geologists and engineers. At the AGM where Sir Anthony Tuke's statement was debated, Joyce Hall from Weipa complained bitterly about the continuing depredations faced by her community, in the aftermath of the forced removals of the early 1960s (see below). Another Aboriginal spokesperson, Les Russell from the Aboriginal Mining Information Centre (AMIC), Melbourne, released an internal document commissioned by RT-Z's Australian subsidiary which proved the company's attempts to subvert Aboriginal land rights.[106] Statements were relayed from other indigenous peoples affected by the corporation's operations, in Namibia, Panama, Canada and elsewhere.

RT-Z's chairman failed to acknowledge the importance of these declarations, no doubt because he barely heard them. A corporation which has flagrantly violated UN Resolutions and a UN Decree on Namibia's natural resources[107] is hardly likely to regard the protests of Aboriginal, or scattered tribal peoples, as more than a minor irritant.

Some other mining companies, however, have been less brash (or well insured) and grudgingly recognised indigenous sacred sites, even where there was no legal duty to do so. Those mining corporations with the biggest operations in indigenous territory — hence the most to lose by disinvestment or withdrawal — seem publicly unmoved by humanitarian submissions, but have been forced to, at least, enter public debates on land rights, and to privately concede some ground to the enemy. True, there are significant exceptions: Lang Hancock, one of Australia's legendary white mining pioneers, counselling the sterilisation of Aborigines, for example,[108] or Hugh Morgan, chairman of the Western Mining Corporation, typifying Aboriginal land claims as 'paganism'.[109] But, while the Australian Mining Industry Council (the other AMIC) mobilises vociferously against an Aboriginal 'veto' on the extractive industry[110] the Australian Petroleum Exploration Association (APEA) has taken pains to conduct open, egalitarian negotiations with Aboriginal organisations.[111] The Tennessee Valley Authority relinquished its major leases in the Paha Sapa (Black Hills) of South Dakota, at least partly because of local joint rancher–Indian actions.[112] Even RT-Z was influenced by an unprecedented international campaign by (and for) the Guaymi people of Panama, to put its Cerro Colorado copper mine 'on hold' for the 1980s.[113]

Elsewhere, indigenous people have proved themselves adept at using government regulations, environmental provisions or direct action, to halt mining operations. The Nasioi in Bougainville failed — despite an armed confrontation with bulldozers — to stop the RT-Z copper mine which is now the world's largest producer.[114] The Aboriginal people of Noonkanbah, succeeded a decade later in routing AMAX from their pastoral station (see below).

Inevitably, mining companies are facing such counter-attacks with a mixture of carrot and stick, heavy-handedness and subtlety. They have taken on board anthropologists to ease their negotiations with north American-Indian tribes, appointed indigenous representatives to their boards of management, sponsored projects of supposed benefit to indigenous communities and, in the final event, helped establish native mining corporations. Under the Alaska Native Claims Act of 1971, Inuit corporations are entitled to comparatively favourable equities in major mining projects.[115] On the other hand, the Council of Energy Resource Tribes (CERT), nominally under the control of western, native American tribal councils, has proved little more than a front for the penetration of Indian natural resources.[116]

There is little evidence that mining companies co-ordinate their responses to indigenous demands. Conzinc Rio Tinto Australia (CRA), negotiated agreements with the Pitjantjatjara people of South Australia, along the lines of its much-vaunted 'Comalco model'.[117] *But, at almost the same time, the parent company was flagrantly violating sacred Aboriginal sites in the Kimberley region of Western Australia.*[118] *What this, and other examples, show, is that corporate power will exploit weaknesses, ignorance, or divisions among indigenous communities, but usually withdraw, or knuckle down to negotiations, when the opposition gets tough.*

A major myth propagated by mining companies and organisations is that native peoples are implacably opposed to all 'natural resource extraction', hence, that they 'irrationally' hold-up projects designed for the greater good. This argument sits uneasily alongside claims that indigenous people overwhelmingly benefit from the jobs, amenities, access to consumer goods and higher standards of living introduced by a wage-labour economy. In fact this last argument is not used very often (the bald, naive statement by Anthony Tuke, quoted above, being an exception) and is, anyway, palpably untrue. Where they are not actually ejected from their land, to make way for a mine, indigenous peoples have certainly had the worse end of the stick: more disease, less safety at work, third class housing, debased food, and the brunt of toxic wastes left after mining.

The utilitarian defence of mining is answered by indigenous peoples in various ways. They point out that they are not necessarily opposed to mining as such: after all the first mines in South America and West Africa were plumbed by native peoples. Scattered communities continue the tradition today.[119]

The largest prospecting force in the rich Pilbara region of western Australia was, until 1960, an Aboriginal group calling itself the 'Nomads'.[120]

What they implacably oppose is mining which — as in the Amazon rain-forest — damages an ecosystem whose balances they are the first to appreciate and preserve; encroaches on sacred sites; pollutes their fishing grounds; disturbs the wildlife they hunt; brings in an alien labour force, with its inevitable alcohol, prostitution and often disease; exploits them as cheap labour in often dangerous work; or which acts as a trojan horse in areas under their own claim.[121]

Where land claims await settlement — as with the Guaymi of Panama — the local community can achieve an unprecedented militancy in fighting off a mining proposal.[122] *Where some land rights have been granted, it becomes much more 'reasonable' in liberal, white, eyes. Several concessions have been granted mining companies in central and southern Australia, as a result of land rights legislation giving negotiating power to the Central and Pitjantjatjara Land Councils.*[123] *In 1983, some of the Oenpelli members of the Northern Land Council even concluded an agreement with Denison Mines to proceed with a uranium mine which the federal government fundamentally opposed.*[124]

Nonetheless, there is no Australian Aboriginal community — and indeed virtually no indigenous community outside of north America — which has a final, legal, veto against mining. Until that is granted as a fundamental right, it is likely that native organisations will dig in their heels against mining projects which, ironically, they might otherwise be prepared to accept as fully informed and equitable partners.

1963. Petition of the Yirrkala people

To the Honourable the Speaker and Members of the House of Representatives in Parliament assembled

The Humble Petition of the Undersigned aboriginal people of Yirrkala, being members of the Balamumu, Narrkala, Gapiny and Miliwurrwurr people and Djapu, Mangalili, Madarrpo, Magarrwanalinirri, Gumaitj, Djambarrpuynu, Marrakula, Galpu, Dhaluayu, Wangurri, Warramirri, Maymil, Rirritjinu tribes, respectfully sheweth—

1. That nearly 500 people of the tribes are residents of the land excised from the Aboriginal Reserve in Arnhem Land.

2. That the procedures of the excision of this land and the fate of the people on it were never explained to them beforehand, and were kept secret from them.

3. That when Welfare Officers and Government officials came to inform them of decisions taken without them and against them, they did not undertake to convey to the Government in Canberra the views and feelings of the Yirrkala aboriginal people.

4. That land in question has been hunting and food gathering land for the Yirrkala tribes from time immemorial; we were all born here.

5. That places sacred to the Yirrkala people, as well as vital to their livelihood are in the excised land, especially Melville Bay.

6. That the people of this area fear that their needs and interests will be completely ignored as they have been ignored in the past, and they fear that the fate which has overtaken the Larrakeah tribe will overtake them.

7. And they humbly pray that the Honourable the House of Representatives will appoint a Committee, accompanied by competent interpreters, to hear the views of the Yirrkala people before permitting the excision of this land.

8. They humbly pray that no arrangements be entered into with any company which will destroy the livelihood and independence of the Yirrkala people.

And your petitioners as in duty bound will ever pray God to help you and us.

(*English translation*)
Certified as a correct translation. Kim E. Beazley

Source: Commonwealth Parliamentary Papers, Vol. iv. 1963. Select Committee on the Grievances of Yirrkala Aborigines, Arnhem Land Reserve, p. 952.

In August 1963 the Yirrkala people protesting against mining on the Arnhemland reserve presented a petition to the Australian House of Representatives; a Select committee favoured buying-off the protestors. Litigation followed, and not until 1971 did the Supreme Court, under Justice Blackburn, rule that, although the clans had established a spiritual relationship with their land, this could not be compensated for as a 'property right' by whitemen's law. [125]

The land rights movement did not attract international attention until 1980 when the Yungngora people of western Australia non-violently ejected representatives of the AMAX mining corporation from their own cattle station at Noonkanbah. The resultant battle brought Australian white trade unions publicly out on the side of Aborigines for the first time; helped bring down the reactionary Charles Court government; stimulated support demonstrations in Europe and the United States [126] *and galvanised independent Aboriginal land councils throughout the country into forming the first National Federation of Land Councils.* [127]

Noonkanbah was acquired for the Yungngora people in 1976 as a pastoral lease from the Aboriginal Lands Fund Commission. [128] *They moved on to the cattle station, pulled it back from the brink of ruin and began to restore community life. Within two years, however, no less than 600 separate mining 'tenements' had been staked by some 30 companies. One of these — AMAX — began preliminary exploration work during which they bulldozed two burial grounds and a ceremonial site.* [129]

The mining company's prospect area was Pea Hill — a Goanna Dreaming site whose importance is explained in the first of the statements below. Although, under Western Australian law, the Aboriginal community had no freehold title to Pea Hill, they nonetheless considered they were entitled to protection under the Western Australian Aboriginal Heritage Act (1972) which on the instructions of anthropologists from the Western Australian Museum, allows the safeguarding of certain sites.

But the Western Australian government ignored the Museum's recommendations, and on 28 March 1980 gave AMAX the go-ahead to drill. Faced with vehement Aboriginal opposition, AMAX was forced to withdraw on 3 April. [130]

Four months later, it was back with a vengeance, after a company spokesman declared '. . . . we have never had these problems before, even with American Indians'. [131] *Protected by police in a 'military style operation'* [132] *the company moved a drilling rig on to Pea Hill, using scab labour. Twenty days later, after numerous arrests of protestors, the Western Australian government itself took over the drilling rig at Noonkanbah employing a front company it had set up virtually overnight.* [133]

For the time being the Aboriginal community had lost. But AMAX eventually pulled out of Noonkanbah, and Aboriginal Australia had discovered a new byword for militancy which would be heard around the globe.

In the first of the Noonkanbah statements, the Yungngora community

*explains the importance of the Goanna Dreaming at Pea Hill. This is
followed by the petition sent from Noonkanbah in Walmajeri — the
Yungngora language — to the West Australian parliament after AMAX's
first desecrations in 1979.*

*After this comes a press statement put out by the community soon afterwards;
the Noonkanbah proclamation which was read out just before the AMAX rig
was established at Pea Hill; and another statement from the community
issued when drilling started. Lastly Bill Wesley — spokesman for people who
have been cruelly dealt with themselves by mining companies, in the Great
Eastern Goldfields[134] expresses what many Aboriginal people felt throughout
Australia when they learned of the 'Battle for Noonkanba'.*

**That area is a goanna place, all around on top of the ground the stones are
really the goanna eggs. The sacred goannas have been living there under the
ground since the dreamtime. If the drill goes down and kills the goanna, it
will kill the spirits of the dead people there too, and it will make all the
goanna leave the country so there will be no more for us to eat. Also we have
a ceremony ground right near there, and if that is messed up we can't have
the initiation ceremony there**

We are sending this letter to you important people who can speak and
who are now sitting down talking in the big house.

We, Aboriginal people of Noonkanbah Station, are sending you this
letter. We truthfully beg you important people that you stop these people,
namely CRA and AMAX, who are going into our land, which is at
Noonkanbah.

These people have already made the place no good with their
bulldozers. Our sacred places they have made no good.

They mess up our land. They expose our sacred objects. This breaks our
spirit. We lose ourselves as a people. What will we as a people do if these
people continue to make all our land no good?

Today we beg you that you truly stop them.

Press Release by Yungngora Aboriginal Community:

Exploration Attempt to Intrude on their Land.

A letter from Amax Exploration has stated that the company intends to enter on an
Aboriginal owned station in the Kimberley, W.A., and drill notwithstanding
opposition by the Aboriginal owners.

The letter was received today by the community's legal advisors, the Aboriginal
Legal Service in Perth.

It stated that the Company had approached the police and the W.A. Government to protect the companys' personnel when they entered the station following statements by tribal leaders that mining personnel would be punished in tribal law if they intruded onto the station.

The letter from Amax followed upon a petition from the Aboriginal community at Noonkanbah which was presented to the W.A. Parliament Thursday, 17th May, by Ron Davies, the leader of the Opposition. In the petition which was in Walmatjari language, the community requested the W.A. Government to stop mining companies, including CRA and Amax from exploring on the station property.

Noonkanbah Station was acquired for the community in late 1976 by the Aboriginal Land Fund Commission. The community is against mining and exploration on their land because of their belief that it will destroy their new found independence. At present, a report from the W.A. Museum on the station's sacred sites is pending.

The Yungngora community has instructed the Aboriginal Legal Service to take all possible steps to prevent Amax from drilling on the station, as the proposed site is in a sacred area.

A spokesperson for the community, Mr Dicky Skinner stated, 'We've been thinking a lot about this problem. The elders and all the communities around here are working on ways in tribal law which will stop Amax coming and drilling on our land.'

Today the community has discovered that Amax is attempting to organize a meeting at the station next Wednesday, with representatives of the W.A. Government, the police, and the W.A. Museum. The community *has not been informed* of these proceedings by Amax.

Speaking for community, Dicky Skinner has said, 'We don't want the gudias (Europeans) coming here in our paddock. They just get whatever stones they find there, rich stones in the ground. They don't worry about Aborigines. We want to talk up for our own citizens, for our own land. We know that we've been losing our ground before and left with nothing. Gudias come along and try to kill people, mining.'

Nipper Tabagee said, "I've been worried about my land, that nobody don't take it away. Doesn't matter what they think. We don't like to have an argument about these sort of things, damaging all our places, running up and down. They don't care that Aborigines have got the country. They only want to come in, looking so worried for money, that's all. Silly idea really, people get mad from thinking about what's going to happen to the country. We don't want it anymore. They make us upset and knock us around. They just don't care."

Noonkanbah Proclamation

Before the coming of white man, there was a law for all men and all time. This law guaranteed the undisputed tenure of the Land from generation to generation. The collective rights, titles and interests of the people were protected by this law. The people lived in a state of virtue and democracy under the Law, without recourse to kings, princes or police.

Let it be known that this Law of the Land continues to guide us up to the present time. Next to the food we eat, it is this thing which keeps us alive and which we cherish most.

Let it be known that, in spite of our misery, the Land and its Law provide hope for us.

The white man has never understood our Law nor taken it seriously. Whereas in 1889 limited sovereign powers were transferred to the State of Western Australia, this transference of power was subject to conditions pertaining to the maintenance of our welfare. These conditions were that a sum amounting to one per cent of the annual gross revenue of the State of Western Australia be placed in a fund beyond the reach of Parliament.

This fund was for our welfare, namely to educate us in order to bring us quickly to equality with the European, to feed and clothe us when we might otherwise be destitute, to promote our general well-being and preservation. This fund was to be expended by a Protector of Natives responsible to the Governor, provision for which was also made within the constitution of 1889.

Thus we legally defined the duties of the State of Western Australia towards ourselves. Yet we, the Beneficial Owners, were given no opportunity to influence the spending of this fund nor to select our own trustee, for almost immediately the State attempted to delete certain sections of the Constitution in breach of its original agreement. This attempt failed to gain the Queen's consent. Thus it was that what has been called the Native Question was born, the same persisting to the present.

Whereas in 1897, the Parliament of Western Australia, without duly consulting the legal entities most directly concerned, passed an Act of Native Affairs, we claim this to be illegal. The setting up of a department and the placing of funds meant for the purpose of promoting our welfare in the hands of a government minister, was contrary to the terms and intent of the 1889 agreement, and therefore we deem it unlawful.

From that time, we, the Beneficial Owners, have been enslaved. In 1905, the Seventieth Section was again removed from the Constitution of Western Australia, the Act of Native Affairs was passed and proclaimed, and an Enabling Bill passed in order to make legal the illegalities proceeding from 1897, at which time the funds were markedly reduced. Thus the State placed itself further in breach of its original agreement pertaining to our welfare.

The circumstances of enslavement and genocide continued. In 1942 we, the Beneficial Owners, elected Donald William McLeod to act and speak on our behalf as we, being illiterate and near destitute, were in no position to continue unassisted. In 1946, the Pilbara section of the Beneficial Owners withdrew their labour in an attempt to establish their credentials as freemen. This action is continuing.

Whereas by way of constitutional referendum in 1967 the State was stripped of its powers to make laws concerning us, yet a series of acts passed by the State of Western Australia since 1970 has further worsened our plight. We believe the responsibility to make atonement for the illegalities perpetuated by the State and to offer us due compensation rests with the Federal Government. Yet they likewise appear reluctant to take the necessary action.

We the Beneficial Owners of this Land, stand prepared to negotiate with Federal authorities at all times, duly recognising their constitutional powers and trusting that through negotiation an acceptable redefinition of our legal status will emerge. Nevertheless, with due consideration of the above history, we hereby resume our titles, rights and interests in this Land, our Estate, by raising our flag, firing a volley and reading this proclamation.

In order that justice be done, we look to the Federal Government or an appropriate impartial authority, to make objective judgement in this matter. We look forward to receiving not only the residue of our Estate but also adequate compensation for damages suffered through the negligence of successive governments, it being apparent that the agreement of 1889 was entered into in bad faith.

Proclaimed at Noonkanbah in the State of Western Australia on the 10th day of August 1980 by:

Donald William McLeod duly elected representative and spokesman for the Beneficial Owners of the Land.

You can't kill Aboriginal Law

Statement by Yungngora Community, Saturday August 30th, on hearing that drilling has started at Noonkanbah.

We had this fight for a long time now, for three years. Charlie Court got round us using a dirty trick. All we can say is that the white man is mad. He doesn't know what he is doing.

They might hurt that sacred Maladku place. But we've still got our law. We live by that law. The white man can't kill the Aboriginal Law no matter how hard he tries.

We can't say any more now. But we know we are not beaten. We are still strong, and we know that we are proud, and that Charlie Court, and Senator Chaney, and the Federal Government, and Ken Colbung are the ones who are weak and shamed.

1. W.A. Government recruited strike breakers through the West Australia Transport Commission.
2. They utilised the services of Midland Brick Company who have a professional strike breaking force for hire.
3. Under heavy Police guard, the trucks moved out early Thursday morning. It is expected to arrive at Noonkanbah late Sunday or early Monday.
4. We understand each driver is being paid $3,500 for the job. There are between 45 and 50 drivers which means a salary bill for drivers alone of between $157,000 and $175,000.
5. Police will guard the convoy and clear the road from Eneabba to Noonkanbah.
6. State Government has gazetted part of the Noonkanbah lease as a public highway and the drill site as a public open space.
7. Road rules and traffic regulations therefore apply.

8. Police are stopping every vehicle to check drivers' licences, vehicle safety, etc.

9. They have fenced the public open space with a 9ft high cyclone fence which is patrolled by the police to keep the community out.

10. I am advised by the community that the earth works, the dam and the camp site which are all within the compound have so desecrated their sacred area as to make it unrecognisable and in traditional sense worthless.

More than millions of dollars
Tribal Aboriginal Spokesman for the Great Eastern Goldfields

The white mans have already taken various sacred sites. They have promised the Aboriginals that they're going to fence the sacred sites and let the Museum take over charge of their sacred sites, and I think that this is wrong, this has gone too far.

We don't want our sacred sites fenced off like the one in the midst of Port Hedland town, like a lone skeleton. We can't hold our tribal ceremonies there.

It will hurt us of thinking that the Premier, Charlie Court, with all his friendly talks that will destroy our tribal customs, our culture; it will, definitely would destroy the entire Aboriginal race because we've lived on these sacred sites — it's not only the sacred sites, the name, it represents our whole heart and soul and mind. It teaches us the way to live, the way to handle our childrens and our childrens childrens after.

Australia's meant more than millions of dollars because that's where our heart lies.

The Aboriginal people of Noonkanbah should not be afraid of what the Government would say because they are not a "group" on their own. The entire Aboriginal race is with them, because this is our sacred sites, this how we was brought up, this how we lived for many thousands of years and we have sang sacred songs that meant lot to us.

If they destroy our sacred sites at Noonkanbah there is no doubt Charlie Court and the mining companies will move from one sacred site to another until our sacred sites there'd be nothing left of them, and I can assure you that this story of Noonkanbah it has hurt me more than in years and I'm a tribesman of Kalgoorlie. I've lived like a white man for a number of years but my heart and soul and my mind are still on my old ways of living, the tribal laws and my tribal culture are still within me and I know that no man, no white man, will ever take away my strong feeling towards my sacred culture.

William James Wesley, whose tribal name is Biluritha.
Kalgoorlie, W. A. 18 June 1980.
Source: Jan Roberts, *Massacres to Mining*, Dove, Blackburn, 1981, p. 145.

Odak Olsen was, in 1978 the (Inuit) President of the Labour Union of Greenland. He attacked AMAX in the context of unacceptable activities by multinational mining companies, during a speech given at a Conference on Non-renewable Resources in Greenland that year. This was just before the country achieved a measure of 'home rule'.

Amax in Greenland

We are usually being told that experienced labour is needed, and the reason why the enterprises do not hire Greenlanders, is that they do not have the required professional training. But we have many experienced mine workers from Qutlissat (abandoned coal mine, Disko Island, N.W. Greenland) living all along the coast, and they have not been used in Marmorilik.

Our experiences in relation to the environmental problems have not been good either. We know now that the fjord at Marmorilik is polluted and that the mining activities are causing a great deal of trouble for the sealers in the area. But the management does not want to do anything about the threatening environmental pollution as long as the pollution is not 'significant'.

This means that the damage has to be done before action will be taken by the Ministry of Greenland and Greenex.*

It is now clear that it is not the people of Greenland and its own development that brought up the exploitation of these resources. It is related to the ever-increasing world-wide search for all kinds of resources, itself the result of an economy based upon a sustained growth. This economy is dominated by very large companies. Particularly in the case of raw materials, where big investments are called for before extraction becomes profitable, the Western world is dominated by a few, large companies. Most of these companies not only control most of the known resources, they also in many cases control the majority of the links in the processing chain, from raw material to the final product.

Let me give an example, which shows how these conditions are related to our own daily situation. The holder of the molybdenum concession is "Arctic Mining Company", a subsidiary of the world's largest producer of molybdenum, American Metal Climax (AMAX) which is also involved in the mining and smelting of a long series of other minerals.

The deposits of Mestersvig (East Greenland) are the third largest in the world and if AMAX had not made an even greater molybdenum find, mining would probably already have been started.

Thus if we open up for the mining of Greenland's raw materials, it will be giants like AMAX that we are letting in.

Source: IWGIA, Copenhagen.

---

*Greenex operates the major Black Angel mine at Marmorilik, west Greenland, and is a majority-owned subsidiary of the Canadian company Cominco.

*Although the world's biggest producer of the world's most prolific metal,
the Aluminium Company of America (ALCOA) is not immediately
identified by indigenous organisations as a flagrant violator of land rights:
certainly not in the league of RT-Z or AMAX.*

*Until the 1970s its biggest crime against native peoples was probably its
involvement in the Brokopondo dam and power plant project in Surinam
which threw more than 5,000 Indians out of their homes.*[135]

*By 1977, a Vice-President of the company was predicting that ALCOA
would move away from its long-standing reliance on bauxite supplies and
smelters in the Caribbean and America, to Brazil and Australia.*[136]

*Since then, ALCOA has been forced to relinquish a project in Costa
Rica,*[137] *which would have uprooted many Boruca Indians; and the effects
of its smelters have been felt by Mohawk communities in southern
Ontario.*[138]

*It has also managed to incense the peasants of Sao Luis, northern Brazil,
with its construction work for a refinery and smelter on their island.*[139] *And
in 1980, its attempts to begin work on a smelter in Portland, Victoria
(Australia) located on sacred land, unleashed Aboriginal direct action
which was as intense as that at Noonkanbah.*[140]

*Despite complex legal moves by Aboriginal groups to halt construction
work*[141] *and an eventual delay in building, thanks to a slump in the market,
electricity prices and other factors, ALCOA in 1984, secured a contract
to proceed with the smelter.*[142]

*The following statements consist of a Declaration by the Gunditj-mara
people delivered as the project went ahead in 1980, and an account by an
Aboriginal participant of the occupation of Portland in December 1980.*

Statement from the Gunditj-Mara at Portland

From as far back as our stories go, we have been a part of this land, as is the soil,
sea, rocks, animals, birds, and all other creations are a part of the land. The entire
natural web of life constitutes our land. The land is sacred to us as it is a part of the
creator. We call the land our mother for she gives birth to us and nurtures us
through our life.

If ownership of the land is by legal occupancy, then the Aborigines are the legal
owners and not the white invaders or their descendants. This land was not
unoccupied, nor was the land taken by conquest, nor was a treaty charter or paper
of conveyance ever signed handing over the land to white invaders.

We, the Gunditj-Mara (as with all the Aboriginal people of Australia), have
never stopped the fight for our land, the land that has been our life since the
Dreaming.

Although all the land is sacred, there are places throughout Australia that are
especially sacred and there are places we hold special, as places of historic
importance. Archaeological sites are also either sacred or special.

Alcoa wish to build on land at Portland that is sacred, special and archaeologically significant (sacred and special) to the Gunditj-Mara people.

The Victorian State Government has so far done little to protect the rights of the Gunditj-Mara people at Portland.

Building at Portland without Aboriginal permission clearly violates the International Covenant on Civil and Political Rights, to which the Australian Government is a signatory.

Article 18: *Everyone shall have the right to freedom of thought, conscience and religion. This right shall include freedom to have or adopt a religion or belief of his choice and freedom, either individually or in community with others and in public or private, to manifest his religion or belief in worship, observance, practice and teaching.*

Article 27: *In those states in which ethnic religious or linguistic minorities exist, persons belonging to such minorities shall not be denied the right, in community with the other members of their group, to enjoy their own culture, to profess and practice their own religion, or to use their own language.*

We do not beg for these rights, we do not beg you to protect our sacred and special places. Why should we; we, as humans, are born with these rights. We demand the Victorian Government to do its duty to aid the Gunditj-Mara and all of Victoria's Aborigines.

Source: North Queensland Messagestick, NQLC, Vol. 6, No. 1, January 1981 p. 1.

Alcoa the destroyer

The Gunditj-Mara people set up a protest camp in the middle of the proposed Alcoa aluminium refinery site about three months ago. It was manned on an alternative basis till they lost their court case on 24th November 1980 for an injunction to stop all work (the wife of the judge who heard the case has numerous shares in Western Mining, which is 30% owned by Alcoa). Justice Brooking, the judge who heard the case, seemed to be on very personal terms with Clive Hildebrand, project manager for Alcoa, and was on a first-name basis while the case was heard. From 24 November the protest camp was fully manned by 30 Aborigines on a full-time basis. The numbers jumped to as many as 100 in the following weeks but never went below the 30. Aboriginals from the camp were continually harassed by Alcoa-paid thugs supposedly employed for security reasons (they were imported from USA).

8 a.m. on 4th December: Clive Hidebrand, the Alcoa thugs and approximately 50 Victorian police turned up at the camp. A car-load of children from the camp were stopped from going to school. Clive read out a message that we were trespassing and we had to vacate the camp-site. An earthmover and a grader moved into the paddock next to the camp and commenced earth work. The people from the camp jumped the fence, leaving Hildebrand, the thugs and the police talking to themselves, and chased after the earthmover. We finally cornered the earthmover when John King and Michael Onus threw themselves under its wheels. Most of the people thought both of them had been run over and the situation nearly got out of hand.

Tina Franklin and Amy Williams stood in front of the grader and stopped it.

The drivers got down from both vehicles very shaken, the wheel of the earth mover was only six inches from Michael Onus.

We knew that this, of course, had been a decoy as the dozers moved into the Heathland, but we were very concerned about the camp site as there were only three people looking after it.

The police put a road block on the main road coming into the Alcoa site.

Aborigines were stopped from coming onto the site. In one case an Aboriginal was removed from a car and the driver, who was white, was allowed on the site.

Whites from Portland treated it as a field day. The road was lined with cars and about 100 whites watched as, in their own words, "the boongs get evicted" — a bit like a public hanging in England in the 1700s, something to do on a Sunday.

At 11.30 we were told by our lawyer that the police could not evict us from the camp site. It is a public road and Alcoa doesn't have exclusive rights over it.

The police told us we were trespassing and if we didn't go we would be charged with trespass, so we decided to go back to the camp. We were informed by police that if we went to the camp we would be still trespassing and they would shift us at 3 pm.

4.30 p.m.: Clive, the Alcoa thugs and police arrived at the camp. We were told we were trespassing and we had to go. Our lawyer informed the police they had no right to shift us and they would be breaking the law if we were arrested.

We sat down in a circle, joined arms around the flag and sang "We shall not be moved".

Clive, looking whiter than ever, hung his head as he asked the police not to arrest us.

Great roars of boos came from the local whites as the police, Clive and his thugs drove away. They felt let down.

7.18, Wednesday, 10th December: Clive, his paid thugs and the police again turned up at the camp, warned us we were trespassing and gave us till 9 a.m. to shift.

8.15: They came again. Our lawyer warned them that if they arrested us they would be breaking the law.

We again sat down and joined arms. It took them half an hour to arrest us.

A fourteen-year-old protester was dragged by her hair to the divvy wagon by a policewoman and batons were used.

When they got us to the police station the whole town could hear our chant "What do we want?".

We were bailed on condition we wouldn't go onto Alcoa land.

That night we set up camp beside the road leading onto the Alcoa site just outside of Alcoa land owned by the Harbour Trust — people have been camping on this land from time to time.

Thursday, 11th: Union leaders Dick Watton, from the Uniting Church, and Reg Blow, Secretary, SE Land Council, came down for an investigation tour.

Police turned up at the new site with the manager of the Harbour Trust. We were told that we had to move or we would be charged with trespass. It was pointed out that whites were camped not far away. The whites were told "We have nothing against you, but we can't shift the protesters unless we ask you to leave as they've been giving us a lot of trouble."

A delegation from the unions went to ask the Harbour Trust if we could camp there. Apparently, the Harbour Trust Commissions could not be contacted (they were quite easily contacted that morning by Alcoa).

The union leaders, Reg Blow and Dick Wotton, inspected the Alcoa site. When they returned to the camp site we were packing up. We had to vacate the camp site by 12 noon. John Halfpenny asked the police if they could give us another hour as he wanted a meeting with us. This was agreed on. Also when the manager could contact the Harbour Trust Commission they would get a decision on whether we could go back to the site.

John Halfpenny told us he was concerned about how many Aboriginal sites had been destroyed and that even our previous camp site had been bulldozed as soon as we were arrested, and that he would be calling for a meeting between Alcoa, the unions and us, the Aboriginal people, and that the destruction of our sites would have to stop until such a meeting was held.

Dick Watton told us we could expect this type of thing in Queensland or Western Australia, but people didn't think it could happen in Victoria. The tactics used by Alcoa at Portland were as bad as those used at Aurukun, Mornington Island and Noonkanbah.

The unions went off to arrange the meeting with Alcoa.

That night we set up another camp on the western side of the Alcoa site on private property.

Friday the 12th, we marched through town to Alcoa office, then on to the Harbour Trust office.

The harbour master said, "I have nothing to say to you." It seems the Harbour Trust Commission still couldn't be contacted (for us anyhow).

We returned to Alcoa office and protested on the foothpath outside their office.

Alcoa had a policeman on duty at the door of their office to stop us from going in.

Bob Daniels, Alcoa's site manager, had been trying to find out whose property we were on so he could get us evicted. When asked by a union official why didn't he leave us alone as he had got us off the Alcoa site, he stated: "I live in this town and I have to think about my children and they are nothing but a health hazard to the town." Bob Daniels was a long-standing member of the Papua New Guinea Police Force (he qualifies for a job in Queensland with the Department of Aboriginal and Island Advancement).

Alcoa failed to meet their deadline with the unions about the proposed meeting.

Friday night, the owners of the property turned up and said, "You can stay here as far as we're concerned. Alcoa *sucks*."

That night we contacted Nareen to try and get a meeting with the PM.

We turned up at Nareen at 7.30 a.m. We told the security guard at 8.30 a.m., that we wished to see the PM to ask him to utilise the powers he has under the 1967 referendum to act on our behalf, as Alcoa has continually broken laws of the State of Victoria and, even though numerous complaints had been made to the Victorian Police, no investigations had been made.

We have been unlawfully arrested, and even while we were waiting to see the PM our sites were being destroyed by Alcoa.

We were told the PM would arrive at 10.30 a.m. and we would have a long wait.

10.45 a.m.: The PM arrived at Nareen by plane.

12.30 p.m.: Mrs Tammie Fraser arrived at the gate. She wished to talk to a delegation of locals.

The press pushed us out of the way and we had to push forward to talk. Mrs Fraser introduced herself to us, told us "Malcolm was resting" and she would take him a message, handed us a phone number and disappeared back into the pine trees on Nareen.

Once again we felt we had been let down after waiting in the wind and rain for five hours. We had been talked down to and pushed out of the way by a news-hungry press. Anyone would think the press had been the ones to have the meeting.

It seems certain that Fraser will not use the powers given to him via the 1967 Referendum, but this is not unusual as he has continually refused to do so in the past.

We wonder who will be the next group to award Fraser a Gold Medal for his work against racism. One thing for certain, it won't be in Australia unless it comes from the KKK.

Five Major Points

1. Alcoa has continually broken the laws of this State.
2. Police have unlawfully been used on one occasion.
3. Police refusal to act on complaints made about Alcoa.
4. The laws of this State have been changed in favour of Alcoa.
5. Alcoa has broken all promises made with unions, Aboriginals, Local Council and the Victorian Government.

One can only ask how much money has Alcoa flashed around the Victorian Cabinet.

It doesn't matter what Alcoa does, the Gunditj-Mara people will still be here and will continue the protest until sacred sites and significant sites are fully protected.

Source: *North Queensland Messagestick*, NQLC, Vol. 6, No. 1, January 1981, pp. 10–11.

If half the material in this chapter concerns the Rio Tinto-Zinc Corporation (RT-Z), it is not simply because this corporation is the most diversified mining company in the world.[143] *Without doubt, RT-Z has been criticised, or opposed, by more indigenous communities for a longer period, than any other mining (or, indeed "natural resource") company.*[144]

Formed in 1962 as a unique conjunction of British city banking interests and two large "old style" mining companies,[145] *RT-Z has become the minerals arm of the British government (of whatever political hue), the world's biggest single producer of uranium*[146] *and an important producer of borax, copper, tin, iron ore, oil and gas. Its operations have concentrated on the "old" Commonwealth, and in particular Australia, and Papua New Guinea where it is the largest holder of leases on Aboriginal land,*[147] *and Canada, where it has participated in two of the largest hydro projects ever sited on Indian territory.*[148] *More recently, as it has increasingly diversified and strengthened its "downstream" interests, the corporation has moved into new fields.*[149] *However, its strengths as a raiser of investment capital, exploiter of huge, low-grade deposits, and provider of mineral technology and services, make it a fundamentally conservative institution, remaining with the metals it knows best, in the areas it has exploited the most.*

Inevitably, it has refined its approach to indigenous peoples over the past 20 years. It is now virtually inconceivable that an entire Aboriginal community could be routed from its traditional land as it was from Mapoon and Weipa without compensation, to make way for the world's largest bauxite mine in the early 1960s. But it was certainly possible for RT-Z to make arrangements to mine the Cerro Colorado deposit on Guaymi land in Panama, knowing that the peoples' comarca *(land base) would probably not be guaranteed by law until mining had gone too far. It was also quite predictable that RT-Z's Australian subsidiary, CRA (Conzinc Rio Tinto of Australia), would attempt to "divide and rule" the Warmun community near its huge kimberlite diamond deposit in north-western Australia (see below), even as it was offering largesse in the form of jeeps and community facilities. Whatever the public face of RT-Z on the question of land rights, its practice was perhaps best summed up in a confidential document, leaked in 1982, just before the most turbulent annual general meeting in its history. Arguing that the so-called Argyle diamond "agreement" should be "isolate[d] . . . from the general debate on Aboriginal land rights", the document recommended a "vigorous lobbying programme in State and Federal [Australian] circles . . . to ensur(e) that our position regarding the Aboriginal issue . . . is fully appreciated among key decision-makers".*[150] *Indirectly, the success of this covert position was borne out in 1984, when the Australian Labor Party government of Bob Hawke finally refused to grant Aboriginal organisations the veto against mining that they had fought for, long and hard, over a decade or more.*[151]

Statement to Rio Tinto–Zinc from the Aborigines of N.E. Australia

The North Queensland Land Council represents the 65,000 Aborigines of N.E. Australia. It is an organization started by Aborigines with the principal aim of fighting for Aboriginal control of Aboriginal Reserves. It is composed of 76 Aboriginal delegates elected by the different communities and towns.

It represents, among others, the communities of Weipa and Mapoon whose lands are already being devastated by the company without these Aborigines being allowed any say in what happens to their much loved lands. It represents the people of Aurukun who have learnt from the devastation of Weipa and are determined to stop the company mining its 300 sq mile lease over Aurukun tribal land.

The people of Weipa are asking for just compensation. They resent being left as beggars, dependent on handouts, confined on a government controlled compound of just 308 acres, while the company makes a fortune from their tribal lands without any payments to them.

The people of Weipa demand that the company restores the vast areas it has mined with native trees so that their animals may return – not with the pines and teak it is planting with a view to extra profit.

The people of Weipa – and those of Mapoon – want the devastation caused by the company to be limited. They want to be able to protect some of their remaining lands from the company so that they may be able to return to live on and from some of the lands that are not yet destroyed.

The people of Aurukun want the company to leave them alone – to leave them with the lands they have lived on for thousands of years so they may control their own lives and develop their communities their own way.

The Aboriginal people are sick and tired of being the easy "target" for the greed of the Western corporations – coveting their few remaining tribal lands.

The North Queensland Land Council has been empowered by the Aboriginal communities to speak on their behalf. It demands that Rio Tinto Zinc listens to them as have companies in Holland and Germany, and that, like Billiton – a company that also has a mining lease at Aurukun, it undertakes "despite what legal documents it holds" not to mine at Aurukun without Aboriginal consent. It also demands the negotiation of proper compensation and the ending of Apartheid practices at Weipa.

20 November 1978

Mick Miller, Chairman NQLC
Jacob Wolmby (Aurukun delegate)
Joyce Hall (Weipa delegate)

Invasion of Mapoon

On 15 November 1963, this is the date of what happen on a Friday night. Government boat brought white police, from Thursday Island; but before their arrival at Mapoon, people of Mapoon who were newly resident of Hidden Valley told us that the Government boat Gelam sailed across to Red Island Point to pick up Saibai police. When the Saibai police went on board the Gelam, they left from Red Island and was on their way for Mapoon; sighted Mapoon after five but orders were given to Captain Mr Tom Dunwoodie to drop anchor.

After seven, the anchor was pulled up and they sailed in for the harbour of Mapoon when it was dark, so that no one can see who arrived on the Government boat Gelam. All police that arrived on the boat waited until everybody was settled down in their homes before all police came ashore.

First home they went to was Mr Robert Reid and family; second home was Mr Andrew Archie, Mrs A. Archie and son; third, Mr Gilbert Jimmy, Mrs Jean Jimmy; fourth, Mr Richard Luff, Mrs Victoria Luff and two girls. And this is what was told to us: "*Pack your suitcases and roll up your swags.*"

Mr Reid added: "It was a big surprise to me, seeing the police right in front of me. I was sitting with the children. I looked up and asked, 'Are you a policeman?' He said, 'Yea,' I asked him, 'Why have you come?' He replied, 'To shift you people!' I said to him, 'Give me the reason.' He said, 'Well, I have no reason to give, but this has been our word from Mr Killoran.' The policeman who came to our house was Mr Hughes.

"I went really mad at the police. I told them they had to walk quietly out the back and call out to me, otherwise I'll damage them." (It seems they walked into his home without asking.) "He walked outside and called out. He asked me if he could come up now. I said yes. The others ran over and stopped me going mad and asked me to cool down. So I cooled off and realized I had to go because my wife was a patient in Thursday Island Hospital and I had to shift to Bamaga for the sake of her." (She would not be allowed to return from hospital to Mapoon.) "It would have been a different story altogether if I had had my wife with me. I did not want to leave old Mapoon."

But this I still remember, police O'Shea's words what he spoke to my husband and myself: 'We have to do our duty because orders were given by authority, that you all are wanted up at Thursday Island to answer question.'

Armed police then walked us along the beach — their revolvers or even their shining handcuffs and clubs they didn't use, though we all seen them hanging on their belts. Police O'Shea helped by taking my suitcase, also our short gun, so I carried our rifle and my hand bag. Mr and Mrs Archie and son rejoined us on the beach; we walked straight along the beach and turn up where the Mission house was, and to our surprise we all seen Mr R. Reid and family standing at the foot of the step under a Saibai police guard. Orders were given by Mr Turner to police that they take us to the Mission cottage where we will leave our suitcases and swags then return back to the Mission house.

Mr Turner took our names down on a book; Mr Turner had the two white police standing on his right and his Saibai police servant on his left, and four Saibai police stood guard at the foot of the step. Mr Turner asked us if we had our tea. We told him most of us didn't have our tea because we came home from duck shooting and was taken by surprise and had to leave our tea hot on our stoves. Mr Billy Miller and his wife Mrs Hazel Miller brought supper for us to eat but we all didn't know whatever happen to the food they brought us.

Mr Turner told his Saibai police servant to cook rice and tinned meat for our tea but the food was so salty to eat one would say, "It's just fit for a dog to eat." Most of us didn't eat, just had a cup of tea. After tea we all were taken across to the Mission cottage to spend the night under police guard. Four families slept with white police above our heads and below our feets. Saibai police sat guard all night until dawn.

Next day was Saturday, 16th November, 1963. Orders were given to us to roll up our swags and to take everything we had down to the beach. While they were unloading the Gelam there was no respect of any kind to let women to have a bath or even use toilet. We sat all day until after five before all four families were given orders to go on board the Gelam. A message was sent by Mr Richard Don to be delivered to Mr William Cooktown and his wife Mrs Constance Cooktown where they took their son and daughter, and also the Wheeler kids, to spend their weekend at Janie Creek.

Message was given to them and they both left on that Saturday night with their engine dinghy. Arrived alongside of the Government boat Gelam, both were ordered to leave their son and daughter, also their swag. And take the Wheeler kids home to their parents.

Both husband and wife went to their house to pack their suitcases. While packing their suitcases they heard their horses crying out for water. They gave their horses the last drink of water and left with their suitcases. Walked into the engine dinghy, arrived near the Gelam, both jumped on board, and they were told not to take their engine dinghy, so it was taken ashore by their nephew. Slept on board the Gelam that night was five families.

Sunday was the next day, 17th November, 1963. Anchor was pulled up and the Gelam sailed around the Gulf Coast, heading for Janie Creek. Arrived at Janie Creek, both white police and two Saibai police went ashore on Gelam's engine dinghy to see Mr Frank Don and his wife Mrs Maggie Don and daughter. Told them that you all wanted up at Thursday Island to answer questions. So Mr Simon Peter's wife, Mrs Rachel Peter, and children came to see their grandparents leave. Arrived at Mapoon, Mr and Mrs Don went ashore to their daughter's place, but Mrs Elsie Cooktown, their daughter, had their suitcase and all packed ready for them. Three married daughters and son-in-law's grandchildren. We all heard their grandchildren from the boat Gelam crying before Frank and Maggie reached the Government boat Gelam.

Mapoon Swamps were disturbed.

You can see the harbour of Mapoon was covered with millions of birds. We didn't see the sun because of birds' wings which covered the sun — the Government boat Gelam was sailing under the shadow of the birds. When Gelam reached Mapoon Point, our people that stayed behind cried so bitterly on our parting day it was sad! To see them crying and throwing up sand to the sky, even the birds felt sad.

Birds followed the Government boat Gelam. Before Gelam left the harbour of Mapoon, to our surprise we all seen the birds form a capital V and then we were on our way to the open sea, heading for Thursday Island. But soon as we reached Crab Island it was a different story. We found out by the way Gelam was sailing that they were taking six families across to Hidden Valley.

After all, Thursday Island didn't want the question to be answered. It was then Gelam reached Red Island Point the question was answered when the four families jumped on the jetty. "What a dirty fat lie".

Our arrival at R.I.P. was at one o'clock but had to wait for about half an hour before we heard the transport trucks engines. The police ordered everybody to jump on the trucks. Arrived at Hidden Valley it was about 2 o'clock. Jumped off. The truck stood under the wattle tree. The first thing we did is to look for the seven homes. (Victoria Luff adds "We were standing out there like a mob of cattle for we didn't know where to go".)

Step right in and light your stove,
Friends and relatives took us into their homes.

Next morning the management came down to see the six families that moved in the night. Manager ask Mrs. Gilbert Jimmy if half of the six families can be divided. Some to stay at Cowel Creek and half here at Hidden Valley. But Jimmy told the manager that his people not going any place.

So this is the truth what I've written, and may our God help us to overcome the evil.

Jean Jimmy
Source: Mapoon Book One (ed.) J. P. Roberts, IDA Melbourne, 1975, pp. 12–13.

Joyce Hall represents the Aboriginal people of Weipa, whose land was stolen by the Comalco company (now majority owned by RTZ's Australian subsidiary) to provide the world's single biggest source of bauxite. The following testimony was delivered at the 1981 International Tribunal on RTZ, held in London before representative shareholders in the parent company.

"What will I get from the dust?"

We're still having problems with Comalco . . . Probably you hear that they are co-operating with us: they are not! All the royalties are given to the State government, they make all the decisions. We are still *no-one*. They still have a lot of problems in Weipa . . . the white man came and destroyed our land, no agreements were made — only between the council, the Comalco bosses and the Manager.

This is a special day for me in Queensland today. It is Mother's Day. I feel I should have been with my mother, but I must go and fight for my people. Mother's Day is important, just as the earth our mother is important. The land was given to us, birds, creatures in the bush — but these things are all forgotten. Now we have mines, airplanes, trucks, the alcohol. The whiteman has brought shame and disgrace to us. He came to our land because he found riches in it — but nothing has been given back to us.

. . . Do you know what happened when I went back to Weipa [in 1978]? The Comalco bosses got TV blokes and reporters to come to Weipa and they invited me to an expensive lunch. The day after the next day, two people from Comalco came around in a truck and picked different people to make a film to cover my story. This is the dirtiest trick they ever did — making me out to be a liar. But I'm not speaking to you people because I come from far away. I'm speaking from my heart, and it is the truth.

. . . They have ripped our whole area, we can't shoot around it. They have planted false trees to make the bush come back — the kind we don't like . . . I think how much they have done to us . . . there is a story. It is of a man, Eddie John, who served Comalco all those years until last year when he finished off. He is the Chief of Weipa. No land was given back to him, no compensation, no house where he can stay. They just looked at him and said: that's it.

. . . One time I sat in our Church, I looked around. It was sunset after the rain. I saw the beautiful sea and the creeks rippling, and thought how wonderful God has created the earth. And I looked out over my land, ripped up by human hands and machines. I thought — what will I get out of that dust? What will I get out of that bauxite? *Nothing.*

Thank you for listening to me.

Joyce Hall
Source: RTZ Benefits the Community, Partizans, London, 1981.

Outside of apartheid South Africa, the world's biggest diamond mine is now on Aboriginal land in the Kimberley region of Western Australia. As chief partner in the Argyle Joint Venture (with a beneficial interest of 56.8%),[152] RT-Z's Australian subsidiary, CRA, has violated sacred sites, "bought off" a small section of the community and wilfully disregarded the views of the Kimberley Land Council (KLC).[153]

In the early days of the project the KLC issued this statement:

Argyle diamond trespass

The Kimberley Land Council (an independent organisation representing Kimberley Aboriginal Communities) believes the Ashton Joint Venture at Argyle* continues to demonstrate callous disregard for the rights, customs and integrity of Aboriginal communities in the East Kimberley.

The Ashton Joint Venture has strong corporate links with South Africa and is believed to be negotiating to enter the South African dominated Central Selling Organisation. Much of the expertise to be used at Argyle will also be South African. But the comparison goes further still. The AJV refuses to recognise the Kimberley Land Council despite its three years independent existence and instead operates on the principle of divide and rule. The effect of its policies is to ensure the separate development of the European economy in the Kimberley, while ignoring the desperate situation of Aboriginal communities unless they sign "agreements" limiting their rights to oppose any aspects of the development.

The terms of the first Argyle agreement involve an annual payment of $100,000 to the small family group at Glen Hill. While the Joint Venturers have thereby tacitly admitted traditional Aboriginal ownership of land in the Kimberley, the financial terms are pathetically inadequate even by Australian standards. The annual operating turnover of the Argyle development will be $400,000,000 (based on annual production figures of 20 million carats). On this basis the terms of the Argyle agreement amount to 0.05% of annual operating turnover. At Ranger in the Northern Territory royalties to Aborigines amount to 4.25% of annual operating turnover.

On the question of Aboriginal sites of significance the Ashton Joint Venture has an atrocious record. At least two sites were desecrated in full knowledge that they were of significance in the rush to prove up the deposit.

We believe that the Argyle development is potentially compatible with Aboriginal interests. But until the mining industry and State and Federal Governments come to terms with the basic issue of human rights involved, recognition of our cultural integrity and of our spiritual link to the land and of our rights to equal access to law and justice, Australia will remain different only in degree to the blatant racism so evident in South Africa.

Part of a Press Release from the Co-Chairman of the Kimberley Land Council, Mr Darryl Kickett, 5 June 1981.

Source: Jan Roberts, *Massacres to Mining*, p. 151.

*The name of the AJV was changed to Argyle Joint Venture in 1983.

The Polynesian inhabitants of Bellona Island, in the Solomons, rejected by a large majority a proposal to mine phosphates on their soil in the early 1960s.[154] *By 1975, however, — with the value of land slumping, traditional crops (copra and seednuts) at a standstill — the larger part of the inhabitants seem to have changed their mind:*[155] *cash had become a prime need over the intervening 15 years, as school fees, taxes, and the cost of travel to relatives made an increasing impact.*[156]

Nonetheless, as another phosphate mining company[157] *prepared to enter the island, a vocal minority protested. One of them was a young Bellonese trained to university level.*

A crazy idea

"Before the arrival of Europeans we were living in a world of our own on the island. We had our own political system, we had our own religion, we had our own economic system, and all these things sum up to a culture. Now we are living in an era of changes in the island, as it is now part of the Solomons, and the Solomons is a part of the world. Now[adays] we believe in development, but we do not believe in destruction. As far as the island is concerned, mining is a form of destruction . . . I don't believe people would be able to live on the island after mining. When we move away from this place we will lose a lot of things. *We lose our own social and cultural identity*, we lose our influence on Solomon politics, we lose our whole existence.

"At the moment things are very like the past, except for the religion, the political system, and other things. But the island is still practising subsistence economy. Now this is one of the problems: the mining will not give us enough money to live generation after generation on the island, because at the moment people [here] are not relying on foreign things to survive on the island. There is some involvement within the island with cash economy, but on the whole the island is still operating under a system of subsistence economy. When something like mining comes, clearly we would not have any place for gardening, we wouldn't be able to live here without money. When we look at what we shall get out of mining it is not enough . . . and people who actually receive the money will spend it, spend all the money, and they will see the problems themselves . . . and it will be worse for the next generation because mining to us is a foreign idea — such as the concept of living in a community where you have to pay for everything . . . water . . . hospitals . . . political leaders. [Before] people used to have many of these things without having to pay — although they had to pay for it in other forms [other than money] . . . Getting involved in cash economy entirely is nowhere near self-reliance. We are more self-reliant at the moment on the island, small though it is, and the style of living is just a style of living. To want to live like *Europeans* or white people is just a *crazy* idea because it is just another style of living."

Source: Torben Monberg, *Mobile in the Trade Wind: the reactions of the people on Bellona Island towards a Mining Project.* Working papers of the National Museum of Denmark, No. 1, Copenhagen, 1976, pp.31–2.

As well as facing the threat of dams (see chapter 5) and deforestation, indigenous Filipinos have been deprived of access to their own minerals — specifically gold — through the intervention of multinational mining companies.

In January 1974 Bontocs from the mountains of Mainit set up walls and barricades against Benguet Consolidated, the country's largest mining corporation, as it moved into their area with survey teams. Led by the women, several attacks were made on prospecting camps.[158] *As one of the leaders of the action graphically recounts, the mining company did withdraw, and a temporary victory was achieved.*

Unfortunately, the following year, eight corporations, headed by Benguet, petitioned the country's dictator, Marcos, to prohibit all Igorot (indigenous) gold panning activities. Marcos eagerly complied, thus depriving thousands of families of their key source of income.[159]

In early 1986, Comote (Kankan-ey and Ibaloi) gold-panners were denied traditional mining rights by Benguet, which sent armed guards on to their land to drive them out. In response to Comote claims that their rivers were being polluted by the company's operations, Benguet filed trespass charges against the indigenous community.

Jaime Ongpin, appointed at the same time by Corazon Aquino to be the country's Minister of Finance was, until this new invasion, the head of Benguet.[160]

"We had to stop the mine"

It happened in 1972. Benguet Consolidated Corporation, a mining interest, entered our mountain area. At that time the people were not organised, because they are clannish people and closely-knit communities. We had to meet and decide to work together.

We first voiced our opposition to the mining by sending a petition letter to the mining firm. This resulted in the barrio captains being called to Baguio where they were offered some money as bribes to consider allowing the mine in their area. These barrio captains accepted the money, and the prospectors came. The rest of us in the community were surprised to see these men with their survey equipment. These prospectors told us that we had no rights because the land had already been sold to the mining firm by the barrio captains. The survey team then proceeded to the area where the mine was to be located.

We women got together and followed the survey team to find out where they were going to put the mine. They had all the equipment — rifles, crowbars, walkie-talkies. They kept telling us the mountains had been sold and we had no right to oppose. We had a confrontation with them, but still they would not listen to us, so we had to think of other ways to stop them. We considered how we could get some of the rifles and crowbars and use them against the survey team — we were so angry at their attitude. Perhaps that is the natural reaction of people confronted with such a situation and expecting that there will be worse things to follow.

There were 19 men in the survey team and more than 100 of us, women. During the confrontation the survey team just kept telling us our lands were sold already. We would grab their rifles, but these were strong men, and after a struggle we would split, and think again how to stop them carrying out their survey. We thought of having teams of five women, and each of them tackling one of the surveyors and not giving up the fight until all their equipment had been won. We felt we had to act to stop the mine being built, even if it meant that some of us would die. A few of the women still have scars to remind them of the fight.

Because I was the leader, my brother was apprehensive that I might have been the one the surveyors would kill first. In this struggle to keep our lands the men had stayed in the community, because they were sure the survey team would kill them. They thought we women would not be badly treated. But some of us were disrobed and injured. The survey men were persistent in fighting us so that they could carry out the orders of the mine owners. Seeing our determination to keep fighting, the survey team finally left, but we stayed on the spot in the mountains. We destroyed the walkie-talkies we had been able to take from the survey men, and we also burned their camp houses. We remained in the mountains overnight.

The next morning we returned home. We did not want the old men to know what had happened for fear they would retaliate and kill the survey team, so we brought our wounded women to Bontoc hospital. The old men only learnt about this later.

The mining firm heard about the injuries and offered some money for the payment of the hospitalisation of the injured women, but we would not accept their money.

Our protest was effective. The mining company withdrew their proposed operations from our area, and after this the old men showed us greater respect.

A short time after this event we women organised ourselves into an Irrigators Association to build an irrigation system for the community. I am the president of this association. We called for the old men to join in our meeting and in the construction of the irrigation system, and they cooperated.

This irrigation system is being built in cooperation with the National Irrigation Association. They gave us a loan. During the work we should be given daily wages, but for some time we had not received any wages so we stopped working. Only now are we starting work again. We have been given a partial payment of the monies due to us.

We will continue with the work because it is for the good of the community. It is hard work, but we will complete the system. We have really lacked water in the past, and this irrigation will be of great benefit to us. No longer will our crops fail, and we will be able to utilise all our fields as there will be sufficient water for them.

In our community the women are the leaders, and we are proud of what we have been able to achieve for the benefit of everyone.

Petra

Source: Alison Wynne, *No Time for Crying: Stories of Philippine women who care for their country and its people*, Resource Centre for Philippine Concerns, Hong Kong, 1980, pp. 15–16.

Big Mountain

Since 1977 traditional Navajo (Diné) and Hopi have been resisting forced removal from their lands in New Mexico, to enable the Peabody Coal company to mine two billion tons of coal on the sacred Black Mesa.[161] *Their actions constitute the most intense and well-organised community direct action currently being carried out in the United States. In the early 1980s the resistors — predominantly women — issued many statements. Here are three of them:*

We the People of Big Mountain, Diné Nation, do hereby declare total resistance to any effort to be removed from our homes. Ancestral lands and to be relocated from the land of Big Mountain. We further declare our right to live in peace and harmony with our Hopi neighbours and cooperation between us will remain unchanged.

We The People of Big Mountain, do hereby recognize that the real purpose of the laws and disputes created is to be removed from our homes and lands to make it possible to mine the coal that lies below the Joint Use Area. The legislators and agencies behind this effort to instigate a dispute between the Navajo and Hopi are the same as those agencies who joined forces to destroy the Diné and Hopi Black Mesa with coal stripmining for the sole benefit of America's selfish wants.

We Further Declare that there is no other justification for the U.S. Government to spend billions of dollars to relocate 6,000 people when a much smaller amount of money could improve the capacity of the land to support the lifestyle of both Diné and Hopi to graze as many animals in this area as they so choose.

We Hereby Resolve that the Diné and Hopi shall maintain traditional ties as did their ancestors against those who seek to destroy the traditional bond of culture and aboriginal ownership of land.

We Resolve that the traditional people will make evidence of their unyielding determination to protect their ancient ways.

*   *   *

We, the Big Mountain people, present not only statements, but questions. From our viewpoint, the basic question is survival of our families. Up to this point we have presented many statements about how we feel, think and understand this serious situation. What we as the Big Mountain people would like today are answers.

The most important answer that might make the issue more clear is this. What will the U.S. Government do to the Big Mountain people when it finally sinks into the government's head that we will not move and that we will resist? Will members of our families be killed or sent to prison? Should death and imprisonment be an eventual result for many of our people, many others, black, white and Indian will ask more questions. They will ask why didn't we hear about this serious issue? They will ask why do Navajo people have to continue suffering and continue to lose their homeland and their livelihood? They will ask why has the U.S. continued its genocidal "Indian policy" while preaching "human rights" to the rest of the world?

Those are the questions that we bring. We have never heard any answers yet that indicate to us that our position is understood.

*   *   *

We are being disturbed by the action of the United States through their courts. Today I know why the government is tearing my people from their place of birth. There is a large subsurface coal deposit and other energy resources where the Big Mountain People live. They want to get rid of us, but we will not leave what our forefathers and the Holy People have given us. We are the caretakers of the area.

The government has strong intentions to dominate and destroy the Navajo way of life. First they reduced our livestock, then fenced the area with barbed wires, and now we are being taken to courts hundreds of miles away for building new housing, but our old homes are ready to collapse on us.

I speak for my children and their children, our Native Indian Culture, our sacred teachings, and our tradition that allows all walks of life to live in harmony and good will side by side. So now I often lay awake at night wondering where I will get a cat that will kill the mouse (the government) that is eating away at our belongings.

Pauline Whitesinger
Maternal Clan: Edgewater
Paternal Clan: Apache Clan

5.   Dams

"Development" plans which destroy Native peoples and lands are often rationalized on the basis that "a few sometimes have to make sacrifices for the larger population." Aside from the questionable morality of placing the "right" of a large people to electric toothbrushes and air conditioners over the right of a small people to survive, there are other considerations which are usually not mentioned. The "6,000 Crees vs. 6,000,000 Quebeckers" rationalization is used to hide the fact that "development" is not promoted for the good of the larger population but for the power and profits of a few, and that in the long run, the larger population pays the penalties as well.

Gayle High Pine, referring specifically to the James Bay hydro-project in Quebec, quoted from *Akwesasne Notes*, Akwesasne, late Spring 1978, p. 24.

After mining, many indigenous communities regard hydro-electric projects and other dams as posing the greatest single threat to their land and culture. Some schemes are linked to the supposed need for cheap electricity for mines themselves – such as Ok Tedi,[162] Teribe–Changuinola in Panama[163] and Tucurui in northern Brazil: this project alone is only one of seven large and 20 smaller dams, designed to power mineral extraction and processing plants, and electrify a new railway, as part of the Great Carajas industrial complex.[164]

Other schemes provide ready electricity for industrial or urban consumers, at the expense of rural dwellers. In this category come the Chico River and Agus River proposals for the Philippines,[165] the Alta–Kautokeino dam on Sami land in northern Norway,[166] the now-shelved Purari project in Papua

New Guinea,[167] *the huge James Bay Development project,*[168] *British Columbia Hydro's plans to flood Kaska Dene land in northern Canada,*[169] *the Kaptai dam in the Chittagong Hill Tracts (see pp. 95–101), the Slave River dam in Alberta,*[170] *the Rejang river project in Sarawak,*[171] *a dam on Salt and Verde rivers, north of Phoenix, Arizona*[172] *and, perhaps most importantly, several massive projects planned for Bihar, Gujarat, Maharashtra, Madhya Pradesh and Andhra Pradesh in tribal India.*

The Inchampalli and Bhopalagnam schemes alone threaten the displacement of 75,000 Madia Gond people.[173] *Further to the north east, multipurpose dams across the river Indrawati, construction for which began in 1978*[174] *will displace 7,770 Penga and Dom people, causing the submersion of no less than 99 tribal villages.*[175] *In addition, the Subarnerekha irrigation scheme, sponsored by the World Bank in Bihar and Orissa*[176] *threatens not only several tribal villages but hundreds of acres of ricefields.*[177]

The most massive Indian hydro scheme is one planned for the Narmada Valley in east-central Indian which could involve the removal of no less than one million tribal people, if implemented at full scale.[178] *In November 1985, after strenuous opposition by environmental groups, the World Bank suspended its funding for Sardar Sarovar.*[179] *Early in 1986, however, the Bank resumed its support.*[180]

The largest hydro project of all, however, is the Itaipu dam, bridging the river Parana between Brazil and Paraguay and opened in November 1983. This has already necessitated the removal of more than 42,000 forest dwellers.[181]

Add to this the flooding of indigenous land to provide irrigation for cash crops and imported livestock;[182] *the drowning of sacred sites;*[183] *proposals to deluge fertile lands to provide cut-price electricity to attract multinational aluminium producers to locate smelters in "deprived" zones*[184] *— and the extent of personal grief, agricultural loss, communal disharmony, religious desecration, caused by "damming", almost beggars description.*

This chapter draws on the eloquent, and often desperate, demands made by indigenous communities, to be protected from the worst devastation possible: the complete *obliteration of that part of themselves which is rooted in a known place, a sacred landscape.*

Goga Kohola is an elder of one of the Maria villages affected by the Indrawati hydro scheme in India. The following is an interview he gave to a member of the Gesellschaft für bedrohte Völker (GfbV) in March 1983 in the village of Gotpadi, after a meeting with a government representative.

"The Land Belongs to the Gods!"

What does the dam construction on the Indrawati mean for you?
Goga Kohola: Even if our village doesn't go down, most of the woods around us and most neighbouring villages will disappear. What sense will it then still have for us to stay here?

We are people of the woods. We need the woods because we manage our livelihood from them. To our belief the land belongs to the gods, not to the government. If it belongs to the gods, how can the government take it away from us? We shall not abandon this land and our houses. If the woods disappear under water, the people will go down, too.

What impressions did you get from the meeting? What did the other village elders say?
This meeting was asked for by our people and they have asked Mr Rao to organise a meeting. The other village elders have also been speaking out against the dams. We have decided to die in front of our houses rather than to let us be driven away. Everybody will fight to save our gods and our land.

What does the population intend to do against the construction of the dams?
First we'll hold council in every village to decide what we can do. We'll lodge a written protest with the Central Government in Delhi. We'll possibly organise demonstrations and road blockades. Should all this be unsuccessful we'd rather die here than go away.

What future do you see for your people?
I think the government wants to kill all of us. The easiest way to get rid of us is to inundate our land.

After the British left our country there was great war in Bastar. Our ruler, the king of all Maria, did not want to give up his rule. A great battle took place. Thousands of Maria fought with arrows and spears against the new Indian army. They could not overcome our people. One night Indian soldiers forced their way into the royal palace and killed everybody they found there. The king was murdered and with him thousands of his men. Now there are not many of us left. As at that time, we're still fighting with arrows and spears. But the government has many guns and it's easy for them to kill us. I think we shall not live for long any more. There is no hope for us.

Source: *Pogrom*, GFbV, Göttingen, No. 107, mid-84.
Translated by Mick Blackstein

Four thousand five hundred Akawaio live in a 1,000 square mile forested area in the upper Mazaruni basin of Guyana. Their traditional land is only 75 miles from the Venezuelan border. Although land rights were supposedly guaranteed prior to Guyana's independence from Britain in 1966, they have never been implemented. The Akawaio also have the misfortune to live in an area hotly disputed between their host government and Venezuela. In the late 1970s the Forbes Burnham government announced a grandiose hydro-electric scheme, to begin operation by 1982 — coincidentally the date for renewal of a treaty of moratorium on the contested region, signed in 1970 between the two governments and the ex-colonial power.[185]

Guyana has almost unlimited energy-generating potential — including a site much closer to the bauxite smelter that was used as an original justification for the project.[186] *It would seem that political, not economic, justifications motivated the government in putting forward a proposal which — so far – has not been implemented.*

"Help us stay where we belong"

Upper Mazaruni River.
5th of Sept. 1976.

**His Excellency The President of the Republic,
Guyana House,
Georgetown**

Dear Comrade President,

I am an old man and cannot write; this my letter is written for you by a young comrade as I have told it to him.

It is well known here that it is hard for the chief men of our country to make journey to see us in our distant villages. Thus I wish to tell you how I feel about this water coming to cover our ancient lands for Hydropower. I take you as my father and the father of all our villages in Guyana. You we must tell the things that are distress to us so you can know to help us find again for our children the happiness we had before.

Two things I heard, but I believe now they are not true. Long years past it was said we would have to fight to keep our lands. When I did not understand, but now I partly understand that Abel received Alleluia from God, and he told us it is an evil to fight and kill one another for we all are brothers. Only now I try to fight in a different way by writing this letter to you. It is my work to tell you how we are living in these lands that God has given us, and to ask that we can keep the ways the old people taught us.

The other thing, it was lately a story that is not for Hydropower but to give our lands to other people, that we must move from our villages. I now understand good that you tried to find some other places for Hydropower but it is only this side in our district that it can be done. We are the people who have been put here a long time ago, and it is a distress to you to tell us that our farms and our hunting lands and our homes must all be made in new places, yet you must know how this thing is hard for us, and so you will think what you can do to help us.

My father and his father told me that our people used to be many and we had to move before like this time, from coast lands and leave our lands there for other people. The names of the places tell you that it was all about the plenty Akawaios used to live. Now to find a place to live quietly in our ways they came back to these mountains where we belong. We are left few only, who were a great nation and there is no other places for us. This is the land and the sky and the air that make us the people of the Upper Mazaruni, you know this true. It is not that we can fool you.

Many of the old people who did not come back up this side, remained among the other men who came to find the diamonds. They die out with new sickness. They lose the language and the way of living good and we do not see them any more. Thus we want to stay quiet in our own place and see our children happy and strong to keep what God gave us.

I do not like it that teachers tell the children it is best to get more money, get diamonds and gold, get job. I want to tell you that the alleluia has been given to our people as the ways to pray and we know God taught this to us, to bring us out of evil and show us how to live in peace and happiness. I do not find the men with money are able to do this better. I have built my house on the earth and my children and grand-children are happy around me. I have built our church on the earth and our naked feet have made the earth hard as we dance alleluia. I kneel on the earth to pray. For God made it good and I am not ashamed. I cut farm and plant on the earth, and it is good that so many things I need for my family come from the earth, and if I am sick the other people will give so that we are not hungry. Now I am old to hunt but my sons and sons in laws go to hunt for me. My wife and I go to fish with our wood skins and some small grand-children. We do not kill unless we need to eat and we are able to have enough to share with friends coming to stay with us. We are happy this way which God showed to us. We are asking you not to tell our children to forget it. Yes, there are good things also which are new. And I am glad for plastic barrel for cassiri and medicine at the hospital and blanket to keep out the cold, but Abel told that we must not lose the good things that we have had long from God, and not let people fool us who are wanting to take away those things.

I am afraid that if we have to move to some far place or among other people who do not live this way, what we have believed and learned here would perhaps fade away. I see that a plant grows in a place where it can be strong and good. If I pull it up and carry it some other place it may not grow well. Sometimes it will die. So God will let us find places to build our houses and cut farms on this Upper Mazaruni where we belong. It is true we may not find land so good as before, but I am asking you to help us stay where we belong. We have learned to move about freely quite often and this way the bush grows back afterwards and the land is still good for children our grandchildren will have. If they are plenty they will not find enough if the place is small. I am saying that this is where we belong. If it is only rocks that are left for us, we will learn from God how to live happy on the rocks. But do not take away what is left when the water comes. It is the place of our people and we will care it well for you and the country of Guyana. Before I die I would like to know that you will not take it away. If the hill where my father lived may become an island it will still be the place where I was born and he was buried. Let my children build how they wish. They are not stupid and they will know what is good for them. They will learn new things and you will be glad to see it. But the way of living in these mountains is a thing we learned from the land. Some day your children could learn it also from my grandchildren, if you help us not

---

"This land keeps us together"

This land is where we belong – it is God's gift to us and has made us as we are.

This land is where we are at home, we know its ways: and the things that happened here are known and remembered, so that the stories the old people told, are still alive here.

This land is needed for those who come after – we are becoming more than before, and we must start new settlements, with new forms around them. If we have to move, it is likely that there will be other people there and we shall not be free to spread out as we need to: and the land will not be enough for our people, so that it will grow poor.

This land is the place where we know where to find all that it provides for us – food from hunting and fishing, and farms, building and tool materials, medicines. Also the spirits around us know us and are friendly and helpful.

This land keeps us together within its mountains – we come to understand that we are not just a few people or separate villages, but one people belonging to a homeland. If we had to move, we would be lost to those who remain in the other villages. This would be a sadness to us all, like the sadness of death. Those who moved would be strangers to the people and spirits and places where they are made to go.

The Akawaio Indians
Upper Mazaruni District
Guyana.
1977

Source: Bennett et al, *The Damned*, op. cit.

to lose it. I would not be here any more, but it is in my mind that God would be glad to see it. Then the land he gave to us would be glad and all Guyana peoples happy as a family should be.

I don't feel to have my name written here for I am afraid about some stories I do not understand. It is no harm to write instead.

Yours co-operatively
Comrade

Source: Gordon Bennett, Dr. Audrey Colson and Stuart Wavell, *The Damned: the Plight of the Akawaio Indians of Guyana*, Survival International, London, 1978.

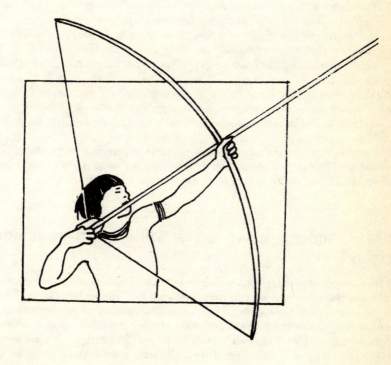

When, in November 1974, the Japanese Prime Minister Tanaka met Michael Somare, Prime Minister of Papua New Guinea, to draw up a joint scheme for harnessing the Purari river for industrial purposes they were cashing in on an idea which had surfaced 20 years before. Then, the newly-formed Australian Aluminium Production Commission (AAPC) and British Aluminium joined the Australian-dominated New Guinea Resources and Prospecting Company, to study the river's power potential for aluminium smelting. Soon afterwards, in 1955, Conzinc (later when merged with Rio Tinto to become Rio Tinto-Zinc) discovered the world's largest bauxite deposits on Aboriginal land in north Queensland. What could be simpler — or more attractive — than linking the two projects together under Australian/British control?[187]

The proposal lay fallow for nearly another two decades, but a lot of restructuring of the western aluminium industry occurred in the meantime.[188] *Japanese companies began to show interest in Purari during the early 1970s. (A tentative proposal by Bechtel, Westinghouse and General Electric of the USA to site a uranium enrichment plant on the Purari seems to have been shelved within a couple of years.) By 1978, there had already been four Purari intergovernmental meetings between possible participants, and the results of a feasibility study had been presented to the Papua New Guinea government.*[189]

At the same time, the local people, drawn from all villages in the Purari delta, and supported by the Purari Action Group (formed in 1974 by Papua New Guinean students) campaigned vigorously against impending environmental and economic disaster.[190] *By 1980 they seem to have succeeded, as the project has not apparently been revived during the past half-dozen years.*

The following are the views of two of the Purari people affected by the dam proposal. The first was given to a member of the Purari Action Group and translated into English. The second was written by a Pastor.

"My children, never, never, lose your traditional rights"

I am one of those people whose origins are in Purari. To many of us *Purari* is a word with special meaning. All the trees, animals, fish, insects, reptiles and even mountains have special meaning for us. These things are our totemic symbols or, in I'ai language, *opa mako*. Long before whitemen came these things were very sacred because they are part of our well-being. I am very sad indeed that whitemen are not respecting the place of our origin. They are disturbing the mountains that are our *opa mako* by building an airstrip and houses on them.

A whiteman or a Papua New Guinean outside our community may laugh at our customs and how we are so closely related to the land and all things that grow on the land. A person travelling up the Purari River may see a landslide on one of these mountains, and to him it will mean nothing but a mere landslide. But to us, those whose totems are mountains, it will indicate this: If you see a landslide on the mountain, you know that a person has died. It is a tribute of the mountain to the dead person.

When we are camping up the river and see a landslide on the mountain we know a Purari person has died. Sometimes we return home and sometimes we stay, hoping that somebody will come up the river and tell us the sad story. This has been observed since time immemorial.

The sad thing now is that the Papua New Guinea Government does not respect our customs and our ties to the land and everything on it. Now they are disturbing some of these sacred mountains, and you will see today that workmen are digging on this mountain. This means that we are losing our traditional values.

We fear for the safety of cassowaries, our most sacred of all animals, the mother and source of the plants, man and the creator of the river. The cassowary mother gave birth to all the trees, and finally gave birth to the first man from whom the people are descended. Many of us today will count up to nine generations and end up at the first man by cassowary mother. The cassowary mother is therefore creator of everything, like Christians think of God as creator of all things.

What makes me feel sad is that for many years we have lived a good happy life as our ancestors had lived before us. We had our own form of government, controlled by chiefs of each clan. We worked together, feasted together and did many things together. Today we cannot maintain the happy life. No longer do we have laws we can rely on because white men's laws can always override traditional laws.

Today, a child goes to school and gets a well paid job in a far away place. As soon as he is settled at his new place of work he forgets about all his relatives who had to work hard to bring him up. The only people he will send gifts or money to are his own parents, and not other relatives. This is really a whiteman way of thinking. As a result some relatives argue with the parents and sometimes fight over these things. What I am trying to tell you is that we cannot live a good communal life as in those good old days.

So when the Government finally agrees to build the hydroelectric dam I personally believe that we will be spoilt in many ways. The great civilization will really swallow our old ways of life. I must agree that this civilisation will mean a lot of change in your life.

Some of these changes will not make you altogether happy, but maybe you will feel a very happy person in this world. What will happen if, for example, this place becomes over-populated because of the development of industrial sites and cities? I am sorry, very sorry to say that you will lose your ancestral lands to land-hungry governments. You will realise that you have lost almost everything that goes with the land once created by the cassowary mother. As an old man who is ready for dying, I would like to say, my children, whatever you do, never, and I repeat never, lose your traditional rights over your ancestral lands.

Source: Purari, Overpowering Papua New Guinea? IDA/PAG, Fitzroy, 1978.

"What will happen when the clever men close the river?"

What I am going to say here is my own views. First I must tell you my schooling is limited. I only completed standard two and later became a Pastor. So my point is, what I will be saying is really a primitive man's view. You can laugh at me if you wish.

I have been listening to the government officers and radio with interest about what will happen here. Sometimes I wonder how the whiteman will be able to close our river to make power for Papua New Guinea. Many of us believe that they will not be able to succeed in their attempt to close the river. To us it is a sacred place. The whole Purari, and especially up stream, is so sacred because that is where our ancestors came from. The trees, animals, birds, and even rivers are the product of our ancestors. If the whitemen close the river it will be only a short period of time before our ancestors will spoil their work and open the river once more. How can our Black government ignore our beliefs?

What is more important, is it money or is it our traditional beliefs and values? I have spent the young years of my life in Port Moresby. I have seen it developed from a little mission station into a city. I have seen many Motuans lose their hunting grounds and gardens. Motuans can no longer hunt or dig the soil for gardens. Instead they have turned to the government for work in office buildings. I do not want this to happen here or to our children.

The land was given to us by our ancestors and we have every right over the land. This also applies to the river. I would like my children to know that the river is part of our life. What will happen to us when the clever men close the river?

Source: Purari, Overpowering Papua New Guinea? Frontisipiece

The Igorots comprise several tribal Filipino communities living in four mountainous provinces in the Philippines. Originally lowland farmers, they were forced into the mountains by settlers from Southeast Asia and by foreign invaders. For about 70 years, they remained relatively untouched by the Americanisation of the region. From the early 1970s, however, US mining, logging, real estate and plantation interests — aided by missionaries, anthropologists, the Peace Corps, US-AID officials, the Green Berets and PANAMIN (Presidential Assistant for National Minorities: Filipino equivalent of Brazil's FUNAI) — began expropriating the Igorots officially "reserved" land.[191]

Initially, the major threat came from mining companies, which affected the Bontoc people in particular.[192] In 1974, then-President Marcos initiated work on the Chico River Dam: a project which had been in circulation for more than ten years, but which required the volatile increase in oil prices, and World Bank and Asian Development Bank funding, to become feasible.[193] The second dam in the huge scheme was to be built on Bontoc land, flooding out 3,000 people and 16 riverside settlements.[194]

Resistance by the Bontoc came swiftly, in the form of statements delivered to the government in Manila, and attacks on survey campsites.[195] The project's focus then shifted to Kalinga territory — the 90,000 Kalinga peoples being considered more pliable than the 130,000 Bontoc. But once again, the local tribespeople resisted with force, and the hills and valleys become a battleground. Within five years, Chico Dams II and IV were officially shelved.[196]

As William Claver, a Bontoc human rights lawyer, has pointed out, the militarisation of the highlands not only hardened Kalinga and Bontoc resistance to the dams — it galvanised them into opposing the Marcos regime on several fronts.[197]

Many of the people joined the National Democratic Front (NDF) and participated in one of the 39 units of the New Peoples Army.[198] The NDF has itself supported the Igorot cause.[199] But most important, in May 1975 150 Bontoc and Kalinga leaders met and signed a Peace Pact (bodong) in Manila which committed the two peoples to unrelenting opposition to the Chico dams and laid the basis for unity, in the face of a lengthy history of attempts — both by Spanish and American colonisers — to divide them.[200]

This was not the last time that tribal Filipinos were to use the bodong as a means of inter-tribal solidarity, or as retribution against members co-operating with government or private corporations. It was employed in 1979 by the Tingguians of the Cordillera, to fight off the Cellophil Resources Corporation (see p. 219)[201] — and again in 1983, in a historic conciliation between the peoples of the Cordillera Sierra Madre and Mindanao.[202]

In the following statements, Wada Taw-il describes how the Marcos regime attempted to implement the Chico project, the peoples' resistance, and consequent oppression; and Gloria, a Kalinga woman, tells of her own community's actions and the vicious military response to them. The section ends with the sanctions of the historic bodong *signed on 13 May 1975.*

"Even Marcos says we are to be sacrificed"

One of the most far reaching and damaging parts of present government policy which affects minorities is its energy program. The government has existing plans to build more than 40 major dams. Almost all of these dams are to be built on lands at present occupied by national minorities. The dams will submerge our best farmland, the settlements, graveyards and sacred sites of many peoples. It is estimated that more than one and a half million minority Filipinos and another half million poor farmers will be impoverished and dislocated by these dams.

These dams would not only displace communities of people, but would destroy the whole tribal economy of some peoples. The government has now passed special regulations empowering the National Power Corporation to restrict or even prevent farming within the watershed of dams, and to forcibly expel anyone breaking these rules. These rules would deny the people the means of basic subsistence that has been theirs for centuries. In my home — the Cordillera — the government has immediate plans for eight dams and further proposals for at least seven more. Already the Ifugao people who number more than 100,000 and live in the watershed of the Magat Dam are being prevented from clearing new mountain farms. They are forced instead to plant trees on their old clearings. This will bring hunger to the Ifugao. But at the very time that the ordinary people are being prevented from continuing their farming practices, new logging concessions are given within the watershed. Local officials, including the governor and assemblyman of Ifugao, now have commercial logging concessions within the area. So, control over the cutting of trees is only imposed on the poor farmers but not on the rich concessionaire.

The energy program for the next ten years was planned to cost more than $14.5 billion but recently Marcos made an announcement that this program must be implemented in only five years. So our situation has become even more critical.

The proposed energy supply increase is not to meet local needs but is planned as an incentive to foreign investment. The whole program is heavily financed and backed by the World Bank, Asian Development Bank and USAID. Most of the Bank money is being spent on construction and equipment paid straight out to foreign heavy engineering contractors. In the Cordillera, on the Ambuklao dam, it was Guy Atkinson and Co of the USA; on the Magat Dam it is Voest Alpine and Brown Boveri from Europe; on the Chico, it is Lahmeyer of Germany.

The government makes propaganda that these dams are a sign of progress and prosperity for the nation and will improve the quality of life, especially for the rural poor. But we in the Cordillera ask, "Whom does it really help?" We know it does not help us and we are the most neglected sector of the rural poor. We gain no share in the benefits of these dams, while our livelihood and culture are to be destroyed.

We are to be sacrificed. Even Marcos says this.

In 1956 the Ambuklao Ibaloy were moved off their land. There was no adequate compensation, no place for relocation. After 25 years when the dam is already choking to death with silt the people still have no land. When they were on their land, they were promised relocation but when the dam was built and they were no longer a threat, there was no relocation.

The government says that dams will bring electricity and irrigation to the lowland peasants but these people still live in poverty. They cannot afford the high costs of electrical appliances or even irrigation pumps and rentals. The benefit is only to rich landlords in the Cagayan Valley, men like Defense Minister Enrile, Local Government and Community Development Minister Rono, President Marcos and a handful of others, all of whom have large tracts of land in the Cagayan Valley that will be irrigated by the Chico and Magat dams.

The dam program that has been worked out for the Philippines by the World Bank has come to be priority only under martial law conditions. When the Chico was first considered for damming in the 1960s the project was indefinitely shelved because of the social costs involved. But by 1973 under martial law when the people had no voice, it was no longer thought necessary to even ask for the people's opinion or even inform them. In Kalinga and Bontoc, we first learned of the project when survey teams invaded the valley. The people angered by such deceit, ejected the teams.

In July 1974 the survey teams came back with a military escort and abused the people, especially in Cagaluan, Kalinga, where three boys were lined up and soldiers used submachine guns to shoot coconuts off their heads.

We tried petitions and legal appeals to the government and the World Bank, thinking that no one would knowingly destroy the culture and livelihood of the 80,000 people of the Chico. But Marcos avoided meeting our delegations. He made excuses and one delegation that went to Manila to plead for their land was turned away because the President was too busy they said "with the preparations of the *Miss Universe* contest"!

Only when it was clear that the people would fight for their land and would have support in Manila and elsewhere did Marcos take notice. The people adopted the tradition of our peace pact which is strong among us to call for unity in the defense of our lands.

It was at this point that the attempts to trick and deceive and divide us really began. Marcos' Minister Melchor announced the suspension of all work in the Chico Valley and the indefinite postponement of Chico II dam in the heart of the mountains. But it is clear now that this was a conscious trick. There has been no attempt to bring the issue of Chico II up for further discussion but plans for its construction have gone ahead. Construction is now scheduled to begin within 3 years.

At the time of Minister Melchor's announcement the government had fears that the Chico would become another minority problem which could spark off an all out war like that of the Muslims in the south. Marcos has an agency, the PANAMIN (Presidential Assistance on National Minorities), to deal with its minority problem but like the government it does not represent the people but the big business that seeks to exploit their lands. Who the PANAMIN serves is very clear by looking at the people who control it. These people are some of the biggest capitalists in the Philippines like Elizalde, Ayala, Soriano & Cabarrus, and working for them are, both serving and retired military officers including those who have been trained in Vietnam in counter-insurgency programs.

PANAMIN was established without even one representative of a national minority as a member. It does not represent or serve the interests of the minority people. Under martial law it has become the government's instrument of repression against minorities. The documents we present show that the PANAMIN, like the state it serves, has had to resort increasingly to armed oppression; and that now, the major item of the PANAMIN Budget is for its own security not for minority development.

Within months of the announcement of suspension of all work at Chico, PANAMIN and its head Manda Elizalde himself showed up in Kalinga, to work on the people. He arrived in November like an early Father Christmas, giving out gifts of basketballs, whisky and blankets; and for the community leaders there was money and the offer of jobs. Elizalde even offered money to satisfy himself with our women. Elizalde expressed concern over our case and promised to help take it to the President. He gathered community leaders together and took them to Manila. But there they were kept under guard and were pressured and tricked into signing their support for the project.

As a result, Marcos announced the creation of Kalinga Special Development Region (KSDR) to give special attention to this poor region. But the whole of the Cordillera is neglected and in need of development; our roads are bad, hospitals few and schools inadequate. Why then did the KSDR only cover the area affected by the dam? KSDR was an attempt to dupe the people into surrendering their land. Within KSDR scholarships were offered to people as long as, and only if, they supported the government.

Worst of all the PANAMIN turned the people against each other. The Basao were armed by PANAMIN in their tribal war with the Butbut people who are well known for their opposition to the dams. The Basao were given more than 40 high-powered rifles. Because of the many guns several Butbut and Basao were killed. As a result the border area between Kalinga and Bontoc was virtually closed by the feuding and the unity of the peoples was badly affected.

But opposition continued even though the PANAMIN, backed by the military, became increasingly abusive and violent. When the troops tried to establish a camp to guard the dam site, 250 Kalingas dismantled the camp and marched 25 kilometers in defiance of martial law curfew regulations to return the camp equipment to the Provincial military HQ. The people also effectively boycotted the 1977 referendum. The elders said that we could not take part because any sign of co-operation with the government would be twisted to make it seem that we supported the dam. Because of these two actions, more than 100 people were arrested and detained without trial. Most of them were held during and over the planting season so that they had nothing to eat. The church had to organise emergency relief for families that had not been able to farm because of the arrests.

We approached World Bank representatives in Manila who repeated the promise of Robert McNamara that the World Bank would not fund the Chico project in the face of opposition from the people; but they lied and they have continued to fund the project despite our opposition. They have also funded other projects like that on the Magat river and elsewhere.

The people's fight for their rights against the Marcos government has taught them many bitter lessons. The resistance of the Kalinga gives hope to other people in the Philippines, thus the government has to send its troops into the province to silence us.

There have been many and horrible abuses against my people. Many of these abuses are documented and show that contrary to the government's assertion that military abuse is rare and incidental, in fact it is common and systematic. None of the soldiers identified to have committed the severest abuses of murder, torture, arson and rape have ever been made to pay.

To cite just a few of the abuses committed:

- 25 October, 1977 in Tanglag Lubuangan, the 55th Infantry Battalion PC led by two identified NCOs burned down two houses and stole or destroyed heirlooms valued in excess of P30,000.
- In January 1978 a farmer, Ruben Ta-ilan, was picked up by identified 55th PC officers. The next day his dead and mutilated body was found by the roadside.
- In April 1978, two elders of Ngibat Tinglayan were shot and killed. And in an operation launched by the 60th battalion, the whole village was subjected to mortar attack causing extensive property damage.
- In June 1978, a 16 year old girl, Norma Kikilaw, sick and confined in Lubuagan hospital, was raped by two identified PC.
- In July 1978, a river ferryman was wounded when he was shot in the mouth by a soldier who refused to pay his fare on the ferry.
- In September 1978, the Chico IV dam site area and all the land around the village of Tomiangan was declared a Free Fire Zone. The people of the village could only enter or leave the village with military permit, and a strict 3.00 p.m.–9.00 a.m. curfew was imposed which effectively stopped the people from working their land. As their fields were within the Free Fire Zone, many were afraid to do any work on their land. For the people there was food shortage and hunger and the PC were able to take advantage of the situation. For food and sport they have shot virtually all the villagers' cows and carabaos grazing in this area.
- In October 1978, in Batong Buhay Pasil, indiscriminate mortar shelling of the community led to the killing of a small child.

In April 1980, Macli-ing Dulag, the spokesman of the Kalingas was murdered by the 44th Infantry Battalion. Macli-ing was a powerful opposition spokesman and the best known of our leaders. He was shot down inside his own house in the night by men since identified and admitted by the government to be members of the 44th Infantry Battalion under the leadership of Lieutenant Adalem. On the same night in the same village an attempt was also made on the life of Pedro Dungoc, another of the Kalinga opposition spokesmen.

Macli-ing was well known to the government for his opposition. His village had hosted two major Peace Pact celebrations called to discuss the dam problem and unite the people and strengthen them in their opposition. He had been offered bribes by Elizalde which he refused.

His murder was a further proof to us that we could not expect justice within the present system where even our most respected spokesmen are just gunned down like animals. The people all know that we must be prepared to defend our land if we are to survive. And we are happy to join the NPA and unite with the other poor Filipinos in fighting for a better society.

We ask this Tribunal to recognise that the struggle of the Tribal Filipinos and other oppressed sectors of Philippine society, is a just struggle and that we have the right to resist the genocide and oppression that we face.

Source: Philippines: Repression and Resistance; Permanent Peoples' Tribunal Session on the Philippines, KSP, London/Utrecht 1981, pp. 185–91. Reprinted with permission.

"We had written letters, but received no response"

The government had decided to build a dam in our mountain region. They began bringing in equipment to carry out a survey. They built temporary camps and erected tents to hold their equipment. The protest of we Kalingas was strong because we did not want the dam to be built.

In our barrio we wondered what to do. We had written letters of protest to the President and the government departments, but we received no response. When we saw the engineering team come with their equipment we thought of meeting them and frightening them away. So our old men went with their spears and bolos [long-bladed knives] to the camp of the engineers. The engineers greeted them in a friendly manner. They told the old men they would not be surveying their exact area. While these talks were going on, some military men arrived and said, "We are ordered to do this survey." So the old men left and went to seek support from other people in the community.

It was decided that the whole community would dismantle the camp, and as a protest we would march with the equipment to the provincial barracks, 40 kilometers away. It was agreed to start at dawn next morning, with the women leading the group, and the men with their weapons behind.

At dawn we approached the camp. There were several hundred of us — old men, young people and children, men and women, and we all took part in dismantling the tents holding the equipment. The engineering team were still asleep in their camp nearby.

We began our march to the office of the provincial governor. We walked without stopping for lunch, and by early afternoon had covered the 40 kilometers and arrived at the barracks of the provincial military commander. We women were the spokespeople, because we intended to show that we were there for peaceful talks. We were met by the commander who said the governor was not around. We repeated again our protests, and explained we had brought the equipment in this way because our words were not being listened to. The provincial commander promised to relay our message to the National Power Corporation administration and the President. He seemed to be sympathetic, so we respected what he told us and returned to our community.

After several days, more military forces arrived at the site on the river. These forces had been sent to pick up some of the leaders in our community who had participated in the protest march. They had some names of the people who were our leaders. The military told our leaders they were being called so the provincial commander could meet them and report what had happened in his negotiations with the President and the National Power Corporation. Our whole community went with them. On arrival at the barracks we discovered it was not a meeting. Instead we were told a Presidential Decree had been issued proclaiming that anyone participating in protest against the dam would be detained. On hearing this, we all entered the detention cells and began singing and making a noise. We were kept overnight, and in the morning the military men sent us home.

One evening about two weeks later, the community leaders were picked up from their houses by the military men. We were not prepared for this, and so 130 of our people were taken by the military to the provincial barracks and detained. Some of the old men were transferred to Camp Olivas detention centre. The other men were sent to various centres. The women were released after three weeks, and due to the intervention of the Civil Liberties Union and other groups, all the men were finally released after a period of five months.

Back in the community, those who had been detained told us that for several days they had been interrogated and had not eaten. They had been told to sign blank sheets of paper and then they would be released. They were also promised houses and cash if they would sign these blank sheets of paper. But our people did not believe the military men, because they had already experienced broken promises of government people so nobody signed.

Now our community is surrounded by military forces. Late last year some National Power Corporation engineers were shot in an encounter by some of our young people who had fled to the mountains for safety, so the government sent more and more men to the area. We are experiencing many abuses by the military who come to our houses and demand we give them supper. They steal our chickens and other food, and we cannot protest because we do not want killing. We have listed down all the abuses against us, with the names of the offenders. Our company of military abusers was withdrawn and replaced by others who behaved for a while, but are now simply becoming just as abusive as the previous soldiers.

It is stalemate situation now. We are like prisoners in our community. We cannot travel on the roads where military check-points are placed, but we have our mountain trails and can visit each other's barrios [village communities].

Gloria

Source: No Time for Crying: Stories of Philippine women who care for their country and its people, Alison Wynne, Resource Centre for Philippine Concerns, Hong Kong, 1980, pp. 10–11.

Pagta Ti Bodong (Sanctions of the Peace Pact)

1. The people of Bontoc and Kalinga affected by the Chico River Basin Development Project are prohibited from working on the dam project.

2. Should a Kalinga or a Bontoc from the dam areas be killed while working on the dam project, the peace pact villages opposed to the dam will not be held responsible, nor will they have to answer for the victim.

3. The parties in this agreement will warn the sons of Bontoc and Kalinga who are in the military not to be hard on the people who oppose the dam project.

4. The villages affected by the dam project are prohibited from selling their goods/products or giving food to the employees or workers of the National Power Corporation.

5. Anybody who is found to have been bribed against the interest of the people in favour of the NPC will be severely dealt with, including death.

6. A peace pact already existing between two barrios will not be affected in any way when one of the members of a peace pact village dies or is killed as a consequence of his working with the NPC. Relatives will claim his body quietly but they are prohibited from taking revenge.

Signed by 150 Bontoc and Kalinga Elders
May 13, 1975

"Are we not also Filipino citizens?"

Petition of the T'Bolis people united against the Lake Sebu dam

Asian Development Bank
Ayala Avenue
Makati, Rizal

Dear Sir:
We the T'boli people of Lake Sebu, Surallah, South Cotabato, after hearing about the forthcoming construction of the Lake Sebu Dam and the subsequent damage and destruction it will bring to our homeland, would like to bring to your attention our strongest opposition to this government project. We would like you to consider the following reasons:

   1. The proposed dam will flood our most precious land and destroy

our food and source of livelihood which we have worked so hard to produce.

2. If this land is flooded and our food supply destroyed, it will certainly kill us and our children. For where shall we go since our Visayan brothers have already taken the choice lands that God has first given us?

3. This land and these lakes God has given us. We do not want this land to be destroyed by flood because it is precious to us, our ancestors were born and were buried here. We would rather kill ourselves and our children than to witness the terrible destruction this dam would bring.

4. We have heard that new lands will be set aside for us in distant and foreign places. We would rather be drowned here and be buried with our ancestors than to live far from our homeland.

5. If we lose this agricultural land, no food production will be made and we can no longer contribute to the national economy.

6. We also have heard that the dam will serve many lowlanders with electric power and irrigation. But we humbly ask, how will the dam serve and assist we T'boli people?

7. In all this, we have never been directly approached, advised or informed regarding the planning of the dam. Do we not have rights? Are we not also Filipino citizens capable of planning for our future?

We do think that real development has to be realized with the free participation of the common people no matter how poor they are.

We have heard that the Asian Development Bank will be funding a major portion of this project. If this be true, we ask only that you reconsider the consequences and moral implications involved in this project.

Very sincerely yours,

T'BOLIS OF LAKE SEBU (This petition was signed by 2,662 T'bolis of Lake Sebu)

Source: The Philippines: Authoritarian government, multinationals and ancestral lands, Anti-slavery Society, London, 1983, pp. 180–81.

The largest contingent of Norwegian military forces to be fielded at any time since the Second World War was deployed in 1981.[203] *Their objective was not to deter a Russian invasion, or put down a threatened coup. Quite simply it was to break up an encampment which Sami families and their supporters from around the world had located at Stilla — "Zero Point" — on the Alta–Kautokeino river. For more than a decade this had been the proposed site for a hydroelectric scheme whose value has been widely disputed, and whose effects — especially on the migration patterns of the Sami's reindeer herds — are incalculable.*[204]

The Sami (or Lapps as they are incorrectly called) are the original people of an arc which stretches through northern Scandinavia to the eastern Soviet Union.[205] *Those in Norway — despite their government's much-vaunted support for the rights of indigenous peoples*[206] *— have never enjoyed the basic cultural and political recognition which Oslo has accorded other national minorities. And, despite a truly heroic resistance — involving the lengthiest non-violent occupation in European history, fasts almost unto death, a mass-occupation of Parliament, and delegations to Rome and the UN*[207] *— they, and their supporters, succumbed to mass arrest and blanket fines. By Spring 1982 the resistance had ended, but not before two of the major Sami organisations issued last-minute statements of defiance (reprinted below) and two Sami activists attempted to blow up a bridge over the Tverr river.*[208]

The latest assault on Norwegian Samiland is a gas pipeline being constructed by the Bechtel Corporation.[209]

Declaration from the Reindeer-Owners

Masi, 5 October 1981

We reindeer-owning Samis, who have used this area since time immemorial, can no longer sit with folded arms and see our pasture lands being steadily reduced. Those of us who have reindeer in the area in which construction work is planned, urge all of you who have come to help us to refuse to comply with Chief of Police Henriksen's order to keep clear of the area.

1) As reindeer Samis, we consider ourselves the landowners in this area, until such time as international law may decree otherwise. Consequently, we cannot allow the Norwegian majority society to use the police to prevent you by means of force from protecting the area which is ours by historic right.

2) We refer to Paragraphs 15 and 28 of the Reindeer Husbandry Act, which the authorities are clearly contravening by their conduct in the present situation. How can we have confidence in those who do not even respect their own laws? At the present time, in the middle of the mating season and a busy autumn migration, we are not in a position to obstruct the construction machines ourselves without external help. It appears to us that the authorities have started up operations at precisely this time for tactical reasons.

3) The majority society must not be allowed to use illegal means to cripple our livelihoods and our culture. The situation is already critical. Our patience is at an end.

This appeal (somewhat shortened here) was read out by one of the Samis immediately before the police went into action early on 5 October. It is signed by representatives of the reindeer owners association.

"We Are Samis . . ."

WE ARE SAMIS – and we intend to remain Samis. We are
neither more nor less than other peoples of the world. We are a
people with a common area of settlement, our own language,
and a cultural and social organization of our own. Throughout
the course of history we have lived our lives in Sami Eadnan
(Samiland). We possess a culture which we wish to expand and
develop.

We have experienced how the land where we and our
forefathers have lived has been taken from us: how that land
has declined and been deprived of its wealth. We have been
pushed aside. Strangers have taxed us, strangers have lied to
us, and strangers have divided our people with their own
national boundaries. We have experienced the decline of our
traditions and our cultural heritage. We have been deprived of
our customs and our way of life, which have been taken from us
and replaced by new and alien ways.

We are one people with a common language, a common
history, and a common culture, and we have a strong sense of
solidarity. We found ourselves on previous generations, whilst
we live and work in the present for the generations to come.

Only when our position has been assured legally, socially
and economically, can our culture develop fully. Consequently,
we demand:

1. that the Samis be given legal status as an indigenous people;
2. that the customary rights of the Samis to land and water be
confirmed by acts of parliament;
3. that Sami livelihoods be protected by laws and regulations;
4. that the Sami language be given the status of official
language;
5. that the Sami order of society and Sami representative bodies
be officially recognized so that we have real opportunities to
debate and make decisions in matters that concern ourselves;
6. that Sami tradition, history, art, knowledge and language be
preserved and taught to our descendants through schools and
other means;
7. to live in peaceful coexistence with our neighbours, and
support and promote world peace, basing ourselves on our own
traditional values.

This program is entirely in accordance with the U.N.
Declaration of Human Rights.

"If the dam is built there, our very life will be nothing to us again with no meanings. The land is our life, and if it's taken away for white man's pleasures, then what are we, the Aboriginals here in Alice Springs? We will be just shadows of the past living in a white man's world."

Rosie (Rice) Ferber[210]

6. Forests

The profound effect of timber felling and other forest exploitation on indigenous peoples should not be gauged by the slenderness of this chapter. The vast majority of all agriculturally-based and food-gathering indigenous peoples depend on forests for nutrition, shelter, fuel, and often clothing, and medicines, as, of course, do many who hunt and fish. For example while only a small proportion of India's adivasi communities (such as the Chenchus, Irulas, Kurumbas and Kadars) subsist wholly on forest produce, many of those who normally practise hill-side "slash and burn" or plains agriculture, will turn to the forests during pre-harvest periods.[211]

Destruction of woodland by commercial timber companies is not only a direct assault on forest dwellers: it can also unleash severe floods on low-lying regions[212] and erode and laterize the soil in tropical environments.[213] But forests are also denuded and drowned as a secondary effect of other developments which have a significant impact on indigenous peoples: road-building for example,[214] hydroelectrification schemes (see chapter 5) cattle-ranching[215] and mining.

National governments and their agencies have often criticised forest peoples for their failure to conserve forest resources, and especially for the negative effects of swidden (shifting, "slash and burn" or jhum) *cultivation.[216] This is a prime example of seeing a mote in the tribal eye, while harbouring (almost literally) a plank in one's own. Under low-population densities, this form of forest use does little permanent damage to the ecosystem. Compounded by commercial logging operations, however, it can prove to be devastating.[217]*

In the case of India — home of the greatest number of forest-dwelling tribal peoples in the world — a contracting land base, aggravated by in-migrating tree-fellers, has effectively reduced the jhumming *cycle from 20 or 30 years, to only five or six. In the north-east Himalayas alone, where more than one and a half million* adivasis *are engaged in* jhum, *the fertility of the soil is diminishing so quickly that vast tracts are becoming barren.[218]*

The response of the country's indigenous communities to such alarming developments has varied. The Angamis of Nagaland, for example, now practise a new form of "bench terracing" even on steep slopes; the Apatani people of Arunchal Pradesh have evolved paddy cultivation, without modern irrigation, at a height of nearly 2,000 metres; tribal people in the Jaintia hills of Meghalaya have "an ingenious bamboo drip irrigation system whereby they harness natural streams at the top of a slope to irrigate betel leaf and areca nut trees which they grow along the slopes".[219]

In the Chamoli region of Uttar Pradesh, where one of the most famous direct actions of recent times began in 1973, when the women began "hugging the trees" (Chipko Andolan), the peoples' two best-known male leaders have evolved very different strategies for forest preservation. While Sundarlal Bahuguna has campaigned against all commercial felling, Chandi Prasad Bhatt argues that the people themselves can be trusted to develop their own local enterprises.[220]

The statements which follow convincingly illustrate that, within certain margins of difference among themselves, indigenous peoples know best how to conserve forest resources, while utilising them ("We respect the forests"). They are not necessarily opposed to some commercial exploitation — but emphatically require it to be under their own aegis (Simione Durutalo), and are the first to perceive the devastating effects of uncontrolled commercialism ("Our gods have left us" and Tiempo, Tubo, Abra).[221]

We Respect the Forest

Madre de Dios is an Amazonian province of south-eastern Peru. The following testimony from a local Amarakaeri Indian was given at a meeting in Lima, in 1983.

We Indians were born, work, live and die in the basin of the Madre de Dios River of Peru. It's our land — the only thing we have, with its plants, animals and small farms: an environment we understand and use well. We are not like those from outside who want to clear everything away, destroying the richness and leaving the forest ruined forever. We respect the forest; we make it produce for us.

Many people ask why we want so much land. They think we do not work all of it. But we work it differently from them, conserving it so that it will continue to produce for our children and grandchildren. Although some people want to take it from us, they then destroy and abandon it, moving on elsewhere. But we can't do that; we were born in our woodlands. Without them we will die.

In contrast to other parts of the Peruvian jungle, Madre de Dios is still relatively sparsely populated. The woodlands are extensive, the soils poor, so we work differently from those in other areas with greater population, less woodland and more fertile soils. Our systems do not work without large expanses of land.

Without destroying

The people who come from outside do not know how to make the best of natural resources here. Instead they devote themselves to taking away what nature gives and leave little or nothing behind. They take wood, nuts and above all gold.

The man from the highlands works all day doing the same thing whether it is washing gold, cutting down trees or something else. Bored, he chews his coca, eats badly, then gets ill and leaves. The engineers just drink their coffee and watch others working.

We also work these things but so as to allow the woodland to replenish itself. We cultivate our farms, hunt, fish and gather woodland fruits, so we do not have to bring in supplies from outside. We also make houses, canoes, educate our children, enjoy ourselves. In short we satisfy almost all our needs with our own work, and without destroying the environment.

In the upper Madre de Dios River wood is more important than gold, and the sawmill of Shintuya is one of the most productive in the region. Wood is also worked in other areas to make canoes and boats to sell, and for building houses for the outsiders. In the lower region of the River we gather nuts — another important part of our economy.

Legal titles

Much is said about Madre de Dios being the forgotten Department of Peru. Yet we are not forgotten by people from outside nor by some national and foreign companies who try to seize our land and resources. Because of this we have formed the *Federation of Indian Peoples of Madre de Dios* to fight for the defence of our lands and resources.

Since 1974 we have been asking for legal property titles to the land we occupy in accordance with the Law of Indian Communities. The authorities always promise them to us, but so far only one of our communities has a title, and that is to barely 5,000 hectares.

"Wild, fierce and savage"

You may ask why we want titles now if we have not had them before. The answer is that we now have to defend our lands from many people who were not threatening us in the past.

In spite of journeys to Puerto Maldonado to demand guarantees from the authorities, they do not support us by removing the people who invade our land. On the contrary, when *we* defend our land, forcing the invaders to retreat, they accuse us of being wild, fierce and savage.

Equally serious are invasions by gold mining companies. The Peruvian State considers the issue of mining rights to be separate from that of land rights, and there are supposed to be laws giving priority to the Indian communities for mining rights on their lands — but the authorities refuse to enforce them. Many people have illegally obtained rights to mine our lands, then they do not allow us to work there. Others, without rights, have simply installed themselves.

There are numerous examples I could give; yet when my community refused entry to a North American adventurer who wanted to install himself on our land, the Lima *Commercio* accused us of being savages, and of attacking him with arrows. Lies! All we did was defend our lands against invaders who didn't even have legal mining rights —

without using any weapons, although these men all carried their own guns.

Prices fixed

We also suffer from forms of economic aggression. The prices of agricultural products we sell to the lorry drivers and other traders in the area have recently been fixed by the authorities. For example, 25lb of yuca used to sell for 800 *soles*. Now we can only get 400 *soles*. Such low prices stop us developing our agriculture further, and we are not going to be able to sell our products outside because we can no longer cover our costs and minimal needs. On the other hand, the authorities have fixed the prices of wood and transport so that the amount that we can earn is continually diminishing. And the prices we have to pay for things we need from outside is always rising.

There are also problems with the National Park Police. They no longer allow us to fish with 'barbasco' (fish poison) in the waters of our communities, although they are outside the National Park. They say that barbasco will destroy the fish. But we have fished this way for as long as we can remember, and the fish have not been destroyed. On the contrary: the fish are destroyed when people come from outside and overfish for commercial sale, especially when they use dynamite.

Our main source of food, after agriculture, is fishing — above all the *boquichico* which we fish with bow and arrow after throwing barbasco. We cannot stop eating, and we are not going to let them stop us from fishing with barbasco either!

Future generation

There are so many more problems. If our economic position is bad, our social situation is even worse. Traders reach the most remote areas, but medical facilities don't, even now with serious epidemics of malaria, measles, tuberculosis and intestinal parasites in the whole region. Our children go to primary schools in some communities, but often the schools are shut. And there are no secondary schools.

The commercial centres in the gold zone are areas of permanent drunkenness. Outsiders deceive and insult us and now some of our people no longer want to be known as Indians or speak our languages: they go to the large towns to hide from their origins and culture.

We are not opposed to others living and benefiting from the jungle, nor are we opposed to its development. On the contrary, what we want is that this development should benefit us, and not just the companies and colonists who come from outside. And we want the resources of the jungle to be conserved so that they can serve future generations of both colonists and Indians.

Source: Survival International News, London, 1983

How BP destroys Fiji's forests

Simione Durutalo, who is interviewed here, is Vice-President of the Fiji Anti-Nuclear Group, an organisation set up by Fijian unions and churches.

What is the impact of multinational corporations in Fiji and the Pacific Islands?
The basic problem that we face in places like Fiji and a few other Pacific islands is the exploitation of our resources, which are very limited in the first place. Not only is land very important to us, but also the marine life and the sea.

Large fishing multinationals with their canneries deplete the fishery resources which the people in the Pacific depend on for their survival.

In small islands, where you have a penetration of multinationals, and they exploit the bigger forests and mineral resources, the impact is triple.

Which are some of the biggest companies in the Pacific, and when did they first start operating?
When the Pacific colonies gained their independence in the late 1960s and 70s, the penetration of the big multinationals really began. Some companies had been there before, but the big ones in international terms — like British Petroleum, which is the most important one in the case of Fiji — only arrived during this period. BP is now into the exploitation of Arabian pine plantations on the main island of Fiji. The company has something like 52 thousand hectares planted.

Why did the government allow the companies to come in and exploit the resources?
The interesting thing about Fiji is that you have a black government which is in power. They are being used as a tool by the multinational, which is not peculiar to Fiji.

The government favoured the multinational because it is based on their development model. They think that foreign investment is great, that we need foreign capital to come in and develop the undeveloped resources, that sort of dependency mentality. They think that multinationals are the greatest thing on earth.

You disagree?
These ideas are mistaken because now a lot of people of Fiji, the native people, are suffering. They are just realising that the coming of the multinationals is not the boon it was supposed to be.

How are the people suffering, as you say?
The people are suffering because now their land is being taken up by mines and forestry, to say nothing of the impact of fisheries. What has happened is they have taken away the resources, the land, the fishing areas, and so on, which was the basis of the native people's subsistence economy. This has caused a total disorientation of the people, a breakdown of their life.

How have the native people responded to the coming of the big international companies?
The native people wanted to control their own resources. They wanted the pine industry to be their own pine industry. This is our land. This is our labour that

planted the thing; why should the government give it out to a multinational? Last year, this struggle resulted in a confrontation between pine forest workers and the police, and some native workers were thrown in jail.

What's the current status of the efforts by native people to oppose the multinationals?
The campaign in Fiji is very confused. The action has always been on the political front, and the government has argued: "How can you form an indigenous association when your government is black native?" So in that sense, you are caught in a contradiction, and it is not like, for example, the situation of natives where you have a white government in charge, or in Brazil where you have a military government where the enemy is always clear.

It is very hard for people to realise that it is their own government that is collaborating with the multinational, that their own black leaders that they elected are screwing them up in the end.

We are just now trying to think in terms of strategy and tactics. We are in an exploratory stage, beginning to fight back, but we have not really organised ourselves.

Source: Multinational Monitor, Washington, December 1982.

The Indian government recently drafted a new Forest Act, to replace legislation which is 80 years old. Under this Act, a state government can designate "reserved forests" in which collecting firewood, flowers and fruit may be punished by three years imprisonment or fines up to Rs 5,000 or both.[222]

If it is implemented, the Act will strike the biggest blow against India's tribal peoples that they have yet sustained. Thirty-six items, currently collected with little harassment from the government, may be proscribed. At the same time, timber corporations and commercial exploiters of bamboo, will be able to denude vast wooded areas for their increased profit. The Act has been widely criticised in India.[223]

The following interview was conducted by a representative of the Gesellschaft für bedrohte Völker *with a village elder of one of the adivasi communities removed from their forest homes to make way for large-scale felling. Goga Gaita's people are from the Bastar region, already threatened by massive hydro-electric projects (see chapter 5). In 1982, 300 tribal people besieged trucks carrying timber from the Mandapal forest, and in the mid-1970s a movement led by Baba Biharidas with the slogan "Bastar timber for the Bastar tribals" had considerable influence on local politics.*[224] *Indigenous opposition to tree felling has, however, been far more extensive in Bihar, where it forms part of the Jharkhand movement. The* Adivasis *of Singhbhum began raiding tree nurseries in 1978: two years later under the banner "Jungle Kato" they started their own tree-felling in selected areas. In 1982, 13 tribal people and three policemen were killed, when police fired on hundreds of* adivasis *who set out to* gherao *the forest range officer, in what has become known as the Gua Massacre.*[225]

"Our Gods have left us"

Rainer Hörig: *What are your problems?*

Goga Gaita: When we lived in the hills we were into migratory agriculture. There we had everything in the same place, food, vegetables and all those other things we need. Here in the plains now we have to clear fields, build dams and level the land. The soil quality of a place changes with time. So we have to clear new fields and build new dams over and over again. Water supplies are not good, sometimes there's enough, sometimes not. We are very dependent on rain. We don't have irrigation works here. So plants don't always grow. Only when there's plenty of rain.

Why have you come here from the hills? What did you expect?

Government brought us down because they didn't want us to fell the woods for our fields.

Were you forced to come?
They came and said: "You're destroying the bamboo we want to fell and sell to the mills. That won't do. You have to go away. There's nothing else to do." Government gave us everything and settled us here in Gotpadi. But our herds aren't growing, cows and oxen are dying. We are not used to ploughing the plains, we are slow in learning. But not even after so many years could we get used to life here, to this hard work. Life wasn't this hard in the hills.

Was there any resistance amongst your people against resettlement? Haven't some people run away?
Yes. Some fled to Bastar. Our main problem is the oxen. Many of us don't have oxen to plough the land. They have to borrow oxen for money. If the harvest isn't good, they get into problems.

What changes did the resettlement make in your life?
Our forefathers have lived in the hills. They had their gods, their prayers and their land, they were short of nothing. We also had a happy life there. There, we had enough to eat, and sometimes we went down to the plains to work in the forests. We had enough to drink, and nobody bothered us. But the new land we came to 20 years ago doesn't bring us luck, or enough to eat. Our gods have left us and the land doesn't want us either.

Why have some families left Gotpadi again?
They left because their oxen died or they had no seed. Sometimes it doesn't rain for three years, and there's no harvest.

What's your relationship to the government? Do you have contacts?
We've often asked government for help. But they don't care for our problems.

When the government is planning a development, roads or dams for example, are you asked about that?
No!

How are families getting on in this village?
Three years ago government people came and sterilised all married men. Since then, we're getting fewer and fewer. Some get ill and die. Some people said in those days, government will care for everything and give us money. But when we go to them and ask for money, they say your name is not registered, you don't have papers to your land and come again later. So they play their evil game with us.

Is there anybody coming to you to offer help? Medical care or schooling?
They say we have to come to them. There's the American hospital Baba Amte in Bamragarh, but that's 12 miles from here. How should a sick man walk that far? They don't come here.

Do you trust Western medicine?
In olden days, we only had our own medicine, and it was very successful. Since government is giving us medicine we have the feeling that our own herbal medicine is getting ineffectual. Perhaps this comes from the poison government is spraying in our villages against malaria.

Have you ever considered how you could put up resistance?

That's not possible. Government wouldn't allow it.

How do you see the future? Your future, that of your family and of your village?
In just a few years it will become impossible even to make a small fire and cook some food. Gotpadi will be no good then. First, government was telling all the woods will be yours, you can build houses and stables. Now government is coming and felling bamboo and trees. We're afraid there'll be nothing left for us in a few years. When we'll not be able even to make fire, we'll have to go.

I'd like to say this: I've made a lot of photographs here without asking people's permission. I'll use them to show my people the problems your people have. And I'll ask my people to help your people. It won't be easy to help you from so far away. But we both have a good friend here and I could give him the money so that he can help you.

This interview with the leader of the people of Gotpadi, is the transcript of a tape recording. Interviewer: Rainer Hörig. Translator: V. S. Patwardhan.

Source: Pogrom (Göttingen) December 1981/January 1982, trans. Mick Blackstein.

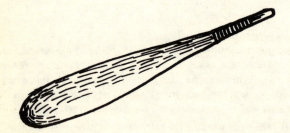

More than half the Philippines is covered by forest classified as "in the public domain", and virtually all the country's indigenous communities live within that domain.[226] *In theory this should mean they are protected from commercial timber operations.*[227] *In practice, they have become the prime victims of a martial law authority which seeks to encourage the logging companies*[228] *— including US and Japanese interests*[229] *— while trampling on tribal livelihood.*

In 1973, the Cellophil Resources Corporation (CRC) was granted nearly 2,000 hectares of Tinggian, Bontoc, Isneg, Kalinga and Kankanais land on which to operate a vast logging concession, establish a pulp mill and run a rayon fibre plant. The Tinggian people conducted the struggle against CRC, first by legal means, then through peace-pact meetings (the second of which, whose resolutions are recorded here, was attended by more than 500 people[230] *and — after increasing military oppression — by joining the New Peoples Army.*[231] *NPA operations — at least in the Abra area — held back the expansion of CRC until 1982,*[232] *but military actions against indigenous villages were stepped up in early 1984.*[233]

Tiempo, Tubo, Abra. 26 January 1979

RESOLUTION of the United Communities of the Cordillera directed to His Excellency Prime Minister Ferdinand E. Marcos, opposing the entry and operation of the Resources Corporation in their Municipalities requesting the President to cancel the CRC's licence covering the said Municipalities:

Whereas, on September 24–25, 1978 the Tingguians of Abra held their historic Inter-Peacepact Partners Gathering in Bangilo, Malibcong, Abra at which a joint resolution was agreed upon demanding the suspension of Cellophil Resources Corporation activities in Tingguian areas until the demands detailed in that resolution were met;

Whereas, little if anything has been accomplished since the September meeting to meet the various demands; for example, Cellophil Resources Corporation has not released any new information regarding its operations, and instead merely repeated the selective information it has given the Tingguians in the past; no serious attempt has been made by either the company or the Bureau of Forest Development to understand why floating logs down our rivers and felling trees in these watersheds feeding our irrigated fields will be devastating to our present way of life; no serious attempt has been made to dialogue with us in good faith, and instead meetings that have been held in our areas between us, the company and government officials, have, for the most part, sought to harass us into submission; and a regrettable development has emerged where the company and some authorities have tried to blame "outsiders" and "individuals" for organizing us which betrays an ignorance of our age-old peace pact system upon which is firmly rooted our tribal communities;

Whereas, after a lapse of four months we have decided to meet again here in Tiempo, Tubo, Abra to carefully deliberate over the many things which have happened since September regarding the problem of Cellophil Resources Corporation with which we are still faced;

Whereas, we tribal Filipinos are assured in the 1973 Constitution of the Philippines that our customs, traditions, beliefs and interests will be taken into account in the formulation and implementation of State policies;

WE REITERATE that:

The entry of the Cellophil Resources Corporation into our municipalities and barangays will destroy our watersheds critical to our water supply for drinking and irrigation; water for our cattle; and will result in the pollution and drying up of our rivers and brooks in which we catch fish and crabs for our daily subsistence;

The cutting of trees from our steep mountains will cause erosion and destroy our fields and farms thereby depriving us of our livelihood as well as the destruction of the natural beauty of our forests;

The entry of Cellophil Resources Corporation in our municipalities will decimate the culture, traditions, customs and other such vital interests of our people;

The operation of the Cellophil Resources Corporation in our municipalities will ruin the strong unity and harmony of our tribal communities which are held together by an extensive peace pact system;

We reaffirm our belief:

That the government must not procure development at the expense of the people in violation of their basic human rights which government is committed to uphold;

The people of these municipalities and barangays are contented and happy, the entry of this company into these areas will cause the moral, cultural, economic as well as physical displacement of people and the loss of their ancestral lands which they have safeguarded for centuries;

That we, Tribal Filipinos, after experiencing centuries of discrimination, exploitation and oppression by a succession of outsiders, now vehemently demand that we be treated with all the due respect as matter of right;

Now therefore, be it **resolved** as it is hereby resolved that His Excellency Prime Minister Ferdinand E. Marcos shall act on the resolution of the United Communities of Cordillera and cancel the license of the Cellophil Resources Corporation and prevent the operation of the Cellophil in the various barangays and municipalities represented in the signatures below;

We further resolve to furnish copies of this resolution to the following:

The President, Cellophil Resources Corporation, Makati
The Director, Bureau of Forest Development, Dagupan City
The Regional Director, Bureau of Forest Development, Dagupan City
The President, National Investment and Development Corporation, Makati
Deputy Minister of National Defense for Civilian Relations, Quezon City
The Bishop of Bangued
The Provincial Governor: Abra, Mt. Province, Kalinga-Apayao

The Provincial PC Command, Abra
Chairman of the Board, World Bank

Signatures of 180 representatives from 17 affected communities

The Compania Administradora Comercial Sociedad Anonima is a
descendant of the Sociedad Agricola y Forestal Suxaola which, with north
American capital, took over lands — abandoned by another company in
1947 — that lay on Talamanca territory, Costa Rica. When the
government granted the company a lease to develop 10,000 acres of forest
in 1983, various Talamanca Indian associations protested to members of
Parliament, many of whom received them favourably. A little later a
government commission was sent to investigate the peoples' complaints.

"Since time immemorial we, indigenous people, have been the object
of the plundering of our lands, of disregard for our basic rights and
all manner of abuses within full sight and tolerance of the
Government, Legislative Assembly and the Judicial Power.
Nevertheless, according to natural law and legitimate right we are
the first inhabitants of this continent.

"Any and every time we have tried to defend this right we have
become victims. We consider that we are human beings and have the
right, at least, to possess land on which we can survive in peace and
tranquillity. For thousands of years we have lived on these lands of
Talamanca and we have survived war with the Spanish and their
diseases. Today we have decided to resist whatever foreign force
intends to deprive us of our lands.

"Apart from this, the Indigenous Law No. 6172 has been a victory
for us and all indigenous peoples of Costa Rica, and we demand the
complete respect and fulfilment of this law.

"Nevertheless, a few days ago (24 May) the indigenous people of
the communities of this reserve had the surprise and unpleasant
news that these lands were not theirs but belonged to a foreign North
American company called Administradora Comercial S.A., who have
mutilated the land for an area of 10,000 hectares.

"At the same time and without the agreement of the Asociación de
Desarollo Integral de la Reserva Indígena, even less the Committees
which exist in the area, the said company brought in lorries, tractors
and workers and immediately began to open roads with the object of
felling trees for lumber and make money out of them
indiscriminately.

"In view of this and seeing the indigenous people so affected by
these North American filibusters we immediately began to speak
with them about the problem and, finding out their aims and
objectives, we told them to leave within 24 hours and get out of the
place. In this way we paralysed the lumber work of this company.

"The company known as Administradora Comercial claimed to
have exploited lumber within the indigenous reservation and alleged
they had owned the rights for 35 years.

"Nevertheless we indigenous people of Talamanca have acquired
this right for many centuries of occupation of the land as the
legitimate owners, for which reason we do not recognise enforced
foreign rights.

"In the light of what has been written above and noting the statements of the said company to show that these lands had been handed over before the reserve had been created and as they think they have a right, we wish to make very clear the following points:

1. This company has violated the Law of Indigenous Reservations No. 6172 of 20 December 1977.
2. They did not appeal on its publication in the Gaceta Oficial.
3. We indigenous people have lived for centuries on these lands and for this reason we are the legitimate owners.
4. The exploitation of lumber will alter the hydrological and ecological balance and other factors which we are not willing to permit.

For this reason:

1. We demand that the Central Government annuls the concessions given to foreign companies within the reserve.
2. We demand that the institutions of the State investigate these matters and give a judgement with respect to them.

"If there is anything at this time which can be called justice there cannot be said to be social justice among those in the reserves without permission and which alter social peace in the ethnic social group.

"It is not possible to speak of respecting human rights because this is not even respecting the fundamental rights of a human being, which in this case is the right we all have to live in peace.

Alejandro Swaby Rodriguez: Comité Pro-Defensa Derechos Indígenas de Talamanca
Guillermo Rodriguez Romero: Presidente Asociación, Reserva Indígena de Talamanca
José Maria Paez Segura: Sindicato Federación de Pequeños Agricultores de Talamanca
Cipriano Mendez: Comité Indígena Pablo Presbere
Severiano Fernandez Torres: Asociación de Educadores Indígenas de Talamanca
Felipa Morales Moralés: Comité de Artesanos de Talamanca
Donald Rojas Maroto: Presidente Asociación Indígena de Costa Rica
José Carlos Maroles: President of the World Council of Indigenous Peoples"

Source: Boletín de la Asociación Indígena de Costa Rica Nos. 4/5 Marzo/Abril 1983, published in IWGIA Newsletter, October/December 1983.

Mataco Co-Op (Aborigines Co-op of Nueva Pompeya)

Nueva Pompeya is in the Chaco province of Argentina, an area of stunted, thorny scrubland occupied by around 5,000 Mataco people — shoved into the area by invading whites. In the late 1970s the Mataco set up a Production and Consumption Co-operative, which was "a completely new experience for an ethnic minority in Argentina".[234]

The Aborigines Department, run by the national government, soon began to impose intolerable restrictions on the venture which was mainly concerned with felling trees and marketing poles. Marketing licences were withheld; revenues had to be spent on food, rather than new equipment.

By mid-1973, with the Co-operative over-producing by two-thirds, but its members determined not to be browbeaten into surrender, the regime, clearly to provoke a disturbance which could be put down by force, sent into the area two administrators whom the people had previously thrown out.

In late 1973, with the Co-operative still over-producing by two-thirds and faced by further ridiculous restrictions (the government maximum was 2,000 poles a year, while Mataco production was closer to 35,000 a year), a large group of Mataco gathered in front of the Governor's office, demanding the dismissal of three men in charge of the "Aborigines Department". Without provocation, members of the paramilitary Organisation Command began machine-gunning the Mataco, claiming that "extremists" had infiltrated the community.

Immediately afterwards the Chaco Indigenous Parliament assembled at Itati, where the secretary-general Mario Agreda Cibila denounced the attack:

This attack is the culmination of a long process which began when the Production and Consumption Co-operative of Nueva Pompeya was created. The purpose of the Co-operative is to achieve self-sufficiency for the community . . . it constitutes an economic entity which soon began to worry the landowners of the area. The thing is that the (indigenous) manpower is the cheapest in the country. If this Co-operative is successful, others will follow its example. And then the exploiters will have no more workers to exploit. The thing is they do not want the Indians to liberate themselves. They are cheap labour. But no exploiter will be able to keep the Argentine Indians from advancing.

The regime's response to this renewed determination was to arrest 10 Mataco, claiming "irregularities" in the license documents of the Co-operative. Two of the (unnamed) prisoners made declarations from gaol:[235]

We were the cheapest manpower, and now our land is ours and so is our work; Governor Bitel and the Government don't want us to make progress. It is unjust, it is clear that they want to be masters of our work. We want the Co-operative, we are going to defend it.

We are not stupid, we are not ignorant as they say. We have suffered a lot to make progress, and now they want to take everything away from us.

Solidarity with the imprisoned Mataco came from all over Argentina, most importantly from other indigenous communities. In October 1973, they were released. But subdued repression of the Mataco continued through 1974; government aid plans glaringly excluded the Nueva Pompeya; the banks refused credit for the sawmill, the Aborigines Department remained extremely tardy in issuing permits for poles.

Finally, in February 1975, the National Institute for Co-operative Action granted the Co-operative a credit of 30 million old pesos: from the context of the gift, it was clear that this was seen simply as a means of controlling "subversive" elements within the community.[236]

7.   Pollution

"Minamata" has become a byword for extreme industrial pollution. The term encompasses a Japanese community poisoned by mercury, its survivors engaged in a 30-year struggle for recognition and redress, the corporations responsible (mainly Chisso and Showa Denko) subjected to international opprobrium and national union action.[237]

A similar scourge, which has affected the Ojibway people of Grassy Narrows, part of the "Treaty Nine" area of north-west Ontario (see Vol. 2, Part 4, ch. 8) is far less well-known outside Canada — and little known inside.[238] *Here, the people have suffered mercury poisoning deriving from effluent poured into the Wabigoon–English River system by Reed Inc. — Britain's largest producer of paper products. The effects of the pollution were graphically described in 1975 by investigative reporter George Hutchinson.*[239] *After Hutchinson's research was published, the Minamata Disease Patients' Alliance (MDPA) invited Indian representatives to come to Japan from Grassy Narrows and Whitedog.*

Concluded the MDPA: "It will be a blessing if our long years of suffering can help you in even one simple way . . . if you rely on [the company] the central government or the provincial government — they will do nothing for you."[240]

These predictions have been borne out in the years since. As graphically described by Joanne Wetelainen, it is clear that the corporations involved (Reed and Great Lakes), and the provincial and the federal government, have all been engaged in a complex process of buck-passing in which the Indians have totally lost out (although $4.4 million was offered towards "community recovery" by the Federal Canadian government in 1984).[241]

Representatives from Grassy Narrows met with participants in the Red Peoples' Long Walk (British Colombia to Akwesasne, May–October 1984) and asked members of the new militant Canadian Indian movement to take up their cause.[242]

A community sold down the river

(Whitedog Reserve) — On 14 November 1983, Minister of Indian Affairs John Munro, issued a 30 day deadline to Great Lakes Forest Products (owners of the Dryden paper mill) to make a settlement offer to Whitedog Reserve for mercury pollution damages. But on 14 December, the last day of the deadline. Great Lakes said they would not make the offer. Whitedog Reserve is now saying they have given up trying for an out-of-court settlement and they will take the company to court.

Since mercury was discovered in the Wabigoon–English River system in 1970, economic, social and cultural deterioration have plagued Whitedog and Grassy Narrows Reserves. That same year, the Ontario government issued a ban on all commercial fishing; a ban that reduced commercial fishing employment at Whitedog from 95 to 15 individuals. Similarly, the ban reduced guiding opportunities from 69 people employed before the ban to 25 positions after the ban was imposed. "Thirty years ago, every able-bodied man on the reserve had some kind of job" says former chief Isaac Mandamin of Whitedog, "Now, there's no work here anymore."

Scientific studies of mercury pollution in the Wabigoon–English River system have shown the Dryden paper mill is responsible for dumping upwards of 20 tonnes of mercury into the river system and they say it could be 90 years before the river system will return to normal.

Meanwhile, the 1982–83 unemployment rate at Whitedog Reserve was 79% and other statistics tell an equally tragic story. In the period of 1971–1977 of all deaths at Grassy Narrows — only 5% were attributed to old age. In a 1978 study of alcoholism, 66 percent of the population ages 16–64 were classified as heavy drinkers, the remaining 34 percent were classified as being close to addiction. Attempts by the bands to seek compensation for damages caused by mercury pollution have met with little success.

The Dryden paper mill was owned by Reed Inc. when mercury was first discovered in the river system. However, all attempts by the bands to get Reed to pay compensation for mercury pollution damages have failed as have requests for assistance to the Ontario government.

The Ministry of the Environment, the government body responsible for policing industrial emissions, issued several pollution control orders to Reed, but the company ignored most orders and little progress was made on the matter.

In 1975, the Whitedog Band presented to Leo Bernier, then Minister of Natural Resources, a series of economic development requests with a view to alleviating the impact of unemployment caused by the pollution. But these too were ignored. In 1976, specific requests were directed to Ontario for assistance in developing wild rice projects. Ontario showed no interest and it wasn't until the Kitchener–Conestoga Rotary Club invested $26,000 of its own funds that Whitedog and three other bands were able to construct a rice control dam one of the few such dams in northwestern Ontario.

For the next seven years Ontario's response to the band's request for assistance was unsympathetic; the reasons Ontario gave for not offering assistance varied, but all told the same story. In 1976 Ontario cabinet minister Rene Brunelle said

"Economic development on Indian reserves is a federal responsibility"; while Leo Bernier said "Ontario's policy is that there will be no compensation for industrial pollution; the court's are open to individuals to take on the polluter." The next year, cabinet minister Dennis Timbrell responding to mercury poisoning said "We don't know if the symptoms (from which the Indians suffer) have been caused by the fish, alcoholism or venereal disease".

Great Lakes: News on the block

While the Whitedog and Grassy Narrows Bands did not receive any money for damages caused by mercury pollution from Reed Inc. or the Ontario government, they were optimistic that things would change when Great Lakes Forest Products bought the Dryden mill and its assets in 1979. According to Whitedog negotiator Bruce Crofts, during the bands first meeting with Great Lakes, the company's vice-president Murray Seely told band members that their approach to resolving the mercury issue would be totally different than Reed's. "He basically said 'We're the new boys on the block and we'll get things settled'" said Crofts.

Whitedog was doubly optimistic because of an Ontario government guarantee to Great Lakes that Ontario would pick up any costs of mercury pollution damages to the bands over 15 million dollars. The Ontario guarantee came after Reed decided to sell its Dryden mill in 1979 but was having difficulty selling because buyers feared potential mercury pollution lawsuits. It wasn't until the Reed president approached Ontario Treasurer Frank Miller and asked him to provide a letter to Great Lakes (one of the potential buyers) assuring them that the province would pick up those liabilities over 15 million dollars, that Ontario agreed and Great Lakes purchased the mill in November 1979.

However, Whitedog's optimism soon faded when, in February 1981, Great Lakes complained of disagreements over the intent of the Ontario government's letter of guarantee. As a result, no offer was tabled by Great Lakes and the Whitedog Band put pressure on the Ontario government to clarify its position regarding the guarantee. In January 1982, the Ontario government issued a new letter which left no doubt as to the 15 million dollar liability ceiling. Great Lakes expressed their thanks to the Bank and promised to make an offer by 15 February 1982. But when the February deadline came, Great Lakes said they were not able to make an offer because of "internal difficulties with Reed" who had at the time they sold the mill, entered into a private agreement with Great Lakes to share the cost of the mercury settlement. Great Lakes told the two Bands that the portion each company was to pay was under dispute and this had created a stalemate in the mediation process.

In an effort to finalize five years of unsuccessful mediation with Great Lakes and Reed Inc., Bruce Crofts, negotiator for the Whitedog Band wrote Reed president J. Peter Williams asking him to clarify the problem. On 6 June 1983 Crofts received a letter from Williams that said "As far as Reed is concerned, the stance that Great Lakes appears to be making . . . that it wishes to settle with Reed before resolving the issue with the Indian bands . . . was not foreseen in the original sale agreement" and Williams went on to say "This approach is inherently unrealistic."

Williams concluded that Reed would make an "appropriate contribution immediately following 'the Great Lakes settlement with the Bands.'" The letter went on to say that in the original sale agreement, Great Lakes was to assume full responsibility for dealing with all pollution-related matters, including the claims of the Bands.

Munro intervenes

At the request of Whitedog, a meeting was called on 14 November 1983 with John Munro, Minister of Indian Affairs, Norm Sterling, Ontario Resources Secretary, the Whitedog and Grassy Narrows Bands and Great Lakes all present. The meeting resulted in Great Lakes promising Munro and the Indian Bands that they would table an offer by 14 December. The offer was to list any conditions Reed felt necessary i.e. the lowering of the provincial liability ceiling; the need for an adequate contribution from Reed Inc. etc. The offer would not be binding until all the impediments listed by Great Lakes were resolved.

On 14 December, the final day of the 30 day deadline, Whitedog heard nothing from Great Lakes. That morning negotiator Bruce Crofts received a phone call from the CBC French radio network saying that the public relations department of Great Lakes had indicated to them that no offer would be tabled. Crofts then called Justice Patrick Hartt of the Indian Commission of Ontario (to whom the offer was to be directed) but no offer, or correspondence had been received. It wasn't until Crofts reached Great Lakes president C.J. Carter that the CBC release was confirmed accurate.

Justice Patrick Hartt later received a letter dated 13 December officially stating Great Lakes would not table an offer. The reason Great Lakes said was "To date, no liability has been established upon Reed or any of its predecessors for the discharge of mercury into the river system in question". The letter went on to say that "No damages have been proven as being caused by such discharge".

On 23 December, Minister John Munro sent an official response to the Great Lakes letter. In it he said he was "perplexed" by the Great Lakes statement that no liability had been established and no damages proven with respect to mercury discharges. He suggested that "No impartial observer would contend that Reed and Great Lakes do not bear major responsibility for the conditions at Whitedog and Grassy Narrows because of mercury poisoning." He called the Great Lakes letter "Nothing more than another callous delaying tactic" that was "abhorrent" to him personally as well as to a great many other Canadians.

Meanwhile, the new chief of Whitedog, Roy McDonald, and his council are quickly moving ahead with legal action. They have called for a meeting with John Munro to determine if the federal government will agree to cover their legal costs. (On 13 December, 1983 the Province of Ontario announced a mercury mediation settlement of $1.5 million with the Whitedog Band.)

Source: Yukon Indian News, Whitehorse, 10 February 1984.

Arsenic, fluoride and 2,4,5-T, are three of the poisons which have blown on to north American Indian people, been found in their water and caused cancer in their blood and bones.

In 1974, Dene and Metis in the Yellowknife area of the North West Territories of Canada woke up one morning to find their water supplies "officially" contaminated with arsenic from mining: despite the fact that the government had known about the pollution for many years. Four years later the Klamath in northern California took action against companies using the defoliant 2,4,5-T along their fishing grounds: a law suit, initiated by the Indian Action Council of Northern California, was dismissed.[243]

After yet another four years, the Mikmaq of Nova Scotia rose up in protest at the continued spraying of the same defoliant, as outlined in a September 1982 press release from the Mikmaq nation.

In 1978, native Canadians living over the border from the Mohawk community at Akwesasne were also sickening from fluoride emissions, upwind from aluminium plants operated by Alcoa and Reynolds Aluminium.[244]

In the late 1970s there were also widespread poisonings among native Guatemalan plantation labourers in the Altiplano region, and unexplained deaths among 78 of the 800 Yucpa Indians of north-west Venezuela — possibly affected by defoliants. By 1980, the Brazil National Indian Foundation (FUNAI) had registered increasing numbers of still-births, miscarriages, infant deformities and adult kidney problems in Indians from the Guapore valley region, where Tordon 155 and 101 (Dow's proprietary defoliants, 2,4,5-T and 2,4-D) had been "massively" employed since 1975.[245]

The following statement is part of a speech delivered by the head of the St Regis Band — the major native community affected — to a Canadian Labour Congress Conference on Jobs and the Environment.

"Our members serve as an Early Warning system"

It is becoming obvious that Indians and Labour share a common problem — the problem of unsafe environments. We also often share the same opponents in our fight to improve environmental health. Both the Labour movement and the Indian movement have run head-long into insensitive industries and foot-dragging governments, when we've pushed for environmental clean ups . . . Even when the scientific evidence documenting the need for drastic action is overwhelming, the victims of environmental pollution have had to wage pitched battles before greedy corporations and irresponsible governments can be jolted out of their complacency. Governments and industries are clearly more interested in covering the tracks of their past environmental mistakes than in taking the bold steps necessary to rectify a particular tragedy.

Simon Fobister, the chief of the mercury-plagued reserve of Grassy Narrows specifically asked me to cite the mercury crisis in Northwestern Ontario as an example of this short-sightedness and procrastination. Reed International has made a fortune in the pulp and paper industry. But Reed has also ruined the economic, social, and physical health of the communities of White Dog and Grassy Narrows. Reed has poisoned the fish of the English–Wabigoon River System with mercury pollution.

. . . Indians and Labour have long been used as guinea pigs to see what level of poison our bodies can withstand before caving in to death and disease. Years ago, coal miners brought canaries into the mines because canaries acted as an early-warning system for the miners. The birds would suffer the effects of deadly vapours in coal mines before humans would. When a bird suddenly keeled over and died, the miners knew it was time to start scrambling for the surface . . . And in many ways, our (Indians) are very much like the canaries the coal miners once carried underground to test the air. Our members unwittingly serve as modern day, toxic-substance early warning systems. Governments and industries continue to conduct human experiments with Indians and Labour. They knowingly allow our people to be exposed to certain levels of industrial contaminants. Then, when human carnage becomes so great the levels of exposure can no longer be justified, the government sets a new exposure limit for the general population.

The St. Regis (Akwesasne) farmers have watched their cattle eat the fluoride-loaded vegetation. They have watched their cattle die. The latest tests conducted by experts from Cornwall University's school of veterinarian medicine, show that practically all of the St. Regis cattle run the risk of becoming ill with fluoride poisoning. Many of our farmers have been forced out of business because of Reynold's fluoride.

Reynolds has robbed us of our natural heritage. The . . . Mohawks have traditionally lived in harmony with nature. We have lived off the land. We have fished, farmed, and hunted in the St. Regis area as long as man can remember. Our culture, religion, and way of life are intimately bound to the land, the animals, and the changing seasons . . . Reynolds is committing cultural genocide in St. Regis.

. . . In closing, let me remind you that all of us are victims when corporate giants are allowed to impose pollutants on us. And it is the victims of this nonsensical arrangement who must apply pressure to force companies to pay the total cost of doing business. Not just their labour, machinery, and manufacturing costs, but also the costs that you and I pay in terms of ruined vegetation, decreasing land values, and deteriorating health. Until we begin to force irresponsible industries to pay the total costs of their operations, there will always be victims.

Source: Akwesasne Notes, Vol. 10, No. 2, Late Spring 1978, p. 12

"Agent Orange" spraying on Mikmaq communities challenged

Two Mikmaq communities in Nova Scotia are fighting to prevent spraying of the herbicide 2,4-D, a suspected cause of cancer and birth defects, in surrounding high forests and watershed areas. The spraying has been proposed by Nova Scotia Forest Industries, the Canadian subsidiary of Stora Kopparbergs Bergslags AB (Sweden), to control the growth of non-commercial shrubs and trees.

The proposed spraying would affect the Afton River, which flows through Afton Reserve, and the Skye River, which flows through Whycocomagh Reserve. At least one other Mikmaq community, Wagmatcook, may be affected by spraying in the vicinity of the Margaree River, a traditional eel and salmon fishery.

The chemical 2,4-D (2,4-dichlorophenoxyacetic acid) belongs to a family of 'phenoxy' herbicides that kill plants by overstimulating growth. Two phenoxy herbicides, 2,4-D and 2,4,5-T, were combined to make the military defoliant Agent Orange, widely used in South-East Asia and now blamed for the health problems of thousands of U.S. military veterans. Phenoxy preparations are commonly contaminated with small amounts of a particularly dangerous poison, dioxin or TCCD (2,3,7,8-tetrachlorodile-*p*-dioxin), which is a confirmed carcinogen.

Phenoxy herbicides are principally produced by the Dow Chemical Corp. (U.S).

Phenoxy herbicides have been linked clinically with cancer in Sweden and with birth defects in Australia (*Lancet*, 1 August and 12 & 13 September 1981). Laboratory studies confirm that phenoxy compounds can cause severe heart and kidney damage to new-born and gestating mammals and fish (*Toxicology* 20(2), 1981). As little as one milligram per litre of water is lethal to young salmon and crabs (*Bulletin of Environmental Contamination Toxicology* 27:877, 1981). The U.S. Environmental Protection Agency banned all use of 2,4,5-T in 1979.

In a recent study of 78 American military veterans who reported health problems after exposure to Agent Orange, 17% had developed cancer, 19% had children with gross birth defects, and more than half suffered from severe neurological problems. Most had severe skin problems (*Journal of the American Medical Association*, 30 November 1980).

The Province of Nova Scotia's Minister of Lands and Forests has publicly denied any health hazard and blames Mikmaq opposition on "outside agitators". On balance, he argues, forest industry jobs for white Canadians outweigh any possible risks.

Leaders of the Afton and Whycocomagh communities won a temporary halt to the spraying program on 7 September by going to the Nova Scotia courts. The court will not decide whether to prevent spraying permanently until December. In the meantime Mikmaq leaders are looking for technical and financial help from environmentalists and other groups concerned about Agent Orange and other hazardous herbicides.

Source: Santeioi Maoaiomi Mikmaoei (Grand Council Mikmaq Nations) press release, 24 September 1982.

Native Hawaiian Cites Ruin of Ocean

"I'd like to share one of the more current concerns of Pacific Island people at this time in 1986. That is the United States effort to build an incinerator on what is called Johnson Island, previously known as Kalama Island when it was under the reign of King Kamehameha. Johnson Island is an atoll in the Pacific that now stores toxic wastes. It is a very small atoll. The Environmental Protection Agency has granted a permit for the U.S. army to build an incinerator to burn these toxic chemicals. This EPA permit was granted without any Pacific Island consultation. No Pacific Island people knew about this hearing. The only people who gave testimony were a few of us in Hawaii. This incinerator is already under construction and it is life-threatening, we believe, to Pacific Island way of life.

"According to studies that have been done, we believe that emissions will fall into the sea and pollute the food chain further than it already has been by the bombings in the 50s of Emoita and Bikini Islands. We see that the United States sees us as being an expendable population of 90,000 people. We may live on small atolls and small islands, but the ocean is also our territory. The Western mindset does not see the ocean as part of the life cycle of indigenous Pacific Island people, so it chooses to use it and commodify it in different ways that really are going to destroy our future . . .

"And I think Hawaii is seen too many times as a part of the West. I think people need to look at Hawaii as a part of the Pacific Islands. That concept has to be deepened and reinforced over and over again. And I think even though we have Congressional delegates in the United States, I think even they have to see themselves as representatives of Pacific Island people and not representing people who belong to the West, because we are in the ocean, and we are thousands of miles from the United States and we are indigenous."

Source: SAIIC Newsletter Vol. 2, No. 3. Spring, 1986. South American Indian Information Center, Berkeley.

Indians Protest Against Aerial Spraying

The Colombian government has approved the use of the herbicide Glifosato in an experimental program to eliminate marijuana cultivation in the Sierra Nevada mountains. In May 1984, the government, under pressure from U.S. drug enforcement agencies, had approved the use of Paraquat in the program, but backed down after a public outcry over its dangers.

The Indians living in the Sierra Nevada region, as well as many others in Colombia, have voiced strong objections to the aerial spraying which began June 25. The Indians are concerned that the herbicide will cause serious damage to the health of the area's inhabitants as well as harm the local plant and animal life.

The Sierra Nevada mountains, a natural park and ecological reserve, are home to the Kogi, Arhuaco and Malayo Indian communities.

The Indians say that while Glifosato has been shown to be effective in killing marijuana plants, no one has investigated its effects on the surrounding environment. The Organizacion Nacional Indigena de Colombia (National Indigenous Organization of Colombia) questions why a densely populated area in which health services are grossly inadequate was targeted for spraying with this experimental product.

Source: UNIDAD INDIGENA, (September 1984) published by Consejo Regional Indigena del Cauca (CRIC), Colombia.

8. Fishing Rights

In 1859 the United States Senate ratified the treaty signed with the Yakima Indians at Walla Walla in 1855. The treaty gave to the Indians the possession of certain land, but ceded other portions of it to the United States. The Supreme Court, on a test case, repudiated the treaty (by a divided vote) in favor of the Indians. Another test case was taken up. In testimony therein Chief Weninock of the Yakimas made the statement (in about 1915) quoted here. Ultimately, the Indians gained their point, which was to be allowed to fish unmolested at their accustomed fishing places.

God created the Indian country and it was like he spread out a big blanket. He put the Indians on it. They were created here in this Country, truly honest, and that was the time this river started to run. Then God created fish in this river and put deer in the mountains and made laws through which has come the increase of fish and game. Then the Creator gave us Indians Life; we walked, and as soon as we saw the game and fish we knew they were made for us. For the women God made roots and berries to gather, and the Indians grew and multiplied as a people.

When we were created we were given our ground to live on and from this time these were our rights. This is all true. We had the fish before the Missionaries came, before the white man came. We were put here by the Creator and these were our rights as far as my memory to my grandfather. This was the food on which we lived. My mother gathered berries; my father fished and killed the game. These words are mine and they are true. My strength is from the fish; my blood is from the fish, from the roots and berries. The fish and game are the essence of my life. I was not brought from a foreign country and did not come here. I was put here by the Creator.

We had no cattle, no hogs, no grain, only berries and roots and game and fish. We never thought that we would be troubled about these things, and I tell you my people, and I believe it, it is not wrong for us to get this food. Whenever the seasons open I raise my heart in thanks to the Creator of His bounty that this food has come.

I want this treaty to show the officers what our fishing rights were. I was at the Council at Walla Walla with my father, who was one of the Chiefs who signed the treaty. I well remember hearing the talk about the treaty. There were more Indians there at Walla Walla than ever came together at any one place in this country. Besides the women and children, there were two thousand Indian Warriors, and they were there for about one moon, during the same part of the year as now, in May and June.

The Indians and Commissioners were many days talking about making the treaty. One day Governor Stevens read what he had written down and had one of the interpreters explain it to the Indians. After everybody had talked and Pu-Pu-Mox-Mox had talked, General Stevens wanted to hear from the head Chief of the Yakimas. He said "Kamiaken, the great Chief of the Yakimas, has not spoken at all. His people have had no voice here today. He is not afraid to speak — let him speak out."

Something has been said about more and more whites coming into the Indian Country and then the Indians would be driven away from their hunting grounds and fishing places. The Governor told the Indians that when the white man came here the rights of the Indians would be protected.

Then Chief Kamiaken said, "I am afraid that the white men are not speaking straight; that their children will not do what is right by our children; that they will not do what you have promised for them."

Source: Touch the Earth: a self-portrait of Indian Existence, (ed.) T.C. McLuhan, Abacus, London 1973.

Marlon Brando, Dick Gregory and Jane Fonda were among several well-known figures who, during the late 1960s, wet their hands in support of native American fishermen and women. They hoisted-in nets, in defiance of sportsmen and state authorities, thus ". . . making the Northwest conflict over fish the first widely publicized [US] treaty-rights defense of modern times".[246]

In fact, Indian fisher-people in the north-west USA have been arrested during similar "fishing wars" since the turn of the century, despite the 1854 Medicine Creek Treaty, which gave them the right to fish ". . . as long as the rivers run".[247]

Hydroelectric projects have disturbed the salmon cycle, and commercial fishing (which increased four-fold between 1947 and 1976) has squeezed the native fisheries even further.[248] *By the late 1950s native people were being accused of "over-fishing" although they took less than 1% of the total catch.*

Through the 1960s and 1970s the police harassed the Indians; native Americans failed to obtain any redress through the courts; women joined the struggle — as did Chicanos and Chicanas.

In 1965 the US Supreme Court agreed that Indians could fish at their "usual and accustomed places" but left it to the States to implement regulations. Finally, in 1974, District Court Judge George Boldt delivered an historic — and momentous — decision which guaranteed native fisher-people half the off-reservation fish from sites at which they were entitled to fish when the treaties were originally signed. State law automatically became unconstitutional,[249] *although the reaction from state officials and commercial catchers became increasingly arbitrary and violent.*

Under new restrictive legislation — the Black Bass Lacey Act — arrests of Indian fisher-people mounted during the early 1980s.[250] *In 1983, 19 native fishermen were indicted in Los Angeles, bringing the total of indictments to 170.*[251] *One of these, David So Happy, describes what the federal offensive has meant to him and his Yakima family. His simple, moving, plea is published here together with a Fishing Rights Resolution passed in 1983 by the General Assembly of the Ninth International Indian Treaty Council (IITC).*

In both 1981 and 1985, legislation was introduced to Congress which sought to abrogate tribal fishing rights. It failed to be passed. Meanwhile, the US and Canadian governments, together with 24 tribes, two intertribal fishing commissions and 24 non-Indian organisations, have ratified the US–Canada Salmon Interception Treaty, which is designed to enhance salmon resources in the north-west region, and enable both commercial and indigenous interests to work together.[252]

"All Indians of the Nation on Trial"

David So Happy Sr.

I am happy to be here. It has been a long struggle in the Northwest for fishing rights. I am a traditional Indian. I have been exercising my rights to fish even though I had to go to jail three and four times. I have been indicted, jailed, chained for fishing, but I still continue to live the way Elders taught me.

We must have salmon for our way of life; for ceremonies in longhouse, for name giving, memorials, first food; we must have salmon. That is the way I have been taught.

Unwritten laws govern Indians, laws that Indians live by, our traditional ways, and always make sure one is living in the nature of things. My Elders say "You will see nature take a hand in getting your rights paid for." You see Mt. St. Helens, tornadoes, hurricanes; nature's way of protecting your denied rights.

I have never registered fishing sites, if I applied I would be conforming. I never wanted to move. They never finished their promised projects, like hatcheries and improved runs. Our sites are retained in spite of dam flooding.

Before Indians are stopped for fishing they have to stop everyone else. Right now they got warehouses of frozen salmon for the government to buy and hand out as commodities.

I continue to resist. I've chased wardens. They wouldn't issue my citations but only take my fish, game, and nets. I documented all this hoping to get help to regain what I've lost. Sometimes "law enforcement" comes at night in riot gear, to take my nets. They come in airplanes and boats to take from my home and hold me there. They beat up my boy and took him to jail. They charged him with assault and resisting arrest, and sentenced him to 10 years in jail and 10 years probation.

For fishing, I was sentenced 5 years in jail and 5 years in prison, and my nephew 20 years in jail and 20 years probation. In our defence case they would not allow use of our treaty. We were found guilty of the Lacey Act, that says you cannot sell fish across state lines. They bought the fish just so we could go to jail.

We are religious people. The Elders come and trade for what we use. If we are asked to give fish to longhouse, we give with no profit. White men are making millions of dollars a year fishing. Indians make maybe $40,000 a year with thirty (30) people depending on him.

White men take three days to wipe out run below Bonneville Dam. Other people fish all year around. Before we see 60 pounds of salmon, but no more. Last nine years the run is depleting. How come the government never fulfilled its promises? (The case might be brought to 9th Circuit Court of Appeals.)

Teach your children Indian ways, talk Indian. I went out fishing 30 years ago with my dad and uncles. The women would divide up the fish, and dry it for winter use. We never asked for pay. Do the things that are Indian. I've taught my children how to fish. I can't go fishing because I'm on probation. All Indians of the nation are on trial. My grandfather knew how to be a real Indian, now they don't want you to be one. My stepfather said, "Never let the white people come in and hunt and fish, soon they will start regulating it." I always remember him saying that. All our problems come from money. That is all I want to say for now.

Source: Janet McCloud, 1983

Fishing Rights Resolution

The General Assembly of the Ninth International Indian Treaty Council and its mandated representation to the United Nations, representing 98 Indian nations in the western hemisphere do declare:

Whereas, recognizing the violation of treaty and constitutional rights against the indigenous people of the Pacific Northwest, citing the recent example of Mr. David So Happy, Sr. of the Tiini, one of the Yakima nation and his nephew, and;

Whereas, charging the U.S. government is in violation for making it a crime for the indigenous population of the Northwest to survive in their traditional and aboriginal way of life through the Black Bass Lacey Amendment Act, and;

Whereas, the Black Bass Lacey Act has been found unconstitutional to the international covenant and aboriginal laws sanctioning our inherent right to sustenance, religious and ceremonial use of land, water, and fish, and interference with the commercial trade of our people which the Black Bass Lacey Act makes it a crime for Indians to exercise, and;

Whereas, the Black Bass Lacey Act which is a continued genocidal and criminal act against the indigenous population, our fishing people never being consulted as to how they utilise the rivers and fish, the Black Bass Lacey Act violates its own intention of conservation by the methods of non-Indian use down river; this is a disguise being used to pave the way and promote commercial and corporate interest, leaving our jobless Indian people in starvation, while the commercial non-Indian fishermen maintain jobs as well as profit from our fish as additional gains, and;

Whereas, our elder Mr. David So Happy, Sr. has been convicted and sentenced to 10 years along with his son, who was sentenced to five years and nephew who was sentenced to forty years for being found in violation of their treaty rights to fish, and;

Therefore let it be resolved that we recommend the Black Bass Lacey Act be immediately explored and reviewed fully, as to its final definitions and implications for the Indian people of the Northwest, as well as its applied implications to all other indigenous people of the western hemisphere, and;

Therefore let it be further resolved to intervene in and support the struggle of Mr. David So Happy, Sr. and family to review the court decisions issued against them and his nation, and provide them with a format to develop a new trial that is just and with proper representation, and;

Therefore be it finally resolved to develop an immediate campaign of support for Mr. David So Happy, Sr. and family and to work together to cease this illegal Black Bass Lacey Act before it's used as a precedent against all indigenous people.

In 1981, another virtual war broke out between the MicMac of Restagouche, Quebec, and the Provincial police who descended with riot gear and tear gas to prevent a minor violation of salmon-fishing regulations. Many MicMac were injured during two assaults by the state, but Indians from all over Canada and the USA arrived to stand in solidarity with their threatened sisters and brothers.[253] *Just after the siege was lifted (but without a promise from the Quebec government that no further force would be used) Chief Alphonse Metallic and the Restagouche Band Council issued the following statement:*

"We will meet with the federal government to discuss the protection of our rights and to explain to them our status and rights as nations. We will consider allowing the provincial government to observe the meeting, so that they will come to the same understanding. We are careful not to call these meetings negotiations, because our rights are non-negotiable. It is this misunderstanding of our rights and status as nations that has caused this situation to develop. The Provincial Government does not recognize our status, and are therefore exceeding their authority in attempting to exercise their power within our territory.

It must be understood that the province has no jurisdiction within the territory of the Micmac Nation. The Canadian government never had jurisdiction on reserves, so they could not have passed such jurisdiction on to the province. The Imperial Crown also did not have jurisdiction within our territory, when they formed and granted powers to Canada, so they could not have passed it on. The only people who could have passed our jurisdiction is the Micmac Nation, and this has never happened.

We entered into a relationship and signed treaties, and we have continued to act as an ally as late as the last world war, when we sent 52 of our warriors into battle to defend the Crown. The Crown, in creating Canada, could only pass to Canada those powers, authorities and jurisdictions which it was the Crown's to pass. They did not have jurisdiction over the Micmac Nation's fishing, or any other aboriginal right, and therefore they could not have passed it to anyone.

It will be said that in entering into previous agreements we recognized the provincial jurisdiction, but this is not true. In entering into those previous agreements, we agreed to co-manage responsibly the resources which our people and the province's people share. We are concerned that they do not take more than they need, and we are conscious not to take more than we need, as we have always been. The ultimate decision as to how much fish were taken, how they were taken, or when they were taken, was always ours to make. But as responsible governments, we deemed it wise to co-manage the resources with our non-Indian neighbors.

Suddenly this year the provincial government decided to tell and to order us what to do. They gave us ultimatums which surprised us, because we thought they understood that they could not do this. Then they sent in an armed force among unarmed people and committed many atrocities and crimes. When we realized that they were determined to continue these violations of our national and human rights, we decided to call upon our brother nations to assist us. We have not been a violent or a military people for many years, and we thought that, with the Crown and Canada as allies, we would not need to be. But Canada showed us this week that they cannot be relied upon to protect and defend our rights and territories. This we must do ourselves, with the help of our brother nations.

Until Canada and the provinces recognize the aboriginal nations of North America, incidents of this nature will continue to happen. We tried to tell this to the federal government at the Constitutional talks, but they refused to listen, and still have not recognized our rights in their highest law."

Source: Akwesasne Notes, Summer 1981.

9. Missionaries

A Cross to Bear

> "The Missionaries asked us to look to heaven.
> While we were looking up, the land was taken from
> beneath our feet."
>
> Maori epithet. (Similar sayings are to be found among native
> north American peoples — and, no doubt, elsewhere!)

At worst, missionaries consciously opened paths for traders, raiders and other colonisers to follow, and which have led to the extermination of aboriginal peoples. At best, they elevated the "savage" into a new, purer kind of being than the rabble who poured off ships with their muskets, rum, venereal disease, and smallpox — and thus saved "him" from genocide.[254] Across the middle ground, however, missionaries were usually bigoted, venal, and often treacherous. They protected their wards from the most vicious impacts of colonisation, only to ensnare them with materialism, facilitate the robbery of their natural resources, exploit their labour, divide their families, remove their children and degrade their culture. Most insidious of all, perhaps, they sequestered the roles of shamans, healers and visionaries, sometimes elevating their own proteges to temporal power and dividing native society.[255]

There have, of course, been missionaries and missionaries. The early Jesuits who entered Paraguay offered the Guarani virtually the only alternative to extinction: their mission-run "reductions", where the power of the caciques was nullified, mass was compulsory and labour appropriated. There was no death penalty, however, and the worst punishment was to be thrown out of the Jesuit encampments and into the merciless hands of the Spanish planters.[256] The Puritan John Eliot, in the mid-17th century, was apparently convinced that the "Mohicans" were one of the lost tribes of Israel. He learned Algonquin, converted many Indians, introduced them to reading and writing and condescendingly provided them with one of north America's first reserves: a tiny plot of four square miles for the "Praying Indians". But these, too, had "taken on a protective coloration to avoid extinction", despite their apparent eagerness to surrender their pagan ways.[257]

By contrast, early missionaries in Australia considered the Aborigines accursed. "They are the most degraded of the human race, and never seem to wish to alter their habits and manner of life" wrote the Reverend Samuel

Marsden who became the colony's first assistant chaplain in 1794: ". . . as they increase in years, they increase in vice".[258] By and large Australia's aboriginal people were regarded as cultureless, completely lacking in spiritual endowment, and fit only for the most patronising kind of protection.[259] By the late 19th century, the missions became the chief vehicles for the indoctrination of Western "values" — above all through legislation which authorised the separation of Aboriginal children from their parents,[260] and compulsory induction into mission schools. Many Aboriginal communities forcibly resisted such ethnocide: hence the establishment of church-run penal reserves, one of which — the notorious Palm Island off the north-east coast of Queensland — exists today,[261] if not as a penal colony. In more isolated parts of the country, missionaries were effectively made into policemen by the colonial administration. With a Bible under one arm and a pistol under the other, they were able to imprison, exile Aborigines and use Aboriginal land in any way they wished.[262]

In Hawaii in the early 19th century the Protestant missionaries (adept at driving out their Catholic competitors) firmly allied themselves with predominantly American traders, and initiated a dependence on them by the Hawaiian royal family which paid handsome dividends by the 1850s. For, it was to the missionaries that the King turned when pressured by foreign powers, and it was the God-merchants who helped introduce constitutional rule, an hereditary kingdom and the other bric-a-brac of a patrimonial society. Polynesian polysexuality was banned, native dress replaced by "clothing", and the private tenure of land came to replace a less rigid, more co-operative system practised under the ali'i (chiefs).[263] In the process, the missionaries themselves gained a great deal of land and, despite their attributing all Hawaii's ills to "alcohol and disease" (caused of course by native promiscuity),[264] they were among the primary agents of the decadence they so vociferously attacked.

It is arguable whether much has changed in the past 100 years, despite the impact of "liberation theology", the UN International Covenant of Human Rights (1966) which unequivocally guaranteed the right of all ethnic minorities to practise their own religion,[265] and the World Council of Churches' decision in 1982 to support indigenous land rights.[266]

True, there are notable examples of missionaries — especially Jesuits — risking their lives, and sometimes dying, for "their" indigenous communities, in south and central America and southern Asia. The church in tribal India has, for the most part, been firmly on the side of indigenous rights, though it has been tardy in empowering adivasis to run their own affairs.[267] After two centuries and more of continual missionary influence there are also inevitably many indigenous leaders who uphold Christian ideals in their struggles.[268]

But old habits die hard: more importantly, assets built up on the land and labour of indigenous peoples, are not surrendered easily. In Australia many of the mission stations have now been handed over to Aborigines. But, in one notorious case — that of Mapoon and Weipa — they were surrendered, with little resistance, to the mining company Comalco which then allowed the government to forcibly evict the indigenous occupants (see p. 177). When the Uniting Church finally did support Aboriginal right to return to their tribal lands, two other missions Aurukun and Mornington Island, were summarily taken over by the State Government led by Joh Bjelke-Petersen.[269] *The Uniting Church still holds shares in companies which trespass on Aboriginal land. Worldwide the picture is little different. Indeed, in some respects it is worse. A most scandalous and cynical situation came to light in Paraguay in the early 1970s, when anthropologists Mark Münzel and Chase Sardi discovered that the Forest Aché were being hunted down like animals. Survivors were "looked after" by the New Tribes Mission in conditions of appalling deprivation and degradation.*[270] *Although Münzel did not accuse the New Tribes Mission of direct involvement in the genocide, they were undoubtedly its beneficiaries. A decade later, the photographer Luke Holland found another Paraguayan Indian people, the Ayoreo — also deprived of their land — living in similar conditions of wretchedness and hopelessness. Carted to the NT Mission, the Indians were stripped of their weapons, feathers, woven bags and musical instruments. Many of them simply gave up their spirits, lay down and sickened until they died.*[271] *The NTM mounted a new "assault" on the Ayoreo in 1983.*[272]

Over the past ten to fifteen years a great deal of information has emerged about the activities of these newer, fanatically evangelical Protestant sects (see below). They have been condemned by a large number of liberal and radical theologians: the historic Declaration of Barbados made a special point of opposing their practises (though not mentioning the sects by name) and dissociating what it called "dissident elements within the churches" from them.[273]

Some modern, radical theologians now argue that the distinction between acceptable Christian intervention in native communities, and objectionable interference, is more apparent than real: that the only way Christians (or an outsider of any other faith) can facilitate indigenous liberation is, paradoxically, by renouncing the theocratic basis of their own religion.[274] *Certainly the most recent demands made by indigenous spokespeople — especially native north Americans defending their right to their own ceremonies, their own sacred sites — admit no place even for the most radical of liberation theologians.*

Sago-yo-watha (Red Jacket) was an Iroquois law-giver, whose name in English means "He who keeps us alert". A contemporary observed that he spoke "with a voice as low, as gentle and caressing, as e'er won a maiden's lips".[275] *In the following piece, delivered in 1905, he explains to a young Moravian missionary why he was being refused permission to open a mission on Indian land.*[276]

A great difference between Red and White

Friend and Brother: It was the will of the Great Spirit that we should meet together this day. He orders all things and has given us a fine day for our council. He has taken his garment from before the sun and caused it to shine with brightness upon us. Our eyes are opened, that we see clearly; our ears are unstopped, that we have been able to hear distinctly the words you have spoken. For all these favours we thank the Great Spirit; and Him *only*.

Brother: This council fire was kindled by you. It was at your request that we came together at this time. We have listened with attention to what you have said. You requested us to speak our minds freely. This gives us great joy, for we now consider that we stand upright before you and can speak what we think. All have heard your voice, and all speak to you now as one man. Our minds are agreed. . . .

There was a time when our forefathers owned this great island. Their seats extended from the rising to the setting sun. The Great Spirit had made it for the use of Indians. He had created the buffalo, the deer, and other animals for food. He had made the bear and the beaver. Their skins served us for clothing. He had scattered them over the country and taught us how to take them. He had caused the earth to produce corn for bread. All this He had done for his red children, because He loved them. If we had some disputes about our hunting ground, they were generally settled without the shedding of much blood. But an evil day came upon us. Your forefathers crossed the great water and landed on this island. Their numbers were small. They found friends and no enemies. They told us they had fled from their own country for fear of wicked men and had come here to enjoy their religion. They asked for a small seat. We took pity on them, granted their request; and they sat down amongst us. We gave them corn and meat, they gave us poison in return.

The white people had now found our country. Tidings were carried back and more came amongst us. Yet, we did not fear them. We took them to be friends. They called us brothers. We believed them and gave them a larger seat. At length, their numbers had greatly increased. They wanted more land; they wanted our country. Our eyes were opened and our minds became uneasy. Wars took place. Indians were hired to fight against Indians and many of our people were destroyed. They also brought strong liquor amongst us. It was strong and powerful and has slain thousands.

Brother: Our seats were once large and yours were small. You have now become a great people and we have scarcely a place left to spread our blankets. You have got our country, but are not satisfied; you want to force your religion upon us.

Brother: Continue to listen.

You say that you are sent to instruct us how to worship the Great Spirit agreeably to His mind, and, if we do not take hold of the religion which you white people teach, we shall be unhappy hereafter. You say that you are right and we are lost. How do we know this to be true? We understand that your religion is written in a book. If it was intended for us as well as you, why has not the Great Spirit given to us, and not only to us, but why did He not give to our forefathers, the knowledge of that book, with the means of understanding it rightly? We only know what you tell us about it. How shall we know when to believe, being so often deceived by the white people?

Brother: You say there is but one way to worship and serve the Great Spirit. If there is but one religion, why do you white people differ so much about it? Why are not all agreed, as you can all read the book?

Brother: We do not understand these things.

We are told that your religion was given to your forefathers, and has been handed down from father to son. We also have a religion, which was given to our forefathers, and has been handed down to us their children. We worship in that way. It teaches us to be thankful for all the favours we receive, to love each other, and to be united. We never quarrel about religion.

Brother: The Great Spirit has made us all, but He has made a great difference between His white and red children. He has given us different complexions and different customs. To you He has given the arts. To these He has not opened our eyes. We know these things to be true. Since He has made so great a difference between us in other things, why may we not conclude that He has given us a different religion according to our understanding? The Great Spirit does right. He knows what is best for His children; we are satisfied.

Brother: We do not wish to destroy your religion, or take it from you. We only want to enjoy our own.

Brother: We are told that you have been preaching to the white people in this place. These people are our neighbors. We are acquainted with them. We will wait a little while and see what effect your preaching has upon them. If we find it does them good, makes them honest and less disposed to cheat Indians, we will then consider again of what you have said.

Brother: You have now heard our answer to your talk and this is all we have to say at present.

As we are going to part, we will come and take you by the hand, and hope the Great Spirit will protect you on your journey and return you safe to your friends.

Source: Samuel G. Drake, *Biography and History of the Indians of North America*, pp. 594 ff, Boston, 1851.

Killing from within

"In Tapuruquara, before the missionaries came, there were many Indians. It was like a city in Tapuruquara. Then the missionaries came and began to change the lives of the Indians, interfering in their customs and religion. But the Indians let them stay. Then the priests said that our most important ritual was no good, and they tried to force the men to play the sacred trumpets that were used in the Dabukuri in the church, in front of everyone — women, children, priests. Women and children are not allowed to see these trumpets — if a woman saw them, in the old days, she was killed. The men became very angry when the priests insisted on this, and so they tied them up and put them in canoes to float downriver. They were all washed up on the banks, and returned to Tapuruquara. When they came, it was in revenge. They distributed amongst the Indians clothing infected with smallpox, and all the Indians of that great village at Tapuruquara died. Now there is no village at Tapuruquara."

(Tariano Indian, Rio Negro, Brazil)

". . . the missions kill us from within, because they forget our traditions, culture and religion. They impose upon us another religion, belittling the values we hold. This decharacterises us to the point where we are ashamed to be Indians."

(Daniel Cabixi, Pareci Indian, Brazil)

Source: Survival International Review, Vol. 4, No. 2, Spring 1979.

The most widely criticised of all missionary organisations working among native communities is undoubtedly the Wycliffe Bible Translators, which functions more extensively, and subversively, as the Summer Institute of Linguistics (SIL). It is the largest Protestant missionary society in the world, in terms of members sent abroad, and although some governments have had the strength to send it packing (notably Mexico and Ecuador[277]), it has also crept back, in places. Its bounty of worldly goods, including airstrips, airplanes, seeds, tools, clothes, livestock, sophisticated communications networks and foreign exchange, are resisted by few temporal powers, and indeed used by some — particularly in south and central America — to pave the way towards assimilation of relatively inaccessible forest Indians.[278] Among the earliest indigenous movements to spell out the dangers posed by the SIL was the Colombian Asociacion Nacional de Usuarios Campesinos (ANUC) — for the most part members of CRIC (the Regional Indian Council of the Cauca). In September 1974, the third Congress of ANUC — an assembly of 4,000 people — issued a wide-ranging statement of aims and policy which included an unequivocal condemnation of SIL's methods:[279]

Summer Institute of Linguistics

As representatives of the Indian communities:

1. We remember the role played by the Catholic missions since the arrival of the Spaniards to change our mentality and make us accept the interests of the "civilizados" (non-Indians); destroying our own civilization; opening the way for the "colonos", merchants and rubber-dealers as well as for the government organisations. In many areas they have succeeded in destroying us and have taken our lands, forcing us to seek refuge in the most remote areas of the hills and forests.

2. We study the way in which the evangelical missions and the Summer Institute of Linguistics works. They claim to be interested only in the Bible and come to study our languages. In this way they can penetrate easier into communities which are already forewarned against the traditional methods of the Church.

But in many areas we have removed the Summer Institute of Linguistics from our lands because we have realised that it is they, also, who are destroying our culture, traditions and customs. As well as this they exploit their knowledge of ourselves, of our lands and the riches of our earth in order to help the 'gringos' (Americans or foreigners in general) who follow them to open oil wells, to extract timber and gold etc.

3. The divisions which have been established within our communities, between Indians who adhere to the missions and to the evangelists, is used to keep us distracted, to keep our eyes covered so that we do not see how our real enemies are depriving us and destroying us.

In many areas we have observed that what we need is unity amongst the Indians whether they be catholic or evangelists; and so we have begun to fight in unity to defend our land and our culture. In other communities, as we begin to organise ourselves, we must understand this issue clearly.

4. Our experience has shown us that we should not attack one another because we profess one or other religion. On the contrary we must reinforce our unity and strengthen the organisation in order to win our struggles.

And in the struggle we shall re-discover the roots of our own beliefs and traditions.

Source: "Hacia la Unidad Indigena" ANUC (Third Congress) September 1–4 1974.

In 1980, the Wangurina Federation of Quichua Indians of the River Napo region of Peru also served unequivocal notice on the SIL to get out of their communities. In a letter to the authorities they said:

Dear Sirs,

We have the honour of addressing you in your official capacities to inform you:

That the Kichwaruna Organisation of the Napo would like to advise you, so that you may bear in mind, that we do not want the people of the SIL to come here. That they are the only ones to depreciate the native communities. We are saying this so that you might advise them not to enter this area. They do this on the Putumayo and elsewhere. They forbid some foods and drinks, they make them sing every day, they tell them not to work because the end of the world is coming.

That the Wangurina Organisation says that they do not want these men to come to the native communities.

So we ask you not to permit, under any circumstances, this SIL with its fantastic and fanatic sects to come to the Napo. We already have our religion and that is enough. We also have bilingual teachers approved by the Ministry of Education itself and we do not need them to come here and cause conflict and division because of religion when there is no need to do so. We also have health promoters and we do not want their health workers or pastors disguised as health workers. We, the Kichwarunas of the Napo, are the only tribes undivided by such sects.

We are relying, in this, on the latest Supreme Decree No. 003-79 AA. Article 16 of this regulation concerning Native Communities which says: "To carry out educational or assistance (including religious) activities on behalf of the Native Communities authorisation must be given by the Ministry of Agriculture which will submit the project to the Native Communities and seek their opinion in agreement in their Assembly."

And article 18: "These authorisations will be cancelled at the request of the communities."

The APU-chiefs of the Kichwaruna communities, gathered in their annual congress of April 1979, are in unanimous agreement in stating that we do not want these people of the SIL to come into our settlements on the river Napo.

God keep you.

Source: Survival International Review, Vol. 5, No. 3, Summer 1980.

*Running a close second to the SIL, in terms of the damage to communities,
is the New Tribes Mission (NTM). Founded in 1942 by Paul W. Fleming, a
north American missionary, it has offices in Britain, Canada, Australia and
New Zealand, and headquarters in Florida.*

*Among its earliest fields of conquest were those in Venezuela where, in
1953, it received permission to carry on its proselytizing indefinitely. By
the late 1970s more than 50 missionaries from the NTM worked among the
Yanomami, Ye'cuana, Piarora, Hoti, Guahibo, Panare and Yaruro.[280]
Unlike the more sophisticated and subtle manipulations of the SIL, NTM's
propaganda is the worst kind of tub-thumping and racism. Its methods
were aptly summarised by a group of Venezuelan intellectuals in 1980 as
". . . ethnocide in its most brutal and direct form by seeking to supplant all
the elements and expressions of native cultures by an evangelizing message
that is fanatical, inquisitorial and sectarian."[281]*

*Here, Simeon Jiminez, a Ye'cuana leader and member of the Venezuelan
Indian Federation, describes at length his, and his peoples', experience of
NFM's brand of evangelicism. He concludes with a condemnation of
Christian missionizing in general.*

"The White man is the problem . . . not the Indian"

I have known the NTM missionaries since 1949/50. They came to learn our
language. They didn't do anything at first except ask us questions, such as what is
the word for water, for food, etc. — words for things. They took notes and others
did interviews with cassettes and tape recorders. Thus they learned our language.

About two years after they began, they started to say things. They began to
convert us and to say that "you have to be evangelist because God prefers that and
because otherwise, you are lost. Everything about the way of life of your ancestors is
a sin. Your life is lost. When you die here and go to heaven, God will not receive you
unless you believe in Jesus Christ. You have to be baptized. You have to think one
thought only, in God, and you have to leave behind what you have thought up until
now.

Because, this world is going to end. It could be 4 o'clock tomorrow, or today. One
doesn't know when this world will end. Thus if you do not believe in Jesus Christ,
you will suffer. There will come a punishment and much suffering. There will be
earthquakes and volcanoes will erupt. Swarms of frogs and locusts will come and
there will be great hurricanes. Thus you will die. But you will not die if you believe in
God. Also, the stars will fall from the sky and many people will die. All the waters
will turn into blood, and you won't be able to drink water anymore. That is the
punishment that God will send."

One of our beliefs was directly opposed to what they were saying. Our belief says
that a person has to conduct himself or herself well. A person cannot lie, a person
cannot kill. One has to respect many things in life, and you have to conduct your life
well. This is our belief. Everyone thinks of all men, of all humans as equal. You

cannot make others suffer, cannot take the things of others and cannot lie.

And someone who dies will reach the middle of a road where there is like a bridge. If you feel that no one will condemn you because of what you have done in this life — because you are guilty if you have acted badly in life — then you will reach the bridge that crosses over a ravine. If you were a good person and acted well in life, then you will cross over the bridge with ease.

This was directly opposed to what the evangelists said about a punishment. Because God, in our belief, does not punish you. In our belief, Wanadi, our God Wanadi, does not punish. Because we already know that we are bad, so we already feel guilty. This is the belief of our ancestors, our true belief.

And against that, the evangelists put fear in us and threatened us. As a result, many people began to convert to evangelism and to lie in public by saying 'I am an evangelist' so that the missionaries would treat them well. But it was a lie, one of the greatest lies one could imagine. While they verbally emphasized their faith in speeches or sermons in church, Ye'cuana evangelists were leading a double life. They would pretend they were fulfilling the high morality demanded of them, but secretly do otherwise. This has brought about division, immorality, disrespect and dishonesty amongst us.

Many other things have been abused by the evangelists. They said that everyone is brothers. So, everyone thought that they were now brothers and sisters to each other. Before, they respected one another because there was a system of restrictions for what you could and could not do with your kin and your in-laws. But the evangelists said that everyone was now a brother and sister to each other.

They treated catholics the opposite way from other evangelists. There was a campaign that the evangelist could not be a friend of the catholics. The entire world was to become purely evangelical. Whoever is not an evangelist is not your brother. You have to be an evangelist in order to be their brothers.

It also reached a point where they got power to say who could marry whom. That is another thing that they have controlled. They say that good evangelists should only marry other good evangelists. The missionary has the power to say who can marry whom. This has destroyed our custom because we believed that your daughter can marry whomsoever wants to marry her but that her mother and father are responsible for her. Hence the evangelists have undermined authority.

They have undermined many of our other customs. They said, you cannot consult shamans because the shaman doesn't do anything, and you cannot confide in medicinal plants. You cannot paint yourselves because to do so is bad, a sin. All of that was prohibited. They began to prohibit drinking ceremonial beer and making festivals. All ceremonies were stopped, and we began to feel and think that what we were doing was bad.

Also, our custom is that certain men, the chiefs, were permitted to have two or three wives. My grandfather had five wives. This is the traditional way among the chiefs. Then the evangelists began to prohibit that and to say it was bad. They said that a man could only live with one woman; to have two wives is a great sin. So they said.

As a result, many people and young women especially, were left without the husbands they had. They are afraid of even saying who the father is because they are meeting them, hidden from the missionaries. And the women who have children and no husbands are punished. Sometimes they do not punish a young woman because she belongs to a family or faction which supports the missionaries. That is, if she belongs to a politically strong group in the village (which means being on good terms with NTM), she may be spared the punishment of isolation.

People do not speak to those who are being punished and do not share food with them. They have to live isolated; that is their punishment, until they repent for what they have done and confess their sins in church. Sharing food (and everything) is very important in Ye'cuana culture; thus the isolation is a terrible psychological and social blow to both the punished person and his/her family.

Another thing is that the missionary does not want an Indian, any evangelical Indian, to venture beyond their domain. Because they do not like Indians to be well-informed about the situation in the country and in the world at large. They don't want evangelists to travel at will; that is dangerous for them. They only want to hear you speaking of Jesus Christ all the time. As a result, the Indian becomes stupid because he doesn't know what is happening in the rest of the world. He doesn't know anything but Jesus Christ and God.

In the beginning, they advised against trading with river merchants, saying that what they charged for the merchandise was so high as to be outright exploitation, which is true. But the missionaries did not teach us how to defend ourselves against economic exploitation. They stopped at the level of saying it was bad.

The missionaries also established the practice that anything, such as a new school or a new teacher, all had to be channelled through them. They ensured that they would be the people to talk to the authorities about new positions or any kind of assistance. So, in a way, people have come to associate any new opportunities, any new openings to the outer world, as being brought by missionaries. Evangelical Ye'cuana, even if they don't believe anymore, remain loyal to the missionaries because they identify them as the source of material wealth. All positions, such as teachers or nurses, bring some kind of wealth to the bearers of these positions.

In 1971/72, there were some people in my community who decided to leave evangelism and they told the missionaries so. The people told the missionaries that although they had converted to evangelicism in good faith, this conversion had brought a lot of confusion in their minds. They felt that they were not doing it right, that they didn't understand it well; so it was better to remain as Ye'cuana (which they know how to be) and the foreigners could remain Christian. Not only were the Ye'cuana not being 'good' Christians, but they were always fighting with their relatives, brothers, and in-laws. All these fights brought division and confusion among people. There was no peace and there were always problems.

Then the missionary said that if we left evangelism, he would communicate to the United States to send a plane to bomb our communities. That caused fear and terror among us. Also, he said that the missionaries were there to help the Indian, to protect the Indian, because the Indians do not know how to speak Spanish but the missionaries do, and they have planes and radio communication. Thus they are there to help the Indians, to intervene against communism.

But what help are they giving to the Indians? They are there to live in our name, in the name of the Indians, as a representative, as an ambassador. But what do they do? Nothing. They are writing their own books. They have an easy life. They have planes and yachts; each has a house that cost 300–400 thousand bolivars. When the government questions them, they say they are helping the Indian but I don't know in what. They don't teach us how to work or what to produce. They don't teach us anything about economics. They don't help us to solve our problems, the problems with criollos, nothing. They are not giving us any help; they are only living there in our name, despite the fact that they have already disorganized our traditional life.

They have also brought hepatitis to the Indians. There was a missionary among the Yanomamo who died of hepatitis. As a result, Yanomamo are dying of hepatitis, and those people are already being finished off . . .

In conclusion, I will now speak in general about Christian missionaries. They do not have any interest in the betterment of Indian people. They cut away, piece by piece, so that Indian people become neutralized, like paralytics, with no history, nothing. Indian people have their own culture, their traditions, customs, etc. But Indian people are dangerous to the missionaries becuase they can stand firm on the basis of their own culture. Christianity does not like that. They talk about 'the poor Indian'. Why are we 'poor'? All of this has come about because evangelists have not solved Indian problems. Because Christianity imposes. It says that if you do not have something, you have to buy it. That is not a solution; it only makes you dependent on material things. That is not a solution. Christianity has not solved the Indian problem. Indians themselves have to solve their own problems by themselves. The missionary can do nothing to solve the Indian problem because they impose.

The only people who can help solve or understand the Indians' problems, or give support to the Indians, must feel like the Indians, live with them, share with them, an understanding such as that. Then they can help, because they are with the Indian. It is no solution if you just live with them, eat their food and speak their language, if you do not share with them. Then you are always imposing on them. That is the problem from which all else follows.

And there is something else that I am not in agreement with. Every time missionaries have reunions, assemblies, conferences, etc., they always speak of 'the Indian problem'. Why is it 'the Indian problem'? All Christians and non-Christians alike talk about 'the Indian problem'. Why? Because full-fledged Indian cultures are strong. Their bearers can stand up because they have a meaningful framework to back them up. Neutralized Indians are something different. Indians with culture and a territorial base stand in the way of industrial expansion.

Indian culture has developed to a point where you do not need books or have to spend money in order to study and to learn. Social scientists today, the doctors and technicians, do not want to know how to develop Indian culture because if they know, they feel betrayed, that the Indian will be superior to them. Hence the white man has to study and to analyse. They study for three years or more, and analyse until they die but with no results. Or with only one result, the destruction of cultures and the environment.

Today, everywhere there are indigenous peoples, they speak of indigenous peoples' problems. The problem isn't with us. The problem is with the conquerors, the colonizers. The white man is the problem because they are the invaders. It is not the Indian. The white people must look on themselves as the problem because they are the invaders. It is not the Indian.

Simeon Jiminez

Source: Native People in Struggle, Cases from the Fourth Russell Tribunal and other international forums, ERIN Publications, New York, 1982, pp. 46–48.

One of the most vocal Sami ("Lapp") activists, Nils-Aslak Valkeapää is an artist, musician, and one of the founders of the World Conference of Indigenous Peoples (WCIP). The following extract is from his voluble and entertaining "spontaneous cry of protest", Greetings from Lappland.

Terror in the name of God

There are already accounts of the preaching of Christianity amongst the Samis from the time of Bishop Adelbert of Bremen (1045–72).

When it came to the ear of King Kristian IV of Denmark that there were still heathens in his kingdom, he gave orders, in 1609, that all Samis who could be proved to live in a state of paganism and would not convert willingly should be punished by death.

The Samis had to submit to baptism under a greater or lesser degree of pressure from early on. The Greek Orthodox Church got a foot in Petsamo when the church which Trifoni had built was enlarged into a monastery in the year 1550 (or 1556). At about the same time the Church got a foothold in the west too, when three brothers built a church two miles south of Kalpisjärvi, in Rounala.

The conversion of Samis often involved violence, for the priests hung on to their privileges, disciplined the people with all sorts of weapons, and introduced spirits into Samiland. The best known is probably "Tuderus, Christ's clergyman, hated here in Samiland". He banished the shaman drums. Sometimes he took his wife with him, and had the Samis give her rides and presents.

Even granting the Church the honour of introducing the art of reading, she still has to answer for many kinds of comportment which one wouldn't have imagined were in place in Christian circles. I'm thinking of the last steps the *dačč̆as* took in their policy of impoverishment. As if it wasn't enough that the Samis had been robbed of their material goods; no, to really finish the job, they had to carry out spiritual devastation as well.

Like other *dačč̆as*, these spiritual men also used violence and alcohol as weapons, and a good deal of psychological pressure into the bargain.

This form of terror isn't merely a matter of history, it exists to this very day.

In times gone by people were condemned to death for *yoiking*, and *yoik* is still not accepted amongst the faithful. Just as a lot of other things are forbidden. Television. Fun.

I don't know whether the preachers themselves realize what sort of activity they are engaged in. They used to go from village to village, holding meetings. The sermons lasted for hours, and didn't end until just about the whole gathering was weeping and screaming in wild hysteria.

Since the preachers were spreading God's word, people often gave them the last joint of smoked meat, because it was important that these spiritual men got something. Of course it wasn't payment, just a little gift; God obviously took care of his own. The preachers might easily return from their sermonizing journeys with a great load of meat.

I cannot call the activities which the faithful engaged in anything but terrorism.

Source: Nils-Aslak Valkeapää *Greetings from Lappland*, Zed Press, London 1983.

An ironic twist to the missionary syndrome has recently been provided in western Australia where — with the help of white evangelists and mining company executives — some Aborigines have set up their own mining and real-estate company.

"Mama Guranpa" has been widely condemned by Aboriginal organisations; this declaration was published by the North Queensland Aboriginal newspaper "Messagestick" in 1982.

Does Jesus want us to rape our Mother?

The plans of "Mama Guranpa Company Pty. Ltd." may amount to just that, the rape of our Land for the benefit of a few enterprising evangelists. Read on — you'll love this story and it is one you *should* know about.

On the 6 October 1981, Robert John Brown, Minister of Religion, put his signature to forms 42, 37 and 17 of the South Australian Companies Act — 1962. Benjamin Wangathanu Mason, Minister of Religion; William Lennon, Evangelist; George Cooley, Community Advisor; Kym Phillip Hand, Solicitor; Peter John Daniels, Land Agent (Leading Light in the Festival of Light and Hon. Colonel in the U.S. State of Kentucky); and Robert Brown were setting up a company. Mama Guranpa Company Pty. Ltd. was born 14 October 1981, born too were innumeral problems for the Pitjantjatjara people and Anangu Pitjantjatjaraku.

What Rev. Brown and his mates had formed was a Black Christian Mining Company. Surely such a company could succeed where a White, money-worshipping mining company could not.

It didn't take long for Mama Guranpa Co. to act, because about 4 weeks after the Pitjantjatjara people received freehold title to some of their Lands in December 1981, the Anangu Pitjantjatjaraku (the Pitjantjatjara people's Incorporation), met at Amata to discuss a number of important issues.

Without invitation a charter plane arrived carrying members of Mama Guranpa Co. Pty. Ltd. They were fronted by Benjamin Mason from Kalgoorlie, Robert Brown from Canberra and Bill Lennon from Coober Pedy, all associated with the Aboriginal Evangelical Fellowship, an extreme Christian body diametrically opposed to Aboriginal traditional beliefs. This group proposed that they should take over the responsibility for the supplies to all of the Pitjantjatjara regional stores and communities and in addition, be the developer for all mining and petroleum activities on the Freehold land. Although many of the Pitjantjatjara people are Christian and had some sympathy for Mama Guranpa views, they felt that the company was not appropriate to handle these matters. Many people thought, (hoped), that this should be the end of their dealings with Mama Guranpa — this was not to be so.

At the Aboriginal Evangelical Conference in Port Augusta over Christmas, Mama Guranpa again attempted to sway Pitjantjatjara opinion and circulated a petition which many Pitjantjatjara signed; the signatories, however, were unable to tell us what they had signed and no copy has been left for Anangu Pitjantjatjaraku to examine. Many of the signatories of the petition were older women and young girls.

On a number of occasions, Brown and others have made illegal trips back on to Pitjantjatjara Lands soliciting support for their company and attacking the executive of Anangu Pitjantjatjaraku and its staff as it carries out its work under the statute.

Mama Guranpa representatives have made some extraordinary claims to have millions of dollars of money for investment to back them. Investigations by Anangu Pitjantjatjaraku and the Aboriginal Mining Information Centre shows that they would not have this much in hand, however, they could attract, (and have attracted), some very heavy investors. Investigations of their backers shows some very interesting people. Peter Daniels, one of the directors of the company (a man with some very extreme religious views), is one of the financial backers of this company. He is closely associated with Craig Spiel, a top ranking Liberal Party supporter in South Australia, who has made his fortune in mushroom growing enterprises and other businesses, (he grew mushrooms in cellars and also 2-up games which have been raided by police). He is said to be a born-again Christian. He stood for the Liberal Party for the seat of Unley, twice and has stood for a senate seat once — all unsuccessful. Both he and Daniels are intent on pursuing their interests through, and at the expense of, the Aboriginal People. The Capital of the Company is $10,000 (10,000 $1 shares).

Mama Guranpa which incidently is a Pitjantjatjara word meaning "The Holy Spirit", in fact in this case "God's own Mining Company", has set itself up as an *everything* company. Amongst the many objects for which the Company was established are; Land Agents, Trustees, Mining, Mineral & Petroleum Exploration, Nominees, Financiers, Patent agents, Share Brokers, Estate Agents, Second-hand dealers and more — much more. Object (26) probably explains how much they are into:— "To buy, sell, manufacture, repair, alter, and exchange, let or hire, export, import and deal in goods, articles and things of whatsoever kind". The Company has a Miners Right, No. 5358 for ordinary minerals which is valid until 1984.

The Pitjantjatjara people are becoming more and more anxious about blatant disregard by Mama Guranpa for their Land Rights Legislation. They are entering lands illegally and are drumming up support in a matter which would contract severe fines should any other non-Aboriginal company attempt to use such techniques.

The executive of Anangu Pitjantjatjaraku met recently at Amata to decide what action to adopt over the Mama Guranpa problem. They resolved by an overwhelming majority to proceed with prosecution of Robert Brown and anybody else requiring a permit under the legislation from entering the lands without first obtaining one. It has been resolved that Brown should be prosecuted under the legislation and police have been contacted in relation to this. In addition the executive members of Anangu Pitjantjatjaraku have travelled with their lawyer through the eastern communities holding meetings in each place describing the activities of Mama Guranpa in detail. They have received strong support from the communities to take firm action against Mama Guranpa should they ever come on to the Lands without approval.

Other Directors have recently been appointed to the company. This seems to be an attempt to get some Pitjantjatjara people on to the board of Mama Guranpa.

Take warning, white orientated, Aboriginal religious bodies may try "Mama Guranpa" type tricks in your area. Be careful of those who use God to gain *their* own ends. Be careful of white Community Advisors or ex-community advisors who are bad — most are highly regarded by the communities in which they work or have worked and have done much for the Aboriginal People in those areas. In fact very few have betrayed our people. But it is that high regard that they are placed in that makes them so dangerous when and if they are bad. Only you can know if they are good but you would be wise to watch them carefully.

Beware of the Evangelist movement, their ideas are not Aboriginal ideas because they have foresaken the traditional beliefs of white man's religion. I do not condemn white religion — everyone has the right to choose in what they believe — what is important to remember is that there are some people within the Christian faith that can and will justify the rape of our Land using that faith which *can* be interpreted in such a way that what is traditionally Sacred to us can be destroyed with Christian sanction.

It would be dangerous to go too deep into this part of this subject at this time, as misunderstandings may eventuate and that would be unfortunate. This warning is simply *beware*, it can be seen how dangerous Mama Guranpa is to the Pitjantjatjara people. It is hard enough for the Land Councils and communities to have to deal with the large multinationals and their dirty tricks let alone having to deal with Bible carrying Aboriginal brothers and sisters, or any Aboriginal brothers and/or sisters for that matter, who have totally lost touch with what the Land is to us and would use their colour as if it gave them automatic rights to do what they like, for their own benefits.

Be wise and call on your Land Council and have their lawyers present at any negotiations you have with *anyone* who proposes anything about your Land.

It has been six years since the Pitjantjatjara became actively campaigning for Land Rights, none of these Mama Guranpa people were seen in any way supporting. Less than four weeks after Land Rights were granted to the Pitjantjatjara, the Company has now rushed forward to seek benefits from the exploitation of Aboriginal Land.

Beware of Mama Guranpa, the Aboriginal Evangelical Fellowship, and the likes thereof.

Source: North Queensland Land Council (NQLC) *Messagestick*, Vol. 7, No. 2, April 1982.

It is not only missionaries who have suppressed indigenous religious practise, but also state agencies and, of course, multinational corporations encroaching (often knowingly) on sacred sites (see Part 3, ch. 4).

In 1984 the traditional Hopi people, one of the most spiritually based of all native American communities,[282] *confronted the Bureau of Indian Affairs as it violated their religious freedom and land.*

Meanwhile, native America and Canadian members of the American Indian Movement (AIM) have been denied the freedom to practise their Sweatlodge and other sacred ceremonies, inside penitentiaries.[283] *Itself violating the 1978 American Indian Freedom of Religion Act, the US Department of Correctional Services has maintained that AIM is a subversive organisation, and must be treated as such in all its manifestations.*[284]

This chapter ends with part of a speech delivered by Gerard Wilkinson (Executive Director of the National Indian Youth Council) in December 1982, calling for a new recognition of the spiritual rights of native American peoples.

"What if someone invaded your churches?"

Mr. William Clark   Sovereign Shungopavi Nation
U.S. Department of the Interior   May 21, 1984
Office of The Secretary
Washington D.C. 20240

Mr. Clark:

We, the Traditional Leaders and People of Shungopavi and other Pueblos of the Hopi Independent Nation, are speaking in behalf of our True Leader and Representative, *Kikmongwi*; he is the one who was invested with the Supreme Power and Authority by the *Great Spirit, Massau'u* to instruct us and to make decisions for us of what is right and good for us in accordance with the sacred instructions.

We are all in agreement; we are requesting you to immediately remove from office Mr. Aleph Secakuku, the Superintendent of the Bureau of Indian Affairs Office at Keams Canyon.

Mr. Secakuku is determined to override the protests of the Traditional Leaders and People. He continues to push his projects in our villages, grazing, fencing and paving roads, projects we do not want.

Mr. Secakuku was presented with a petition from the spokesperson for the *Kikmongwi* of Shungopavi and Traditional People against the paving of roads in their pueblo. Mr. Secakuku said, "It doesn't matter. I'm going to do it anyway!"

At Hotevilla and Second Mesa, Mr. Secakuku forced the fencing of their grazing lands, overriding their objections and disregarding their petitions. He said, "I'm willing to take all responsibility."

When work-crews and surveyors come into our village they have walkie-talkies. If we ask them to leave, they call the BIA and police come in to protect the intruders, not the people of the Pueblo.

Therefore, because Mr. Secakuku has absolutely no respect or regard for our most sacred leader, *Kikmongwi*, or Traditional Leaders, or our religion, we want him forever removed from his position as superintendant; we do not want him to be in any position to make decisions for or about us or our lands!

We have written many letters to Mr. Secakuku and others to object and oppose their interference with our pueblo life and we are ignored. They only listen to a small group of dissidents who are attempting to usurp the rightful authority of *Kikmongwi*. They call themselves the Shungopavi Board of Directors; they claim to be working for the betterment of the people, but they were set up without the knowledge or consent of *Kikmongwi* or Religious Leaders. Although they are recognized by the Bureau of Indian Affairs and the so-called Hopi Tribal Council, *they do not represent us!*

We only recognize the clan and religious leaders who were first admitted into the Shungopavi pueblo and who *have made a sacred oath to help Kikmongwi to preserve and protect the Hopi way of life and religion at all times, both now and in the future!*

These *Kikmongwis* have historically been recognized as the True Leaders of the Hopi People. Oliver LaFarge, who deceived the people into accepting a puppet tribal council, said afterward in his report: ". . . the *Kikmongwi* is the true leadership in the conservative villages, seven out of nine . . . at no time is there any doubt in the minds of the Indians as to just who is *Kikmongwi* in a given village."

We still know who Kikmongwi is and we respect and listen to him!

We have resided peacefully upon our homelands for thousands of years; we have been able to provide for ourselves, until you began to disturb our way of life. You know we have our own language, religion, our own traditional government.

Our traditional pueblo is our sacred center, our church, our mother. It is against our religion to have our mother's body desecrated. We do not want water, sewer or electrical lines put into our mother's body. This is according to our sacred law and instructions laid down for us by *Massau'u*.

We know that you have laws that are supposed to protect basic human rights and liberties and to allow for religious freedom, but you have always interfered with our Native Traditional Hopi People's religious freedom! You have recently passed a new law called the "American Indian Religious Freedom Act", (1978) number S.J. RES 102. This law is supposed to protect our right to freely practice our religion. We ask you: Are these merely words again on a piece of paper??? Or will you enforce this law against those like Mr. Secakuku who is violating our exercise of religion??

We know that you too have religions. We ask you. What if someone invaded the sanctity of your churches, and attempted to make

unwanted changes in the structure of your religions? What if
someone with government authority told your priests and ministers
they will not respect their religious authority within their churches?
What would you do? We are merely requesting the same
consideration!

As original indigenous inhabitants of Shungopavi and other
Pueblos, we are still an independent and sovereign nation and
people. We have never made any treaty or agreement with any
nation, including the United States, to cede, relinquish or convey any
of our lands, original rights or liberties. You have forced everything
upon us, tricked and deceived us. Now we feel that we are threatened
with the loss of everything.

We have heard from other Native people that you have destroyed
their traditional life. They report that they have greatly suffered
because of the loss of their land, language and religion. Their
traditional family life is broken down. Many are in prisons, many
suffer from alcoholism and drug use. The men and women no longer
respect one another, children are abused and abandoned.

The United States government, through the Bureau of Indian
Affairs, have created this destruction, through the so-called Hopi
Tribal Council and now the so-called Shungopovi Board of Directors,
groups put in place without the consent of the majority of the people.
We do not recognize the Tribal Council and the Board, who are
leasing our sacred homelands for mining and bringing unwanted
projects into our Pueblo. We do not recognize the many laws, rules,
regulations and guide lines for your programs you say are intended
to benefit and help us. That is your opinion from your perspective.
Not ours.

Our religion tells us to live a simple and hard way of life, growing
corn and praying for rain; you are destroying all possibility of this
with your laws. We are opposed to this destruction of our way of life,
and we are opposed to the forced relocation of the traditional Dine
People at Big Mountain and Teesto, or land exchanges, for that same
reason. We want a total *Repeal* of P.L. 93-531! Our peace and your
peace is at stake.

You must correct, change, stop these actions and put things back in
the natural order before it is too late. We have tried to warn you again
and again that some white men will cause great suffering for all life if
they continue to violate and desecrate the Great Spirit's Laws for this
land and life. Already the forces of nature are hitting your cities and
towns with greater intensity and violence. Big winds, earthquakes,
tornadoes, volcanoes, severity of seasons changing, droughts, floods,
fires, freezing cold weather, blazing heat waves. All your scientists
have not been able to predict these natural forces, nor can they stop
them!

The forces of nature are angry because of all the suffering and
harm your system has caused the true native people of this land,
people who were placed here by the Great Spirit. Whether you
believe us or not will not alter the truth of what we say. You will soon
see for yourself that we are speaking the truth!

We are a peaceful people and we can only bring this to your attention and request in a humble way that you will truly respect *your own laws* and the laws of the Great Spirit, who is the true owner of this land. We are placed here to guard and take care of this land for the Great Spirit and future generations. We can only inform and warn you; after that *it is up to you*! But because this concerns all people living on this land, we also have the duty to publicize and alert all peaceful people of this land and the entire world as to what is happening to us. *You are destroying us! We urge you to stop!*

We are told that it is your duty to keep the internal peace and to watch over your employees that are working for you. That is why we are sending this urgent request to you. We have a long list of grievances and complaints. It is important to you and us that you come to Hopi land, you and no one else, as it is your duty to see and hear for yourself all the problems and suffering your government is causing us!

By Bah Saw Ah.

Signed by four members of the Shungopavi (Hopi) nation.

AIM statements

Gary Butler, an American Indian Movement (AIM) leader, was told in 1983 that he was being transferred from Millhaven penitentiary to Laval (see p. 338). He addressed the Keeper in the following terms:

I understand why you fear me. It is not because i am physically dangerous, but because i work for the people. It is because i continue to speak out about my spiritual beliefs no matter what you do to me. You are afraid of me because you can not break my spirit, but i pray for you . . . Ever since Dino and me came to canada, you people have denied us the basic human right of Freedom of Religion. First in your court rooms where you would not allow the Sacred Pipe to be present. We can not swear on your bible. When the pipe is there, we speak the truth — but you denied us the right to use what the Creator gave to our people as a way to communicate with Him. You denied us our way of life. For this reason we did not present a defense. In your prisons, we have fought for the right to pray with the Pipe, Sweetgrass, Sage, and Cedar. We have fought to have Sweatlodge Ceremonies. You did all you could to stop our words of truth. But you can not and that is why you are afraid. Now you have charged me with suspicion of conspiracy to escape with the use of explosives and firearms or weapons. Reality is that i have escaped before but i have never harmed one person in doing so, including guards. And i have never used outside help which would be necessary to get the articles you accuse me of planning to use . . . I intend to take every legal stand i can. I want you to justify your actions and accusations in a court of law. Because you can not. Ever since i was in what you call canada, you people have put me in a higher and higher security rating. What for? What have i done? All i have done is speak the truth.

Source: Society of the People Struggling to be Free, Vancouver, October 1983.

In April 1984, Leonard Peltier, with two other native American prisoners, began a Sacred Life Fast in protest at conditions in Marion prison, Illinois. This statement was sent as a "request for administrative remedy" to the US Bureau of Prisons at the start of the fast.

The United States refuses to allow me to practice my religion in any form. They do this to me knowing full well that they violate their own laws and constitutions. I have been granted an evidentiary hearing. And the next few months are the most important challenge I have ever faced because I am fighting for my "Freedom"; I am fighting for justice in a country where justice for my people is *nearly impossible* to obtain. Against these impossible odds I can only win if I have the power of *The Great Spirit* fully in my life. You will not allow me to pray with the *Sacred Pipe*; you will not allow me to purify at the Uwipe; you deny me the drum, feathers, rattles, gourds, medicine bag, sage, sweetgrass and everything else that is sacred to me. You will not permit me to pray with my Indian brothers and you will not even allow me to visit with my outside Spiritual advisers except through a plexiglass window and talking over a telephone. My religion is a burning within my heart and the illegal denial leaves a disharmony that can only be remedied by a Sacred Life Fast. Therefore, this is to inform you that on April 10th, 1984 I will begin a ·Life Fast. I will eat absolutely no food until the prison officials remove the ban from the practice of my religion.

Source: Leonard Peltier Defense Committee, Washington, May 1984.

Religious Freedom and Survival

There is no more important issue before American Indians today than the preservation of their rights to worship in their traditional way.

The basic problem arises from the fact that Indian places of worship are natural sites rather than church buildings. These natural sites are now being threatened or destroyed at an alarming rate by economic and tourist developments. If you destroy a church building, as undesirable as that might be, you can rebuild the structure and the worship practices can go on. If you destroy Rainbow Bridge in Utah, a natural sandstone arch used by Indians for centuries, you can never replace it. The religious ceremonies performed there will be gone forever. This has happened already, despite the legal efforts of the National Indian Youth Council (NIYC) and others.

A particularly damaging setback was the loss of the Little Tennessee Valley in east Tennessee. The Little Tennessee Valley is the Cherokee Nation's most sacred area. Cherokees have used the valley continuously for at least 12,000 years. In the 1960s, it was slated to be flooded by the Tennessee Valley Authority's (TVA) Tellico Dam, a $120 million flood control project. The environmentalists filed a lawsuit under the Endangered Species Act claiming that the snail darter, a small rare fish, would be destroyed. The Eastern Band of Cherokees wished to intervene on religious grounds, but they were literally laughed at by the environmentalists.

The environmentalists won their case. However, since many prominent people had bought land cheaply around the valley hoping to make a lot of money when it became lakefront property, Congress acted to overturn the decision. NIYC then filed a lawsuit on behalf of the Eastern Band of Cherokee Indians on religious grounds. We went to the Supreme Court twice but were rejected.

Before flooding the valley, the TVA dug up about 15,000 Indian graves. The Indian remains are now in shoe boxes in the basement of the Frank McClung

Museum at the University of Tennessee. There was also a small non-Indian cemetery of about 300 people, whose remains were reinterred elsewhere. It is ironic that a great many of the Indian remains are more recent than the non-Indian ones they reburied.

After the flooding, the chairperson of the TVA told the *New York Times* that the Tellico Dam was a mistake. Recent efforts to bring tourism to the lake and to attract industry have failed. As a result, the TVA has proposed to turn the lake into a chemical dump.

To the Cherokees, this is the depths of obscenity. It is as if the Moslems had lost their mosque at Mecca to a strip mine or that Christians had seen Jerusalem flooded.

To deal with this situation, NIYC has launched a national campaign to make the public and political decision-makers sensitive to the issue of Indian religious freedom. NIYC is forming a national coalition of church groups, civil rights organizations, Indian tribes and Indian organizations in support of Indian people's rights to worship in their traditional way. We will soon be filing more suits. Model legislation may be introduced in Congress to replace or make functional the American Indian Freedom of Religion Act, which was enacted in 1978 to protect Indian religious rights but which has no enforcement power and has been systematically ignored by the government.

We invite all who live in this land to get involved in the struggle for Indian religious freedom. It is everybody's issue.

As in the time of Columbus, these are hard times for Indian people. But we cannot write off what happened then and what is happening now to the "times". If this planet is to survive, we must make moral judgments on what has been done. People who have been part of the "times" have done this. Pedro Margarit, who travelled with Columbus on his second voyage to the New World, was so outraged by the treatment of Indians on Hispanola that he returned home as soon as possible and denounced what was happening. This incurred the wrath of both church and state, and he died a disgraced pauper. A number of young engineers and executives of TVA have called us to express the anguish they are going through over what the TVA has done to the Cherokees. Until these people are running the world, we have no chance of surviving.

D. H. Lawrence, the English writer, lived in New Mexico for a large part of his life. From his observations of Indians and non-Indians he wrote:

> There it is, the newest democracy ousting the oldest religion. And once the oldest religion is ousted one feels that the democracy and all its paraphernalia will collapse and the oldest religion which comes down to us from man's prewar days will start again. The skyscrapers will scatter to the winds like thistledown and the genuine America . . . will start on its course again. This is an interregnum.

The "oldest religion" and the "newest democracy" are on a collision course. The Pedro Margarits of this world who are sensitive to humanity and believe in justice must join hands with Indian people and actively strive to set a new direction towards respect and brotherhood. I think that this is the only reasonable course for rational human beings.

Gerald Wilkinson

Source: Speech by Gerald Wilkinson to the Indian Rights Association reprinted in *ARC Bulletin*, Cambridge (Mass) Fall, 1982.

10. Schools

We couldn't do anything we wanted. If we stirred ourselves up, they put us down. We were forbidden to go out after classes, and had to be quiet. All the time, they were shouting after us. The master and the Father beat us. We didn't have enough to eat. We were always having to scratch because our wrists and ankles got covered in sores. We were sent to the kitchen to wash the dishes. One day, while I was there, the master entered, pretended not to notice me, approached the cook, and began touching her sex. I didn't know that Whites (*nabe*) were capable of playing with the sexes of women.[285]

The prime method used by missionaries to destroy indigenous culture was schooling: if you couldn't catch the adults, at least you could capture the hearts and minds of the children. In some instances, this meant literally physical capture; in others, blackmail and gross deception.

This is not, of course, the whole story, though it is the fundamental one. Some pupils forged close and affectionate relationships with their mission teachers; others were at least able to speak their own language under the patronage of the church, while government-administered institutions robbed them of the very basis of their "Indian-ness". By and large, however, native spokespeople today reject any form of imposed education. It has become an unacceptably high price to pay for their articulateness in the white world.

Granddaughter of William Longshem, chief of the Soda Creek Indians, and of a part-French ("Meti") paternal grandfather, Mary Augusta Tappage was born in the Cariboo country of British Colombia in 1888.

When she was four, Augusta was taken to the Catholic St. Joseph's Mission in the Onward Valley, near Williams Lake, where she remained until discharged at the age of thirteen.[286] In conversations with Jean E. Speare in the early 1970s, she recalled her conflicting feelings about being a Mission ward. Her own children, Joseph and George never went to school: "taxpayers children couldn't go to the Mission". Instead she educated them herself.[287]

At Mission School

Yes, I remember my days at the Mission school. It was fun, once you got used to it.

I was a small girl to start — I can't remember when my mother dumped me there. I know mama was there with me, but when she left, I never saw her.

There were no Sisters at that time. The Sisters of St. Anne must have shut down, closed down, I don't know why. But that's what they were saying.

When I started, there were white women there. You see, the next time they opened the doors, two white women were teaching us —Mrs. Lancaster and Mrs. Richardson. Mrs. Harry Horne was the cook. They were good and kind. I don't know where they came from to tell the truth, but they stayed and stayed for years. Yes, they stayed and stayed.

The Fathers were there too. I guess they got paid, you know; I guess they all got paid.

The old lady was old — Mrs. Richardson was old. Mrs. Lancaster wasn't old; neither was Mrs. Harry Horne. She used to cook for us, cook for everybody. She used to do it all alone. After she left, the bigger girls took the cooking on, yes. Three of them. One cooks, one serves. I guess one helps peel potatoes and sets the tables and everything.

We went to school in the mornings about ten o'clock. The bell would ring. I would go to school. I would stay there till dinner time. Twelve o'clock.

They taught us everything, everything; reading, writing, figuring — not sewing — no, not during school hours. The sewing was from four o'clock till six. We had to patch. We had to patch the boys' clothes. We had to wash and iron Mondays, Tuesdays. We had to patch and keep on patching till Saturday and all their bags would be lined up. They had numbers, see. They had numbers. Each bag had a number. All the clothes that goes into this bag had the same number. Every pupil a number.

It wasn't bad, patching. But we liked to be out instead of staying in the school.

Now as I see it, as I see it now, I didn't learn enough. No I didn't learn enough. Should have looked after my book instead of closing it when it got hot. I'd close the arithmetic. I'd close the grammar book. And I'd turn my face to the wall. And they'd punish me. They'd make me kneel down in a corner with my book — but I'd never open my book. I'd just kneel there and get punished. Oh, my knees used to get sore, but I never looked at my book, No, not till the next day at school.

We all slept in one big room. Bigger than this house, the room. It took all the children, all the grades. Girls in one, boys in another, sleeping rooms.

The children came from all over the reserves, Sugar Cane, Soda Creek, Alkali, Canoe Creek, Dog Creek, Canim Lake, Quesnel, in those days. Yes. They came by stage if their parents couldn't bring them. Horse stage — the stages, yes, were driven by horses. And they'd get down to the Mission with the stage. If their parents couldn't come, the stage would take them home.

There was no one from Chilcotin, no — too far away, out there, far away.

We didn't have vacation for a long time. They didn't give us vacation. We'd stay there all year. Pick berries in the summertime from July to September. Then we'd go back to school. We'd use the berries at the mission in the winter. We'd be there all winter.

Little kids used to be homesick for their homes. Oh, yes, they used to cry at night. They were small, like this. Toward the end we got used to the Mission, we used to play, recreation time, they called it, all run in the yard and play, run and play, do everything.

I didn't see my mother and father much. Sometimes they'd come and see us. Maybe three times a year. Sometimes we'd get lonesome for them, but what could we do? We couldn't do nothing. No phones, there was nothing those days. Messages by mouth is all.

I guess they missed us, after we grew up. But they never missed us while I was small and useless. I know they didn't, I don't just think so!

It was compulsory I guess in those days to go to the Mission school. It's worse now. Compulsory education everywhere now, you know. They put you to jail if you don't put your children to school, and who wants to be put to jail?

But it was nice.

We had little gardens. They had a board fence around and we used to raise flowers, pansies and sweet williams. I like that. We used to have a ditch full of water running down there, and we'd water our gardens till they bloomed. It used to be nice yes, nice to see some flowers in those dry hills — sand and sage — and then some flowers.

But we didn't have many seeds. Just pansies and sweet williams, but no roses. When the sisters came, they had lilacs. Lots of lilacs. We had to dry up the pansy seeds and save them. The Sister used to make us pick them for her and she would dry them for another year.

It was nice there at the Mission school. I liked it but I think now I didn't learn enough. I didn't keep my books open enough!

Source: The Days of Augusta, (ed) Jean E. Speare, J. J. Douglas Ltd, Vancouver, 1973.

Combating 'Finnecizing': Sami young

Today there are teachers whose native language is Sami, but by no means all of them get positions in schools where there's really a use for them. Knowledge of Sami is not considered a qualification when the school council considers applicants, and teachers with another background may easily be appointed instead of the Sami speakers.

The school inspectors can't be blamed for everything. Often the Sami parents themselves don't want their children to learn Sami. This is the result of the language policy which has been pursued. These parents have themselves had the experience of falling short in competition with the majority, so they want to spare their children the same thing. Many believe that the best thing to do is to suppress Sami in favour of Finnish. The parents' reaction is understandable, but one must put the question of whether society has the right to lead people into such a dilemma.

By the end of the 1960s it was possible to start noticing an improvement in the position of Sami. It has now become a teaching subject in many schools, and there are more Sami teachers. All the same, instruction in reindeer husbandry and in other special subjects could be arranged by appointing peripatetic teachers. In autumn 1970 the State appointed a committee to investigate the school question in Sami districts.

In addition to deficient education, Sami children have to go into the strait-jacket of boarding school life. The staff always come from outside and only speak Finnish. Clothing and conduct are not what the children are used to from home. Boarding school life is so unlike the home environment that it's not surprising if the adjustment process leaves its mark, at worst in the form of psychological disorders. From the point of view of the Finnecizing ideology, boarding schools are an effective means in the struggle against everything Sami. In fact these institutions can even promote a hostile attitude to Sami language and culture.

Great distances and scattered settlements can of course be used as an argument for not extending the vocational schools in Samiland. It gets too expensive. It's also true that a certain amount of courage is required to move away in order to get vocational training, not least for those who have only bad school experiences behind them. All the same, the Christian college of further education at Anar has had every place filled by pupils each year. This shows that despite everything, people do have initiative. If the school had some vocationally oriented courses the number of pupils would probably increase. There can't be any doubt that there's room here for vocational schools.*

Source: Nils Aslak Valkeapää, *Greetings from Lappland*, Zed Press, 1983, p. 75.

*In 1979 a technical college was established at Anar ("Inari" in Finnish). It's purpose is first and foremost to cater for livelihoods in Sami areas, and Sami handcrafts.

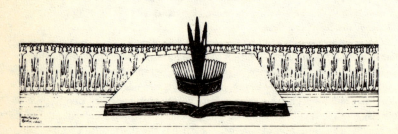

Kept in Ignorance

"There are more and more Whites here in Pond Inlet. Teachers came here. When our children were first made to go to school, we were scared. And I was very scared. Because my child was told he had to go to school. The child I loved so much, when the one I loved best had to go to school, he was so small. Although I really wanted to say no, I said yes. I felt intimidated. The little one had never been away from home. I loved him tremendously. I so wanted to refuse, but I agreed. Because of being afraid. Yes. If it were now, I'd just ignore them. It's as if our minds were weak. Now we're getting to understand it was like this: Those Whites who were often here, policemen and government officials, they wanted to hear the truth about life here. But in those days it seems they didn't tell their superiors. I think they wrote lies and sent them South. We're getting to realise now.

"Yes, that's what we understand about them now. The policemen and traders were like this: they did things here they were never supposed to do. Eskimos were kept in ignorance."

Anaviapik

Source: "Pond Inlet", produced by Michael Grigson for Granada TV in the "Disappearing World" series, Spring 1975.

Annibal Weypygi was about 16 years old when he gave this account of his childhood to a sympathetic priest, four years ago. He was then living at the Chupapou plantation, a new settlement on the Jejui Guasu River, under the Catholic missionaries of the Divine Word Congregation.

My name is Weypygi: I am Âché

My name is Annibal Weypygi. Weypi is a kind of frog, my first name is a White name. I am an Aché-Guayakí, one of the Indian tribes of the country. I like it better when people call me Aché, because that means a person and I like to be treated as such.

I used to live naked in the forest with my parents and other Aché. We lived a good life. In the forest there were lots of things to eat, we ate everything. Our friend the forest offered us all sorts of fruit: palm-hearts, and also meat, lots of meat.

We used to eat, and still eat today, the meat of big and small animals and various kinds of fat grubs such as kracha, pichu, mbuchu, chakaacho.

We were never afraid in the forest for he was our friend and gave us many things, we sold none of those things, we honoured only the spirits "Ajave" and "Werendy" who sometimes would carry away an Aché, then we would fetch him back.

Away from the forest we were frightened for we know from experience that there are people who do not love us, who kill our parents and steal our brothers. Yes, steal. Why and what for? We do not know, we run away from them.

Sometimes crossing the forest we came across roads, then we would follow them. But when we heard the noise of a car or a truck the women would abandon their children on the road and we would run all together. Why did the women abandon their children? Not because they didn't love them, but because we knew all too well that cars move fast but that the bullets from their guns move even faster.

When the noise had passed what did we do? We would wait in the forest and the mothers would return to the road, crying, thinking that their children were no longer there. That's the way it was, that mysterious and terrifying noise swallowed us up.

Every encounter with "civilised" people was a sad one. I don't want to think about it. After one tragedy of this sort we were left very sad for many youngsters were no longer children for they were left without parents, and many women were no longer mothers for they were left without children. We were no longer Aché, we were sad people.

They fired at my father twice with a gun, he has a scar on his left shoulder and another on his left arm. I wasn't even born when he was wounded the first time, but the last time, when he was wounded on the arm, I knew about it all right.

I remember it well, I was walking along with them in the forest. We had walked quickly and a long way, soon I became tired and my father carried me on his shoulders. At the moment of the tragedy I was on my Papa's neck, the gunshot hit him and so he ran off.

Many Aché died after this incident. We had with us as well baby lions, tigers, wild boar and other animals. We left them all behind.

The cause of the tragedy was that we had been hunting the cattle of the Paraguayans. We did not understand why they were so mean about their cattle since we were used to sharing everything we had, and we still do but they do not.

One day, when we lived near the Parana River, some Aché whom we did not know came near to us. They were sent by Señor Pereira from Arroyo Moroti (this we learned later).

Then we left the forest and lived with Señor Pereira. One day we wanted to eat as we used to eat when we lived in the forest, we were still hungry after being given food by our friend. We told Señor Pereira and set off.

We no longer run away from cars but still the White people take advantage of us. One day we were following a road and we met a lorry coming towards us.

My father wanted to eat some bread biscuits. He stopped the lorry and asked the driver for some. The driver was a Paraguayan and first he said to my father, "Give me your son and I will give you this", showing him a sackful. My papa pressed me to go with the man but I began to cry because I didn't want to . . . and I didn't go.

After this encounter we left the red earth of the road, here nobody gives you anything. And we began to walk on the fresh, green leaves of the forest. We killed many tatú, coati and birds.

Then after walking a long time through the forest, we arrived at the house of Señor González at Punto Cuarto. This man told us that very soon the "Apawachu" was coming (this means the "great father", he was referring to Father Nicolas da Cunha, SVD) and indeed he did come. He said prayers, he celebrated the Mass and then we got into his lorry and went to a place called La Paloma. There we met up with various other Aché.

Later we lived in Manduvi and then in "Chupapou" where we are now. Even after leaving the forest, we still are in danger of being treated like animals.

I had a friend of my own age . . . we were inseparable when we were living in the forest. His name was Julio Wachúgy (a deer). He came here with me but then he went off with Señor Benitez to Yvyrarovana, from there they took him away to "Paraguay" (To us that means Asunción but to them it means something else).[1]

I don't know what the price was: usually it is an empty promise and a lie. I never saw my friend again.

And not only Wachúgy but also many other Aché were taken to "Paraguay". On another occasion they wanted to take me too.

I went down to a stream with two Aché to fish. A lorry appeared with some men

[1] Paraguay is a Guarani term and is the name usually given to Asunción. But for the Aché "Paraguay" is not Asunción. For the following two reasons "Paraguay" represents for them some kind of unknown hell: firstly because nobody knows what it is and secondly nobody knows where it is. They know only that those who go there never return. For the Aché "Paraguay" is a spot somewhere in their country but it could also be a place somewhere on their continent.

in it. They called to us. My cousin got there first, his name is Felipe Jakúgi,[2] they lifted him into the vehicle. I wanted to escape and ran away from them. He was taken to "Paraguay" and up until now we have had no news of him.

Source: SENDERO, Asunción, 24 April 1981, translated and reprinted in *Survival International Review,* No. 37, 1982.

[2] Felipe Jakúgi has been in detention for the last 3 years. He is at present in the Borstal at Villa Hayes. He is accused of having committed a criminal act. He is now fifteen years old.

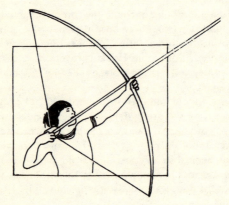

Even before the full force of government-inspired genocide was launched against the Indians of Guatemala, (see pp. 104–15), USAID and CARE-supported castellanizacion *teaching programmes were using Spanish instruction to help wipe out indigenous language and culture. Between 1966 and 1972 less than one-fifth of such classes were bilingual.*[288] *The following account was given in 1968 by a Mayan teacher — the only Indian instructor working in more than 20 national schools in his community.*

We need to teach our people

The basic problem here in Guatemala is one of educating the *gente indigena* (the Indian people). We need to teach our people, so they will be a force to obtain what they want.

Let us say that we want a clinic here. The people know that there is a great deal of sickness, and often they ask: "Why don't we have a hospital?" But, maybe the Minister of Public Health hasn't considered putting a hospital in every community. Yes, he is able, but only with the collaboration of the *pueblo*. For this, the *pueblo* only waits, and as one of the proverbs says: they wait for the bread to fall from the sky. Without work, though, nothing will fall. So we are trying to teach our people to fight, to better the *pueblo* through their own efforts.

The people need to understand. They need to organize into groups, into committees, into clubs for the betterment of the *pueblo*. They must be the ones who do the educating, who give classes in literacy, who resolve the problems of sickness, hunger, and poverty.

Some people here in Guatemala say that this unity that I speak of will come from the school teachers in the national system, from the *magisterio*. In reality, though, I do not believe this.

For many years, I have seen the teachers in the national schools, and now I am the only Indian who teaches in one. For years, the progress of the *pueblos* has been in the hands of these teachers. This is what the Minister of Education says, but I do not know what these teachers are doing. In reality, I haven't seen them do anything. They are only teachers in their schools, in their classrooms. But, a teacher who leaves his classroom, who goes to talk with the villagers or municipal authorities, I have never seen one.

I have never seen one of them say: "I am a teacher. I have the obligation to teach things. Please let me organize a group of youths for this or that." Maybe this happens in other departments, but not here. Here the teachers are like those in San Antonio. "If we teach them," they say, "then later they will command. They will wake up. It is better not to teach them too much."

In San Antonio, I remember the teachers saying: "We should not teach these Indians too much, for they are clever, and they will rise up." This attitude keeps us the same. It keeps us from progressing. "Only teach them a little of each subject," they say. This is the idea, both here and in San Antonio.

When the parochial school began to function here, these teachers felt crushed.

They saw that the Indian students in the parochial school learned well. One time I remember one of my fellow teachers said to them: "You did not want to teach us, but we learned on our own. Now we are going to teach our own children." Tomas had courage. He threw this in the face of the *ladino* (non-Indian) teachers in San Antonio. This is my idea also.

Yes, there are many things which are good about education in Guatemala: the Ministry, the program, the laws, etc. They say concretely that all citizens have the right to education. But, the teachers also have their customs. "Why should we teach them to read?" they say.

Look at the teachers in the villages. Yes, maybe they teach a little now, because they have shame. Maybe, they teach a little. But, take Concho in the village of Nanwits. He is typical. How many students does he have in his school? Four, they say. And, the law says that one should have at least twenty-five students in each school. But, who knows? Maybe, he is tired or lazy, and no one controls him, so he doesn't care how many children there are in his school. Surely, this would be different if the community were made up entirely of *ladinos*. Then, he would really feel shame. But, he doesn't respect the rights of Indians. The rights of Indians to an education.

What we need here are ten Indians like myself, who are teachers in the villages. What we need is a group of residents who are preoccupied with the progress of the *pueblo*. If we had more people who finished six grades of school, and then returned to their *pueblo* to teach, things would be different. If the people fought for Indians to teach in their schools. If there were ten of us in the villages, then things would be different.

But, we must fight for this. We cannot wait, as they say, for the bread to fall from the sky.

Source: Indigena, Berkeley, Fall, 1974, Vol. 1, No. 2, p. 7.

The following letter was written by Saul Rojas Panduro on behalf of numerous Shipibo and Conibo Indian communities in Peru, represented by the Agrarian League of Juan Santos Atahualpa, of which Panduro was president in 1978.[289]

It is a retort to statements by Dr Gabriela Porto de Power, representing the right-wing Popular Christian party, which were delivered to the Constituent Assembly.

Education for inferiority

1. Dr Porto declared that in frontier areas of the forest, where there were five or six potential pupils, schools should be set up.

In the province of Coronel Portillo there are several Native Communities recognised by the State – including Sipiria, San Juan, Fatima, San Fernando de Vainilla, Aruya, Jaticza (Amahuaca), Nuevo Peru, Atahualpa, Samaria and Nueve de Octubre. These communities have, through the combined efforts of their members, built themselves schools, each providing for over 40 pupils; and incurred considerable hardship in order to pay for the teachers. This situation is the result of the refusal of the Education Authority to appoint any teachers, on the grounds that the State cannot afford to pay for such things.

2. Dr Porto presumably possesses a "culture far superior to that of our native populations". She ought to know that, although Europe tried to impose, by brute force, its culture and civilisation upon Latin America, the era of barbarism instigated by these "cultured" people did not possess the spiritual force necessary to destroy the indigenous culture of *Tahuantinsuyo* (the Andean Indians) which survives, waiting for changes in the social, economic and political situation which will give it the opportunity to develop. Our condition is similar. We were conquered by the fire and sword of the *Huiracocha* (white man) who tried to impose on us his customs, language and mercantile practices, at the same time as he irresponsibly exploited our natural resources. With the passing of the years the white man has changed his tactics. Instead of murdering our brothers physically, and buying our women and children as slaves for his homes, he now makes us work in return for a pittance, or nothing. We have been left hardly any trees for our canoes, the pools and even the rivers are emptied of fish, and there are hardly any animals left to hunt. Whatever "civilised" name is attached to it, it cannot be denied that mass-murder is slowly being perpetrated.

3. Dr Porto reduces our problems to the need for education and linguistic training. This scheme oversimplifies a complex phenomenon. Although we know that education and language can provide us with vehicles for the expression of ideas about freedom and oppression, the education provided by the white man is designed to convince us of the superiority of his culture, to accustom us to a

feeling of inferiority, to devalue us, to categorise us even lower in the social scale, to label us, to destroy us as a group – which must result in the permanent dissolution of any sense of collective identity.

4. Dr Porto's arguments are alien to our experience. Although we have been educated as white men, we possess a level of culture without which no white man could survive in the forest. We know how to hunt and fish, and to apply medicines of which you know nothing. We know the forest as the townsman knows his streets: and we are convinced that it is not education or the use of Spanish that will resolve our problems of hunger and misery. We look on, with distress and mounting anger, as the arrival of the white men on to our land destroys the life of the community; every day more of our people starve and more become sick from diseases which were virtually unknown to us until they were introduced together with the culture and civilisation of the white man. For these reasons, we can have no faith in the solution proposed as "National Integration and Culture", founded, as it is, on the assumption that the Indian is inferior.

5. The problems of the forest and the native peoples call for a deeper analysis. We believe that our active participation in the discussion of this problem is essential – although, probably, we will be denied the right to have any ideas on the grounds that we are illiterate. That is why we hasten to declare that we do have ideas – how to build our houses and boats, how to fish and plant, forecast the weather, cure diseases, distinguish a good white man from a bad and judge whether particular work imposed on us is likely to be beneficial or harmful. We have had long experiences of the white man and the *mestizo*, which is why we wish to be no longer their slaves but only their friends. But, for that, fundamental change is required – not intellectual change, not the learning of their concepts and language, and especially not the establishment of schools for five or six children and the refusal of teachers for Native Communities with more than 40 pupils.

Source: This statement was originally published in *Marka*, Peru, November 1978. Trans. Stephen Corry.

Two years later native teachers were removed by the Peruvian Ministry for Education from Shipibo-Conibo schools. Supported by Survival International the community protested against the arbitrary action. The offending teachers were replaced by bilingual instructors.
The Shipibo-Conibo wrote to the President thanking him for his intervention but warning that the struggle was far from over.

A different process of extinction

Caco-Macaya 14 April 1980

Mr President,

We are writing to you to acknowledge and thank you for your effective action regarding the replacement of our bilingual teachers. The letter you made known to public opinion and to the Government of our country, the Minister of Education and Mr Carlos Moreno Quinones himself, had the desired effect, which shows how timely it was, for the teachers who had been discharged in an assault against our culture are now back at their jobs.

This, Mr President, is the reason for our letter, together with the desire that our relations be permanent.

Traditionally, our problems have not been known, not even by our Governments themselves who, because they did not identify us, years ago fiscally exterminated many native groups of our jungle; the process continues even today, although in a different way. Today extermination is manifested by the violations of our culture and the Government's refusal to acknowledge that as far as language is concerned, our country is multilingual.

Mr President, we wish to express our continued concern regarding the attitude of the Minister of Education of our country in promoting Professor Carlos Moreno Quinones to the position of Regional Director of Education for all the Loreto District, since we are sure this is part of a Government plan.

Mr President, we would appreciate your making our problems known and supporting us in our future struggle to defend a bilingual form of education such as the programme drawn up by the Sixth Education Region.

We also wish to submit our protest against the Bilingual Education policy laid down by the Summer Institute of Linguistics (SIL). We will fight so that this Institute, which does so much to harm our culture, disappears from our country. It works in accordance with the interests of North American capitalists who sell us an education that doesn't consider our customs, in exchange for spying on and appraising our natural resources so that they can later remove them when it fancies them.

We also denounce Multinational Firms that attempt to enter our jungle and those that already have reserves in it, such as Occidental Petroleum, and Belcon Petroleum in Madre de Dios; the Pacocha industry, a subsidiary of an Imperialist Yankee Firm that has obtained "reserves" in the San Martin District; and the Indu Peru Firm that comes in Peruvian disguise but we know they are Imperialist subsidiaries that want to take possession of the riches of our Ucayali river.

We denounce these things before you, Mr President, in order to make our voices heard and we reiterate our desire to make our relationship a permanent one.

We take this opportunity to assure you of our highest consideration.

Yours faithfully,
Gilberto Silvano González, Secretary , LAJSA.
Saul Rojas Panduro, General Secretary, LAJSA.

Source: Survival International Review. London. Vol. 4, No. 3, Summer 1980.

11.   Racism

There is an anti-imperialist analysis which sees racism not so much in the contemporary context of competing social groups as in the historical context of naked aggression, the theft of land and resources, and the demands of the slave trade.[290] In this view, the Spanish Conquistadores, who ravaged central and south America, and the English, Dutch, Portuguese and French who plundered their way into other territories in the "New World" actually constructed what we now term "racism". Assisted by devilish clerics and pseudo-philosophers, they could justify the wholesale slaughter of indigenous peoples, the seizure of their gold, spices, crops, medicines, women, children — above all their land and sacred places — by arguing a savage, sometimes satanic, divinely-ordained difference in the people they encountered.[291] Only in areas where native labour could be enslaved was it appropriated, and its traditional forms adapted to suit the convenience of the colonists; thus giving rise to the encomienda *system through ladino-ized America between the 16th and 19th centuries.[292] Elsewhere — in territories where indigenous communities proved more intractable — the fire and the sword, later the musket and gatling gun, wiped the landscape clean both of its inhabitants and their agriculture, enabling the settlement of millions of black labourers ripped from their own tribal communities in West Africa.[293]*

Thus, the early centuries of colonialism were not simply a trilateral trade between three continents, resulting in horrors of which the academic world has long been broadly aware. More accurately, there was a quadrilateral process, to which the destruction, terrorising and colonisation of indigenous peoples were paramount. The reason Western history books — even enlightened ones — rarely tell the true story, is simple: in areas where there was the greatest concentration of enslaved African labour, such as the Caribbean, the original inhabitants were among the first to be eliminated, in all but a few strongholds.

This historical experience of racism-as-destruction (physical, cultural and economic) rather than exploitation (of labour, fertility, political aspirations) means that there is comparatively little analysis by indigenous people of racial discrimination in the sense understood by black and Asian communities. What has emerged is strong and incisive: especially from urban Aborigines who know that they are disregarded, impoverished, spat upon and sometimes murdered because they are black, as well as being Aboriginal.[294] This is stated, so clearly in "Blackism . . ." that any further comment would be superfluous. Following this is an account by Lionel G. Lacey of his experience "Under the Act" — the Queensland Aborigines Act — which immediately evokes conditions governed by the infamous contract labour system of South Africa.

The black power movement in north America and Western Europe has not always been regarded favourably by indigenous people, including black Australians.[295] Nor have black African states exactly rushed to the support of indigenous movements or their land claims.[296] The reasons for this are complex, and certainly include a lingering suspicion that indigenous peoples would settle for a form of apartheid in meeting their demands for self-determination, or hold back modernization of the industrial economy, by "returning to the earth" rather than organising on the factory floor. (The first misconception is firmly rebutted by Pat Dodson in the contribution which follows.)

By and large, then, condemnations of racism by indigenous communities have been subsumed under declarations against genocide, land-theft, forcible sterilisation — in other words, as an assault upon culture — or (as in the case of the Yellowknifer newspaper editorial, condemned by the Dene *Native Press) on identity.*

Land Rights and Apartheid

It is an anti-Aboriginal political tactic to suggest that Aboriginal Land Rights is a version of Apartheid. It is as despicable as it is clever.

Worse is the often confused and defensive response often exhibited by non-Aboriginal people. It makes us both angry and ashamed that other Australians are not quick to defend our right for separate cultural development, one that is recognised as essential in any multi-cultural society.

Apartheid is a word for a gross and cruel system where power is distributed on the basis of race.

Apartheid is a dictatorship designed to protect a strong, wealthy and privileged minority from the legitimate needs of the majority it oppresses.

Apartheid is a way of putting a wall around the privileged few and attempting to justify this dictatorship in the name of religion and racism.

Land Rights protects the numerically weak against the strong. It is the antithesis of Apartheid.

Land Rights gives to us, Australia's indigenous minority, a way of fending off cultural genocide, of protecting the few against the onslaught of the many.

Land Rights is not a privilege but a belated and limited measure of justice. It returns to us some of the land that was brutally taken from us. After 188 years of massacre, dispossession and neglect, the *Aboriginal Land Rights (Northern Territory) Act, 1976*, was the first and only bi-partisan, national recognition of our prior ownership of the Australian Continent.

Land Rights is about justice and life. Our land is our life. It is the basis of our cultural, social, spiritual and political systems.

We, the custodians of the oldest living culture on Earth, have prevailed against all odds. Land Rights gives us a chance to rebuild and regenerate from the ravages of the last 200 years. Land Rights is partial compensation for the Apartheid-like practices of Australia's colonising governments. Land Rights gives all other Australians the chance to come to terms with the past, and gives Australians the opportunity to make justice the basis of this country's nationhood.

It goes without saying that present day Australians cannot be held responsible for the initial injustices suffered by Aboriginal people at the hands of the initial non-Aboriginal invasions. But there is a clear obligation on non-Aboriginal Australians to ensure that our rights continue to be recognised, and that no government or vested interest group is allowed to turn the clock back or to continue the process of dispossession and alienation that has befallen us since 1788.

As the Western Australian Chamber of Mines anti-Aboriginal campaign clearly demonstrated, ignorance can be quickly fanned into prejudice and racism. The only defence against this is education and knowledge.

And now all Aboriginal people face another million dollar disinformation campaign from the Australian Mining Industry Council. The benchmark rights, so far only achieved in the Northern Territory, are the focus of this unscrupulous campaign.

The Public will be told that we are privileged, that we lock up the land, in short that the small measure of justice we have achieved must be taken away.

But what is the real situation?

The 1976 Act gave Northern Territory Aboriginal people the right to a title over some lands called "inalienable freehold" — this means the land cannot be bought or sold.

This title was immediately given with respect to land that governments had "reserved" for Aboriginal people — mission lands and other reserved areas; many had become concentration camps for thousands of dispossessed people. This land comprised 19% of the Northern Territory. It is the most unproductive land in the Northern Territory.

The Act also meant that any "unalienated" crown land in the Territory could be claimed by us, if we could prove our cultural and spiritual bonds to this land. "Unalienated" simply meant land that no-one else wanted — not governments, pastoralists or the mining industry.

Thus, in this most secular country, a court to test religious beliefs and affiliations was set up to determine the grant of title to Aborigines. As a result, a small fraction of the land we belonged to for 40,000 years was returned to us.

The 1976 law also had a vital built-in protective measure. It gave us the right to control entry to the land we regained —that like other private land we could refuse entry, not by trespass notices as the pastoralists do, but by asking outsiders to apply for permission. The penalty for being on Aboriginal land without a permit is the same as that under the *Summary Offenses Act* for trespass on private land.

Most importantly of all, the Act gave us the right to say no to tourist, mining or other development, where it is not worth the resulting cultural dislocation, or to negotiate the terms and conditions under which such development would take place.

If development did seem worth it, the Act gave Aboriginal traditional owners the ability to bargain with equality, to meet the outside forces of capital and enterprise on an equal footing.

And if Aboriginal decision-making in this area was deemed not to be "in the national interest", the law said the Australian Government can override their decisions. In fact Aboriginal people do not have the final veto at all — the Australian people have it through the Federal Government they elect.

In short, the law which finally recognised our prior ownership and right to restitution gave us rights over strictly limited areas of land and has built-in mechanisms to balance the interests of the ruling government.

Indeed, it guaranteed the preservation of mining interests on Aboriginal land at the time the 1976 Act was enacted. The delays in dealing with these prior interests are in large degree the result of administrative arrangements made by the Federal Government and the Northern Territory Government, particularly the decision to impose a moratorium on the processing of exploration licence applications. This moratorium which was not lifted until 1982 meant that exploration applications were frozen by the government for six years.

In the meantime negotiation took place between the Land Councils and those with prior interests on Aboriginal land over the terms and conditions for exploration and mining. These negotiations have been satisfactorily concluded without the need for arbitration.

The moral value of the 1976 Act lies in its attempt to correct the first gross injustice, and this far outweighs its practical implications.

I believe the forces lined up against us are dangerous, not only in the immediate sense, but that they represent a challenge to moral fabric of this society.

Apartheid exists in South Africa, because enough people believed in its dictatorial and basically fascist philosophy. Concepts of justice, fair play and democracy, have not been the priorities of enough South Africans.

Australia, one of the world's wealthiest countries, is being put on trial. In its own backyard is our third world, one where the greatest hope is Land Rights, and with it the dignity to exercise control over our lives, and regenerate our cultural and spiritual lives. This hope for Land Rights is in the face of Aboriginal adult morbidity rates 20 times higher than non-aboriginal rates (the highest in the world). This rate of morbidity is similar to that as experienced by such impoverished countries as Haiti, India and Bolivia.

Australia, like any nation with a history of colonisation, and invasion, is morally bound to come to terms with us, the indigenous people.

The history of this colonisation is only just becoming known. It was denied for hundreds of years, and based on the convenient legal fiction that Australia was "terra nullius": an uninhabited land.

The British used this to justify massacres, to deny re-telling the stories of the forebears heroic guerilla warfare against their invasion. There are no war memorials to our people who died defending their country.

Indeed when we were the majority, and ruled by a non-aboriginal minority, the practices were those of Apartheid. Our people were separated out, put into "black areas" run by missions and government superintendents. Children were taken away from their parents and raised by institutions.

Immigration, massacres, decimation from imported diseases, reduced us to a minority, but it has not reduced the justice of our call for recognition, restitution and justice.

The British and other migrants who have come here since, have exercised a free choice. They are not like the first uninvited wave of colonisers.

They have come here in the knowledge that the basis of race relations in this country is unreconciled and unresolved.

To the extent that this represents a free choice, there is a responsibility on all Australians to ensure just reconciliation with the rights of us, the prior owners of this country.

In fact, our so called "special" position in this country, is that of being the only indigenous people living in a former British colony where there has been no proper national settlement with us.

And what partial restitution there is, is under ferocious challenge by vested interest — many of the multi-national companies with no stake in Australia's long term future.

Groups such as the Australian Mining Industry Council use their financial muscle to use the media to tell to other Australians that our rights claim to justice is somehow a threat.

But 95 percent of the land available to claim is desert or wetlands, places where few non-aboriginal people can live without air conditioned life support systems.

Our land makes up around 23 percent of the Territory's barren areas — and we are a quarter of the Territory's population. Elsewhere in the Territory, cattle properties, owned by about 50 families and 200 companies, cover 52 percent of the Territory.

Land Rights does not threaten one centimetre of private land anywhere in Australia.

Where our land includes National Parks, it is leased back to governments for all people to enjoy.

If mining companies want to mine our land, they are required to negotiate with that land's traditional owners, but they are forced to do so on an equal footing, and required to respect our right to say no.

It is this the mining industry has decided to put on public trial.

At stake is our just demand right for restitution, justice and cultural survival. Their demand is that, in place of this, Australians give the mining industry an unfettered right to develop, exploit and destroy.

The debate will determine moral fabric of this society, and indeed whether Australia is able, with any credibility, to challenge the ideology of any other country's racial policies.

Pat Dodson

Pat Dodson is chair of the National Federation of (Aboriginal) Land Councils.

This article is reprinted from *CARE* (Campaign against Racial Exploitation) *Newsletter* No. 74, Adelaide, December 1985.

"Without stereotyping, racism has no basis"

'Politicians responsible for "cold air"?' was the cute headline over an editorial in the August 25 edition of the Yellow-knifer newspaper. And what followed the title was another attempt at humour, a purportedly tongue-in-cheek comment on an August cold snap that brought snow to the territorial capital two days in a row.

The premise of the would-be joke was that native politicians were "with-holding" Indian summer and importing snow and cold from the high Arctic to Yellowknife in order to "put the pressure on for the settlement of land claims" and to force acceptance of the Denendeh proposal for public government.

It is probable that there was no conscious malicious intent behind this ill-conceived piece of fatuity. Nevertheless, no matter what the intentions of the writer, the editorial was racist primarily because it re-inforces and perpetuates a stereotype of native people.

Now, a stereotype, in this instance, is the image that one group of people has of individuals from another group. That image may have some small basis in reality, or rather a group's perception of reality, but it is usually grossly over-simplified and distorted.

There are two basic stereotypes of

native people popular in North American culture. One is the stereotype of the "noble Redman", the primitive who lives in harmony with nature. You've seen these guys in the movies. Chief Dan George played one, Old Lodge Skins, in the film Little Big Man.

And the other stereotype is that of the sneaky, guileful savage who is dishonest, treacherous and just basically can't be trusted. You've seen guys like this too. They're the ones who, after they have been invited inside the fort to receive gifts and smoke the peace-pipe, pull the Winchesters out from under their blankets and murder all the trusting settlers.

The editorial refers to native leaders as "culprits" and describes Dene Nation president Georges Erasmus as "cunning" and "the one behind it all". What native people are doing to Yellowknifers is called a "conspiracy", "attempting a new ploy" and "all this trickery".

Every one of these words is heavy-laden with connotations of deceit and/or wrong-doing. Granted, any one of these words by itself might not amount to much but when you string them all together, they carry a certain weight. They help to keep alive the image of the sly, duplicitous "redskin".

And to perpetuate a racial stereotype is to perpetuate racism since without stereotyping, racism has no base. How would it be possible for a bigot to hate every Black, for instance, as an individual?

A sad footnote to this is the degree to which a lot of native people have swallowed the stereotyped definition of who they are. It's not so surprising, I suppose, given the pervasiveness of the images. Interestingly, the "good Indian" stereotype seems to be gaining in popularity these days in some circles but it doesn't cancel out the damage wreaked by the negative image. It only works to a different end, assimilation rather than exploitation.

The editorial writer sees native people as a clannish bunch who stick together since, basically, they are all the same. Don't think so? Check this out. Quote: "Erasmus, Stevenson *and company* . . ." and ". . . *such people* as Richard Nerysoo and Jim Bourque." (Italics mine).

In this editorial it is taken for granted that they will know exactly who "and company" and "such people" are. Since their nativeness is the most salient feature for the editorial writer, what else could those phrases mean but all the rest of the Dene and Metis?

So what's the matter? Can't we take a joke? Well, a joke is one thing and a racist joke is something else. Freud has posited that humour can be used to mask aggression. And there is certainly evidence to suggest that is what is happening in the Yellowknifer editorial.

The closest thing to a punch-line in the editorial appears in the final paragraph: "As we write this the sun is peeking out from the clouds; the wind is dropping. Could it be that both warmth and sanity are returning to the north or are we just being buttered up prior to the imposition of a permanent freeze on everything?"

"A permanent freeze on everything" alludes to the slowdown of economic development for which the native people are seen as being responsible. And in the view of the editorial writer, it is this "freeze" and not the snow and cold weather that is causing Yellowknifers to "suffer most". So the real thrust of the piece is an attack on native people who, because of their recalcitrant attitude towards development, are causing Yellowknifers to suffer.

O.K., a foolish editorial in the Yellowknifer is scarcely on the order of the gunning down of Black teenagers in Soweto or the virtual genocide being visited upon the indigenous people of the Amazon rain-forests. But those violent acts of racist oppression have their basis in the same types of attitudes expressed in the editorial. Simply put, those attitudes are that native people are all the same, that they stick together and that they are somehow responsible for the problems of the non-native community.

These attitudes don't belong on the editorial page of a newspaper. Or on any other page, for that matter.

Source: Native Press, 10 September 1982.

Blackisms

Black is, being an expert at the pick and shovel.

> **Black is,** being lied to by Gubbs in as many ways as possible.

Black is, not knowing what the Governments next promise will be.

> **Black is,** being called "boy" when you're over thirty years of age.

Black is, going to Camp Jungai and having whites cook for you and loving it.

> **Black is,** having a Gub marry you so they can get the $1,500 housing grant.

> **Black is,** being adopted as a child, and kicked out as a teenager.

> **Black is,** knowing this land is our land.

Black is, a way of life.

> **Black is,** no one caring.

> > **Black is,** an enemy of capitalism.

> **Black is,** paying twice as much as Gubbs.
> **Black is,** getting twice as little as Gubbs.

Black is, something you will never get out of your system.

> **Black is,** being born a fighter and dying a fighter.

> > **Black is,** wearing chains that are invisible.

> **Black is,** never having to get a suntan.
> **Black is,** watching Gubbas get sunburnt and loving it.

Black is, making do with what you've got.

> **Black is,** owning Australia and having to pay rent.

Black is, never having a full garbage bin.

> **Black is,** hating Captain Cook.

> > **Black is,** being called Jacky.

> **Black is,** always having an open house.

Black is, always knowing you are being stared at.
Black is, lending a helping hand.

> **Black is,** wronged at white schools but righted by experience.

Black is, being barred from hotels, bashed by pigs and having our land taken from us.

> **Black is,** standing up for our rights.

Black is, living in Fitzroy and labouring in Toorak.

Black is, getting knocked down but getting up again.
Black is, taking a risk of a fat lip if you open your mouth.

Black is, realising at an early age that you will never be Prime Minister.

Black is, crying when you see some other black trying to be white.

Black is, being sued for trespassing on your own land.

Black is, knowing you're right but told you're wrong.

Black is, having a communal wardrobe.
Black is, smoking on the sly.
Black is, not being seen at night.

Black is, "being put down", but always getting up and having another go.

Black is, sitting around an open fire and sharing a drink.

Black is, fighting for what's right.
Black is, understanding each other.

Black is, not a colour but a way of life.

Black is, a never ending struggle against white's so called supremacy.

Black is, never wasting bread on suntan lotion.

Black is, some Gub saying that you're not because they can't notice it.

Black is, being loved on Cummera and hated in Canberra.

Black is, to want and fight.

Black is, being told you've got enough and still having a hungry gut.

Black is, always having a full teapot.

Black is, bashed by whites then thrown in jail.

Black is, wearing hand-me-downs and being put down.

Black is, barracking for the Indians, and booing John Wayne.

Black is, being tried by twelve white people and told that you are receiving justice.

Black is, knowing that (John) Batman was Robbin' (our land).

Black is, going to white school and coming home again no wiser.

Black is, talking a lot, but nobody listens.

Black is, always looking behind you.

Black is, knocked back for a job and called a bludger when you're on the dole.

Black is, never having any friends except for your cousins.

      Black is, having a crowded car.
      Black is, opening a new packet of cigarettes and closing with two left.

Black is, seeing Robbie Muir (Mad Dog) bashing the Gubbs at their own game.

      Black is, respecting your elders and listening and learning.

            Black is, identifying with brothers and sisters.

      Black is, being hassled.
      Black is, defending your own.
      Black is, knowing the struggle to survive.

Black is, talking to the press but never getting it said.

      Black is, being put down but always getting up and having another go.

Black is, to die fighting.
Black is, to know how to love.

      Black is, sticking together when the chips are down.
      Black is, always hoping for a better day tomorrow.
      Black is, living in a tent in Canberra.

Black is, loving thy black brother and sister.
Black is, being lost in their own land.

      Black is, mutton flaps every Sunday.

Black is, wanting to be a boxer, knowing its one way of being able to legally punch up a Gub.

      Black is, Lionel Rose winning the world title.
      Black is, me.

Source: Mureena (Aboriginal Student newspaper) Vol. 2, No. 2, Sydney, December 1972.

Jerry Gambill, a Mohawk scholar and former editor of Akwesasne Notes *described how to "recuperate" the Indian in a speech delivered at a conference on human rights at Tobique Reservation, in August 1968. Introducing this succinct and witty appraisal to a north American readership in 1972, Shirley Hill Witt and Stan Steiner pointed out that the earliest laws prohibiting marriage between whites and non-whites in America were applied against Indians, not blacks. "Since the 1600s the legal and social acts of discrimination originally established to exclude Indians have served as the basis for many racist practices facing new minorities".[297]*

Similarly, the Queensland Aborigines Act (revised, refined and enhanced in the 1970s) initially inspired early discriminatory legislation against blacks in South Africa.[298]

Although the Queensland government proposed cosmetic "liberal" changes in the early 1980s, life on the reserves remains substantially as described by Lionel G. Lacey in the following piece.[299] Robert Smallwood, a prominent member of the council of the Yarrabah reserve in north Queensland then pinpoints a specific aspect of white rule in Queensland — the payment of discriminatory wages — which bears clear comparison with labour practices in South Africa.

Twenty-one ways to "scalp" an Indian

Methods must coincide with the type of problem and, in the case of human rights, the reception or resistance which the majority have toward your aims. The Indian has problems peculiar to *Indians alone* and deals with a very receptive society.

The Indian's problem in solution has much of its roots in a lack of communication. As soon as the Indians become articulate enough as a people, and signs indicate they are fast becoming that way, their aims will become clear and society will become receptive to our wants.

One fact is clear to the Indian. He does not go where he is not wanted. You can't force people to accept you. Nothing is ever gained by anything destructive. At least, if acceptance is what you are seeking.

The Indian's interests are locked within himself, his proud past, his country, and his own destiny as shaped by himself.

Being other than white isn't common cause enough to justify civil disobedience.

The art of denying Indians their human rights has been refined to a science. The following list of commonly used techniques will be helpful in "burglar-proofing" your reserves and *your rights.*

Gain the Indians' Co-operation — It is much easier to steal someone's human rights if you can do it with his **own** co-operation, so . . .

1. Make him a non-person. Human rights are for people. Convince Indians their ancestors were savages, that they were pagan, that Indians are drunkards. Make

them wards of the government. Make a legal distinction, as in the Indian Act, between Indians and persons. Write history books that tell half the story.

2. Convince the Indian that he should be patient, that these things take time. Tell him that we are making progress, and that progress takes time.

3. Make him believe that things are being done for his own good. Tell him that you're sure that after he has experienced your laws and actions that he will realize how good they have been. Tell the Indian he has to take a little of the bad in order to enjoy the benefits you are conferring on him.

4. Get some Indian people to do the dirty work. There are always those who will act for you to the disadvantage of their own people. Just give them a little honor and praise. This is generally the function of band councils, chiefs, and advisory councils: They have little legal power, but can handle the tough decisions such as welfare, allocation of housing, etc.

5. Consult the Indian, but do not act on the basis of what you hear. Tell the Indian he has a voice and go through the motions of listening. Then interpret what you have heard to suit your own needs.

6. Insist that the Indian **"Goes through the Proper Channels"**. Make the channels and the procedures so difficult that he won't bother to do anything. When he

7. Make the Indian believe that you are working hard for him, putting in much overtime and at a great sacrifice, and imply that he should be appreciative. This is the ultimate in skills in stealing human rights: When you obtain the thanks of your victim.

8. Allow a few individuals to **"Make the Grade"** and then point to them as examples. Say that the "Hardworkers" and the "good" Indians have made it, and that therefore it is a person's own fault if he doesn't succeed.

9. Appeal to the Indian's sense of fairness, and tell him that, even though things are pretty bad, it is not right for him to make strong protests. Keep the argument going on his form of protest and avoid talking about the real issue. Refuse to deal with him while he is protesting. Take all the fire out of his efforts.

10. Encourage the Indian to take his case to court. This is very expensive, takes lots of time and energy, and is very safe because the laws are stacked against him. The court's ruling will defeat the Indian's cause, but makes him think he has obtained justice.

11. Make the Indian believe that things could be worse, and that, instead of complaining about the loss of human rights, to be grateful for the human rights we do have. In fact, convince him that to attempt to regain a right he has lost is likely to jeopardize the rights that he still has.

12. Set yourself up as the protector of the Indian's human rights, and then you can choose to act on only those violations you wish to act upon. By getting successful action on a few minor violations of human rights, you can point to these as examples of your devotion to his cause. The burglar who is also the doorman is the perfect combination.

13. Pretend that the reason for the loss of human rights is for some other reason than that the person is an Indian. Tell him some of your best friends are Indians, and that his loss of rights is because of his housekeeping, his drinking, his clothing. If he improves in these areas, it will be necessary for you to adopt another technique

of stealing his rights.

14. Make the situation more complicated than is necessary. Tell the Indian you will have to take a survey to find out just how many other Indians are being discriminated against. Hire a group of professors to make a year-long research project.

15. Insist on unanimity. Let the Indian know that when all the Indians in Canada can make up their minds about just what they want as a group, then you will act. Play one group's special situation against another group's wishes.

16. Select very limited alternatives, neither of which has much merit, and then tell the Indian that he indeed has a choice. Ask, for instance, if he could or would rather have council elections in June or December, instead of asking if he wants them at all.

17. Convince the Indian that the leaders who are the most beneficial and powerful are dangerous and not to be trusted. Or simply lock them up on some charge like driving with no lights. Or refuse to listen to the real leaders and spend much time with the weak ones. Keep the people split from their leaders by sowing rumor. Attempt to get the best leaders into high-paying jobs where they have to keep quiet to keep their paycheck coming in.

18. Speak of the common good. Tell the Indian that you can't consider yourselves when there is the whole nation to think of. Tell him that he can't think only of himself. For instance, in regard to hunting rights, tell him we have to think of all the hunters, or the sporting-goods industry.

19. Remove rights so gradually that people don't realize what has happened until it is too late. Again, in regard to hunting rights, first restrict the geographical area where hunting is permitted, then cut the season to certain times of the year, then cut the limits down gradually, then insist on licensing, and then Indians will be on the same grounds as white sportsmen.

20. Rely on reason and logic (your reason and logic) instead of rightness and morality. Give thousands of reasons for things, but do not get trapped into arguments about what is right.

21. Hold a conference on **Human Rights**, have everyone blow off steam and tension, and go home feeling that things are well in hand.

Jerry Gambill

Source: Akwesasne Notes, Vol. 1, No. 7, July 1979.

Life under the Queensland Act

> *I come from Cherbourg Aboriginal Reserve, about 200 miles from Brisbane, Queensland. I would like to tell a little story about how the Queensland Acts affect me and my people.*

Well, in the Reserve or community there has to be a white manager. We have one on Cherbourg. The people have got to see the Manager if they want a job, because he says and tells you where you will work. When I was little I knew the Manager was the boss because he had an office of his own and I used to see my uncles and aunts or some other blacks sitting outside for hours. They were waiting for him to call them in. Then he would ask them questions like: What can you do? How long did you go to school? Who do you live with . . . ? and so on. The people would wait for something like two weeks and then he would give them jobs like Hygiene or some other shit job that pays $24 to $42 per fortnight.

On Cherbourg there are things that are really bad, like the people have only the right to vote for two of the Aboriginal councillors. But the big man, the Director (Pat Killoran), who is white, can appoint three councillors of his choosing. If the Director doesn't like the two Councillors that the people pick he can then appoint all of the councillors.

At Cherbourg there was, and still is, hardly anything to do. There is no pub, no pool tables, no swimming pools. In the law of the Queensland Acts, no grog is allowed on the Reserve anyway. When I got a job the pay was $24 a fortnight. A lot of people will say that things have changed now. Well things may have changed a little bit in the cities, but on the Reserves the country blacks are still pushed down and can't control their own affairs and the wages are still the same. The wages might have been raised by $1 to $2, but this is fuck all. There are still bad housing conditions, and medical [treatment] and education are not given to us in the way that they should be given. The Queensland Acts are fucking our minds, we don't know which way to move.

When we go away from the Reserve into the city, when we want to come back home the whites put the laws in the way, like you have to have a permit to go back on the Reserve. If you learn something from the city or are involved in the Black Power movement, you will not be allowed back home. Why? Because the white man is scared about blacks learning about how to fight these laws. The white man wants to keep control because there is profit in it for him, and also he thinks that blacks are like kids and cannot control their own affairs.

The white Manager is there to explain to the Aboriginal Council about the laws; in other words, to set up Uncle Toms. Uncle Toms love their controller and will do anything for the white man. The Council on the Reserves are Uncle Toms. Also the Aboriginal Council is there to keep control of the black police. Some of the laws are worth looking at.

One law is "That a person shall not carry tales about any person so as to cause domestic trouble or annoyance to such person." That means to me that I can't joke about my mates or talk about the whites that live in good houses and get good wages and good food, while we have fuck all.

Another law is "That a person using a gate or any other opening in a fence, capable of being closed, shall close it unless instructed by an authorised person to leave it open." First of all, in most Reserves the only decent fences and gates are those that are around the white Manager and staff houses.

Then there is the law "That a person swimming or bathing shall be dressed in a manner approved by the Manager." What it means is that before a black person can go down to the creek for a swim he has got to stand up in front of the Manager to get approval of what clothes he or she is wearing. We couldn't afford to have good swimming togs anyway because of the wages.

We have got to get permission to use electrical goods, such as a hot water jug, electrical radio, iron or electrical razors. Also no person on a Reserve can ever own their own home; this will always be owned by the Director. So if a wife and husband are asleep in bed, the Director has the power to wake them up if he wants to. One law is "That parents shall bring up their children with love and care and shall teach them good behaviour and conduct and shall ensure their compliance with these By-laws." What right have these bastards got to tell us blacks how to live our lives? When you look into the Queensland Acts it is very hard to understand. Just think how hard it is for us blacks to understand when most of us don't even know what is in these Acts. We are just forced to live under them. We have got no right to the land as far as the Director and others think; they own every square inch of it. .

Under the Queensland Acts they even have the right to shift us off the Reserve and our homes, if they want to. And they do it. In North Queensland at Mapoon in the Cape York area, they forced the black people off Mapoon with guns. The people went back last year, though, to reclaim their tribal land. This shows that some blacks are starting to wake up to what is going on and are fighting against it.

When a black person is born in Queensland the Director has the full power to decide everything that will happen to that child. I only just mentioned a few of the laws. There are hundreds of laws just like the ones I said. They have put it in their language and so it is very long. With these Queensland Acts we are never treated like people, we are treated like animals. I remember that we never saw anyone except for the tourist buses full of whites that used to come around to have a gig at us.

Blacks all over Australia have had demonstrations and have written things about these Acts; some people have gone to jail too, over these Acts. People have fought on almost all angles and got the support of some whites to try to get rid of these Acts, and bring about awareness to everyone about what is happening. But as soon as blacks do these things, the Government sends in the police to jail them or frame them up. I was framed up by the pigs because I was fighting against these Acts and spoke to a lot of people about them.

The Government and all the white bosses don't want the people to know about the shit conditions that blacks are living in. The Queensland Acts are still there. Blacks are getting killed, raped and pushed down every day because of it.

This is our land. It was taken off us and we want it back. We want to have control over our lives instead of some pig pushing us down or some white Manager or black Uncle Tom telling us what to do. We must push up now. We will keep on fighting anyway. I hope you understand it a bit more too, because it is very hard to write about the Queensland Acts. What I wanted to do was to give you a feeling to get up and fight against them now.

Lionel G. Lacey

Source: Cheryl Buchanan, *We have Bugger All*, The Kulaluk story, Black Resource Centre Collective, 1974.

One of the prime measures of discrimination against blacks on Queensland Reserves has been the payment of wages which fall well below the level set by the Federal government. The Queensland government, until 1979, chose simply to ignore the ruling.[300] *That year the Industrial Court in Canberra ruled that the treatment of Aborigines must not differ from that of whites in this regard. The Queensland government simply retorted that it could not find the money.*[301] *The Australian Council of Trade Unions also came out in support of the Aborigines of Yarrabah — the Queensland Reserve which had been the source of the original protest — and demanded a year's back pay.*[302]

In August 1983, the Canberra-based Human Rights Commission confirmed that Australia's 1975 Racial Discrimination Act continued to be violated, because award wages were not paid on reserves in Queensland, and when they were, conditions applied to them were not always observed.[303]

In September 1979, Robert Smallwood, one of the Yarrabah workers subject to this blatant discrimination, addressed a letter to "all members of trade unions in Melbourne" after his own union, the AWU, had failed to support him and his fellow black workers.

"We are only asking for support"

To all members of Trade Unions in Melbourne   17 September 1979

We, the members of the AWU on Yarrabah Reserve, North Queensland, request your support in our struggle to get award wages for our people. The Queensland Department of Aboriginal and Islander Advancement [DAIA] claims that we are working under a Training Wage Program and therefore it does not have to pay us full wages. Yet there are no instructors and we work 48 hours a week.

On 19 and 20 July, 15 of us joined the AWU believing we would have the same benefits as any other AWU member. On 23 July 11 of us were sacked and a further two were sacked on the following day. On 2 August we were reinstated at the old wage of less than half the award rate.

On 6 August the AWU agreed with a decision of the Queensland Industrial Court that the DAIA, our *employers*, should do a survey on Aboriginal reserves in Queensland *to find out who is entitled to be paid award wages*. Also they have agreed not to let any more aborigines on reserves join the AWU until after an agreement has been reached with DAIA.

The AWU agrees with the *false* statement from the DAIA that if they paid us award wages then there would be mass sackings of Aborigines on reserves as they claim they can't afford it. Yet to pay all Aborigines on reserves award wages would only cost the Queensland Government 1/5th of one percent of their total budget.

We still have to pay full prices for all commodities. We don't get enough wages to clothe and feed our children properly.

Unfortunately, as we have never received a proper wage, we have no strike fund to support ourselves and our families while on strike. Also, if we are sacked, which is quite likely to happen, there is a waiting period of 3-6 weeks before we can receive unemployment benefits. We do not like to ask for financial assistance but we will be in serious trouble if we go out on strike without financial support.

We are only asking for support the same as any other union member in Australia is entitled to.

Robert Smallwood.

Blacks who stand up with pride, stand up and fight against racism such as that contained in the Queensland Acts, are described as "violent" no matter what they've done. When the Gwalwa Daraniki Association fought for the Kulaluk land claim a few years ago they answered the accusation of "violence" this way:

The real violence

"People have said that the Gwalwa Daraniki wanted violence. Violence, they say! These same people who for years and years have continued to keep their feet on the backs of black people, these same people who let our babies die at a rate faster than any other country in the world, these people who tell us what we should do, where we should live, how we should live, who give us wages that makes sure that we starve, that our bellies are pinching, these people who make us live in houses not fit for pigs let alone people, who treat us like dogs, who are nice to us if we wear the right clothes and talk proper English, and stab us in the back when we aren't looking, who keep most of our people locked up in prisons for many years for crimes caused because of frustration with the white man. These people who rape our culture, take photos of us throwing boomerangs, doing corroborees, singing, smiling, then take them to their nice cosy homes and laugh at us. These are the same people who have to hide to scream — *violence* — who say, 'We do so much for those natives, they just don't want to learn', and wonder why we hate them.

"Let me say this, brothers and sisters. When an Aboriginal man or woman cannot walk into a hotel or a shop or anywhere without getting stared at, without getting called, 'black bastards, coons, heathens, savages, lazy, shiftless, stupid, dirty, filthy niggers' — this is *violence*. When every day of our lives black people are made to feel that we are 'inferior' to white men and women, when every day some black person is thinking 'When are we going to get some food for our children', 'Why don't they give us jobs', 'Why do they call us names', this is *violence*. When black children have to go to school to learn that Captain Cook discovered Australia — this is *violence*. When black people of this country are put onto Reserves and told what to do and how to do it by the big white boss, when black people have to drink in separate bars — this is *violence*. When black people go to jail and get a sentence of three years, five years, or whatever for doing little more than trying to survive — this is *violence*. As soon as they see that black face you can be sure that those magistrates will send you to jail, 'to teach you a lesson'. No matter what they say, they are the ones that are using the *violence*."

Source: Cheryl Buchanan, *We have Bugger All! – the Kulaluk story*, Race Relations Department, Australian Union of Students, Carlton, 1974.

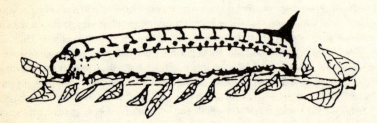

Nazis fleeing from Europe are not the only "refugees" to have found a welcome in Bolivia in recent years. In 1977, the Banzer dictatorship's Under-Secretary for Immigration, Dr Guido Strauss (his forebears are German) announced the government's intention to encourage into Bolivia ". . . a large and important number of white immigrants . . . especially from Namibia, Rhodesia and South Africa."[304]

These 20th century vortrekkers, it was envisaged, would take over large tracts of land in the eastern half of the country, drawing on cheap labour from the Indians.[305] In the event, the scheme fell through — but no thanks to the chief "protectors" of Indians in eastern Bolivia, namely the foreign missions including the Summer Institute of Linguistics (see chapter 9).[306]

This monstrous proposal was greeted with alarm and anger by indigenous organisations. The Council of Amaut'as and Coordinating Centre of the major Indian group, MINK'A issued a trenchant condemnation which took the opportunity to vilify racism at both ends: in southern Africa as well as Bolivia itself.

Kollasuyu: No to the Racist Invasion

The timely publication by brave people in the oral and written media, and the statements made by intellectuals concerned with the Indian and *mestizo* peoples of the Kollasuyu region, warn us against the sinister conspiracy, the countless shady deals and contemptuous remarks set forth by our European-minded enemies who, in order to save their distant racial cousins who are finding themselves in hot water in Africa because of their racist intolerance, want to transplant "apartheid" into the very heart of this dark skinned continent, thus worsening our social and economic situation by sending us the burden of the most hard-line racists in the whole world.

This new assault by the inheritors of the times of hatred on the Indians (peasants, miners and factory workers) forces us to raise our voice in protest, calling on public opinion in the free countries of the world, on international organisations who watch over human rights, on public and patriotic institutions, on students and academics of this country, asking them to express their viewpoint and say if this is not an invidious new invasion by racist Europeans.

Nature has arranged for every ethnic group to have its place of origin and every colour its continent: America belongs to the American Indian, Africa to the black man, Asia to the Mongol and Europe to the white man.

Being the inheritor of the slave-based Roman Empire, Europe has produced monstrous racial theories and invented death machines; its thinking is ethnocentric and racist, its science is the nuclear bomb, and its culture, wars.

The Mongolic peoples, directed wisely by people of their own race, have become considerable powers in a short time, being able to sing hymns of victory over their white European and North American oppressors.

The peoples of Africa show us another example of great physical and spiritual struggle for their total liberation from European racism.

However, the peoples of indigenous America have had a very different experience, because ever since that *day of misfortune* occurred we have been living between the Devil and the deep, blue sea; either relegated to indigenous reservations (anthropological parks) or assimilated with the white minority, impotently mourning the physical extermination of our people, the destruction of our monuments and the murder of our *mallcus* and *amaut'as*.

For the indigenous people of the Kollasuyu region, the War of Independence, which has been so effusively praised, was no more than a pantomime civil war between Creoles and Spaniards, in other words between children and their parents. Thus, the foundation of the Republic of Bolivia meant a mere change of label to the Colony and imposition of new masters, with the resulting senseless bloodshed of Indians and half-breeds on the battlefields. In fact, to the Creoles it was enough to declare political independence from Spain, and the Republic has not, for over a century, begun to see the social and economic liberation of our indigenous and *mestizo* people.

For more than 300 years of colonial rule and over 150 years of Republic, in other words for 500 years of exploitation and robbery, racism and genocide, the Spaniards and the would-be Spaniards have kept our country in a shameful state of backwardness; and now, to cover up their total incapacity, this "ruling class so proud of its white Spanish ancestors" is brazenly granting itself another span of between 400 and 500 years to develop Bolivia by the arrival of 150,000 Anglo-German families from Southern Africa.

To this generation of outsiders, who once more have released their hatred against the Indians, we say:

Is Bolivia backward because the Indians are lazy?

These gratuitous slanderers of ours know nothing of the history of the Kollasuyu region and Bolivia; they do not know that it was the Aymara and the Quechua who built up great empires based on a philosophy of equality, and that Spanish barbarity demolished them. They are unaware of the fact that the *mit'ayo* [Indians conscripted for work in the mines], *yanacuna* [Indians conscripted for work at the farms and plantations of the conquistadores] and *obrajeros* [craftsmen] have accumulated wealth for colonialist Spain and for the mine-owners and feudalist landowners of the Republic. At present, we, the Indians, are forced to work at the bottom of the mines, are scattered all over vast cotton fields, exploited in the sugar-cane plantations, kept in confusion in the factories, segregated in the cities and confined to inhospitable border tracts.

The Indians living in the cities make the machines go round in the factories, pave the streets, build the roads, sports grounds, skyscrapers, villas, etc., enabling others to use and take unfair advantage of the fruits of our constantly underpaid labour. To tell the truth, *in Bolivia the Indians are the only ones who work*. So what is then the reason for the backwardness of Bolivia? — It is the constant surges of *colonialists* who have come to this country as *technical experts* to plunder our rich resources and take advantage of our extremely cheap labour.

Indians cost more than beasts, for they eat more and work less?

Another example of incredible ignorance, another insult made up by some racist colonizers who are handling public affairs in this country as if it were their personal property. Anywhere in Bolivia it is only too easy to watch ordinary people, seeing the pain of men and women who are always hunger-ridden, starving and undernourished children and old people striving to keep their humanity afloat begging alms of those they happen to meet. Evidently the Indians are in no way favoured by the State, so — who is spending money on them? Why do some people boast about keeping well-fed but lazy Indians? The Indian peasant has been the object of economic exploitation and fragmentation of his farmland, and the Indians living in the cities constantly face underemployment and undernourishment — can't they see that the Indians subsist only thanks to coca leaves and papaya, bread and bananas?

The immigrants will bring new blood to the human capital of this country?

Those Anglo-German potential immigrants from Africa are not going to contribute with one drop of their blood to the human capital of this country, for ethnically speaking they are fanatical *racists*, in social terms they are a *caste*, politically they mean *apartheid*, and on the moral level, South African laws punish with imprisonment mere sexual relations between persons of different races.

Why do some want to give the eastern paradise to strangers?

The northern part of the province of La Paz, the Chapare region of Cochabamba, the Izozog and other regions of the eastern paradise, all of which have been made accessible thanks to the unpaid labour of our Indian soldiers and equipped with the resources produced by our brothers working in the mines, factories, agriculture, the oil industry, together with Indian and half-breed professionals — *that land is ours*, it was defended by our fathers in wars with other nations; that land is in store for us and for our children and *never* for other undesirable people to come and set up their own garden of Eden in the territory that we have made sacrifices for.

Do we need racist colonizers?

The English Mennonites who have a colony in Vallegrande have been given a vast farmland area on which they are making a fortune. What have these people with their anachronistic and racist lifestyle done to deserve being presented with this "promised land"? They have transferred no technology and certainly made no capital investments to develop Bolivia; they exclusively employ their earnings in making it possible for their fellow Mennonites to come over and settle down as they are thrown out of other parts of the world.

"Thanks to the Japanese to whom we owe the virtue of having become consumers of our own rice"? — To those alienated groups who believe this kind of thing we say: the Aymara, Quechua, and others have colonized Caranavi, Santa Fe, Chapare, Alto Beni, Yapacaní and many other regions without any protection whatsoever, and now we are able to enjoy a great variety of products; what great achievements could we not reach if only we had the moral and material support! For how much longer are we going to hear foreign virtues being praised and only contempt for the creative and productive capacity of our people? There is also the invidious colonization of South Koreans in our cities, who monopolize the black market, and the few German immigrants who are fortunate enough to be endowed with large cattle ranches and farming estates in the eastern part of Bolivia where our Indian brothers and sisters are being exploited (Camba, Mojo, Chiquitano, Guarayo, Ayoreo, Chiriguano, etc.).

How can the Bolivian Government continue to allow dangerous *small states of expatriates* to be established in these territories which are notoriously coveted by the sub-imperialists of Brazil? At this present time they still want colonization to take place with none other than those distinguished *representatives of apartheid* that are the Anglo-Germans who are to receive the eastern paradise pretending to be *agricultural experts*.

Why is nothing done to make return possible for those of our people who are living in foreign lands?

Thousands of Bolivian families have emigrated to neighbouring countries, to the USA and Europe, due to lack of farmland, places to work and to the absence of guaranteed civil rights, and so they create shanty towns and offer their cheap labour in factories, on building sites, at sugar harvests, etc. Instead of facilitating an invasion of undesirable people, the Bolivian Government should seriously endeavour to bring our people back to the place where they belong.

The Altiplano (high plateau) and the valleys are over-populated, and in agriculture a total fragmentation of the farmland into tiny lots has taken place as an effect of the Agrarian Reform, and the only hope lies with a systematic transfer of the labour force to Eastern Bolivia. Why have the requests of those peasant organizations which have applied for the permission to colonize land there been turned down? What have citizens of foreign countries done to deserve being presented with extensive farming estates in the hot valleys and in Eastern Bolivia?

If Bolivia has vast unpopulated regions and does not have a sufficient population, what aim is birth control then meant to fulfil?

We know the Anglo-racist policy of McNamara, President of the World Bank, who has expressed the following opinion: "*The population explosion* (of Indians and half-breeds?) *Is the greatest obstacle to progress in Latin America*", and he goes on to announce that "*in its granting of loans the World Bank will give priority to the countries which implement birth control schemes*". So we know why McNamara and Kissinger visited Bolivia and later decided to lend millions of dollars to our country.

In fact we do know that Bolivia does not have a sufficient population, but why then can the dismal hosts of the Peace Corps, Friends of the Americas, Food for Peace as well as other groups and religious Protestant sects, operate as they wish and please in the campaigns to sterilize women and children under the labels of vaccination and philanthropy?

We have had enough of *gifts from the people of the United State of America*, such as vaccines, food, and especially sterilizers about which Lyndon Johnson in his wisdom stated, "*five dollars invested against population growth are more efficient than a hundred dollars invested in economic growth*".

To the best of our knowledge it has been scientifically proved that all mankind (including the racists) are born with a creative ability; only the white racists, however, think that their race has the key to cultural development, or that we, only by intermarrying with them, can improve our quality as human beings. This way of thinking is a totally outrageous offence to the dignity of our people.

America is Amerindian — there is **no room here for the white racists.**

Remembering Tupac Katari, we say: better die than carry on living on our knees.

Chuquiapu, June 1977
Council of Amaut'as
Centro de Coordinación y Promoción Campesina MINK'A
La Paz, Bolivia.

Source: IWGIA Document No. 30, Copenhagen 1978.

The use of "Native-American"

The single most oppressive reality facing native peoples in North America has been the conscious and persistent unwillingness of United States people to recognize that native people are members of native nations. The argument that native people are not members of their own nations has long been used as a rationalization for the denial of native rights to land, water, and a way of life (and livelihood). In fact, the legal machineries of the United States and Canada have asserted repeatedly that native peoples either do not have status as nations or that their nations exist in a special relationship to the United States under which all rights to land and resources and even culture is less than those rights would be to any other people. There have even been standing policies in this hemisphere that assert that native people are not legally human beings because they do not possess a status as recognized nationalities, and therefore have no rights whatsoever.

Young people in the United States need to be sensitized also to the racist policies which have oppressed native people throughout the world, and encouraged to be able to identify those policies. The term Native American, in and of itself, is a seemingly harmless term, but it is used in a way that infers, however innocent its author, that native people are somehow exactly the same as other hyphenated Americans (Chinese-Americans, Polish-Americans, etc.) That would not be objectionable, except that native peoples are in fact members of their respective nations, and the denial of their rights as distinct and separate nations with their own territories, sovereignty, cultures, and power over their own lives has been the basis of much racialist policy in the Western Hemisphere. Because of that history, our own preferences lead us to use terms such as "native people" rather than Native Americans because we feel that it is a more accurate term.

Source: Akwesasne Notes, Late Spring 1977.

Darling of some of the international cocktail circuit, the West German film-maker Werner Herzog is execrated by many others, not least two of the communities in which he has attempted to make films. But while the citizens of Delft found his intentions merely obnoxious (letting loose rats in their streets for the making of Nosferatu*),*[307] *the Aguaruna of north Peru were virtually terrorised in 1979 and 1980, as the Teutonic megalomaniac tried to begin shooting* Fitzcarraldo.

Wawaim is an Aguaruna community of about 280 people on the Cenepe river; legally recognised by the Peruvian government, the settlement has had title to its lands since 1974. (Due to colonisation schemes, road-building programmes and the activities of forest traders, many communities formed assemblies to resist outside pressures, and in 1977 these federated as the Aguaruna-Huambisa Council.)[308]

In July 1979, Herzog chose the Wawaim village as the site for the now-famous "boat raising" scene in his fantasy around the life of the infamous rubber-baron and opera-lover, Fitzgerald. (It was the forest Indians of Fitzgerald's day who "corrupted" his name into "Fitzcarraldo".) On an initial visit to Wawaim, Herzog ascertained that the Aguaruna were far from overjoyed at resurrecting any myths surrounding Fitzcarraldo, let alone having their village cut in two, so that a dirty old river steamer could be hauled over a mountain.[309]

He left the village, only to return eight days later with a small detachment of Peruvian soldiers. Members of the community were threatened, some shots were fired, four Wawaim Aguaruna were apparently thrown into jail, and Herzog got a few Indians to sign an agreement. On 15 July however, the assembly met to discuss these events, and unanimously withdrew permission for the film to be made.[310] *A month afterwards, the General Assembly of the Aguaruna Council endorsed the decisions of the Wawaim with the statement reproduced below.*

Neither this — nor a Peruvian government statement that the Aguaruna had every right to resist Herzog's intentions[311] *— deterred the film-maker. He proceeded with his intentions, until 1 December 1979, when a group of Aguarunas raided his camp, forced his crew to take to boats, and burned some of his installations.*[312]

Herzog then turned to the Machiguenga who also tried to resist — but with less militancy.[313] *Disgruntled by their "uncooperativeness" the director drafted in Campa Indians and managed to complete his project around two years behind schedule.*

Herzog's racism — and that of his white co-workers, notably Klaus Kinski — pervaded all his dealings with Peru's native inhabitants. While ostensibly upholding their "identity" and "dignity",[314] *in truth he showed contempt for indigenous organisations, risking Indian lives (three did die during the shooting) and grossly violated native land. In Les Blank's adulatory film biography of Herzog, he is observed remarking "We will probably have one of the last films with natives in it. It's a tragedy that is going on. We are losing . . . mythologies."*[315]

Most recently, Herzog has returned from Australia with "Where the green ants dream", a film made with a minimum of fanfare (for probably obvious reasons) and similar lack of reference to Aboriginal organisations. The making of that film has been specifically condemned by Maori film-maker Merata Mita, as an example of deplorable neo-colonialism.[316]

Ironically, the Fitzcarrald Isthmus, site of the rubber baron's operatic boat-lifting exploit, was also attacked in 1984 by a group of Indians, protesting at the construction of a heliport — the first stage in a canal to link the Urubamba and Manu rivers. This is a pet project of Peru's President Belaunde, and constitutes part of the huge Manu National Park, which threatens many native occupants of the region, including the Machiguenga.[317]

"Fitzcarrald, whose methods are repeated by Herzog"

In the face of this deed [Herzog's invasion of Wawaim] we have called a General Assembly of all the communities, so as to release this document which is the first to be produced in a proper form, without pressure and with adequate representation.

What follows is the unanimous position of the Aguaruna and Huambisa communities.

a) Considering that, even while carrying out work in the Wawaim community, the [film] company uses people and forest resources from several communities; considering that the materials are limited and of a prime necessity, and considering that there already exist internal sanctions in these communities against selling the said resources to foreigners, and considering that the company has pressed its demands for these;

b) Considering that in its short period of occupation and bearing in mind that it is still in the preparatory stages, the [film] company has had a traumatic effect on communal life — not only that of Wawaim, but also all nearby communities and the majority of valley communities, including those of the Cenepa and Maranon — and, in conclusion, on the entire Aguaruna and Huambisa population, in view of the slanders against its delegates and organisations;

c) Considering that the company's action has produced divisions and disrupted all the communal and inter-communal work, as well as producing a strong monetarisation of social relationships;

d) Considering that the company has solicited the "massive and voluntary participation" of the various inhabitants of the community of Cenepa and Maranon, in particular of around 1,500 working Indians (preferably those with long hair for the shooting, thus commercialising our dress) to haul up the boat, a number of people not to be found either at Wawaim or throughout the Cenepa;

e) Considering that, with its denunciations and intrigues, the company has sustained prejudice towards all the communities and to the organisation which groups together the communities of the four rivers, calling into question their leaders and thereby producing a general nervousness and legitimate disquiet from the Indian people in the area;

f) Considering that, for Indians, the fact of collaborating in a work which, for commercial reasons, intends to reconstruct —if not apologise for — the actions of Fitzcarrald who was one of our worst exploiters and assassins, means we cannot admit him, nor haul the boat, interpreting, for financial ends, the sufferings and death of our Machiguenga and Campa comrades, who at that time were victims of the exploiter Fitzcarrald, whose methods one might say are repeated by Herzog: he also having distributed guns and ammunition to the Indians working for his company;

g) Considering the passivity and, in certain cases, the complicity of representatives of the Ministry of Agriculture and Food, as well as some officers — whose action, we believe, isn't isolated — and considering that these are the soldiers who made and signed the law for our defence and that it was the Ministry of Agriculture which worked out the ruling; that they are obliged to ensure that this law is respected, since we have neither invited, nor given our permission to the company to come in, and since neither its works nor gifts interest us;

Considering all this and all the reasons, and all our disquiet, the signatories underneath declare that which follows:

1) That the activities of the film company don't simply affect one community but all the Aguaruna and Huambisa peoples.

2) That the Aguaruna and Huambisa Council, representing the greatest voice among the people united in an extraordinary General Assembly, refuses vigorously the works of the "Wild Life Films in Peru" company. We ask the authorities to ensure respect for our rights according to article 23 of D.L. No. 22175.

Naputuka, 19 August 1979.

"Our decision is total, unanimous and irrevocable"

After a vigorous rejoinder to the Aguaruna declaration, made by Herzog on 25 August, the leader of the Aguaruna-Huambisa Council in Peru (himself subjected to personal slanders by the German) issued the following statement:

The Wildlife Films S.A. company has undertaken a new press campaign against the Aguaruna people. It would be useless to demonstrate once again how slanderous and false all their accusations are.

So we would like, before public opinion, to reduce the problem to the simplest terms:

1) The Decree Law 22175 article 13 declares: "Territorial ownership of indigenous communities is inalienable, indefensable and not distrainable". This means that we have rights, which we can make valid, when it is necessary.

2) The form of the legitimate right for the Wawaim community has been to demonstrate its absolute refusal that the Wildlife Films company should occupy one metre of their territory. This decision was first communicated to the competent authorities before the company had installed itself, and again when it began its activities.

3) Our right has been recognised by all the official bodies to whom we have addressed ourselves, as witnessed by unappealed documents of the Ministry of Agriculture, the Cabinet of Information and Communications, and the Ministry of the Interior.

In summary, we prevail upon rights recognised in law, reinforced by official decision, and we make use of these rights within limits prescribed by law. Peru is a state of rights, and it is not necessary that each citizen should be obliged to find arguments, each time that they exercise a legitimate, acquired, right.

We don't have to respond with arguments, of which some are our own, but others of which have been attributed to us by outsiders, the press, or indeed our accusers.

In this conflict, our decision is total, unanimous and irrevocable. All the manipulations of Wildlife Films are only desperate bids to reach its own ends. And in order to get there, they lie, denigrate us, and even go so far as provoking an intervention by the authorities against us.

Evaristo Nugkuag Ikanan, President of CAH, 10 December 1979, Lima.
(Both the Aguaruna documents quoted here are to be found in *Journal de la Societé des Americanistes*, Vol. 67, Paris 1980–81, pp. 4.2. and 4.3, trans. Roger Moody.)

As already mentioned, after making "Fitzcarraldo" Herzog moved into Australia where he gained the co-operation of a few Aboriginal groups to construct another allegory of neo-colonialism — this time, of small black people up against a mining colossus. Although the Mutitjulu Community of Central Australia — the custodians of famed Ayers Rock (now properly called Uluru) — may not have been aware of Herzog's activities, they have certainly been blighted by other cinematic visitors. The following statement was issued by the Community in mid-1984:

Statement by Mutitjulu Community

The Mutitjulu Community welcomes representatives from the Australian National Parks and Wildlife Service, the Conservation Commission of the Northern Territory, the Tourist Commissions, the Film Industry, the Department of Aboriginal Affairs and other interested parties to this meeting today. We are happy you have come. It is a very important meeting and we hope it will help to make rules for filming at Uluru (Ayers Rock). We want to make some things clear first. There have been many wrong stories told in the newspapers recently about past film applications. All decisions about film applications have been made by the Mutitjulu Community. Our lawyers and other advisors have only been doing what we have told them to do. They have been advising us not to stop film companies, but we have been angry because some film companies have been mucking us around or have not been complying with reasonable conditions about filming. At the same time we were very busy with meetings about the handover of freehold title.

That is why we called for this meeting. We wanted this meeting to fix up the rules for filming. When we were waiting too long we wanted to stop film crews from coming until after this meeting.

We have already said before and we say it again today that filming of a tourist or scenic nature can go ahead, we only want to make sure film crews do not try to film our sacred place.

If the companies want to film members of the Mutitjulu Community they should discuss their ideas first with the Community Council. That's only fair.

We know that some people in Australia are a bit worried about what will happen after freehold titles have been handed over. We want to put their minds at rest.

At the same time as the freehold title is given, we will be giving the people of Australia a long lease through the Australian National Parks and Wildlife Service. Tourists will continue to be able to come to the Uluru National Park in accordance with the plan of management approved by the Parliament. We are looking forward to working with the Australian National Parks and Wildlife Service and the Conservation Commission of the Northern Territory in jointly managing this Park, not just for the benefit of Aboriginal people but for all Australians, and for overseas visitors also. We are pleased that the tourists are going to be accommodated at Yulara, because it will reduce the pressure on our Community.

Cassidy Uluru Chairman, Mutitjulu Community.

Source: Land Rights News, Central Land Council, Alice Springs, Australia, No. 20, August 1984.

Lastly, a few reflections by some Mapuche, exiled in Paris, on the way in which they are regarded by some of their trade union colleagues. What they experience is more specifically racialism *than racism, though no less pervasive for that.*

A stupid Indian who could speak

It may seem rather a paradox, that while being discriminated against on grounds of race, there are some who are allowed to assume responsibilities as union members.

In the continual struggle, carried on by the unions, the participation of all members is needed, and on those occasions when the need for unity, which strengthens the continuance of the struggle is greatest, *racism* becomes a matter of only secondary importance or at least is disguised.

Within this body the Mapuche is regarded as a "comrade in battle", equal to the rest, and on many occasions can be found at the head of the unions.

But there are contradictions. On the one hand he is respected and his authority observed as a union official while in his official capacity, but at the end of the day he is still regarded as that "stupid Indian". And it is here that we see the Mapuche's daily two-fold struggle: against the exploitation of the ruling class and against the aggression shown towards him by his own colleagues.

For example:

> Being the Union President in the factory where I worked I was not, as an official, asked about my Mapuche origin. (May I point out that most of my colleagues had started working there at the same time as me and many were from the same school or district. What I'm trying to say is that it has been a long road of struggling, working and being friends together).
>
> As I was taking part in the TUC campaign for the party for which I was candidate, I had to visit a number of industries in which I was surprised to be considered as "the Indian" and not the Union leader. In fact the only thing I had going for me, so it seemed, according to those who listened to me, was that a "stupid Indian" knew how to speak.

These are but a few of the problems we constantly face. However we do not feel malice or vengeance towards our colleagues of the same social rank as ourselves. We understand that many of these racialist attitudes are subconscious and not premeditated, but nevertheless they reflect how deeply dominant ideology has penetrated society. We are well aware of the identity of our enemy and the reasons why we should fight him. Today more than ever unity is needed among the lower classes of the rural and urban areas — the social class to which the Mapuche belong.

Moreover, we believe that this unity must turn into an ideological task based upon destroying racism (one of the bourgeois tools in the division of class) and the quest for the path towards building a just society, in which the common people and the Mapuche people are the principal protagonists, and there is a unanimous agreement of respect and recognition for our people.

The Mapuche people:
> were not brought into the world to be bakers or maids.
> are not second-class citizens.
> are not rough, weak, ignorant or drunkards.
> have never been on the fringe of social struggles.
> fought for 300 years for independence against the Spanish invasion and continued their fight against the middle-class usurpers of the islands.

Today **the Mapuche people** are still fighting against the fascism that wants to wipe them out.

The Mapuche people are a race and should be recognized and respected as such.

Source: Amuleayn, Traru, Paris, June 1980; translated and published in English in *Survival International Review*, Nos. 37 and 38, pp. 9/10 by Manda Denton, Heather Weller and Christine Pettit.

12. Workers and Slaves

While the image of indigenous peoples, as food-gatherers, herders, or agriculturists, applies to many communities all over the world, there are others whose immediate survival (at least) depends on wage labour, or indentured labour, inherited over several generations. In particular this applies to campesino *Indian communities in south and central America whose land was invaded around 100 or more years ago*[318] *and whose foreparents were subjected to* encomienda. *But is is also true for Indian "tribals", for many Australian reserve Aborigines (see p. 298), reservation American Indians and northern native bands, whose land-base is being fast eroded through pipelines, hydro-projects, and mining.*[319]

The first statement in this chapter is part of an interview, in the late 1970s, with a 15-year-old native Bolivian sugar cane-cutter from the Santa Cruz area. This is followed by extracts from a speech by a leader of the Izozeno-Chiriguano peoples from the same region, which graphically shows how indebtedness to the cane contractors prevents indigenous labourers tilling their own land, and hence contributes to the cycle of increasing dependency.[320]

Next, is part of an article from a Peruvian Indian journal, depicting a parallel servitude: the use of young (and often older) Indian women as domestic servants. The chapter concludes with a spirited account of several actions taken by indigenous participants in the 1977 National General Strike in Colombia. Although many grievances attached to specific government malpractice (and broken promises) a major motive for the very well-coordinated action (much of it in the hands of CRIC — see p. 364) was to protest against discrimination against indigenous plantation workers. The CRIC journal Unidad Indigena *concluded that "... participation in the general strike on a national level was something new and unknown for the rural Indian population, nonetheless, it was successful and a useful experience, thanks to good preparation work."*[321]

You always have to work

I was nine or ten when I came to work for the first time. I was working then. As a day labourer, weeding, watching, and the like. Since I was working every day, I had pains all over my body: at night I couldn't lie on my side. Later it got better: I learned how to work. I just turned 14, and this year the boss saw me working and said, "All right, boy. They're going to teach you how to cut cane, so you'll learn to do a good job," he said. So when next year comes, God willing, I'll return to the harvest, but as a harvester. I'll know how to cut cane, I'll be in. My brother told me, too . . .

One year later:

Now I'm working as a harvester. My brother – I've got a brother – taught me. He taught me how to cut cane; I didn't know how to cut it. I cut it too high. "Cut it real low," he said. Okay, I cut it this low. "Lower, lower yet!" I got down to the ground. "That's good. That's the way to cut." I had a backache all morning. "Lower, lower!" The sweat was running off me; my hands were opened. Cane is hard, hard to cut. Early in the morning, at around five, my brother brought me; and since I was hungry by 10 o'clock, I couldn't do any more work. I went to sit down under the *motacú*. "What's the matter?" my brother said, "Come on and work." "No, I'm tired," I told him. "Is that why you wanted to cut cane?" he said. "No, no," I said, "I didn't want to cut cane; I just came to look!" "Come on and work." And I went back to work; I worked until five. When I got home I was tired, really tired! I hurt all over; I couldn't go to the field. The next day they brought me by force. Yes, that's how they brought me. I worked and fell asleep in the cane. I woke up in the field. I couldn't take it; I just went to sleep right in the middle of the cane. But later when I knew how to cut, it was easier; I could cut. Cut, strip, bundle, load, cut, strip: it's the same over and over. Loading is even harder. When I tried they made me a little bundle, but I couldn't lift it. The cane was heavy, real heavy. I couldn't lift it; you need a lot of strength.

We don't rest here; we work night and day, night and day. Every week, night and day: we hardly rest on Sundays. So I tell you, I won't be able to get used to this: it's a lot of work. For example, when the truck comes you have to go; whether you're tired or not, you just have to go; even if it's at night or not, you just have to go; even if it's raining, you just have to go.

In Izozog we work too; we work hard; but if you're tired you don't go to the field right then. But when you've rested well, five or six hours, I don't know, then you go to work. So you yourself can say: "Now, I'm going to work." "Now I'm not."

Here in the harvest you always have to work, all the time. That's the way it is. We worked all night over there: from dawn to evening to dawn to evening again: two nights without sleeping. I can't take it any more: I'm tired of it. But I have debts: 5,000 pesos of debts. Tomorrow we'll rest a bit, do some shopping. I like to sit a while in the square and watch the trucks and the people walking around. I return for half an hour and then go back to the market. We spend an hour or two there and then return to the camp. Sometimes I stay at the camp, I stay there to sleep, you know. When the others come back we go back to work. I waited to see the procession in Montero [on August 6, the national holiday], but I've never seen it. It's supposed to be nice, but what can I do? I don't have the time. We have the sugar-cane procession!

Source: I sold myself; I was bought.

"The Bosses have bought us"

Speech by Victor Vaca, representing Grand Captain Bonifacio Barrientos of the Communities of the Izozeño-Chiriguanos:

Greetings, dear brothers who are present here: my Ayoréode brothers and my Aymara brothers.

Dear brothers, for almost a month now we have heard that there was going to be a meeting, but we didn't know how many kinds of people would attend: but thank God and thanks to our brothers who have come from all sides: because of them we could hold this meeting.

The first thing I can tell you, my Ayoréode brothers, is that at one time, not long ago, we were enemies. But what has happened now? Now we are united with you: I am not afraid of you and you are not afraid of us. That's how it seems to me. We are giving each other our hands.

You well know that before, we killed each other. You killed our fathers, and our fathers killed you. But now we can look each other in the face.

Dear brothers, let this meeting be to our benefit; let this meeting which we are holding here continue every year so we can consider our problems. You want to know so much about us and we about you.

What I am going to tell you is the problem of the Izozog area. After the war [the Chaco War between Bolivia and Paraguay 1932-38], this Izozog was lost: it was taken prisoner by the Paraguayans, but thanks to Grand Captain Bonifacio Barrientos, he remained alone with 400 men, fighting in favour of Bolivia with the Izozeño people. But the women and old people were all taken by the Paraguayans.

Because of Bonifacio Barrientos, again after the war, the people were able to settle in the land of Izozog, to form their own nation. But after the war there were many killings: a lot of us died. But Bonifacio Barrientos fought hard to be able to defend his people, the Izozeño people. Bonifacio Barrientos was not afraid although his brother died from a gun. They killed him: the Bolivians killed him because his brother had had to go to Paraguay, with the Pilas. But the brother of Bonifacio Barrientos didn't know where Bolivia was because at that time no one was interested in where the peasant people were.

After they left the war, the Bolivians shot the brother of Bonifacio Barrientos in order to frighten the entire Izozeño people as well, but Bonifacio had to stand up like a man and went to La Paz. He went to La Paz to ask that we again be allowed to live in our country, Izozog. Now he has liberated us, and he placed our boundary stone so that we can live on our own land. This boundary stone means that it is our land, the land of the Izozeños. Now we are on our own land, but what is happening? The land is beautiful. The land is productive: it produces everything: yuca, camote, rice, cane: everything, and besides we have irrigation. The problem was that we do not have people to guide us: we don't know how to raise our families or progress. For this reason so many Izozeño people have gone to Argentina, since at that time there was no work here in Bolivia. But later, when Paz Estensoro came in, he built the Guabirá refinery, and now we can all leave to work, leave to make money, and we don't have to go to Argentina any more. Those who are in Argentina are fifty per cent of our people. I have seen several communities of our people in Argentina, and they will not return any more.

Now the problem with our work here in Bolivia is that the bosses have bought us, all the Izozeños, by means of the advance, and we hardly work at all for our land, Izozog. Before, we did not have these advances, but now we are getting along very poorly because of these advances, because we don't have time to work for our land any more. There are some people who owe up to five and six thousand, and they cannot pay it back any more. And there are so many Izozeño people who remain here, near Santa Cruz de la Sierra, because of their debts. This year the bosses don't want to let the people go who owe a lot, and there remain few in Izozog to work in the fields. There is no time, and no strength left.

There are so many Izozeño people who don't want to come here to Santa Cruz any more, because they have so much debt, and there are also some Izozeños who owe ten or fifteen thousand. Only the boss now seeks their life, not to pay but their life. This year there was a boss who left here with soldiers to kill, just to kill an Izozeño.

May we from this meeting be able to draw some benefit for our problems, for our problems which you have as well as we.

This was my speech. Thank you, and I'll say more later. Thank you.

Source: Brigitte Simon, Barbara Schuchard, Barbara Riester, Jurgen Riester *I sold myself: I was bought*, IWGIA Document No. 42, Copenhagen, 1980.

"A stinking labyrinth"

At the present time, the problem of exploitation suffered by women household workers is something which matters least to the political organisations; it's what they keep quiet about and hide simply because for those who hold the reins it is not in their interests that these be made clear. But here I should like that my voice resounds in the mountains and vibrates in the deepest places about the feelings of all the women household workers in Peru; we must grab the guts of the 'mistresses' who read this article.

Today in the main cities of Peru, those assimilated into western culture enslave Indian women as servants. This is the concrete situation of thousands of youngsters who leave their communities and are drawn to the cities in search of 'advancement'. They are lured by western propaganda which in its devouring mission repeats lies saying that the communities are 'cultural orphans'; that scientific and technological advances are only found in the big cities; where one can 'live better'; furthermore, that we should integrate ourselves and be like 'decent' folk; that it is easier to earn money; that we stop speaking Indian languages, eating Indian food, wearing our traditional wide skirts; that we must improve the race, etc.

Full of these illusions and hopes, one goes off abandoning the community by a tortuous path, leaving behind the flowering fields bathed in dew . . . What will the fate of this young girl be? She crosses mountains and valleys and still everything is beautiful until she reaches the asphalt motorway which leads to the big cities. It is an enormous surprise to discover a stinking labyrinth full of the unnatural smells of the process of modernisation, worm-eaten, scarred by misery and corruption. A nest of vipers ready to devour the pure and innocent.

On arriving in the city, women household workers are alone, uprooted in a culture that is the opposite of their own, without resources to survive; then one is forced to seek work and it's here that one begins to feel the difference between women in the cities and women in the communities. This last point we can only understand if we bear in mind that among the evils brought by Europeans was slavery, servitude, exploitation of man by man, their colonial policy and with that capitalism and class division. In Latin America, we do not know slavery or servility, on the contrary before the Europeans came our peoples were happy.

Source: "Women Household Workers" by Adela Principe Diego, in *Pueblo Indio*, No. 1, Lima, Sept./Oct. 1981.

"Notwithstanding repression, we let our protests be felt"

The Indian Communities in the General Strike

Indians of the Department Cauca supported the General Strike of last 14 September by massive participation. Preparations started as soon as CRIC had decided to participate in the strike.

Meetings, conferences and lectures of the organisation were used to explain reasons and aims of the strike and the tasks to be accomplished. In most areas and districts responding to the strike appeal, popular support was far-reaching.

The General Strike in various Indian areas: San Ignacio, San Isidro and El Camelo

On 14 September we, Indian village communities of San Ignacio, San Isidro and El Camelo, assembled for the General Strike, not to find wonderful solutions for our problems but to give an example of our fighting solidarity with other people's organisations in struggle. At the same time we denounced INCORA [the State Land Reform Agency] and demanded it facilitate land acquisition and cope with the "Quintana plan" as promised to us by the Director of INCORA during a recent visit by representatives of our three communities. According to his words the plan lacked then only the board's approval to start transferring land; still, there has not been a step of progress in this matter since. Another problem we denounced was the lack of adequate and advantageous credits, as well as technical support by INCORA functionaries. They are visiting and leaving us with only directives we should follow, without showing us how we should do this. They keep forgetting that Indians do not have those new techniques and theories they know about.

These problems, as well as suppression and the high cost of living, made us to mobilise for the General Strike and participate in the common protest. Notwithstanding repression and threats by the department authorities against the exploited class participating in the strike, we were successfully able to conclude the agreed task: to put up road-blocks on the streets to Guacas and Quintana. These became free again only at around 2 p.m., as we positioned a truck there throughout the whole of the morning. The government showed its fear of the organisation by early militarisation of the Cedelca plantation. Some three truckloads of soldiers arrived and stayed at the plantation until the 17th. The military was not satisfied with just observing us. On the day of the strike they went for our comrade Dionision Lamé at his own house where he was sleeping, took him to the plantation, submitted him there to an extensive interrogation and tried to force him to denounce those who had put up the road-blocks. Realising that the comrade could not tell them anything they let him go at 7 p.m. on the same day. Notwithstanding this hard repression we carried on with our fight in firm determination.

Caldono

In the reservations of Caldono, Pueblo Nuevo and Siberia, meetings were held in all localities to get ready for the strike. At these, the idea of the strike was explained and suggestions gathered as to how to carry through the strike and what the problems of the village community were. We also discussed problems of the community council and of the common land property it owns in the Cooperative Enterprise.

As agreed, some 300 comrades marched on Wednesday at 8 a.m. in discipline and order down to the park of Caldono. They applauded CRIC, waved flags and carried banners protesting against the high cost of living and demanding recognition of the community council and respect for the reservation, denied it by white population and government functionaries.

Demands were raised to solve the problems of *agave* cultivation, and repression was condemned. Having marched several times around the central park they assembled at the town hall and used the stage in front of it as a platform for Indian speakers.

The governor of the Party opened the meeting with a speech, followed by comrades from the reservations of Pueblo Nuevo, La Aguada and the village community of Siberia, and then by the other participants from all places on the reservation of Caldono.

This mobilisation of Indians made the town administration and especially the mayor's office tremble and appeal, four times, to the military for help, although they had already concentrated police from Siberia and Pueblo Nuevo. Twenty policemen stood on the ready from the previous day. Local militia armed themselves to the teeth on the pretext that Indians would seize the village during Tuesday night, plunder and burn down the Caja Agraria and the shops and free prisoners. Also, some heavies from other places arrived, made their armed rounds from 9 p.m. on, and guarded the access roads to the village. Nor did the Caja Agraria employees sleep as they were worried.

Both roads leading to Caldono were blocked. The road from Siberia to Pescador was blocked with steel spikes so that all cars coming from Caldono got stuck. The road from Caldono to Mondomo was also blocked with two large trees. Six policemen had to be called to try to free the approach. They met there with the military on its way to the village. They all had to swing their axes to free the road. Reaching the village, finally, they found only children playing in the park, as the meeting had ended and the comrades had already dispersed. Several policemen pursued the comrades to arrest putative leaders but, as all walked close together, they could not achieve anything. Somewhat later 12 policemen arrived in a car and arrested an Indian in the road. They accused him of not belonging to the village community. Ultimately they could not prove anything against him and had to let him go.

Toribio, Tacueyo and San Francisco

On 14 September we, comrades from Toribio, Tacueyo and San Francisco followed the strike appeal agreed upon by CRIC as a form of protest common to all other sectors of the people of the country.

The roads of Tacueyo and Toribio were blocked from 4 a.m. on. This crippled merchants and agents, exploiters of the village community, in their activities. Many cars got stuck, and one of the great landowners of the area, who was on his way to his *finca* in the firm belief that there could not be a strike in the countryside, arrived at a spot where the road was blocked with large rocks placed there by 40 people. He turned and fired shots in all directions as he started his car to go back.

During the day we had a meeting with 400 Indians at the road-blocks, applauded the strike, listened to the scarce news about it from other parts of the country and discussed our problems. We demanded that the lands, which by rights are ours, be made over to us, and that coffee be purchased from us at adequate prices. We protested against the high cost of living and succeeded in demonstrating to our enemies and to those not recognising our organisation that we are prepared to stand up and declare war on them wherever they do not want to recognise us.

Another road-block was organised by 80 young girls who went there with banners and stopped all cars.

In the afternoon police came and wanted to arrest five comrades, guns ready to fire. Bad luck to them that two of the comrades could get away! But the comrades Marino Mestizo, Enrique Musicué and Corpus Ul were brought to prison and roughly beaten up. This escalated until comrade Enrique Musicué was kicked so that he fainted and almost died. Until now, only comrade Corpus Ul has been released.

The launch of the strike in this area was a good experience for us, though the radio of the rich and the olígarchs told the Colombian people that in the Cauca Valley nothing whatsoever was happening — but this they can ask of "Miguelito Andrade".

Tierradentro

We Indians in Tierradentro upheld the promise agreed with all sectors of the people, to organise a General Strike as a protest against repression and the high cost of living which make the whole Colombian population suffer under recent governments and especially under President Dópez's administration, and we mobilised as well as possible.

Our intention was to hold a peaceful meeting in Belalcázar, in which village people also could have taken part. But we had (as everywhere in the country) to face the fact that authorities, military and police, were once again prepared to suppress the right of the people to express their protest against injustice. Four truckloads of military and police were brought to Belalcázar to stop the demonstration.

Great landowners started a terror campaign by saying that the Indians wanted to raid the village, to murder and plunder the shops. Several days earlier, the strike authorities were busy arresting any strangers coming to Belalcázar or Inza, and on the day preceding the strike they declared a curfew for both villages from 6 p.m. on. Notwithstanding all this, on Wednesday 14 September, the day of the National General Strike, we fulfilled our task as agreed upon on national level, even though we did not hold the meeting. Normal activities in Belalcázar and Inza stopped. Just a few cars were made to move, and the presence of such great numbers of military, as well as the curfew order itself, made everybody aware of our protest. The authorities felt the weight of our organisation, and the great landowners' rumours only added to their fears.

As for us, we organised mobilisation: Comrades from high-lying reservation assembled the night before at the arranged place and marched on the day of the strike towards Belalcázar until stopped by the military. As it was agreed to avoid useless confrontations with, and provocations by, the powers of repression, the comrades turned back and tried to hold the meeting in Toez. There, however, they were again confronted by military so that, after they had had discussions with the soldiers and made clear the reasons and justification for the public protest against the government to them, the comrades decided to disperse.

Comrades of the reservation near to the road to Inza assembled and marched towards Belalcázar. As the news arrived that the comrades from the high-lying parts had turned back, they decided to go to the Guadulejo road crossing and succeeded in holding their meeting there before the suppressive powers learned about it. Six comrades made speeches. We were already on our march back as two truckloads of soldiers arrived to pursue us. They managed to arrest one single

Indian only. Next day they let him go as they could not prove him guilty of anything.

The marches were carried through in excellent order, with our flags, banners, slogans and our own demonstration stewards. Notwithstanding repression we let our protest be felt and honoured our promise to go through with the General Strike in a region as far way as Tierradentro at the same time as comrades amongst peasants, workers, students and employees and other groups of the people did the same in different regions and towns of the country.

To cut it short, the strike initiative concretised itself in action. In various places where adequate basic preparation had been carried through, communities participated in a well-organised way and gave an example of their interest in the development of the organisation and in the alliance with other groups of the population in towns and in the countryside.

The strike resulted in an understanding of the power of organisation as a fundamentally new way of struggle. On the national level some mistakes of preparation may have been made out of lack of experience, judged by the way the struggle went on 14 September, as nobody was expecting the scale of repression let loose by the government. Notorious was the panic-mongering, too; still, the intimidation of all great landowners and agents was positive as they are the most direct exploiters of the Indian communities in the Cauca Valley.

Source: Unidad Indigena, No. 25, October 1977, trans. Mick Licarpa.

13.   Sterilisation

First accounts of the forcible sterilisation of indigenous women circulated in the 1960s, when missionaries (particularly from the Summer Institute of Linguistics (SIL) — see chapter 9) were accused of carrying out hysterectomies on south American Indians against their will.[322]

Within a decade several reports were circulating which alleged enforced sterilisation by missionaries in Amazonas,[323] the Cundinamarca department of Colombia[324] and among both native American women and men in Oklahoma.[325]

By the 1980s, so-called "family planning" programmes aimed at potentially subversive peoples (usually of low fertility, even compared with Western Europe) were so prevalent as to be protested against only in passing; for example in Guatemala, West Papua and East Timor.[326] In the United States, however, the work of a Cherokee/Choctaw physician, Dr Connie Uri, identified the genocide, and it became increasingly difficult for foundations such as Ford and Rockefeller to justify their sterilisation programmes as either voluntary or beneficial. At about the same time, in an article in Montreal's Sunday Express, Father Robert Lechat, a Catholic priest working among the Inuit of Canada's North West Territories (NWT) accused the federal government of ethnocide: according to his figures, between 23% and 45% of women in eight Inuit communities had received hysterectomies.[327]

Since 1974, Depo-provera has come to join surgery as a prime method of preventing indigenous women bearing children. Its main testing ground has been northern Thailand among the hill tribespeople of Chiang Mai, where the US-funded McCormick Family Planning programme has used the drug extensively on Akha and Lanu women.[328] It has also found its way to Aotearoa (New Zealand) and Polynesia. In Western Australia it is targeted especially for use by "mentally retarded" women — and elsewhere in Australia by Aborigines.[329]

Cheryl Buchanan — a leading Aboriginal activist — explains the context in which sterilisation against Aboriginal women has been carried out in Australia. Dee Fairbanks is an Anishinabe woman, and was in 1977

Director of the Adult Education Program of the San Francisco Indian Center in California. She summarises the evidence on enforced sterilisation of native American women.

A Depo-Provera survey was initiated by the North Queensland Land Council in 1982, and announced in its newspaper, the N.Q. Messagestick:

"A threat to millions of women"

This so-called miracle drug is a threat to millions of women — particularly native women — in the Third World. Depo-Provera is injected in a single dose into the arms or buttocks of women. It provides women with three to six months infertility. It seems so easy, just one jab and no more worries about having children.

In 1968 the manufacturers of DP were ordered to test their drug on monkeys and beagles. The tests revealed breast cancer, diabetes and cancer of the womb. DP was banned in America and Britain by responsible health bodies. Astonishingly, the FDA which banned use of the drug in America, allowed export of the drug to other countries. DP side effects are notorious. The drug completely disrupts the menstrual cycle, causes heavy bleeding and irregular bleeding of the vagina. It also makes women more prone to diabetes. Given to breast feeding mums, DP passes in large quantities to the baby where its effects, although unknown at this stage, may cause deformed bone growth.

None of these risks seem to worry the manufacturers who have admitted paying bribes of $2,710,000 to employees of foreign governments. We advise women not to use it. Jan Mayman of the National Times overheard Family Planning Association tell inquirers about DP that the drug was used only for "mentally retarded women and those who forget to take the pill".

The West Australian Government is giving this drug to Aboriginal women in that State through the State Community Health Service. If West Australia is doing it, then what is the possibility of the Queensland government doing the same through its State Aboriginal Health Program.

Source: North Queensland Messagestick, Vol. 7, No. 1, February 1982.

"Like lambs to the slaughter"

In the black community of Australia it is a known fact that on an average the number of Aboriginal children being born per population is about 3 or 4 times greater than the white population. But let us look at the reality of these births. The children are born into social conditions that are against everything we would want to see our children have. They don't get proper food — mostly kids drink powdered milk which may be okay but it hasn't got added vitamins and minerals to boost your child's milk. This is because a large tin of Sunshine Milk is $2.50 and Enfamil Lactogen and these formulas researched to suit a baby's diet are $5.50. A big difference when you are feeding 2 or 3 small children. Then as the child gets older and needs solids like potatoes, pumpkin, brains etc. the normal black child is given a bottle to suck on, because the family just doesn't have the food. On Aboriginal Reserves especially, the father finds it difficult to get employment and where they do the wages per week are well below the basic wage. This is caused by the notorious Queensland *"act"* and its regulations. The mother say if she has been deserted (which is pretty common) is in a worse position to keep the children because there are very few jobs for unskilled women. Recently there was publicity relating to women on the Reserves where they found that most women are denied social service benefits such as Supporting Mothers Benefit and Family Assistance. The Social Service people justify their position by putting the onus back onto the Department of Aboriginal Affairs. It's a good position for them because they can kick claims from one Department to the next without having to take full responsibility. Less likely would they ever think that the black women and kids were **people** that they were dealing with. And so the black woman is left with the responsibility of listening to her childrens cries of hunger and wondering how in the hell she is going to feed them. After two or three children now the black woman is offered to be *"done"* by the white doctors. The doctors hardly explain the operation of being *"tied"* of what its effects are on a young woman's body — and I'm talking about women that are 19 or 20. The doctor offers it because (generally) he thinks she's had too many kids or that she can't look after them. I know of a number of cases where the operation was done without the consent of the women — who were told that the operation was something completely different. And in anyone's looks this is what I see as **forced sterilization**. It's just too common to hear black women say, *"Oh after that last one the Doctor says I can't have any more"*. When you ask why, they don't know, because they haven't been told. Many a black woman has been un-mothered by the cut of some doctor who decided to *"experiment"*. Then the other side to the matter of Forced Sterilization relates to contraceptive pills. As soon as you are a single black woman and you have a baby, you are offered (forcefully) the *"Pill"*. Again there is no education as to how it works, its effects, its dangers. Instead you are told to take it every day and come back when you run out. It was a long time before I found out that taking a "Pill" consistently that is reacting to your body, can and has caused sterilization. Most black women have permanent headaches and drop Vincent and other powders like they're going out of style. So you wouldn't even give a headache a second thought. Yet headaches can mean that the "Pill" you're on is no good for you. The important things, the average doctor just wouldn't bother telling you. It's the pill popping world, where a pill a day keeps the doctor in pay (a little rhyme I made up). But who knows what is in those little white and pink capsules, or green bombs or anything else — but — *"doctor's orders you know"*. We must get out of the habit of *always accepting* what the doctor says as the *absolute* truth. Mostly they aren't sure of what's wrong with you or what your needs are. We have to start demanding to know *what* they give us in terms of pills and *WHY*. Otherwise we're like lambs going to be slaughtered — we don't even know let alone care.

Mooladani
Cheryl Buchanan

Our children are our wealth

Many, many years ago, before the White Man came to North America and before the Anishinabe People (Chippewa or Ojibwa) knew about another type of man, a prophet came to the Anishinabe People and told them that another type of people would be coming to them. The prophet told the Anishinabe People that they must beware, because this new people would try to destroy their religion and culture, and their life as they knew it.

The Anishinabe People took their ceremonies and religion, which was recorded on birch bark scrolls, and hid them inside a hollow Ironwood log. Then they took this log and buried it deep inside the side of a cliff, where no one would find it. It was hidden there to keep it safe until the time came that the Anishinabe could practice their culture and religion without fear from any man.

The prophet also said that when that time came, a baby would be born — this baby would be a boy. When he got older, he would dream where the Ironwood Log would be hidden and lead his people to it. The Anishinabe People would live in peace once again.

Many Anishinabe Mothers ask themselves, will their little one be the one to lead the people with his dreams. I am an Anishinabe Mother, and I ask myself that question when I look upon my son

at night . . . "Will he be the one?"

Many Indian women will never ask themselves that question, and never have the hopes that I have for my son — for they will never be mothers. The hope and pride of being an Indian Mother has been taken from them with a slash of a surgeon's scalpel. It's called Sterilization . . .

Government Investigation

Two major reports have been released recently. The first was that of Dr Connie Uri, a Cherokee/Choctaw physician from the Los Angeles area. Dr. Uri came across the first case of this method of genocide against our people in November 1972. It was a young woman 26 years old. This young Indian woman had her uterus removed when she was 20. She already had two children, but because she was an alcoholic, and in the doctor's eyes, incurable — he performed a hysterectomy. A very radical operation for so young a woman.

After that, Dr Uri led an investigation in Claremore, Oklahoma. She discovered that 48 sterilization operations were performed in a one-month period (July 1974) at this Indian Health Service Hospital (IHS) in Claremore, Oklahoma. Some of these operations were hysterectomies performed on women as young as eighteen.

Dr. Uri finally got someone to listen to her, Senator Abourezk of South Dakota. He asked the government to investigate her charges; the Government Accounting Office (GAO) handled the investigation. It took GAO two years to complete their investigation.

The GAO report revealed that in four Indian Health Service hospitals — Aberdeen, Phoenix, Oklahoma City and Albuquerque — there were 3,406 sterilization operations performed in a three-year period of time. This was for the fiscal years 1973 to 1976. (According to government census, Indians are about half of one percent of the population of the United States. The sterilizations among Indians would be equivalent to about 452,000 sterilizations among the national population. — Ed.)

Of the 3,406 sterilizations, 3,001 were performed on Indian Women of child bearing age (15–44) and 142 of these operations were performed on Indian Men. 1,024 operations were performed outside the IHS hospitals by doctors and facilities under contract from IHS for this purpose.

The GAO report also revealed that IHS was still sterilizing individuals under the age of 21, although a moratorium was, and still is, in effect on sterilizing minors. According to the report, 36 individuals under the age of 21 were sterilized.

The GAO report dealt only with informed consent. This was their only real concern when compiling the report, but in every case that they studied, true informed consent was lacking for one reason or another. Informed consent is only a legal term . . . not a moral term.

Exporting sterilization

So what is IHS doing now? Well, according to *Akwesasne Notes*, IHS has been accused of sending medical teams to Liberia on funds meant for Indian Health needs. These medical teams are supposedly going there for consultation, but investigators report that once in Liberia, the surgeons (experts in sterilization techniques) are being dispersed to racist South Africa's training centers. At the training centers, they are consulting with doctors on sterilization techniques to use on Black Women in South Africa's "Reservations". This report is unconfirmed; however, IHS has admitted to sending medical personnel to Liberia.

Sterilization Abuse or Forced sterilization is by no means limited to Indian people. One-fifth of all married Black women in the U.S. are sterilized. One-third of all women of child bearing age in Puerto Rico are sterilized. Figures are now running as high as 42 percent of American Indian women sterilized in certain areas.

According to Dr. Uri, "We have only about 100,000 women of child-bearing age — total . . . The Indian population of this country is dwindling, no matter what government statistics say to the contrary."

Dr. Uri also states that voluntary sterilization among a "population of 200 million people isn't going to wipe out the country, but in such a small group, it will wipe out Indians. Sterilization cannot be the preferred form of birth control for minority groups."

Dr. Uri said at the Sterilization Hearings in Los Angeles, "They admitted to one sterilization on Indians for every seven births. Actually, it was one in every four — they didn't admit that."

But according to Dr Emery Johnson, IHS Director, "The Indian sterilization rate is no higher than in the general populations." He also stated that sterilization of American Indians "had nothing to do with genocide".

Our children — Our future

The sterilization of the American Indian woman is not a matter of medical ethics or experimentation. It is an act of genocide, the murder of the unborn Indian child. Genocide is part of the American Indian's history since the onslaught of so-called "civilization".

The System tells us that we are poor because we have so many children. It tries to leave us with the opinion that when we have no children, we will be wealthy . . . we will be surrounded by flower beds and white picket fences around our own homes — this is not so.

Our children are our future. Our children are our wealth. When the system starts sharing some of its money with us, we can live in material comfort. Until that time comes, our comfort is with our families.

And, my hope lies with my son or another Anishinabe son to lead us to our future.

Dee FairBanks

Source: Indigena, Berkeley, California, Summer 1977.

14. Prison

Introduction

Indigenous people are among the most imprisoned in the world; indeed a recent Australian survey declared that one group of Aborigines may be the most incarcerated group on this planet.[330] *The pattern holds on many US reservations and in parts of northern Canada.*

At one level, there are men and women, hounded by the FBI and other federal US agencies since Wounded Knee (1973), who have been thrown behind bars on trumped-up charges for political reasons, motives of fear — Leonard Peltier is the most renowned, but not the only representative of these. Then there are many others — usually unknown and unremembered — who in a moment of anger and frustration at an injustice done by whites, resort to violence and end up behind bars. But the largest number are those who turn to alcohol, get drunk, throw a few punches, and fall foul of whiteman's law; or who resort to apparently meaningless violence (and often self-inflicted injuries) because they have been marginalized, forcibly separated from their land, compelled to repudiate their culture, live apart from their Elders or their own children.[331]

It would be as invidious to distinguish which of these are "political prisoners" and which "social casualties" as it would be to draw a dividing line between the black "criminals" of a South African bantustan, the "rioters" of Soweto, and the Mandelas.

On 26 June 1975, barely two years after the historic defence of traditional Indian sovereignty at Wounded Knee (see Vol. 2, p. 107, n 72), Dick Wilson — the corrupt tribal chief of the Pine Ridge reservation, South Dakota — signed away 133,000 acres of "his" peoples' land to mining companies (notably, Union Carbide which has since become notorious for the Bhopal disaster in India).

That day the reservation was flooded with FBI agents, US marshals, SWAT teams, and agents of COINTELPRO — an FBI operation which for some years had tried to undermine both the black and the American Indian resurgence using all manner of illegal methods.[332]

In the confrontation that followed, one native American and two FBI agents were killed. Three hundred and sixty five members of the

*community were arrested in the ensuing hunt. Among these were Rob
Robideau, Dino Butler, Jimmy Eagle and Leonard Peltier.*[333] *The first two
pleaded self-defence and were acquitted; charges against Jimmy Eagle were
dropped. Peltier escaped to Canada from where he was extradited on the
basis of an affidavit signed by a native American woman, Myrtle Poor
Bear. Although Poor Bear recanted and offered to turn defence witness,
Peltier was hauled into court and on 18 April 1977, sentenced to two life
imprisonments. These are the bare facts in a case which has achieved
international notoriety (even a protest from the Soviet Union)*[334] *and
demonstrated unequivocally the threat posed by the American Indian
Movement (AIM) to agencies of the US Federal government.*

*Leonard Peltier, an Ojibway-Lakota, with a long history of militant
activism for his people, is certainly the most renowned American Indian
political prisoner of recent times; arguably of all time. His statement to
Judge Benson, before sentence in 1977, marks a watershed in relationships
between native Americans and their oppressors.*

*However, many other AIM supporters have been persecuted by the FBI:
a partial list would include Dave Madera, Skyhorse, Leonard Crow Dog,
Russell Means, Yvonne Wanrow, Herb Powles — and Dennis Banks.*[335]
*One of the founders of AIM, Banks was convicted of riot and assault in
1975, in Custer, South Dakota: he fled before sentencing but, after taking
refuge on the Onondaga reservation in New York State, surrendered, in
1984 for the sake of his family.*[336]

*Anna Mae Aqash, also arrested in 1975 and charged with possession of
an explosive device, was found murdered on the Pine Ridge reservation only
four months after her release on bail.*[337] *Her statement to the Court of South
Dakota is printed below.*

*Leonard Peltier meanwhile sits, in fear of his life (there have already
been two attempts to murder him), in one of America's most notorious
jails, the Marion penitentiary of Illinois, whose special control unit was
constructed to break the spirit of "recalcitrant inmates". While awaiting a
possible retrial, with evidence showing he was innocent of the charges made
against him*[338] *he, and two other native American prisoners, conducted a
Sacred Life Fast, in protest against the prison authorities' refusal to allow
native American religious practices behind prison walls (see ch. 9).*

"Convicted for being Chippewa and Sioux blood"

Judge Benson:

There is no doubt in my mind or my
people's minds you are going to sentence
me to two consecutive life terms! You

are, and have always been prejudiced
against me and any Native Americans
who have stood before you, you have

openly favored the government all through this trial and you are happy to do whatever the FBI would want you to do in this case.

I did not always believe this to be so! When I first saw you in the courtroom in Sioux Falls, your dignified appearance misled me into thinking that you were a fair-minded person who knew something of the law and who would act in accordance with the law! Which meant that you would be impartial and not favor one side or the other in this law suit; that has not been the case and I now firmly believe that you will impose consecutive life terms solely because that's what you think will avoid the displeasures of the FBI. Yet neither my people nor myself know why you would be so concerned about an organization that has brought so much shame to the American people. But you are! Your conduct during this trial leaves no doubt that you will do the bidding of the FBI without any hesitation!

You are about to perform an act which will close one more chapter in the history of the failure of the United States courts and the failure of the people of the United States to do justice in the case of a Native American. After centuries of murder of millions of my Brothers and Sister by white racist America, could I have been wise in thinking that you would break that tradition and commit an act of justice? Obviously not! Because I should have realized that what I detected was only a very thin layer of dignity and surely not of fine character. If you think my accusations have been harsh and unfounded, I will explain why I have reached these conclusions and why I think my criticism has not been harsh enough:

First, Each time my defense team tried to expose FBI misconduct in their investigation of this law suit and tried to present evidence of this, you claimed it was irrelevant to this trial. But the prosecution was allowed to present their case with evidence that was in no way relevant to this law suit — for example, an automobile blowing up on a freeway in Wichita, Kansas; an attempted murder in Milwaukee, Wisconsin, for which I have not been found innocent or guilty; or a van loaded with legally-sold firearms and a policeman who claims someone fired at him in Oregon state. The Supreme Court of the United States tried to prevent convictions of this sort by passing into law that only past convictions may be presented as evidence if it is not prejudicial to the law suit, and only evidence of the said case may be used. This court knows very well I have no prior convictions, nor am I even charged with some of these alleged crimes; therefore, they cannot be used as evidence in order to receive a conviction in this farce called a trial. This is why I strongly believe you will impose two life terms, running consecutively, on me.

Second, You could not make a reasonable decision about my sentence because you suffer from at least one of three defects that prevent a rational conclusion: you plainly demonstrated this in your decision about the Jimmy Eagle and Myrtle Poor Bear aspects of this case. In Jimmy's case, for some unfounded reason that only a judge who consciously and openly ignores the law would call it irrelevant to my trial; in the mental torture of Myrtle Poor Bear you said her testimony would shock the conscience of the American people if believed! But *you* decided what was to be believed and what was not to be believed — not the jury! Your conduct shocks the conscience of what the American legal system stands for! — *the search for the truth!* by a jury of citizens. What was it that made you so afraid to let that testimony in? Your own guilt at being part of a corrupt pre-planned trial to get a conviction no matter how your reputation would be tarnished? For these reasons, I strongly believe you will do the bidding of the FBI and give me two consecutive life terms.

Third, In my opinion, anyone who failed to see the relationship between the undisputed facts of these events surrounding the investigation used by the FBI in their interrogation of the Navajo youths: Wilford Draper, who was tied to a chair for three hours and denied access to his attorney; the outright threats to Norman Brown's life; the bodily harm threatened to Mike Anderson; and finally, the murder of Anna Mae Aquash — must be blind, stupid, or without human feelings so there is no doubt and little chance that you have the ability to avoid doing today what the FBI wants you to do — which is to sentence me to two life terms running consecutively.

Fourth, You do not have the ability to see that the conviction of an AIM activist helps to cover up what the government's own evidence showed: that large numbers of Indian people engaged in that fire fight on June 26, 1975.

You do not have the ability to see that the government must suppress the fact that there is a growing anger amongst Indian people and that Native Americans will resist any further encroachment by the military forces of the capitalistic Americans, which is evidenced by the large number of Pine Ridge residents who took up arms on June 26, 1975, to defend themselves. Therefore, you do not have the ability to carry out your responsibility towards me in an impartial way and will run my two life terms consecutively.

Fifth, I stand before you as a proud man; I feel no guilt! I have done nothing to feel guilty about! I have no regrets of being a Native American activist — thousands of people in the United States, Canada and around the world have and will continue to support me to expose the injustices that have occurred in this courtroom. I do feel pity for your people that they must live under such an ugly system. Under your system, you are taught greed, racism and corruption — and most serious of all, the destruction of Mother Earth. Under the Native American system, we are taught all people are Brothers and Sisters; to share the wealth with the poor and needy. But the most important of all is to respect and preserve the Earth, who we consider to be our Mother. We feed from her breast; our Mother gives us life from birth and when it's time to leave this world, she again takes us back into her womb. But the main thing we are taught is to preserve her for our children and our grandchildren, because they are the next who will live upon her.

No, I'm not the guilty one here; I'm not the one who should be called a criminal — white racist America is the criminal for the destruction of our lands and my people; to hide your guilt from the decent human beings in America and around the world, you will sentence me to two consecutive life terms without any hesitation.

Sixth, There are less than 400 federal judges for a population of over 200 million Americans. Therefore, you have a very powerful and important responsibility which should be carried out impartially. But you have never been impartial where I was concerned. You have the responsibility of protecting constitutional rights and laws, but where I was concerned, you neglected to even consider my or Native Americans' constitutional rights. But, the most important of all — you neglected our human rights.

If you were impartial, you would have had an open mind on all the factual disputes in this case. But, you were unwilling to allow even the slightest possibility that a law enforcement officer would lie on the stand. Then, how could you possibly be impartial enough to let my lawyers prove how important it is to the FBI to convict a Native American activist in this case? You do not have the ability to see that such a conviction is an important part of the efforts to discredit those who are trying to alert their Brothers and Sisters to the new threat from the white man, and the attempt to destroy what little Indian land remains in the process of extracting our uranium, oil, and other minerals. Again, to cover up your part in this, you will call me heartless, cold-blooded murderer who deserves two life sentences consecutively.

Seventh, I cannot expect a judge who has openly tolerated the conditions I have been jailed under to make an impartial decision on whether I should be sentenced to concurrent or consecutive life terms. You have been made aware of the following conditions which I had to endure at the Grand Forks County jail, since the time of the verdict:

1) I was denied access to a phone to call my attorneys concerning my appeal;

2) I was locked in solitary confinement without shower facilities, soap, towels, sheets or pillow;

3) the food was inedible; what little there was of it;

4) my family — brothers, sisters, mother and father — who travelled long distances from the reservation, was denied visitation.

No human being should be subjected to such treatment; and while you parade around pretending to be decent, impartial, and law-abiding, you knowingly allowed your fascist chief deputy marshal to play storm-trooper. Again, the only conclusion that comes to mind is that you know and always knew you would sentence me to two consecutive life terms.

Finally, I honestly believe that you made up your mind long ago that I was guilty and that you were going to sentence me to the maximum sentence permitted under the law. But this does not surprise me, because you are a high-ranking member of the white racist American establishment which has consistently said, "In God we Trust," while they went about their business of murdering my people and attempting to destroy our culture.

The only thing I'm guilty of and which I was convicted for was being Chippewa and Sioux blood and for believing in our sacred religion.

Leonard Peltier

Source: Free the People, Leonard Peltier Defense Committee, St Paul, (Minnesota) 1977.

"I believe in the laws of Nature"

As indigenous people we look at our relationship to the United States government and we look at our relationship to the land, our obligations to the land. Our obligations to our people are stronger than our obligations to the United States government. The United States government is barely 200 years old, the land and our people go back 100 thousand years. The federal government chose to prosecute us because we will not betray our culture, our identity. The federal government chose to prosecute us because we chose not to betray the People.

We are surprised the American public can sit back and accept the conduct of various agencies of the federal government such as the Federal Bureau of Investigation. All we must do is look at the conduct of the Federal Bureau of Investigation in the last 10 to 15 years, the attacks against the Blacks, the attacks against Martin Luther King, Jr., were of the same nature as the attacks against the so-called Black militant, Fred Hampton, the attack against the Communist Party and the Socialist Workers Party.

Look at the Congress, the elected government of the United States. They are thoroughly intimidated by the Federal Bureau of Investigation because the Federal Bureau of Investigation has investigated all of them. They are powerless to stand up to the lawlessness. They are victims of their own hypocrisy. Look at the burglaries and the murders and the suicide notes and the death threats. Look at the conduct of this activity. We watch a non-political election take place in 1976 when the politicians were saying that the public was apathetic and they didn't know why. What could they do about this apathetic public? They claimed innocence, ignorance of the reasons.

Look back over the history of the Federal Bureau of Investigation, the civil rights movement, that was a political alternative to racial equality economically. Coming from the people. The federal government through the FBI and paid provocateurs infiltrated the civil rights movement and waged political warfare. The anti-war movement was again another political alternative to war. It was the people expressing themselves and the FBI chose to attack. The American Indian Movement is a religious political alternative to our people and the government chooses to attack. *We view this as no more than repressive activity designed and implemented to prevent the growth of new political and social ideas from the people.* To make the people afraid to stand up and speak their ideas and their minds. We take all things into consideration and we think it is time the people of the United States, the people of America evaluate their position. It is time a decision be made as to whose rights are more important: the rights of the people or the rights of the government. It is time to be realistic about the future.

As the indigenous people of the Western Hemisphere, we look at our land and we look at the technology, and we understand the technology needs things like uranium and coal and oil and we know many of these things are on our land. We know this is a justification and a reason for the federal government to attack us, because by attacking us, they intend to get these natural resources. They want to take them by destroying our resistance. They want to destroy our culture. They want to destroy the idea of freedom. They want to make us the same as the white people. They want to make us the same as black people. They want to make us feel powerless. They want to destroy our spirit. They want us to not understand our natural relationship to the earth and our relationship to our spirit. They want us to continue to give respect and validity to their forms of power, their laws and their guns and their bombs. They want us to continue to look at these things as being power. They do not want us to ever recognize that these things are not things of power, these are tools of repression. These are instruments of violence.

True power is natural. A blizzard is true natural power, a tornado and a hurricane and an earthquake. These things of natural power that come from earth are powers that man cannot control. The federal government does not want us to recognize that as people we carry this natural power within us. They do not want us to recognize collectively our natural power is as strong as the artificial power they possess. They want us to be intimidated. They want to separate us by race. They want to separate us by class. They want to separate us by sex. That is why they put Leonard Peltier on trial and convicted him. That is why there have been 562 indictments from Wounded Knee. That is why every member of the American Indian Movement has been to court in the last five years.

It is time for the people to stand for what they believe in. It is time to bring to a halt the criminal practices of federal agencies such as the Federal Bureau of Investigation. It is time to bring back honour and respect. It is time to bring truth back into our daily lives.

It is time for us to understand the problems that confront us are not problems created by color of skin. Our race is a thing that is used. The problems that we must deal with, the problems that we must confront, are ones of values. It is the values that make us what we are. The white people have not practiced the manifest destiny mentality because they have white skin. They practiced this and they believed it because their Christian values told them that it was alright. So it is time that we look at our values.

It is time that we think of liberation. It is time to pray for the People. It is time to make a decision on what we morally believe to be right and what we morally believe to be wrong. It is time to live by those moral beliefs even if it means we must be unpopular, even if it means we will be attacked.

It is time to show strength for what we believe to be right. We ask the people who read this, we ask that they support us. We ask that they be fair. We ask that they be objective. We ask that the people who read this help us to find justice. For by helping us, they can help themselves, and by helping themselves, we can save the People. We ask the people reading this to help us free Leonard Peltier. We ask that the people reading this help us to free the Indigenous People.

I am a part of this creation as you are, no more and no less than each and every one of you within the sound of my voice. I am the generation of generations before me and the generations to come. I was born and cut free from my umbilical cord. I was nurtured by my Mother. I learned to walk, run and speak. I have travelled throughout this Universe and have been only a minute part of this Creation. And from this I have learned what is my freedom.

For every agreement made between the societies of this Universe, I have made but only one to this Federal Court of Pierre, South Dakota, that being: that I shall return on the 3rd day of the month of October in the year of 1975 to enter my "plea", which I consider is a belief rather than a "plea".

I am being denied my right to participate in this Creation. That right being the freedom to come and go as I please in this Universe. The reason given for this being that I have violated a Federal Law which is the illegal possession of a firearm whose serial numbers have been obliterated and/or removed. I shall contest the Federal Government of the United States for I feel that there is no law of governing that I have agreed to in this country with anyone.

I refuse to accept any man-made governing laws that cannot be enforced with fairness to everyone and their freedom. I believe in the laws of Nature which are being enforced without man himself. I do not believe in having to succumb to social, state, federal, or national laws unless I agree to recognize them first. I recognize the laws of Nature put before me in this Universe. If I fail to obey these laws of Nature then I shall face my punishment. My greatest punishment forced on me today is to be denied my right to participate in this Creation. To restrict my travel within your cement "block" is severing my participation.

If I have gone against this Creation — no man on this Universe holds the power to punish me other than the Creator himself. I have but only one power and it is my beliefs, which will exist among the confines of your "blocks" and into a world beyond yesterday and today.

You have been confining me and allowing your servants to strike me since I was the age of 7 years old. Yes, I have been beaten, ridiculed, and restricted since that age. You are continuing to control my life with your violent materialistic needs. I do not realize your need to survive and be a part of this Creation — but you do not understand mine and therefore I refuse to and I will not issue a plea of "guilty" because you are in the majority. My Creator is not the majority.

I have disciplined myself for 30 years and have altered by participation in this Creation so that you can also exist. You have no discipline over yourself in allowing others to survive. I have travelled throughout this country and I have observed your undisciplined military servants provoke those whose rights are the same as yours. I shall continue to discipline myself and appear before you against my desire of unrestricted travel. I shall not ignore you but will face you and I expect the same guarantee that I agreed to before in returning here again to settle this. I want to review the indictment passed by the GRAND JURY and to request that the Government of the Dominion of Canada in my court, if you are considering me a federal violater.

I am not a citizen of the United States or a ward of the Federal Government. Neither am I a ward of the Canadian Government. If I have taken from the United States or Canadian Government anything for my survival it was only in respect for the disciplinary restrictions I have maintained for 30 years to allow you to survive too. I refuse to be punished because of your inability to enforce a governing system that I have not agreed to.

Your preconceived or premeditated acts of establishing power to control this Universe should never be enforced by weapons with serial numbers.

I have a right to continue my cycle in this Universe undisturbed. I have never denied your right to survival.

Anna Mae Aquash
Statement to the Court of South Dakota
September, 1975

Source: Free the People 1977.

Statement of the Haudenosaunee in defense of political prisoners

We, the Council of Chiefs of the Haudenosaunee (also known as the Six Nations Confederacy), express our support of and solidarity with all those men and women who are held prisoners in the United States because of their actions in defense of the sovereignty of Native Nations. The United States is an outlaw in the community of nations. The United States Government has violated every principle of international law and human decency. That government has broken every agreement and every treaty ever made with Native peoples.

It has stolen Native lands and then passed laws and invented policies to enforce those laws which have upheld the oppression of our people. Almost all the Native peoples are political prisoners in their own land. The sovereignty of Native Nations has been stolen as a national policy of the United States.

We express solidarity with Leonard Peltier who is incarcerated on purely political grounds for his action in self-defense and in the defense of the sovereignty of the Lakota Nation. We express our solidarity with the Chiefs and people of the Mohawk Nation who are suffering under indictments and a state of virtual siege by the police forces of New York State for their rightful acts in defending the government of the Haudenosaunee, and we extend our support of and solidarity with all those men and women in United States jails as a result of the extreme political repression directed against those who have participated in actions in support of the sovereignty of their Nations in California, Nebraska, Washington, Oregon, Nevada, New Mexico, Arizona, North and South Dakota, Wisconsin, Montana, Minnesota, Michigan and the many other territories dominated by the United States Government.

The Council of Chiefs
1979

Activists of the American Indian Movement (AIM) are also incarcerated in Canada. One of these, Stuart Stonechild (along with Gary Butler) was transferred in 1984 from his English-speaking prison to a French-speaking prison, presumably to intimidate him.

A recent statement from prison by Stuart Stonechild is followed by a powerful declaration condemning the treatment of native Canadians — as if they were prisoners of society as a whole — which was submitted by the Association of Metis and Non-Status Indians of Saskatchewan, to the Moore Inquiry (into prison reform) in 1977.

Prison as persecution

My name is Stuart Stonechild. I am a Cree prisoner-of-war inside this Canadian prison system.

I am one man, one spirit. I'm a follower of the sacred pipe, the sweatlodge is my church. These ways are "the common heart" of my people; the heart that has sustained us through all persecution of time past. And the heart that sustains me today.

I did not ask for a transfer to this prison! It was a step taken by this prison system to isolate me from my people. And an act designed to silence my personal involvement in the struggle for spiritual freedom for my people inside these prisons.

Today these prison are only an extension of the christian persecution and genocide that my people resisted for centuries. The struggle is a war. A war that is being declared non-existent because the piece of paper this society covers their eyes with states otherwise; Charter of Rights, section 2–2. Yet a war being waged that is still taking a toll in human spirit and life. And a war still intent on the complete annihilation of my people — the aboriginal people of this continent! In my heart, these "paper rights" aren't felt as strongly as the persecution I am subjected to on a day to day basis. I see this war clearly. I see my place in this war clearly. Physically I'm a prisoner, but my spirit remains free to resist.

For the survival of my people, I'm an AIM warrior and a Brotherhood soldier. I retain the spiritual teachings of my elders intact for the future, as they have retained it intact for me. For this I am called a "militant Indian"; a rather redundant and archaic reference used by this system and government to belittle my integrity and avoid the issue.

Yet [this is] all the justification needed for them to continue their attacks.

Militant because I believe in the sanctity of Mother Earth as opposed to her complete destruction?

Militant because I follow the traditional ways of my people instead of the "cargo doctrine" of christianity?

Militant because I speak the truth from the heart as opposed to just making sounds with the mouth?

No. — For those who see, I share my strength. For those who don't, I share my prayers.

This statement is short for now. Further information will be forwarded as my situation transpires.

In the Spirit of Crazy Horse
Stuart Stonechild
Nehiyawak (Cree) P.O.W.

Source: AIM (Canada) Montreal, 1984.

"Our People are Canada's Political Prisoners"

Submission to the Moore Inquiry
by Association of Metis & Non-Status Indians of Sask.

Amongst other things, your inquiry has been charged to look into the causes of the alleged "riot" at the Prince Albert Correctional Centre and into any other associated matters, which you deem to be worth looking into. Such terms of reference can be interpreted very narrowly, or very widely. To date, the former interpretation seems to have been taken. Our Association is not surprised by this decision because we know that a sincere look at the real causes of the disturbance in the Prince Albert Correctional Centre on June 21 and 22 would raise questions about the century of genocide committed against our people that would demand answers far beyond the jurisdiction of a judicial inquiry.

The typical attitude taken towards the massive atrocities committed against Native people was expressed at your inquiry by Mr. Clyne Harradance when he told Mr. Thompson that "it seems strange to me that he [Mr. Thompson] would spend so much time running around to help an inmate he doesn't even know the violent background of", in his legal battle against one of Mr. Thompson's own longtime staff members. While the attitude expressed by Mr. Harradance typifies the attitude of the white establishment towards Native people, and while we would not have used the word 'strange', we would certainly agree with Mr. Harradance that it is very unusual for a government bureaucrat to assist a Native person whose most basic human rights have been brutally violated in seeking justice from those violations. The norm is quite the contrary. The establishment generally rushes to hide any suggestion of misdeeds by their employees, in spite of the fact that the atrocities committed against Native people are a secret to no one. This observation, however is extremely ironic coming from Mr. Harradance, who is a member of the profession of people who earn their livelihood by helping all manners of people in seeking compensation for, or defense against, all forms of real or imagined injustices; so long as they have the money to pay for this help. Native people, however, generally do not have the money necessary to use the services of this profession.

During the course of this investigation you have heard stories of prisoners taking massive doses of drugs in quantities sufficient to take the lives of two of them. It must have crossed your minds, at some point, that there must be a reason why these people would be so willing to consume drugs in this quantity. Why we would be willing to risk our health, even our own life, to seek momentary relief from the nightmare in which we live?

This phenomena is not restricted to our prison population. Drug and alcohol addiction is at a crisis level for our entire people, both inside and outside jail. We were not born a suicidal race. Before the white conquest of North America we did not hang ourselves, slash our wrists or blow out our brains with bullets, alcohol or airplane glue. No — these things are a recent part of our history. They are part of our existence under the oppression of the Canadian government that has robbed us of our land, our culture, our identity and our dignity. Without closely examining this fact, your inquiry will only scratch the surface in your attempt to understand the disturbance that occurred in Prince Albert on June 21 and 22.

It has been mentioned at this inquiry that 67% of the jail population in the P.A. Correctional Centre is Native. This figure must be examined in light of the fact that we represent only 10% of the population in Saskatchewan; this over-representation in jail population is common for Native people.

We are presently the most incarcerated people in the entire world. Can you accept this as a normal situation in a country that brags to the world that it is free and democratic? Our people are political prisoners. The Canadian government is presently planning 27 new federal penitentiaries, while the Saskatchewan government is planning 3 new jails. Who will occupy these new institutions? Our experience with your system has already given us a reasonably good idea as to who will make up the inmate population. Our people are doing life on the instalment plan.

Your histories tell you that we were savages, inhabiting the North American wastelands before your ancestors discovered us. Perhaps this lie allows Canadians to sleep with a lighter conscience, given your government's treatment of us. After all, you brought us civilization and modern medicine but your ancestors also brought us diseases, including tuberculosis and gonorrhoea, which are still epidemical amongst our people. One out of every 3 Blackfoot Indians alive in 1860 died of smallpox, and it is only now that we are coming to learn that much of this disease was spread by deliberately giving us infected blankets. If this was an act of civilization then we would have gladly remained being savages. But, our people were not savages and North America was not a wasteland. We lived here with our own culture and our own institutions of government. We did not have police because we did not require them. Our culture and our laws prohibited anti-social behavior. We did not permit one man to steal another man's land, deprive him of his means of a livelihood and leave him and his family to starve to death.

Those laws were part of the civilization which your ancestors brought to us. The barbarities committed by your civilization against our people are part of your civilization — not ours. But you had to force your civilization upon us and destroy our culture, which was based on values of sharing and brotherhood. Instead of allowing us our own schools you violated your own laws and denied us this right. You broke up our families and dragged our children off to your "Indian schools" to learn your values of greed and competitiveness. But those schools did not teach us the technical competences that were necessary to earn a livelihood in modern industrial society. Academic inequalities between "Indian schools" and the rest of the public school system were so great that to have called those institutions "schools" was a joke. They were concentration camps for Native children.

Having deprived us of our land and livelihood, having broken up our families and our social organizations, having destroyed our culture and our identity, having been cast aside by your civilization as being just so many objects standing in the way of Canadian development that you call progress, many Canadians cannot understand why we act in a self-destructive manner. Our behavior is no different than any other people who are facing genocide. Our people are becoming a violent people. At first, this violence will be turned inward — against ourselves. This phenomena always accompanies cultural disintegration. But the violence does not remain inward. Eventually, more rational targets will be found for our frustration and despair. This is beginning to happen. This is what was happening in the Prince Albert Correctional Centre on June 21 and 22.

Much has been said at your inquiry about who led the riots. Was it the New Native Perspective Society? Was it the American Indian Movement? These questions seem to suggest that if you know the leaders you know who caused the disturbance. What nonsense! The cause of the disturbance was not inside the Prince Albert jail but within Canadian society. The disturbance was a result of people striking back against years of injustice. Do you really believe that leaders start, or are capable of holding back, such uprisings?

Inside the jail is a reflection of society at large and your justice system, which affects us both inside and outside of jail. You have heard Mr. Bryshyn admit to brutally attacking a prisoner and explaining away this atrocity with an apology in which he said he only wanted to show the prisoner what it felt like to be on the receiving end. Our people have been on the receiving end for a 100 years and we know what it feels like to be there. Sometimes we are even tempted to retaliate. You have heard Mr. Bryshyn testify that 2 of his fellow guards stood by and encouraged this vicious attack. These men are civil servants paid to ensure that incidents like this do not happen. Not only are they accomplices to Mr. Bryshyn's assault, but they are committing theft every time they accept their paycheck. Most of our people are in jail for far lesser crimes. You have been told that Mr. Chester was removed from his job for reason of assault, but actually he was promoted. Under your law he should have been incarcerated. Had he been a native and his victim white, incarceration surely would have resulted. The crimes that cause us to be incarcerated are usually the crime of being Indian or the crime of being poor. The self-confessed assaulters are hired as our guards.

Your inquiry has heard much discussion about Native organizations within the jail. Some of your authorities are concerned. Your leaders, who allow or even encourage the racist brutality we face every day, are called statesmen. Our leaders are called "heavies". The newspapers have been full of these discussions. Isolate the "heavies". Restrict the privileges of the "heavies". Confine the "heavies" somewhere else. More nonsense.

Our leaders are sincerely seeking solutions to the desperate situation which we face. If the limited parameters in which they have to work causes them to act in a manner that threatens the system then the parameters should be widened — not narrowed. Our people will develop leaders, and if the system represses those leaders, then new leaders with more militant solutions will emerge.

Mr. Stubbs, Mr. Waller and a host of other "authorities" have told your inquiry that tighter security and more discipline are required to keep our people in line. Mr. Bryshyn even suggested that we should be worked so hard we would be too tired to cause trouble. What absurdities! You cannot kill the spark that exists within our people to resist racist oppression. You can only cause that spark to find more desperate means of fighting for our liberation. The answer to dealing with our people lies either in the elimination of the oppression under which we live, or the completion of genocide, which was started by your forefathers.

Source: New Breed, Saskatchewan, September–October 1977.

The concluding statements in this chapter were presented to the Fourth Russell Tribunal (Rotterdam, November 1980) and drafted by the Presidential Office of the High Court of the Chamber of Representatives of West Papua (Dewan Tertinggi Perwakilan Rajkat Papua Barat). They were signed by Ms. Kaisiëpo and D.S. Ayamiseba "on behalf of the people of West/Papua/Melanesia and the allies in the Operasi Papoea Merdeka (Free Papua Movement or OPM)" — the latter being the liberation movement which since 1965 has struggled to liberate West Papua from a genocidal Indonesian occupation.[339]*

"Not wanting to keep silent"
Detention and Banishment

In the early years of the Indonesian Administration in West Papua (New Guinea) many people, who don't want to keep silent about their opinion, were detained. Even now this is still happening.

See the list of Papuan people, whom some even died in prison of torture etc. The most well known are Johan Ariks (Manokwari) and not so long ago Baldus Mofu (Biak). The story of first mentioned person can be found in this documentation. Several others, like Dirk S. Ayamiseba (escaped in 1980 to the Netherlands), Eliazer Bonay (who is at the moment in Papua New Guinea living in a refugee camp), Menasse Suwai (escaped to Holland in 1979), escaped on fear of their lives to other countries.

And all this because of their support to their people in West Papua New Guinea. Dirk S. Ayamiseba is escaped to the Netherlands and asked the Government for political asylum.

The following statement was announced by Dirk S. Ayamiseba, his son Andy Ayamiseba manager of the Papuan Popgroup the Black Brothers and Markus Wonggor, Kaisiëpo Ms:

"Being political refugees we declare:

We fled into the Netherlands because of our political differences with Indonesia. These political differences are the results of the political repression and the exceptional violations of the Human Rights by the Indonesian Republic in our country, West Papua New Guinea (West Irian). Under the administration of Indonesia many ten thousands of our people found their death in the past 17 years. The presence of the Indonesian Republic in our country is also caused by the Netherlands and the United States of America. We therefore deem the Netherlands and the United States of America also responsible for the death of many ten thousands of innocent people in our country. So we demand that the Netherlands and the United States of America look after the retreat of the Indonesian Republic out of West Papua New Guinea (West Irian).

Not only Russia has to get out of Afghanistan, but Indonesia too has to retreat from West Papua New Guinea and East-Timor.

We demand therefore that both countries — the Netherlands and the United States of America — to get Indonesia out of our country in the same way they have helped Indonesia to get into our country; because of the killing in both West Papua New Guinea and in East Timor by the Indonesians.

Message from the Home-Country   31-10-1980

Be Greeted,
When possible, I ask for help in order to spread the delayed information from our country by radio and press.

1. The ABRI (Angkatan Bersenjatah Republik Indonesia) has killed this year in Irian Jaya (West Papua) – by capturing and torturing of political prisoners at Biak and Jayapura – the following persons:

Baldus Mofu (at Biak, 7-2-1980)
Michael Wajoi, and
Mathias Tata-Rawajai (both at Jayapura, in the beginning of this year)

2. Six women who hoisted the Papuan-flag in front of the building of the Government of Irian Jaya (West Irian), Dok 2, in Jayapura at 4 August 1980 are still in prison in the KODIM-prison, Jayapura. These female political prisoners are raped and humiliated by members of the ABRI.

3. Marten Tabu, Jareth Wajoi, Joël Worumi and Abner May have to stand their trials at the Military Court at Jayapura.
In spite of his surrender at 16 April 1980 and his amnesty by the president of the Republic of Indonesia, the case against Marten Tabu is not cancelled. Also Jereth Wajoi and Abner May who did sign a co-operation declaration and became members of the ABRI.

4. The arresting and the detention of Freedom-fighters in Irian Jaya (West Papua) is still going on.
At least 500 Papuan fighters – who are fighting for the Independence of their country – are detained in prison all over Irian Jaya (West Papua).

So far and thank you in advance.

We are the sovereign people of this land

It is impossible to find an Indian family who doesn't have an immediate member in jail or being processed by the courts, or a young one in foster care, some loved one bouncing from the gutter to the treatment center and around again.

This is the real everyday life environment of our present day young generation — what they are learning from — their example of a way of life. There are still a lot of us not now in prison or totally consumed by these other problems but we are living with and are horrified at these symptoms of programmed genocide.

It is the constant regulating of us by Congress and the courts for the benefit of those who profit by these political manipulations and is accomplished through our inability to determine our own direction in our lives. They have kept us so split up that enough of us haven't gathered together to decide a truly proper course of action for our own benefit.

Our politics is out of our hands and in the hands of our greatest enemy . . . we are all truly political prisoners.

We must oppose this devastating control lest our children become like them and totally abandon their future generations for their present personal gains. If we cannot come together to decide for ourselves a proper course of action, a proper direction as a race, then this present continuing genocide must eventually lead to total annihilation, we will cease to exist.

Source: 1978 Statement from "The Longest Walk", (see Part 4, ch. 10).

15. Tourism

Tourist/Home Movies

"And here's one of an Indian
Selling Ralph a trinket —
I suppose he'll use the money
To buy some wine and drink it."
Tourist, do you also
Tour the Black Man's slums
Photographing winos,
Photographing bums?
Do you really think you're welcome,
Do you really think it's funny
The things that starving people do
For little bits of money?
Do you see the anger?
Do you see the pain?
That says in silence "Go away
And don't come back again."

Bob Bacon.
Source: Akwesasne Notes.

Compared with the other depredations and indignities suffered by
indigenous peoples, tourism might seem a minor irritant. In fact, the
usually ignorant, often arrogant, loud-mouthed, heavy-footed European or
American, swinging camera and flashing dollars, ploughing into native
communities by charabanc and river steamer, has to many indigenous
people come to signify the ugliest kind of invasion. This is especially true
of the Pacific where island nations such as Hawaii, Fiji and Tahiti are
virtually in hock to tourist interests, and where, relative to overseas visits,
robbery, rape, drug-pushing and prostitution are increasing.

But these are only the most obvious signs of malaise. In order to keep
tourists coming some governments – notably Fiji and the Philippines – offer
development corporations tax holidays, cheap indigenous labour, and in
many cases, indigenous peoples' land or fishing and hunting reserves.[340]

Hydroelectric schemes power tourist complexes, drawing on local water

*supplies or flooding native forest and paddy. Roads are driven through
fields and villages, often endangering sacred sites. Most drastic of all,
families are kicked off "development" tracts and forced to earn a
subsistence living by caricaturing the rituals and ceremonies which bound
them to their evacuated land.*

*Organised tourism in Peru was, until quite recently, confined to areas close
to the mainstream of the Ucayali-Amazonas: the Shipibo-Conibo near
Pucallpa, and the Yagua and Ticuna people near Iquitos and Leticia were
its principal victims. Contracted by entrepreneurs, the Indians are paid to
await the tourists, take off their western-style clothes, abandon their
shotguns and act the "primitive" for the cameras. The blurb for one of the
tourist agencies using the region evinces a barely-concealed racialism:*

*". . . these strange jungle people dress now as they did long before the
Conquistadores even dreamed of the New World; grass skirts are the basic
dress for both men and women. Friendly and chatty, they talk freely and
giggle frequently with all visitors. Often the men will bring out their long
blow-guns and put on an exhibition that would command respect from any
marksman . . . We can also acquire some of their native produce."[341]*

*Of late, more "adventurous" tours have been organised in the form of
pseudo-scientific expeditions, often advertised in leftist American and
European journals. The Peruvian Manu National Park – allegedly a
conservation area – may well have originally been conceived as a vast
tourist stamping ground.[342] And, indeed, a 1985/86 brochure, produced by
one London-based tourist company, lists trips to Manu — in conjunction with
the World Wildlife Fund – as one of its major attractions.[343]*

Our culture will belong to the tourists
Shipibo-Conibo Declaration Against Tourism

At the present time, the indigenous communities are confronting a new type of
penetration and exploitation on the part of groups who are dominating them
through tourism. Many companies organise tourist trips to the communities, and
make a large profit from them.

The object of these journeys is to display the life and customs of the people,
distorted and adapted to the tastes of the tourists. Native peoples are presented as
groups of "savages" and "uncivilised", as people still living in former eras and now
overpowered by history. In order to make their journeys interesting, tour
companies that organise them distort, ridicule and disparage the indigenous people.
They are treated as mere objects.

The tourist companies make huge profits at the expense of the communities; but
the people reap no reward. Recently, companies on the Ucayali have been making
$10,000 for each day trip from each tourist, but the communities receive nothing.

For the indigenous people tourism signifies the breakdown of, or a change in,
traditional life and traditional forms of production, work and interchange. They

abandon their traditional lifestyle in order to carry out work for tourists. In this way they devote themselves to making *things* that can be sold, or doing their traditional dances but modified so as to make them more agreeable to the tourists. But the tourists are not interested in the dances or the songs of the people. The only thing that interests them is to amuse themselves and laugh at the expense of the people; to take photos to show in their own countries that they were with "savages" in the real jungle.

In this way, little by little, the dances, festivals, beliefs and ways of life of the people are losing their significance. There will come a time when these dances, songs and beliefs have become so modified that they no longer belong to indigenous culture — but to that of the tourists. This is another form of theft.

In order to gain the trust of some people, the tourist companies often economically favour one or two members of the community, so as to ease their entrance into the communities. In this way some members of the community are converted into exploiters of their own people. This breaks down unity, something which up till now has always existed.

Tourism also means a new way of distracting the indigenous people and making them forget the social, economic, health, political and cultural problems that face them.

The tourist companies create new "necessities" causing a greater dependency on consumer goods that, owing to their low wages and the low prices paid for their products, the people cannot buy. At the same time, the artistic and cultural creativity of the communities comes to be affected — in that they imitate the production of objects attractive to tourists in order to sell them.

In some communities, the members think that, to allow the entrance of tourists could be beneficial, because it is a way of having better outlets for the sale of their artefacts. In other communities the possibility of charging the companies, and also making the individual tourist pay an entrance fee, has been considered.

These proposals in the long term will bring negative consequences even though there will be some economic improvements initially. With time, tourism will destroy the indigenous culture and will contribute towards the final disappearance of the group.

In other communities it is considered that no tourists at all should be allowed into the communities. This could be achieved through organised opposition, through assemblies and meetings to study the problem. The communities must also look for help to peasant and other indigenous organisations, so they can put pressure on the state organisms responsible for the regulation of the tourist companies.

In the face of all the problems caused by the tourist agencies, in the indigenous communities of Rio Ucayali, some of them have agreed the following:

Paoyhan community: Total rejection of the tourist agencies because the Communities don't benefit by their presence. We won't allow the entry of tourists because they bring other ways of living and in general a culture different from our own reality.

Tentiboya community: We don't want the people from these highly developed countries coming and viewing us as tourist objects.

Calleria community: We totally reject the appearance of tourist companies because we are not touristic objects, but human beings.

Patria Nueva community: A total rejection of the tourist agencies. The entrance of tourists won't be allowed, so as to ensure that tourists have more respect for indigenous people.

Flor Naciente community: We reject the new forms of financial exploitation by the capitalists creating touristic companies. The entrance of tourists won't be allowed, as the first action taken, as a form of protest, on the part of the community.

Shambo community: We do not subscribe to the presence of tourist enterprises because it benefits only a very few people.

Pamaillo community: The tourist companies trample on the rights of indigenous peoples looking for new ways to enrich themselves. Tourism is one of the new methods that these "*sabidos*" use to make money at our expense. They look for help from progressive organisations in order to gain respect for their existence.

Source: Grupo Aquinmis, Shipibo, Rio Ucayali, 1978.

Indigenous Filipinos suffer profoundly from the worst effects of tourism. In June 1979 a whole village of Dumagat people was uprooted in Dingalan, Aurora, to make way for a multi-million peso resort along the sea coast. Four years earlier hundreds of Ifugao families lost rice fields, orchards and watersheds, thanks to the construction of the Lamut-Banaue national highway, intended to boost tourism in the province. Early in 1980 the entire Ibaloi Igorot community of Taloy Sur in Tuba, Benguet, was removed so that the Ministry of Tourism and the Philippine Tourist Authority could construct Marcos Park (which features a model Igorot village as one of its attractions!).

Bontoc and Matuksa "cultural reservations" in Baguio — the country's largest tourist attraction next to Manila — house tribal people without electricity or other amenities, while the government squanders public money on convention centres, hotels, parks and city streets.[344]

"Cultural festivals", largely engineered by tourist interests, take place throughout the Philippines. One of the most renowned is the Grand Canao of Baguio intended to "showcase the culture of the different Cordilleran tribes".[345] The reality behind the razzmatazz was made clear by a group of Igorot students from the Cordillera in a statement issued in late 1980.

A masquerade to hide injustice

Since ancient times, the *cañao* has been a ritual dance of the people of the Cordillera to appease the spirit-gods. It is held only in times of death, marriage, or thanksgiving. Now, the Igorots in the "Grand Cañao" are unaware that their customs and traditions are being used in praise of a new god — Tourism.

The objectives of the "Grand Cañao", according to its organizers, are "to boost the tourism industry and preserve the culture of the Igorots".

What does that mean?

First, there is an anxious desire to build up the tourist industry as a means of increasing the dollar reserve of the country, since the Philippines is in heavy debt because of multi-billion dollar loans from foreign countries.

Second, the "Grand Cañao" is offered as a commercial item or market commodity, not for the interests and welfare of the Igorots, but for the interest of business establishments, hotels, restaurants, tour guides, etc. What do the Igorot dancers get out of the "Grand Cañao"? Cultural prestige? No, but cultural exploitation.

Third, the "Grand Cañao" is an attempt of the government to show that the Philippines is a "big, beautiful, entertaining country, with smiling and dancing people". The "Grand Cañao" is actually a façade, a masquerade which hides the social ills and injustices which many Igorots are suffering from.

The attention of the tourist, some unenlightened Filipinos, and even most of the Igorot participants to the "Grand Cañao", is diverted from the racial discrimination against and exploitation and oppression of the Igorots: the Ibaloi, Kankana-ey, Bontoc, Ifugao, Kalinga and Apayao people.

1. In the 1950s, two giant hydroelectric dams were built in Benguet, dislocating Ibaloi families living there. Up till now, the dislocated families have not yet received just compensation for their expropriated lands.

2. At present, the government is forcing thousands of Bontocs and Kalingas to leave their ancestral lands and give way to the erection of hydroelectric dams. Many Igorots have died in the struggle against the dams, which threaten to destroy hundreds of hectares of rice terraces and fruit plantations. The province of Kalinga is under the tyranny of the military.

3. Eighty-one Ibaloi families in Taloy Sur have been ejected from their lands to give way to Marcos Park, a tourist complex which is under construction.

4. In Apayao, 6,000 Isnegs will be forced out of their lands when the waters of four hydroelectric dams will rise. The government started constructing the dams without first informing the people that their lands and homes will be submerged.

5. Many Igorots all over the Mountain Provinces are prohibited by the government from cutting down trees for firewood or construction, but huge foreign-controlled logging corporations are allowed to wipe out centuries-old forests of pine trees.

6. The land of the Cordillera is rich in mineral resources: gold, copper, silver, even uranium. Foreign-controlled mining corporations now monopolize the mining industry, with huge million dollar profits. Igorot mine workers receive an average salary of only P35 a day or less.

7. Some Ibaloi families were dislocated by the establishment of the Baguio City Export Processing Zone, a commercial paradise for multi-national corporations.

8. In the last typhoon, Igorot farmers suffered millions of pesos in damages on their vegetable farms.

9. About 600 Ibalois and Kankana-eys are being forced out of their lands in Daklan, Bukod, to give way to a geothermal plant.

The fact that many people are unaware of these things is reflective of the repressive measures of the present government.

The list goes on — economic dislocations, ejection from ancestral lands, exploitation of the Cordillera natural resources where the Igorots are not beneficiaries. All in the name of infrastructure and technical development. All in the mad scramble to cope with foreign standards of economic advancement. All in a sick desire for international publicity while the broad masses of the Philippine society, the supposed beneficiaries of development, are overlooked and their rights trampled upon.

Now, even the cultural practices of the people are being used for the benefit of the tourists and the privileged few.

Still, the "Grand Cañao" organizers have the audacity to claim an annual showcase of native songs and dances will preserve the culture of the people! How will you preserve the culture of a people if you are destroying their lives? Is singing and dancing all there is to culture? In the first place, their use of the term "culture" is perverted. The "Grand Cañao" is *not* the culture of the Igorots. The whole affair is out of context. Its purpose has been divorced from the traditional beliefs and customs, values and ideas of the people.

Therefore, we students from the different provinces of the Cordillera hereby denounce and oppose the "Grand Cañao" as just another form of exploiting our people.

We believe that the people must have the right to self-determination, and that they should not be subjected to the whims of a privileged few.

To the public, we exhort you to open your minds, and realize that in the land of the true *cañao*, in the mountains, there are people who are suffering from oppression; that this is no time to hold a "Grand Cañao"; that an authentic Grand Cañao will only happen when the people have finally achieved freedom and justice!!

Concerned students from the Cordillera 1980

Australia's most renowned tourist attraction, Ayer's Rock, was handed back to its Aboriginal owners in 1983. The move generally won approval though it was long overdue (much of this sacred site having been eroded by the countless boots of thoughtless visitors) and largely token: the Aborigines would lease back the "site" to the government, so that some form of tourism could continue.[346] *The following year another sacred Aboriginal area, coveted by a motley of "leisure interests", was temporarily saved from flooding to make a marina.*[347]

Though the encroachment of tourism on Aboriginal land is much less than mining, some Aboriginal areas — for example in northern Queensland — have become favourite targets for state and private tourist interests. This is especially true of Palm Island, the notorious former penal colony for recalcitrant Aborigines (see Chapter 14) which in 1971 was put out to tender by the right-wing Queensland government as a tourist centre.[348] *That particular proposal was apparently shelved, but in 1977 Palm Aborigines discovered that Orpheus, a small island in the Palm group, was being put up for tourist lease.*

In response to this threat North Queensland Aborigines, and academics from the Pacific, hosted a seminar called "Tourism and the future: Coordination or Chaos?" Mick Miller delivered a statement on behalf of the North Queensland Land Council — the country's largest Aboriginal organisation — setting the terms under which his people were prepared to countenance tourism.[349]

No risk for a quick buck

Aborigines must participate fully in the establishment of any tourism on Aboriginal reserves. For far too long we have been the forgotten people in deals between governments and commercial interests — e.g. mining — to Australia's shame, and now we are beginning to make ourselves heard.

It is time Aboriginal people are consulted before any development takes place on Aboriginal reserves. Tourist operators often have secret meetings with Chairmen of Aboriginal reserves without the knowledge of the people.

There must be effective Aboriginal control and participation in planning of any tourist enterprise on Aboriginal reserves by the Council and Community to protect the culture of the people and their environment. A good percentage of the profits should go to the Aboriginal Communities concerned. Tourism would be good for the reserves in Queensland if and only if Aboriginals had the major say in the business; in that way they could benefit.

Aboriginal people must be employed not only as cooks and yardmen but must be trained in the managerial side of tourism so they can effectively have a say in running tourist complexes.

Tourism must be controlled instead of having a mad race into nowhere when we don't know where it will end up. We are particularly concerned about the effects on the environment and on Aboriginal culture. At the same time there are advantages in improved communications, transport, health and education on the reserves which are very far away from the mainstream of society.

Rather than see private enterprise develop a tourist project on an Aboriginal reserve, even if it is in liaison with the people, it would be better if the government funded the Aboriginal Council or Co-operative to initiate a Tourist enterprise and provide managerial training for local Aborigines plus perhaps some white advisers answerable to the Aboriginal Council.

We must not however risk our culture for the sake of a quick buck.

Source: Messagestick (NQLC) Vol. 3, No. 1, 1978.

16.   The Land is not for Sale

Underscoring virtually every contemporary struggle by indigenous peoples — be it against specific damage, or for cultural and political self-determination — is the demand for land rights. The demand is couched in varying terms, depending on whether treaties have been violated (as in the USA and New Zealand) or never signed (as in Canada; see Volume 2, Part 4, ch. 7); on whether traditional land has been progressively usurped from its original custodians (as in Australia and Amazonia), or is threatened by identifiable contemporary aggressors.

This chapter includes declarations by land-based peoples suffering from each of these varieties of theft. Inevitably their concerns are both general and specific — and for that reason, might have been included elsewhere in this book. (By the same token, many statements printed in other chapters could have found a place here.) In addition, other peoples who thought they enjoyed an implicit right to their territory — as in Ecuador, the Philippines, Chile before the dictatorship, parts of Brazil, or in Costa Rica — have recently suffered the brunt of arbitrary legislation, designed to privatise their holdings, or "emancipate" them.

WHAT TREATY THAT THE WHITES HAVE KEPT HAS THE RED MAN BROKEN? Not one. What treaty that the white man ever made with us have they kept? Not one. When I was a boy the Sioux owned the world; the sun rose and set on their land; they sent ten thousand men to battle. Where are the warriors today? Who slew them? Where are our lands? Who owns them? What white man can say I ever stole his land or a penny of his money? Yet, they say I am a thief. What white woman, however lonely, was ever captive or insulted by me? Yet they say I am a bad Indian. What white man has ever seen me drunk? Who has ever come to me hungry and unfed? Who has ever seen me beat my wives or abuse my children? What law have I broken? Is it wrong for me to love my own? Is it wicked for me because my skin is red? Because I am a Sioux; because I was born where my father lived; because I would die for my people and my country?

Sitting Bull

Day of the Indian

"Today, the 19th of April, is the day dedicated to the Indians all over Brazil. We know neither when nor why the Day of the Indian was created, but we wish to take advantage of the opportunity to make public our message of the Day of the Indian.

First we want to say that the 22nd of April, 1500, when Pedro Alvares Cabral stepped for the first time on these lands, was the beginning of the expansion of western civilisation and the beginning of the end of the indigenous societies.

With the passage of the years, our destruction was intensified, carried out by western civilisation. The most diverse instruments of degradation were used in the massacre of the indigenous groups. Factors contributing to this process were sicknesses brought by the white man which had until then been unknown to us, the plundering of our lands, and the application of colonialist and ethnocentric educational methods which did not respect our political, economic and religious structure.

So much so that in the 16th century the Indians were considered irrational animals, and it was necessary for Pope Paul III to declare to the public of the time that we were human beings, with body and soul. But in spite of this, the destruction of the indigenous people continued."

(From Message of the Day of the Indian 19.4.1977, signed by representatives of the Xavante, Bororo, Pareci, Apiaká, Guarany, Kaingang, Kayabi, Terena & Kaiowá tribes)

Source: Survival International

Brazil's 1973 Indian Statute has as its main purpose "preserv(ing)
[Indians] culture and integrating them, progressively and harmoniously into
the national community.''[350] *Apart from the implicit contradiction in this*
aim, FUNAI, the main body set up to protect the country's indigenous
communities during this process, is itself "subordinated to the overall
policy of economic development for the country".[351]

In the last ten years the world's biggest colonisation projects have taken
place on the Indian lands of Brazil, and FUNAI has quite clearly become a
prime agent in the process. Even the vestige of protection for native
Brazilians which FUNAI has been able to afford is now threatened, with the
promulgation of new Decrees allowing other state bodies and mining
companies access to indigenous lands.[352]

In 1978 the tribal people of Brazil were faced with a Draft Emancipation
Decree which, in many respects, was the very opposite and was intended to
be the rubric for the final integration of the Indian.[353] *An Assembly of*
native leaders forcefully rejected a form of "emancipation" which would
finally rob them of their land rights.

Emancipation which means Destruction

Declarations and Demands of the Assembly of Native Leaders
(*27 December 1978*)

As we are on the verge of seeing the new draft for the Decree for Emancipation
which will "regularize" the Statutes respecting the Indian signed by Your
Excellency, we would inform The President of the problems which have been raised,
studied and resolved in this Assembly.

Having sent to your Excellency the Draft Decree for Emancipation, we are
hereby setting forth our opinion — the opinion of the Indian, the only individual
who was not invited to give his opinion with regard to the emancipation which he is
about to attain.

In the first place, we would like to call to mind a passage from the letter by Andila
Inácio Kaingang, with which Your Excellency must be acquainted. We have in this
Assembly today repeated the same things and have merely adopted some of his
thoughts as our own.

We are taking the liberty of sending this Document in the name of the Indians
who inhabit the immense territory of Brazil.

Mr. President, it would not perhaps be possible for our people merely to speak
and understand their mother tongue without their understanding these cries for
peace, love and understanding. No, Mr. President, we are sure that our people will
understand this message, even though it be in other languages, as it has understood
the word "patience" which has up to now been shouted in our ears — a patience
which has now reached its limits, as would happen with any nation whatever might
be the stage of its civilization.

Mr. President, Your Excellency, you must agree that the passions of our people can no longer be contained within limits when they look at the lands remaining to them in comparison with the vast territories of Brazil over which we used in the past to have full dominion and which have been unlawfully taken from us by the White Man.

What puzzles us most is that it is in these conditions that the Draft Decree for Emancipation is being launched, when we know that various Articles of our Law, the Statutes respecting the Indian, have not been included.

What most calls for attention and which has been the subject of arguments and complaints within the various organisations with a Brazilian National field of action is the following: "The Executive Authority will carry out, within the period of five years, the demarcation of the Native Territories which have not yet been demarcated".   (Article 65.)

Just as public opinion condemned this emancipation, so we, in the name of the Native Brazilian Community, reject this emancipation. May it be dismissed by your Council and may our demands be taken into consideration. May that article of the Law be fulfilled, that article appearing to be one of the vital points which the new Law avoids. May the Indian be acknowledged as the heir to and lawful owner of his own lands and may the reservations be recognised as the collective property of the Native Communities. Any omission or lack of concern regarding this aspect of the matter will constitute an attitude which will lead us to conclude that the emancipation proclaimed by the Minister of the Interior forms nothing more or less than a hostile attitude and ill-intentioned as regards the Native Communities, and therefore worthy of censure.

Another Article in the Statutes respecting the Indian states the following: "The native lands may not be subject to leasing or any legal Deed or transaction which might restrict the full exercise of immediate tenure by the Native Community or by the forest-dwelling aboriginals".   (Article 18.)

Mr. President, we are well aware of the grave problem which confronts the Native Communities who have had their lands leased out by the FUNAI itself and who now find themselves unable to move intruders which the FUNAI has allowed into our zones. Other lands are encroached upon in a peaceful manner, although without the opportune support of the Post Chiefs or of the regional representatives of the Organisation for the protection of the Indian. A concrete case is that of Roraima, where the representative of the FUNAI permitted interlopers to encroach upon the native areas, according to the statements of the Native Leaders who met in the Assembly of Surumu.

But the most serious case was the one in which an act of coercion was suffered by a Native Community which now has no prospect of seeing their lands returned, as happened to the Kadiweu of Mato Grosso do Sul who had their land snatched from them with the permission of the competent body (the FUNAI), by means of leasing. These same interlopers now form the Association of the Lessees of the Kadiweu Reserve, which has a powerful regional sway.

The Statutes for the Indian, in Article 66, states: "The Organisation for the Protection of the forest-dwelling aboriginals will make public and observe the regulations of Convention 107." This Convention protects our most elementary rights and, as Brazil is one of the signatories of this Convention, it is under the obligation of carrying it out, especially as regards our freedom of communication and expression. This is to the point, because we are now complaining about the police activities which the FUNAI is exercising over the Native Communities, forbidding the Indians to take part in meetings and assemblies. It seems that the FUNAI is afraid of what is said at these meetings, where we do nothing more than report on our struggles and failures and the crimes carried out by the White Man in the communities of which every one of us forms a part. A fact which is deeply imprinted on our memory came from the breaking up of the Assembly of Surumu in Roraima, which is in contradiction to special Law No. 5.371 of 5th December, 1967, which authorises the founding of the National Institution for the Indian, as stated in Article 1, sub-clause I thereof, which empowers the FUNAI "to establish the policy and guarantee the fulfilment of the policy for the natives based on the following principles:— respect for the person of the Indian and for the tribal institutions and communities."

Mr. President, we are not seeking to lay down regulations and laws because we are neither pedagogues, jurists nor theologians, but we simply wish clearly to state our immediate demands, as guaranteed to us by the Statutes respecting the Indian.

We are not impressed by the statements made by the Minister on behalf of the President of the FUNAI, in the Press, in defence of the emancipation, because we, who are the victims of this policy, are the only ones who can give a sincere opinion as to what this emancipation represents; for if fine words could solve our problem, we should not today be in a situation which is so different from that which the Statutes respecting the Indian upholds, since the emancipation desired by the Minister will bring about the destruction of the tribal system for the Native Communities, and consequently to the collective and individual destruction of its elements, in as much as the Indian must live in his own community, with the full liberty to continue his cultural traditions and with the freedom to own his own land.

Mr. President, the period for the demarcation of the native areas having expired, we wish to inform Your Excellency that the Native Communities believe that they have every right to defend and rid their zones of interlopers should the competent body, the FUNAI, not complete the demarcation of the native zones. As we conclude that it is on this date that the period for the demarcation of the native areas expires, we demand that what you have ordered should be carried out and that the proposed law for emancipation, for which the Minister, Rangel Reis, is responsible, should be scrapped.

These are the opinions of the Brazilian Indian, expressed through their representatives present this day: Karipuna, Palikur, Galibi, Dessana, Apurina, Jamamadi, Tapirapé, Xavante, Rikbaktsa, Pareci, Kaiwa, Kaingang and Guarani, at the meeting held in Goiás on the 17th and 19th of December, by the native representatives of Amapá, Amazonas, Mato Grosso, Mato Grosso do Sul, Espírito Santo, Santa Catarina and Rio Grande do Sul.

Goiás, 19 December, 1978.

Source: Survival International Review (London) 1979.

During the 1982 Commonwealth Games, Aborigines and their supporters massed — and marched — in their thousands against the racism of the Queensland state which hosted sportspeople from all over the world. Musgrave Park, in Brisbane — a former burial ground and haunt for down-and-out blacks[354] — was occupied by a tent city. This was one of the Declarations to come from the People in occupation.

Statement of Protest

Now Hear This
We, are the indigenous people of this country, now called Australia.

Our people lived here for (approx) fifty thousand years, divided into about 500 district groups in their own areas that had recognised and stable borders. Our society was stable, our still unrelinquished sovereignty over our land was absolute.

Our ancestors evolved a basic and just system of laws. Laws that allowed all individuals to experience the ultimate of reasonable positive pleasures and allowed the achievement of their ultimate human potential. The dignity of the individual is maintained by these Laws else they would have been unmaintainable.

Our society was stable. We had not the need of monarchies, prisons or armies. We did not have the need to invade and colonise other countries because our technology was not destructive to the land and our culture was not destructive to the human experience.

Since the White invasion, destruction has been wrought on our homeland and her children. We have been, and still are, the victims of genocide, racism and exploitation. Our lands are being destroyed by a technology that is destructive to the planet and thus to human existence on the planet.

We have lost much. Injustice is forced upon us. Our humanity is being degraded and our history distorted by strangers. We wish no more of this.

We are taking another step in the process of decolonisation. Before the World, we accuse White Australia (and her Mother, England) of crimes against humanity and the planet. The past two centuries of colonisation is proof of our accusation.

We hereby demand yet again recognition of our humanity and our land rights. Hear us, White Australia, we are the spirit of our land. Our name is

humanity. Our aims are self-determination and
justice.
We will not be defeated.
We are our history, we are our culture, we are our land.
We are now.

Authorised by the People of Musgrave Park, 1982.

Ed Bernstick, a Cree Indian from Canada, delivered this statement to the Economic Commission of the Geneva International NGO Conference on Discrimination against Indigenous Populations in the Americas, 1977.

A future where everyone can survive

I have been involved in many things concerning the economic situation of Indian people in Canada. The situation that exists for Native people in Canada is that we have been categorised by Canada as Eastern or Western or Northern Canadian Indians, and treaty and non-treaty Indians, registered and non-registered, status Indians and non-status Indians, Metis, half-breed. Economically each category is affected differently. The responsibility of the Canadian government lies in the control they have gained over all Indian peoples. We have one document, the Indian Act, an act passed to control the treaties of Indian people in Canada. Indian people have not had a say in the economic situation of their communities. The government has said we are farmers, but to this day they have not achieved this goal, for we have never been farmers.

When the people took over the Bureau of Indian Affairs offices in Washington, there was a contract paper that was discovered there between the Department of Indian Affairs in Canada and the BIA in the U.S. This White Paper policy was introduced by the Canadian Government. At the same time there was a new economic development program set up called the Mid-Canada Corridor. This is the Northern Development Plan. This was a plan to take all economic basis away from Indian people. It involves the Department of Northern Saskatchewan and Northlands in Alberta, the Department of Northern Manitoba where there is a huge hydrodevelopment project going on, and the development programs in Northern Ontario, Quebec, British Columbia and the Territories.

These programs are developed without consultation with the native people, who are extremely isolated and out of touch. This adds up to genocide against the native people of Canada —culturally and physically.

It is estimated that in this country all oil and gas in Eastern Canada will be depleted, so there are pipeline proposals. Each province and territory exerts control of the native people within its claimed boundaries. We are affected by such laws as the Migratory Bird Act, and yet in our treaties we have fishing and hunting rights. We have court cases where our people have been put in court for shooting a duck to feed their family because it infringed on the Migratory Bird Act. In many areas, there are no jobs, and people must rely on hunting and fishing to survive.

A lot of our land areas have been subjected to manipulation. For years, the ranchers have cleared land around the reservations with the cheap labor of native people. Today most of our reserves are faced with dealing with timber mills, paper mills around the reserves. There are power plants which destroy the fish around reserves.

The Government uses "legal" tactics to keep Indian people in poverty. They try to assimilate entire reserves, and have succeeded on some in destroying the language, education and livelihood of the people, and the Canadian government is responsible.

The corporations are looking for resources and look more and more to Indian land. We need protection. The death rate has climbed threefold in the last 10 years. Our elders tell us from their oral history, that land that was ceded through treaties included only one foot down, and does not include water and most minerals. The timber and water that exists would be enough for all if shared equally. The world community should think of the human rights of Indian people. We are not saying we do not want to share our resources, but we are saying that we must think of a future where everyone can survive.

Source: Saskatoon Environmental Society Newsletter, Saskatoon (date unknown).

*Colombia's major Indian organisation, CRIC, was founded in the early
1970s. The following — extracted from their first Bulletin published in
1973 — remains the principal programme around which they have
organised, with growing strength, for land rights over the last twelve years.*

We are peasants . . . we are Indians

We are Peasants

1. We, the Paeces, Guambianos, Coconucos and the rest of the Indians of the Cauca
live in the mountains, on the haciendas and the reservations. We are peasants.

2. Many of us work cultivating the big haciendas of the rich people. We live there as
"terrajeros", paying to live on the land on which we were born, and on which our
grandfathers and fathers worked and died. We live on small plots on these farms
which were stolen from us with lies and deception.

3. Many others of us work as peons, earning no more than a little weak soup or a few
pesos. Because we have no land left. Because the rich took away the reservations or
because the land that is left is too small. We, the "terrajeros" and peons are
exploited.

4. Other Indians live on reservations. But the majority of them have been invaded
by the rich. They took the best lands, leaving us only rocky outcrops. For this
reason the Indian Councils have no land to share out and most of us live in misery.

5. We, who have no more than half a square of land, or even a quarter; we, who live
as "terrajeros" or as peons on the haciendas; we, who have a small plot of land on
one of the few remaining reservations; and others, who live crammed next to their
neighbours, making only enough to eat, we represent most of the peasants of the
Cauca. We are the majority of the population of the Cauca. There are 200,000 of us.

6. . . . . But we do not have enough schools, nor health centres, nor roads, nor land
on which to work. Or, if we do have a plot of land, it is too small even to feed our
children.

7. On the other hand, the rich for whom we work have all that, and much more.
They have all that because they live from the work which we do.

8. The Indians who have tiny plots of land, the "terrajeros", the peons and the
"comuneros" we are all exploited. Just like the peasants everywhere. Just like the
peasants in all Colombia.

We are Indians

1. We, the Paeces, Guambianos and the rest of us, are Indians. Because we are
descendants of the indigenous nations who inhabited these lands centuries before
the invaders from Spain ever arrived. We are of those peoples who in Colombia and
in the other countries of America were destroyed and submitted to servitude in the
mines, on the lands and on the haciendas. Because we share the spirit of those
peasants and soldiers of the Guambiano and Paez peoples who fought and died in
so many battles against the invaders. We are "natural" Indians, as they call us, and
we have a right to our lands.

2. We are Indians, and we have our own customs. We are Indians and we speak our own language. We love our Indian music. Many of us dress in traditional dress, some of us because we like it, and some of us because it is cheaper that way, or more comfortable. There are also some who dress as white people do, when it is cheaper or more comfortable for them to dress that way. Our women have their own ways of preparing food. And all of us have different ways of working, according to the type of land on which we live. We appreciate these customs, these languages, this history which unites and strengthens us. We are Indians, and we believe that it is good to be an Indian.

3. These things which make us Indians can be seen. But there is another thing which cannot be seen and which we should remember: we are Indians because we believe that the things of this world are made for everyone. It is like saying that since we are all equal, the means of living should also be equal.

4. Because of this, we believe that the land, just as the air, the water and all the other things which keep us alive should not be only for the few. The land should not be owned, but should be communal: just like the water, just like the air. So that we can all cultivate it and reap fruit from it to feed the rest, and so that we can escape from this misery and better our lives.

5. This is why we like the reservations. Because there, the lands must all be shared out between all the members of the community. And, as the land cannot be sold, if the members of the Indian Council are good, deceptive people cannot impoverish anyone. Because of this too, we like to work communally, because all of us can work. All of us.

Our Problems

1. We, the Indian peasants, as we are peasants, have the same problems as all the other peasants in Colombia. We do not have land to work, or if we do have any, the plots are too small or worked out. We do not have the means to take our goods to the market, and the truck drivers and intermediaries rob us. We do not have credit in order to be able to better and extend our crops. Every day we get hungrier, we have fewer clothes with which to cover ourselves, and we suffer from more illness which stops us working and kills us. We suffer from having to pay rent for our land, from having to sell our crops very cheaply because of pressure from the authorities, from being thrown out by the police when we try to recuperate the lands which the rich stole from us and which we need in order that our families do not die of hunger. And so many more things.

Our problems of land, health, housing, dress, schools, markets, are the same as those of all peasants.

However, the landowners and other rich people have all this and a lot more, because they live from our work. And because they have the government, the police and the prisons on their side to punish. Because their interest is in staying rich, they fight to keep us exploited. Therefore we must always struggle to defend ourselves. There are those who say that in the world there is always fighting. The rich fight to keep the land and to keep the poor working for them; and we, the poor, fight to keep them from doing this so as to be able to better our lives.

2. We, the Indian peasants, being Indians, have other problems too. After the wars

against the invading Spaniards the indigenous population diminished so much that it seemed that we were going to die out. So the Spaniards sent us to live in the mountains in reservations; and they passed many laws which they said were to protect us. And the other governments right up to today have said the same thing. But they did not protect anyone. What the rich wanted was that we should not die out so that we would be able to work for them. Then the rich realised that the Indian does not let himself be humiliated and exploited as long as he has his land, his own government and his customs. For this reason, from that moment they set about making us ashamed of our languages, our clothes, our customs and everything else that belongs to us. They have made many people believe that we are like animals, so that we would abandon our way of life and so that, as we ceased to be Indians, they could exploit us better as "terrajeros" and peons. So, for this very reason, in order to humiliate us and to make us work for them, they have always tried to control the Indian Councils which govern us, and have abolished many of the reservations and appropriated many more. Thus they have gone on persecuting us, even to the point of declaring us minors-in-law, because minors-in-law cannot defend themselves. But in spite of all this we, the Indian peasants, know that we are not like animals, and that we are not minors, and that we can defend ourselves. So we support our Indian Councils and fight to keep our reservations.

3. But even though we still have some reservations we, the Indian peasants, suffer from the same problems as all the other peasants of Colombia. The main problem is that of land, there are many others. We are travellers along the same path. The same remedy must be applied to the same sickness. We must learn to fight together. To put things right.

Our Struggles

We, the Indians of the Cauca have been struggling for centuries to keep our land, our own governments and our customs. Almost always we have fought together.

1. The oldest struggle that we can remember is the war against the invading Spaniards. That was in about 1535 when they arrived with Sebastián de Balalcazar. In those days the Pubenses who lived in the region of Popayán were ruled by the "chiefs" Calambás and Payán. But when they were attacked they were not alone; the Paeces came with the "chief" Gaitana, and the Guambías with the "chief" Piendamú, to help them defend themselves. Thus, united the three great Indian nations were able to resist the foreigners' attacks on Popayán for twenty months and then defeat them in many other battles.

The Spanish captain Pedro de Añasco paid with his life for the lives of so many Indians he had murdered in order to rob them of their riches. In the end we were defeated because the weapons of the Spaniards were more powerful and caused so much death. But we, the Pubenses, Paeces, Guambías and other Indians carry on defending ourselves with the same courage that the whites recount in their histories.

2. Then, from 1700 onwards the rich started encroaching on the reservations in order to exploit the gold in the rivers and the gold and silver in the mountains; and they enslaved us. So we rebelled again and the invaders were defeated. It was then that the village of Caloto was destroyed by the "chief" Juan Tama, and La Plata was burned down by the "chiefs" Tumbichucué and Calambás. And the mines were

shut so that the ambitions of the rich did not go on causing death and enslavement. This time all the Indians of the Cordillera united in the fight, even those of Ecuador.

3. Another hundred years went by, and the oppressors began to take away from us the reservation lands which they had left us. They began making laws to abolish the reservations. They began in 1822 and they are still at it today. Many reservations were divided up, many Indian Councils were terminated and the landlords made many more Indians pay the "land-rent". Nevertheless many of us resisted and a hundred years ago there were rebellions in Tierrandentro, Jambáló, Pitayó and Guambía. And the invaders were not able to take the reservations in these regions. Because we had fought we kept the lands.

4. Then, at the beginning of this century, the landlords invaded again. Other fighters appeared on the scene, to defend. In Guambía, Marcelion Ulé and Julio Yaquibá. In Totoró, José Gonzalo Sánchez. In Tierrandentro, Rosalino Yajimbo. They all joined up with Manuel Quintín Lame to organise the struggle; they called it the "Quintinada". They wanted everything to be better for the Indians, but they were unable to explain things very well and many did not understand that the struggle was for the Indian cause; so they went to defend the white parties, the Liberals and the Conservatives. There were also peasants and priests who did not understand the justice of the struggle and who aligned themselves with the landlords and betrayed the Indian cause. They accused those who were fighting, and Quintín Lame and the others were taken prisoner and judged. This particular fight was lost but the struggle went on. Quintín Lame went to Tolima to organise the Indians there, and with them he confronted the landlords and the corrupt officials. He was put in jail many times, but he kept on fighting at the side of his Indian brothers. Many others did this too, like Rosalino Yajimbo who died in prison, like José Gonzalo Sánchez who was poisoned by the landlords. For this: for defending themselves.

5. "History is the mother of truth", Quintín Lame used to say, and there is truth in it. So we should always remember what our struggles teach us: That a people who struggle cannot be exterminated by war, nor by persecution, nor by exploitation. That we, ourselves, many of our reservations and Indian Councils, are still alive because our forefathers fought for us. That if we are united we can strive to overcome our enemies with our arms. And our principal arms are: clarity and organisation. Clarity is knowing why we are fighting, what we are fighting for, and how to fight. That our struggles of yesterday and today have been to keep our land, but also to govern ourselves and to advance our customs. That this struggle helps us to remedy a little our poverty, exploitation and our hunger. But just as we know that food which was enough for yesterday is not enough for tomorrow, we must prepare ourselves for renewed struggles to better our lives. Better than yesterday, better than ever. And also that our struggle is long. It began centuries ago and it is not over. That our defeats have not put an end to our patience as Indians, and that we continue to fight. As the saying goes: "Those who are exploited will rebel".

What our Grandfathers tell us

We, the Paeces and Guambíanos have also been through legal struggles along with our wars. For example that of EL CHIMÁN in Guambía. This is how our grandfathers tell the story.

"Many years ago, our forefathers lived on the plains near Popayán. But the whites harassed them and the Guambíanos began to clear land and sow further away. But each time they had cleared some land, the whites followed them and took it away. So they arrived at the village of Silvia which used to be Guambía. All the Guambíanos used to live there, but they were expelled from there. That was when some white people hired houses in which to live.

Then the whites wanted to put a stone mill there, so they became friends with some of the Guambíanos. And they said, 'Come on, my friend, rent me a little plot on which I can install my mill'. And because they were friends the Indians gave them a plot for the mill in El Chimán. Straight away they needed another plot for pasture as the whites did not have anywhere to keep the animals which carried their grain."

And our grandfathers told us that each time the newcomers came to visit their new friends they brought clothes and things to eat, they said that these were presents, but they made the Indians sign receipts saying that they had bought the land.

Then it was after about twenty years that the Indians realised that their new friends had become their landlords and that they were being forced into paying them the "land-rent". At that time, in about 1880, two comrades Felipe Beltrán and Calambás, began the struggle.

But the whites who were stealing the land were already looking for a way of putting an end to the comrades. When they were ready to celebrate their triumph they went to Silvia and bought poisoned rum to give to the two comrades who were organising their brothers. They gave it to them and they became very ill and went crazy and were lost. They died.

After a long time Feliciano Ulluné, governor Guambía, and Luciano Muelas, a member of the community at El Chimán, started the struggle again with José Antonio Tumiñá as secretary. They went to Bogotá to ask for the copies of the titles which established the boundaries of the reservation at Guambía. They found them. And they demanded their lands be returned.

Then one of those who had stolen the lands, one of the landlords proposed that they leave him a part of it because he had children. Luciano Muelas and Feliciano Ulluné said that they would not accept that, as they had won the whole area of land and that they were going to get the whole of it, not only a part. Then the landlord said, "then we shall fight to see who wins". And this they did.

But, unfortunately, the secretary of the two comrades, Tumiñá, took all the papers they had brought back from Bogotá and, hiding them, handed them over for the sum of 500,000 pesos, which today would be 500 pesos.

So the landlords began to make them pay the "land-rent" again. Those who lived there had to pay. They threatened to remove those who were fighting and they left alone those who did not fight.

Besides all this the invaders of Popayán and of Cali made an agreement and called together all the people of Guambía so that they could kill large numbers of them, so they would not fight any more. So they killed the poor people and sent one man to jail for twenty years. But in spite of all this the fight still went on.

In 1935 four comrades began to fight again and sorted out the business of the papers in Bogotá. In this struggle were the comrades Quintín Lame from

Tierrandentro, Sr Correa from Pitayó and José Gonzalo Sánchez from Totoró as well as a group of comrades from Guambía. Then the fight was sealed for other comrades, but the Indian Council did not support them at all, they said they were alright and that those over in El Chimán could go to hell . . .

The struggle of 1935 only clarified what had been stolen, in what way and by whom. But they could not get anything done about it. Then, in 1942, two comrades travelled to Quito to look into the land titles; they found another title to the reservation which showed the boundaries of Chimán to be inside the reservation of Guambía itself. This fight hardly gained anything in the way of land. But as the Indians from Tierrandentro, Totoró, from Guambía and Pitayó were united; and as José Gonzalo Sánchez was also speaking out against paying the "land-rent" — the rent was decreased a little bit. Also the hours of work on the haciendas was reduced from twelve to eight.

So that is the way it is . . . That is the story of El Chimán, the story of a struggle from 1880 up to the present day. Recently, since 1960, the struggle has begun again — but this time it is more organised. This is what our grandfathers have told us. The rest we know because we, ourselves, have seen how the comrades of Chimán, by continuing their legal struggle, have won back part of their lands in 1971.

In this way this story shows us how our enemies attack us: with corruption, making one of us betray the rest for money; by dividing us, rewarding those who humiliate themselves and pursuing those who fight; by setting traps and accusing the Indians of crimes which they themselves have committed; with repression, by poisoning our leaders, imprisoning some of us and having others killed in order to instill fear in us.

We know all these things and we have not forgotten them. Now we understand and bear in mind what Quintín Lame said: "Now the Indian youth must awaken and seek its path. We must carry on the struggle and not let ourselves fall into obscurity".

How CRIC was Born

1. In the last few years the rich and the landlords have been exploiting us more and more. It was to protest about this that we assembled in Toribío on February 24 1971. The Indians of the Cauca organised a large meeting because we wanted to win back our lands and to abolish the payment of "land-rent". To this assembly came more than 2,000 delegates from the areas of Toribío, Totoró, Guambía, Pitayó, Jambaló, San Francisco , San José, Tacueyó, Quisgó and Quinchaya. Besides these, the farm workers unions of the eastern Cauca, the Committee for the Recuperation of the lands of Silvia and the Agrarian Socia Federation of Corinto were present.

There, in Toribío, the CRIC (The Regional Indian Council of the Cauca) was born. Now, with this organisation we the "comuneros", the "terrajeros", the "parceleros" and the peons, are carrying forward our struggle. We, who are all Indian peasants.

2. Then, on the 6 September 1971, the second assembly was called in La Susana, on the reservation of Tacueyó. This time delegations from the following reservations were present as well as those who were at the first meeting; Paniquitá, Poblazón, Rioblanco, Alto del Rey, Guachicono, Puracé, Pancitará and representatives from

the Peasant Associations of Silvia and the Cauca, the Indian Committee of the farmworkers of Purace and a delegation from Tolima.

3. So the CRIC is an organisation controlled by Indian peasants who were elected at the Assembly. Thus it is independent of the political parties and of the government. It is directed by an Executive Committee of three members and a governing board formed by two delegates from each reservations: one from the Indian Council and the other from the other groups of Indian peasants which exist in the area.

4. CRIC's programme sets out our struggles of today in seven points:

1. To recuperate the reservation lands.
2. To increase the size of the reservations.
3. To strengthen the Indian Councils.
4. To stop paying the land-rents.
5. To make known the laws concerning Indians and to insist on their proper application.
6. To defend the history, language and customs of the Indians.
7. To form Indian teachers to teach in the Indian languages in ways which are applicable to the present situation of the people.

5. Today many reservations support this programme. Already 45 Indian Councils have united with the CRIC. By extending the CRIC we are showing the interest we have in organising ourselves. Today's struggles, like those of yesterday, have caused us much suffering, imprisonment and persecution. And they will cause us much more before we win. But we are becoming stronger as we go and we will carry on the fight without fear.

CRIC's Programme

Let us read again the seven points of CRIC's programme and consider them.

1. To recuperate the reservation lands.

This is a most justified struggle and one which has caused us the most suffering and death in our history. It is the struggle of our fatherland which we inherited from our grandfathers and ancestors. And it is what we most need. For that reason it is the principal task. Starting with the land we can shake ourselves free of the exploitation and domination of the rich invaders of our territory and their middlemen. The poor peasants who live and work alongside us and who marry our children are not enemies. They came to our land and we welcomed them as friends; they too were victims of violence and exploitation. If they acknowledge the authority of the Indian Councils they are with us. We have already seen some fruits from our struggles: land has been recuperated in Chimán, Paniquitá, Zumbico and San Francisco, and we are recuperating more in Pitayó, Coconuco and Jambaló.

2. To increase the size of the reservations.

Because many were measured out on bad land and now the area is too small or the soil is exhausted. In some cases they are surrounded by large haciendas and the reservations would be extended into these. CRIC proposes that the "concentrations of the plots of land" as mentioned in the law, should be applied to extend the reservations which are too small or to make new ones. Because we should preserve the form of the reservations which has been of so much use to many of us. And the Indian Councils should carry on their work of supervising the land and regulating the kind of work which most suits it.

3. To strengthen the Indian Councils.

Because the Indian Councils have been and still are the representatives of our form of working the land and are the basis of our own organisation. They know, as we do, our needs, and they can act to halt the ambitions of the landlords, the business-men and the politicians, all of whom are the exploiters of the Indians. By electing good Councils and supporting them in their struggles, we can strengthen ourselves.

4. To stop paying the land-rents.

Just as the stealing of our lands is still the "Conquest", our paying the land-rents is a continuation of the "Colony", from which we have not yet escaped. And as the laws say that neither of these things should exist in our country — all the more reason to fight against them. Ever since CRIC put forward, in the first assembly, the refusal to pay the land-rent, many communities have already shaken off this slavery and others are in the process of doing so. But the struggle of the "terrajeros" and the peons cannot remain there. It should continue so that they might get better land, work and living conditions.

5. To make known the laws concerning Indians and to insist on their proper application.

We already know that there are many bad hypocritical laws which state that they are to defend us, but which say that we are minors-in-law and that the reservations should be terminated. But there are also some laws which have served to defend us. CRIC believes that we should keep as much as possible of our customs, but that the Indian Councils should learn those laws which serve to better our situation. And we should all struggle so that one day these laws might become more just and give the people what they want and that they are fulfilled.

6. To defend the history, language and customs of the Indians.

Because these help to keep us united and strong. With these we learn to fight and not to be humiliated. For these reasons it is important to know them and not to lose them. Just as CRIC has done in this little book: we have taken up the stories told us by our grandfathers, learned the value of our struggles and demonstrated how we understand and feel about life.

7. To form Indian teachers to teach in the Indian languages in ways which are applicable to the present situation of the people.

As our languages and traditions are so important, our children should be educated in them. The government itself recognises that this should be done when it pays bilingual teachers. But even if they are bilingual they are not teachers. Because they do not let them teach. They just make them repeat what the white teacher says. So CRIC fights for the training of Indian teachers who teach in our own languages, our own truths and our own knowledge, just as other truths and other knowledge. Because the CRIC knows that only by developing ourselves in our own way in education, in economics, in our communities and in technical aspects, only by doing this can we win our struggles. For this reason we must not believe what our oppressors teach us. Just as the saying, "you must expect to be wounded by thorns", so we can only expect exploitation from the exploiters. It is better then to keep our distance from what the exploiters teach just as we do from thorns.

We are already on the Path

These struggles of CRIC are our own struggles. It was the same struggle yesterday as it is today and now it is affecting us. It is a struggle against the oppression which wants to bury us in misery, disease and ignorance.

1. But this struggle is not only that of the Indian peasants of the Cauca, but of all who live in Colombia.

The Guajiros who are fighting against the exploiters who have stolen their salt beds, their fish and their pearls.

The Arhuacos of the Sierra Nevada who fight against the landlords who are pushing them up against the snow peaks.

The Motilones of the Department of Northern Santander who are fighting against the petrol companies who have taken their best lands from them.

The Cuivas and Guahibos of the Eastern Plains, fighting the millionaire cattle-ranchers who pursue and kill them as "irrational beings".

The communities of the Vaupés struggling against the rubber-men and the middle-men who enslave them.

The Ingas and Sibundoyes of the Putumayo, struggling to survive in the face of the government institute which has taken over their valley.

Thus, in all parts of Colombia, half a million Indian peasants, like us, are fighting to defend themselves against their exploiters. They are struggling, like us, to win back what they need. Because we have begun to open our eyes. Because we have begun to understand the true situation. Because now we can distinguish the reasons which make us how we are, and we can now see who are our real enemies.

2. But this struggle is not only that of half a million Indian peasants, but of all the exploited peasants of Colombia. They have pushed us into little corners and have surrounded all of us. But the fences cannot prevent us from seeing. Many of us are different from one another. But the problem is not in our differences but in that which bring us all together: the exploitation which is punishing and killing us.

3. To put an end to so many miseries we are organising ourselves in different ways. In some places in Agricultural Unions, in others in cooperatives; in many others in communal councils or in the National Peasant Association (ANUC).

And now the Indian peasants, the "terrajeros", the "parceleros" and the "comuneros" and the Indian Councils are organising in the CRIC.

Because from union comes strength and from strength will come our victory.

We will reap this harvest when we have all of the mountains behind us. When the peasant population has become strong through its own clarity and organisation and when we can do the thing which our exploiters are afraid of: when we can all meet together and retrace the steps which have brought us this far.

Source: Stephen Corry: *Towards Indian Self-determination in Colombia*, Survival International Document No. 11, London, 1976.

*A decade before Lakota people reoccupied the Paha Sapa ("Black Hills")
of South Dakota, a number of Sioux climbed Mount Rushmore to "sit on
Top of Teddy Roosevelt's Head" — as Lame Deer graphically put it.*[355]
*They were protesting against not only the grotesque misuse of a sacred
mountain and the proposal to carve an effigy of Crazy Horse on
Thunderhead Mountain, but the theft of native American land. Just like the
occupation of Big Mountain in the early eighties, the Mount Rushmore
action was started by women:*

Sitting on Teddy Roosevelt's head

"This idea of coming up here originated from a woman in Pine
Ridge, South Dakota. And first they started a demonstration
down on Sheep Mountain, near Scenic. The Government took
two hundred thousand acres of Indian land for a bombing
range. They promised to give it back after World War Two
ended and they haven't given it back yet. So we printed up some
handbills about the movement, told them everything that was
happening. Then we took those handbills from home to home
and gave them out, and we told the Indians who we gave them
to not to say anything. So the Indian population of Rapid City
knew about occupying Mount Rushmore a month before it
happened. But the white people never knew it. We just didn't let
it out.

"So we started in on a Monday morning, the twenty-fourth
of August. There were only us three women. We thought other
people were coming up, but they didn't. I guess they were
scared. And it lightninged all the way up, so we thought about
Crazy Horse and we knew he was with us. We were really scared
that the rangers would arrest us. For a few days we were
handing out handbills to the tourists in the parking lot. Then
Lee Brightman came to support us, and then the Indian
students came in. We got braver and braver and now we're not
afraid of anyone."

Muriel Waukazoo and **Lizzy Fast Horse.**

Source: John Fire/Lame Deer and Richard Erdoes, *Lame Deer: Sioux Medicine Man*, Davis
Poynter, London, 1973.

Black control of black affairs

We, the undersigned X Citizens, support
the following demands of Aborigines, as
authorised by Members of the "Black
Embassy and Information Centre".

1. To **abolish** the Queensland Aborigines and Islanders Acts of 1971 and their Regulations and By-Laws.

2. **Land rights now!**

A. Immediate ownership rights by Tribal Groups of land they are now living on.

B. All lands that are now set aside as Aboriginal Communities should be owned and controlled by the same Community.

C. That Aboriginal lands include **total rights to all natural resources**.

D. That any mining or prospecting that is going on now should be stopped until Aboriginal communities are told the **truth** about what is happening, and that every man, woman and child of that community should make the final decisions about mining and compensation — **not** the mining companies, the State Government, Church bodies or anyone else.

E. Where land has been taken by the State Government, the Black Community should be given money as compensation.

F. That any Crown Lands which have traditional meaning to Blacks be given back to them.

G. That **all sites where there are sacred objects** or **sacred places** be controlled by the local Elders.

H. **That all mining and fishing rights and all areas** be open to the use of Aborigines without money having to be paid or other conditions being placed on us.

I. Where an Aboriginal Tribe has been taken away from their Tribal Land and forced to live on "Yunbas" or in the cities (i.e. St. George, Cunnamulla and Urban Cities such as Brisbane, Townsville, etc.) these communities be given ownership and control of land and that they get **compensation**.

3. **Black control of black affairs**

A. **No more financial cutbacks** to the Aboriginal Community Services in Queensland or any other State by the Commonwealth Government and that **total monies are given immediately to all submitted budgets**.

B. We want more money made available to **programs** started by the Blacks.

C. **No more sacking of Aborigines employed by the Commonwealth Department of Aboriginal Affairs**.

Source: Rabelais (Black issue), Sydney, June 1976.

". . . We planted corn, beans, squash, cotton, having received these gifts from the earth. The plants provided for us over generations and generations as long as we also provided for their care and gave back to the earth what it had given us. And we gave back, in work, song, prayer, replanted seed, a system of thought and practice that spoke and acted upon the responsibility that we had learned we must have for the land and its fertility and for the People and their vital health. The land is not just dirt, stones, clay; over generations and generations, our People learned they must care for it because it provides food, clothing, and shelter, and we know we are part of the land; and we are responsible for ourselves in caring for the land . . ."

Simon Ortiz, Acoma Pueblo, 1979

Source: Winona La Duke, unpublished thesis, 1980.

"Built on the blood of Africans, Asians, Indians and Chicanos"

In June 1846 the United States invaded Mexico. In 1848 the invading forces reached the capital and obliged Mexico to surrender.

Under the "Peace Treaty" signed between the two countries, Mexico was obliged to cede a third of its territory to the United States.

Since this sad time, the descendants of the Mexicans and the Indians who occupy this territory (today known as the south-west of the United States) live like a people oppressed and colonised.

The Treaty of Guadalupe Hidalgo, signed 136 years ago, guaranteed to the inhabitants at the time, as well as their descendants, the right to preserve their own culture and language. At the same time, it also guaranteed all the land rights of "those who were the first occupants".

None of the stipulated promises in the Treaty has been honoured.

Our people have been victimised: by the theft of land, murders, cultural oppression, enforced deportation, brutal work conditions, and inhuman and brutal violence from the police, inadequate medical care, compulsory sterilisation of women, and participation against their will in the US military.

When heroes like Tribucio Vasquez, Geronimo, and Joaquin Murieta tried to defend their peoples and their land, they were brutally murdered and became, in US history, bandits and "renegades".

The Chicano-Mexican people of the South-West accuse the government of the United States of genocide. This country has been built on the blood of Africans, Asians, Indians and Chicanos.

We demand freedom and self-determination for all the colonised peoples who find themselves on land which today is called the United States; especially the peoples of Indian nations, of Puerto Rico, Hawaii, the Pacific islands and the Chicanos of Aztlan of the South-West USA.

A. G. Gonzales (Chicano)

Source: (translated): Diffusion Inti, Paris, April 1984.

Land owners since time immemorial

The First Memorandum Presented to the Government by the Amuesha Congress 1969

We, the undersigned, representatives of 20 communities (510 families) of the Amuesha tribe who met on 1–3 July in the Community of Miraflores (Oxapampa) to participate in the first Amuesha Leaders Conference, unanimously agreed to send this memorandum to the Government of Peru in order to bring to its attention the problems which afflict us.

The main points which were discussed were:

1) The insecurity of our landholdings due to the lack of titles which guarantee them. This has allowed invasions of our land by colonists and large landowners.

2) The groups which hold land have so little that, as a result, their socio-economic position is very precarious.

3) The total lack of legislation regarding forest tribes. It was pointed out that the last Agrarian Reform Law made no reference to our position but merely referred to problems of technical and social assistance.

During the course of the meeting the following resolutions were passed:

1) To demand that the Government fulfil its obligation to give titles to the lands which we presently hold for the following reasons:

a) We have been the owners of this land from time immemorial.

b) To protect us from the advance of the colonists who constantly threaten to take our land from us.

c) To enable us to take advantage of the programmes of Technical Assistance and Credit.

d) To allow us the security of permanent crops.

e) To permit us to form cooperatives for production and commercialisation as a means of incorporating ourselves into the national system of production.

f) To request the creation and construction of schools.

2) To request that more land be ceded to us and that the amount should be in a just proportion to the number of people who live on it. In deciding on the quantity of land that shall be awarded to us, the government should take into account the following factors:

a) The poor quality of the soils which demands that a large amount of land be granted in order that future generations are not faced with the problem of its infertility.

b) The population's decision to concentrate on the raising of livestock which needs a greater area.

c) The lack of money amongst the Amuesha and the distance of their reserves which means they must have guaranteed areas reserved for hunting and fishing.

3) To make known our wish that land be granted to us in the form of communal reserves and not in individual plots.

4) To make known the need for technical assistance and credit to develop the land which we are requesting.

5) To request the help of State institutions in the founding and building of schools in the communities which need them.

6) To ask that the legal procedures for obtaining personal documents be made more accessible and that we be excused the fines as it is only recently that we have learnt of the need for these documents.

Since about 1958 we have sent requests to the Delegation of Forest regions and the Agrarian Reform office in attempts to legalise our possession of our land. Unfortunately, up until the present time we have had no success. The present memorandum is a united effort on the part of the Amuesha to expose the problem and to draw the government's attention to it so that it can take the necessary measures in accordance with its just and effective agrarian policy.

We hope that you will attend to this matter with the urgency that it requires, given that we are the legitimate owners of these lands from time immemorial.

Miraflores (Oxapampa), 3 July 1969.

Source: Stephen Corry: unpublished MSS, Survival International, London.

Statement of the Cordillera Consultative Committee on P.D. 410, the Ancestral Land Decree

9 March 1984

The Cordillera Consultative Committee is a group of Igorot professionals committed to upholding the rights and welfare of the Cordillera national minorities. We manifest our strong objections to Presidential Decree 410, the Ancestral Land Decree, which would cause the loss of the ancestral lands of minority groups all over the country, including the Igorots, by Sunday, March 11, 1984. In the Cordillera, the provinces included in the decree are Mountain Province, Kalinga-Apayao and Ifugao. Benguet and Abra do not fall within the coverage of the decree.

P.D. 410 was signed into law by President Marcos on March 11, 1974. From this date, the decree sets a 10-year grace period within which we national minorities should file application for ownership of our ancestral lands. Otherwise, if we fail to perfect paper titles to our lands within this period, we stand to "lose preferential right thereto and the land shall be declared open for allocation to other deserving applicants."

The grace period ends on March 11, 1984. After this, without paper titles, we national minorities shall lose all prior claim and vested rights to the lands which we have occupied and defended for generations. Our lands shall then be set up for grabbing by any individual immigrant or corporation who abides by the rules of land registration. Furthermore, our lands may also now be given away by the President, at his own discretion, as land grants, by virtue of the "passage" in last January's referendum of an amendment to the Constitution to this effect (Plebiscite Question No. 3).

We Igorots of Mountain Province, Ifugao and Kalinga-Apayao have not filed for registration or application of ownership over our ancestral lands. Why should we? We have no doubts about our ownership. We know that we are people of the land, and that the land belongs to us. We have established this territorial prerogative to our home villages through prior occupancy, tillage and continued use since time immemorial.

Our custom law defines our tribal territories over which the different communities have communal ownership, and the collective responsibility for their preservation and defense. Our tribal boundaries are clearly delineated. Individual rights to parcels of land within the tribal territory are open only to members of our communities, and are subject to the prior collective rights.

By our custom law, our vested tenurial rights are quite clear to all of us, and to anyone else with sensitivity of observation. Why should we still need to register our lands and acquire paper title, when these are complicated and expensive procedures which most of our people do not have the inclination nor the capacity for? Why should we be forced to comply with the difficult requirements of the government when this same government has not been responsive to our needs, and instead has been the source of many of the problems we face today?

The government has neglected even basic social services in the Cordillera. It has displaced many Igorot communities to make way for dams, tourism projects, mines, logging concessions and other development projects. It has politically divided the Cordillera by arbitrarily splitting up the Cordillera provinces into unequal status in two separate regions: Region 1 — the Ilocos Region, and Region 2 — the Cagayan Region. It has even sponsored the prostitution and commercialization of sacred Igorot culture in such activities as the Grand Cañao. It has militarized the Cordillera in the face of the people's mounting anger at these abuses.

Over and above all of these however, the government has sought to legitimize such national oppression of the Cordillera minorities by passing laws inimical to the peoples' interests. P.D. 410 is in this category, as also is P.D. 705, or the Revised Forest Code, which declares almost the whole of the Cordillera as forest reserve. These two together, along with other unjust land laws, have made us, the Igorots, squatters in our own lands.

P.D. 410 is thus part of a pattern of discriminatory policy and legislation which violate our human right as national minorities to our ancestral lands, which is the foundation of our distinct indigenous cultures and lifestyles. The private individual titling which the decree encourages would subvert our primary communal relations of people and land, and would open up our ancestral lands even to outsiders. Such discriminatory legislation, together with other oppressive structures imposed over the peoples of the Cordillera, will, in the long-term, and if we allow it, lead to the dismemberment of the physical land base of our societies, and therefore also the disintegration of our cultures — a form of ethnocide.

We therefore call for the repeal of P.D. 410, P.D. 705 and other unjust land laws. We call for the end of national oppression and discrimination against the peoples of the Cordillera. We call on all freedom-loving Igorots to unite and persevere in the assertion of our right to self-determination whereby we may freely determine our political status and freely pursue our economic, social and cultural development. Finally, we call for a broader unity with the rest of the Filipino people in our common struggle for national freedom and genuine democracy, and with equality for the Igorots and other national minorities.

Source: Tribal Forum (Episcopal Commission on Tribal Filipinos) Vol. V, No. 2, March–April 1984.

A band of 2,500 native Canadians have waged one of the longest consistent battles for land. In 1869, two years before British Columbia entered the Canadian Confederation, the Nishga of the Naas River travelled to Victoria to present formal claims on their territory and fishing waters. Two years afterwards, they hired an English law firm, Fox and Preece, to take their case to the British Crown: the monarch and privy council declined to listen. Throughout the early years of the 20th century they consistently refused to "extinguish" their aboriginal land rights, in exchange for compensation and a reservation. Finally, in 1973, they won the right to be recognised: more than a decade later, the highly ambivalent attitude of the Federal government to land claims negotiations, and the dissenting voices of various Provinces means the Nishga are still battling for what, in all justice, is theirs.[356]

On top of this, they have for some years confronted the AMAX mining corporation (see p. 163) which insists on dumping toxic heavy metals in their fishing waters at Alice Arm.[357]

Nishga Declaration

The Nishga People is a distinct and unique society within the many faceted cultural mosaic that is Canada. The issue is whether the Nishga element within this mosaic will be allowed to face the "difficulties", will be allowed to become full participants contributing in a positive way to the well being of the Naas Valley in particular and the country in general. The positive aspect of this participation, we feel, must be through self-determination, self-determination that is dependent on the shared and mutual responsibility of governments and Nishga People.

If Canadian Society and Nishga Society of which it is part, is to be truly free, we as a distinct people and as citizens, must be allowed to face the difficulties and find the answers, answers that can only be found by determining our own social, economic and political participation in Canadian life. Governments, both Federal and Provincial, must be persuaded that Nishga self-determination is the path that will lead to a fuller and richer life for Nishga People and all Canadians.

We, as Nishgas, are living in a world where dynamic initiatives must be taken to achieve self-determination especially in respect to the natural resources of the Naas Valley, in order to control our own process of development within the larger Canadian society and to make decisions that affect our lives and the lives of our children. We realize that our struggle for self-determination will be a difficult one, but we refuse to believe that it is in vain, if governments and the Nishga People agree to their mutual responsibility for that growth and development. Nishga self-determination of resource development within the Naas Valley is the economic base that will allow for self-determination of the other aspects of modern 20th Century society that makes up this Canada of ours.

In 1969, N.T.C. agreed in principle with the "statement of the Government of

Canada on Indian Policy", in the face of strong opposition from other Native Peoples across the nation. That agreed principle was incorporated in the policy statement: "true equality presupposes that the Indian people have the right to full and equal participation in the cultural, social, economic and political life of Canada". Such an agreement in principle, however, does not necessarily mean the acceptance of the steps to implement as suggested by the 1969 Policy Statement. Co-existent with the N.T.C. agreement of the stated principle is also the N.T.C. agreement with the Hawthorne Report, that "Indians should be regarded as Citizens. Plus, in addition to the normal rights and duties of citizenship, Indians possess certain rights as charter members of the Canadian Community".

Undergirding the whole of the above, is the demand that, as the inhabitants since time immemoriam of the Naas Valley, all plans for resource extraction and "development" must cease until aboriginal title is accepted by the Provincial Government. Also, we, the Nishga People, believe that both the Government of B.C. and the Government of Canada must be prepared to negotiate with the Nishga on the basis that we, as Nishgas, are inseparable from our land; that it cannot be bought or sold in exchange for "extinguishing of title".

Conclusion

What we seek is the right to survive as a People and a Culture. This, we believe, can only be accomplished through free, open-minded and just negotiations with the provincial and federal authorities, negotiations that are based on the understanding that self-determination is the "answer" that government seeks to the "difficulties" as they apply to the Nishga People.

Source: Citizens Plus: The Nishga People of the Naas River in Northwestern British Colombia, Nishga Tribal Council, New Aryansh, 1975.

Blacks for Australian Independence

The history of Aboriginal resistance against imperialism goes back almost 200 years. Australian Blacks at first viewed the coming of the Europeans without malice. They thought of land occupation in terms of common use and sharing. When, to their dismay, they realised the exploitation intentions of the English colonialists, the Blacks began a struggle which they have valiantly continued to this day.

English laws refused to acknowledge the land rights of the Blacks (the original inhabitants and rightful owners of Australia), thus no treaties were made. Genocide of the whole Aboriginal population was attempted. One-third of the pre-1788 population was herded into concentration camps known as "reserves" or "missions". School history text books ignore or distort this period of Australian history. They ignore the heroic guerrilla warfare which the Blacks waged against their dispossessors. This war of resistance continued throughout the 19th Century, and it has been estimated that more Aborigines died in active defence of their land than Maoris in their better known wars against the English invaders.

While the Aboriginal people were being systemically slaughtered and the survivors imprisoned on "reserves", the British capitalists and local squatters grew fat on the fruits of black land. To add insult to injury, Blacks were now forced to work for starvation wages, or rations of salted beef, tea, flour and sugar. They were denied citizenship and freedom of movement, and until well into this century numerous "punitive raids" were made on any Black groups who tried to resist the continuing racial exploitation and oppression.

The decline of British imperialism made room for the inroads of American pastoral and mining companies, in northern, western and central Australia. This has heightened the exploitation and increased the dispossession of Blacks. Even Aboriginal "reserves" are not safe from their encroachment. The current attempts by the multinationals to mine uranium in the Northern Territory are but recent cases in point. Not only do the multinationals wish to rip up and despoil sacred tribal land and deprive the inhabitants of essential hunting areas, but they even make the suggestion that nuclear waste can be dumped in the inland — of course, only Blacks live there, so it is called "uninhabited"!

Blacks took a significant role in the preparations for the anti-uranium mining Moratorium (1st April). The anti-uranium movement is a clear example of where white and black Australians can, should and will stand together in a united struggle to control our country and our destiny, ourselves. We all know the environmental dangers associated with the mining, refining and use of uranium. We are aware that this is a further example of a quarry and a dump. And we can see that the headlong rush of the uranium lobby is another link in the involvement of Australia directly in the two superpowers' nuclear race for global supremacy. The devastation of Aboriginal land could be equalled all over the world by the madness of nuclear competition between the US and USSR.

The current struggle between the US and Soviet superpowers has brought about the intensification of political and economic pressure on the working class, working and progressive people of Australia. We are being forced to bear the burden of US imperialism's fight for survival. Nobody is suffering more in this crisis than the Blacks. For 200 years at the bottom of the socio-economic ladder, they are now being crushed even further. Fraser, co-operating in US imperialism's moves, has slashed the Aboriginal Affairs budget to the stage where many Black housing, health, legal and cultural organisations are finding it impossible to operate successfully. More spending cuts are expected.

In the capital cities and country towns, the Black unemployment rate is literally ten times the rate of white workers — and that is shocking in itself. Through the imperialist ideology of racism, Blacks are kept at the bottom of the ever-growing pool of unemployed, which serves and makes things easier for the foreign multinationals to attack the people and reduce our living standards.

The Black struggle against the foreign pastoralists and miners and the obscene doctrine of racism which they never fail to promote has continued through the century to the present day. The Gurindji people struck in 1966 against the inhuman working conditions at Wave Hill station. After years of valiant struggle they have succeeded in winning back part of their land and a degree of self-determination. In the Pilbara, at Yirrkala, Weipa and Aurukun there have been big struggles recently. In the cities and towns Blacks have demonstrated and resisted police harassment, gaolings and beatings, and have fought to set up and maintain their support services in health, education, law, housing and for freedom from the tyrannical Queensland Acts. People will remember the courage of the Aboriginal Embassy in Canberra, its brutal suppression by the Federal Government in McMahon's time, and its re-construction by a united group of Blacks and whites.

Land rights for Black Australians!!
Oppose the foreign exploitation of Australian people!!
Oppose US and Soviet ownership of Australia!!
Fight for independent socialist Australia!!
Support the Australian independence movement!

Authorised **Gary Foley** (Black Student Union)

Source: Identity, Canberra, July 1977.

The following statement was drawn up by the indigenous Association of Central Llangahua, Ecuador, after a series of manoeuvres which enabled ranchers to take over their best land.

"We Cannot Eat Good Will"

"March 18, 1974. A dialogue with the Provincial Governor takes place. We thank him for his manifestation of good will in assuring us that he will take actions to bring about a satisfactory end to the litigation within thirty days. But in thirty days, we cannot eat good will. Our decision is:

"To Work the Land for which we are ready to pay a fair price. We are a people and we have the right to life. They forbid us to work for ourselves and counsel us to work for the hacienda. We have decided the contrary. If the police come against us, we will not go against the police, we will offer them our last plate of food, we will make our situation known to the world. We have respected the law which has been declared to be in favor of the people, but the law that is administered by the oligarchy has not respected us. We will no longer yield before threats, and if we die our children will continue the fight. We hope for the endorsement of all those who understand the justice of our cause."

Source: Indigena, Berkeley, Winter 1974–75, p. 8.

"You just can't hold us up again!"

Utopia
16 October 1980

Mr. Everingham,

We have been told that you are going to the High Court to stop the Aboriginal Land Commission from hearing the Utopia claim.

We are very angry and worried about this. You are trying to rob us of our land. We have to hang on to this place. We don't want you and the Northern Territory Government to take this place away.

We showed the judge this country. That's enough. He saw all that place. We told him about our stories and songs from the Dreaming, and about our sacred places. We showed him our sacred places and our tjuringas. The Northern Territory Government does not have tjuringas for this place.

We have been here all our lives and our fathers and grandfathers lives. We have been following that business.

The Northern Territory Government lawyer has seen this country. He knows that what we say is true.

Mr. Everingham, we don't like what you are doing to stop our claim to make Utopia Aboriginal land. We hold the land in a stronger way than white fellers. We hold it from our fathers and grandfathers. We hold it as Kurtingurla.

We can't leave our country behind. If we go away bad things will happen. Somebody might get killed if we go some where else. We can't live if we leave this country. We have to hold this land. It has our dreamings and sacred places. We've got sacred everything here.

We are looking after the cattle. We keep working and looking after the bores. We can't leave.

If mining companies came, they might mess around with our sacred land. There are not many minerals country here but mining people have come and they have broken sacred things. Aboriginal people should have the say whether mining people can come.

It is not only Aboriginal people at Utopia who are worried about what you are doing in fighting Aboriginal land claims. People at Tea Tree and Willowra, and Chilla Well and Mt. Allan are worried too. And those Gurindji at Wave Hill too. You are fighting all of us. Roger Vale is the member for the Legislative Assembly for us. He should be helping us. That's his job, that one. He should be fighting for us and for Tea Tree and Willowra and Chilla Well and Mt. Allan, or he might get kicked out.

Senator Chaney has been pushing for us. He has been here and knows about this country. He should help us. The Land Fund Commission want Utopia to be Aboriginal land. Senator Chaney should make sure that his lawyers push for us in the High Court.

That's what we want to say to you. It is very important for us. We ask you to think again about trying to stop the claim, and listen to us. We are not just worried for bullocks but we are worried about our sacred country. This has been our land, it has been our food, for a long long time, this country. You just can't hold us up again, like whitefellers did before.

Jacob Pitjarra
Old Fred Kamarra
Sandy Riley Ngala
Biddy Kamarra
Myrtle Pitjarra
Gloria Ngala
Mary Kamarra
Lena Purla
Lena Skinner Purla
Voilet Pitjarra
Lily Kngwarriya
Emily Kama Kngwarriya
Lucky Kngwarriya
Maggy Kamarra
Audrey Kngwarriya
Alice Kngwarriya
Diana Kngwarriya
Wendy Purla
Betty Skinner Kngwarriya
Patsy Kamarra
Lily Pitjarra
Kathleen Kamarra
Katy Kamarra
Ruby Kngwarriya
Sarah Kngwarriya
Janet Kngwarriya
Joy Kngwarriya
Lily Kngwarriya
Hazel Kngwarriya
Polly Ngala
Abie Ampitjana
Susan Kngwarriya
Mary Pitjarra
June Ampitjana
Betty Pitjarra
Aileen Ampitjana
Minnie Purla
Nora Pitjarra
Barbara Kngwarriya
Dora Pitjarra
Joy Kngwarriya
Katie Pitjarra
Kathleen Pitjarra
Judy Kngwarriya
Mary Ngala
Margaret Loy
Amy Kamarra
Kaye Haywood
Biddy Beasley
Rita Pitjarra
Jannie Kamarra
Joanne Kamarra
Minnie Kngwarriya
Elsie Kngwarriya

Jeannie Beasley
Daisy Kamarra
Betty Purla
Johnny Skinner
Toby Paul
Marnie Lewis Kamarra
Sammy Morton Ngala
Muscley Tommy Purla
Dave Ross Purla
Paddy Webb Kamarra
Dick Mill Kamarra
Motor Car Jimmy Ngala
Alec Kngwarriya
Louis Purla
Roy Loy Purla
George Kamarra
Motor Bike Ngala
Billy Dempsey Purla
Ted Ngala
Don Onion Purla
Michael Kngwarriya
Jerry Kngwarriya
Donald Jones Kngwarriya
Billy Morton Pitjarra
Billy Morton Pitjarra (2)
Two Bob Kngwarriya
Greeny Pitjarra
Sam Kngwarriya
Don Young Ngala
Kupitji Kngwarriya
Albert Morton Pitjarra
Slippery Morton Pitjarra
Frank Morton Pitjarra
Banjo Morton Pitjarra
William Pitjarra
George Pitjarra
Jacky Kamarra
Frank Kamarra
William Purla
Kenny Pitjarra
Peter Kamarra
Fred Kamarra
Hector Purla
David Purla
Albie Dixon Ngala
Ray Nelson Pananka
Dick Purvis Pungarta
Long Paddy Pitjarra
Ronny Price Ampitjana
Tommy Bird Ampitjana
Glory Pitjarra
Reggie Purla
Lennie Jones Kngwarriya

Source: Central Land Council, Alice Springs, October 1980.

The Murui of the Caqueta relate their true history
The struggle against the rubber workers of Amazonas

Our Murui Indian nation has always occupied the forest region of the Caraparaná and Igaraparaná rivers in the Comisaría del Amazonas. In 1900, at the start of this century, the rubber workers from the Casa Arana set foot on our lands and began to exploit us. Fleeing from their crimes and outrages, we moved our settlements up the Caquetá as far as Florencia and across the Putumayo down to Leticia. In no way could we understand the exploitation and cruelty shown by the rubber workers. We did not know how to defend ourselves. While the workers were on our land they slaughtered more than 40,000 of our people.

The rubber workers used the traditional animosities between the different Indian groups of the region such as the Andoques, Mirañas, Boras and Muinanes — to weaken any resistance on our part. They sent us to watch some and pursue others. We did not realise that we were brothers, that if we had been united we would have overcome those exploiting us.

However, our grandparents often put up a valiant fight against such manipulation. As time passed we began to recognise the value of unity and organisation. In 1913 a group of villains murdered the son of the chief of Menajé who had flatly refused to cooperate with the white men. To avenge his death he brought together the leaders of four Murui tribes.

He proposed that they go with his people to the white rubber workers' camp using the false excuse of discussing the "contract" for the collection of rubber — forty arrobas per month per family under the threat of death [an arroba is a measure of weight; approx. 25 lbs. — Ed. note] — but they lay in ambush and, when the white men came to the meeting, they killed six rubber workers and wounded others.

Due to so much forced labour, our fields were abandoned and we were in danger of starving. For this reason everyone gathered in Yarocamena (a village which the missionaries have decided to call "Santa Maria") and there the leaders prepared coca and tobacco paste, the sacred symbols of our traditions, to unite the people and to discuss the situation. They recognised the need to be organised and we were collecting weapons for three years, preparing ourselves and attracting more and more Indian comrades to the resistance movement. But there are always those who are afraid, there are always spies and traitors. In 1916 the Peruvian army began to surround us and so we moved to another village called Atenas and there we set about building trenches and underground escape tunnels. When the army did arrive there were 1,500 Murui Indians ready to fight to the death. The battle lasted four hours. We fought bravely, but the enemy had the advantage in weapons. Almost all our people died that day. The army mercilessly killed women and children, burning them with fires inside the tunnels. A few who did not die where taken as prisoners to Iquitos. It was not a total defeat. We had shown our strength and the white men felt obliged to treat us with less cruelty, partly because their labour force, in other words the Indians, were disappearing. The order was no longer to kill us, but to correct us, putting an end only to the revolutionary elements.

By the end of 1918 we were living in relative calm. The tribes were regrouping, we were cultivating our chagras and we reconstructed our malocas or sacred houses.

But again in 1926 we saw our life threatened. The rubber was becoming exhausted on the Colombian side and the workers began to take us away to Peru by the dozens. Once more we were forced to flee into the forests. Nobody remained on our traditional land save a few elders.

When the conflict between Colombia and Peru began we saw the possibilities of escaping and sometimes groups of entire families walked for months putting up with terrible shortages. Little by little, many died from diseases or were killed by rubber workers. We all possessed the hope of reorganising our ruined way of life, but we were bitterly disappointed.

In 1939 the Penal Colony of Araracuara was established on the Caquetá. There we were forced to work as labourers or guards to earn the money to pay the debts with which the traders deceived us, while the Penal Colony began to take possession of our lands.

In the years 1934–36 the Capuchin mission was founded in La Chorrera its aim being (according to them) to gather up the "poor Indian children and put them in an orphanage . . ." — as if the Murui infants did not have any parents — "in order to make them civilised". In the missionaries' school everything was a sin; we were prohibited from speaking our language, they made us lose respect for the teaching of our grandparents, and they forced us to pray. So that the youth would not return to our communities, they married us by force establishing villages around the mission. In 1934, the same Capuchin missionaries arrived at the Caquetá, baptising us, marrying us, and collecting the children for the school, thereby destroying our culture; our physical exploitation continued.

The traders arrived at the Indian settlements and in exchange for machetes, axes and clothes made us work the rubber again (we received 2 centavos per kilo of rubber which was later sold in Manaus at 50 or 60 centavos).

The authorities began to bother us in the Penal Colony. The white guards sent for us for no reason. We were unable to walk in peace. They abused our women. They accused us of hiding weapons. They made our young people drunk and corrupt. They beat us. They treated us worse than the prisoners. But when we complained and when we wanted to organise ourselves, the white authorities split us up by buying off our leaders and creating an atmosphere of fear. Some of us decided to increase their harvests or to cut timber to sell these products, but then the white men thwarted that using threats or deceit. They bought us drinks in the bars, then they took advantage of the general drunken state to fight and afterwards they blamed us for all the damage.

It was always us, the Indians, who were put in jail. The police and the judges were always on the side of their white friends.

At the end of 1967, the white authorities met the traders and decided that each one of them would "sponsor" a tribe to assist progress in the region and help us. Lisardo Zumaeta was in charge of the Muinane; Alberto Zumaeta was entrusted with the Andoque; Aniceto Fajardo with the Indians of Puerto Sábalo; and Miguel Vargas with those of Monochoa. But it is clear that far from protecting us, slavery was still rife.

They put us back to work on the rubber and under the new contract the employers would be responsible for everything: food, medicines, etc. for their

Indian rubber workers. But quite the reverse occurred, and they weighed the rubber collected by us in scales which were "fixed" so that they would show a lower weight than the true one. Those of us from Mocochoa did not want to go on working, and they looked for another way of "using" us: they began to buy manioc from us — the basic foodstuff of the region — at very low prices for them to sell it later at a more inflated rate. Coupled with that, they pushed up the price of commodities they sold us. So we organised an economic bloc. We did not want to sell them any more manioc, and because of that they called us revolutionaries. In turn they ceased to sell goods to us and we suffered severely, but we held firm to our principles and since they could not buy manioc in Brazil, they had no other choice but to pay us a just price. Thus we gained some experience: it is necessary to be firm and not let oneself be exploited.

The politicians have also exploited us, deceiving us with promises of assistance with tools and local hospitals and making us more flexible with large feasts. But now we are determined to fight on. The politician, Fajardo, when he saw that he could do nothing to stop us, petitioned the government and denounced us as being revolutionaries, and since he is a merchant he threatened us with an economic bloc again. However, we accused him of making our Indian comrades drunk and taking them by force to vote in the polls. They sent a judge to investigate, but he was Fajardo's nephew, and so no progress was made. They sacked a police official who acted in our favour.

Our situation today has not really improved. We have requested assistance from the Ministry of Agriculture and the government, but to no avail. We have not yet realised that one cannot expect any great assistance from the wealthy. If we wish to improve our position it is we, the poor, who must organise ourselves. Those of us from Monochoa have already stressed among the people the importance of uniting all the Indians of the region into an Indian League. The poor settlers, who in the majority of cases were prisoners of the Penal Colony, are equally defenceless and exploited by the authorities and traders. Over the last years they have always supported us in our campaign. And now we consider it to be of the greatest importance that we should unite not only amongst ourselves but also with the poor white settlers, thereby possessing more support to improve the situation of the poor in Colombia.

Source: Unidad Indigena No. 3, CRIC, Colombia, 2 March 1975.

Ken Gunbuku and Bill Manydjarri are custodians of the Yolnggus people of north-eastern Arnhemland (Australia) who, in 1983 held a special meeting at their outstation of Gapuwiyak, to discuss the threat posed by a road corridor through their land.

Ken Gunbuku: We Yolnggus, we have been here in Australia since a long time. Before there were our *gathus, wawas, marimus* and here we are, from them, who died here long ago. We are not visitors like *balandhas* (whites) who came from over there, from England, and then started to go after us vigorously. But they did not bother to see what we need. We want this very strongly, namely our land. No tree is going to be chopped down, and there is going to be no big road; no rock is going to be blasted off and our homeland is not going to be made miserable. This is in our eye and in our heart and in our life.

Bill Manydjarri: Every year your *rom* (law) you turn it around. Then you come after us with your *rom*. Our old people, the *maris, bapas, gathus*, they were not like that. And we lay down the *rom* the same way as when they died. There is no *rom* right of yours for drilling or to bring in the bulldozers. We are not going to grant you rights for drilling, or whatever no, you got no permit for this here . . . Where are you from? From over there, wherever your home may be. Your *miri, gathus* are from way over there. Go back to your place! There is no tree, no ground, no water of yours here. You *balandhas*, you are without manners, like the birds who are going to fly around and sit down and perch . . . Whether you come after us this year and another year and yet another year . . . and another Christmas . . . and we will still say: No, no, no, no, no, no! And this until I die!

Source: Cameron Forbes, "Aboriginal Australia" in *The Age*, Melbourne, 17 March 1984. Reprinted with permission.

This letter to you was written by tribal elder, Guboo Ted Thomas

My name is Guboo Ted Thomas. I am a Tribal Elder of the Yuin Tribe on the South Coast of New South Wales. I am writing to you about Mumbulla Mountain, which is of vital importance to the culture and dignity of the 3,500 Aborigines living on the South Coast today. The Mountain is about 30 kilometres south-west of where many of us live at Wallaga Lake, not all that far from Bega.

For us Aborigines, it is a sacred mountain where initiations used to take place. These took place at sacred sites on the Mountain.

When they were old enough, the boys of our tribe were taken away to these special sacred sites. Here they were taught the special secrets of our Culture. So, you see, the Law comes from the Mountain.

They had to spend a long time on the Mountain away from their people, and they were put through special tests to prove that they were men. Then they were initiated and brought back to the tribe as young men who respected their Tribal Law and Culture. The Law has been handed down from one generation to the next, ever since the Dreamtime.

I was told about these things when I was young. I was told by my grandfather, my father and my uncle. Near Wallaga Lake where we live there is another important mountain called Goolaga – or, by white people, Mt. Dromedary. When I was a boy, I used to walk with my people from Wallaga Lake over Mumbulla Mountain to Bega. From Goolaga to Mumbulla is all part of the one walkabout.

When we were walking, the old people would sometimes point to places on Mumbulla Mountain and tell me there were special sites there. They told me that one day I would be taken there and have them shown to me. This would be when I would be initiated. They said that then I would have to help look after the Law and the Culture.

But the last initiations were about 1918, when I was still too young. These were done by our Tribal Elders. One of these was Jack Mumbulla, who has the same name as the Mountain. Some of the men initiated there were Percy Davis (my grandfather), Murrum Alf Carter (whose descendants still live at Wallaga Lake), Bukel Albert Thomas (my cousin) and Eric Roberts (who still lives at Wreck Bay).

We hope to bring back initiations on the Mountain in the near future. This will be very good. It will help make our Law and our Culture strong once again.

So I hope you can see now why Mumbulla Mountain is an important part of our Culture and why it should be protected. It is important to us Aborigines, but we think it should also be important to white Australians as well. It is something that should be important to our Australian heritage.

Source: A-I-M (Aboriginal Islander Message). Glebe, July 1979.

While we have breath . . .

His Excellency Ferdinand E. Marcos   8 December 1983
President of the Republic of the Philippines
Manila, Philippines

Dear Mr. President:

We, the undersigned T'boli, Ubo, Manobo and Visayan residents of the barangays of the Municipality of Lake Sebu created by Batas Pambansa Bilang 249 and approved by Your Excellency on November 11, 1982 do hereby petition Your Excellency to reconsider your appointment of Jose F. Sison, Jr. as first mayor of our Municipality. We see this appointment as a disregard of the clear will of the overwhelming majority of the residents of Lake Sebu whose petition and signatures were presented to your Excellency at Malacanang on November 17, 1983 by tribal representatives of our group.

Your appointee, Mr. Jose F. Sison, Jr., has no experience of our tribal customs. He does not speak our language and he is not even a resident of Lake Sebu. We see his appointment as Mayor and those of his council as further impoverishing and oppressing the tribal peoples of Lake Sebu.

Mr. President, these are the same men who, either themselves or through their families have divided our lakes among themselves, who have helped drive T'bolis from their ancestral lands, who have tried to deny us our right to vote, who have consistently used armed force in an attempt to intimidate us. We therefore find these appointments distasteful, intolerable and unjust.

We therefore reiterate our petition of November 1, 1983 which we quote in part.

"... we want to bring to your attention the following considerations:

1. That the area covered by the proposed municipality in fact comprises the ancestral lands of T'boli, Ubo and Manobo tribes which from time immemorial they have occupied.

2. And that therefore the tribal citizens of this area feel that they have prior claim to the lands and other resources of this area without prejudice to the legitimate rights of settlers.

3. That the overwhelming majority of the population are T'bolis, Ubos and Manobos.

4. That in a previous petition to your Excellency dated August 1982, we requested that the chief executive of the municipality of Lake Sebu come from the T'boli tribe. However to prepare greater tribal unity we revise our former petition to request simply that the choice of the majority be honored.

5. That we wish to state that we maintain our original desire to have a T'boli mayor in the near future, and T'boli candidates are preparing themselves for this position.

Therefore, we the undersigned have agreed to the creation of the new municipality of Lake Sebu on the condition that the majority have the right to choose the municipal officials.

We trust in your continuous support for our cause, which will bring justice to all our people."

Mr. President, we trust that you will not take this our second petition as a sign of disrespect for you and your office. That is far from our intention. However, you must understand that we are in anguish over that appears to us to be an attempt to wrest our ancestral lands from us, destroy our culture, and endanger our very survival. While we have breath in us we can never give up this struggle.

We remain,

Yours sincerely,

T'Boli-Ubo-Manobo-Visayan concerned citizens of the newly created
Municipality of Lake Sebu
13,747 Signatures

Source: Tribal Forum, Manila, Vol. 5, No. I, February 1984.

*Paitan is a small reservation belonging to the Mangyan people of the
Philippines. Although nominally owning 220 hectares, the people have been
forced out of their homes into the mountains, due to encroachment from
settlers. The following Open Letter was drafted during a meeting at the
reservation in May 1976.*

A Small Flame

To the Filipino People:
We are 200 representatives of the Alangan Tribe of the Mangyan
people of Mindoro who have met for two days here in the sitio of
Paitan, Calapan, Mindoro, at the foot of the Halcon mountain.

We have discussed many things which we wish to share with all the
Filipino people.

At one time our tribe was the only people in this fertile plain
around Calapan that is said to be as big as the province of Bulacan.
We planted and harvested in peace. We thought we were the only
people in the world (Mangyan means Man) and we were proud and
contented. A hundred years or so ago the Tagalog and later Ilocano
settlers came to take our land. We retreated because it seemed to us
there was enough land for all and we are not a warrior people as
everyone can tell you.

But the land is not unlimited. We have been forced up into the
mountains. Still the settlers come. If we plant a few trees, a Tagalog or
Ilocano will come and claim them.

There is no place for us to settle down. Don't believe that we are
contented roaming the mountains building temporary huts, living by
kaingin. We are not a nomadic mountain people. We have been
forced up to the mountains. We know such a life is no life for our
families: half the children die, there are no schools, no medicine.

We have met these days to discuss our problems, not as a small
group but as a whole tribe, for we know that a solution is possible
only if we have union. These days together we have felt the warmth
and strength our tribal unity brings. We are happy to be Mangyans.

Here are our needs:
1. We want land for our tribe, enough for all of us, a piece of land
that is titled and secure, that others cannot steal. We are willing to
take any land, provided it is secure and adequate for our families. We
will not retreat any more.

2. We want our own way of life. We are willing to live side by side with others but we want to live our own culture and traditions. We are losing these since we live as isolated small groups browbeaten by Christians. We want our own secure land, our own place, where we can come together and find again what are really our way of life, our beliefs and traditions. We want to protect what is left of our culture, as you protect a small flame till it grows into a strong fire.

Our traditions are peaceful as everyone can tell you. To us they are like life itself. If we lose our own way, what are we? We need our own place to become the people we are supposed to be. Time is running out.

3. Lastly, we need schools for our children where they can study in peace and not be insulted as they are now in the lowland schools. We want them to learn your ways which have so much to offer, but we want them to be true Mangyans also. We want your schools, but on our terms, in our place.

We older Mangyans are illiterate. Of the 200 meeting here only 26 can sign their names. We do not want to stay this way because such ignorance is harmful to us. We want adult education courses. We want to learn. But above all, we want to know our rights.

Source: The Philippine Times, Manila, 1–15 January 1977.

This declaration, made by the Mapuche of Jose Jineo, Chile, gives an example of the kind of land-grabbing which is attempted on indigenous territory, with the connivance of the military junta — even though the community has legal title, and no single member has requested sale or division of the land.[358]

Accusation by the Mapuche community of Jose Jineo

The members of the community of Jose Jineo, Rofue, department of Temuco, who are the present occupiers of the community's land, inform the authorities and public opinion:

That the communal estate of 104 hectares, Deed of Gift no. 1026, dated October 14th 1905, inheritance number 359A, registered in the General Archive of Indian Resources, has never been divided, nor have the present occupants asked for any division.

That they have always been troubled by individuals presenting legal documents which declare them to be the owners of properties which have resulted from division.

That, when the matter is brought to court, they present documents of purchase and sale to people who have never belonged to the community nor are heirs of those settled there.

This has happened in the case brought by Dona Ana Maria Ulbrich Cravero and Guillermo German Ulbrich Whal, who are presenting legal documents relating to an estate of 80 hectares in the Jineo community, Rofue.

They accuse the owner of the land, Robustiano Gineo Calfuman, and Dona Leonor Reyes Valdes, widow of Jose Gineo, of being in illegal occupation of the land, and request the court to restore it to them. The document, a deed of sale and purchase, gives as boundaries the inheritances no. 36–37–38–39–40 to the North, and nos. 33–34–35 to the West. This shows that legal apportion- ment of the land to its occupiers has been granted without the knowledge of interested parties.

The entire community asks for the cancellation of the verdict of the Second Court of Temuco, which allowed the claim of the individual, because there has never been division within this community.

No member of the community has signed an assignment of inheritance, so there cannot be any property belonging to individuals.

For division to have taken place, the community would have had to ask for the application of some article of the law of that date.

The Community has never asked for division, nor been informed that any such request was made; the acts of granting inheritance which are now being invoked have not been made known to, still less accepted by, the community.

Consequently, it is dishonest to demand a free loan (*comodato precario*) from Robustiano Gineo and Leonor Reyes. They live on their land in accordance with the Deed of Gift, having inherited from their parents. If there has been no division, there cannot have been a granting of inheritances, still less the sale of land.

This is not a new attempt to dispossess them under the government of Jorge Alessandri, another individual land claim to the same estate; the authorities at Temuco supported him, as they are doing today. Gineo and his family were held in custody while his house was burned and its surroundings wrecked.

Robustiano Gineo's mother, Dona Bartola Calfumao de Gineo, went to Santiago in defence of her land and her children. She saw the Minister of Land and Colonies, Julio Filipi, and demonstrated to him that her community had never been divided and none of its heirs had sold any estate.

The deed of sale and purchase made out for this individual was demonstrably invalid, because the seller belonged to another community and had no connection — by inheritance, kinship, or in any other way — with this community.

By order of the then President, Sr. Alessandri, and his minister Sr. Julio Filipi, Gineo and his family were restored to their land and have remained there to this day, on land which belongs to them. As it is a very serious matter to try to impose legal documents on a community which has never been divided, and claim sale and purchase which has never been made by the Mapuche, we ask the Government to intervene and to give us JUSTICE.

An attempt is being made today to drive from their land members of the community who have never sold their rights, and who have lived in the community since the time of settlement in 1905.

We look to the Chilean government to correct the mistakes which have been made, and to all authorities to ensure justice.

Signed by all members of the community of Jose Jineo currently occupying land there.

Source: Boletin Informativo Mapuche, Chile, date unknown, quoted in *Survival International Review*, Spring 1982.

About 40 years after colonists peddling British imperialism began to exploit New Zealand in earnest, they were forced to sign a unique concession, the Treaty of Waitangi. It was the only Treaty (as such) which the British government concluded with an indigenous nation. But although in the 1870s, Prime Minister Gladstone invoked it as a sacred trust ("There is no Treaty more binding on Britain than that of Waitangi") he himself refused to meet the Maori king Tawhiao when he arrived in Britain with a petition urging that it be honoured.[359]

In recent years, a boycott of Waitangi Day, combined with militant demonstrations, like that of 1984,[360] has become the keystone of the radical new Maori movement. The same year, a number of Maori organisations came together in Ngaruawahia to draw up a position paper on the Treaty and initiate a broad campaign for Maori land rights. Following is the programme agreed by that Hui *(gathering).*

The dignity of the land

● *Kia whaka kotahi tatou — tera te wairua o tenei hui.* (Let us make ourselves one — that is the spirit of this hui.)

The purpose of the hui was to bring together collective opinions from Maori people, to talk about and seek points of healing and reconciliation, in regard to the Treaty of Waitangi.

Throughout the hui came repeated calls for the unity of our people. In essence we heeded our own calls and practised what must always be a constant and progressing means for achieving our vision as *tangata whenua* (people of the land) of Aotearoa.

● *Te mana wairua, te mana whenua, te mana tangata me tuku iho ki a tatou e nga matua, e nga tupuna.* (The dignity of the spirit, the dignity of the land, the dignity of the people is released to us by our parents, by our ancestors.)

Status of Treaty

1. The Treaty of Waitangi is a document which articulates the status of Maori as tangata whenua of Aotearoa.
2. The Treaty of Waitangi shall be the basis for claims in respect to the land, forests, water, fisheries and human rights of Maori people.
3. The Treaty of Waitangi is a symbol which reflects *Te Mana Maori Motuhake* (The distinction of being specially Maori). We declare that our *Mana Tangata Mana Wairua, Mana Whenua*, supersedes the Treaty of Waitangi.

Celebrations, 1985

1. That this hui supports the cessation of the celebration of the Treaty of Waitangi, at Waitangi, and throughout Aotearoa, on February 6, 1985.
2. Accordingly, this hui recommends to the Waitangi Trust Board and the Government that they withdraw the Navy, the military, police and other Government organisations and representatives from participation in the Treaty of Waitangi celebrations at Waitangi 1985.

3. That this hui endorses the calling of a hui by the four Maori elected MPs, to be held at Waitangi on February 4, 5 and 6, 1985, and that the MPs work with a collective *tangata whenua* from throughout Aotearoa.

Waitangi Tribunal

1. That the Waitangi Tribunal be given retrospective powers to 1840 to hear grievances and that adequate resources be made available to the tribunal and to applicants (complainants) to ensure the grievances are fully researched.
2. The Maori Land Court be given wider powers — not less than equal to the High Court of New Zealand.
3. The Maori Land Court and Maori Affairs should follow recommendations of royal commissions to do with Maori issues.
4. Not only should the beds of lakes and rivers be returned to the owners, but also all rights in respect to the water should belong to the owners.
5. There should be changes in procedures of the Maori Land Court *vis à vis*, the prevention of Maori land from being alienated.
6. That a body 50 per cent elected by Maori people and 50 per cent elected by the remainder be established: (a) to sit between Parliament and the Governor General to ensure that all proposed legislation is consistent with the Treaty of Waitangi; and (b) to rule on recommendations from the Waitangi Tribunal and to formulate any compensation programmes to be implemented by the Government.
7. That a law be introduced to require that all proposed legislation be consistent with the Treaty of Waitangi.

Department of Maori Affairs and Maori Trustee

1. That the Department of Maori Affairs be required to account to the people for its actions, especially for the year-by-year practice of underspending its appropriation — thereby handing millions of dollars back to the Government while Maori needs are so widespread and critical.
2. We challenge Maori people to take a wider interest in the way the Maori Trust Office functions. This would ensure that the fullest possible benefits are made to the Maori people.

Maoris in Parliament

1. We urge a greater monitoring of the political performance of Maori Parliamentarians acting on behalf of the Maori people.

Maoris in Government Administration

1. We urge the establishment of a real Maori dimension within the Department of Education — then throughout the educational system.
2. We urge the establishment of a real Maori dimension from top to bottom of the Department of Justice.
3. We call for the establishment of a real and active dimension within every Government department, especially with Health, Social Welfare and Treasury.

Proposed Bill of Rights

1. This hui is suspicious of the passing of a Bill of Rights because we believe we already have one — the Treaty of Waitangi.

2. That part of the work of the proposed commission include the investigation of the relevance of the Bill of Rights for Maori people. We request that the Government ensure adequate Maori representation on the preparatory committee of Government.

Proposed Commission

1. This hui endorses the establishment of a commission to implement the recommendations of this hui.

2. This commission shall be comprised of members of the present planning committee, with power to co-opt other representatives.

3. That the work of this commission be funded by the Government.

Role of Maori Women

1. On the principles of equality and justice enunciated in many submissions made to this hui, we submit that recognition of these principles be also applied to Maori women as follows:

That because Maori women constitute over 50 per cent of the *tangata whenua* there must be equal representation in all areas of decision-making in the future.

The hui, which ran from September 14 to 16, had been called for by these organisations:

Te Runanga Whakawhanaunga i nga Hahi o Aotearoa (the Maori Council of Churches), *Te Kotahitanga* (New Zealand Maori Council), Maori Women's Welfare League, The Race Relations Conciliator, Maori Wardens' Association, Maori writers and artists, Mana Motuhake, Maori university students, Maori Battalion and Maori members of parliament.

Source: Auckland Star, 19 September 1984.

This section continues with a presentation made in 1981 at the Geneva NGO conference on the rights of Indigenous peoples and their land, by Chief Hilary Frederick, chief of the "Caribs" (Kwaib). A community of between 2,000 and 3,000 Kwaib and part-Kwaib in the Dominican Republic is all that is left of the 35 million Amerindian inhabitants of the Caribbean islands — apart from a few small villages elsewhere in the region which can claim some Arawak descent.

Virtually all Chief Frederick's speech is reproduced here. It encapsulates many of the issues highlighted in the rest of this anthology, and puts them in the context of a prolonged struggle for land rights, conducted by a single people whose very existence is barely recognised today outside of the Lesser Antilles. Hilary Frederick takes us succinctly — but with necessary detail — through the mythology of original "discovery", the merciless extermination by successive imperial invaders of the vast majority of original Caribbean peoples, the extempore self-protecting alliances formed by the remnant communities with the oppressors, and the final appropriation of Carib territory through colonial deceit and cartographic jiggery-pokery.

The Kwaib people — like the Dine of New Mexico, the Aboriginal "fringe-dwellers" of western Australia[361] or the refugees from hi-jacked Diego Garcia (see p. 126) — now suffer the worst consequences of internal colonisation and de-development. No amount of external aid could redress the wrongs they have suffered. For, as Hilary Frederick puts it: "The issue of Kwaib lands is nothing but that of the material requirements of a people who have an undisputed right . . . to prepare the future of their children on an island on which they have more claims than any other human beings".

The Caribs and their Colonizers: The problem of land

Pre-European Invasions

The Caribbean archipelago stretches itself along a 2,500 mile arc which ties the southern tip of Florida to the eastern coast of Venezuela, and circumscribes the Caribbean sea on the western end of the Atlantic. The region inherited its name from one group of native inhabitants, the Caribs, who occupied the Lesser Antilles and whose northward drive was cut short by the European invasions. The Arawaks of the Greater Antilles have now completely disappeared, and of the 35 million people who inhabit the 50 or so Caribbean islands, less than 3,000 can claim that their ancestors were indigenous to the region prior to its subjugation by European powers. Clusters of population with some Amerindian features have been noted in Guadeloupe and most particularly, in St. Vincent. But the only substantial group of native Amerindians left in the Caribbean resides in the now independent Commonwealth of Dominica, one of the Windward Islands of the Lesser Antilles. There are now about 500 people now caged by cultural, political and economic deprivation on a "reservation" that they share with some 1,500 neighbors and/or relatives of Carib and mixed ancestry.

The early Caribs were the third group of migrants who left the north-eastern shores of South America to make their way northward through the archipelago. The Ciboneys had preceded them by at least a millenary but Ciboney culture seems to have died when these early discoverers reached the larger northern islands. What was left of the Ciboney civilization was most probably appropriated by the Arawaks, the second group of Amerindians to follow the path, some three thousand years ago. In the larger islands, especially in the alluvial plains of Cuba and Haiti, the Taino branch of the Arawaks had established a flourishing civilization, producing cotton, manioc, corn and fruits, making pottery and enjoying sports, particularly ball games. Not more than two centuries before Arawak development in the Greater Antilles was curtailed by Columbus' arrival, a third group of Amerindians took the northward path through the Antilles. They called themselves Callinago and had long been engaged in warfare against the Arawaks on the South American continent. Their venture in the Lesser Antilles was carried out against that background of enmity. Mostly males had come for the long trip, the women remaining among the Callinago Balouaboum, that is, those of the continent. As they conquered the Arawaks of the small southern islands of the archipelago, the Callinago took spouses among them and the new wives referred to their tribe Karipuna. Other indians referred to them as Galibi or Garibi and it is perhaps a deformation of this latter name which led the Spaniards to call them Caribales from which are derived the words Carib, Caraibes, etc . . . under which descendants of the Callinago are known to the outside world. Today we call ourselves Kwaib, however all of the terms Carib, Kwaib and Callinago (which means harmless people) will be used interchangeably.

European Invasions

All the peoples of the Caribbean have come to know that Columbus did not discover the New World. Chinese, Vikings and West African traders preceded him.

Columbus' intentions were primarily to amass wealth, new territory and slaves. Spain had already been inspired by earlier Portuguese successes in enslaving Africans. At the time of the first voyage of Columbus, there was in operation a renowned Portuguese sugar factory by slaves in the Guinea coast of Africa. It is not surprising therefore that Columbus would record his primary observations about the people whom he met in the Bahamas on October 12th 1492 that "they should be good servants and intelligent, for I observed them to be timid and unwarlike," and was of the opinion that with their superior Spanish artillery a very small force of Spaniards could overrun and capture all of the Islands. "So that," he continued, "they are good to be ordered about, to work, to sow, and to do all that is necessary." He also recorded in his first diary that he "was attentive and took trouble to ascertain if there was gold."

He returned to Spain with a few slaves, leaving a settlement behind on the island of Hispaniola.

On his second voyage in September of 1492 between twelve to fifteen thousand European settler/colonizers accompanied him. They established a colony on a different site on the island of Hispaniola, the ancestor Arawak nation warriors having annihilated the group expedition that Columbus had left behind on his first journey.

By the middle of the 16th century, Spain had established the first colonial empire in the Americas. At the same time the Portuguese were exploring the great trading opportunities offered by the African route to India. In 1494, the Treaty of Tordesillas divided the world between these two countries in an agreement to settle anxiety over fixing of the boundaries of their prospective empires.

The other European nations, determined to share in this new found wealth, disregarded this treaty and established colonies on the basis of effective occupation. In 1605, the English made their first attempt to settle in the West Indies, in St. Lucia. This attempt failed as a result of the heroic defensive efforts of the Callinago nation. They tried similarly to settle in Grenada four years later, but failed for the same reason. In 1623 the English occupied St. Kitts, and Barbados in 1625. In 1625, the French also landed in St. Kitts and the two nations decided to partition the island between themselves. In almost every island efforts to invade the territory were faced by defensive warfare from the Callinago and Arawak warriors. Superior arms and ruthless methods of warfare, however, eventually gave the settler/colonizers the upper hand.

In Grenada, after effectively occupying the island, the French exterminated the Callinago nation, the last group of which, rather than submit to enslavement, threw themselves headlong over a cliff which has since been called, "le morne des sauters" (Leapers Hill, or The Jumpers). In Dominica and St. Vincent, Callinago resistance made the English and the French sign a treaty with the Callinago nation that these two islands would not be colonized but would remain nonaligned Carib territory. In the meantime the Arawak people were being systematically enslaved, if they were submissive, and punished if they resisted, as they often did, until they were all finally exterminated. So complete was the devastation of the Indian civilization in the West Indies and Latin America that even some humanitarian Europeans, like the Catholic Bishop, Bartolome de Las Cases, arose in defense of the native peoples attempting to arrest the genocide that was taking place.

In one historical pamphlet entitled *Very Brief Account of the Destruction of the Indies*, the Bishop charged that 15 million had perished to lay the foundation of the Spanish empire in the New World. Dominica and St. Vincent remained the final refuge of Callinago nation. In 1655 Phillipe de Beaumot, a French cleric in Dominica was asked "What is to become of the poor Carib, must he go and live with the fish in the sea?" Not only were the people being exterminated but the hemisphere also suffered the loss of the rich cultural, political, economical and social methods of adaptation to the tropical West Indian environment; adoption of which would have only enhanced and graced successive civilizations in the region.

Desecration of a culture

Kwaib people organized their lives in an extended family arrangement. Each clan shared a piece of land which was cooperatively owned. The chief was elected by universal adult suffrage. He was elected for his bravery, courage, endurance and will power in addition to his qualities of truthfulness and honesty and especially his powers of persuasion since his rule was exercised through persuasion rather than through force. Wealth and family origin did not figure much in the election of chiefs. Each chief usually exercised authority only over his own clan though sometimes, especially during warfare, a regional chief was recognized, or sometimes even a supreme national chief.

Land was the common domain of all. Still today, in spite of Government's persistent efforts to encourage Caribs to individual ownership title of lands on the territory, land remains vested in the total community. The basis of Callinago diet was manioc; which is poisonous unless prepared in a special way. Women tended to planting this and other tubers, fruits, berries and cotton; in addition to pottery making, weaving, making of hammocks and other crafts. Kwaib people carried on interisland and intercontinental trade. Their 60 foot dug out kanawa (from which the English word canoe is derived) fetched a good barter price. Fishing was the main activity of the men who experienced no fear in venturing far out into the ocean.

They were able generals and commanders. They were known not to destroy property for the sake of vandalism when making raids, but to preserve it so that they could make use of it in the future. The Kwaib people had a special proclivity for languages, speaking the native language, the Arawak language (which many of their captured wives retained and passed on to the children), and a special secret council language spoken by the elders. The European languages were quickly learnt in the interest of our own defense. Kwaib people have since then been forced to abandon their original language. Ancestral traditions and history were passed on orally and the people possessed retentive memories. Our people also had a strong religious tradition with a conception of good and evil forces. The French colonizers in spite of concentrated efforts did not succeed in converting Callinago tribes people to Christianity until they had totally subdued us physically and began the process of imposition of their values.

The final stage

Dominica and St. Vincent because of their mountainous nature provided impenetrable protection against foreign incursion, continued to be the last refuge of Callinago tribespeople. However, these islands remained valuable, Dominica more so, as a rest stop for fresh water and wood, for ships coming to the new world. In spite of the treaty with the Caribs of 1660 the French, firstly through missionaries, began to settle the island and establish small homesteads. Though they encroached on Carib land they were allowed to stay if only because they pledged peaceful coexistence.

France and Britain remained in constant dispute over Dominica until 1805 when the French were finally driven out never to return. The Kwaib nation, the real owners of the land, in order to save their own interests usually had to form alliances with either of these two parties. Often through hypocrisy, doubledealing and treachery they would end up being the worst loser. Perhaps the most destructive effort in this regard was the murder of Chief Indian Warner at Massacre by his half brother Colonel Phillip Warner both sons of a former colonial English Governor of St. Kitts (General Thomas Warner). After the death of his father, Indian Warner, Thomas, son by a Carib woman, fled ill treatment in St. Kitts to live among the Kwaibs on the leeward side of the island. The French had settled and formed loose alliances with the Kwaib people on the windward side.

Indian Warner eventually became chief and remained fairly sympathetic to the English cause against the French. In 1664 he assisted them in a successful attack on the French settlement in St. Lucia by organising an expedition of 600 Kwaibs and 17 canoes to aid the British militia. For this deed he was later captured by the French, imprisoned, tortured and then released. In 1674, after the Kwaib warriors launched a counteroffensive against English settlements in Antigua, a militia of six companies under Phillip Warner was sent to revenge. The Kwaibs were massacred after feasting on brandy supplied by Phillip who gave the signal for beginning the massacre by stabbing to death his own half brother.

With the decline of Spain as a colonial power through the 17th and 18th centuries, France and England increased their efforts to effectively occupy many of the islands that heretofore Spaniards had formally laid claim to. Dominica, however, remained the last stronghold of ancestor warriors. Indeed the island was again declared neutral by the Treaty of Aix la Chapelle in 1748. However, in spite of this treaty the French still made further encroachment on Kwaib land in order to cultivate its rich well watered soil. The Kwaib nation was being exterminated and those who escaped treacherous death sought refuge in the more remote and inaccessible northeastern parts of the country. Finally in 1759, the British captured Dominica, possession being formally recognized by the Treaty of Paris in 1763. After the British takeover the French settlers were especially anxious about the possibility of their estates being appropriated by their new rulers. Their fears were assuaged; the British exacting a "quit rent" from them instead.

This period marks the beginning of the modern stage of misappropriation of the Kwaib nation's lands. It is to be noted that no mention of Carib lands or rights was made in the treaty of 1763. The French who had more or less peacefully coexisted with the Kwaib nation through a series of unwritten treaties and alliances assured and promised the ancestors at the time of the British takeover that they (the Kwaib nation) were to be given the northern half of the island by the new conquerors; from sea to sea or 'lamma pour lamma' as it is said in patois. Many elders today will corroborate this treaty. Britain however commissioned its Chief surveyor John Byres to survey the island, make a map and subsequently divide the country into lots which were eventually sold in England. On the Byres map produced in 1764, a small area in Salibia, the sight of the present reserve of less than 250 acres was delineated for the entire Carib nation. The Kwaib nation, however, though much reduced in number never lost the indomitable spirit of the ancestors. We continued to resist all efforts by the British to cultivate any of the lots in the interior. Sometimes in allegiance with African brother runaway slaves the Kwaib nations successfully defended the forested and mountainous northern half of the island in particular against all newcomers. Many of the expeditions dispatched by the Crown representatives from Roseau ended in disaster. Constant warfare however takes its toll. By 1800 few Kwaibs remained alive and a de facto peace was agreed to however the indomitable spirit of the ancestors still reverberates and the struggle for the divine and human rights of Kwaib people will evermore continue.

Now, is as good a time as any to raise a very important issue, that has a very direct bearing on the rest of this presentation. Hereinafter, the question of Kwaib land rights will be discussed according to treaties, documents, maps and written documents of the European colonizers and successors neocolonizers in office. The fact that our attention will be turned to the European concept of "legitimate" thinking; (i.e. what is written has an importance that is denied the spoken) does not mean that we accept the written process only as legitimate. This is one of the white world's ways of usurping the legitimate rights of people and destroying the culture of non-white people. Kwaib culture has an oral tradition. The treaty of our ancestors made with the French subsequent to the imposition of British rule is in our view legal, real, and binding even though we may have come to accept new treaties and new realities. Similarly, our history, our oral tradition teaches us that during the illegal raid and subsequent defensive efforts of our people on the territory in 1930, the plan of the reserve together with other important articles relating to the history, security and cultural tradition was taken from Chief Jolly Johns office. Inspector Branch has admitted to taking the Chief's Staff and "the plan of the Reserve" in his testimony to the commission appointed by His Excellency The Governor of the Leeward Islands to look into the conditions of the Carib Reserve and the disturbance of 19 September 1930. Our local oral tradition states that this plan has everything to do with the disputed borders of the present reserve and we demand that the authorities produce it. So while we approach the issue of Carib land rights from the modernist legalist perspective, we want to remind all that the oral tradition of the Kwaib nation is indeed ample testimony of the injustices committed and the usurption of the national lands of our people. The oral tradition also remains the best evidence of the heroic efforts of our people to defend these lands since 1800.

Land problem — Legal history

The legal history — as far as "official" records are concerned — shows that in the late 1860's the British Crown granted lands to Posner, Bishop of Roseau and his successors in office, with the understanding that these lands would be used by and for the Caribs of Salybia and its surroundings. The documents accompanying that grant do not emphasize Carib rights nor the necessity of retribution on the part of the British. From the outset, the Caribs were treated as subhuman beings, immature or otherwise irresponsible, at best children of a sort since they needed a tutor to supervise the use of their land: Salybia was granted *to the Bishop* for the Caribs! The granter and the tutor failed to realize that Caribs had long been able to manage a territory which had always been theirs in the first place!

The 1903 notice of H. H. Bell and the 1901 Skeat Map

The same paternalism and condescendence impregnate the document which fixed in 1903 for the first time perhaps, the boundaries of the so-called Carib Reserve. The notice, signed by then Administrator H. Hesketh Bell, and which appeared in the official Gazette, Volume XXVI, Saturday, July 4, 1903, Government Notice No. 30, reads as follows: "Whereas it is considered expedient to delimit the Carib Reserve and to set out the boundaries of their settlement or territory in the Parish of St. David in this Presidency, notice is hereby given that with the approbation of the Secretary of State of the Colonies, the Government of Dominica desires to reserve to the Caribs for their use, all that certain portion of land situated in the Parish of St. David and bounded:

Northerly by the Big River, by lot 63 and the Ballata Ravine;

Easterly by the sea;

Southerly by the Raymond River and Crown land; and

Westerly by the Pegoua River, by Concord Estate and by

.lots 61 and 63.

All as the same are set out or delineated on a plan or diagram of the said lands drawn by Arthur Percival Skeat, licensed Surveyor, and filed in the Registrar's Office in this Presidency where the same may be inspected at any time during office hours.

Any person who has any objection to make to the said plan or who claims any land within the boundaries above set forth, must, within forty days from the date of this notice, lodge such objection with the Registrar for the consideration of the government otherwise the land so delineated and described will hereafter be taken and considered as the Carib Reserve and will be recognized accordingly. Dated this 30th day of June, 1903.

H. Hesketh Bell

Administrator"

We will come back more than once to this important document, but let us simply note for now that the land was only that which "the government of Dominica desires to reserve to the Caribs for their use." There is no mention of Caribs rights over the land, of the modalities of the usufruct, no title, and no guidelines nor procedure for entering in actual possession and use of territories not yet occupied. In light of Carib illiteracy, of actual conditions of communication between Salybia and Roseau then and now, the 1903 notice can be read as a memo the government sent to itself. Caribs are implicitly treated as irresponsible: no effort is made to accommodate their participation in the proceedings. Yet, it was the same land they had total control of at least two centuries before any British ever set foot on it!

The Bell notice of 1903 is the first British legal document pertaining to the Carib Reserve as an entity, and though it does not clarify the question of Carib rights, it sets out at least the boundaries of the territory they could use. Yet, when we read the notice, it becomes clear that the written text is meant to be accompanied by the Skeat map. While the Northern and Eastern boundaries can be easily identified, the Southern and Western ones are blurred and imprecise without the map. The land of which use was given by Bell to the Caribs are *"as set out or delineated on a Plan or Diagram"* by Arthur Percival Skeat which itself should be kept in the Registrar's Office where it *"may be inspected at any time during office hours"*.

It is very troubling then that neither the Registrar nor the Lands and Survey Offices of the Dominica government can produce the signed copy of the Skeat map, presumably dated 1901 and without which the notice remains imprecise especially as far as the Southern and Eastern boundaries are concerned. An employee who has handled maps during ten years at the Lands and Surveys Office has revealed to us that *in 10 years, he never saw an original version of the Skeat map!*

What happened to the Skeat map? Can the question of boundaries of the Carib territory be settled without it? Is its disappearance a consequence of foul play? Who would have interest in such disappearance? These are questions that the Carib people of Dominica submit today to the International Community of Human Rights Fighters.

Of course, there could have been reliable copies of the original map drawn by A. P. Skeat in 1901. And indeed, one such copy may have been that made by the then Surveyor General W. A. Miller in 1906. But again, our queries reveal that the Miller map of 1906 has also disappeared! In other words, the Carib territory is delineated by a notice itself almost useless without the map on which it is based. Furthermore, the government of Dominica is telling the Carib people that the only available version of this map is a 1978 copy, itself based on a 1906 copy of the 1901 original which the 1906 copy is based have disappeared!

The 1903 notice is also remarkably silent on the acreage of the territory. The figure of 3700 acres seem to have first appeared on the Skeat map from where it was reproduced on a communication by Bell to the Secretary of Colonies in which he submitted the proposal for the "Reserve". Paragraph 38 of the communication reads: "38. I attach hereto the plan of the survey made by Mr. Skeat. It will be seen that the Carib Reserve, within the boundaries now proposed will include 3700 acres."

This paragraph then tells us that there must be a copy of the original map in British colonial records and that this copy may have contained indications of size. The map that the Carib people were finally granted with a title for the territory in 1978 has no indication of scale but simply bears the inscription: "contents 3700". That map was copied and certified by Jerome A. Robinson then Crown Surveyor and now head of the Lands and Survey Office of the Commonwealth of Dominica. Without questioning the integrity or the competence of Mr. Robinson, we believe that, in view of the fuzziness of the record and the disappearance of its certified predecessors, this map alone cannot serve as a reliable basis to establish the limits of the Carib territory. There is no way to prove that this map actually replicates the Skeat map or that it represents an area of 3700 acres. Two major areas of contention taint the reliability of the 1978 map:

    a. the southern boundaries of the Reserve

    b. the line of separation between the Concord Estate and the Reserve.

These two points will be discussed separately hereunder.

A—The Question of the Southern Boundaries: The 1978 map places the south-eastern corner of the Carib territory at that point where the Raymond River flows into the Atlantic, and in that regard it seems in accordance with the 1903 notice. The problem starts when one does not notice Raymond River on any map of Dominica that we have seen. In fact, the map which is the official map of Dominica, published by the British government's Directorate of Overseas Surveys (D.O.S. 351, series E 803, 1978 edition) does *not* identify Raymond River. Rather, it shows two streams of water of relatively equal size flowing into Raymond Bay. Is the Raymond River of the 1978 Robinson map the Aratouri or Madjini River? There is no clear answer to that question in the Robinson map but the difference means a lot of valuable acres of land for the Carib people, land on which we can build our homes and feed our families. The Carib Act of 1978 fixed the "Raymond *or* Madjini River" as a southern boundary and denies those lands to the Carib people. But we are asking the writers of this Act on what evidence they can identify the Madjini River as Raymond River? There is no such evidence! The 1903 notice just says "Raymond River". Moreover, in repeated instances prior to 1978 Misters Wynski and/or Pascal surveying for the government on lands situated on the Northern side of Aratouri River felt obliged to inform the Carib Chief and Council (as can testify a number of Caribs, including the very respected Jerome A. Francis, who was chief of the Carib people from 1959 to 1972 and the one to hold that office for the longest period in recent years until ill-health forced him to resign his office). Why would surveyors, then working for the Crown feel compelled to inform the Caribs of their activities if they did not know that they were working on land which duly belonged to the Carib people? Furthermore, the D.O.S. map referred to above, clearly puts the boundaries of the Carib Reserve on the Southern side of the Aratouri River which seems to indicate that the Raymond River is actually the Richmond River. The various boundaries of the D.O.S. map must of course be based on the Bryers map of 1764 mentioned earlier. Last but not least on the question of Southern boundaries: both Madjini and Aratouri run only a few miles. There is absolutely no marker westward of their sources as to where the Carib territory ends, and the Carib people have again been denied valuable land on the basis of an imaginary line which appears on the Robinson map but of which the origins are unknown. It is primary school knowledge that a line needs at least two defining points. Yet, the Southern border of the Carib territory has only a point of departure — itself dubious — and no other markers. Why then is the line going from "Raymond River" northward? This is not a rhetorical question. Good acres of land on which Carib children can be fed are being wiped out by one stroke of the pen! Squatters have taken over and are still invading large stretches of land between Aratouri and Madjini Rivers and Westward of both. In some cases, the Dominican government has sold land which we know to be Carib property. Not just for historical reasons the original boundaries of the Skeat map must be discovered and verified and related concretely for Caribs to know the limits of the territory affected to their use in 1903.

B — The Concord Estate: The encroachment on Carib Lands is not only on the southern side of the territory but also from the west. Heirs to the Concord Estate claim that it spreads on both sides of the Pegoua River far into land that the Caribs consider their own. The 1978 Robinson map shows the estate spreading on the east of the Pegoua River, but we have already shown that this map alone does not constitute reliable evidence. Two questions could be asked:

i. Did the Concord estate originally spread on both sides of Pegoua River?

ii. If it spread on both sides of Pegoua, how far from the river did it spread?

We believe strongly that the first question can be answered once and for all with evidence coming from the memo sent by Bell to the Secretary of the Colonies. Part of paragraph 35 of the memo reads:

Some months ago, however, it was brought to my notice that a good many Caribs were working plots of land in a valley that appeared to be outside the northern boundary of their reserve, and that they already possessed several flourishing patches of cocoa in that locality. The matter was brought to light through Mr Wm. Davies, the owner of the adjacent plantation "Concord" who submitted an application for a block of what he described as "Crown Lands adjoining his estate". Mr Government Officer Robinson was sent to inspect the locality and he returned with the report that the land applied for by Mr. Davies was in actual occupation of the Caribs and was being well cultivated by them. The Caribs moreover, claimed that the valley does form part of their original reserve, and they would, I believe strenuously resist eviction.

Three simple but important facts emerge from this statement;
1. Davies, the owner of Concord, was *applying* for more land around 1903:
2. this land was *already* being used by the Carib people:
3. Bell, who set the boundaries of the "Reserve" was of the opinion that the Caribs should *keep* this land. One is forced to ask them by what miracle the Concord Estate now finds itself on both sides of the Pagoua River and still seems to keep on expanding ever since 1903? Whose land is Concord assimilating if not that flourishing patch referred to by Bell and on which the original owner of the estate, the powerful William Davies had put his eyes on?

To help the international community understand what powerful foes the Carib people are facing on the Concord Estate affair, it is necessary to sketch William Davies.

William Davies can be considered as one of the five most powerful Dominicans who ever lived. A light-skinned member of the so-called "Mulatto Ascendency" of the late nineteenth and early twentieth centuries, an ally of the Potter, Falconer, Bellot, Riviere and Hamilton families, the owner of numerous estates including the famous Bath Estate of which *part* was taken to build the Melville Hall Airport, Davies once put a notice in the 31 May 1983 issue of the journal *The Dominican* to inform the public that he kept "Two six-shooter derringers; 1 shot gun; 1 Winchester Repeater (13 consecutive shots); 2 Colts Revolvers-5 cartridges each; cutlass by the score, well sharpened" to "ensure a warm reception" to intruders on his Bath Estate! (See Joseph Broome, *How Crown Colony Came to Dominica*, from Institute of Caribbean Studies, University of Puerto Rico).

We do not believe that Bell, who was no "friend" of Davies gave up to his pressures, but we can say loud and clear that if he did, the documents quoted above indicate that restitution should be legally granted to the Carib people for a land unjustly taken from them by a man who did not need such additional holding to assure his subsistence. But moreover, as we have shown, there is nothing in Bell's texts which suggest that he gave the land to Davies instead of leaving it to the Caribs. Quite the contrary! The Pagoua River would then run through Concord Estate, and Bell's instructions to Skeat as he summated there in paragraph 36 of the memo to the Secretary of the Colonies, were clear and formal:

"He (Skeat) was instructed to follow the recognised boundaries of the Reserve and to adopt, whenever possible, streams, cliffs and other national landmarks". And further, in paragraph 38:

"The inclusion of the Valley lands, whose ownership has hitherto been opened to doubt, will probably add three or four hundred acres to the area heretofore held by the Caribs".

But there is even additional evidence that the disputed stretch of land now labelled Concord Estate on the east of Pagoua River belongs to the Caribs. Let us unfold the story . . .

Davies died as eventually do even the most powerful. Concord Estate was later claimed by A. C. Shillingford and after Shillingford's death by his heirs. Shillingford, his heirs or executors seem to have even obtained a certificate of title for the land. (We have not seen such a certificate, but, as we shall prove, its existence would still be meaningless). In the early 1970's the executors of Shillingford were represented by Alleyne & Company Barristers at Law and Solicitors, who wrote to the then Carib Chief Masclem Frederick a letter we are reproducing in its entirety as Appendix B. [Not reproduced here. Ed.]

N. V. is a Carib in his late fifties. He has lived on Lagly, part of the disputed territory since a little boy. His grandmother worked land there, his great-grandmother worked land there. He, himself built his house there in the late thirties. He once asked Miss Johnson, (the Miss Johnson referred to in the above quoted letter) a question which, he told us, remained unanswered and that we paraphrase here:

"If you have a right on this land as you say you have and I have lived and worked on this land for most of my life, how come you cannot show me a piece of paper proving that I paid rent, or that I owe you rent or any other return for your land?"

If the intention of the letter is that the Johnson family should relinquish any claim they may have to that part of the Concord Estate which lies within the Carib reserve in return for land to be given to that family by the Government, one would think that the Government should, if necessary, adopt this solution in order to solve this problem which affects the lives of the Carib people.

Perhaps it will be possible for Mr Brian Alleyne who is now the Minister of Home Affairs of the Commonwealth of Dominica and has the most direct executive authority on Carib affairs, to find the equitable solution for this problem, particularly since he has already submitted a memorandum to the Committee of Twenty-four, the Committee on De-Colonisation and the Committee on Human Rights of the United Nations, sent on 20th July 1970 on behalf of the Carib Chief and Councillors for whom he was the Solicitor:

"The result of the absence of the title in the Caribs has been that they have been unable to protect the land from encroachment by outsiders, and the area reserved for them has consequently been reduced over the years to a considerable extent. In some instances, title actually passed to squatters, and in others, due to the legal inability of the Caribs to eject the squatters, the Caribs have been effectively deprived of the land of which the squatters have acquired possession."

Oral history and conclusion

We do not want to give the impression that we consider the 1903 notice and the 1901 map as being the only parameters of Carib rights over land. Even if there were no allegations of violation of the 1903 agreement, indeed even if there was no map at all, the question of Carib lands rights would need to be exposed to the international community, for it is not simply a legal matter: it is a matter of justice and both, legality and justice, are not always equivalent. Justice, human justice; that is respect for human beings regardless of their race and origin requires that one looks beyond Bell's achievements. For not to do so would infer that the Bell notice was just. Yet it was not only unjust but unfair and its "legality" rests on centuries of genocide. The issue of Carib lands cannot be discussed without the light of history and especially the history of the Caribs themselves.

Carib history teaches us that all the land of Dominica once belonged to the Carib. At a time that decolonisation is much spoken about, we have to ask ourselves how and why all the land of Dominica does not belong to Caribs anymore? Carib history teaches us that when the interpower struggle turned to British advantage and the French decided to leave Dominica forever, they made an agreement with the British that roughly half of the area of the island (from sea to sea) would belong to the Caribs. Even Bell in his memo to the Secretary of Colonies admits the possibility of a first delimitation of Carib territory dating back to French times. During the so called 1930 disturbances — when police invaded the Carib Reserve on a false pretext killed two Caribs, arrested and wounded numerous others — the office of Carib Chief Jolly John was ransacked and important papers and documents among them the plan of the "Reserve" were taken away. Where is this plan? What were the other documents? Where are they? Do they reveal more than what the Skeat map can tell us?

More recent Carib history teaches us that the admitted boundaries of the territory merged in the South with Wakaman point, a much more Southern point than both Madjini and Aratouri. In fact, all the Kwaib people over thirty believe that their officially recognized boundary passes there. One cannot dismiss such belief as collective hallucination. But all Caribs over thirty readily admit also that they saw a continuous shrinking of the southern part of their land with successive governments sanctioning the taking over of large parcels of land as squatters invaded them. As one old woman argues; "Since I was little, the boundaries were at Wakaman. Then they told us it was Richmond. Then it was Aratouri, and now it's Madjini. Little more and they will send us to the sea".

But of course, the issue goes beyond documentary evidence of boundaries set a long time ago. The whole matter of the "Reserve" limits are now getting Caribs increasingly concerned because of contemporary conditions. Poverty, illiteracy, and other endemic features of underdevelopment are widely visible on the whole of Dominica but they reach their peak among the Kwaib people. There is no electricity in Carib territory except at the police station. The illiteracy rate among Caribs is much higher than in the rest of Dominica. Even if the full 3,700 acres are considered, population density on the reserve is much higher than the national population density. One has to ask, in the light of this: What are 3,700 acres anyway, for 2,300 people directly linked to the original owners of the whole island? What are 5.78 square miles? The issue of Kwaib lands is nothing but that of the material requirements of a people who have an undisputed right to preserve their historical heritage, their uniqueness and prepare the future of their children on an island on which they have more claims than any other human beings.

Source: Presentation by Chief Hilary Frederick at the NGO Conference on the Rights of Indigenous Peoples and their Land, Geneva, 15–18 September 1981. Reprinted with permission from paper no. 23 of the International Organisation for the Elimination of All forms of Racial Discrimination (EAFORD), London 1983.

The World Council of Indigenous Peoples made a presentation to the NGO Conference on Indigenous Peoples and the Land, held in Geneva in 1981 which ended with the following statement

- While colonial governments have, in most cases, allotted lands to Indigenous Peoples which are barren and marginal in agricultural productivity, imperialist actions have forced them to make their living from the most inhospitable areas of the earth.
- These lands are now found to contain valuable minerals and resources which transnationals argue are needed to accommodate the increasing demand for materials, continued corporate growth and industrial "progress".
- Realizing the necessity of establishing economies independent from the world economic system based on their rights to self-determination, Indigenous Peoples are increasingly being seen as a nuisance to governments and transnational corporations.
- To promote corporate investment the Indigenous People must be removed or silenced to make way for mines, dams, plantations and factories.
- Indigenous Nations today are suffering economically more than ever before and are not in control of sufficient resources to protect their interests and maintain their traditional forms of life.
- Rapid industrialization has done little to raise the standard of living, provide adequate food, housing or education.
- For the most part, Indigenous communities are now too poorly equipped to respond to the devious attacks launched against them by transnationals and are inevitably headed for the slums and ghettos of the starving millions.

In conclusion, the WCIP urges the international community to recognize and respect our rights, as Indigenous Peoples, to self-determination. Our right to own and manage our land and natural resources is the fundamental element in order for us to survive as Indigenous Nations.

In closing, I would like to take this opportunity, on behalf of the World Council of Indigenous Peoples, to commend the Sub-Committee on Racism, Racial Discrimination, Apartheid and Decolonization of the Special NGO Committee on Human Rights in Geneva for taking the initiative to organize this Conference. We have deeply appreciated this opportunity to illustrate the effects of the industrialized world upon the Indigenous Nations throughout the world.

Notes Part 3

Chapter 1

1. See "The Most Violent Conflicts" chart in *A World At War* 1983 published by the US Center for Defense Information and quoted in *Tapol* Bulletin No. 57, London, May 1983.

2. "The population of East Timor has been reduced by 200,000 since the invasion. About 60,000 were killed and about 140,000 died as a result of starvation caused by economic disruption and inability to grow food." Mgr. Martinu da Costa Lopes, Bishop of Dili, *Irish Times*, 8 September 1983.

3. Carmel Budiardjo and Leim Soei Liong, *The War Against East Timor*, Zed Press and Marram Books, London, 1984 pp. 33–4 and 134–5. See also part 2, pp. 169–244, of this excellent work, reproducing large parts of the Indonesian army's secret plans to implement their occupation of East Timor. One of the most comprehensive indictments of Indonesia's reign of terror over East Timor was provided at the UN Decolonization Committee in September 1983, by Margo Picken of Amnesty International. (Quoted in Torben Retbøll, (ed.) *East Timor: The Struggle Continues,* IWGIA document No. 50, Copenhagen, October 1984, pp. 82–96.

4. Budiardjo and Liong, pp. 76–9.

5. Ibid., p. xv.

6. Ibid., pp. 3–8.

7. The Timor Papers, *National Times*, Australia, 30 May–5 June 1982.

8. Budiardjo and Liong, p. 146.

9. Ibid., p. 22.

10. Ibid., pp. 74–95.

11. Ibid., p. xi.

12. Ibid., p. 109.

13. Ibid., p. xiii.

14. In 1983 Britain abstained, leading the *Guardian* of London (21 February 1983) to scorn, in an editorial, that the Thatcher government's "renewed interest in self-determination for small island communities" didn't stretch very far.

15. The former Australian Labor leader, Gough Whitlam, self-appointed champion of Aboriginal causes, was the chief architect of his country's pro-Indonesian policy; a line followed by the current Australian Labor Prime Minister, Bob Hawke, despite the Australian Labor Party (ALP) condemning Indonesia's invasion of East Timor.

16. Budiardjo and Liong, p. 153.

17. *Native Peoples News,* Summer 1983, London, p. 3.

18. *Tribal Forum,* Episcopal Commission on Tribal Filipinos, Manila, Vol. IV, No. 7, November/December 1983.

19. IWGIA press release, Copenhagen, 6 August 1984.

20. See "Tribals bombed", in *Survival International News,* London, No. 7, late 1984.

21. *Tribal Forum*, Manila, Vol. VII, No. 2, March–April 1986, p. 9. *Kasama,* the newsletter of the London-based Philippines Support Group also reported in mid-1986, that Kalingas were still being forced into "strategic hamlets", and indigenous leaders being murdered by the military (*Kasama*, No. 19, May–June 1986).

22. According to a recent survey by a Norwegian missionary, there are no less than 150 "ethnic groups" represented in the Sylhet tea gardens, while between 20 and 30 tribal communities live in Bangladesh as a whole. From an informant in Bangladesh to Roger Moody, October 1984.

23. *The Chittagong Hill Tracts: Militarization, Oppression and the Hill tribes,* Anti-Slavery Society Indigenous Peoples and Development Series, No. 2. London, 1984, p. 15.

24. Ibid., p. 23.

25. Ibid., p. 24. In the second phase of "resettlement" families were given 700 *taka*, between five and seven and a half acres of land, 200 *takas* a month for five months and around 24 lbs of wheat monthly for six months.

26. Shelton H. Davis, *Victims of the Miracle: Development and the Indians of Brazil*, (Cambridge University Press, 1977) pp. 38–40.

27. *Chittagong Hill Tracts*, Anti-Slavery Society, pp. 29–30.

28. See in particular M. M. Huq, *Government Institutions and Underdevelopment: a Study of Tribal Peoples of the Chittagong Hill Tracts, Bangladesh,* (Institute of Local Government Studies, University of Birmingham), December 1982.

29. *Chittagong Hill Tracts*, Anti-Slavery Society, pp. 38–40. See also Wolfgang Mey, "Development Strategies and Social Resistance in the Third World: The Chittagong Hill Tracts Case: Genocide in Context", International Conference on Development Strategies and the Third World, University of Copenhagen, April 1983.

30. I was based in Chittagong in March and April 1972, and made several trips into the Hill Tracts. Virtually every day, armed units thundered up the Rangamati road, supported by helicopters: The official pretext (only to a small extent justified) for this activity was that remnants of the Pakistani army and Pakistani-supported Mizo tribal fighters had found refuge in the region.

31. *Chittagong Hill Tracts,* Anti-Slavery Society, p. 61.

32. See Press statement by Upendra Lal Chakma, Member of Parliament, Bangladesh, Dhaka, 1 April 1980.

33. Atiqul Alam, reporting from Dhaka, Bangladesh, in the *Guardian*, 29 February 1981.

34. Report for 1984 to the UN Working Group on Indigenous Populations, Anti-Slavery Society, London, 1984.

35. *Chittagong Hill Tracts*, Anti-Slavery Society, 1984, p. 44.

36. Ibid.

37. *New Nation,* Dhaka, Bangladesh, 11 November 1983.

38. Ibid., 26 April 1984.

39. *Bangladesh Observer*, 4 June 1984.

40. Urgent Action Bulletin BAN/Ib/Sept/1984, Survival International, London, 1984.

41. Urgent Action Bulletin BAN/Ic/Jun/1986. Survival International, London, 1986.

42. The most comprehensive collection of statements by indigenous Guatemalans is contained — together with numerous smaller pieces — in the excellent four volume *Guatemala! The Horror and the Hope*, edited by Rarihokwats for Four Arrows, and published in 1982. Other books with a strong bias toward presenting indigenous points of view are George Black's *Garrison Guatemala* (Zed Press/NACLA, London and New York, 1984) and the superlative documentary collection *Guatemala in Rebellion: Unfinished History* (Grove Press Inc., New York 1983) ed. by Jonathan L. Fried, Marvin E. Gettleman, Deborah T. Levenson and Nancy Peckenham. The most compelling autobiographical essay is *I, Rigoberta Menchu* (ed.) by Elisabeth Burgos-Debray (Verso, London, 1983). The only full-length study I know of, representing the points of view of a contemporary Guatemalan Indian who has *supported* the military regime is *Son of Tecun Uman, A Maya Indian tells his life story*, (ed.) James D. Sexton, (University of Arizona Press, Tucson 1981). Written in the form of a diary, at the editor's request, by Ignacio Bizarro Ujpan, a Tzutguhil Mayan, it covers the years 1972–7 in minute detail.

Although this was a period of mounting military repression, Ignacio seems blithely unaware of (or unconcerned by) the murder and torture of other native Guatemalans. The only deaths — apart from a few cases of internecine murder — which concern him, are those from drowning in nearby Lake Atitlan (pp. 209–11). His chief concerns range from gaining lucrative work (he is made an organiser of cotton-picking crews and labours as a day-labourer (pp. 63, 93–103, 77), fights at soccer matches (pp. 85–6), disputing the power of shamans (p. 212) to carrying out his devotions as a Catholic (pp. 158–61), combating his alcoholism (p. 207) and minimising the effects of the devastating earthquakes of 1976 (pp. 135–42, 148). He becomes a force in his local municipality (*acalde*) despite squabbles with the mayor (pp. 111–12), and zealously defends the territorial rights of the people of San Jose (Joseños) against those of neighbouring San Martin (pp. 59–63). Otherwise he finds little to take issue with against external forces: not wanting to supply Joseños to the military reserve, only because this would deplete the resources of the town, (pp. 193–4). Indeed, Ignacio is very in favour of military service in the "proper army" (pp. 35–8, 40–6); hardly surprising, considering he is also local director of the Partido Institucional Democratico (PID) which won the 1976 local elections (pp. 169–85). The PID was the army party, on whose ticket Lucas Garcia came to power in 1978 (see George Black, p. 48).

43. This was one of the most horrendous military assaults on unarmed people of the 20th Century, comparable with Amritsar, Sharpeville and Sabra and Chatila. On 29 May 1978, about 800 Kekchi Indians assembled in the village of Panzos, to await the official reply to their petition against land seizures. After a momentary scuffle between two soldiers and a man who did not understand Spanish, the army, assisted by white landowners, opened fire, killing at least 140 women, children and men, and injuring more than 130 others. Tens of thousands of protesters took to the streets of Guatemala City, when news of the massacre reached them, crying "Cowards! Assassins". The regime countered with a statement that "38 subversives, agitated by Fidel Castro, leftist guerrillas and the clergy, attacked an Army garrison at Panzos, and were killed". In fact, Panzos had no military garrison. (See *Guatemala! The Horror and the Hope* p. 39).

44. An example of appropriation is afforded in the film *When the Mountains Tremble* (USA, 1983) when glamorous *ladino* women "model" costumes of the Mayan people, in front of an audience containing some of those who have done their utmost to wipe their culture from the face of the earth.

45. *Economist*, London, 2 February 1985, p. 85, and *Guatemala Update* (Guatemala Working Group, London, Winter 1984/85).

46. The *Grupo de Apoyo Mutuo Por la Aparacimiento Con Vida de Nuestraos Hijos, Esposos, Padres y Hermanos* (Mutual support group for the Safe Return of our Children, Spouses, Parents, Brothers and Sisters), whose own spokesperson, Hector Orlando Gomez, was kidnapped in March 1984 (*Information Sheet*, Washington Office on Latin America, 2 April 1984).

47. *Guatemala Update*, Winter 1986.

48. The figures and the quote come from *Bitter and Cruel: Report of a Mission to Guatemala by the British Parliamentary Human Rights Group, October 1984*, London, 1985.

49. *Little Hope: Human Rights in Guatemala*, published by Americas Watch Committee, New York, January 1985.

50. *Financial Times,* London, 13 May 1985.

51. *Washington in Focus*, Washington Office on Latin America, Vol. II, No. 8, 17

December 1984.

52. *¡Guatemala!* July/August 1984, Vol. 5, No. 3, published by Guatemala News and Information Bureau, Oakland. See also *Guatemala Update!* London, Spring 1983.

53. A recent visitor to Guatemala has described the formation of the civilian militia as "probably . . . the most sustained attack on indigenous lifestyles since the Spanish conquest" *Guatemala Watch*, early 1984, quoted in *Native Peoples News*, No. 10, Spring 1984, London, p. 11.

54. While *campesinos* in southern Mexico have generally taken warmly to the refugees, the Mexican government's policy has varied from appeasement to Guatemala (and some instances of forcible return) to threats and inducements to refugees to move from border areas to less hospitable camps 250 miles away at Campeche (see *Guatemalan Refugees in Mexico — 1980–84*, Americas Watch Committee, New York, 1984; also *Cultural Survival Quarterly*, Vol. 8, No. 4, December 1984, pp. 81–2; *Native Peoples News*, No. 9, Autumn 1983; and *Out of the Ashes, the Lives and Hopes of Refugees from El Salvador and Guatemala*, El Salvador and Guatemala Committees for Human Rights and War on Want (WOW) Campaigns, London, 1985.

55. *Guatemala! the Horror and the Hope*, Vol. I, pp. 42–5.

56. See *Guatemala in Rebellion; Unfinished History*, especially pp. 42–111.

57. George Black, pp. 155–72.

58. See, for example, *South American Indian Information Center (SAIIC) Newsletter* Vol. I, No. 3, Berkeley, p. 3; also *Huerrquen*, published by the Comité Exterior Mapuche, Belgium, March 1982 quoted in *IWGIA Newsletter* No. 31/32, Copenhagen, June/Oct. 1982 pp. 26–9. See also "The Mapuche of Chile" in *Native Peoples in Struggle*, ERIN publications, Bombay, New York, 1982, pp. 60–63.

Chapter 2

59. *Chronology of low level military aircraft activities over Innu Territory (Ntesinan)*. Naskapi–Mintaais Innu Association, Sheshatshit, (Labrador) October 1984.

60. Ibid. — See also, *Pogrom* Gesellschaft für bedrohte Völker, No. 102/103, late 1983; and *Native Peoples News*, London, No. 10, Spring 1984, "How Nato Buzzes the Inuit", p. 18.

61. *Low level Fighter Bomber Training over Ntesinan; the issues in the words of Innu people, the Military, Biologists and Canadian government officials*, NMIA, Sheshatshit, October 1984, *passim*.

62. *Project North Journal* Toronto Vol. 8, No. 4, Winter 1984, pp. 5–6.

63. *Low level fighter/bomber training*, p. 7

64. *Project North Journal*, Vol. 8, No. 4, p. 3, and statement by Fran Williams President of the Labrador Inuit Association quoted in *Pogrom*, op. cit.

65. *Low level fighter/bomber training* p. 7.

66. Statement by Innu Kanantuapatshet, Sheshatshit, 11 September 1984 and see *Project North Journal*, op.cit. p. 3.

67. E.g. by Survival International and Friends of the Earth (see UAB CAN/1/MAY/1986, Survival International, London.)

68. A detailed account of the betrayal of the Ilois is contained in Minority Right's Group Report No. 54, *Diego Garcia: A contrast to the Falklands*, by John Madeley, MRG, London 1983.

69. See *Native Peoples News,* London, No. 9, Summer 1983 p. 16.

70. Information from the Diego Garcia Support Group, London, 1984. Published in *IWGIA Newsletter,* No. 34, Copenhagen, July 1984, p. 76.

71. *Native Peoples News,* London, No. 10, Spring 1984, p. 20.

72. *Guardian,* London, 26 July 1984.

73. Friends of Kaho'olawe *Newsletter* (undated) Honolulu, 1982.

Chapter 3

74. *Guardian,* London, 5 January 1985, p. 2.

75. *Native Press,* Yellowknife, 9 March 1984.

76. Protests against these impending tests were mounted in Yellowknife, by the Dene Nations and others in April 1986. (*Native Press,* Yellowknife, 27 March 1986).

77. See statement by Thomas Berger, chair of the Berger Commission, in *Committee for Justice and Liberty Newsletter,* Toronto, Special issue, 15 April 1977, pp. 2–9.

78. *Native Press,* op. cit.

79. *ICC Arctic Policy Review,* Nuuk, No. 3, 1983, pp. 6–7.

80. See *Native Peoples News,* Spring 1982.

81. *Vanua-Aku Viewpoints,* Vila, Vol. II, No. 66, January–February 1982, p. 7.

82. "Palau defends No-Nuke Constitution in fifth plebiscite", Belau Pacific Centre press release, Koror, 10 September 1984; and Roger Clark and Sue Rabbitt Roff: *Micronesia: the Problem of Palau,* Minority Rights Group Report No. 63, London, 1984, pp. 5–8.

83. *Micronesia: the Problem of Palau,* especially pp. 16–18.

84. See also Leonie Caldicott, "Between the Crocodiles", interview with Roman Bedor, *New Statesman,* London, 25 February 1983, pp. 19–20.

85. Teresa Lieber, "The Indians against the Missile", special supplement p. 4 *Native Peoples News,* No. 6, Winter 1981; see also: *Akwesasne Notes,* Spring 1981, pp. 6–7.

86. *Native Peoples News,* No. 10, Spring 1984 p. 19.

87. *Supreme Court of the US Syllabus, US vs Dann,* Washington, February 1985.

88. Through the experimental years of the 1930s and into the 1950s uranium was primarily directly used for weapons purposes (see Norman Moss, *The Politics of Uranium,* André Deutsch, London, 1981 pp. 19–37). Much of this came from indigenous lands, notably in Canada and Australia.

89. See David Weiss, *The Hour is Late,* mimeographed thesis, (University of California at Santa Cruz) 9 March 1979, pp. 102–128 also, *Uranium Development in the San Juan Basin, Region, Final Report of SJBR Uranium Study* (US Dept of the Interior, Albuqerque, 1980) especially pp. I–II, I–17, X–12.

90. The world's largest uranium mine, at Key Lake, Saskatchewan, is on Indian territory, while Canada's second largest worked deposits, at Elliot Lake Ontario, though not on native-claimed land, deliver "tailings" and effluent into a river system fished by the Serpent River Band. (See entries for *Denison Mines* and *Rio Algom* in Roger Moody, *The Gulliver File,* CIMRA and WISE, London and Glen Aplin, 1985). For the impact of the mines on native health, see *Dirty Bizness,* Partizans, London, 1986 pp. 7–8.

91. Background to these mines is contained in *Ground for Concern,* edited Mary Elliott for Friends of the Earth, (Penguin, Australia 1977) pp. 25–63.

92. The Roxby Downs mine is owned 51% by Western Mining of Australia (WMC) and 49% by British Petroleum (BP); both companies' attitude towards the

Kokatha claims have been disparaging, to say the least. (See *Western Mining Corporation* entry in *The Gulliver File*.)

93. In 1982 a British TV producer, Chris Olgiati, when researching for a "Panorama" programme on the Libyan bomb project, discovered boys of 15 and 16 working, entirely without radiation protection, in the Arlit mine. (See Roger Moody, "Uranium Scandal in Niger", *WISE Bulletin*, Amsterdam, Vol. 4, No. 5, June 1982) pp. 1–2.

94. See Uranium Institute, *Uranium Supply and Demand, Perspectives to 1995*, London, May 1984.

95. *Mining Annual Review*, London, 1985, p. 109.

96. This is my own guesstimate, based on figures from the IAEA/OECD biannual "Red Books" on uranium, published in Paris, from the Uranium Institute, and the mining corporations.

97. For example, the US Department of Energy (DoE) assessment report, *Uranium in the United States of America*, (USDoE, Grand Junction) October 1980 (GJO-III(80)) envisages new American uranium production essentially coming from mines constructed in established uranium zones.

98. The breakthrough came with the Copenhagen international conference in 1979 (see p. 158). Until then, not even the American Indian Movement (AIM) ". . . understood that the demand for energy resources was [the] primary cause [of] federal and corporate encroachment on Native lands . . ." ("Uranium Mines Threaten Native Americans" in *Pacific Research Bulletin*, Mountain View, California, Vol. 10, No. 1, 1979) p. 33.

99. For example, the Lomex Corporation's operations planned in San Luis Obispo County, California, and resisted by the Red Wind native American community (*Keep it in the ground bulletin*, WISE Amsterdam, January 1983); the Honeymoon uranium leaching project, defeated by an Aboriginal and environmental coalition in 1983 (see *Honeymoon* entry in *The Gulliver File*); and all uranium mining in British Columbia, headed-off by a broad alliance of interests, including the British Columbia Chiefs, (see article by Roger Moody, *The Vole*, London, Spring 1980).

100. This statement was one of many made by Aboriginal Australians in support of their countrypeople, fighting against the invasion of Noonkanbah, by Amax and other mining corporations (see Part 3, ch. 4).

Yeelirrie is a potentially very large uranium mine, situated on Aboriginal land in Western Australia and 75% held by the Western Mining Corporation, headed by the virulently anti-Aboriginal Hugh Morgan.

Esso, a division of the world's largest corporation, Exxon, withdrew from the venture in 1982; though the West German company UG (*Urangesellschaft*) holds a tenth of the equity. (See *Western Mining Corporation*, Gulliver File, WISE/CIMRA, Glen Aplin, 1988.)

101. Winona La Duke, in her unpublished paper *Nuclear Exploitation: Impact on a People*, US 1978, points out that the Trojan Power Plant in northern Oregon is situated on top of what was once a Tchinook burial ground: the remains of the dead were dug up by Portland General Electric and carted to another site. In 1981, the Tarascan Indians of Mexico were being threatened with a nuclear reactor which could completely destroy their fishing waters. (*Washington Post*, Washington, 18 May 1981.)

102. Under Public Law 97–425 the governing body of a tribe can object to designation as a nuclear-waste site, but must register its objections within only 60

days, and would have to rely on a Congress veto before its designated status was removed. (See Carol Cornelius Mohawk, "Will there be high-level nuclear waste disposal sites on native land?" *Akwesasne Notes*, Summer 1983, p. 20.)

103. Winona La Duke, *The Council of Energy Resource Tribes (CERT): An outsiders view* in WARN (Women of All Red Nations) Rapid City, 1980, p. 9. (See also *Akwesasne Notes*, Winter 1983).

Chapter 4

104. *Guardian, Financial Times, Daily Telegraph, Times*, et al 4 June 1982.

105. Statement by the chairman, Rio Tinto-Zinc Corporation plc, *Annual Report and Accounts, 1981*, pp. 7–8.

106. David Simpson, "Diamonds maybe forever but not Aborigine land rights", *Guardian*, London, 23 June 1982.

107. Amid the plethora of UN-originated material on multinational corporations in Namibia, Alun Roberts *The Rossing File*, (Canuc, London, 1979), stands out for its conciseness, and the *Hearings on Namibian Uranium* (mimeographed transcripts) (United Nations, New York, 1981) for their breadth.

108. *Native Peoples News*, CIMRA, London, No. 6, 1981.

109. *Land Rights News*, Central Land Council, Alice Springs, No. 20, August 1983, p. 3.

110. As this book goes to press, the whole future of land rights legislation in Australia is an open book, with virtually every Aboriginal organisation and many support groups condemning the intentions of the Federal (Labor) government. Although there are many issues involved — notably Aboriginal claims to pastoral land usurped by white business interests — the battle centres on plans by a growing coalition of Federal-state-mining interests to abolish even the small gains won in the Northern Territory and South Australia, since 1976. Rejecting the findings of the Seaman Inquiry into land rights (*Age*, Melbourne, 28 September 1984) which were generally welcomed by Aboriginal organisations, the Burke government in Western Australia has proposed new legislation which is "clearly music to the ears of the mining industry" (*Financial Review*, Sydney, 24 January 1985). The proposals include withholding an Aboriginal power of veto, abolishing mining royalties for Aborigines, granting compensation which is unrelated to the value of the mined product; severe restrictions on the types of other land which Aborigines will be able to claim (*Aboriginal Law Bulletin*, Sydney, February 1985). At the beginning of 1986, it seemed clear that the Federal government was prepared to renege on its election promises and introduce so-called "land rights" legislation, on a country-wide basis, which would reflect the unacceptable restrictions proposed by Burke.

111. APEA proposed in 1981 "proper face to face negotiations disclosing exploration programmes in full, and most important, dealing through land councils". APEA is strongly influenced by Royal Dutch Shell. (See Daniel Vachon and Phillip Toyne, "Mining and the Challenge of Land Rights", in *Aborigines, Land and Land Rights*, Nic Petersen and Marcia Langton, Australian Institute of Aboriginal Studies, Canberra 1983, p. 3235.)

112. See speech by Gerald Wilkinson, excerpted in this anthology, p. 266.

113. Of course RT-Z did not openly admit to this, and indeed, in 1985, when Alastair Frame took over as company chair, prospects for opening the mine appeared better than for two years. In 1983, however, the then chair Anthony Tuke admitted privately to a delegation from Survival International that the company had received more international protests over Cerro Colorado than any other

project and that this was of considerable concern to him.

114. See Bougainville: Company Town in the Soloman Islands, in Anthropology Resource Center (*ARC*) *Bulletin*, Boston, March 1979, p. 2; also *RTZ Uncovered*, (Partizans, London, 1985) p. 3.

115. Although the Native Claims Act granted title for local Inuit, Aleut and other native Alaskans to no less than 44,000,000 acres, nearly a decade later the transfer was only one eighth complete, and other supposedly safeguarded lands were passing into multinational control. Most notably this involved the Quartz Hill molybdenum deposit, which was excised from the surrounding National Monument area, after considerable pressure was exerted by mining interests. Key among these was the operator of the Quartz Hill mine, US Borax, a majority-owned subsidiary of RT-Z (*Financial Times* London, 20 November 1979). In 1984, the Inuit Circumpolar Conference formed a Native Review Commission to investigate the effects of the 1971 Act, headed by Thomas Berger, one of the few unequivocal non-native champions of indigenous rights in Canada (see *Arctic Policy Review*, ICC, Nuuk, No. 1, 1984).

116. See Winona La Duke, *The Council of Energy Resource Tribes: an Outsider's view* in, Women of All Red Nations (WARN) Rapid City, 1980.

117. The "Comalco model" was developed initially around negotiations between the bauxite company (now majority owned by CRA, RT-Z's Australian subsidiary) and the Pitjantjatjara Land Council in the early 1980s: it established the principles that only Aborigines know the significance of the land and specific sacred sites, and that the companies must be completely open in their intentions. While the Comalco model largely worked in South Australia (see Phillip Toyne and Daniel Vachon, *Growing Up the Country; the Pitjantjatjara struggle for their land*, McPhee/Gribble and Penguin, Victoria, 1984, pp. 111–16: the authors call the negotiation procedure the "Pitjantjatjara model", but it is virtually the same), it has been criticised for over-relying on the company's integrity, not having legal sanction behind it, and not being relevant in situations where precise sites cannot be revealed for security reasons (e.g. diamond deposits). (See Ritchie Howitt and John Douglas *Aborigines and Mining Companies in Northern Australia*, APCOL, Chippendale, 1983, pp. 72–3.) Boolidt Boolidtba of the Aboriginal Mining Information Centre criticised the model in 1981, at the International Tribunal on RT-Z, for legitimising a basically fraudulent process: i.e. "tell us where your dreaming sites are, we'll avoid these, and do what we like with the rest of the land".

118. Howitt and Douglas pp. 46–50; Jan Roberts, pp. 160–3.

119. The Igorot of the Philippines, with their gold-panning, for example (see Felix Razon and Richard Hensman, *The Oppression of the Indigenous Peoples of the Philippines*, IWGIA document No. 25, Copenhagen, 1976, pp. 35–6) Kenneth and Julie Slavin's *The Tuareg*, (Gentry Books, London, 1973) briefly portrays tin-mining among the Tuareg in the Air Mountains of Niger — ironically a region where their labour is exploited in some of the world's biggest uranium mines (Slavin, ibid, p. 96). See also Andrew Gray's *And after the Gold Rush . . . ? Human Rights and Self-Development among the Amarakaeri of Southeastern Peru* — a vivid study of the ways in which speculators and multinationals have threatened the recent, human-scale gold-mining activities of the peoples of the Madre de Dios region of Peru. IWGIA Document No. 55, Copenhagen, March 1986.

120. Jan Roberts, pp. 64, 90, 175, 189.

121. See editorial "Now for the companies!" in *Native Peoples News*, No. 5, Spring 1981, CIMRA, London, p. 3.

122. This huge copper deposit, in which RT-Z has a minority share but controls management options, pays the salaries of the national mining corporation, Codemin, and stands to profit while the Panamanian people bear the major financial risks, has received more attention than any other mining project affecting indigenous people in recent times. The possible exception being the Ok Tedi mine in Papua New Guinea which, though not yet officially producing, has already been the subject of two major studies. R. Jackson's *Ok Tedi; The Pot of Gold*, (University of Papua New Guinea, 1983) reveals many dangers inherent in this project, including the probable total disappearance of the Min's (local tribespeople) fish resources (p. 135) and a devastating effect were the tailings dam to collapse (p. 136). William S. Pintz's thorough study *Ok Tedi; evolution of a Third World mining project* (Mining Journal Books 1984) also highlights the potential dangers of river sedimentation and the Papua New Guinea government's ambivalent attitude to a huge, untried, scheme which might, or might not, fill the national coffers, and might or might not ruin the environment.

Background to the Cerro Colorado mine and the resistance of the Guaymi people is contained in: *Panama's Copper and Canadian Capital*, Latin American Working Group Newsletter, Vol. V, No. 4/5 (Toronto, 1981); Chris N. Gjording, S.J., *The Cerro Colorado Copper Project and the Guaymi Indians of Panama* Cultural Survival Occasional Paper No. 3, (Cambridge, Mass., March 1981); Survival International's *Cerro Colorado Copper Project Background paper*, (London, October 1986); and issues of *Survival International Review, 1980–84 passim*); Robert Carty, *RTZ Comes to Panama*, (LAWG, Toronto, 1982). The Guaymi Congress' Panamanian support committee publishes *Guaypress* news communiques from Panama City. Some of these articles, and other contributions from Guaymi objectors, are published in Spanish in *El Pueblo Guaymi Y su futuro*, by CEASPA (Centro de Estudios Y Accion Social — Panama) El Dorado, 1982.

123. Both Mobil and Esso, among the multinationals, have amicably concluded oil-drilling agreements with Aboriginal communities (Jan Roberts, p. 150), while several Australian companies have entered successful negotiations with the Central Land Council (*Land Rights News*, CLC, Alice Springs, 1982–84, *passim*). Oil and gas exploration are potentially less destructive than mining, however. Probably the best example of close co-operation between company and community remains that of Ngaanyatjara Council and Shell Oil in South Australia in 1980 (Toyne and Vachon, pp. 116–19).

124. *Financial Review*, Sydney, 7 July 1983.

125. Lorna Lippmann, *Generations of Resistance; The Aboriginal Struggle for Justice*, (Longman Cheshire, Melbourne 1981) pp. 49–50.

126. Winona La Duke of Women of All Red Nations, along with members of the American Indian Movement, demonstrated outside AMAX headquarters in the USA.

127. At one of the Federation's first meetings, Father Pat Dodson of the Central Land Council said it would try "to show the world that Noonkanbah is not just an isolated event, that it is part of an on-going system of oppression and exploitation." *Age*, Melbourne, 11 November 1981.

128. Roger Moody, "Killing Dreamtime" *Native Peoples News*, No. 5, Spring 1981, p. 16.

129. Ibid.

130. Ibid.

131. *Tribune*, Sydney, 9 April 1980, p. 8.

132. *West Australian*, Perth, 8 August 1980, p. 1.

133. Roger Moody, "Killing Dreamtime", p. 17. Other short accounts of the Noonkanbah confrontation can be found in: Jan Roberts, *Massacres to Mining*, (Dove, Blackburn 1981) esp. pp. 137–45; and Ritchie Howitt and John Douglas, *Aborigines and Mining Companies in Northern Australia*, (APCOL, Chippendale, 1983) pp. 60–65, 90–96.

134. See "Munda Nyuringu". Film, directed by Bob Bropho and Jan Roberts, Melbourne 1984; available from Contemporary Films, London.

135. See *The Global Reporter*, ARC Boston, Fall 1983.

136. International Bauxite Association Newsletter, No. 29, October 1977, p. 5.

137. *Global Reporter*, op.cit.

138. *Akwesasne Notes*, Vol. 10, No. 1, Early Spring 1978, p. 17; and Vol. 10, No. 2, Late Spring 1978, pp. 12–13.

139. Amanda Milligan, "Kicking the canner", *Guardian*, London 29 July 1983.

140. See *Native Peoples News*, No. 5, Spring 1981, p. 23.

141. Ibid., No. 8, Winter 1982, p. 18.

142. *The Age*, Melbourne, 1 August 1984, p. 4.

143. *RT-Z Uncovered*, Partizans, London, 1985.

144. After the Black Hills Survival Gathering of 1980, RT-Z was targeted by a "further action group" of participants for special campaigns around the world in a backhanded recognition of its unique role as a violator of indigenous lands. In 1981 the action coalition Partizans (People against Rio Tinto Zinc and its Subsidiaries) held the world's first "victims" tribunal of a multinational corporation, and stimulated or co-ordinated actions by the North Queensland and Kimberley Land Councils in Australia, CEASPA in Panama, CAFCINZ in New Zealand and several other organisations. See *RTZ Benefits the Community: report of the International Tribunal*, Partizans, London June 1981; also various issues from 1981–1984 of Partizans' journal *Parting Company*.

145. Robert Carty, "RTZ comes to Panama", unpublished study on RT-Z for the Latin American Working Group (LAWG) reproduced in part in *Dialogo Social*, no. 134, Panama City, May 1981. pp. 16–31.

146. *RTZ Uncovered*, 1985, p. 7.

147. See Jan Roberts, *Massacres to Mining*, Dove, 1985, Blackburn, 1981 especially chapter 23: "CRA and the international struggle for Aboriginal land", pp. 153–63; also AMIC newsletters, Melbourne 1981/82.

148. Diane Hooper, *The Rio Tinto Zinc Corporation, A case study of a Multinational Corporation*, Peace Research Institute, Oslo, 1977, pp. 48–52.

149. For example, Brazil and the Arctic: see *Native Peoples News*, No. 9. Summer 1983, pp. 4, 12.

150. Jan Roberts, *Massacres to Mining*, pp. 161–2.

151. For summary of 1985 Australian draft land rights legislature, see Survival International Urgent Action Bulletin, London SI Aus/5/FEB/1985.

152. Annual Report of CRA, Melbourne, 1983.

153. Several well-documented accounts of CRA's duplicity and violations have been published. Ritchie Howitt's excellent unpublished paper on the corporation is summarised in Ritchie Howitt and John Douglas, *Aborigines and Mining Companies in Northern Australia*, APCOL Chippendale, 1983 pp. 47–50. Marcia Langton, an Aboriginal researcher, has also performed a very good "dissection" of the AJV, and CRA's manipulative role, in Langton, "A National Strategy to deal with Exploration and Mining on or near Aboriginal land", Nic Petersen and Marcia

Langton, (eds.) *Aborigines, Land and Land rights*, Australian Institute of Aboriginal Studies, Canberra, 1983, see pp. 390–402. See also: *CRA, The Western Australian Museum and Aboriginal Sacred Sites in the Argyle Diamond Prospect*, Kimberley Land Council, Turkey Creek, privately printed, July 1980; also *Dirty Bizness*, Partizans, London 1986.

154. Torben Monberg, *Mobile in the Trade Wind: the reactions of the people on Bellona Island towards a mining project.* Working papers of the National Museum of Denmark, No. 1 Copenhagen 1976, p. 17.

155. Ibid., p. 30.

156. Ibid., pp. 17–27

157. Called simply "ABCD" in Monberg's *Mobile in the Trade Wind.*

158. Felix Razon, Native Peoples struggles against US Imperialism in the Philippines, in *The Oppression of the Indigenous Peoples of the Philippines*, IWGIA document No. 25, Copenhagen, 1976, p. 35.

159. Ibid., p. 36.

160. UAB/PHIL/36/APR/1986, Survival International, London.

161. Peabody Coal is now predominantly controlled by Newmont Mining, a company within the GFSA/Consolidated Gold Fields camp run by British and South African investors.

For further details of the Navajo-Hopi "dispute" and the relocation see Vol. 2, p. 156.

Chapter 5

162. *Ok Tedi: The Pot of Gold*, R. Jackson, University of Papua New Guinea, 1982, especially p. 118; and William S. Pintz, *Ok Tedi: the evolution of a third world mining project*, Mining Journal Books, London 1984, especially p. 116.

163. *Documentos de Congresos Guaymies sobre los Proyectos de Cerro Colorado y de las Hydroelectricas Teribe y Changuinola*, Guaymi Presiding Committee of the Canquintu and Soloy Congresses, Panama 1980. See also Chris N. Gjording, *The Cerro Colorado Copper project and the Guaymi Indians of Panama*, Cultural Survival Occasional paper No. 3, March 1981, Cambridge, Mass, pp. 8, 25, 34.

164. Robin M. Wright, "The Great Carajas: Brazil's Mega-Program for the 1980s" in *The Global Reporter*, ARC Boston, Vol. 1, No. 1, March 1983, pp. 3–6. In the past years there have been reports of extreme violence used by landowners against peasant farmers in the Carajas region, to secure land which can then be resold for agribusiness. Villages have been burnt, at least 30 people killed, and some 2,500 smallholders threatened with eviction. In most cases these are *campesinos* who have not materially threatened Indian land — as distinct from the commercial/judicial/police alliance ranged against them; see "Peasants tell EEC team of murder on Amazon" *Guardian*, London 12 December 1984.

165. Much has been written on the Chico dams, and the Kalinga and Bontoc peoples' resistance to their construction. See, especially, *The Philippines; authoritarian government, multinationals and ancestral lands*, Anti-Slavery Society London, 1983, pp. 101–19 and *Tribal Forum*, published by the Episcopal Commission on Tribal Filipinos, monthly, Manila: Vols. IV and V, 1983 and 1984; also Alison Wynne *No Time for Crying: Stories of Philippine women who care for their country and its people*, Resource Centre for Philippine Concerns, Hong Kong, 1980, pp. 8–11.

166. Robert Paine, *Dam a River, Damn a People: Saami (Lapp) Livelihood and the*

Alta/Kautokeino Hydro-Electric Project and the Norwegian Parliament, IWGIA document No. 45, Copenhagen, June 1982; *Charta 77*, edited Beverley Wahl; and Nils-Aslak Valkeapää *Greetings from Lappland; the Sami — Europe's Forgotten People*, Zed Press, London, 1983.

A graphic and comprehensive account of the struggle against the Alta-Kautokeino project is also given (both in Norwegian and English) in *Alta Bilder*, Jan Borring, Britt Hveem, Asmund Lindal and Helge Sunde, Pax forlga ås, Oslo 1981.

167. *Purari: overpowering Papua New Guinea?* Rob Pardy, Mike Parsons, Don Siemon, Ann Wigglesworth, International Development Action, for Purari Action Group, Melbourne 1978.

168. Boyce Richardson's devoted chronicle of the valiant attempts of James Bay Cree and Inuit to halt the scheme contains numerous statements by its antagonists: Boyce Richardson *Strangers Devour the land, a chronicle of the assault upon the last hunting culture in North America, the Cree Indians of northern Quebec and their vast primeval homelands*, Alfred A. Knopf, New York 1976. See also "Lessons from James Bay" in *Project North Journal*, Vol. 8. No. 1, Toronto, Winter 1984; and Peter A. Cumming, *Canada: Native land rights and Northern Development*, IWGIA document No. 26, Copenhagen 1977, pp. 31–3.

169. *Project North Newsletter*, Toronto, Vol. 7, No. 1, January–February 1984.

170. Sally Swenson "The Slave River debate: what direction for Canadian development?" in *The Global Reporter*, ARC Boston, Vol. 1, No. 2, Summer 1982, pp. 7–8; also *Native Press*, Yellowknife, 10 November 1978.

171. The largest dam on the Rejang would displace or severely affect more than 4,000 people, primarily Kenyah, Kayan, Ukit and Penang. (*Ecoforum news alert*, Nairobi, Vol. 1, No. 4 , Vol. 2, No. 1, January 1985. See also *Survival International News* London, No. 7, late 1984.

As this book went to press, opposition to the project — usually now called the Bakun dam, and reckoned to displace more than 17,000 native people — was mounting around the world. See *Bakun, Between Energy and Tragedy*, the February 1986 issue of *Utusan Konsumer*, Penang; also *International Dams Newsletter*, Vol. 1 No. 2 San Francisco April 1986; UAB/MAL/1/JUN/1986, Survival International, London: "South East Asia's Biggest Dam Threatens to Displace 5,000 Natives" *Third World Features* (undated) 1986.

In an article in *Cultural Survival Quarterly*, Vol. 10, No. 1 (Cultural Survival, Cambridge, USA, 1986 pp. 42–4) Ruth Taswell points out that the Bakun project is not the first to have displaced indigenous Sarawakans: in 1982, the Batan Ai Dam necessitated the removal of more than 3,000 Iban people.

172. The whole Yavapi Indian community at Fort McDowell risks losing its land if this project proceeds (see *Cultural Survival Newsletter*, Cambridge, Mass, No. 3, Summer 1981, p. 24).

173. See Marcus Colchester's introduction to the Bhopalagnam and Inchampalli Hydel projects, *An end to laughter? Hydropower projects in Central India*, Working paper for Survival International, 1984. Marcus Colchester points out that "more land will be lost through inundation [by these schemes] than will benefit from the irrigation" produced by them (p. 6).

174. *Pogrom*, No. 107, March 1984, *Gesellschaft für bedrohte Volker*, Gottingen, p. 24.

175. Centre for Science and Environment, New Delhi, *The State of India's Environment, A citizens Report*, 1982, p. 70.

176. World Bank/IDA News release, No. 83/11, Washington DC, 19 August 1982.

177. Xavier Dias, "Reign of Terror on tribals", *Blitz*, Bombay, 19 February 1983, p. 7.

178. Estimate by the Indian National Institute of Urban Planning, quoted in UAB/IND/1/OCT/1985, Survival International, London.

179. Two international Labor Unions filed protests with the International Labour Organisation (ILO) while Survival International mounted an international write-in campaign (*International Dams Newsletter*, Vol. 1, No. 3, San Francisco, June 1986).

180. *International Dams Newsletter*, ibid.

181. *Survival International News*, Survival International, No. 1, London, late 1983 p. 5.
An excellent survey of current hydro-electric projects in Brazil which directly affect native communities is provided by Paul D. Aspelin and Silvio Coelho dos Santos in *Indian Areas threatened by Hydroelectric Projects in Brazil*, IWGIA document No. 44, Copenhagen, October 1981.
Impoverished peasants have joined with Indians in protesting against the impact of the Carajas project. In early 1984 a group of farmers, opposition MPs and trade unionists demonstrated against the siting of the Itaparica dam on the Tocantins river, and a government plan to seize the land and homes of 40,000 peasants. This constitutes one of the early stages in Carajas intended to power an Alcoa/Shell alumina and aluminium plant near the northern port of Sao Luis. Said Joao Regis, one of the demonstration organisers, "The Government has been supplying electricity on the cheap by building dams without compensating anyone other than big landowners who hold title deeds. Everyone wants energy, including us, but this project would change the whole life of thousands of families and they're not the sort of people who have the resources to set up somewhere else." *Guardian*, London 30 January 1984.

182. Alicia Baranas and Miguel Bartolome, *Hydraulic Development and Ethnocide: the Mazatec and Chinantec People of Oaxaca, Mexico*, IWGIA document No. 15, Copenhagen, 1973.

183. Mayan sites — especially the city of Yaxchilan, still sacred to the Lacandon people — will be flooded along the Rio Usumacinta, if a joint Mexican/Guatemalan proposal is given the go-ahead in the near future: see "Archaeological and Ecological Implications of Proposed Hydroelectric Projects on the Rio Usumacinta", S. Jeffrey, K. Wilkerson, in IWGIA newsletter, No. 38, Copenhagen, July 1984.
One of the biggest struggles in recent years to prevent the flooding of sacred Aboriginal sites involved thousands of non-violent protesters and many Aboriginal people on the site of the Gordon-below-Franklin dam in Tasmania. The project was halted by the Federal government in 1983. A full account of the struggle to save the Franklin River can be read in Roger Green, *Battle for the Franklin*, Fontana, Australia, 1984.

184. A good introduction to the manipulative rationale of aluminium companies in locating smelters in de-developed countries is provided by Ronald Graham's *The Aluminium Industry and the Third World: Multinational Corporations and Underdevelopment*, Zed Press, London 1982. See also Gordon Bennett, Audrey Colson, Stuart Wavell, *The Damned: the plight of the Akawaio Indians of Guayana*, Survival International Document VI, London, undated. A crisp summary of other hydro/smelter schemes during the 1970s is contained in *Purari: Overpowering Papua New Guinea?* (1978) pp. 131–82.

Other useful insights into the impact of dams on indigenous peoples are to be found in: "Saving Rivers, Saving Lives", special section on hydroelectrics and native peoples, *The Global Reporter*, Vol. 1, No. 2, Summer 1983, ARC, Boston; also Patricia Adams, *Third World Energy Myths*, Energy Probe, Toronto, 1984.

185. See Gordon Bennett, Audrey Colson, Stuart Wavell, *The Damned: the Plight of the Akawaio Indians of Guyana*, Survival International Document VI, London, 1979, p. 3.

186. Ibid., pp. 5–6; see also "An Update", Survival International, London (undated), p. 2.

187. See *Purari — Who Needs it?* produced by the Purari Action Group, Boroko, 1978.

188. See Ronald Graham, *The Aluminium Industry and the Third World, Multinational Corporations and Underdevelopment*, Zed Press, 1982, pp. 78–110.

189. *Purari: Overpowering Papua New Guinea?* by International Development Action and Purari Action Group, IDA, Fitzroy, 1978 p. 221.

190. *Purari: Overpowering Papua New Guinea?* pp. 7–9.

191. Felix Razon, "Native Peoples Struggle Against US Imperialism in the Philippines", in *The Oppression of Indigenous Peoples of the Philippines* IWGIA document No. 25, Copenhagen, 1976, pp. 33–4.

192. Ibid., pp. 35–6.

193. Submission by National Congress of American Indians (NCAI) to US Congress House Banking Committee's Subcommittee on International Development Institute and Finance, June 1983, quoted in World Council of Indigenous Peoples (WCIP) Newsletter, Lethbridge, No. 3, August 1983, p. 28.

194. Razon, (1976) p. 37

195. NCAI submission, in WCIP Newsletter, No. 3, p. 29.

196. Ibid.

197. Quoted by Charles Drucker, The Chico River dams: The Power of Indigenous Peoples, in *The Global Reporter*, ARC Boston, Vol. 1, No. 2, Summer 1983, p. 6.

198. Ibid.

199. Testimony by NDF spokesman to the Permanent Peoples' Tribunal Session on the Philippines, in *Philippines: Repression and Resistance*, Komite ng Sambayanang Pilipino (KSG), Utrecht and London, 1981, p. 201.

200. Razon, (1976) p. 38.

201. Ben and Nilo Langa-an, *Squatters in their own land*, cyclostyled manuscript, Philippines, May 1980, p. 3.

202. *Tribal Forum*, Episcopal Commission on Tribal Filipinos, Vol. IV, No. 7, November/December 1983.

203. Asmund Lindal, Helge Sunde (eds) *Alta Bilder, 12 years struggle for the Alta Kautokeino watercourse* (Norwegian/English text) Pax forlag, Oslo, 1981, p. 97.

204. The Norwegian government claimed in official statements that only 21 animals would be affected (Bjartmar Gjerde, Storting, Oslo, 6 June 1979); other surveys maintained that many thousands would be affected, as well as migration patterns and Sami livelihood over a very wide area (see Robert Paine, *Dam a River, Damn a People* IWGIA document No. 45, Copenhagen, June 1982.

205. How "original" might be a matter for academic debate, since they were forced northwards over several hundred years, but their claim to Samiland on the basis of "first occupancy" is beyond dispute. See Nils-Aslak Valkeapää, *Greetings from Lappland: The Sami — Europe's Forgotten People*, Zed Press, London, 1983,

pp. 13–21.

206. *IWGIA Newsletter*, No. 27, Copenhagen, June 1981, pp. 66–8.

207. Ibid. pp. 63–6. See also *Charta 79. The Sami People and Human Rights*, Oslo, 1982, pp. 36–9.

208. *Charta 79*, p. 43.

209. *Pogrom*, Gesellschaft für bedrohte Völker, Göttingen, No. 107 mid-1984 pp. 8–9. Bechtel is the world's biggest constructor of nuclear plant: it also has the dubious merit of having built (*inter alia*) RT-Z's Bougainville copper mine, on Nasioi land; Freeport's copper concentrate pipeline in West Papua (which was severed by the OPM indigenous liberation movement in 1977); the Ok Tedi mine on Min land in Papua New Guinea; Cominco's Red Dog mine in the Canadian High Arctic; and the Da Nang airforce base used for US assaults on North Vietnam. Future contracted projects include the Alcoa smelter (trespassing on Gunditj-Mara sacred sites in Victoria, Australia); the Jabiluka mine in Aboriginal Arnhemland; RT-Z/Borax's Quartz Hill molybdenum mine in an Alaskan National Park area. (See Bechtel entry in *The Gulliver File*, WISE/CIMRA, Glen Aplin, London, 1985.) As if this unique record wasn't sufficient, Bechtel also has nearly a 17% interest in the world's biggest stripminer of Indian territory: Peabody Coal.

210. In 1983 the Northern Territory government of Australia proposed flooding the "Old Telegraph Station" near Alice Springs, to create a recreational lake. Aboriginal groups fought vehemently against the desecration of the sacred sites at Welatye-Therre (see *Native Peoples News*, No. 9, Summer 1983, p. 6 "A Flood of Protest"). The following year an independent committee sat to hear evidence on alternative locations for the lake (*Central Land Council News*, No. 20, August 1984). The scheme is currently shelved.

Chapter 6

211. *The State of India's Environment, 1982, A Citizens Report*, Centre for Science and Environment, New Delhi, 1982, p. 120.

212. Ibid. p. 39.

213. Shelton H. Davis, *Victims of the Miracle: Development and the Indians of Brazil*, Cambridge University Press, 1977, pp. 143–4.

214. Ernesto C. Miglizza, *The Integration of the Indigenous Peoples of the Territory of Roraima, Brazil*, IWGIA document No. 32, Copenhagen, 1978, pp. 17–18.

215. See, for example, Shelton Davis (1977) pp. 142–3; *State of India's Environment*, p. 122.

216. As Catherine Caufield points out in her excellent book *In the Rainforest* (Heinemann, London, 1985) there is a real difference between tribally-initiated "shifting" cultivation, and slash-and-burn which is often introduced by outsiders. However, many indigenous forest dwellers are being forced to turn to slash-and-burn, and there are effective means of reducing its negative impact. Caufield, pp. 131–42.

217. Nigel Dudley, *The Death of Trees* Pluto Press, London, 1985, pp.29–31; see also Caufield, pp. 150–83. The destruction of forest is often associated with other environmental depredation, such as mining and flooding for hydro-electric schemes. For example, some of the tribal peoples threatened by the Bakun dam in Sarawak (see previous chapter, *n* 171) have recently had their customary felling rights pulled from under their feet by logging companies. ("Native Customary Rights Felled by Timber" *SAM Features*, Sahabat Alam Malaysia, Penang, no date, 1985.)

218. *State of India's Environment*, pp. 40, 44.

219. Ibid., p. 45.

220. Ibid., pp. 42–3.

221. A major campaign launched by the Friends of the Earth International in 1984, to conserve tropical forests, initially failed even to mention the pivotal role of forest dwellers in determining their own economies. During 1985 and early 1986, however, the campaign was broadened. "Forests for Survival" was launched as a coalition of a number of groups, including FoE International, the Kenyan Green Belt Movement, the National Park Service of Nicaragua, the Environment Liaison Centre in Nairobi, Agapan (Brazil) and the largely indigenous Chipko Movement of India (*Ecoforum*, Vol. 10, No. 6, Environment Liaison Centre, Nairobi, December 1985).

222. *The State of India's Environment*, p. 54, contains a summary of the new Act.

223. For example, Walter Fernandes, "Forest Resources and Forest Dweller Economy" (pp. 16–24), Dinanath Manohar, "Tribals, Forest Policy and Forest Legislation" (pp. 34–41) in *Samata*, No. 1, 1984, published by the Caste-Class Study Programme of the Christian Institute for the Study of Religion and Society and the William Carey Study and Research Centre, Bangalore.

224. *State of India's Environment*, p. 47.

225. Ibid.

226. *The Philippines: Authoritarian government, multinationals and ancestral lands*, Anti-Slavery Society, Indigenous Peoples and Development Series: 1, London, 1983, p. 61.

227. Wada Taw-il "Logging Operations in Cultural Minority Homelands", in *Philippines: Repression and Resistance; Permanent Peoples' Tribunal Session on the Philippines*, KSP London and Utrecht, 1980, p. 194.

228. *The Philippines*, A-SS, p. 67.

229. Ibid. pp. 63, 68–73.

230. Ibid. p. 84.

231. Wada Taw-il, "Logging Operations in Cultural Minority Homelands", p. 195.

232. *The Philippines*, A-SS, p. 90.

233. "Abra Militarisation intensifies", *Tribal Forum*, Episcopal Commission on Tribal Filipinos, Manila, Vol. V, No. 3, May–June 1984, p. 15.

234. Nemesio J. Rodriguez *Oppression in Argentina: the Mataco Case*, IWGIA, Copenhagen, 1975, p. 27.

235. *El Mundo*, 22 October 1973, Buenos Aires.

236. Rodriguez, (1975) p. 25.

Chapter 7

237. *Minamata the story of the poisoning of a city, and of the people who choose to carry the burden of courage:* words and pictures by W. Eugene Smith and Aileen M. Smith. Alskog-Sensorium Book, Holt, Rinehart and Winston, New York, 1975. See especially pp. 26–33.

238. The Ontario Public Interest Research Group (OPIRG) has published a model critical study of Reed International covering not only the "Minamata" poisoning, but Reed's grabbing of other land for timber operations in the Treaty 9 area, and its operations in South Africa and Zimbabwe (Rhodesia) which violated UN sanctions. See *Reed International: profile of a transnational corporation*, OPIRG, Peterborough, 1977. *The Sunday Times* also covered the "Scandal of

Wabigoon River" in three pages of quite penetrating reportage: *Sunday Times*, 1 May 1977, pp. 1, 17, 18. See also *Akwesasne Notes*, Vol. 8, No. 5, early Winter 1976, pp. 10–15.

239. George Hutchinson, *Grassy Narrows*, Van. Nostrand Reinhold Ltd, Toronto, 1975.

240. *Watawat News*, reprinted by *Yukon Indian News*, 10 February 1984.

241. *Akwesasne Notes*, Summer 1984, p. 26.

242. *Red Peoples Long Walk bulletin*, Canada, October 1984.

243. *Akwesasne Notes*, Winter 1978. p. 21.

244. See *Akwesasne Notes*, Vol. 10, No. 1, Early Spring 1978, p. 17 (quoting *Klainai News*); also *Akwesasne Notes*, Vol. 10, No. 2, late Spring 1978 pp. 12–13.

245. *Cultural Survival Newsletter*, Cambridge (Mass), Vol. 5, No. 3, Summer 1981 pp. 4–5.

Chapter 8

246. Bruce Johansen and Roberto Maetas, *Wasi'chu: the continuing Indian Wars* Monthly Review Press, New York 1979, p. 187.

247. Ibid.

248. Ibid., p. 190.

249. Ibid., p. 188.

250. Ibid., p. 191. See also "Klamath Fishing Struggle" in *Akwesasne Notes*, Autumn 1978, p. 17.

251. Press release from Janet McCloud, Colombia River Fishing Rights Update, 7 November 1983. See also press statement from the National Lawyers Guild, New York, in *Akwesasne Notes*, late summer 1984, p. 25.

252. *Indian Report*, 1–23 Spring 1985, Friends Committee on National Legislation, Washington, p. 6.

253. See *Akwesasne Notes*, Summer 1981, p. 20. "MicMacs defend fishing Rights; Assaulted by Quebec Provincial Police". Further information on the Restigouche struggle is to be found in IWGIA Newsletter Nos. 28/29, Copenhagen Oct/Dec 1981, pp. 41–8.

Chapter 9

254. See Jack Beeching, *An Open Path: Christian Missionaries 1515–1914*, Hutchinson, London 1979, especially pp. 16–81.

255. For example, the evangelists who followed Captain Bligh (of *Bounty* fame) to Tahiti, according to Jack Beeching wanted to "impose on the Tahitians the moral values which, in England, had made the factory system possible". They took up with Pomare, a kingly pretender who was quite willing to hitch his falling star to their wagon, and precipitated a destructive civil war. Through Pomare, the islanders were forcibly introduced to "schools, guns and trade": see Beeching, ibid, pps. 92–6.

256. Beeching, pp. 24–35.

257. Ibid. pp. 45–7.

258. Letter to Secretary of New Zealand Mission, 24 February 1819.

259. Jan Roberts: *Massacres to Mining; the colonisation of Aboriginal Australia*, Dove Communications, Victoria, 1981 pp. 38–43.

260. This appalling practise has been graphically portrayed by the Aboriginal writer/director Gerry Bostock in the film *Lousy Little Sixpence*, Sydney, 1983.

261. Among several telling portraits of this notorious penal colony, see in

particular, Bill Rosser, *This is Palm Island*, Australian Institute of Aboriginal Studies, Canberra 1978.

262. Jan Roberts, (1981) p. 41.

263. Paul Jacobs and Saul Landau, with Eve Pell, *To Serve the Devil*, Vol. 2. *Colonials and Sojourners* Vintage Books, New York, 1971, pp. 18–27.

264. See, for example, "An Inquiry into the Causes of Decrease in the Population of the Sandwich Islands" by Rev. Artemas Bishop, in *The Hawaiian Spectator*, January 1838, pp. 52 ff. quoted in Jacobs, Landau and Pell, p. 26.

265. See John H. Bodley, *Victims of Progress*, Cummings Publishing, Menlo Park California, 1975.

266. The World Council of Churches statement "on land rights for indigenous people" focused primarily on the Americas, Australia and New Zealand and original inhabitants dispossessed by largely Christian invaders. This statement cited several examples of contemporary Christian groups adopting a pro-indigenous position, notably Project North (Canada) and churches which had intervened with shareholder resolutions to oppose the activities of Canadian mining companies; the meeting of 27 missionaries from five countries in Brazil in 1980, which "confessed their mistakes and the wrongs committed against the indigenous people" and the WCC team visit to Aboriginal Australia in 1981. (*Statement by the WCC Sixth Assembly Central Committee*, July 1982 WCC. Geneva, 1982.)

267. Revolutionary priests and nuns have been especially courageous in support of the Indians of Guatemala (see *I, Rigoberta Menchu*, Verso, London 1984, pp. 234–5). A good recent example of pro-tribal missionary writing from India is Michael Van den Bogaert's *The Tribal my brother*. Xavier Institute of Social Service, Ranchi, 1983.

268. For example (and fairly at random), Pastor Walter Lini, the first Prime Minister of independent Vanuatu; Father Pat Dodson, chair of the National Federation of (Aboriginal) Land Councils in Australia; Joyce Hall of Weipa (see chapter 7); many tribal Filipinos (see chapter 5); N. E. Horo, former President of the Jharkand party in India, Rigoberta Menchu of Guatemala.

269. Jan Roberts, (1981). pp. 56–7.

270. Mark Münzel *The Aché Indians: Genocide in Paraguay*, IWGIA Document No. 11. Copenhagen 1973.

271. Luke Holland, *Pig Hunt*, Survival International, London 1981 (also available as a mobile exhibition from Survival International, 310 Edgware Rd, London W2). See also p. 274 of this anthology "My name is Weypygi. I am Aché".

272. See "Bolivia-Colombia-Paraguay: Missionary Manhunts Continue", in *Survival International News* No. 2, 1983, pp. 1–2. In this article Luke Holland makes a direct link between the New Tribes Mission and the US-inspired campaign against Che Guevara's guerrilla forces in the same area in 1967.

273. *Declaration of Barbados*, signed by *inter alia*, Victor Daniel Bonilla, Miguel Chase Sardi, Darcy Ribeiro, Stefan Varese and Guillermo Bonfil Batalla, Barbados, 30 January 1971. Reprinted widely; for example by IWGIA as the first document in its invaluable documentation series (IWGIA, Copenhagen). Despite the ringing condemnation of missionaries in the Declaration, the signatories acknowledged their pervasive power by proposing ten steps they could take to minimise their negative impact on indigenous communities (see IWGIA document No. 1, pp. 5, 6).

274. "L'Evangelisation Coloniale et le Desarroi du Père Adolfo" (Colonialist

evangelisation and the confusion of Father Adolfo) in Robert Jaulin's *La Paix Blanche: Introduction a l'ethnocide*, Editions du Seuil, Paris 1970, (pp. 336–401) admirably develops the contradiction in an argument that Indian "religion" by its nature cannot come to terms with even the most benevolent and humane God seen as "out there", inevitably separated from the spiritualisation of everyday life.

275. *The Indian and the White Man*, (ed) Wilcomb E. Washburn, Doubleday and Co., New York 1964 pp. 211–13.

276. Paul Jacobs and Saul Landau with Eve Pell, *To Serve the Devil*, Vol. 1 *Natives and Slaves*, Random House, New York 1971, p. 50. See also, "The Indians Rebuff a Missionary" in *The American Spirit: United States History as seen by Contemporaries*, Vol. 1 (ed) Thomas A. Bailey. D. C. Heath and Co. Boston 1963 and 1968.

277. The SIL was ordered out of Mexico in 1975 (*Survival International News*, London, No. 2, 1983) and Decree No. 1159 was signed in 1981 giving the organisation a year to leave Ecuador (IWGIA Newsletter, Copenhagen, No. 28/29, October/December 1981 pp. 14–16).

278. See in particular, *Die frohe Botschaft unserer Zivilisation; Evangelikale Indianermission in Lateinamerika; eine Dokumentation über den Einfluss protestantisch-fundamentalistischer Mission am Beispeil des Summer Institute of Linguistics*, Mark Münzel et. al., Reihe pogrom, Göttingen and Vienna, July 1979. Also, Soren Hvalkof and Peter Aaby (eds): *Is God An American? an anthropological perspective on the missionary work of the Summer Institute of Linguistics*, IWGIA/Survival International, London and Copenhagen, 1982. A very detailed account of SIL's work in south America, especially Peru, is contained in *Fishers of Men or Founders of Empire? The Wycliffe Bible Translators in Latin America*, David Stoll, Zed Press and Cultural Survival, London 1982. A valuable summary of the SIL's encroachment on other indigenous areas is contained in this book: see especially pp. 237–48.

279. Stephen Corry, *Towards Indian Self-Determination in Colombia*, Survival International Document 11, March 1976, London.

280. *Native Peoples in Struggle, Cases from the Fourth Russell Tribunal and other international forums*, ERIN publications, New York, 1982, p. 46.

281. The full statement was published in *El Nacional*, Venezuela, on 19 September 1980, and in English translation in *Survival International Review*, No. 34. It was submitted to the Fourth Russell Tribunal in 1980 and signed by Carlos Azpurua, Esteban, Emilio Mosonyi and Beatriz Bermudez. For a detailed study of the negative impact of the NTM on the Yanomami of Venezuela and neighbouring Brazil, see Jacques Lizot, *The Yanomami in the Face of Ethnocide*, IWGIA document No. 22, Copenhagen, 1976.

282. See for example, "Statement in Support of the Sovereign Shungopavi Nation" sent to the US Department of the Interior by the Northwest Indian Women's Circle, Tacoma, in June 1984.

283. *Akwesasne Notes*, Mohawk Nation, Spring 1984, p. 19.

284. Phyllis Fischer, *Traditional Aboriginal Spirituality within the Prison system*, Quaker Committee on Jails and Justice, Toronto, 1984, includes recent information on the violation of native prisoners rights at Kent Penitentiary, British Colombia.

Chapter 10

285. This statement was made by a young Yanomami to the anthropologist Jacques

Lizot, and is quoted in Lizot's *The Yanomami in the face of ethnocide*, IWGIA document No. 22, Copenhagen 1976, p. 20. Lizot describes the process by which the missionaries kidnapped the young:

". . . Indians were enlisted with scant regard for the methods. The missionaries busied themselves, clothing the children and adolescents, putting flaps into their outfits; they were then enticed into boats, with sweets and dry cakes sprinkled with pepsi cola, and promises of an easy future. That wasn't all: they went into neighbouring communities and came back with batches of naked children. The parents were not warned . . . They tied up at the bank, and without entering the houses, called the youngsters to come into the boats. The children, thrilled at travelling in a motor-boat, didn't need to be asked twice. Off they went to an unknown destination, without dreaming they wouldn't return quite soon." (Lizot, 1976 p. 19).

286. *The Days of Augusta*, (ed) Jean E. Speare (photographs Robert Keziere) J. J. Douglas Ltd, Vancouver, 1973. p. 7.

287. Ibid. p. 8.

288. *Indigena*, Berkeley, California, Fall 1974, Vol. 1, No. 2, p. 7.

289. Stephen Corry, unpublished documentation on Peru, London 1983.

Chapter 11

290. See, for example, the excellent two-volume study *Roots of Racism* and *Patterns of Racism*, Institute of Race Relations, London, 1982.

291. Of course there were noble exceptions, such as Bartolomé de Las Casas, who repudiated activities of the Conquistadores. In the early years of colonialism both the Kings of Spain and England ordained a measured, benign response to the heathens of the New World. Their commands were rarely heeded on the ground. A worthy attempt has been made by the scholar Karen Ordahl Kupperman to refute the idea that early English colonists of North America "were abruptly dismissive of Indian culture, that they were either totally uninterested or else saw it as something to be shunned or even destroyed as the work of the devil". (Karen Ordahl Kupperman, *Settling with the Indians: the meeting of English and Indian cultures in America, 1580–1640*, J. M. Dent, London, 1980 p. vii). Quoting an impressive range of sources, she convincingly demonstrates that some Puritans, though censorious of Indian customs, adopted a similar attitude towards the lower echelons of English society of the same day (pp. 26–7). Many observers, though critical of Indian "primitiveness", recognised their excellence as food-growers (ibid. pp. 83, 86): "the early colonists were dependant on Indian aid in so many ways and were so vulnerable that they could not afford to be contemptuous of native accomplishments" (p. 106). Indian moderation, justice, loyalty, love of children, and above all temperance were much admired (pp. 143–7). Unfortunately, Kupperman's thesis depends on certain assumptions which are untested and probably untestable: that the widely applied term "savage" did not originally have its modern connotation at all, but meant something akin to "natural" or "native" (pp. 111–13); that, though Indians were often viewed as "treacherous", this had more to do with the Puritan view of human relationships than "a quality especially inherent in the Indian character" (pp. 127–9). Her general conclusion is worthy of respect, however, and indeed confirms the view that, after the initial period of contact and commerce, colonial avarice and fear dictated a new stereotype of the native American: "It was the ultimate powerlessness of the Indians, not their racial inferiority which made it possible to see them as people without rights . . . If, in the

period after 1640, the American Indians were the subject of racism by English people, the conclusion must be that this racism was a product of, not the cause of, the treatment of Indians by colonists." (p. 188).

A less flattering view of Puritan perceptions is contained in Keith Thomas, *Man and the Natural World, Changing attitudes in England 1500–1800* Allen Lane, London, 1983. While conceding that American Indians (unlike, for example the "Hottentots") were not normally considered by the Puritans to be "brutish", several writers did refer to their "beastly" characteristics (p. 42). Since "the ethic of human domination removed animals from the sphere of human concern . . . it also legitimised the ill-treatment of those humans who were in a supposedly animal condition". (ibid. p. 44).

For a more conventional view of the early settlements in north America, see David N. Durant, *Raleigh's Lost Colony: The story of the first English settlement in America*, Weidenfeld and Nicholson, London, 1981. Here the colonists are shown as initially curious and benign towards the Chesepian and Roanoac nations, then suspicious, finally distrustful and aggressive. The Indians suffer disease and starvation, and after diplomacy has apparently failed, the Powhatan Confederacy attacks the colony: its final fate is still unknown. (pp. 67–85, 117–20, 159–64).

292. This system is described in detail in *The Conquest of the Incas*, John Hemming, revised edition, Penguin, 1983, pp. 145–8, 353–4, 399–400.

293. Recent heated debate about the extent and impact of the slave trade on indigenous African societies is summarised in *Forced Migration: the impact of the export slave trade on African Societies*, (ed) J. E. Inikori, Hutchinson Library for Africa, London, 1982. Inikori concludes that, during the whole period of slave trafficking (including "exports" to Muslim states which began early in the Christian era) some 15,800,000 girls and women, and 13,900,000 boys and men were seized in sub-Saharan Africa (p. 25). This compares with Galeano's estimate that nearly 70,000,000 Aztecs, Incas and Mayas died — many from disease — in the first 150 years of the conquest of South and Central America (Eduardo Galeano, *Open Veins of Latin America*, Monthly Review Press, New York and London 1972, p. 50.)

294. For example on 28 September 1983, 16-year-old John Pat was murdered by police at Roebourne, Western Australia, after five off-duty police provoked a fight with another Aborigine, Ashley James, in a local off-licence, calling him a "black bastard". In court, one of the policemen excused grabbing John Pat by the hair with the words "It's a natural thing . . . When they are stirred up, they tend to get greasy and slippery." An all-white jury acquitted the police, to an outcry from Aboriginal organisations and civil liberties groups throughout Australia. (See "Defend Black Rights" pamphlet from the Aboriginal Support Group, London, September 1984.)

295. See, for example, discussions featured in the film *Ningla-a-Na*, (Strachan and Cavadini, Sydney Filmmakers Coop, 1978) and between Maoris and visiting members of the Keskidee Centre, north London, in the film *Keskidee Aroha* (Sanderson and Mita, New Zealand 1982).

296. Black Australian activists created a furore during the 1981 Commonwealth Heads of Government Meeting (CHOGM) in Canberra, when Gary Foley, leader of the National Aboriginal and Islander Health Organisation (NAIHO) accused black African leaders of deliberately snubbing grass-roots Aboriginal organisations and accepting only the Fraser government's version of the situation. "Mugabe really pissed us off by going to a fucking white woman Susan Ryan, to hear the Opposition's version of Aboriginal affairs. If we get to fucking Zimbabwe to ask about black Zimbabweans, we wouldn't go to Ian Smith or any of that mob,"

ejaculated Foley (*Age*, Melbourne, 7 October 1981). A more moderated protest came from the convenor of the NAIHO (*Age* 9 October 1981). Robert Mugabe promised to "study" the Aboriginal situation and, "I can assure you when we have the facts we will stand up." ("Zimbabwe Leader gives pledge to Aborigines", *The Age*, Melbourne, 8 October 1981). No known statement has yet been made by the Zimbabwean Prime Minister.

297. Shirley Hill Witt and Stan Steiner (eds.) *The Way*, An Anthology of American Indian Literature, Random House, New York 1972.

298. Shorty O'Neill, in speech delivered in London, 1982.

299. In October 1980 the Queensland government announced that it would repeal the infamous Aborigines Act and Torres Strait Islanders Act of 1971. Legislation to replace these, put forward in April 1984, would grant "deeds in trust" to Aborigines in place of the old reserves. Although certain new "rights" are given Aborigines — such as less patronising community self-management, control of entry to reserves and access to fauna and flora — the 1984 Bill was drafted without any consultation with Aboriginal organisations; says nothing about vetos on mining; does not give Aborigines free access to plants and other natural products on their land. It also leaves the status of the two "hijacked" shires — Mornington Island and Aurukun — very unclear. For a summary of the new Act see Garth Nettheim, "Queensland's New Legislation, Letting go?" in *Aboriginal Law Bulletin*, NSW, No. 11, August 1984.

300. Garth Nettheim, *The Age*, Melbourne 26 September 1977; see also, *Discrimination against Aborigines and Islanders in North Queensland; the case of Townsville*, Larsen, Dwyer, Harrtwig, Whop and Wyles, AGPS, Canberra, 1977.

301. *Financial Review*, Australia, 30 May 1979.

302. Ibid. 13 June 1979.

303. "Payment of Award Wages on Aboriginal Reserves in Queensland", draft Human Rights Commission Discussion paper No. 2, prepared by Dr John Hookey, Canberra, August 1983.

304. Quoted in Norman Lewis, "Eastern Bolivia: the White Promised Land", *Observer*, London 5 March 1978, reprinted as IWGIA document No. 31, Copenhagen, May 1978.

305. Brigitte Simon, Barbara Schuchard, Barbara Riester and Jurgen Riester, *I sold myself; I was bought*, IWGIA document No. 42, Copenhagen, 1980.

306. In 1979 the charity Food for the Hungry International, with the co-operation of the Bolivian regime, proposed settling 100 Hmong refugee families from Thailand on Indian land in the Yucumu area of Bolivia: it was intended to demonstrate the feasibility of a much bigger scheme, and was assisted by two members of the Summer Institute of Linguistics (SIL). (*IWGIA Newsletter*, June 1979, Copenhagen, pp. 40–41.)

307. *Native Peoples News*, Nos. 2/3 CIMRA London, 1979, p. 39.

308. *Survival International Review*, No. 27, London, Autumn 1979, p. 28.

309. Stephen Corry, unpublished manuscript on the Indian organisations of Peru, Survival International, London 1979, p. 168.

310. *Survival International Review*, No. 27, p. 28.

311. Corry, p. 168.

312. *Survival International Review*, No. 28. Winter 1979 p. 31.

313. "Werner Herzog up to his old tricks with Peruvian Indians" *Lima Times*, Peru, 26 September 1980, translated into English and published in *Survival International Review*, No. 34. Among other documents prepared by native Peruvians to refute Herzog's view of the "Fitzcarraldo affair" are: Evaristo

Nugkuag, "Nostromos los Aguaranuas", in *Tarea*, May 1980, pp. 49–54; and a statement by the Sepahua community "Documentos" in *CETA*, Peru 1981 pp. 250–251.

314. Werner Herzog, Statement made to the Press in Lima, Peru on August 25th 1979 reprinted in *Survival International Review*, No. 27, Autumn 1979, p. 29.

315. Roger Moody, "Ego and Illusion", *The Leveller*, London, 3–16 September 1982.

316. Merata Mita interviewed by *Framework*, No. 24, London, 1984.

317. Survival International, London, Urgent Action Bulletin PRU/Oct 3/1984: "Peru: Indians Killed. Park no protection as development encroaches".

Chapter 12

318. See, for example Stefano Varese, *The Forest Indians in the Present Political Situation in Peru*, IWGIA document No. 8, Copenhagen, 1972, especially pp. 9–10; also Nicolas Inigo Carrera, *Violence as an economic force: the process of proletarianisation among the indigenous people of the Argentinian Chaco, 1884–1930*, IWGIA document No. 46, 1982, especially pp. 4–42.

319. This has applied particularly in northern Saskatchewan, where initially, the Federation of Saskatchewan Indians strongly supported a new wave of uranium mines, because of the immediate employment they would bring. By 1983, however, with some hopes unfulfilled and Indians being delegated the most dangerous jobs in the new mines, the Federation modified its uncritical stand.

320. These extracts come from a very powerful and comprehensive account of the struggles of the Santa Cruz sugar workers, Brigitte Simon, Barbara Schuchard, Barbara Riester and Jurgen Riester: *I sold Myself; I was bought*, IWGIA document No. 42, Copenhagen, 1980.

321. *Unidad Indigena*, No. 25, October 1977.

Chapter 13

322. *Indigena*, Berkeley, California, Summer 1977.

323. Eduardo Galeano, *Open Veins of Latin America*, Monthly Review Press, New York, 1973, p. 16.

324. The accusations were made by a priest, Guillermo Manrique Lopez. See *Indigena*, Berkeley, Winter 1974–75.

325. In addition to the article by Dee Fairbanks reprinted in this chapter (p. 326) see also Marie-Helene Laraque and William Meyer, "Sterilizations and Experiments: in Guatemala, Colombia and Oklahoma", *Indigena* Berkeley, California, Winter 1975–77.

326. For instance in the Declaration of Iximche made by a group of indigenous leaders in February 1980 (see *Guatemala! the Horror and the Hope*, Four Arrows, Pennsylvania, 1982 p. 226); in documentation provided by the High Court of the Chamber of Representatives of West Papua to the Russell Tribunal, Rotterdam, 1980 (see Fourth Russell Tribunal documentation No. 15, *West Papua* p. 3); testimony by the former Bishop of Dili, East Timor, Mgr. da Costa Lopes (in Budiardjo and Soei Liong, *The War Against East Timor*, Zed Books & Marram Books, London 1984 p. 116). Rigoberta Menchu mentions, in passing, the "scandal" of enforced sterilisation in Guatemala during the late 1960s in *I, Rigoberta Menchu An Indian Woman in Guatemala*, edited and introduced by Elisabeth Burgos-Debray, Verso Editions, London 1984. p. 61: '. . . to us, using medicine to stop having children is like killing your own children".

327. Quoted in *Indigena*, Summer 1977. See also *Akwesasne Notes*, early Spring 1977 Vol. 9, No. 1, pp. 4–6.

328. *Depo Provera; a report by the Campaign against Depo-Provera*, ICAS, 374 Gray's Inn Rd., London WC1, 1981.

329. As late as 1981 Aboriginal young women at Oodnadatta were being given Depo-Provera against their will, while in 1984 a former research worker at the Bamyili settlement in the Northern Territory, revealed that Aboriginal girls as young as 12, had been provided with contraceptive pills, under the guise of "vitamins". (*The Advertiser*, Adelaide, 26 December 1984. See also Jan Mayman in the *National Times*, Sydney, 15 March 1981.)

Chapter 14

330. According to Darwin lawyer Colin McDonald in *Australian Society* (1 February 1984), Aboriginal residents of Groote Eylandt, a reserve off the north Australian coast, probably have the highest imprisonment rate in the world: 25 times the national average. A large number of crimes are attributed to alcohol consumption, which markedly increased when the mining company BHP (Broken Hill Proprietary) built a mining town and opened a manganese mine in the late 1960s.

During his 1981 John Barry memorial lecture in criminology at Melbourne University, the director of the country's Institute of Criminology, William Clifford, also claimed that imprisonment levels for Aborigines "may be the highest in the world for a minority group". (*Age*, Melbourne, 1 October 1981.)

331. A unique study on the effects of dispossession was carried out by sociologist Paul Wilson in the early 1980s, after he was asked to help defend Alwyn Peter, an Aboriginal man accused of stabbing his girl friend to death (Paul R. Wilson, *Black Death, White Hands*, George Allen and Unwin, Sydney 1982, p. 1). Alwyn lived on Weipa South reserve (see chapter 5). Wilson found that the homicide rate for Aborigines living on Queensland reserves was ten times the state and national average (ibid. p. 4) while "Not only are Aborigines imprisoned at a rate far exceeding any other group in the nation but they are also dying more frequently and at an earlier age than other Australians." (ibid. p. 72). In addition, the frustration and hopelessness of life in Aboriginal camps gave rise to a frightening degree of self-mutilation (ibid, pp. 22–34). Wilson concluded that Queensland reserve Aborigines were victims of a deliberate policy of dislocation, victimisation and the sacrifice of "Aboriginality" (ibid. pp. 43–7). Justice Dunn acknowledged the influence of these "historical factors" over which Peter had no control, and passed a lenient sentence, with a recommendation for immediate consideration for parole (ibid. p. 115).

Albert Namatjira was, until lately, perhaps Australia's most celebrated Aboriginal personality: the painter of watercolours which brought him international fame. In 1958 he was arrested and charged in Alice Springs, with supplying liquor to Aborigines — in fact he was simply sharing a bottle of rum with a local tribesman. He was sentenced to 6 months imprisonment (reduced on appeal to three months) and released after two months, with what writer Frank Clune called "a broken heart". He died soon after his release. According to Len Fox in his simple, well-written history *The Aboriginals* "These events probably caused more heart-searching among Australians as to our attitudes to Aboriginals than any other event in our history." (Len Fox, *The Aboriginals*, Nelson, Melbourne, 1978, p. 69.)

332. *Hearing Board Report, Minnesota Citizens Review Commission on the FBI*,

Minnesota, 1977; and *General Hearings*, MCRC 1978, Minnesota, 1978.

333. The finest account of the Peltier case and surrounding events is to be found in Peter Matthiessen, *In the Spirit of Crazy Horse*, Viking Press, New York, 1983. Good summaries are contained in many native American publications, notably *Akwesasne Notes*; in material published continually by the Leonard Peltier Defense Committee, (Washington) and in two articles by Rex Weyler: "Leonard Peltier", *New Age*, January 1981, pp. 44–9 and "America's Own Hostages", *New Age*, December 1980, pp. 30–38.

334. *Rocky Mountain News*, 7 June 1984.

335. *Leonard Peltier Convicted*; publication of Leonard Peltier Defense Committee, Washington (no date) p. 4.

336. See "Leonard Peltier and the Contemporary Indian Resistance in the United States" by Richard Wexler, *City* newspaper, Vol. 13, No. 9, 23 November 1983, also "Peltier Gets New Hearing", *Guardian* (New York) 16 May 1984, p. 4. Peltier was refused a new trial in May 1985, *Akwesasne Notes*, Vol. 17 No. 4, late summer 1985.

337. *Free the People*, Leonard Peltier Defense Group, St Paul, Minnesota, 1977, p. 4.

338. *New York Times*, 14 September 1984. See also: *Indian leader Dennis Banks Surrenders*, published by Dennis Banks Defense Committee, San Francisco, September 1984. Banks received a 3-year sentence in 1985, (*Indigenous Peoples' News* — Emergency Bulletin No. 7, February 1985, Rochester), but was released in early 1986 (*Pogrom*, Göttingen, No. 120, 1986).

339. *West Papua: Obliteration of a People*, Tapol, London, 1983, pp. 94–102.

Chapter 15

340. See, for example, Cynthia Z. Biddlecomb, in *Pandanus Periodical*, Micronesia Support Committee, Honolulu, No. 5, December 1983, pp. 1–4.

341. Stephen Corry, "Don't go down to the woods today", in *Native Peoples News*, London, No. 7, Summer 1982, pp. 8–10.

342. Ibid. The enormous negative implications of the Manu National Park for Indian communities have been dealt with by Survival International (Urgent Action Bulletin PRU/3 Oct/1984) and the International Youth Federation for Environmental Studies and Conservation, in its magazine *Taraxacum*, Denmark, Vol. 3, No. 2, 1984. Among the tourist agencies operating in this region are the Amazon Safari Company, (see *Boletin Copal*, Peru, March 1980), Andean Outfitters and Angels Camp (sic) of California (Corry, op cit), Twickenham Travel of Middlesex, England and the shipping company Union Lloyd (*Native Peoples News*, No. 7, Summer 1982, p. 10).

343. *Twickers' World, wildlife, cultural and wilderness Journeys*, 1985–1986. London 1984, p. 9.

344. "A Case Against Tourism" from *Tribal Forum*, Episcopal Commission on Tribal Filipinos, Manila, November 1984.

345. Ibid.

346. Aboriginal Land Rights Support Group *Newsletter*, Sydney, Vol. 22, December 1983, p. 6. See also *Land Rights News* (Central Land Council) No. 20, August 1983 and *Land Rights News* (CLC) No. 19 Summer 1983.

347. *Land Rights News* (Central Land Council) No. 20 pp. 7, 8.

348. "Palm Islands in Danger again" and "No tourists on Palms" from *North Queensland Messagestick*, Vol. 2, No. 2, Cairns, 1977.

349. *North Queensland Messagestick*, NQLC, Cairns, Vol. 2, No. 5, 1977. See

also: "What do the Palm Islanders own?" *North Queensland Messagestick*, Vol. 5, No. 2, July 1980; and "Money Might buy Palm Island, but its people can't" in *North Queensland Messagestick* Vol. 6, No. 1, January 1981.

Chapter 16

350. Estatuto do Indio, title 1, Article 1, in Legislacao, Brasilia Ministerio do Interior/FUNAI 1975.

351. *Jornal do Brasil*, Rio de Janeiro, 28 January 1975.

352. "Death Blows", *Native Peoples News* No. 10, Spring 1984, quoting Brazilian government Decree No. 18.118 (February 1983) and Decree 88.985 (November 1983).

353. *Survival International Review*, London, Spring 1979, pp. 34–5.

354. *Native Peoples News*, No. 8, Spring 1982, p. 7.

355. John Fire/Lame Deer and Richard Edoes *Lame Deer: Sioux Medicine Men*, Davis Poynter, London 1973 p. 98.

356. "The Nishga — a Century-long struggle" in *Project North Newsletter*, Toronto Vol. 5 No. 8 October–November 1980.

357. See *Project North Newsletter*, op cit, November 1981, October 1982 and December 1982.

358. For an account of land legislation introduced by the Chilean junta to dilute and destroy collective land-holdings by indigenous communities, see *Survival International Review*, No. 30, pp. 32–42 and *Survival International Review* No. 28, pp. 25–6.

359. Waitangi Treaty, statement by Waitangi Action Committee, Otara, in *North Queensland Messagestick*, 1981, p. 3.

360. See "6,000 Maoris, Whites march for land rights", report by the Pacific Concerns Resource Center, Hawaii, reproduced in *Native Peoples News*, No. 10, Spring 1984, p. 10.

361. See *Fringedweller* Robert Bropho (son of Nyinda), Alternative Publishing Cooperative Ltd, Chippendale, 1980; a superlative account of what it means to be a dispossessed black Australian. Bob Bropho is also co-director (with Jan Roberts) of *Mundu Nyurungu* (1984) filmed among the fringe-dwellers of the Western Australian desert.

Postscript

An anthology of this size is inevitably prepared and typeset some time in advance of publication. Although I hope that the majority of contributions will be of abiding interest and importance, it is only by examining and supporting ongoing struggles that we can really determine if there is a global indigenous movement, with common aims and values; and, if so, where it is taking both its members and their supporters. While the rejection of ethnocentrism, especially in its most concretized, pseudo-scientific form as anthropology, is implicit in all the pieces that follow there is now a danger that such collections will popularize new myths, new tautologies. To paraphrase Edward Said's critique of "orientalism" as a self-perpetuating system, managed by Westerners: "Indigenism [may become] knowledge of the Indigenous World that places things Indigenous in class, court, prison, or manual for scrutiny, study, judgment, discipline or governing"[1].

What follows is a brief account – drawing wherever possible on indigenous sources – of events since 1986 which update issues dealt with in the main body of the text. It is by no means comprehensive and itself risks being overtaken by events. Nonetheless, it should be of value in filling some of the gaps in a work of this kind. Readers who want more details (and I hope many will) should refer to the Notes that follow each section, including those following this Postscript.

Part 3

Chapter 1: Invasions and Genocide

Since 1986, Indonesia's *transmigration* policy – aimed not only at the indigenous Timorese but also West Papuans – has been the subject of an international campaign by Survival International, Friends of the Earth, Tapol, and other organizations worldwide, aimed at forcing the World Bank to withdraw its financial support, and for certain governments (notably the British) to pressure the Indonesian regime into halting the programme.[2] In 1987 the Indonesian government announced a 65% cut in funding for the programme.[3]

In the Philippines, the advent of a democratic government has failed to prevent the army's attacks on tribal peoples, particularly in the northern Cordillera where an "all out offensive" against the New Peoples Army (NPA) has actually intensified the oppression that characterized the Marcos regime.[4] Vigilante groups, supported by the army, have initiated a reign of terror in many indigenous communities[5] while the much-publicized land reform decree, unlike previous drafts, fails to guarantee the integrity of indigenous areas.[6]

From April 1986 to mid-1987, Bangladesh army attacks on the Chittagong Hill Tracts tribal communities also intensified, creating a major refugee exodus to India.[7] Under international pressure the Indian government reversed an earlier decision to return the refugees to Bangladesh against their will.[8]

Another cosmetic change – this time in the governing regime of Guatemala – has had no favourable effect on the life of the indigenous majority. Under Vinicio Cerezo, who came to power in 1986, one commentator wryly put it that: "they [now] kill the Indians democratically".[9] The terrorist Committees for National Defence have not been disbanded, the strategic hamlet programme continues, the assassination of indigenous leaders continues, agrarian reform has been abandoned, and a longstanding plan to sterilize indigenous women, supported by the University of Colorado and the British International Planned Parenthood Federation, was recently exposed.[10]

Chapter 2: Militarization

Low-level "strafing" of Nitassinan (Ntesinan) – now with American B-52 bombers and F-18 aircraft – continues to disrupt communal life over a wide area of Labrador–Quebec,[11] despite the fact that an Environmental Impact Assessment Study, commissioned by the Canadian government, will not report until the end of 1988 at the earliest.[12]

Chapter 3: The Nuclear State

In 1987, as the people of the Republic of Belau went to the polls for the tenth time, their unique nuclear-free Constitution looked like being abolished. The island's 15,000 citizens – under intense US pressure and interference – have now taken their third vote on the Constitution, their fifth vote on the compact, and one vote on amending the Constitution, to allow a reduction from 75% to 50% in the proportion of the electorate required to consent to a change.[13]

While the French continued to test nuclear weapons in the Pacific in the face of virtually united opposition from Pacific peoples, they made plans to transfer testing from Mororoa (where cracks have appeared in the atoll and radiation releases have reached horrendous levels) to Kerguelen Islands, which might also be used as a nuclear waste dump.[14]

Better prospects await the Lakota in the Black Hills of South Dakota. This area was targetted for intense multinational mining activity, but most of the companies have now withdrawn. In late 1986, the Sioux Nation Black Hills Act was introduced into the US Senate: if passed, it would restore 1.3 million acres of Federal (not private) land to the Lakota (Sioux) nation.[15]

Chapter 4: Mining and Multinationals

Britain's Rio Tinto-Zinc Corporation (renamed RTZ in 1987) continues to maintain its unenviable status as the world's most profligate encroacher on indigenous lands. Its associate Australian company CRA (49% owned by RTZ) is now test-drilling for uranium in the Rudall River National Park in Western Australia, despite united opposition from the Aboriginal-run Western Desert Land Council.[16] The Portland smelter, managed by Alcoa, went on stream on Gunditjmara land near Portland, Victoria.[17]

Chapter 5: Dams

The Tucurui dam – part of the Grande Carajas project in Brazil, which is the single biggest threat to South American Indians' survival – advances, despite numerous protests against the entire scheme from inside and outside Brazil.[18] After twelve years resistance by the Kalinga and Bontoc of the northern Cordillera, however, Filipino President Aquino cancelled the Chico River dams project in September 1986.[19] And, after an unprecedented campaign by indigenous organizations in Malaysia and their supporters around the world,[20] the Bakun dam in Sarawak seems to have been shelved – at least until 1990.[21] In 1987, despite a similar international campaign, several demonstrations by tribal peoples,[22] and intensive lobbying within India by scientists and environmentalists,[23] the Indian government precipitately gave the go-ahead to the Narmada Valley project – potentially the most devastating hydro-electric scheme ever devised for Asia.[24] With World Bank endorsement, a newly drafted loan agreement classifies the majority of people to be displaced by the scheme as "landless", hence with no automatic right to compensatory land.[25]

In 1986 and throughout 1987 the Sami ("Lapps") of northern Scandinavia experienced an even greater threat to their caribou (reindeer) herds than that posed by the Alta-Kautokeino dam in the late 1970s. Radioactive fall-out from the Chernobyl disaster necessitated many thousands of caribou being condemned as unfit for human consumption.[26] Increased Sami autonomy has been put at risk, and longstanding differences between northern Sami (with their commercialized reindeer herding) and the southern Sami (with their smaller-scale economy) have been exacerbated.[27] At the 13th Nordic Sami Conference in Sweden in 1986, a resolution calling on all Scandinavian governments to give special assistance to the Sami, in the aftermath of Chernobyl, was passed overwhelmingly.[28]

Chapter 6: Forests

At the time of writing, the new Forest Act has still not been implemented by the Indian government. Meanwhile, indigenous communities in Sarawak have engaged in a blockade to halt commercial timber logging;[29] many tribal people protesting against the scheme were arrested during the Malaysian government's arbitrary crackdown on its opponents in late 1987.[30]

Chapter 8: Fishing Rights

David So Happy Sr. was ordered to prison in 1987 for trying to assert his peoples' traditional fishing rights.[31]

Chapter 9: Missionaries
In 1986 and early 1987 the New Tribes Mission (NTM) resumed the "manhunts" which had first brought Paraguay's Aché and Ayoreo people to international attention some years before. "Missionized" Ayoreo were used by the NTM to track down and bring in forest Ayoreo. Five people died in resulting conflicts[32] and the British Parliamentary Human Rights Group called for "a proper enquiry" into the NTM's activities.[33] A long-running campaign by Asociacion Nacional de Usuanos Campesinos (ANUC) in Colombia, to expel the Summer Institute of Linguistics (SIL) from indigenous territory, bore fruit in late 1986, when this highly suspect band of hi-tech evangelicals was replaced by a new committee of professional linguists, as announced by the Colombian government at the second meeting of the National Indigenous Council (CONI).[34]

Chapter 11: Racism
The Queensland government has still not compensated Aboriginal workers for discriminatory wages. Aboriginal organizations, backed by ten trade unions, have now demanded $Aus 4 million in backdated claims.[35] Werner Herzog released his film "Where the Green Ants Dream", with its portrayal of Aboriginal Australians as a victimized, isolated people – then went on to shoot "Cobra Verde", in Ghana, which is an attempt to resurrect the all-woman "Amazon" kingdom of Dahomey.[36]

Chapter 13: Sterilization
According to a Queensland researcher, Australian Aboriginal girls, some as young as 13, continue to be injected with Depo-Provera, under the guise of rubella immunization.[37]

Chapter 14: Prison
Leonard Peltier remains in prison in the USA. In late 1987, a senior Australian criminologist announced that 23 times more Aborigines than whites were in gaol; no less than one in twelve Western Australian Aboriginal people in the 20–29 year old age group were incarcerated at any one time.[38] As the deaths of black Australians in custody since 1982 rose to more than 100 by late 1987,[39] a Royal Commission was set up to investigate,[40] and Aboriginal organizations launched their own Black Deaths in Custody action group.

Chapter 15: Tourism
In 1987 the British tourist agency Twickers' World, responsible for encouraging encroachment on indigenous land in the Manu National Park, sponsored a reconstruction of the First Fleet voyage from Portsmouth, England, to Australia's Sydney Cove. This re-enactment (which also profited from visits to South Africa and Namibia) was heavily criticized by Aboriginal organizations, anti-apartheid groups, and others in Britain and Australia.[41]

Chapter 14: The Land is not for sale
Late in 1987, the Brazilian government introduced constitutional changes which would secure tenure only for Indians "permanently located" on lands enjoyed

"since time immemorial". Even this measure – which clearly excludes a large number of displaced indigenous communities – will not safeguard Indian territory from mining, for which 2.000 claims were awaiting approval at the beginning of 1988 alone. The new decree will also cease to protect the rights of Indians "with a high degree of acculturation". When the legislation was introduced, Ailton Krenak, head of UNI, stood in silence before the Constituent Assembly, his face dyed black in the traditional demonstration of mourning "for the Indian peoples whose death sentences are being passed".[42]

In March 1987, after several meetings to define constitutional rights for Canada's indigenous peoples, and to restore their self-government (under the terms of the 1982 repatriated constitution) the Federal government and native Canadian leaders recorded failure and frustration. Major opposition to the entrenchment of self-government in the constitution has come from some provincial premiers who fear the loss of resources and the burden of costs in settling land claims and instituting some measure of indigenous control.[43]

The Labor government in Australia has also abandoned any attempts to institute a national model for Aboriginal land rights, as a result of bitter opposition from mining and pastoral interests. Although in 1987 the Federal government announced that it would be introducing a "treaty" recognizing Aboriginal first occupation of Australia, and acknowledging the wrongs done to Aborigines over the past 200 years, it has become clear that this measure is at best a palliative, at worst a cynical ploy.[44]

The Maori people of New Zealand have fared better. The Waitangi Tribunal, set up in 1979, declared in 1986 that the Treaty of Waitangi was a quasi-constitutional document which must be honoured by the New Zealand government. Although legislation introduced that year fell short of the Tribunal's recommendations,[45] the following year the Tribunal was given the power to decide on the restoration to Maori ownership of millions of hectares of government-owned land (more than 50% of the country's surface) currently controlled by new state corporations.[46]

Notes

1. The original quote is from Edward W. Said's *Orientalism*, Routledge and Kegan Paul (1978) reprinted Penguin Books, London (1985) p. 41.

2. Survival International Press Release, London, 31 July 1986; *Tapol* No. 75 (May 1986), No. 76 (July 1986) London.

3. *Survival International News*, No. 16, London 1987.

4. Survival International Press Release, London 13 June 1987.

5. *Kasama* (Philippines Support Group Newsletter) No. 27 Nov.–Dec. 1987, p. 3. See also "Life is even worse under Aquino" Statement of Delegation of Philippine Indigenous Organisations to the UN Working Groups on Indigenous Populations, in *IWGIA Newsletter* No. 51/52 Copenhagen, Oct./Dec. 1987.

6. *Kasama*, No. 25, June–August 1987, pp. 8–9.

7. Amnesty International Bangladesh: *Unlawful Killings and Torture in the Chittagong Hill Tracts*, Amnesty International, London, September 1986; International Workgroup for Indigenous Affairs (IWGIA) *Urgent Action Bulletin*, Copenhagen, 17 November 1986.

8. *Survival International News*, No. 16, London, 1987, p. 3.

9. Javier Farje in *IWGIA Newsletter*, No. 10, Copenhagen, 1986, pp. 44–57.

10. Ibid. See also Report by Americas Watch and the British Parliamentary Human Rights Group, London, February 1987.

11. *Native Press*, Somba K'e (Yellowknife) 15 May 1987.

12. *Project North Journal*, Toronto, Vol. 10, No. 4, Winter 1986.

13. *Pacific News Bulletin*, Sydney, Vol. 2, No. 4, Sept.–Oct. 1987.

14. *Peace News*, Nottingham, 17 April 1987.

15. Friends Committee on National Legislation (FCNL) *Newsletter*, Washington, No. 496, Nov. 1986.

16. Western Desert Land Council, *Uranium Exploration in the Rudall River National Park, An Aboriginal Perspective*, photocopied, undated (1987). See also: *Times on Sunday*, Western Australia, South Hedland, 4 April 1987; and *Parting Company* (People against RTZ and Subsidiaries), London, November 1987.

17. *The Age*, Melbourne, 10 October 1986.

18. See *Bound in Misery and Iron, The Impact of the Grande Carajas Programme on the Indians of Brazil*, Report from Survival International with an environmental assessment by Friends of the Earth, Survival International, London, 1987; also Survival International *UAB/BRZ/II/OCT/87* and *International Dams Newsletter*, San Francisco, Vol. I, No. 5, Sept. 1986.

19. *Survival International News*, London, No. 16, 1987, p. 6.

20. For example, a major article in the *New Scientist*, London, 15 January 1987, pp. 37–42.

21. *Survival International News*, No. 16, 1987.

22. *International Dams Newsletter*, Vol. 1, No. 6, Nov.–Dec. 1986, p. 9.

23. Ibid., Vol. 2, No. 2, March–April 1987.

24. Ibid., Vol. 2, No. 4, July–Aug. 1987, pp. 1 and 5.

25. *Survival International News*, No. 15, 1987.

26. Alan Whitaker "Radiation in Lappland" in *Anti-Slavery Newsletter*, London, Vol. 2, No. 7, 1986, p. 1.

27. *Cultural Survival Quarterly*, Cambridge, Mass., Vol. II, No. 2, 1987, pp. 69–70; also *IWGIA Newsletter*, No. 48, Dec. 1986, pp. 71–3.

28. *SAIIC (South American Indian Information Centre) Newsletter*, Berkeley, Vol. 3, No. 2, Winter 1987.

29. *Utusan Konsumer*, Malaysia, June 1987; Survival International *UAB/MAL/2/ JUL/87*.

30. Survival International *UAB/MAL/2a/NOV/87*.

31. *Native Self-Sufficiency*, Forestville, Vol. 8, No. 3, 1987.

32. Survival International *UAB/PGY/I/FEB/87*; and *Observer*, London, 1 February 1987.

33. *Survival International News*, No. 17, 1987, p. 5.

34. *IWGIA Newsletter*, No. 42, Oct. 1986, p. 22.

35. *Direct Action*, Australia, 28 May 1986.

36. *AfricAsia*, London, No. 40, April 1987.

37. *New Scientist*, London, 3 Sept. 1987.

38. *Age*, Melbourne, 19 November 1987; and *Times on Sunday*, 22 November 1987.

39. *The Australian*, Perth, 20 November 1987.

40. *Age*, 20 November 1987.

41. *Portsmouth Points*, Partizans, London, Nos. 1–3, June–Sept. 1987.

42. Survival International Press Release, London, 25 November 1987.

43. *Project North Newsletter*, Vol. II, No. 3, Fall 1987, pp. 1, 2, 7; see also *Project North Newsletter*, Vol. 10, No. 1, Spring 1986; Vol. II, No. 1, Spring 1987.

44. *Land Rights News*, Darwin, Vol. 2, No. 2, March 1987; Vol. 2, No. 3, June 1987; and *Age*, 11 December 1987.

45. *Peace News*, Nottingham, 20 March 1987.

46. *Financial Review*, Canberra, 11 December 1987; *New Zealand News*, London, 6 January 1988; *Nuclear Free and Independent Pacific Bulletin*, England, No. 8, Summer 1987. See also Sue Stover "Stumbling towards Aotearoa: Race Relations in New Zealand" in *National Outlook*, Vol. 8, No. 5, Sydney, June 1986, pp. 11–13; and *IWGIA Newsletter*, No. 50, July 1987, pp. 15–24.

IWGIA

INTERNATIONAL
WORK GROUP FOR
INDIGENOUS AFFAIRS

IWGIA publicises and campaigns against the oppression of indigenous peoples and actively supports their right to determine their own future in concurrence with their own efforts and desires:

(1) By organizing research, examining their situation and publishing the information to a world-wide readership.

(2) Thereby furthering international understanding, knowledge and involvement in the cause of indigenous peoples.

(3) By fighting racism and securing political, economical and social rights, as well as establishing the indigenous peoples' right to self-determination.

(4) By arranging humanitarian projects and other forms of support to indigenous peoples and ethnic groups with a view to strengthening their social, cultural and political position. This includes practical and economic support for seminars and conferences.

Through the information given directly to us by indigenous peoples, and through reports by scholars living or working in the relevant areas, IWGIA seeks to inform and exert influence on governments, international organizations and on the public opinion.

IWGIA's publications appear in both English and Spanish. Each Document/Documento (published approximately 4 times a year) treats a special theme concerning the situation of a particular indigenous people. The Newsletters/Boletins contain news, articles and book reviews. The new IWGIA Yearbook provides a global view of events in the indigenous world, accounts of developments, comments and analysis.

IWGIA invites you to subscribe to its publications, and to enter the world-wide network of indigenous peoples and concerned scholars who constantly share information on indigenous affairs. Personal cheques are accepted and should be made payable to: IWGIA, Fiolstræde 10, DK 1171 Copenhagen K, Denmark.

▫ Personal Subscription: £16
▫ Institutional Subscription: £25

NAME: _____

ADDRESS: _____

Back issues of more than 50 different documents are available. Please write for more details.

FIOLSTRÆDE 10
DK1171 COPENHAGEN K
TELEPHONE 01 12 47 24 DENMARK